HOW TO CONQUER YOUR ALCOHOLISM

A Complete and Useable Program and Reference Guide to Getting & Staying Sober

D.H. WILLIAMS

Conquer Your Addiction LLC
O'Fallon, MO

The information provided in this book is designed to provide helpful information on the subjects discussed. This book is not meant to be used, nor should it be used, to diagnose or treat any medical condition. For the diagnosis or treatment of any medical problem, consult your own physician or practitioner. The author is not responsible for any specific health needs that may require medical attention or supervision and is not liable for any damages or negative consequences from any treatment, action, application, or preparation given to any person reading or following the information in this book. References are provided for informational purposes only and do not constitute endorsement of any websites or other sources. Readers should be aware that the websites listed in this book may change.

Conquer Your Addiction LLC
P.O. Box 1509
O'Fallon, Missouri
www.ConquerYourAlcoholism.com
www.ConquerYourAddiction.com

ISBN: 978-0-69236189-4

Cover and interior design: Gary A. Rosenberg • www.thebookcouple.com

Printed in the United States of America

To My Children:
Adam, Anna, Michael, and Maria,
who became fantastic adults
despite a "challenging" childhood.
Well done! I Love You!

To Mom:
For being there
in the worst of times.
Thanks!

Contents

Preface, xiii

Introduction: Why You Should Read This Book, 1

The Conquer Program Overview, 6

An Important Note for Those under Age 25, 17

Women and Alcohol—Extra Problems for You, 23

PHASE 1: LAY THE FOUNDATION FOR SOBRIETY

Level 1—Admit You Have an Addiction to Alcohol, 31

The Evolution from "Normal" to a Problem Drinker, 33

Could You Be a "Functional" Alcoholic?, 37

Are You an Alcoholic?, 39

Interventions: A Good Idea?, 50
    What Is an Intervention and How Is It Done?, 51
    Possible Intervention Scenarios—Is the Alcoholic In Denial?, 54
    Planning an Intervention, 58
    The Role of Family and the Impact of an Intervention, 65

The Conquer Quiz: You May Be an Alcoholic If . . . , 68

Level 2—Know Your Triggers, 82

Why Knowing Your Triggers Is So Critical to Being Sober, 85

Trigger Interrelationships—A Missing Link in Alcoholism
    Treatment?, 88

Starting to Build Your Trigger Defenses, 89

DRINKING TRIGGERS FROM A TO Z

Anger, 94

Anxiety (Includes Worry), 100

Boredom, 107

Change, 113

Depression, 117

Disorder, 120

Envy (includes Jealousy), 124

Escape, 127

Extreme Emotions (includes Grief), 130

Frustration, 133

Fun, 136

Guilt (includes Embarrassment, Remorse), 142

Health Problems (particularly Pain), 148

Holidays (includes Special Occasions), 151

Hungry (includes Eating Disorders), 153

Insomnia, 158

Job, 162

Kids (Children), 169

Loneliness, 174

Media, 181

Midlife Crisis (includes Elderly Drinking), 186

Money, 191

Music, 194

Noise, 196

Overconfidence (includes Ego, "Pink Cloud"), 198

Peer Pressure ("Friends"), 202

Powerlessness (including Being Controlled), 206

Proximity, 209

Quitting (Fear of), 213

Relationships, 217

Relatives, 223

Reminders, 226

Sex, 230

Smell, 235

Social Situations, 237

Stress (Physical Stress), 240

Taste, 245

Times of Day, 247

Tired, 251

Unfun/Uninteresting, 253

Victim-Mentality (includes Child and Sexual Abuse, Low Self-Esteem), 257

Weather (includes Seasons), 264

X's—Ex-spouse/Ex-partner, 267

Yelling (includes Arguments, Conflict, Confrontation), 273

Zeal (includes Excitement, High Energy), 276

Level 3—Listen to Your Body!, 283

Alcohol-Related Health Problems from A to Z, 284

The Joint Progression of Disease and Alcoholism—
  Age Doesn't Matter!, 288

The Role of Genetics in Alcoholism, 303

How Alcohol Can Destroy Your Body—A Sampling, 305

Suicide and Painful Death by Alcohol, 320

The Conquer Program Health Assessment Guide, 327

PHASE 2: BUILD YOUR NEW DEFENSES

Level 4—Engage Friends and Family, 339

You Can't Do It Alone, 340

Who and How to Ask for Help, 340

Using Friends and Family as an Alcohol Defense, 344

Level 5—Detox, 347

Intro to Detoxification, 347

The Possible Side Effects of Detox, 351

Types of Medically Supervised Detox, 354

What to Expect Step By Step, 357
  Selecting the Treatment Facility, 357
  Making Arrangements, 358
  Preparation and Check-In, 359
  After Check-In, 360
  Day One, Two, 360
  Day Two+, 361
  Checkout and the Next Few Days, 363

Level 6—Rehab and Therapy, 364

Rehabilitation Treatment Programs, 365
   Inpatient Rehab, 366
   Outpatient Treatment Programs, 369
   Key Legal and Regulatory Protections, 372
   How Do I Select a Facility and Program?, 380

Traditional Therapy, 382
   Behavioral Couples Therapy, 384
   Cognitive-Behavioral Therapy, 385
   Motivational Enhancement Therapy, 387
   Step Facilitation Therapy, 387
   Time Perspective Therapy, 387
   How Do I Select a Therapist?, 390

Alternative/Unconventional Treatment Approaches, 391
   Acupuncture, 392
   Aversion Therapy, 393
   Hypnosis, 396
   Meditation, 397
   Salvation Army Rehab, 405

Level 7—Join a Community, 408

What to Look for in a Community, 410
   "Relatability," 410
   Demographics, 411
   Convenience, 411
   Variety, 411

Community Examples, 412
   Alcoholics Anonymous—The Gorilla in the Support Room, 413
   Rational Recovery, 426
   Secular Organizations for Sobriety (SOS), 429

SMART Recovery, 430

Women for Sobriety (WFS), 432

Online Communities, 434

Level 8—Break Bad Habits, 436

Alcohol-Related Bad Habits, 437

Ideas for Breaking Bad Habits Post-Sobriety, 438

Deliberately (or Unconsciously) Alienated Others, 438

Chronic Lateness, Procrastination, 439

Constantly Complaining, Being Critical, Argumentative, Interrupting, and Nitpicking, 440

Lying and Exaggeration, 440

Reacting Without Thinking, 441

Smoking, 442

Tea: A Possible Substitute for Alcohol?, 443

Kava Kava, 443

L-Theanine, 444

Chamomile, 445

Valerian Root, 445

Rhodiola Rosea, 445

Magnolia Bark, 446

Level 9—Develop New Hobbies, 447

Why Developing New Hobbies Is So Important, 447

Potential Hobbies from A to Z, 448

"Extra-Special" Hobbies, 451

Exercise, 451

Pets, 453

Volunteer Work, 455

Potential for Addiction to New Activities, 457

PHASE 3: COMPLETE YOUR FORTIFICATIONS

Level 10—Consider Spirituality, 468

Organized Religion and Alcoholism, 469

The Concept of a "Higher Power," 471

Ways to "Get Spiritual," 473

    Religious Literature, Teaching, and Testimonials, 475

    Spiritual "Event" or Epiphany (includes rock bottom), 478

    Preponderance of the Evidence, 481

Level 11—Make Yourself Sick of Alcohol, 484

Moderation, Relapses, and The Conquer Program, 484

Proximity, Smell and Taste—The Axis of Evil, 485

What's The Buzz? What It Is and Why We Want It, 487

How and Why Alcohol Affects Your Brain and Body, 492

Drugs To "Treat" Alcoholism, 495

Aversion Therapy Revisited—What It Is and How It Might Help, 498

    The Importance of Pavlov's Dog, 499

    Proximity Trigger Aversion Therapy, 500

    Smell and Taste Aversion Therapy, 501

Level 12—The Last Detox, 506

The Trick: Do It While You're Sick, 507

Other Tricks to Help Detox, 509

Level 13—Develop Your Defense Progressions, 512

The Stages of Alcoholism and Sobriety, 514

    Early, Middle, and Late Alcoholism, 515

    Early Sobriety, 518

    "Tuning" Sobriety, 519

Ongoing Sobriety, 520

What Do You Do If You Relapse?, 521

The Concept of Progressions, 522

Develop Your Defense Progressions, 523

Step #1—Inventory and Prioritize Your Triggers, 524

Step #2—Identify Your "Floor" Defenses, 526

Step #3—Identify Related Triggers, 527

Step #4—Identify Key "Tips," 527

Step #5—Identify Key Levels of Defense; Get Specific!, 528

Step #6—Order Your Tips and Defenses, 530

Step #7—Test and Adjust Your Tips and Defenses, 532

Step #8—Develop a "Generic" Trigger Defense Progression, 533

Step #9—Periodically Refresh Everything, 535

Examples of Progressions, 536

Conclusion, 555

APPENDICES

A. Learning to Sleep in Early Sobriety, 557

B. The Conquer Program Checklists, 575

Website Resources, 602

Endnotes, 608

About the Author, 640

Preface

My name is D.H. Williams. I am not a doctor, psychologist, or any professional service provider. What I *am* is someone who was an alcoholic for over 20 years, and tried everything out there to overcome it, and failed.

On the surface, I was a highly accomplished professional in the technology field, with a degree in Electrical Engineering from a top 5 school and an MBA from a top 20 school, graduating near or at the top of my class, respectively. I worked for many years at three of the top tier management consulting firms in the world, earning a lucrative living, despite being a "functional" alcoholic for many years. I have written four books and have been published and quoted in several national newspapers and magazines.

Despite this lucrative resume, my drinking caught up to me, with foreclosure, bankruptcy, major health problems, unemployment, and divorce being the result. I despaired of any way out of the hole I had dug for myself, but I did not know what else to try, as I had done multiple rehabs, dozens of therapy sessions, hundreds of AA meetings, and untold thousands of days when I tried to figure out how to stop drinking and stay that way were futile.

Finally, in a perfect storm of circumstances, I developed a program that *does* work, which I call the Conquer Program. This book describes this program and all associated information you need to do it successfully yourself, including being a self-contained, one-stop-shop reference guide that concisely provides what you need to know about alcoholism, along with hundreds of links to more sources of detailed information and analysis.

To repeat, I am not a medical or a psychiatric doctor, or anything remotely resembling one. I *am* a greatly "experienced" alcoholic who has run the gauntlet of most types of existing programs—some several times. I have come to the conclusion that many self-help books on alcoholism and nearly all existing programs and therapies take a "top-down," academic theory-based approach to helping alcoholics, *greatly* underutilizing the actual experiences and perspectives of the people on the ground—us, the alcoholics. This book is different: it is based on many years of alcoholic real-life experiences—mine and many others—turning those ugly pasts into a new, positive, and above all *useable* way to get and stay sober.

This book and program focuses on alcoholism as that has always been my albatross. It is very possible that a great deal of this program can be used to conquer other addictions, particularly various legal and illegal drug addictions, and even to others such as eating. This is conjecture on my part, as I never had those addictions, but there are promising signs and feedback that this may be so. Since I cannot personally vouch for such applications; it is up to the user of these other addictions to draw their own conclusions.

Finally, all opinions and recommendations in this book are my own. If you are expecting a program based on years-long medical studies and the like, go somewhere else. I do cite, *extensively,* numerous medical and non-medical sources and references, usually to illustrate and explain key experiences or support key viewpoints, and also to recognize that an incredible amount of time and effort has gone into trying to understand alcoholism and ways to get sober. Instead of dismissing these past efforts, I've tried to bring out the best, most salient and most *useable* aspects of that research and writings in this program.

Since many self-help books and treatment programs tend to be fun-free and even boring, I have tried to take a light-hearted, even humorous approach wherever possible, and to keep it interesting and engaging throughout. Above all, this book continually strives to be *practical* and *useable,* on a daily and even hourly basis. That is probably the biggest single distinction of the Conquer Program—that you can be confident in incorporating it into your everyday life seamlessly, simply, and effectively—so you can break the stranglehold this hideous disease has on your life, and live the remainder to its fullest!

Introduction

Why You Should Read This Book

Alcoholism *sucks*—no ifs, ands, or buts about it. If you are an alcoholic, alcoholism is condemning you to an early death—maybe fast by drunk driving or sudden arrhythmic cardiac death, or slowly as it gradually disintegrates your personal, professional, and physical well-being. For your loved ones, it is killing them as well but in a different way: they are watching the alcohol train wreck getting closer and closer to taking out everything associated with you, not the least the hope for sanity and happiness.

Maybe you've tried everything you can think of: rehabs, therapy, 12-Steps—nothing seems to work for very long, if at all. You are at your wits end. *Why* don't they work? Everybody does them. They are all over the press, yet they seem only to work for only a select few, and most importantly, NOT for you. What to do? Give up and accept this as your lot in life? **NO.**

As a twenty-plus year alcoholic who tried nearly *everything,* often multiple times, I had accepted that alcoholism was my lot in life. Why not? I had already lost nearly everything: money, marriage, jobs, and health. Death was probably lurking around somewhere, but I didn't care. However, a kind of perfect storm of factors came together to help me to sobriety, or as I like to put it—*Conquer* Alcoholism.

This book covers the 13 Levels that will help you do this, too, with the end result hopefully being that you are able not only to successfully *resist* the temptations about, dependence on, and cravings for alcohol, but to *do it without consuming a large part of the rest of your life.* Instead, within a few weeks of reading this book and building a new set of defenses to replace the ones destroyed by alcoholism, you will be able to live a life where alcohol is no longer the center of your daily universe. Not only will you be able to resist alcohol successfully, you may well be able to *ignore* it, as being irrelevant to your new life.

● ●

Why Is This Book So Long?

There are three reasons why this book is so long: First, alcoholism is a very complicated issue—if it were easy, then you wouldn't have so many problems overcoming it, right? There is no quick fix, miracle cure, or doctor magic that will do for you—the onus is on you. However, armed with the right knowledge and structure that this book provides you can eliminate ignorance as a weakness in your defenses against alcohol attacks.

Second, a full one-third of the book is dedicated to your possible drinking triggers, e.g. what causes you to want to drink—what they are, understanding them in detail, seeing if they are applicable for you personally, and if so figuring out how to deal with them *without alcohol.* There are *hundreds of specific tips, ideas, and defenses* on how to not drink, addressing over forty possible triggers, so that is a lot of ground to cover.

Most alcoholics will have somewhere in the range of 6–12 major drinking triggers. But each of these can have one or more "related triggers" that can sometimes come along for the ride when a major one is "activated." A good rule of thumb is that you will have as many unique related triggers as you do major ones. So someone with 6 major triggers will also have something close to 6 additional related triggers to worry about. Bottom line there is a great deal of ground for you to cover, as it is critical to understand how collectively *all* of these triggers can contribute to your desire to drink.

Third, this book is intended to be a self-contained reference guide, meaning if there is something that might help you conquer your alcoholism, it is covered here, instead of sending you off to some other source (which often causes people to stop reading and at a minimum is distracting). That said, there are hundreds of links to find out more on a particular topic that you can drill down to your heart's content. But if you just want the basics, each topic is covered concisely yet thoroughly in this book—at least enough for you to determine whether it is worth your time to pursue it further (then using the links to help you do so). This can help you save dozens if not hundreds of hours of research by itself. But since there are literally dozens of alcoholism-related topics to cover, it takes up a lot of pages no matter how concisely they are written.

● ●

There are a few things you should know before reading further. First, I am painfully aware that most self-help books *suck,* particularly those on alcoholism. Double the pain! They are written in academic jargon, or so generally that they serve mostly as eye candy—looking good on paper but useless when it comes to trying to put them into practice. Or they are just plain poorly written and extremely boring or, in a nightmare world, a combination of all of the above.

I fully recognize this looming self-help nightmare, and go to great lengths to make the material **interesting, entertaining, and even fun** wherever possible—no easy feat given the subject matter. To achieve this, I use humor, lots of interesting facts, a touch of profanity, and many individual testimonials from alcoholics, among other methods. The testimonials are particularly important in illustrating key concepts and as a whole, making the discussions *relatable and engaging*.

But the key goal is to *keep you reading.* It does no one any good to throw down the book (or fall asleep) in boredom after a few chapters or pitch it in the real or virtual garbage, which is the number-two danger of self-help books (the number one is that they don't help you at all). So keep reading—if a certain section is depressing, then frankly there is probably no way to avoid it, but the next section could be highly entertaining. ALL of the sections are as practical and useful as I could make them.

● ●

A Note to Nonalcoholics

Most of the nonalcoholics I talk to cannot understand at all why we drink, or why we can't stop. This book should *greatly* help with both of these. Pay particular attention to Levels 1 and 2; Level 1 provides an intensive analysis of what alcoholism is and why it is so difficult to overcome, and Level 2 provides literally an A to Z primer on the *specific* reasons that we drink—and ways for the alcoholic to overcome them. Hopefully, this will provide you with invaluable insights to help your alcoholic as he or she *will* need your help. How you can provide it is spelled out *in detail* throughout the book.

● ●

So why should you read this book, specifically? First and foremost is probably because either you or someone you know has an addiction— specifically to alcohol—or at least you strongly suspect it, and it worries the hell out of you. According to the annual (2011) National Survey on Drug Use and Health (A study by the *Substance Abuse and Mental Health Services Administration*[1]), 23.5 million Americans are addicted to alcohol and drugs. That's approximately one in every ten Americans over the age of twelve—roughly equal to the entire population of Texas! But only 11 percent of those with an addiction receive treatment. Statistics vary widely on treatment effectiveness, but at least one treatment program states that overall only *1 in 35* succeeds. Others put it closer to 1 in 10.

In other words, less than 2% of addicts are successfully treated. Scary math indeed—so apparently most existing addiction treatment programs also suck, despite all their press. Bottom line: *Existing alcoholism treatment programs are not designed well enough to get the addict into treatment most of the time, and when they do they rarely succeed!* That is why you are reading this book—**you are looking for a program that actually works!**

In the February 4, 2013 issue of *The New York Times*, an article titled "Effective Addiction Treatment,[2] states: *"Many of these [addiction treatment] programs fail to use proven methods to deal with the factors that underlie addiction and set off relapse."* The article quotes one of the authors of the study on addiction treatments as saying: *"There are exceptions, but of the many thousands of treatment programs out there, most use exactly the same kind of treatment you would have received in 1950, not modern scientific approaches."* The study goes on to bemoan the lack of competence and use of "modern" scientific methods in much of the addiction treatment world.

Unfortunately, even programs that use "proven methods" seem more apt to fail the addict than not, as noted by the unpleasant statistics above. In this book I discuss many of the reasons for those failures *from an alcoholic's point of view* and, more importantly, detail a program that looks to address those failures. Most importantly the program also articulates new steps that, collectively, have an excellent chance of **helping you get sober and stay that way** and, once reached, *maintain* **that sobriety in a way that doesn't consume large parts of your life and mindset.**

● ●

"But I Don't *Want* to Stop Drinking!"

Believe me, I understand *completely*. My best guess is that I spent far more time *not* wanting to stop drinking than I did over the course of twenty-plus years as an alcoholic, even when I *knew*—logically, emotionally, and intuitively—that it was ruining my life. Failed marriage. Financial destruction. Job loss. Major health problems. Frankly, it was only when I was *forced* to stop (due to major surgery and long hospital stay) that I started thinking about *why* I drank (the genesis of Level 2—Know Your Triggers). In my case it was (Fear of) Quitting, Boredom, a general desire to Escape the pressures of life, and a few others that I finally figured out were driving me to drink. And some of these had changed over time.

Does it matter for you to understand how your triggers have changed over time?

My answer is a definite Yes. It is very important to understand the history of your triggers and their individual impact on your drinking as it forces you to get to their root causes, by going back to the beginning so to speak. Not only does it help with the "Why Do I Drink" question, it helps you to understand how you got to be an alcoholic in the first place—something that mystifies many alcoholics and is often a big factor for many in denial of their addiction. Understanding this history and how to use that knowledge is specifically spelled out in various Levels in this book (particularly Level 2), as well as a checklist to help the process in Appendix B.

I make no other guarantees in this book, but I will make this one: If you don't want to stop drinking, at least read Level 2—Know Your Triggers. I guarantee that you *will* have a much better understanding of why you drink and why you don't want to stop.

• •

As discussed and referred to many times throughout this book, *alcoholism is a disease,* and by all accounts one that cannot be "cured," like say a bacterial infection can be with antibiotics. Various terms are typically used to address dealing with alcoholism as a disease, such as "recovering," "arrested," "abstaining," "rehabbing," etc., with the term "recovery" being the most used and well known. I try not to use these words in reference to the Conquer Program for a variety of reasons, mostly to do with their constant implication that dealing with alcoholism is an intensive, never-ending life process.

Don't get me wrong; dealing with alcoholism IS a never-ending process, and I absolutely agree there is no true cure. However, in my view, staying sober *does not* have to be an intense, *all-consuming process for the rest of your life,* as nearly all other treatment programs are whether they admit it or not. I prefer the word "Conquer," as indicated by the title of this book and program, since its definition gets to the heart of the best possible outcome when it comes to alcoholism:

Conquer: to successfully overcome a problem or weakness

Conquer implies a degree of completeness that is not present in the word "recovery" for example. Again, it does not say or imply "cure," but it does indicate a way that we can deal with alcoholism and get on with our lives; always keeping it in the back of our minds but *not* letting dealing with it play a huge ongoing role in our daily activities. That is the goal of this program—to help you *Conquer Your Alcoholism* and get on with a much happier, healthier life for you and your loved ones—sooner rather than later, *possibly* as fast as a few weeks. However, how fast the

Conquer Program will start to show results will depend on *many* factors, such as whether you have truly admitted to yourself you are an alcoholic; how many major drinking triggers you have; how fast you can detox, enter rehab, and/or arrange therapy; and most of all how much time you dedicate to building and refining your new defenses.

Certainly progress can start to be realized almost immediately upon reading any Level, particularly Level 2—Know Your Triggers, which is the heart of the Conquer Program. Once you truly understand your triggers and begin building your defenses to deal with them, it can be a few weeks to several months before you reach a full "conquered" state. More detailed time estimates for each phase are included in The Conquer Program Overview chapter later in this Introduction. At the end of the day, it is all up to you.

A Note on Footnotes

In this book I take an unorthodox view towards the use of footnotes/endnotes. In addition to citing references and research, I also use them to more fully explain mini-topic areas that can be highly interesting to some (but not all), thereby avoiding disrupting the flow for the majority. There are also many interesting, even amusing "asides" that hopefully contribute to the overall entertainment value of the book, an important goal mentioned earlier.

Another goal is to provide pointers to more information on the many subtopics in the complex world of alcoholism. Ignorance of these topics can stop sobriety in its tracks. There are hundreds of web resources—don't hesitate to use them! Additional sources can be found at www.ConquerYourAddiction.com.[3]

THE CONQUER PROGRAM OVERVIEW

According to the *National Institute on Alcohol Abuse and Alcoholism*,[4] there are four key elements to the disease of alcoholism:

- **Craving**—A strong need, or urge, to drink.

- **Loss of control**—Not being able to stop drinking once drinking has begun.

- **Physical dependence**—Withdrawal symptoms, such as nausea, sweating, shakiness, and anxiety after stopping drinking.

- **Tolerance**—The need to drink greater amounts of alcohol to feel the same effect.

These four "cornerstones" of alcoholism are discussed in *great* detail throughout this book. Their definitions and overall relationship with each other are discussed in Level 1—Admit You Have An Addiction To Alcohol. The mental/psychological "craving" for alcohol is the premise of Level 2— Know Your Triggers. Loss of Control is analyzed in Level 1 and incorporated into the various "tips" and other key defense Levels against alcohol provided throughout this book, culminating in Level 13—Develop Your Defense Progressions. Physical dependence and tolerance are dissected in Level 5—Detox, Level 11—Make Yourself Sick of Alcohol, and Level 12—The LAST Detox.

It is these elements—or to use a war analogy, these strategies of attack and their associated weapons—that alcohol uses to break through our meager defenses and cause us to surrender to alcohol and alcoholism. Since our natural defenses have proven to be vulnerable, ineffective, weak, or even nonexistent because of the disease of alcoholism, *we need to develop new, better, stronger, more effective defenses* that will cover and repel **all** possible methods of attack **all** of the time. ***This is the goal of the Conquer Program.***

The 13 Levels of the Conquer Program address each of these elements in a logical, intuitive, *and useable* way through methodically building up levels of defense that in the end will serve as a practical fortress to defend against the various ways alcohol can attack you.

The Levels are:

Level 1—Admit You Have an Addiction to Alcohol

Level 2—Know Your Triggers

Level 3—Listen to Your Body!

Level 4—Engage Friends and Family

Level 5—Detox

Level 6—Rehab and Therapy

Level 7—Join a Community

Level 8—Break Bad Habits

Level 9—Develop New Hobbies

Level 10—Consider Spirituality

Level 11—Make Yourself Sick of Alcohol

Level 12—The LAST Detox

Level 13—Develop Your Defense Progressions

These Levels are organized into three Phases:

Phase 1—*Lay the Foundation* for your sobriety (Levels 1–3)

Phase 2—*Build New Defenses* using the best of what is out there (Levels 4–9)

Phase 3—*Complete Your Fortifications* for repelling alcohol attacks (Levels 10–13)

Figure 1 illustrates these Phases and the Levels in each Phase. The stacking of the Levels is not an accident; it is intended to show a progressive building up of defenses.

Each Phase has a model that illustrates and reinforces the Lev-

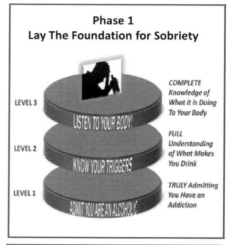

Figure 1: The Conquer Program Phases and Levels

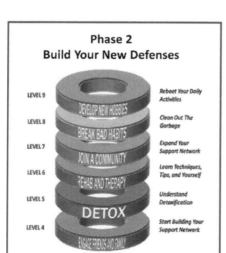

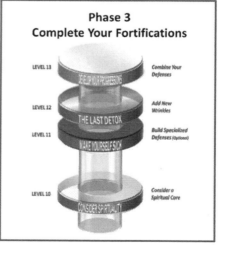

els of defense concept, with the result being an extremely strong, multi-level fortress built on a rock-solid foundation that together can enable you to successfully withstand the multitude of ways that alcohol can attack you.

Phase 1—Lay the Foundation for Sobriety

Phase 1 looks to lay a rock-solid foundation for sobriety through a combination of self-admission (*truly* admitting you are an alcoholic), self-understanding (*thoroughly* understanding what causes you to drink) and physical assessment (*completely* determining the toll that alcohol is taking on your body). Figure 2 below illustrates this multiple Level foundation building approach with Levels 1 through 3.

Why is this so important? Well, just as trying to erect a building on a sandy foundation is doomed to have it crumble around you, so is trying to build a solid fortress against alcohol doomed if it is built on a foundation of ignorance, self-delusion, and outright lies. *Nothing* is going to help you if you don't truly admit deep in your heart and mind that you have a problem—and a big one—and you need help.

Phase 1—Lay the Foundation for Sobriety

LEVEL 3

LISTEN TO YOUR BODY!

COMPLETE Knowledge of What it is Doing To Your Body

LEVEL 2

KNOW YOUR TRIGGERS

FULL Understanding of What Makes You Drink

LEVEL 1

ADMIT YOU ARE AN ALCOHOLIC

TRULY Admitting You Have an Addiction

Figure 2: The Three Levels of Phase 1—Lay the Foundation for Sobriety

This bit of insight may seem obvious, particularly if you are a nonalcoholic, but getting to that state of clarity is very, Very, VERY hard for most alcoholics. Why is it so hard, you ask? The answer is easy: *no one* wants to admit that they are flawed, have a major weakness, or are (negatively) different from most other people. Sure nobody is perfect, but who wants to seemingly be *that* imperfect? Nobody. Thus lays the core of denial for the addict. This core must be removed for any treatment program to be truly effective, replaced instead by a solid foundation of acceptance, self-knowledge, and mental and physical readiness to be helped.

Phase 1 consists of three Levels:

- **Level 1**—(Getting you to) Admit You Have an Addiction to Alcohol

- **Level 2**—(Getting to truly) Know Your Triggers

- **Level 3**—(Understand your health situation by) Listening to Your Body!

When you have completed Phase 1, you will have a foundation for sobriety that will underlay and support all the subsequent Levels of defenses that you will build in Phase 2 and (if necessary) Phase 3. Of all the Phases, Phase 1 will be the fastest to complete, possibly in as little as a few hours, as it is primarily reading and taking time to think through your triggers.

Phase 2—Build New Defenses

Phase 2 builds on the Level 1 foundation by taking the best of (often fragmented) existing approaches to achieving sobriety and integrating them together in a logical yet intuitive manner, continuing to build up a solid and united set of defenses against alcohol. Figure 3 below illustrates how these Levels "stack" together. The Levels with different colors indicate a significant physical aspect to that Level's activities.

Phase 2 covers the importance of building various types of support networks, as well as "traditional" methods such as rehabilitation programs, therapy, Alcoholics Anonymous–type meetings, and discusses how areas such as alcohol-related bad habits and the importance of developing new hobbies.

One key difference in these topics versus other programs that are out there is that they are discussed and analyzed in a different and *more practical light*. As I experienced going through many of these (multiple times),

Phase 2—Build New Defenses

LEVEL 9 — Reboot Your Daily Activities

DEVELOP NEW HOBBIES

LEVEL 8 — Clean Out The Garbage

BREAK BAD HABITS

LEVEL 7 — Expand Your Support Network

JOIN A COMMUNITY

LEVEL 6 — Learn Techniques, Tips, and Yourself

REHAB AND THERAPY

LEVEL 5 — Understand Detoxification

DETOX

LEVEL 4 — Start Building Your Support Network

ENGAGE FRIENDS AND FAMILY

Figure 3: The Six Levels of Phase 2—Build New Defenses

one of my biggest complaints was how little of the methods discussed was actually *practical and useful* on a daily basis in combating my alcoholism. Much of it was general—"ear candy" that sounded good at the time but was a distant memory within days if not hours—and mostly useless when it came to helping me change my thinking or actions.

Phase 2 consists of six Levels:

- **Level 4**—*Engage Friends and Family* to begin developing your support network
- **Level 5**—(Fully understanding and getting the most out of) *Detox*
- **Level 6**—(Getting the most out of) *Rehab and Therapy*
- **Level 7**—*Join a Community* of fellow alcoholics to extend your support network
- **Level 8**—*Break Bad Habits* that developed while you were drinking
- **Level 9**—*Develop New Hobbies* to fill the new free time you have from not drinking

By the end of Phase 2 (anywhere from a few weeks to a few months) you will have gained a new appreciation for how you can use "traditional" methods to help you get and stay sober. If it gets you all the way there, wonderful! If not, then at a minimum you will have developed many of the tools and defenses that in combination with the additional defenses of Phase 3 will hopefully provide you with everything you need to Conquer Your Alcoholism.

Phase 3—Complete Your Fortifications

Phase 3 looks to add some unconventional defenses to those you built in Phases 1 and 2. Those earlier phases may well serve to help many alcoholics to a life of sobriety. But it may not be enough for some—"something else" may be needed. Phase 3 takes the premise that "traditional" methods, no matter how well structured and integrated, may not be enough for some of you. **Phase 3 is not a standalone approach—Doing Phases 1 and 2 are absolutely critical for the success of Phase 3.**

Phase 3 is *non-traditional, unorthodox, perhaps even radical* in some ways, as it looks to build those final levels of defense needed for alcoholics who just haven't been able to "get over the hump" and get traditional methods to succeed, no matter how well-crafted and executed. Figure 4 (right) has a variety of coloring indicating the variety of physical, mental, and even spiritual dimensions of life that come into play in new ways to help even those most challenging of alcoholics to a life of sobriety.[5]

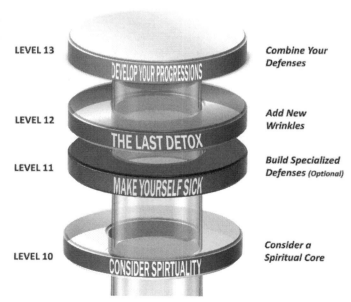

LEVEL 13 — DEVELOP YOUR PROGRESSIONS — Combine Your Defenses

LEVEL 12 — THE LAST DETOX — Add New Wrinkles

LEVEL 11 — MAKE YOURSELF SICK — Build Specialized Defenses (Optional)

LEVEL 10 — CONSIDER SPIRITUALITY — Consider a Spiritual Core

Figure 4: The Four Levels of Phase 3—Complete Your Fortifications

Phase 3 consists of four Levels:

• **Level 10**—*Consider Spirituality* as a core defense to your sobriety

• **Level 11**—*Make Yourself Sick of Alcohol*, particularly to its proximity, smell, and taste (this level is Optional)

• **Level 12**—(Make this) *The LAST Detox* by approaching it in unconventional ways

• **Level 13**—*Develop Your Defense Progressions* that combine and structure all the defenses you have built.

It is this last Level 13 that provides exceptional strength to your new defenses and is the real power of The Conquer Program, through integrating and layering multiple defenses together so that if one does not work well for some reason, there are others ready to go to prevent an alcohol attack from being successful and causing a relapse or worse.

How Long Will The Conquer Program Take?

How fast you can incorporate the full Conquer Program into your life is completely dependent on the individual—how much chaos your life is currently in, whether you have already done and are "up-to-date" on some of the Levels (e.g. Detox), and most of all how much effort you are prepared to invest mentally and even physically into following the program. The good news is once you achieve a basic understanding of the overall Conquer Program, **you will begin to see positive results in some areas almost immediately**. You can also do some Levels in parallel, such as developing new hobbies (Level 9) while you explore the possibility of introducing spirituality into your life (Level 10).

The ranges of timeframes that each Level can take are as follows:

Level 1 (Admit You Have an Addiction to Alcohol) —As you might suspect, this can be very easy or very hard, with timeframes to match. In an ideal world, you already know in your heart that you are an alcoholic, and this Level is "merely" confirming it with a few hours of reading. However, if you or your loved one is still in denial, this may take a long (and impossible to estimate) time to achieve the goal of admitting the addiction. This hopefully will not be the case; the whole point of The Conquer Quiz in Level 1 is to overcome this denial by being faced with hard facts of observable behaviors and end results. If the alcoholic takes the results to heart, then the time range for Level 1 could be measured in days and even hours. Hours, days, or weeks: however long it takes, it is *essential* that they admit they are an alcoholic, as the rest of the program (indeed *any* program) will be of limited value if the addict does not truly admit the addiction.

Level 2 (Know Your Triggers)—The description of possible drinking triggers takes up a full one-third of the book, so it is serious reading (a few hours) in itself. But what is likely to take longer—likely days—is *accurately* identifying what your major triggers are, as well as key related triggers. **A major trigger is a circumstance, situation, event, or state of mind that drives you to want to drink more often than not and can do so independently of any other triggers. A major trigger can also set off or "activate" other "related triggers" that in combination can quickly increase the desire to drink.** You will then need to identify the key tips and defenses you want to employ to defend against all of those triggers.

Level 3 (Listening to Your Body!)—This Level is primarily for information purposes only (and read in an hour or less), *unless* you think you have an alcohol-related ailment. In that case you will need to see your doctor to explore that ailment further, including how you are using this program to quit. Seeing your doctor may take a couple of weeks to setup and complete.

Level 4 (Engage Friends and Family)—Determining who you want to take under your wing (and vice versa) in helping you through this program can be done in as little as a couple of hours if you already have in mind who you want to help you and whether they are very aware of your problem. In that case, all you need is to introduce them to this program, and possibly (re)convince them of your determination to quit drinking. However, if there are no obvious candidates, or you have trouble summoning up the courage to ask someone and to explain how you might need help, it may take several days to explore who might be the right person(s) and approach them asking for their help.

Level 5 (Detox)—This will, of course, depend on whether you are still drinking or not. If you are, then obviously this will need to be at the top of your list in terms of immediate time commitment—two to three days at least. However, it will also likely be part of a broader Rehabilitation effort.

Level 6 (Rehab and Therapy)—A stay in a Rehabilitation program can take days or even weeks to set up (e.g. identify a facility and book a bed) and weeks or even months to complete. If you have done Rehab in the past, it may or may not be necessary to do it again; read that Level before deciding.

Therapy, if you choose to pursue it, usually can take a number of months to achieve real results. However, this is a perfect example of a part of the program that can be done in parallel with other Levels. Its primary goal is to help you understand key triggers that may be eluding your understanding otherwise. Some people may decide to not do Therapy as part of this program, which is understandable particularly if there are cost/availability issues and/or you have tried it in the past with no success.[6]

Level 7 (Join a Community)—You can easily join an alcoholic community such as Alcoholics Anonymous; it just takes finding a meeting in your area at a time that works for you. Online communities are even easier. The (possible time-consuming) trick will be finding one that works for your personality and overall convenience.

Level 8 (Break Bad Habits)—This Level is another example of one that can a) take a little time to identify, yet take a long time to implement fully, b) achieve *some* immediate results, and c) be done in parallel with other program activities. Identifying your bad habits will be easy; it is breaking them that will take time and practice.

Level 9 (Develop New Hobbies)—New hobbies may also be easily identifiable, but take some time to get into a rhythm of doing. Some may require a lot of lead-time while others can be done at the spur of the moment. Try a mix to achieve some immediate benefits while planning for the longer-term.

Level 10 (Consider Spirituality)—I don't expect anyone who is not spiritual to instantly become so upon reading this Level, if at all. But it may plant seeds that will grow over time into something resembling reality. So don't expect immediate results; it is another activity that can be done in parallel with other Levels.

Level 11 (Make Yourself Sick of Alcohol)—Since this is an optional Level, it may not take any time at all. If you choose to do it in the manner that the author did, it may take several weeks.

Level 12 (The LAST Detox)—The activities described here do not necessarily take any more time than a "regular" detox, though some may require some advanced planning depending on what extra "wrinkles" you choose to add to this last attempt to get sober. Since one of the core wrinkles is combining detox with another illness, you may have to wait to get sick to attempt it.

Level 13 (Develop Your Defense Progressions)—Designing your progressions for all your triggers may take a few hours; adjusting, modifying, and perfecting them could take several weeks. Indeed this is a set of activities that you will need to revisit every few months for the rest of your life to make sure they are aligned with what else is going on in your life.

So, all told you could be looking at a few weeks to several months to *fully* implement the Conquer Program, depending on your particular circumstances and effort. Unfortunately, there is no silver bullet, no magical cure, which you can do quickly and easily—you will need to make a very large personal investment in time, effort, and possibly even money.

The *very* good news is that you won't have to wait all that time to start to see results; they should start *almost immediately.* Just getting to the point of admitting you have an addiction (Level 1) is a huge breakthrough in itself, starting you on a new, positive path. Understanding *why* you drink like you do (Level 2), even if you haven't stopped drinking yet, will start to work in your favor as you start catching yourself (and perhaps even not) drinking in circumstances where you automatically drank before. Consulting with your doctor (Level 3) may put you immediately on a path to feeling better overall. Confiding in a key friend and family member (Level 4) and having them help you *by itself* will feel like a huge monkey is off your back, believe me. And so on—each Level will have parts that can be done immediately and with immediate results, even if the full results may take much longer to achieve. This is NOT a program where you have to wait to the end for things to get better!

The time you spend will be well worth it; and the result of that investment may be a brand new life. ***The end result of the Conquer Program will be a new way of being able to think and act towards alcohol, with it taking only a small part—NOT center stage—in the play called the rest of your life.*** Talk about a return on your investment!

AN IMPORTANT NOTE FOR THOSE UNDER AGE 25

This program was developed by a fifty-one-year-old guy, based on over twenty years of "experience" abusing alcohol. Many of the premises and examples of the Conquer Program are based on having been around long enough to really screw up your life, which for the most part, I assume will mostly be people around twenty-five years of age and older. My mid to late twenties are when I believe my alcohol use started spiraling out of control.

This program is also premised on the idea that you do not drink for fun, or at least that is not the *main* reason you drink, but instead drink to "deal with" your accumulating life's pressures. This again tends to skew the age range to later years, well after the teens and early twenties. It also can take several months or even years to progressively drink enough every day to bring on *physical* addiction (mental addiction can come far faster). The relatively slow pace of addiction is one key reason I believe many youths become drug addicts before they become alcoholics.

Most young problem drinkers/alcoholics are likely still in the "drinking is fun" stage of life, at least in part. But even if this is true for you, yet you recognize you have a problem, then this program may very well work for you. However, your triggers may or may not exactly fall under those discussed in Level 2. Many trigger discussions assume an older age, such as Job, having Kids (children), Money, Midlife Crisis, Health problems, and eXs. If you feel some of your triggers are not covered in Level 2, please follow the process to identify additional triggers described in that section. While many triggers are covered, it is by no means a complete list, as every individual is unique, and youths often have more than their fair share of highly unusual problems.

Does that mean this book and are not for you? **NO.** It *is* applicable to you for two very important reasons:

• Screwing up your life with alcohol is not some sort of reserved seat for older generations. Many people in their early teens and twenties can really get a jump on doing as well as older ones—the only difference is the amount of time and opportunities to do so.

• Even if you haven't done major, obvious damage to your life by your early to mid-twenties, odds are many of the foundations of how you may use alcohol in the future have already started to be built. NOW is the time to recognize any early warning signs that your mind, body, and life are starting to throw your way. To use a bit of a cliché, if you are trying to change the direction of a large ship, it is far easier when you are miles away from shore than when you are about to crash into the dock. Use this program to help you identify how your life may already be starting to spiral out of control when it comes to alcohol. Some of it may be obvious, but much of it probably isn't. It certainly wasn't to somebody like me who managed to chart a path of destruction over a long period of time, barely getting sober before it killed me (and almost did).

"Tips" for dealing with and/or addressing various dimensions of alcohol (ab)use is a central theme running through this book. With that in mind, I'd like to provide some tips that I wish I had heard and taken to heart when I was younger, particularly in my late teens to mid-twenties, when, like nearly everyone else around that age at one point or another, I thought I was invincible and life would go on forever. These include:

• **Understand the difference between drinking to have "fun" and something else.** As you'll see in Level 1, alcohol can very subtly change from being something to have "fun" doing to something that is much more of a crutch to escape the pressures of life. Worse, it can do so over so much time and so gradually that you may well not notice it until it blows up in your face. Very much a kind of ambush. Just being aware of this kind of insidious sneak attack may help you avoid it.

• **Look for early warning signs.** There is a "test" in Level 1 (called The Conquer Quiz) to help you decide for yourself whether or not you have an alcohol problem. It is based primarily on your personal behaviors and results associated with alcohol. Many of those behaviors/results essentially require a bit of time to come about, such as a failed marriage (question #23), whether your appearance is changing disproportionally to your age (question #17), and going out of your way to disguise your alcohol purchases and discards (question #4). All of those generally require a fair amount of time on this earth to really start being apparent. However, one that does not is whether you have a tendency to "binge" drink (question #5).

● ●

The "Importance" of Binge Drinking for Young Adults

One of the questions in "The Conquer Quiz" is about whether (and how often) you "binge" when you drink. Binging is defined as having 4 drinks (for females) or 5 drinks (for males) in a two-hour period.[7] Put more usefully, do you often drink until you pass out, run out of money, the party or bar shuts down, or until there is no more alcohol left? If you do this often, it may be an early indicator of a susceptibility to alcoholism. One of the key elements of this disease is that you *lack control* when it comes to managing your drinking, and binging most of the time you drink when you are younger—particularly when others around you are not—is not a good sign, meaning you cannot blame it on Peer Pressure. This trigger is discussed in Level 2. **If you binge drink, it may be an early warning sign to you that you cannot control alcohol**, and thus you should avoid it (or at least try harder to drink less). Being a binge drinker is not necessarily a "requirement" to be an alcoholic, but it is safe to say that most alcoholics (particularly male[8]) *are* binge drinkers.[9]

● ●

Binger or no, there are other questions that, while in total may not add up to a score that screams alcoholic, may well starting ringing alarm bells in your head. These include whether your personality *dramatically* changes when you drink (questions #1 and #2), whether you feel an intense pressure to get other people around you to drink (question #14), and whether you usually are one of the last people to leave a bar or party (question #8). In my view if you say "I Agree" to more than a few of these and others in "The Conquer Quiz," you should start asking yourself a *lot* of questions about your relationship with alcohol, including "Am I taking it too far?"

Pretty much everybody expects "young people" to sow their oats, act crazy, and say or do stupid things. It's a part of growing up, and arguably it is not a bad thing, as you may regret later in life things that you didn't do when you were younger. One HUGE caveat: in this day of social networking, ubiquitous camera phones, and 24/7 internet, and the fact that *anything* you post there can be counted on to *always* be there, this former fact of life that "you were young, stupid and no one will remember" is no longer true. Not all dumb things are created equal, and that is definitely true when it comes to your behavior and drinking:

> I once shared a train ride with a loquacious college student who told me she was "practicing drinking" in advance of her planned spring break in Mexico. "It was my mom's idea, after I got sick

over Christmas break from mixing rum with beer," she explained. "She doesn't want me making a fool of myself in Cabo, so we're working on getting my tolerance up."
—*Her Best Kept Secret* by Gabrielle Glaser[10]

There are dumb things, and then there are *really* dumb things. This makes my all-time top ten list—on the part of the mom, not the daughter. Why is this so especially dumb? First, your body rejecting alcohol is a *good* thing; after everything is said and done it is a toxin, even a poison, which your body does *not* like. Hangovers are no accident after all. Second, tolerance to alcohol is one of the four main dimensions of alcoholism (cravings, tolerance, physical dependence, and loss of control— detailed in Level 1). "Building up" your tolerance means you are deliberately putting your head in the potential alcoholism noose and kicking out one of the legs of the stool you are standing on. That in turn can lead directly to physical dependence, leg 2 of 4. So mom in her wisdom is already pushing daughter halfway to the point of the stool dropping out completely from under her.

• **Understand your emotional and environmental triggers**. *Everyone* has something that sets them off into a particularly bad state of mind— the vast majority of us have several. This is true at *any* age. People who abuse alcohol nearly always do it wholly or in large part in reaction to these triggers. Level 2—Know Your Triggers is dedicated to helping you understand this in detail, including how they can combine together to be *much* worse than just the sum of their individual parts. Even if you are not an alcoholic-in-training, you may well find that knowing what your personal triggers are will help make you a more positive and even happier person in general.

In Level 2, I literally go through an A-to-Z discussion of major drinking triggers. While every person is different of course, arguably you can say some triggers impact certain age groups disproportionally. Health and marriage problems have an obvious bias toward older generations for example.

But there are others that are equal-opportunity triggers when it comes to age, such as Guilt (fighting with a friend, sleeping with an undesirable person while wasted, etc.), so you start becoming more wasted to forget about it, to attempt to deal with it, or to excuse that behavior because you were drunk so it doesn't matter so you can keep doing it.

The "Job" trigger is another. One of the most dangerous times in life is being under twenty-five and not having a job. It is no stretch to argue that for an under twenty-five-year-old anything involving a job is one of their main priorities. How could it not? Constant pressure from parents to get one, friends for having one, and the future calling to ask, "Where the hell *are* you?" This in turn can activate other related triggers, such as Boredom, Depression, and Frustration. **Watch out for related triggers!** They can often cause far more distress and complications than the original one.

Certainly a related trigger to not having a Job, a low-paying Job, or one for not very long is not having much Money. In any of these circumstances and you're under twenty-five, what's the first thing that hits you after a long day of work (or lack thereof)—HAPPY HOUR! Be careful of these sultry low prices on everything that you love: "beer, wings, and more beer." While they are quite enjoyable, they can also set the stage of starting to drink more days than you don't. NOT a good trend.

• **Learn *in detail* about how alcohol affects your brain and body.** This is discussed extensively in Level 3—Listen to Your Body! And Level 11—Make Yourself Sick of Alcohol. Besides (hopefully) scaring the hell out of you about how alcohol can wreak havoc on your body at *any* age, you may be *very* surprised how drinking *more* alcohol actually works *against* what you are trying to achieve by getting drunk in the first place! Hint: It's not just hangovers; it is also how at a certain point in your blood alcohol content (BAC) level the chemical effect turns from an euphoria-inducing result to a dysphoria-causing one.[11]

• **Adopt some helpful rules of thumb you can always remember, even if you are trashed.** These include:

  • NEVER post anything on the Internet when you are drunk. Never, never, never. This includes not leaving drunken voicemails or any other "permanent record." Even texts are borderline.

  • Never make a major life decision while intoxicated—do not "DUI" (decision-making under the influence)." To state the obvious, don't drink and drive. But this can be *far* more subtle. Many of us, particularly when we are younger, have little perspective about how much (and how fast) is too much to drink in terms of its impact on our coordination and reflexes. This is true for any early drinker, even if you are not on a path to be an alcoholic.

Finally, remember that the impact of alcohol varies *significantly* by gender. For example, the rate of hospitalizations for alcohol overdose jumped 50 percent between 1999 and 2008 for women between 18 and 24 (males the same age only jumped 8%). Much more on this in the next section: Women and Alcohol—Extra Problems for You.

• •

What Is Alcohol Poisoning?

Acute alcohol intoxication, or alcohol poisoning, can occur after the ingestion of a large amount of alcohol. **Inexperienced drinkers, or those sensitive to alcohol, may become acutely intoxicated and suffer serious consequences after ingesting smaller amounts of alcohol.**

When ingested in larger quantities, alcohol slows body functions, including heart rate, blood pressure, and breathing. When alcohol significantly depresses these vital centers, unconsciousness results, this is one step away from a coma and possible death.

Many people are surprised to find out that death can occur from too much alcohol. Most think that the worst that can happen is they will vomit or pass out, with a hangover the next day.

Symptoms of alcohol positioning include:

- Repeated episodes of vomiting

- Unconsciousness or semi-unconsciousness

- Slowed or irregular breathing. Slow respiration, eight or fewer breaths per minute or lapses of more than 10 seconds

- Cold clammy or pale or bluish skin

- Vomiting while "sleeping" or passed out, and not waking up after vomiting.[12]

- If you encounter a person who exhibits one or more of these symptoms, call 911. **This is a medical emergency.**[13]

• •

One additional note: Level 2 discusses drinking "triggers" in great detail. Triggers are what make you want to drink, even when you don't want to! One of them is Peer Pressure, such as when your friends are drinking, and you feel that you should be also—to "fit in," "be cool," accepted as one of the gang, or even just so you don't stand out. This trigger and over forty others are discussed in great detail in this Level, including *ways to help you not drink* when you are faced with the trigger and others like them.

WOMEN AND ALCOHOL—EXTRA PROBLEMS FOR YOU

My original drafts of this book were based on my personal observations and experiences, both individually as a long-term alcoholic and as a male. As I delved into scientific research and in particular other critiques and self-help writings on existing alcohol treatment issues and programs, I became very, very aware of distinct differences in how various "demographics" viewed alcohol, and (strange as it sounds) vice versa. This was most notable in the differences between men and women. Two recent publications in particular were very eye opening on how women view alcohol and their alcohol problems—and how little attention has been paid to it in formal research historically. The first was an article in the *Wall Street Journal*, titled "Why She Drinks—Women and Alcohol Abuse"[14] and the second is a book titled *Her Best Kept Secret: Why Women Drink—and How They Can Regain Control*[15] by Gabrielle Glaser.

Studies starting in 1970 "discovered" that alcohol generated different moods in men and women. Men reported feeling increasingly aggressive and powerful as they drank, while women said they "felt calmer, less inhibited, and more easy-going."[16] But this was just the tip of the iceberg.

While in general I try to keep this book and in particular the trigger discussions in Level 2 as broad-based as I can in order to relate to as many people as possible, those publications opened my eyes on the very distinct differences between women and men on how they view alcohol. Certain triggers in particular—including Anxiety, Powerlessness, and Victim-Mentality—and their related triggers seem to manifest themselves very differently in "methods" and frequency between genders. Other very important and distinct triggers for women include the particular challenges in raising children, physical (un)comfortableness with their bodies at various times of lives, and perspectives and issues regarding sex.

It doesn't end there; these differences do not just manifest themselves mentally or emotionally—there are also very real differences between women and men *medically* when it comes to alcohol. Not only do certain medically analyzed triggers such as Anxiety and Depression manifest themselves differently for women—but women are *twice* as susceptible to them, and *twice* as likely as men to "deal with" them by using alcohol.[17] Adding injury to insult, alcohol has a greatly different impact on women *physically* than it does to men. Unfortunately *much* worse.

I have an engineering degree, go to work every day, and I am a FEMALE alcoholic. I gave birth 2 months ago to a baby—that meant 10 months of sobriety. But I am back. Drunk as I write this. Have experienced the DT's: basically, I was IN HELL. The DTs are the worst. Am 36 years now. Why can't I stop? Have a loving husband, new daughter, good family. I'm killing myself and I don't know why.

shawtyler73, alcoholism.about.com

Shawtyler73's emphasis on her gender is interesting but *very* relevant. Roughly there are twice as many male alcoholics than female, if you use the CDC's statistics (*www.cdc.gov/alcohol/fact-sheets/mens-health.htm*) for binge drinking as a proxy. Other studies concur: *females make up "only" one-third of the alcoholic-abusing population.*

But what women lack in members they make up in terms of consequences: **Women *are twice as likely to die* from alcoholism as men.**[18] There are a huge number of factors that go into why alcohol hits women so much harder, but can be partly summarized as follows:

Women are affected by alcohol more rapidly because they tend to have a higher proportion of body fat than men. As fat cannot absorb alcohol, it is concentrated at higher levels in the blood. Women also have less of a gastric or stomach enzyme (dehydrogenase) that metabolizes or breaks down alcohol before it enters the bloodstream. Because of this, women absorb up to nearly 30% more alcohol into their bloodstream than men of the same height and weight who drink the same amount of alcohol. Women are also usually shorter and lighter than men, further concentrating alcohol in their blood. Therefore, when women of average size consume one drink, it will have almost the same effect as two drinks do for the average-size man. If women eat little or skip food entirely, that compounds the effects of drinking alcohol.[19]

Higher Risk for Disease

There are more problems ahead; women who abuse or are dependent on alcohol are more vulnerable than men to have or contract:

• **Liver disease.** Women are more likely to contract alcoholic liver disease, such as hepatitis (an inflammation of the liver), and are more likely to die from liver cirrhosis (a chronic disease that progressively destroys the liver's ability to aid in digestion and detoxification).

- **Brain damage.** Women are more likely than men to suffer alcohol-induced brain damage, such as loss of mental function and reduced brain size.

- **Breast cancer.** Alcohol may also raise a woman's chance of developing breast cancer. Each additional 10 grams of alcohol (the amount in about one 4-oz glass of wine) per day raises the relative risk of developing breast cancer over a lifetime by about 10%.

To put this in perspective: A woman's overall lifetime risk of breast cancer is almost 9 in 100 if she drinks no alcohol. Two drinks per day increase the risk to just over 10 in 100, while six drinks a day ups her risk to about 13 in 100.

Compared with women who don't drink or who drink in moderation, women who drink heavily also have an increased risk of:

- Osteoporosis (a thinning of the bones).

- Falls and hip fractures.

- Premature menopause.

- Infertility and miscarriages.

- High blood pressure and heart disease.[20]

• •

Key Sources for Women-specific Alcohol Issues

Once I had my eyes opened to female-specific drinking issues by the above publications, I sought out more potential sources. Thanks to discussions with *Women For Sobriety*[21] (WFS, discussed in Level 7—Join a Community), I became aware of several other key sources, including *Turnabout: Help for a New Life* by Jean Kirkpatrick (founder of WFS); *Goodbye Hangovers, Hello Life* (published by WFS); *A Woman's Way through the Twelve Steps and Drinking* by Stephanie S. Covington; *Drinking: A Love Story* by Carolyn Knapp; *Smashed—A Story of a Drunken Girlhood* by Koren Zailckas; and *The Adverse Childhood Experiences Study* (*http://acestudy.org/*). All of these are referenced in various sections of this book, but I would encourage you to read them in their entirety if you have the opportunity; they provided numerous unique insights into specific female gender-specific issues regarding alcohol.[22]

• •

As you progress through the rest of this book and develop your new defenses against alcohol, it will be very beneficial to keep these increased risks in mind. The good news is that the attention to gender differences in addiction has become much greater over the last few years, and the rise of support groups such as Women For Sobriety has helped address women-specific issues much more pointedly and effectively. Hopefully, this book will help as well.

Regardless of whether or not you are male or female, under or over age twenty-five, it is now time to begin your path to sobriety via the Conquer Program. In the remainder of this book, you'll learn everything you need to know to set you on the path to conquering your alcoholism. It will also serve as a one-stop-shop for additional information, references, and links to specific alcoholism topics. This approach (particularly in electronic form) makes it easy to follow up on nearly any alcohol-related topic.

Here are some practical suggestions in approaching the remainder of the book. There is a *lot* of information included here—even to the point of being a bit overwhelming. If this is your initial reaction, then you might first skim through the entire book, trying to get a feel for its content and structure. From there take a Phase-by-Phase approach, concentrating on the Levels within each Phase. In particular I recommend you read Level 2—Know Your Triggers, completely and in detail *at least* twice. This Level is the key to the overall Conquer Program.

In Appendix B, there are checklists and other tools that can be useful as you progress through each Level. Print out (or copy) these and have them handy to take notes and write down ideas.

Last but not least, enjoy yourself as much as possible as you work this program! You are embarking in many ways on a way to a whole new life. While some of the Levels in the program have some unpleasant aspects, there are others that can be highly interesting, entertaining, and even outright fun. The end result will be one well worth the time and effort—a life where you have Conquered Your Alcoholism!

PHASE 1

LAY THE FOUNDATION FOR SOBRIETY

Phase 1 looks to lay a deep foundation for sobriety through a combination of self-admission (truly admitting you are an alcoholic), self-understanding (thoroughly understanding what causes you to drink), and physical assessment (determining the toll that alcohol is taking on your body). As illustrated in Figure 5 below, the first three Levels of the 13-Level Conquer Program focus on developing this foundation.

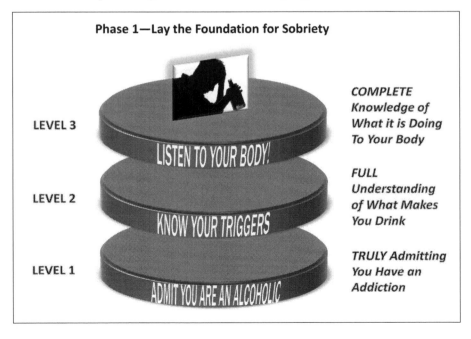

Figure 5: The Three Levels of Phase 1

LEVEL 1—ADMIT YOU HAVE AN ADDICTION TO ALCOHOL

If the foundation of a fortress is weak, then whatever is built on top of it will eventually become worthless and crumble to the ground. The analogy is equally apt when trying to become sober. If you don't *TRULY* admit in your mind and heart that you have a serious alcohol problem, anything else you do to try to treat it is just for show and eventually worthless.

The Conquer Program looks to truly convince the severe problem drinker of the reality of their situation by a different sort of test that is not general, not subjective, but based on a person's real life experiences and behaviors. The "Conquer Quiz" uses a point system based on 25 statements that will help convince you or a loved one of the situation once and for all.

LEVEL 2—KNOW YOUR TRIGGERS

The events, situations, and/or states of mind that make you want to drink or be particularly vulnerable to drinking situations, cravings, or states of mind are called "triggers." While most programs spend a significant amount of time on triggers, it is often not comprehensive in terms of number of triggers or level of detail. Instead, they usually focus on only a subset of the ones listed in Figure 6 below (which is not itself an exhaustive list), such as ones that have a catchy acronym like HALT (Hungry, Angry, Lonely, Tired). Most alcoholics have several triggers, and certainly not the same ones. Nor does a high-level trigger description come close to capturing the essence of what drives a person to drink—much more detail is needed.

For example, many alcoholics cite "Stress" as a major trigger. Well, that's great on the surface, but what does stress really mean? There are, of course, many, many causes of stress, from job problems to money to a noisy neighbor to a bad commute and so on. Determining the *specifics* of those causes—in particular the "root" causes—is what this program emphasizes over and over, particularly in this Level.

In addition, those triggers are often not "stand-alone," meaning they do not always occur by themselves. For example, Boredom and Loneliness are often tightly coupled when it comes to drinking triggers. Another example is how Relatives, Holidays, and Stress often go together during certain times of the year. And they can cascade, with

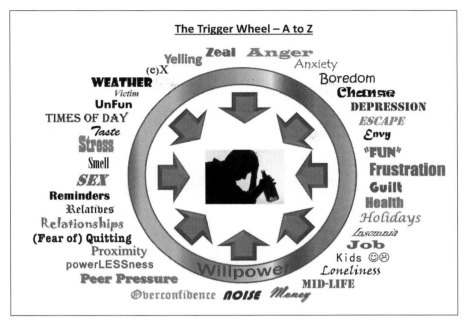

Figure 6: The Conquer Program Trigger Wheel

one trigger activating/triggering another one making successfully defending against alcohol attacks *incredibly* difficult.

Finally, not all triggers are created equal in terms of the ability of your natural willpower to deal with them. You may be able to handle the worst Job stress that comes your way without blinking an eye, but any problems with your in-laws may have you eyeing a bottle instead. Truly understanding your triggers means understanding where your willpower defenses need extra support, which in turn enables you to intelligently, logically, and emotionally find ways to develop and enhance that support. Reinforcements!

LEVEL 3—LISTEN TO YOUR BODY!

Too often an alcoholic's health plays little or no role in his or her thinking about their alcoholism disease (which is very ironic if you think about it). When attention finally turns that way—often many years into the descent into alcoholism—they find a great deal of unpleasantness await-ing them. Some of this is obvious, such as major skin problems and loss of memory, while others are not, such as cirrhosis of the liver. But there are many, **MANY** health problems that alcohol can cause, as shown in Figure 7 below.

Figure 7: Alcohol-Related Diseases from A to Z

This program in total, and Level 3 in particular, place great emphasis on understanding your physical health in general and how it relates to alcohol as you embark on the journey of sobriety. This consists of knowledge (the many ways that alcohol can screw you up physically) and diagnostics (an unbiased self-assessment of your physical situation combined with that of your medical doctor). This knowledge will help you tailor many of the defenses you will build in future steps.

LEVEL 1

Admit You Have an Addiction to Alcohol

Admitting you are an alcoholic is absolutely one of the hardest things you will ever do in your life. If you have already done so, then congratulations! I do not say this to be funny, but to recognize a *very* real accomplishment, and one for which you should be proud. Truly admitting your alcoholism lays the foundation for conquering it.

Even if you have admitted you are an alcoholic, I'd encourage you to read this level in its entirety before moving on to Level 2—Know Your Triggers. It will provide information that will give you much more insight into the nature of your disease, and help reinforce any doubts you have about the need to continue with the broader program.

If you haven't reached that point, however, or know you have problems with alcohol but just don't know how concerned you should be, Level 1 will be a critical resource for you. Unlike many other alcoholism programs, the Conquer Program doesn't just jump in with some test. There *is* a test (the "Conquer Quiz"), but not until we cover essential information about what alcoholism is, is not, and how it is possible that you can actually *be* one in the first place.

The realization that you are an alcoholic, or even that you have a drinking problem, is hard on every dimension possible—mentally, physically, and even spiritually. I guarantee that every single person who finally admitted to him or herself that they had an addiction spent several months and more likely several years denying it. After all, your mind and body didn't just wake up one day and decide to be an alcoholic—it was usually years in the making and so gradual that it seemed almost normal, like it was a part of expected everyday life. An abrupt change in thinking after such a long, slow descent into alcoholism is problematic to say the least.

Indeed, making the jump from viewing your drinking as being some version of "normal" to that of an actual addiction is anguishing, even traumatic. I think nearly all not-yet-admitted alcoholics sense this in some way and, as a result, delay "facing the music" about their drinking as long as they can. They sense that once they do, their life will have to change **dramatically** if they want to live effectively and positively from that point forward. Thus, denial becomes a kind of self-preservation strategy for the person to avoid having to make this kind of wrenching upheaval in his or her life. People for the most part hate major change— for good or bad, that is just a fact of human behavior, and alcoholics are no different. This mindset is addressed in the (Fear of) Quitting trigger in Level 2.

Very often it takes other kinds of traumatic events in one's life to finally get through and over this denial. A marriage failed, jobs lost, legal nightmares, even near-death or death itself—these kinds of events and situations are often referred to "bottoming out," where the alcoholic's life is stripped so bare as to make it impossible to deny reality anymore.

Level 1 is dedicated to trying to awaken the alcoholic to the reality of their situation *before* they "bottom out" or cause or experience some life-shattering event. The sooner a person can do this— truly admit that he or she is an alcoholic—the sooner they will potentially save themselves and their loved ones, friends, and even complete strangers untold disruptions in their lives and even actual lives themselves.

To do this—to condense the learning from what might otherwise be years of pain—into an *effective* part of a self-help book requires a different way of thinking about how to convince the alcoholic of their reality. External pressures such as constantly nagging at the person about their drinking or even interventions can sometimes work, but for the most part the alcoholic needs to be convinced *from within* that they truly have an addiction.

To do this, Level 1 first focuses on "opening up" to the possibility of being an alcohol addict, by methodically understanding the following:

• **Your History.** "I know I didn't start out an alcoholic, so how could I get from there to here?" Understanding how it is possible to go from a "fun-loving" person to an out-of-control drunk is a key to start accepting the reality of your situation.

- **The Masks of Alcoholism.** How you can hide that you are an alcoholic, even from yourself. Not recognizing such masks can add years of denying you have a problem.

- **The Disease of Alcoholism.** What "alcoholism" means, from both theoretical and practical viewpoints. A full and realistic perspective of how alcohol is slowly but *truly* ruining your life on many dimensions will take away ignorance as an excuse for doing nothing.

The above information helps turn the issue about whether you are an alcoholic from an *emotional* question (one full of subjectivity and easy to deny) to a *logical* one (one that has to be looked square in the face that you can't evade). The next step is to use that logical approach in providing a new kind of test—called The Conquer Quiz—which focuses on a person's *specific* behaviors and results involving alcohol rather than subjective, touchy-feely questions that are vague, general, or open to interpretation. With the results of this quiz, you can face the facts of your situation with a cool, logical eye, to clearly, cleanly, and truly deep in your mind and heart convince yourself and others—**one way or the other**—about whether or not you are an alcoholic. **Without that *total* conviction that you are indeed addicted to alcohol, ANY treatment program is bound to fail.**

THE EVOLUTION FROM "NORMAL" TO A PROBLEM DRINKER

None of us started drinking with the intent of being alcoholics, and most of us, if we even thought about it, would have attributed a zero percent chance of that happening. Sure there are some of us that may have a higher risk of alcoholism due to some genetic patterns or environmental factors, but as a whole no one thinks they will "grow up" to be an alcoholic.

Many, if not most people who abuse alcohol—indeed most people in general—start drinking in the course of having "fun," whether it's out with their high school friends, in campus bars, out after work, etc. For most people, the relationship between alcohol and these kinds of "having fun" situations is limited to just that, not intruding into other parts of their life.

But for the vast majority of people who evolve into problem drinkers/ alcoholics (this distinction is discussed later in this section), being able to put significant limitations on where, when, and how much they drink is very, Very, VERY difficult. In time, drinking alcohol will start to be done for reasons other than fun—to escape from, cope with, or numb ourselves to the pressures of everyday life. That is the "tipping point," where drinking to have fun starts to mutate into something else and puts you on the path to alcoholism.

Understanding *how* this can happen over time helps provide a historical context that can greatly help us in our battle with addiction—most importantly, getting us to truly accept that we are indeed alcoholics. There are a seemingly endless number of testimonials showing how it is possible to "mutate" from being a normal fun-loving person to a person addicted to alcohol, such as the below, based on a generalization of my personal experiences:

> *In my case, and I strongly suspect in the experience of most other alcoholics, drinking started out as a way to have "fun" with your friends in your teenage years or early twenties: sneaking booze from your parent's liquor cabinet on Friday night, hitting the bars looking for a hookup, watching the game, etc. Certainly taste was not part of it, at least for me at the start. Beer and wine are unpleasant at best the first time you taste it, and downright gross or literally sickening at worst (Mad Dog 20/20 or Southern Comfort anyone?).*
>
> *So why do it? With a nod to peer pressure, the most common answer is to have fun, of course. But why would we think it is fun to start with?*
>
> *I suspect for many the association between fun and drinking was formed in our early teenage years, as we saw our parent(s)—normally so proper, tense, logical, etc., when sober—loosen up and become much more friendly and outgoing after a few drinks, particularly at parties. At least that is how we perceived them; in all likelihood it was their personality change that stuck with us. They were different than they normally were. Older brothers and sisters coming home drunk probably struck us with the same reaction, though in their case head rubs and giggles and maybe strange smells in the bathroom were added treats . . .*
>
> *Another great association (both growing up and constantly reinforced in our later years) between drinking and "fun" was and is the media, particularly TV shows, commercials, and movies. Where there is one show/movie/commercial that shows the downside of drinking (think Flight with Denzel Washington or the occasional "Don't Drink or This-Is-Your-Brain-On-Drugs" public service ads), there are probably at least five dozen*

others that portray drinking as cool, manly, or sexy (think James Bond movies and every beer commercial ever made except those with animals— those are just funny; one more way of associating fun and alcohol).

In the meantime, we were growing up: college, new jobs, developing careers, marrying, children, children out of nest, divorces, mid-life crises, health problems, and other events and stages of life that did all they could to Fuck With USs (FUSS). But the desire to have Fun along the way was always there of course, and unfortunately so was its association with alcohol.

As we progressed through our "carefree" teenage years, the association of Fun with alcohol was embedded, even if we didn't actually drink much at that point. Once we got to college, of course all bets were off; everybody was doing it or some other substance. There was the famous Freshman Fifteen, where you put on at least 15 pounds, and it wasn't because of your normal food intake—it was alcohol. Some of you partied till you flunked out; others sobered up enough to graduate. And then you got a job, or were unem- ployed—either being stressful. Those who didn't go to college skipped right to the full-time work stage. Any and all of those being a big, big change in our lives.

A new job meant a new set of responsibilities, bosses, and coworkers, and other changes such as a new city, finding (and paying for) housing and transportation, new friends, even new habits. Fun came in new forms and environments: drinks after work, company softball games, girl's night out, holiday parties and the like. Booze was there all along the way.

But there were also the new pressures—high workloads, unpleasant bosses, massive travel, new financial demands—even though you were making more money than you ever had in your life, it just wasn't enough. Taxes, insurance, (high cost of) dating, car payments—these new or expanded pressures needed a release, and what was there to provide it? Alcohol. This was a "tipping point," where alcohol started to transition from being Fun to a new role in "dealing with" newly formed (or formerly ignored) triggers: Job problems. Money problems. Relationship Issues. Change in general. For some, serious dating became a serious stress point, and a new "Fun" challenge. Alcohol was there to "help" of course, but often caused more problems, such as passing out (and other things) prematurely, vomiting on dates, and in general turning off girls as much as not.

And so it went; you found a partner, got married, had kids. Promotions came, which meant more money but also more responsibility and more kinds of stress—politics for example. Money troubles did not ease, they just became different—the "need" for a bigger house in a better neighborhood;

the "need" for more, newer, better cars; the "need" for more toys—RVs and boats; the "need" for pricy educations and activities for the kids; the "need" for vacation homes and expensive vacations. And on and on and on it went.

Actual true fun, if it ever truly existed in your adult working life, started becoming more infrequent, particularly as those new, bigger, and more improved triggers decided to join the party. Life became a bit of a blur, and before you knew it your daily habits started to mutate, with alcohol a key participant in many of them. Times that you drank went from Friday and Saturday nights (the official "Fun" nights), to Sunday (game times), and to maybe Wednesday (hump day) and then Thursday (one more work day till the weekend!). You were now drinking on more calendar days than you were not. You were now not just tipping towards alcoholism, you were falling— Big Time.

Time went on, yet few if any of the pressures of life were lessening. Instead there were new ones, growing ones, mutating pressures: troubled teens, legal problems of one sort or another, deteriorating relationships, job upheavals, health problems, with alcohol increasingly seeming the only thing that would help take your mind off them—provide some "Fun" as it were—if only for a little while. Even your sex life took a toll, as drinking became more important than intimacy, and your ability to "perform" diminished the more you drank . . .

With the platoon of daily pressures you were now "dealing with," you abandoned any pretense of drinking being mainly for Fun, whether you realized it at first or not. Instead it became your Escape from these pressures. It was so much easier to sink into the comfort of an alcoholic haze than it was to deal with stress and unpleasantness. Drinking expanded to nearly all days of the week and in higher volumes. You started to experience more and more indicators of addiction—changing personality and appearance, professional misadventures, personal breakups and trauma. You were no longer that fun-loving guy or gal; instead you had mutated and become an Alcoholic, whether you realized it or not.

Every individual's story is different of course, but I encourage you to reach back into your memory and see if you can chart your own "mutation." In particular try and determine the point where drinking changed from being less "Fun" to more of a way to deal with the pressures of everyday life. It will provide valuable context as you try to determine your drinking triggers, both now and how they have changed over time.

COULD YOU BE A "FUNCTIONAL" ALCOHOLIC?

Admitting you have an addiction is one of the most painful thought processes and conclusions imaginable. It can turn your world upside down, destroying many of the underpinnings that made up the foundation of your life. **This process and conclusion can become even more difficult if you are a "Functional" Addict.**

The common stereotype of an addict involves people who are obviously making a mess of their life and are often associated with criminality, poverty, and being physically unpleasant. Alcoholics and drug addicts are often perceived as such.

The reality is that many addicts do not fit this stereotype. There are plenty of individuals who on the surface are considered successful in life, yet they are hiding an addiction to alcohol or drugs. These people are usually referred to as *high-functioning addicts,* and they may account for as many as *half* of all addicts. *The fact that these people are so successful at camouflaging their problem can mean that they ultimately cause more harm to their mental and physical health and others around them in the long-term.*[1]

Having lived this to a large degree, I definitely agree with this last sentence, particularly with respect to my physical health. And of course it gave me more time to *"royally fuck up"* most of the other dimensions of my life (this phrase is dissected later in this Level).

Specifically, a functioning addict can be defined as someone who can hide the excesses of their alcohol or drug use. They may have a good job (for a time), a secure home life (for a time), and be respected in the community (for a time) despite consuming an excessive amount of alcohol or drugs most days. To an outsider this individual is functioning at a high level, but this is often hiding the reality that internally the addict's life is falling apart. The functioning addict is sometimes able to maintain their balancing act for many years but eventually things *will* fall apart— sometimes gradually but often in dramatic and tragic ways.

> *I too was a functioning alcoholic. I had a successful career, a Mother, worked out all of the time (sometimes with hangovers so bad I thought I would pass out) but then one day it all fell on top of me like an earthquake takes down a small city. I have friends approach me about how to get sober or whether or not I think they have a drinking problem. My answer . . . the only answer is . . . when it starts to create problems in your life . . . you need*

to take a long hard look at the destruction it is causing . . . especially to those that you love. I eventually lost everything.

Anonymous, cryingoutloud.com

Functioning alcoholics can seem to be in great physical shape; they can work out often and eat well enough that their body on the outside seemingly shakes off the alcohol. Thus, it makes it even harder to spot and easier for the addict to deny the problem.

I think you're me—highly functional, workout, eat healthy (saves calories for alcohol), great family, husband and daughter—not even a question, happy clients. Endlessly reading blogs waiting for the right inspiration to quit but really wanting to moderate because the idea of quitting is painful, really painful. Feeling envious of others who have made the decision and now find joy and peace and a better life. I don't know what it will take . . .

Anonymous, cryingoutloud.com

The particular dangers facing the functioning addict include:

• The fact that they do not fit the typical stereotype of an addict makes it easier for them to deny that they have a problem.

• They have fewer obvious reasons to stop than other addicts and thus are less likely to stop. This gives them much more time to do damage to their body and mind.

• Frequently a functioning addict belongs to a profession with a culture of hard partying, making it seem like a "normal" part of life. They might even believe that failure to engage in this behavior would mean that they would not be able to do their job.

• They can put on an outward show of success that may result in less pressure on them to change their behavior. The alcoholic can even use their successes as justification to keep on drinking because their achievements give them a sense that they are already doing well enough in life. Family and friends may excuse the excesses for this reason as well. As a corollary, the functional alcoholic may feel that they've too much to lose by admitting that they have a problem. The apparent successes and excuses can mean that they remain addicted even though they accept that it would be better for them to stop.[2]

The functional addict will have the same indicators of addiction as other addicts albeit better hidden or easier to rationalize which prolongs and deepens the damage alcoholism is having on them and their family. So even if the functional addict can string together more "successful" years until they finally admit addiction, this is *always* offset by the higher difficulty in achieving sobriety and the damage that had been built up over that time, waiting to be unleashed. It is a ticking bomb that just gets more powerful over time while you progressively get weaker in your "functionality."

The late sportscaster Pat Summerall—very much a functional alcoholic for many years—said it eloquently:

> "As the years and the parties passed," he said, "I became more erratic in my judgment and less patient as I drank more frequently and recovered more slowly. In addition, I had lowered my standards along the way—professionally, personally and physically. To my shame, I had become a practiced liar and a seasoned cover-up man. I was spending more and more time on the road just to be around the party scene, always to the detriment of my family. I had walked away from my marriage and alienated my three kids. They didn't deserve that treatment.[3]

The key takeaway here: if you believe that since you are a well-functioning alcoholic now, you always will be, you are wrong—**IT WON'T LAST**. Just as an elite athlete will fall victim to age, wear, and tear, so will the "professional alcoholic." Sooner or later, your mind and/or body will break down, threatening to take everything with it. So the time to do something is *before* that happens. Do not think you can't be a well-functioning person without alcohol. Instead, you will find that you will be able to think better and more clearly than you have in years if not decades, and the "functioning" you did while drinking will be much more so after you Conquer Your Alcoholism!

ARE YOU AN ALCOHOLIC?

That's really the million-dollar question, isn't it? Because if you are, and you don't do anything about it, it is going to cost you $—*lots* of it. Some of it is obvious, some of it intuitive, and some you just don't think about:

- **Lost income.** Job income (see next); investment income (stupid decisions); entrepreneur income (lost productivity, missed opportunities); multiple earner incomes (spouse can't work/work as much due to your alcoholism)

- **Your job.** Not getting a job, missed promotions, losing a job, missing work, lost productivity

- **Health care costs.** Medical treatments, psychiatric treatments, rehabs, escalating insurance costs, deductibles, co-pays, lost/cancelled insurance

- **Alcohol consumption cost.** Retail store purchases, liquor stores, bar bills, parties, even "lost" alcohol (you forgot where you hid it)

- **Relationship costs.** Marriage counseling, divorce lawyers, child counseling, alimony and child support, maintaining multiple households

- **Miscellaneous.** DUI lawyers; ripple effect costs of jail time; higher auto and life insurance.

For many of us, we need to add these dollar costs to our "incentives" to get sober. No, this is not mercenary, or selfish. Instead, it is a real, reasonable, and potentially powerful incentive for an alcoholic to make an alcohol treatment program work.

But first, you have to figure out for yourself whether you are an alcoholic or not. Perhaps you are just a problem drinker?

Problem Drinking versus Alcoholism

The distinction between "problem drinking" and being an alcoholic is not at all clear, at least according to historical studies. Not only does it depend upon the source, it is further complicated by there being no truly useable definition of what an alcoholic actually is (discussed next) that would enable you to make such a comparison! Some sources view the distinction as more of a labeling than as anything else (e.g., that they essentially mean the same thing), whereas others view them as distinct categories. My view is that while both are major problems, there *is* a distinction.

As introduced in the Conquer Program Overview, there are four cornerstones to alcoholism. These are:

- **Craving.** A strong need, or urge, to drink.

- **Loss of control.** Not being able to stop drinking once drinking has begun.

- **Physical dependence.** Withdrawal symptoms, such as nausea, sweating, shakiness, and anxiety after stopping drinking.

- **Tolerance.** The need to drink greater amounts of alcohol to feel the same effect.

The National Institute on Alcohol Abuse and Alcoholism (NIAAA) website[4] puts these in the order I listed them above, which I think perhaps confuses some people (including me). In my opinion, it does not imply any order of progression (other than alphabetically) since I believe if it did, then Tolerance is out of place. Why?

As discussed earlier, no one thinks they will grow up to be an alcoholic, and the vast majority certainly don't do it deliberately. One very important dimension to understanding your alcoholism is *how you got that way*. The mutation of "Fun" into an addiction to alcohol illustrates this "process" at a high level and only from one perspective. But it would be more helpful to think about the above "four cornerstones" in terms of the process, such as in Figure 8 below.

The Alcoholism Cycle

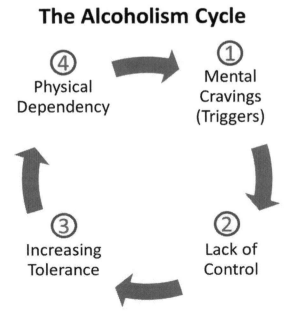

④ Physical Dependency → ① Mental Cravings (Triggers)

③ Increasing Tolerance ← ② Lack of Control

Figure 8:
The Ongoing
Alcoholism Cycle

To me, this process flow makes much more sense than just reading the words. First, you get beyond the idea of "Fun" as a reason for drinking (think about it as Step Zero). The next step is using alcohol as a "crutch," "release," "diversion"—or whatever word makes sense to you—as a way of dealing with those triggers, at least some of the time; maybe even occasionally at first. This is Step 1 in the diagram above.

The second step in the process is what degree of control a person has on their drinking—particularly their ability to *stop* drinking. Most "normal" people know when they have reached their limit, or have had too much, and can *stop there.* Alcoholics *cannot.* "Stopping" is not just your drinking on any given day; it also means not drinking "on command" on any given day, as well as not drinking in response to your worst triggers. To me, *that gets at the crux of the difference between a "Problem Drinker" and an Alcoholic.*

One good "definition" of problem drinking that I came across in my research was the following:

> *A problem drinker if given a sufficient reason to stop, can and will stop. An Alcoholic on the other hand will keep drinking despite the consequences; they have lost the power of choice when it comes to drink.*[5]

I like this definition because it focuses on the *actions* of the person drinking. Instead of using the term "willpower"—which strongly implies the decision to stop is purely a conscious, logical one—it uses the term "lost the power of choice," which to me means that it was something largely beyond their control mentally and/or emotionally. *In other words, it is the Lack of Control—the inability to manage drinking once you start—that is the critical element distinguishing the Problem Drinker from the Alcoholic.* This view is also consistent with the predominant view in medical and psychiatric research that *alcoholism is a disease,* which we will get into shortly.

●　●

"Willpower" Versus Lack of Control and Alcoholism

Willpower in the context of addiction has a variety of different definitions; among them the "self-discipline" or" self-control" of the individual; the ability to "resist temptation," including not being influenced by other people; or even the "inner strength" and resolve that a person has. Many definitions have some version of "strength of character" in them. Some "experts" feel that overcoming addiction is "simply" a matter of willpower. I believe that all of these "definitions" are complete bullshit to one degree or another.

All humans have willpower to some degree, but each of us is different in that our willpower can be strong for some things, average for many things, and almost non-existent for a few. Whether it is substance abuse, gambling, shopping, eating, sex, obsessive compulsive behaviors, or just biting our fingernails, we all lack the willpower or control to do or stop doing *something.* It's just most obvious and destructive when it comes to alcohol abuse.

To me this *lack of control*—or lack of willpower if you prefer—**is at the heart of alcoholism** and addiction in general. Interestingly there is little medical research on how this lack of control manifests itself chemically in our brains and bodies, though there is a ton of it in describing the effects alcohol has on us (discussed much more in Level 11—Make Yourself Sick of Alcohol).

If you stop to think about it, you will find *many* examples of how you can make yourself do something or stop doing something you know you shouldn't be doing. In my case it is obvious that I have no control over drinking—once I started doing it on any given day I didn't stop until I effectively passed out. I drank when circumstances clearly screamed "don't drink!"—but I did it anyway. I completely lost any semblance of control when it came to alcohol.

However, alcohol was the only "thing" I did where I behaved this way. I've used marijuana in the past, and stopped. I've enjoyed the feeling of other drugs, yet did not feel compelled to seek out sources for them so I could continue the feelings. I even have a bottle full of oxycodone (prescribed) sitting on my shelf for episodes of severe pain I've had in the past or can expect in the future, but I have no desire to take it in general even though I like how it makes me feel—in fact it has to be severe pain to make me finally decide to take even one. Other minor "addictions" (particularly candy) I've been able to stop doing with relatively little trouble.

In all of these, I exhibit a strong degree of control—or more than one flavor of willpower as defined above—yet I have none when it comes to alcohol.

• •

Clearly there are many people who can stop an addiction-like habit all on their own, whether it is drinking, smoking, drugs or non-substance-related behaviors such as excessive shopping, eating, gambling, etc. What they seemed to lack prior to stopping was a large enough incentive to do so.

Probably the most famous example of this was problem-drinker President George W. Bush. A famous (but incorrect) incentive supposedly was an ultimatum by Laura Bush that "It's either Jim Beam or me." Not so she said; instead, he made the decision to quit after a "wild drunken weekend" to celebrate his 40th birthday.[6]

As Mrs. Bush said in an interview: *"George just woke up and he knew he wanted to quit. And he stopped and he was able to stop. A lot of people can't. A lot of people need help to stop. He just stopped cold turkey."*[7]

• •

Can You Use The Conquer Program to *Moderate* Your Drinking?

This question can be very tricky to answer. The simplest answer is *possibly,* IF you are a Problem Drinker and NOT an alcoholic. Again, *control* is the key distinguishing factor. In my judgment, if you lack this control element, you have to stop drinking **completely.** No if, ands, or buts.

However, if you think you are "just" a problem drinker, and your Conquer Quiz results (discussed next) support this view, then it is entirely possible. Level 2—Know Your Triggers in particular will help you understand the underlying reasons why you drink. However, that by itself may not be enough to truly motivate you to cut back, at least consistently and in the long-term. It will depend on that individual's personality, personal circumstances, and specific triggers. For example, if one of the problem drinker's major triggers is Peer Pressure, then changing your circle of friends may well do the trick (of course that is far easier said than done). If, however, periodic Money problems throw you into a drinking funk, you may want to drink in those circumstances and nothing will motivate you otherwise. So it depends.

• •

The next step in the Alcoholism Cycle is Tolerance. To me this should go before Physical Dependency. Why? Because it is the Tolerance that we build up over time—primarily due to our Lack of Control—that results in our drinking increasing amounts of alcohol to get to the same "state of mind." We desire the "rush" we experience in the first one or two drinks; the "buzz" that comes after a few more; the "numbness" that we desire to allow us to not think about specific problems; or the desire to "checkout" completely from the world so we don't have to feel or think about *anything.* We chase these desired states like a dog chases a cat, and it gets harder and harder to achieve over time or last as long— making us drink even more.

The "final" step in the cycle is the Physical Dependency that results from our increasing alcohol intake. When we reach a state of physical addiction, it in turn increases our desire to include alcohol in how we "deal" with more and more problems (triggers). This desire results in our drinking more and more/frequently; and—since we lack the control to stop—ever increasing our tolerance, which makes our physical dependency even more pronounced, which . . . If ever there was a "vicious circle," this has to be right up there with the worst of them. *Once you have "completed" a full cycle, it becomes incredibly hard to stop drinking, and will get progressively worse with time as you repeat the cycle.*[8]

Not convinced? Admittedly this is my interpretation of the four elements of alcoholism as defined by the NIAAA. But how do other institutions see alcoholism? Answer: they view it as a *disease.*

Alcoholism as a Disease—What Does It Really Mean?

It took me years to recognize the possibility of my being an addict; even more to then finally admit it out loud, and longer still to really, truly believe it in my mind and heart. A lot of years wasted, but that's the nature of the disease. **And alcoholism IS a disease.** But what kind?

According to *mayoclinic.com:*

> "Alcoholism is a chronic and often progressive disease that includes problems controlling your drinking, being preoccupied with alcohol, continuing to use alcohol even when it causes problems, having to drink more to get the same effect (*Tolerance*), or having withdrawal symptoms when you rapidly decrease or stop drinking (*physical dependence*). **If you have alcoholism, you can't consistently predict how much you'll drink, how long you'll drink, or what consequences will occur from your drinking."**

From *The National Council on Alcoholism:*

> Alcoholism is "A chronic, progressive and potentially fatal disease characterized by tolerance and physical dependency or organ changes, or both. Generally, alcoholism is repeated drinking that causes trouble in the drinker's personal, professional, or family life. When they drink, alcoholics can't always predict when they'll stop, how much they'll drink, or what the consequences of their drinking will be. Denial of the negative effects alcohol has in their lives is common in alcoholics and those close to them."

And from *Wikipedia.org:*

> Alcoholism is a broad term for problems with alcohol, and is generally used to mean compulsive and uncontrolled consumption of alcoholic beverages, usually to the detriment of the drinker's health, personal relationships, and social standing. It is medically considered a disease, specifically an addictive illness."

I read the words above, and I nod my head and say to myself, *Yes, this sounds right.* The mayoclinic.com one sounds particularly good, and all emphasize lack of control in one way or another. BUT does it get me as a still-in-denial alcoholic any closer to admitting that yes, this applies to me? Probably not, since those definitions are A) very general for the most part, and B) even those "specific" parts are open to interpretation and thus easily able to fall into a "that doesn't apply to me" mindset. For example, what do the words "compulsive" or "consistently predict" really mean?

For me, the simplest—or at least shortest—definition of alcoholism is:

Alcoholism: an addiction to alcohol

But while we can all nod our heads at that definition as well, it doesn't really help us either as that leaves us to deal with the word "addiction." And it turns out there is no useful, *actionable* definition of addiction either!

According to the American Society of Addiction Medicine:

> Addiction is a primary, chronic disease of brain reward, motivation, memory, and related circuitry. Dysfunction in these circuits leads to characteristic biological, psychological, social and spiritual manifestations. This is reflected in an individual pathologically pursuing reward and/or relief by substance use and other behaviors.
>
> Addiction is characterized by inability to consistently abstain, impairment in behavioral control, craving[s], diminished recognition of significant problems with one's behaviors and interpersonal relationships, and a dysfunctional emotional response. Like other chronic diseases, addiction often involves cycles of relapse and remission. Without treatment or engagement in recovery activities, addiction is progressive and can result in disability or premature death.

Analysis: no wonder you can't read your doctor's prescriptions! These guys' writing prose is second only to patent lawyers in their ability to send your brain fleeing for the exit. While the definition may be technically correct and well put in medical terms, it is certainly not one where after reading you have an "Ah Ha!" moment that says, "That's me!"

Dictionary.com has it as:

> The state of being enslaved to a habit or practice or to something that is psychologically or physically habit-forming, as narcotics, to such an extent that its cessation causes severe trauma

Analysis: The use of the words "enslaved" and "severe trauma" seem a bit overdramatic as well as limiting. More importantly, if I had strictly used this definition, it might have taken me years longer to admit I had an addiction, as no one wants to admit they are "enslaved," and many people (including myself) do not experience "severe trauma" upon "cessation" (see the Detox Level in Phase 2 for some statistics). Maybe I experience extreme discomfort, but not severe trauma. A more generally accurate statement would be "they feel a lot better when using," or a lot worse when not, but certainly not "severe trauma" like being in a bad car crash or knifed in a gang fight.

Merriam-Webster sees it as:

> A compulsive need for and use of a habit-forming substance (as heroin, nicotine, or alcohol) characterized by tolerance and by well-defined physiological symptoms upon withdrawal; *broadly:* persistent compulsive use of a substance known by the user to be harmful.

Analysis: The use of "habit-forming" in the definition of "addiction" seems kind of circular to me. Isn't a habit a very close cousin to an addiction, at least when used in the context of things that are bad for you in general? Not helpful.

I also have a problem with its limitation to the use of substances (hello gambling addicts!), and the implication that the substances are harmful in any amount. Many, many studies have extolled the benefits of moderate usage of several potentially addictive substances, including alcohol. Unfortunately, this just muddies the waters, much to the delight of non-declared addicts: "Look! It says red wine is good for you!" two glasses into the two bottle daily intake . . .

Based on the above definitions of alcoholism and addiction, I have synthesized my own formal definition of alcoholism:

> A disease of addiction that destroys the mental and physical defenses normally used to manage alcohol—resulting in the inability to control and resist the desire to consume alcohol, eventually creating a physical dependency that maintains and accelerates the addiction.

I believe this definition gets closer to the heart of what substance addiction is about, in this case alcoholism. Still, it doesn't exactly roll off the tongue nor stick in your brain in any relatable manner. This definition and nearly all of the earlier ones for both alcoholism and addiction are not ones that the typical person, let alone addict, can identify with or compare themselves to. You need something spiffier and simpler—a definition that you intuitively know fits you or not. Here's my take on a truly usable definition:

> **Addiction: Something you use or do so much that you CAN'T stop doing it, even when it is royally fucking up your life.**

Feel free to embellish to make it even more meaningful to your personal situation, but I think that gets to the heart of it. But how to judge if this describes us *personally?*

Alcoholism "Tests" Versus The Conquer Quiz

Most of us—even the most illogical—can recognize when we are doing an unusual amount of a certain activity, such as trimming our nails twice a day, playing seventy-two rounds of golf every weekend, etc. We can also "see," if pushed, that certain kinds of behavior can be so unusual as to be unhealthy in some manner—mentally, physically, or environmentally to those around us and ourselves. And, if we can be convinced that those unhealthy behaviors are moving in a negative direction, such as a beer drinking habit migrating from a weekend 5 pm to 8 pm activity to a daily 5 pm to 11 pm one, you might finally be convinced that yes, but you can't stop. BUT.

But it is easy to write it off as a quirk if there seem to be few ill effects in a person's daily living and quality of life. Or the change from an occasional two-hour drinking period to a daily eight-hour one took place over so many years that you didn't notice it happening. It just seemed "normal," even if the new normal was radically different from the old one. So that leaves defining *"royally fucking up your life"* to get at the question as to whether or not you have an addiction.

Like the "definitions" of *addiction* and *alcoholism* presented earlier, there is no single be-all, end-all description that everyone can agree upon to determine if a person is an alcoholic—not even close. Likewise, there is, unfortunately, no foolproof test that will definitively say yes or no that you are alcoholic. But that doesn't stop people from trying, and in fairness, it is a worthy goal.

There are a number of "tests" that are supposed to help identify potential abuse problems, such as the Short Michigan Alcohol Screening Test (SMAST) and the Drug Abuse Screening Test (DAST), which more broadly seeks to identify all forms of chemical dependency. But there are major problems with these kinds of tests, particularly the ones that seem plastered all over articles starting with some variation of "Are You an Addict?"

Take the SMAST for example. In my opinion, it is a good example of the subjective and laughably presumptive attitude about what constitutes an addict. Copyright laws prohibit me from showing the list verbatim. But 8 of the 12 questions start with "Have you ever . . . ?" Do you ever . . . ?" or "Has your drinking ever . . . ?"

Answered at face value, it means you would have to answer yes if you only did the action *once,* such as feeling guilty about your drinking. Who hasn't at one time or another, particularly after some embarrassing incident? If you reasonably decided to replace the word "ever" with "often" or "frequently," then it becomes a question as to what defines those new thresholds—replacing the "ever" part of the question with one with a far more subjective phrasing. And the whole purpose and integrity of the test starts to break down.

The other four questions are also highly subjective, such as the one that asks if you *feel* you are a "normal" drinker, or another that asks if your friends or relatives *think* you are or not.

There is even a geriatric version[9] that is similarly subjective if not more so, and fairly insulting (asking if drinking helps decrease your shakiness or tremors, or makes it hard for you to remember parts of the day or night). Plus these "tests" look like they haven't been updated in a while; the geriatric version copyright was in 1991, and the original one years earlier.

But the age of these tests doesn't appear to matter. In a recent article about whether you are an addict[10], the author listed addiction "indicators" that essentially cover the same general ground with the same subjective phrasing. Questions such as whether you have had *"increased"* tolerance (to alcohol); *"unsuccessful"* efforts (to reduce drinking); and if you have spent *"significantly large"* amounts of time getting, using, and recovering from the substance. Again, come on! While headed in the right direction, it is still way off from the destination. If I'm an addict in denial, it would be easy to say no to these indicators *and believe it* with selected examples of how these did not apply.

Thus, I've come to the conclusion *that actual behavior and end results are the only reliable indicators of alcoholism* available, at least right now. So I developed my own test—partly based on personal experience, partly based on conversations with other alcoholics, others married to or reared by alcoholics, as well as the surprising little research there is on this *specific* type of approach.

Most of the statements on The Conquer Quiz have an obvious "fucking up your life" element to them. Others are not as direct but are clearly negative, and if you extrapolate, the behavior can easily be seen to be destructive and in the clear direction of addiction.

The point of The Conquer Quiz is to convince the alcoholic that he or she truly has a big problem, and motivate them enough to begin treatment—via this program or perhaps another. But what if that is not enough? What if it seems like nothing can convince the alcoholic that they have a problem and need help? They deny they have a problem, or if they acknowledge it they think that they can fix the problem by themselves (and never do)? For loved ones facing these mindsets, it may well be tempting to try an *Intervention*.

INTERVENTIONS: A GOOD IDEA?

As a (possible) alcoholic you may have zero interest in reading about interventions. If so skip to the next section on The Conquer Quiz to see if you *are* an alcoholic (however, reading it you may find some interesting insights into what your loved ones might be thinking). If you are a loved one of a (possible) alcoholic, you may have heard a lot about interventions and are considering doing one. If so this section is for you.

Prior to researching and writing this book, I had a strong bias against interventions, as I believed (and still do) it is pointless to try and force an alcoholic into treatment if he or she does not believe they have an alcohol addiction. However, further research indicates that interventions *can* be effective in certain circumstances *if* they are planned and executed properly. However, many people have different ideas about what is involved in an intervention, and even what it is to begin with. So let's set the record straight.

What Is an Intervention and How Is It Done?

An intervention is an *organized* encounter between a person who has a serious alcohol (or other substance) problem and a group of people consisting of various loved ones and possibly other concerned parties. The intervention—usually at a time /place (and purpose) unknown to the alcoholic—provides a safe, neutral environment for those concerned to voice their opinions/feelings about how the person's drinking concerns/affects them, creates issues in their lives, and finally why/how they think the person should seek help.

The goal of any successful intervention is to raise awareness that there is a serious problem that needs immediate attention and, most importantly, to get the addict into a treatment program *as soon as possible*. This means *immediately*; no waiting a day to "get their stuff" together, or for the alcoholic to "think about it." If you, the loved ones, are going to do an intervention, then in my opinion to have any reasonable chance in succeeding the alcoholic needs to go to a treatment center *minutes* after the intervention has concluded. This immediacy causes great logistical and planning problems as you might imagine, discussed shortly.

Interventions can have various formats and degree of formality. All interventions need a leader, to coordinate everyone involved, direct the planning, and make key decisions. Sometimes this person can be a more-trusted-than-average family member or friend, or it can be a relatively neutral 3rd party such as a pastor or family counselor. Increasingly professional intervention counselors ("interventionists") are becoming involved, spurred by TV reality shows such as *Intervention*.

Should A Trained Intervention Counselor Be Used?

In an ideal world, the answer to this question would an easy yes. Besides training and experience, such a counselor can provide an impartial set of eyes on all the parties involved. By the time an intervention has to be considered, the loved ones' relationship with the alcoholic has become so strained as to make normal conversation almost impossible, let alone a serious discussion regarding addiction treatment. The interventionist's primary responsibilities not only include facilitating the intervention, but also providing support, direction, and detailed planning assistance to friends and family prior to the intervention in a relatively unemotional and unbiased way detached from real and perceived wrongs of the alcoholic's past. The interventionist's responsibilities include managing the overall process, coaching the participants on key Do's and Don'ts, providing general guidance on what to say and not to say. The intervention must be conducted in a calm, collected fashion that gets the alcoholic to agree that he or she has a problem that needs treatment—*now.*

The downside of using such a paid counselor is usually the cost. The alcoholic's insurance may or may not cover an intervention. If the selected treatment center does not supply one (included with overall treatment cost and thus potentially billable to insurance), it may cost the participants significant dollars out of pocket (though this can be spread among all participants).

While the cost of this service varies by the individual professional and the specific services provided, you can expect to pay a flat fee for the intervention as well as cover the costs for the interventionist's travel, lodging and meals. Some interventionists opt to charge an hourly fee rather than a flat fee. If charged a flat fee, it should cover all planning aspects as well as potentially follow-up care (keeping tabs on how the treatment is going, arranging the first post-treatment meeting, etc.). While prices vary based on the location and complexity, various sources I researched had a "basic" intervention (including all meetings and preparations leading up to and including the intervention itself) in the $1,500 to $2,000 range, with interventions requiring travel adding another $500 to $2,000.

Transportation for the alcoholic to the treatment facility is also not covered by the cost of the intervention. Indeed, the family is responsible for either transporting the alcoholic to the treatment center or paying an additional daily rate to the interventionist if they are going to accompany the alcoholic to the treatment facility. This travel can sometimes include air travel, hotel, and meals.

The cost of the actual treatment is also not included in the price of an intervention. Again, in some instances, insurance may cover a portion of the intervention-related costs, and many facilities offer financing plans to help the financial burden become more feasible.[11]

Are interventionists worth the money? In assessing success rates of such interventions, an informal poll taken at the National Association of Independent Interventionists Conference (AIS) in 1995 revealed that 90% of professionally facilitated interventions resulted in the identified patient entering treatment as a direct result of the intervention.[12] However, it should be noted that there were no comparable statistics available for *non*-professionally facilitated interventions. It should also be stressed that there are no studies that I am aware of that indicate that the subsequent treatment success is any better for intervention-initiated admissions than non-intervention admissions (called "self-referrals"). Viewed from a different perspective this observation *may* indicate that effectively "forcing" someone into rehab is not necessarily worse than those "freely" admitted. However, the research on this is far from clear and makes no distinction between those who are in denial about their alcoholism versus those who acknowledge the problem, but resist treatment. Again in my opinion it is very unlikely that someone who does not truly admit they are an alcoholic can successfully conquer their alcoholism in any treatment setting, no matter *how* they got there.

A site for finding an interventionist can be found at www.interventionsupport.com/interventionists/. Key criteria for selecting one can be found at www.interventioninfo.org/research/family.php.

Where Do You Hold an Intervention?

The setting for an intervention is surprisingly important, as it can greatly help (or disturb) the tone of a naturally delicate situation. Interventions should take place in a large, open yet private space that can accommodate several people comfortably. However, since interventions are nearly always a surprise to the alcoholic, where the intervention physically takes place usually has to fit a scenario to get the alcoholic there in the first place, among other factors.

When deciding where to hold an intervention for someone you care about, try to avoid:

• *A public place.* Interventions can get emotional and loud. Some family members believe that holding an intervention in a public place may decrease the chances that their addicted loved one will make a scene, but this is unlikely. It's better to avoid public places and opt for a private one instead.

• *A place that your loved one is unlikely to go.* Since you don't give the subject of the intervention an invitation to the event, holding it at a place they are unlikely to go limits the chances that they will even attend. Unlikely venues may tip them off to the intervention and give them a chance to avoid it completely.

• *A place that has a negative association for your addicted loved one.* Certain places, including the home of a family member, can have a negative association for your loved one. He or she may already be on guard or in a poor frame of mind if you attempt to hold an intervention in this place, making it difficult for your words to get through.

Instead, choose a location that is:

• *Convenient for the participants.* It's not just your addicted family member who must be able to get to the location with ease. You and everyone involved should not only be able to get there easily but feel comfortable discussing personal and emotional issues at the location you choose as well.

• *Comfortable for your addicted loved one.* The location you pick should also be a place where your loved one feels at ease and in control. Nowhere that is intimidating or uncomfortable will be appropriate.

• *Private.* Your home, the addict's home, or the home of someone else in the family might be one of the better choices because it affords the privacy necessary to share this very personal discussion. Make sure, however, that all those in the house are included in the intervention in order to ensure total privacy. If certain family members are not part of the event, a different location may be more appropriate.[13] Also, if the private residence is disorderly (e.g. a pig sty), is where the alcoholic has drank before, or if there is evidence of alcohol (particularly a bar), that residence is probably not a good choice.

Possible Intervention Scenarios—Is The Alcoholic In Denial?

To fully understand what you can anticipate for in terms of intervention expectations and outcomes, you need to determine what kind of intervention scenario you are facing. There are two basic intervention scenarios:

1. When an alcoholic is *in complete denial* about his addiction, and no hints, criticisms, or individual pleas to the person to admit his/her addiction and get help have had any impact; or

2. When an alcoholic knows and even readily admits he or she has a serious problem, but refuses to get any help, for whatever reason.

The Complete Denial Alcoholic

When the alcoholic is in complete denial about their addiction, the odds are highly stacked against having a successful intervention.[14] An intervention is nearly always a one-shot deal,[15] and there is generally only an hour or two for everyone to get their views out on the table and convince the addict through logic, guilt, and/or some other set of emotions to come out of their denial cave and consider the worst truth—that they are in deep, deep trouble and need to get help *immediately.*

Unfortunately, the alcoholic has doubtless heard all the concerns, complaints, and pleas about his or her drinking before—multiple times—and is highly unlikely to suddenly say "Yes, I have a problem; send me to treatment!" If the intervention does happen to succeed (e.g. the alcoholic agrees to go to treatment), it will likely be solely due to the combined peer pressure of the intervention participants and the collective guilt heaped on the alcoholic. He or she will likely still enter treatment in denial, which in turn will greatly limit the effectiveness of whatever treatment they receive. If the alcoholic does make it through treatment/rehab "successfully" (e.g. comes out sober and not kicked out[16]), in my opinion they are still very unlikely to last any length of time before relapse, unless the treatment program was unusually successful in convincing the alcoholic that they truly had an addiction.[17]

One of the "tools" that can be used to "convince" the in-denial alcoholic that they must go into treatment is the threats of loved ones to completely remove their support from the alcoholic. This could mean very harsh measures, such as no longer giving money to the alcoholic or no longer allowing him or her to live in their home. It could even mean divorce (e.g. immediately filing papers the next day), and/or taking custody of children and denying access to them. It could even mean sending the alcoholic to jail (depending on the legal status of the person and applicable state laws). Interventionists refer to these measures as "bottom lines." As you might expect, these are very serious threats, and must be carefully thought out, planned and orchestrated or they could make the overall situation *much* worse. But there is evidence to show that following-through on these bottom lines can be effective, even if the alcoholic refuses treatment at the intervention, by making their lives untenable in the subsequent months until they give in and accept treatment. However, even when this happens it usually falls under the definition of "forced," which unless the alcoholic is no longer in denial is unlikely to improve the chances of treatment success.

The "I Know I Have A Problem, But . . . " Alcoholic

When the alcoholic knows he or she has the problem, and admits it to others to at least some degree, then the odds of an intervention success become more favorable.[18] In these circumstances they also have very likely considered that they need some sort of help, and possibly have even looked into getting help at some point.

However there are many reasons for an admitted alcoholic not to have followed through on these impulses for help. They may be afraid of asking for help in getting the help (men in particular).[19] They may be a bit lazy—getting treatment is not a simple thing to arrange. Do *not* underestimate the role laziness (or to be more charitable, lack of energy) plays in not getting treatment. As you will see, much planning is involved, even if there is no intervention. Addicts usually intuitively understand this at some level, and even if they start looking into treatment on their own they will often stop at the first or second obstacle they encounter, as they often lack the energy or mental focus to overcome these planning obstacles on their own, particularly if they think there are many more to follow.

Other reasons for the alcoholic not pursuing treatment include cost, as well as worrying about how they will keep their job while they are in treatment. Very practical concerns such as who will care for their children or even pets may dissuade their getting treatment, as could concerns about how and when the rent and other bills will be paid. Sometimes the addict thinks they can fix the problem themselves, such as by going cold turkey for a few days, or trying to gradually cut back on their consumption (both approaches rarely work of course). Finally, the biggest reason for not pursuing treatment may be just flat out Fear of Quitting (discussed in Level 2—Know Your Triggers), which is *greatly* underestimated as a drinking trigger and reason to not want to quit in my opinion. All of these reasons/obstacles and excuses must be anticipated and planned for by the people involved in the intervention.

Thus, in the circumstances where the alcoholic has already admitted to some degree that they have a problem, the challenge for the intervention organizers is not so much getting the alcoholic into an intervention room or even getting them to agree to go to treatment as much it is making and handling all the arrangements and managing the "regular" day-to-day activities and responsibilities of the alcoholic. One goal for the intervention planner is to take care of the alcoholic's life responsibilities such that they have only one responsibility left: to get off the couch, walk out the door, and into a car for travel to the rehabilitation center—*immediately.* No delays, no sleeping on it, no finishing the work week—instead, going to treatment *now.* This includes the alcoholic *not* having to worry about the rest of their life crashing while they are away for several weeks.

It is this *immediacy* aspect that is often what makes or breaks the intervention for the alcoholic resisting treatment, for both those in denial and those who know they have a problem. A vague promise by the alcoholic in the intervention to go to treatment at some later date is worth practically nothing—a million things can happen to prevent it, not the least of which is the addict changing his mind about the need for (or ability to practically do) treatment, or even going back to full-blown denial.[20] The intervention becomes useless when this happens—indeed, worse than useless, as another intervention will likely be impossible to successfully pull off.

Preferred Approach

For an intervention to have a chance to be successful in either scenario, it is essential to have plans in place to take the addict to treatment *immediately* after the intervention, as in almost that very next minute after they say "Yes, I'll go to treatment." No next week or next day stuff, or even a delay of a couple of hours—NOW. *Many* arrangements will need to be made beforehand, including arranging to have a treatment slot open and waiting at a facility, and a car outside the intervention to immediately take the alcoholic to rehab.

Of course it is not that simple; to pull something like that off requires tremendous planning on the part of at least one of the addict's family members or friends. Level 4 talks about the importance of engaging at least one friend and/or family member to assist the addict as he or she goes through the Conquer Program. While the typical relative or friend can expect to put in a lot of effort as they help the alcoholic progress through the program, that overall effort can pale in comparison to the pre-intervention planning and during-treatment effort needed to get the alcoholic's life in order (and keep it that way)— enough at least for them to suddenly go off to a treatment facility for a month or more and not have their "regular" daily life in total chaos when they return. If the alcoholic is in any way worrying about this kind of chaos awaiting them, the treatment is almost guaranteed to be far less effective than it otherwise would be. Thus to have any chance of success, a great deal of planning must be done, both for the actual treatment as well as the intervention that precedes it.

Planning an Intervention

An effective intervention requires a great deal of *detailed* planning. You have 1) to get the alcoholic's life in order for them (as much as it is possible to do) while they are separated from their regular daily life, *and do this without them realizing it before hand;* 2) arrange for treatment at a rehab center that is *timed exactly* with your intervention; and 3) figure out how to do the intervention itself. This means a 3-part plan consisting of:

• *Alcoholic Separation Planning*—A plan for managing the alcoholic's daily life while they are in treatment so the person doesn't have to do anything or worry about anything other than getting better;

• *Treatment Planning*—Setting up the actual treatment for the alcoholic to be admitted to (assuming the intervention is successful); and

• *Intervention Planning*—Figuring out the blow-by-blow, hour-by-hour plan for the actual intervention event.

Each of these could be led by different people, but they have to be in coordination with each other.

Alcoholic Separation Planning

Unless the addict is homeless or nearly so, it is very likely that the addict will lead some sort of quasi-normal life that cannot be just dropped at a moment's notice to be not thought about for 30, 60, or even 90 days or more.[21]

There is no special laundry list for planning an alcoholic's extended absence; each person will have unique circumstances. However, you will most likely need to pay particular planning attention to:

• Existing living arrangements (making sure the rent and utilities are paid for the duration of the alcoholic's treatment stay and a month or two after they return);

• Key bills (e.g. medical insurance, to make sure it is not cancelled in the middle of treatment for non-payment);

• Key responsibilities (e.g. children, pets, even plants); and

• Job (making sure that an extended arrangement is reached with the alcoholic's employer).

All of these require a very high degree of "inside knowledge" into the alcoholic's life, even going so far as needing someone to snoop around in the person's mail and personal files. This is usually best done by the spouse/partner (if applicable), mother/father, or (close) roommate.

Much of the above is greatly simplified if the addict already lives with a family member. However, it is complicated if the addict is single/isolated, has children (living with the alcoholic), pets, is totally responsible for where they live, or any mix of those. For children and pets, daily care arrangements must be made, and if there is no close relative or friend that can provide this care continually and at a high quality, the addict will understandably become very reluctant to go to treatment. If the alcoholic is in a relationship with another alcoholic (which happens surprisingly often), this can also complicate matters as often the person is reluctant to leave the other because of their worries about the other's ability to take care of themselves.

Most alcoholics will have some kind of job that will need to be managed, particularly if they are a functional alcoholic. Convincing a boss that the addict needs an extended time off—without the alcoholic knowing about it—can be extremely difficult. While laws provide some protection against discrimination and firing based on substance abuse, that is still possible, particularly if the person has been poorly performing (a significant possibility obviously). If the addict is not convinced their job is safe it is highly unlikely that he or she will agree to treatment let alone stay there for an extended time. In general, covering for the alcoholic's missing time if they do not want the company (or specific coworkers) to know about the problem is also extremely difficult, as using a bunch of general sick time and/or vacation time may be very difficult to get approval for and will likely raise eyebrows anyway. It will likely be simpler for all concerned that the alcoholic take extended sick time or short-term disability time off from the company. But planning and setting this up *before* the intervention may not be possible. Instead, a family member will need to contact the company to inform them of the situation after they have been admitted for treatment to arrange for the appropriate time off. Level 6 (Rehabilitation Treatment Programs—Key Legal and Regulatory Protections) discusses key possible job protections for alcoholics seeking treatment as well as strategies for dealing with employers.

Treatment Planning

Planning for entering a treatment center is discussed in great detail in Level 5—Detox and Level 6—Rehab and Therapy. At a summary level the steps required include:

• **Identify a Treatment Center.** There are a variety of factors that need to be considered when selecting a treatment center (discussed in the later Levels). However, besides cost/insurance coverage, the biggest factor with respect to an intervention is *when* they can formally admit your alcoholic as a patient. As you might expect, the better clinics tend to have longer waiting times for a "bed" (as they call patient slots), and even if one is available it may be difficult to precisely time the admission to coordinate with the end of your intervention.

That said, if the clinic has relationships with "professional interventionists" then this step can become much easier. Even if they do not, the treatment facility may have significant experience with patients who come in through that process, so this experience may be an important factor to consider if other more preferred clinics are not working out from a timing standpoint. Be aware that they may require detailed and personal information regarding the person who is struggling with alcoholism before they commit to admitting that person.

• **Examine Options for Treatment.** As discussed in later Levels, there are a number of options for treatment, depending on the specific circumstances of the alcoholic. In some cases, a person may require hospitalization for medical detox, or may need special transportation (though this is unlikely if the alcoholic is coherent and medically stable enough to go through an intervention). Different options are available depending on the severity of the problem, the background of the person, and the involvement in other alcohol treatment programs in the past, among other factors.

• **Coordinate Entry into the Facility.** This is the probably the trickiest part, as it needs to coordinate with the broader intervention execution (discussed next). If the facility/clinic is familiar with interventions, they should be prepared to work with the intervention coordinator, within reason. However, since interventions are not always successful, e.g. the alcoholic will not always agree to go to treatment, it is conceivable that the facility will require some sort of non-refundable deposit in case the alcoholic refuses.

- **Plan Family Support "Treatment."** Watching several dozen episodes of *Intervention* convinced me of one important treatment element often neglected—the need for very close family members/key friends to change *their* behavior as well as the alcoholic. Many treatment centers have some degree of family education available; it varies mostly by level of intensity. An example of high-intensity is the family program at the *Betty Ford Center*. It "offers an intensive five-day (Monday-Friday) educational program with group work, lectures and presentations addressing various dynamics of the disease of addiction. By addressing the physical, emotional, mental and spiritual dimensions of those impacted by the disease of addiction, this program helps family members and loved ones begin their own recovery."[22]

While such intense family "treatment" is not always available (or necessarily needed), it does point to an aspect that *is* needed—for the people around the alcoholic to change *themselves* to better support the alcoholic when they return from treatment. It is illogical if not naïve to expect the newly sober alcoholic to come back into the same uneducated, probably chaotic environment that existed before they went away for treatment and not be negatively affected by it. The risk of relapse increases if those around the alcoholic have: not become better educated about alcoholism; not modified some of their negative attitudes towards the alcoholic; not become equipped with their own tools to deal with past history; and above all learned to stop being enablers[23] for the alcoholic. Hopefully this book will help significantly in reducing the typical ignorance of non-alcoholics about what this disease is and in particular what goes on in the mind of a typical alcoholic.

Intervention Planning

An actual intervention session is not just some people getting together in a room on a whim to confront the addict; it requires a lot of planning. There are several sources of intervention planning guidance including Wikihow (www.wikihow.com/Perform-an-Intervention), Hazelden (www.hazelden.org/web/public/hff80302.page), Livestrong (www.live-

strong.com/article/225707-how-to-conduct-a-family-intervention/),
and the Mayo Clinic (www.mayoclinic.org/diseases-conditions/mental-
illness/in-depth/intervention/art-20047451).

While each of these tutorials has its nuances and areas of emphasis,
they share many of the same qualities. These include:

• **Carefully choose the participants.** Obviously not just anyone should
be part of the intervention. Depending on the history and personality of
the alcoholic (and how widely known their alcoholism is and who has
warning of a possible intervention), you may find many people volunteering to be part of it, or practically none at all!

Who the leader of the intervention is (from a family member/friend
standpoint) is a key designation, as they may be the one to make key
who/what/when/where intervention decisions. That person will likely
depend on how the idea of an intervention came to be in the first place.
Since very often the person with the most motivation and means (money
and time) really starts pursuing the idea of an intervention, they are
often the defacto leader.

Selecting who else should be part of the intervention can be difficult.
Experts say the ideal number of participants (excluding the alcoholic and
the interventionist, if any) should be five or six, and no more than
eight.[24] Children may or may not be considered in this number; an intervention can be an extremely disturbing event for all concerned, so there
are obvious issues with involving children directly. However reading letters from the alcoholic's children can be a very effective tool. Indeed
research indicates that sharing the children's grief and concern in the
right forum, in the right way, can be the straws that tip an alcoholic
towards treatment in an intervention.

• **Collect and write down your thoughts.** Each participant will be
expected to write down thoughts on why they think the addict needs to
get help, how important they are to them, and what will happen if the
alcoholic continues on their current path. This letter is then read to the
alcoholic during the intervention to describe how the alcoholism is hurt-
ing everyone. The point is to give alcoholics a crystal clear picture of
how they are not just destroying themselves, but also those who care
about them. The letter should be succinct and comprehensively detail
how the person cares about them, is scared for them, and how they want
to help them on their road to sobriety. Writing a letter ensures that each

person can clearly say what they want without being distracted by the emotions of the intervention.

Try to keep each letter short (less than 10 minutes), as everyone's attention span will be frazzled due to nerves and anxiety, and may be subject to interruptions (crying, denials, arguments, etc.). It is up to the interventionist/moderator to keep things progressing steadily and chaos-free.

• **Figure out the logistics.** Set the specific time and place and have an excuse planned to get the alcoholic to that place at a certain time. Depending on the schedule of the participants and the daily life of the alcoholic this can be very complex or somewhat straightforward. Sort of like planning a surprise party. Arrange transportation to a treatment center, which in addition to timing it to an open bed slot, may require extensive car and possibly even plane travel.

• **Decide on consequences and ultimatums.** At the end of the intervention day, the intervention will be judged on one simple question: Did the alcoholic go to treatment? Since by many measures an intervention is a last resort, most interventions have a hard list of demands that the alcoholic must meet (mostly around going to treatment), and consequences that will result if the alcoholic does not agree, ranging from refusing to be an enabler (e.g. not purchasing alcohol or other related items) anymore to flat out never seeing the alcoholic again. Most important here is the willingness to *follow through* on these promised consequences. Do not state consequences that you are not willing to enforce!

• **Prepare.** Much like a wedding, holding a dress rehearsal is a critical part of the intervention. Work out who is doing what, and when, in getting the alcoholic to the intervention site. Pretend that the alcoholic is sitting there as you read your letters. Practice what you will do (individually and as a group) if the alcoholic's decision is A) agree to get treatment, or B) no. If an interventionist is used, it is the interventionist who will orchestrate the pre-meeting and the intervention itself. The intervention itself should be planned to be about 90 minutes, with an extra 30 for contingencies.

• **Execute.** The intervention will ideally follow along a clearly and carefully constructed plan that the family leader/interventionist has developed. The leader will open up with why everyone is here, and then direct the other participants to read their letters, including ultimatums ("bottom lines"). The leader will ask the alcoholic what his or her decision is—sometimes after the first reading, sometimes after several. Often the alcoholic will start with an initial "no," but after additional readings will turn to a "Yes." For this reason the order of who reads first, second, etc. can be very important, as is persistence on part of the leader. As long as the alcoholic stays in the room, there is a chance for a Yes.

The leader of the intervention will need to judge when it is appropriate to ask the person if they will go to treatment. It could be after the first reader, or after several. It may need to be asked several times before the alcoholic agrees. Reading the body language of the alcoholic is very important in this process. It is possible that the alcoholic will say (or yell) "No!" and leave the intervention. Having a person designated beforehand for this possibility of chasing after the alcoholic is usually a good idea. That person will need to be someone particularly close to the alcoholic (and also in good shape; sometimes it is necessary to run). Usually encouraging words and affection will bring the person back to the room, where readings can resume.

Once the alcoholic says Yes, then bring the intervention to a close quickly, with hugs and encouraging words, and then get the alcoholic into the car to go treatment. Do not give them an opportunity to rethink their answer.

So there you have it: interventions are difficult to pull off, but can be done successfully with a great deal of detailed planning. Strongly consider hiring a professional interventionist if you can afford it. Recognize that an intervention will be much more likely to be successful if the alcoholic has already recognized to some degree that they have a problem.

However, if the alcoholic is still in denial, an intervention may be a waste of time, as 90 minutes of a guilt-trip is not enough to change a hard-core denial mindset into one that truly recognizes the alcoholism. Indeed, it may even be counterproductive as the alcoholic may highly resent the intervention and go out of their way to drink even more, much like a 10-year old will do something deliberately because he is told not to do so.

A much better way is for the alcoholic to convince him or herself that he has a problem—in effect a "self-intervention." How can this be done?

That is the purpose of the following Conquer Quiz. It has the same goals of traditional interventions: e.g. trying to get you to realize you have a serious problem and that you need help. The distinction is that the Conquer Quiz encourages the possible alcoholic to step back and look at her life through a series of practical observations about activities and the end results, in a way that cannot be manipulated or open to subjectivity, nor done through a collective highly emotional guilt trip by others. To the alcoholic in denial, the Conquer Quiz provides you uncontestable, fact-based proof of their problem. To the alcoholic that has accepted the reality of the problem, but has not yet done anything about it, the quiz will help reinforce just how much of a problem it is, hopefully increasing the motivation to do something about it. In either case, the possible alcoholic has to convince themselves—logically and most of all in his or her heart.

This doesn't mean that the alcoholics have to do it completely by themselves. In fact, they *can't* do it all by themselves. Level 4 (Engage Friends and Family) describes the importance of friends and family in the Conquer Program. In the context of an intervention, the family's role plays a critical part in its potential success and can also have a big impact on the participants as well.

The Role of Family and the Impact of an Intervention

As strange as it sounds, in some ways an intervention is actually more for the benefit of friends and family than the alcoholic. Those loved ones over time have become increasingly frustrated, frightened, alarmed and/or angry at what the addict is doing to himself and his refusal to acknowledge that there is a serious and harmful problem. Friends and family often become depressed and even feel that there is no hope left for themselves and the future of their family. With no effective outlet for that frustration, to them an intervention can seem like a great way of venting that disappointment, sadness, anxiety and anger, becoming a seemingly nothing-left-to-lose option. Many participants report that even after an unsuccessful intervention or subsequent treatment that they feel a sense of closure, with which they can go on with their lives since they have essentially written the alcoholic out of their lives.

Even if an intervention does not go well, there are some positive benefits that can be gleaned from a complete failure. These include:

• *The alcoholic's enabling system is destroyed.* People who have helped the alcoholic pursue his addiction in the past, such as through giving money, buying booze, providing a safe haven to drink, or just looking the other way, may no longer do this after an intervention. It becomes difficult for many addicts to continue their addiction without the support of their chief enablers, which may drive them to seek treatment sooner than they might have otherwise.

• *Family and friends receive basic alcohol and drug education.* When the people that are closest to the addicted person understand the disease, they are better able to deal with it. Indeed, one of the key goals of this book is to help nonalcoholics have a much better understanding of the alcoholic mind; this knowledge can only help everyone involved.

• *Participants are exposed to the local treatment resources.* The family becomes aware of and may even visit the local treatment centers. If/when the addicted person reaches out for help in the future, he or she will be able to act more quickly.

• *The conspiracy of silence is broken.* Just the fact that the family can sit together and speak openly about the problems that have occurred over the years is very important. Often there have been incidents that were kept secret.

• *The family is exposed to support communities such as Alcoholics Anonymous and Al Anon.* These are the twelve-step groups that are free and widely available that act as support for the addict and his or her family. Alcoholics Anonymous is discussed in great detail in Level 7—Join a Community. Al Anon is a support community for alcoholic family members.[25]

Arguably the biggest benefit of an intervention for the participants is that it allows them to start taking their lives back. The alcoholic has likely destroyed huge amounts of family time and money while generating huge amounts of stress.. The problems of the alcoholic are often heaped on the loved ones, and even multiplied, to the point that they are often frazzled to the point of physical and/or emotional collapse. Usually the alcoholic is totally oblivious to this chaos, and even if not they won't care—certainly not enough to make changes. It may be the shock of an intervention that is required to wake the alcoholic up to reality. But how big a shock is needed?

One of the key questions that loved ones are asked by interventionists in preparing for an intervention is "What are you prepared to do?" or "What is your bottom line?" Meaning, if the alcoholic refuses to go to treatment, what harsh measures are the family members prepared to take? Will the spouse file divorce papers tomorrow, and take sole custody of the children? Will the caring mother refuse to give money to an alcoholic, to stop paying his or her rent, or even kick the alcoholic out of their home? Will the sister refuse to allow the alcoholic to see her nieces and nephews anymore? The theory is that unless the alcoholic is faced with those harsh consequences of refusing treatment, there will be no "incentive" to do anything different, including going to treatment.

This is obviously a high-risk approach, with potentially disastrous results if the alcoholic calls the family on it and refuses treatment. Either the family reneges on their threats (totally destroying their credibility and any possible effectiveness of future threats) or if they follow through the alcoholic is suddenly faced with no support. In that latter scenario, the alcoholic *could* reconsider and go to treatment. Or they might deteriorate completely, resulting in completely cutting themselves off from all positive influences and even resulting in homelessness or possibly even death. In my view this "all-in" high stakes approach should be avoided, unless the family is nearly 100% convinced that the person will agree to treatment.

One of the key mistakes many people who are considering staging an intervention make is that if they pull it off life will be finally back on the right track, with a normal life just around the corner. Unfortunately this is a far cry from reality. Even a successful intervention should be viewed as a *direction changer* rather than as a solution, for both the alcoholic and the intervention participants. You are trying to get the ship turned at least somewhat before it crashes into the shore; you don't necessarily care at this point about the new specific direction and destination. The effectiveness of treatment is assumed, as is a back to a normal life when the alcoholic returns. This rosy picture will almost never happen. The newly sober alcoholic will be very vulnerable and possibly even needing more (hopefully more educated) support from family and friend. At a minimum everyone concerned needs to recognize that the interrelationships between the alcoholic and the loved ones will be far different after an intervention than before.

Intervention or no, it is critical for the loved ones of the alcoholic to realize that they have a role to play in the alcoholic's treatment. This role doesn't stop with just getting the person into treatment; in fact, most of the work will come *after* formal rehabilitation treatment is completed.

Many loved ones will need to become more educated about the addiction, and realize the impact their attitudes and (lack of) knowledge about alcoholism plays into the alcoholic's sobriety. Rehab is only *one* part of the sobriety puzzle. Unfortunately many if not most people (including those in treatment) do not realize that unfortunate reality—they think Rehab will take care of all the problems, forever. It will not of course: many additional levels of defense must be built, which again is the objective of the Conquer Program.

As I stated at the beginning of this section, I have a large degree of skepticism about the effectiveness and even the wisdom of doing interventions, particularly for those in denial about their problems with alcohol. It is *far* better for alcoholics to convince themselves that they have a very serious problem. That is the purpose of The Conquer Quiz.

THE CONQUER QUIZ—YOU MAY BE AN ALCOHOLIC IF . . .

There are 25 statements in The Conquer Quiz. If you say "Yes," or "I Do," or "I Agree" to a statement, you earn points. They each have a value ranging from 1 to 3 points, for a possible total of 45 points. A few have more than one possible score depending on the specifics and/or frequency of that behavior.

I leave it to the test taker to judge how many points are "enough" for you to be convinced you have a serious problem. My personal recommendation is that **7 points is enough to consider yourself a problem drinker**, if you haven't recognized that already. At **12 points the evidence strongly points to an addiction to alcohol.** You exhibit enough behaviors and are racking up enough problems in your life to start meeting the "fucking up your life" definition introduced earlier.

At **20+ points**—well, to get to this place in the scorecard you have to demonstrate so many behaviors and results from your drinking that you may want to seriously consider the possibility that you may not have all that much longer to live unless you do something to stop your drinking *now*. At a minimum your overall life is rapidly going into the dumpster if it isn't there already.

But these are just my personal recommendations; guidelines as it were. These thresholds are subjective—believe me I know—but the questions/statements are NOT *to the extent possible*. Again, at the end of the day there is no magic formula that will say Yes you are addicted to alcohol or No you are just a problem drinker or a person who just likes to have a lot of "Fun." *You* have to recognize the severity of your drinking. **This quiz is a tool to help you do so—to get away from emotional mudslinging and confusing medical verbiage and focus on what it is you are doing when it comes to alcohol, and what its impact is on your life.**

Some statements in The Conquer Quiz, such as those for job loss and health problems, can be subjective since they can be caused by more than one factor. And unfortunately they are also relatively easy for the alcoholic-in-denial to put the blame on something else other than alcohol, even if drinking is the obvious reason to everyone else. That said, for all statements there are descriptions, explanations, and examples to provide you with more detail, so you *cannot* claim to misunderstand the statement. A scorecard can be found in Appendix B so you can easily tally up your points.

THE CONQUER QUIZ: YOU MAY BE AN ALCOHOLIC IF . . .

1. **Your friends and/or family comment frequently on "the kind of person" you are when you are drinking, e.g., you dramatically change personalities, and *in particular,* you become very unpleasant.** In my opinion and experience, being a "nasty drunk" is a strong indicator of susceptibility for alcohol abuse for a significant number of people. Even if there is no *direct* statistical or medical proof linking being an angry drunk to being an alcoholic, there is a *boatload* of medical, statistical, and anecdotal evidence of why and how drinking makes some people more prone to nastiness and/or anger, and in particular how anger directly or indirectly turns negative.

For example, according to a Minnesota Prevention Resource Center study, 40% of rape offenders were drinking at the time of the incident, and in 44 to 70 percent of the *reported* cases of battered women the offender was drunk. Various studies on homicides cite similarly disturbing statistics. *So even if you or someone you love is not truly an alcoholic but IS an angry drunk, you have something to worry about, and that person has a major reason not to drink just on this one dimension alone.*

POINTS: 1 point if you erupt in anger while drinking once a month, 2 points if twice a month, and 3 points if you do it three or more times a month, OR you have *ever* had the police come to your house because of arguments you were having when you were drinking. If you score 3 points here you should strongly consider Anger Management or other types of specialized counseling.

If however you don't necessarily get angry but *do* become a very unpleasant person, you are not off the hook.[26] This may be more nuanced, so you may have to ask a friend or family member their opinion. In this case if you are *consistently* (defined here as happening more often than not) nasty or unpleasant (but *not* angry) when you drink, you should score 1 point regardless of how often you drink.

YOUR SCORE: _____

2. **Your behavior materially and consistently changes when you drink.** You become loud when you are normally quiet (or vice versa), are irrational when you are normally logical, irritable when normally patient, become confrontational when you are generally passive, or take risks while drinking that you would *never* do if sober are some common indications of this kind of changed behavior. Another is that you can't socialize effectively with adults except when drinking, or can't communicate with children except when drinking. Isolating yourself while drinking (and more and more in general over time) is another indicator. This statement is a more subtle manifestation of the angry drunk personality change, and may be harder to detect unless you are looking for it, but I've been told by many spouses and close family members of alcoholics that they recognized this behavior pretty easily.

One theory is that this kind of *consistent* dramatic change of behavior is a result of an allergic reaction to alcohol, which if true is a different form of a lack of control over alcohol.

POINTS: 1   **YOUR SCORE:** _____

3. **You plan your day/night around drinking.** If it is a choice between getting that alcohol fix (even if you refuse to call it that) and doing other, more productive things like picking up the dry cleaning, getting to your kid's soccer game on time, etc., and you usually choose getting the fix, well there you go. This includes you regularly worrying that you won't have enough alcohol for the night or weekend, or drinking on your way to/during that activity.

POINTS: 1   **YOUR SCORE:** _____

4. **You "rotate" your alcohol purchases through different stores to avoid a perception by the cashiers that you drink a lot (even if you don't think you do). This includes deliberately hiding your alcohol bottles in the garbage.** If you start consciously doing this, it is a bad sign of a pickup in your drinking intake, particularly if you are not counting otherwise. Easily recognizing the liquor store cashiers in other settings is also not a good sign. Putting your wine bottles in someone else's trash is not either.

POINTS: 1   **YOUR SCORE:** _____

5. **Even if you don't drink most of the time, when you do, you "binge,"** e.g., drink everything in sight until you pass out, run out of money, get arrested, etc. Or to put some numbers to it, you have more than 4–5 drinks in a short period of time (about two hours), depending on your gender and particularly your body weight given that is the key factor in determining blood alcohol concentration.

The National Institute on Alcohol Abuse and Alcoholism defines binge drinking as a pattern of drinking that brings a person's blood alcohol concentration (BAC) to 0.08 grams percent or above. This typically happens when men consume 5 or more drinks, and when women consume 4 or more drinks, in about 2 hours. Note: More interesting facts and subtleties on binge drinking can be found on the Center for Disease Control website at www.cdc.gov/alcohol/fact-sheets/binge-drinking.htm.

Note: this question can be a *very* tricky one to truthfully answer, and not just because no one runs around doing BAC tests every time they drink. I knew a number of people, particularly in college, who obviously binged every time they drank (I think downing a twelve-pack in one evening by yourself qualifies) but did not turn into alcoholics. But as best as I can tell this is the exception rather than the rule, particularly if it occurs regularly over a period of years.

> *I've been a binge drinker for 20 years. I have every reason in the world to quit drinking. A great husband, 3 kids that I love like crazy, my own business, friends, and I have the desire to quit—to be a sober person—but I can't seem to accomplish this.*
>
> Ariel, cryingoutloud.com

> *When I was busted my BAC was almost three times the legal limit. Now, everyone is accustomed to hearing about BAC levels, but until you have to face it, it doesn't mean much. I was in the "death" level! And, I drank like that for years.*
>
> anonymous, cryingoutloud.com

Indeed, binge drinking has a significant amount of medical research about it, to the point that some professionals come close to directly equating being a binge drinker with being an alcoholic (e.g., no other test questions required).

I do not take such a hard line. To me, frequency and total volume of alcohol consumption are more important than infrequent blasts of alcohol intake when it comes to talking numbers. The number of points awarded here is dependent upon how *often* you binge.

POINTS: 1 point if you do it twice a month, 2 points if you do it three or four times a month, and 3 points if you do it five or more times a month.   **YOUR SCORE:** _____

6. **One of your favorite mantras is "I can stop anytime I want to." You become very defensive when someone questions your alcohol consumption.** Just saying "I can stop anytime I want to" should make your tongue fall off and your nose grow, and usually is one of the earlier denials on the road to finally admitting you have an addiction. Virulent defensiveness, even to the point of anger, is another powerful indicator of addiction, to others if not to you. To minimize subjectivity, give yourself a point if you say this (or something similar) once every two months. *It is an early indicator of an emerging alcohol problem that people are even talking to you such that you are "forced" to respond this way.*

POINTS: 1   **YOUR SCORE:** _____

7. **You drink in the morning.** This should be self-explanatory, but let's make it crystal clear. This means you drink something with alcohol in it during the morning hours after you wake up. You drink it either before, during, in place of, and/or after breakfast and before lunch. This includes exceptionally smart activities such as putting alcohol in your coffee on your way to work. I suppose you could also EAT something with alcohol in it, but if you are having Jell-O shots for breakfast then you don't need a damn quiz to tell you that you have a major alcohol problem.

I've left this statement as being worth 1 point, but if you are honest with yourself it should be at least a 2. Definitely give yourself 2 points if you do it at least once a month. For the life of me, I can't see any excuse to drink in the morning, unless you are just coming off the night shift.

POINTS 1 or 2   **YOUR SCORE:** _____

8. **You can't drink alone—you try to coerce others into drinking with you. Conversely, you usually (more often than not) have a specific desire to drink alone.** These may seem like polar-opposite behaviors, and they actually are, but they both cover the extreme ends of social drinking patterns, and are (in my opinion) unhealthy indicators of alcoholic behavior. I was the latter—couldn't wait to get alone so I could drink in peace with no one looking over my shoulder. Drinking to dispel major discomfort in social settings is a common drinking trigger, and discussed more in Level 2—Know Your Triggers.

POINTS: 1   **YOUR SCORE:** _____

9. **You become irritable when your usual drinking time nears, especially if alcohol isn't available, or it looks like you will be delayed getting to it. You make a ritual of having (starting) drinks at certain times and become annoyed when this ritual is disturbed or questioned.** This certainly applied to me. My body and mind would not think of alcohol the whole day, but when 5:30 pm rolled around

it suddenly, out of the blue, was all I could think about. Even if I did not know what time it was!

If I was not in a position to drink, say in a traffic jam, I would become progressively irritable and unpleasant. Interestingly enough if I could get to around 9 pm without a drink, the craving would usually pass. I'm still not sure what this meant. The best I can come up with is that it was too late to start serious drinking and still be able to enjoy it, so I bucked up and checked one in the good guy column of "I didn't drink last night" that could be used in future arguments and rationalizations.

POINTS: 1   **YOUR SCORE:** _____

10. **You start hiding empty alcohol bottles from other people in your household or even other "interested" parties such as the garbage man.** This was my personal specialty. I've occasionally thought of starting a business helping suffering wives/husbands find their spouse's alcohol bottles—empty or full—to assist them in producing intervention material (even though I'm not much of a fan of interventions). It is actually quite amazing (particularly to nonalcoholics) the places where an alcoholic can hide booze. I imagine drugs would be much tougher.

POINTS: 1 or 2 (This really should be worth 2 points
in general, but definitely give yourself 2 points if you
start *forgetting* where you put them.)   **YOUR SCORE:** _____

11. **You Smell. A lot. Often.** You reek of booze much of the time, even hours or days after your last drink. When you wake up (whenever that is) the bedroom stinks. Maybe it smells of alcohol, maybe of strong body odor, some mixture of the two, or something else. Whatever it is, it doesn't smell good.

This odor is one of your body's ways of desperately telling you to slow down on drinking. You are consuming it more than the rest of your organs (particularly liver) can process it, so it tries to get rid of it through your skin pores.[27]

POINTS: 1, 2, or 3. If this happens to you (by your
partner complaining about it, for example) at least
once a week, give yourself 1 Point. Twice a week,
2 points. Pretty much all the time: 3 points.   **YOUR SCORE:** _____

12. **You Sneak. You Lie. About Booze.** You sneak to the refrigerator or bar or wherever booze is usually stored after "drinking time" is supposedly over to get more booze, and do it in a way that your spouse, partner, children, roommates, whoever else does not know about it (supposedly). While there may be some valid reasons why you might do this—say you don't want your in-laws bitching at you while they are visiting—if you are doing this on a frequent basis it is generally a bad sign. So if

you do this more than twice a month without any *clearly* valid reasons (e.g., your in-laws) award yourself a point.

Similarly, *regularly* lying (to *anyone* except maybe your mother) about how much you drink, drank, intend to drink, or what you drank and how fast deserves a point. There could *easily* be more than the 1 point allotted here, **since lying about drinking is very often the first behavioral indicator of being on the road to alcoholism.** But it can be very subjective—not in the lie itself but the reasons behind doing so—so I kept it to 1 point. But the test is the same for sneaking—a point if you lie about your drinking more than twice a month.

NOTE: both of these behaviors are very often precursors to the hiding of booze behavior discussed earlier; if you both sneak/lie *and* hide booze *even occasionally* (say once every three months) then awarding yourself a point here is a no brainer.

POINTS: 1   **YOUR SCORE: _____**

13. **You have a great deal of trouble going to sleep, or staying asleep, without a certain amount of alcohol in your system.** There is a trigger chapter and then a whole appendix dedicated to alcohol-related sleep issues later in this book, as I found it one of the hardest parts of my post-alcohol life. If you can get to sleep BUT you have very bad nightmares consistently, also award yourself a point, as this is also an indicator of a type of intense short-term withdrawal.

POINTS: 1   **YOUR SCORE: _____**

14. **You are usually one of the last persons to leave a bar or party.** "Usually" means you do it more often than you do not. A corollary to this (and worth a point) is your panicking when you hear the words "last call" and trying to down as many drinks as you can (without being noticed, or equally as bad not caring) in the time remaining.

POINTS: 1   **YOUR SCORE: _____**

15. **You have a history of alcoholism in your immediate family and/or biological grandparents.** Unlike every other question in this quiz, this is one question you have absolutely no control over. As they say, "You can choose your friends, but not your family." However, it can be a very important indicator of susceptibility to alcohol abuse. Genetic issues are discussed in Level 3 (Listen to Your Body!).

So if someone in your immediate family (parents, siblings, biological aunts/uncles) is a *clear* alcohol abuser, give yourself 1 point. If one of your biological grandparents is/was an alcohol abuser, give yourself 1 point (to be clear, if you have alcohol abuse in both your immediate family as well as one of your biological grandparents, that is a total of 2 points). Again, this is not your fault, but the research shows that you have a much higher risk of alcoholism with this genetic background.

POINTS: 1 or 2   **YOUR SCORE: _____**

16. You're convinced that there are certain activities that you do "better" drunk or high than you do sober. You think you are a much more interesting person drunk than sober. This is a tricky one to prove. In my case, I felt that I was significantly more creative and an out-of-the-box thinker when drinking than when I was sober (usually when developing management consulting presentations and reports). I still occasionally think that in my younger days this was true to some extent; however, as I got older, I would increasingly wake up the next day to find what I had written the night before to be so much gibberish. The singer/guitarist Joe Walsh recently had a great quote on this topic (albeit one you have to read carefully to understand):

> "It's a great denial for an artist to say that we need to experience the entire spectrum of emotions [from abusing drugs or alcohol], blah, blah, blah. Could (Jimi) Hendrix have played like that if he wasn't on acid? Probably not. Could (Ernest) Hemingway or (William) Faulkner have written all that literature if they weren't alcoholics? Probably not. Y'know, so I justified me with that kind of talkin' and reasoning—[with it] not really occurring to me that they're all dead because of it."[28]

Let's face facts—the vast, vast majority of people do NOT do anything better while drinking, so give yourself a point if you think so. Period.

A bit trickier part is the second sentence about being *more interesting* when drinking. Many people feel they are much more interesting and particularly funny when drinking. Here it may actually be true, particularly if confirmed by friends and colleagues ("Gee Ralph, you really are a great guy once you loosen up a bit" with drinks, etc.). Even if it is true on the surface, in my view it is usually a function of pent up innate charm or charisma being released by alcohol, *not* the creation of a personal characteristic that was never there. This is a very important distinction, and one to emphasize to yourself as you become sober. But in the meantime give yourself a point, as it indicates an extreme personality change, at least outwardly, and cause for concern.

POINTS: 1   **YOUR SCORE: _____**

17. Your appearance has materially changed in a way that cannot be wholly explained by aging. In particular you feel you have become uglier and/or fatter (or even much, much thinner, depending on circumstances) compared to your peers or how you seemed to be until relatively recently. Your skin seems permanently "*flushed*." You refuse to have your picture taken. Since this statement is subjective, look in the mirror, and then look at pictures before you started drinking heavily. Compare these photos with photos of your parents when they were your age (assuming they were not alcoholics) and try to reconcile the differences with and without alcohol. I would score this statement as more than one point if it were not, unfortunately, so subjective.[29]

POINTS: 1   **YOUR SCORE:** _____

18. **One or two days a week not drinking, or for special occasions, is considered a major accomplishment by you or your key loved one.**Your ability to abstain for this short period is usually used as ammunition in arguments with your spouse about how you are not an alcoholic and can "quit anytime I want to." Be honest as you can here, as it is one of those unavoidably subjective statements. A good mini-test is that you go to bed thinking "Hey, I can do this not-drinking thing" and then you drink the next day, often despite your best efforts.

POINTS: 1   **YOUR SCORE:** _____

19. **You buy more than two drinks on an airplane, or you get antsy when the flight attendant hasn't shown up for a while so you can buy your next one.** This might seem somewhat silly, but I'm convinced it is a valid indicator for road warrior alcoholics. Using the excuse of going to the bathroom to corner the attendant in the back and buying or begging more drinks also qualifies. Assaulting or abusing your flight attendant because she wouldn't serve you another drink earns you an instant "Addict" brand on your forehead with this one. I'd mention several celebrities that this happened to, but don't want to get sued.

POINTS: 1   **YOUR SCORE:** _____

20. **When you go out of town, you spend a great deal of time figuring out how to get your alcohol supply.** Sample questions to self in arriving: Where the hell is the closest liquor store to my hotel in Chicago? Is Illinois a "state" package store, or can I get vodka at a 7–11? Are there days of week/time of day restrictions for buying alcohol?

If you go wandering in an unfamiliar town at night regardless of the neighborhood or weather, this is another (and particularly bad) sign. If you **pre-planned or did research** about drinking *before* you even got on the plane or in the car that is even more troubling, **and worth 2 points. So is taking booze *with you* on the trip.**

POINTS: 1 or 2   **YOUR SCORE:** _____

Now for the Biggies—the "Big Five" as I call them in "Royally Fucking Up Your Life" —covering the truly fun aspects of alcoholism of legal problems, marriage loss, job loss, financial loss, and health problems. Most of these have some degree of subjectivity—it is, unfortunately, unavoidable. I can only use my personal experience and opinions to illustrate these points; everyone will have to decide for themselves if they are applicable, as they are extremely personal to the particulars of the alcoholic's life.

21. **You have *more* than one DUI *arrest* or equivalent (includes arrest for drunken behavior, etc.).** One DUI is "understandable." You were just dumb that night, or honestly thought you were ok. But more than one—come on! Besides not having the *Scared Straight* experience of a DUI arrest and prosecution to make you avoid drinking and driving, my view is that if you got caught two or more times, there are probably at least 10 (50? 100?) times that many where you drove drunk— *unable to control yourself and having whatever brains you possess going completely out the window.* I emphasize the word *arrest,* as it *still* counts even if you avoided conviction because of a good lawyer or on a technicality that had nothing to do with your blood alcohol level. No subjectivity at all on this one folks.[30]

POINTS: 3   **YOUR SCORE:** _____

22.   **More than one job lost directly or indirectly due to alcohol.** This is a tough one to prove, short of actual dismissal for being drunk on the job. Even if an employer suspects alcoholism in general, they legally are often constrained as to citing that as a cause for dismissal, particularly if it is viewed as a handicap by the applicable federal or state laws or union rules.

As a functional alcoholic (discussed earlier), the reasons for losing a job were difficult for me to discern in real-time, particularly since much of my work was project-based. Such projects were rarely cancelled once started, though they could easily not be renewed for a variety of reasons (budget, shifting priorities, future work could be done by internal resources, etc.) as well as dissatisfaction with the original work. In hindsight, I would say my alcoholism led to the loss of three or four projects and at least one job at a cost of tens of thousands of dollars in personal income. But I did not recognize/admit this until many years after the fact.

POINTS: 3   **YOUR SCORE:** _____

23.   **Marriage (or long relationship) breakup directly or indirectly due to alcohol.** This is easier to determine, at least if you accept the various declarations ("You are drinking too much") and ultimatums ("You need to stop drinking or I'm leaving you") by your partner.

However, these can easily be muddled at the time with the rationalization that your drinking is *due to* marital problems (e.g., an *effect*), and not the *cause of* the marital problems. I certainly thought this was true while my marriage was dissolving, and it wasn't until much later (after the divorce) that I recognized that my spouse might have been partially (but by no means completely) right (see, I'm in denial even after I'm sober!). I could write a whole novella on this topic alone, but it is not germane to this being a high potential indicator of addiction. Suffice it to say, you can often find many of your triggers if you dig deep down into the reasons for a serious relationship breakup.

POINTS: 3   **YOUR SCORE: _____**

24.   **Major financial loss, including bankruptcy or foreclosure directly or indirectly due to alcohol. OR you spend *a lot* of money on alcohol.** Includes making breathtakingly stupid investments that you knew were doomed but did anyway while you were under the influence. This financial loss can also obviously be tied to job loss to some degree as indicated above.

Financial loss is probably the most difficult to prove of the Big Five, particularly to an addict deep in denial. However, calculating how much each month was spent on alcohol is a quantifiable substitute and can be quite illuminating and impactful to the person, even if it barely scratches the financial surface. For me, it was approximately $400–$600 a month (you would be amazed at how liquor prices for the same brand/size can vary by store and state).Think about it: $5,000 to $7,000 a year is nothing to sneeze at, particularly if you are unemployed at the time. This figure is probably low if most of the drinking happens in a bar. Mini-test: If you spend more than $300 a month on your *personal* alcohol *consumption* (e.g., $10 a day or more) then you need to agree with this statement.

POINTS: 3   **YOUR SCORE: _____**

25.   **Major health issues attributable to alcohol, at least in part.** The bottom line is that most addicts' bodies (in my non-medical opinion) send their mind all sorts of messages that alcohol is fucking it up. But the mind says, "Message Undeliverable" much of the time—unfortunately often up until the time it is too late. I was very, very fortunate that I finally received the message (involuntarily), just before that happened.

"Proving" that alcohol is a major contributor to a significant health problem *should* be relatively easy—if you accept such statements from your doctor, that it is. However, many ailments where alcohol can be a major factor (again, see Level 4-Listen to Your Body! for the long list) can also be influenced by many other factors. So it is often difficult for the doctor to say *definitively* that alcohol is causing the affliction or moving it into very serious territory. Without that kind of absolute statement, it is easy to dismiss or ignore health as an "I Agree" to this statement.

The above also presumes that you actually *tell* your doctor how much and how often you drink. And do NOT shave a third off the quantity that you say you drink because you are embarrassed—been there, done that. A big challenge for many no doubt, but if you are not going to tell anyone else about how much you drink, **tell your doctor.** It may save your life. See Level 3—Listen to Your Body! for more information on different alcohol-related ailments.

POINTS: 3   **YOUR SCORE:** _____

                                               YOUR TOTAL: _____

DETERMINING YOUR QUIZ RESULTS

Total up all the points you recorded on a piece of paper or the scorecard provided in Appendix B. My view of the results is as follows:

• **7 Points or more**—A problem drinker, at least. Should be considered a wake-up call that you may be on the road to alcoholism.

• **12 Points or more**—Very likely have an addiction to alcohol. If you haven't crossed that line yet you are very, very close.

• **20 Points or more**—Absolutely no doubt about addiction, with extremely serious problems in your life very soon if not here already.

• **30+ Points**—If you don't find a way to stop drinking *immediately* you are headed to disastrous results within months.

Unfortunately, I easily answered "I Agree" to the majority of statements on the quiz. I won't tell you exactly how many points I scored, but it was definitely north of 12. I say that now that I am sober. But even though I would have answered differently to a few of the questions when I was drinking—e.g., I would have tried to weasel my way around the statements concerning job loss and health problems, for example. Despite all evidence to the contrary, I still would have easily racked up more than 12 points. I firmly believe that if I had such a checklist in my younger days, I would have admitted to being an alcoholic years earlier than I did. Who knows what would have happened then?

What Should You Do With the Results?

Ok, you've taken the quiz. Now what? While different people may react differently to an unpleasant score, my first suggestion is to step back and reflect on it for a while. If you've been thinking in the back of your mind that you *might* have a problem, your score may not come as a complete shock, but disturbing nonetheless. If you are (were), in complete denial, a high score may be far more of one. In both cases thinking about the results for a day or two, might be the best way to come to terms with the reality of your situation. You might even take the test again, though I would caution you to not change any of your initial answers unless there are clear-cut reasons to do so. Above all be honest—you have worked up the strength and courage to take the test, so why lie now?

If you already *knew* you were an alcoholic going into the test, use the results to validate how you came to that conclusion. More importantly you can use the results to fortify your determination when times get tough in later Levels where you may start to wonder if you really are an alcoholic. The best (worst) of us will wonder this occasionally, even if all the evidence in the world to the contrary is beating us on the head.

If you scored in the "Problem Drinker" territory, from about 7 points to 12, then I would strongly suggest taking the quiz again being as honest as you possibly can be. The big danger is that this can be a kind of no-mans-land, where you say "yes I drink a lot but I can control it if I need to." That would be fine if you actually *did* control it, but those who can yet don't are little different than actual alcoholics. The real tragedy would be using a low score to justify continued heavy drinking.

If your score was very low, say 5 or less, then again the first thing you should do is ask yourself if you were honest when taking the quiz. While it was very deliberately designed to avoid subjectivity (e.g. being able to weasel out of an honest answer), some questions are unavoidably so, such as the questions about job loss, marriage breakup, and financial problems. Since those questions are worth many points, answering "No" when reality shouts "Yes! will make a big difference in your total score. After all, it's very possible the direction you take in your life may depend on how you answer the questions, so why not do it honestly?

If you do believe a low score is accurate, then congratulations! But if you scored *some* points, use it as an early-warning mechanism and start to pay more attention to how much and why you drink, and in the process hopefully avoid the spiraling descent into alcoholism many of us have already taken.

Finally, in all scoring scenarios, you might talk over the results with a close friend or family member (in essence getting a jump on Level 4— Engage Friends and Family). You might even ask them to take the test acting like they were you, then comparing the results. It will set off an interesting conversation, I promise you, particularly if you scored yourself low and they do not.

This concludes the first and most important Level of the Conquer Program. Again, any program is bound to fail if you do not truly admit in your heart that you have a serious problem and need help. That was the goal of Level 1. Level 2, next, intends to get you to understand *why* you drink like you do.

LEVEL 2

Know Your Triggers

After accepting (however reluctantly and whatever the process that got you there) that you have an addiction to alcohol, *knowing* what triggers your drinking is the **SINGLE** most important Level toward Conquering Your Alcoholism. If you do not understand, *in detail*, what causes or motivates you to want to drink, how can you figure out how to stop? You can't develop a solution to a problem unless you know the underlying causes. In the context of alcoholism, these root causes are called your drinking "triggers." To figure what these triggers are, is the goal of this level, and to repeat: it is *absolutely critical* to the usefulness of the remaining levels and the Conquer Program overall.

In a nutshell, a "trigger" is someone, something, or some situation or circumstance that causes you to drink or want to drink. In essence, triggers are the "cravings" for the "relief" that alcohol can bring. There are two types of triggers:

• **External triggers** are people, places, things, times of day, days of the week, or situations and conditions that offer drinking opportunities or cause you to want to drink. These types of triggers are more obvious, predictable, and avoidable than internal triggers.

• **Internal triggers** can be puzzling because the urge to drink can seem to "pop up" in your head, sometimes before you are even aware of the actual reason. The urge may have been set off by a veritable legion of possibilities: a passing thought, deep reflection on something, outside influences that cause a reminder about something else in your head, all types of emotions—both positive and negative—such as excitement or frustration, a physical sensation such as a headache, tension, or nervousness, etc. These are particularly tough to deal with since, as they say, "It's all in your head."

● ●

A Note on Triggers (Mental Cravings) and Physical Dependence (Physical Cravings)

Cravings caused by the triggers described in this Level are distinct from physical-dependency "cravings" that start to occur once you are actually *physically dependent* on the chemical compounds within alcohol, where your mind and body have become so used to alcohol that it comes to view it as "necessary" to function "normally." Physical dependence generally requires consistent drinking of substantial amounts of alcohol over a substantial period. It is very likely your strongest trigger-based/mental cravings started well before you became physically addicted to alcohol. Detoxification—discussed extensively in Levels 5 and 11—is the process by which you break this physical dependence. The *mental* cravings for alcohol—those that you *associate* with it being used or "needed" to "deal with" various personal problems, issues, situations, and circumstances—are what are generally referred to as triggers throughout this book.

● ●

The above definitions are good to keep in mind. I don't distinguish between external and internal triggers in the rest of this book as they often tend to blur as you drill down on why a particular trigger makes you want to drink, which is a critical part of this program and the core goal of this Level. The definitions are good to keep in the back of your mind though, particular that of internal triggers, which can be irritating if not maddening because they can be so difficult to avoid.

There are MANY possible triggers for your drinking, or *really* making you want to drink. Here's a starter list: *anger, anxiety, boredom, change, children, chaos, death, depression, ego, envy, excitement, food, friends, frustration, fun, guilt, health problems, holidays, hunger, inertia, insomnia, job, loneliness, media, mid-life crisis, money, music, noise, overconfidence, pain, powerlessness, proximity, relationships, relatives, reminders, self-esteem, shame, smell, sex, social situations, special occasions, stress, taste, times of day, tired, unhappiness, eX (wife, etc.), weather,* and *yelling.*

Crap.

Yes, *everybody* encounters all or nearly all of these in one form or another, at one time or another. But to alcoholics, the first impulse, and second, and third is to "deal with" them by drinking. How in the hell are you supposed to stop drinking when you have to somehow deal with those every day, and alcohol has been your first, second, and third choice for who knows how many years? Well, the first thing you need to do is figure out which ones make you want to drink the most—in terms of frequency, amounts consumed, and above all the underlying *reasons* why they hit you particularly hard. That is what this Level is all about, and why it is the second most important foundational part in your program to stop drinking, right after admitting you actually have a real problem.

Hopefully, most if not all of your triggers will become apparent after you go through this trigger discussion. If not, re-read it in its entirety; there is a *lot* of detail and observations within each trigger discussion that may not be apparent in the first read. If after a re-read you still feel you somehow can't articulate all of the triggers—like you have missed one or two, but can't explain why—do not be discouraged. Continue through the rest of the program on how to deal with the triggers you *can* identify; it very well may help you to figure out what those missing ones are (or perhaps they are "hidden" by the more obvious ones). In addition, in Level 6—Rehab and Therapy, we discuss various types of therapies that may be useful in "uncovering" those triggers and/or delving deeper into the ones you "cleanly" identified. Even for people who feel that they nailed all their triggers after reading this Level, you might strongly consider finding a therapy/therapist for a few sessions where you can explore them in even greater detail.

An Important Note on Trigger and Level Capitalization

Throughout the remainder of this book, when referring to specific triggers introduced in this Level, the first letter of the trigger will usually be capitalized, as in Angry, Boredom, Frustration, etc. This capitalization is to make clear that I am referring to the trigger and all associated information discussed in that trigger's respective chapter. The purpose is also to reinforce the importance of those triggers and to, in effect, make them subject areas (in effect making them nouns if they were not already) versus a typical verb, adjective, or non-capitalized noun that might otherwise be lost or misinterpreted in the broader sentence or paragraph. I also use this approach to the term "Level," where capitalization denotes reference to that chapter/defense Level as a whole, versus lower case "level" that could mean a measure of something, like "some level of satisfaction."

WHY KNOWING YOUR TRIGGERS IS SO CRITICAL
TO BEING SOBER

One analogy I use is comparing alcoholism to a deep body wound, and that triggers are infections that keep it from healing. In my opinion, the vast majority of alcohol treatment programs take a "Band-Aid" approach to the alcoholism wound; they try to patch-up the wound while not doing an adequate job of treating the underlying infection.

A very similar way of looking at it is using the "levels of defense" concept introduced at the beginning of this book. Since alcoholics have little in the way of "natural" defenses to alcohol (e.g., akin to your immune system being compromised in the infected wound analogy), we have to build up a new set of defenses against the "attacks" of alcohol. The forms of alcohol attack—and the wounds and infections they can inflict—come in the forms of triggers.

If you don't know your enemy, and are not prepared for the huge variety of weapons it will use to attack you, then you stand a very good chance of being defeated. *Truly* knowing your triggers is essential in any long-term defense against alcoholism and is a core tenet of The Conquer Program.

Thus, as you go through the rest of this book/program beyond this Level, triggers will *repeatedly* come up in various ways, particularly in avoiding them, minimizing their impact, and even occasionally using them to your advantage. Once you accomplish this, you stand a *much* better chance of living a life without having to obsess about not drinking on a daily basis. Unless you plan on becoming a monk and living in a Tibetan cave the rest of your days, *you will NEVER be able to get away from all of your triggers all of the time.*

So your defenses need to be prepared for and ready to go at any time! But first you have to understand the types of attacks—triggers—that you are vulnerable to having.

As Figure 9 on the next page indicates, there are dozens of triggers that can attack an alcoholic over the course of their day, week, month, and life. For different people, some of the triggers may not be applicable at all; other times they may only occasionally occur; and for still others the alcoholic may feel they are constantly under attack. *It will vary greatly person by person.*

Figure 9: The Conquer Program Trigger Wheel

Most alcoholics will have somewhere between 6 and 12 very significant or "major" triggers. These are triggers that *really* make you want to drink, *more often than not*. They can make you want to drink *all by themselves*, e.g. independently of anything else going on in your life, but they also can set off a number of "related" triggers (discussed shortly). Since most of us can come up with past situations where nearly all of the triggers listed here came into play in some form or another, sorting out which ones are truly *major* can be challenging.

To add to the complexity, an alcoholic's defenses may be weaker for some triggers than others (indicated by the different color levels). Worse still the strength of the defense may vary depending on the hour of the day, day of the week, personal living environment at any given time, how their day at the job went, and on and on and on. This complexity and variability makes it almost impossible to build ONE set of defenses against an alcohol attack; thus, *a multiple-level defense is essential to deal with all the possible attacks all of the time in all possible situations and circumstances.*

These triggers are by no means mutually exclusive (e.g., there is some overlap in their definitions and impact), nor do all triggers impact large portions of alcoholics. Frustration, for example, is arguably a trigger for many people in some form—either directly or via a related trigger—but

Times of Day may only affect a small percentage of alcoholics. But it is very likely that nearly every alcoholic has more than one, possibly several. What they are *specifically* is what we are trying to get to the bottom of in this Level.

To add to this incredible diversity of possible attacks and needed defenses, many of these can occur at the same time. For example, Job problems can occur at the same time you are having Relationship difficulties with Money and Health problems preying on your mind as well, requiring simultaneous (and often different) defenses. Or one trigger can cause or "activate" other triggers, often multiple ones in a kind of chain reaction. These are called "related triggers" and are discussed more in the next section.

Finally, *it is very important to understand how your triggers can change over time, both while you are drinking and after you get sober.* The triggers themselves may change, the number of triggers may increase or decrease, and/or their priorities may change.

For example, it is very possible the number of triggers will increase as you "progress" in your alcoholism. This increase is consistent with the Alcoholism and Trigger Cycle introduced in Level 1. You may also find that the number of your triggers *decrease,* and become less severe overall, once you are sober. This decrease is illustrated in my personal experience in Figure 10 below and discussed more in Level 13—Develop Your Defense Progressions, particularly as it relates to multiple "stages" of sobriety.

Example of Alcoholism Triggers Evolution

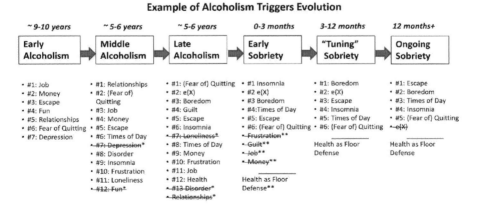

~ 9-10 years	~ 5-6 years	~ 5-6 years	0-3 months	3-12 months	12 months+
Early Alcoholism	**Middle Alcoholism**	**Late Alcoholism**	**Early Sobriety**	**"Tuning" Sobriety**	**Ongoing Sobriety**
• #1: Job	• #1: Relationships	• #1: (Fear of) Quitting	• #1 Insomnia	• #1: Boredom	• #1: Escape
• #2: Money	• #2: (Fear of) Quitting	• #2: e(X)	• #2 e(X)	• #2: e(X)	• #2: Boredom
• #3: Escape	• #3: Job	• #3: Boredom	• #3 Boredom	• #3: Escape	• #3: Times of Day
• #4: Fun	• #4: Money	• #4: Guilt	• #4:Times of Day	• #4: Insomnia	• #4: Insomnia
• #5: Relationships	• #5: Escape	• #5: Escape	• #5: Escape	• #5: Times of Day	• #5: (Fear of) Quitting
• #6: Fear of Quitting	• #6: Times of Day	• #6: Insomnia	• #6: (Fear of) Quitting	• #6: (Fear of) Quitting	• e(X)
• #7: Depression	• #7: Depression*	• #7: Loneliness*	• Frustration**		
	• #8: Disorder	• #8: Times of Day	• Guilt**	Health as Floor Defense	Health as Floor Defense
	• #9: Insomnia	• #9: Money	• Job**		
	• #10: Frustration	• #10: Frustration	• Money**		
	• #11: Loneliness	• #11: Job			
	• #12: Fun*	• #12: Health	Health as Floor Defense**		
		• #13 Disorder*			
		• Relationships*			

Figure 10: Example of Trigger Evolution

As of this publication I have 5 triggers, whereas I once had more than double that number—up to 13 in the years just before I became sober. Using this program, I was able to whittle them down, with those remaining becoming much less "intense" as time goes on, and my defenses perfected. With this reduction in number and intensity of major triggers also means that their *related triggers* are also much fewer and less intense, the importance of which is discussed next.

TRIGGER INTERRELATIONSHIPS— A MISSING LINK IN ALCOHOLISM TREATMENT?

Even when traditional treatment programs go through some degree of extensive trigger discussion, they nearly always "treat" these triggers as "standalone," that is, that the effects that that trigger has on your drinking habits is due to that trigger *all by itself.*

To a certain degree that is understandable, as many triggers such as Anger, Anxiety and Depression have legions of doctors, numerous medications, and untold millions of dollars dedicated to understanding and treating those disorders. Many other triggers have similar, if not as well-known (and funded) professional and medical attention given to them. For the vast majority of triggers, we will discuss I have tried to research the latest medical viewpoints on the root of these conditions and potential ways of dealing with them medically or otherwise. But for each trigger that you feel applies to you, I would strongly encourage you to do your own research as there is a huge amount of material out there to consider—even for "smaller" triggers.

And perhaps even worse, certain situations in an alcoholic's daily, historical, or ongoing life can "activate" or trigger other triggers! For example, Boredom can make you Lonely, which in turn might make you want to go out with friends who drink (causing direct or indirect Peer Pressure), which may take you to a place where Proximity and Smell of nearby alcohol has you drooling for a Taste of alcohol to help you Escape from other problems in your life. It is ***incredibly*** difficult to defend against alcohol in these circumstances! Figure 11 at right illustrates some of the possible relationships between triggers. There are dozens.

Unfortunately there is relatively little in existing alcohol treatment literature that addresses the nature of these multiple/cascading types of relationships; most multi-condition analysis is focused on what is called *Dual-Diagnosis*[1] conditions, such as having clinical Depression and alco-

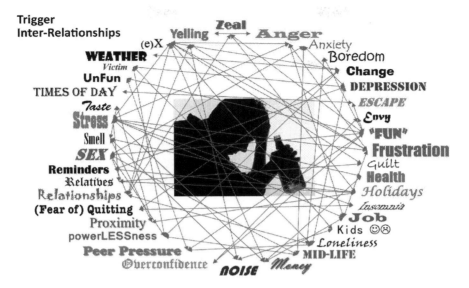

Figure 11: The Complexity of Trigger Inter-Relationships

hol dependency at the same time. While helpful to those suffering both of (or only) those conditions simultaneously, it hardly scrapes the surface of all the other possible combinations. Particularly when they don't occur very often—but when they do they are an extremely serious threat to your sobriety.

But knowledge is power as they say, and knowing about how these triggers and their inter-relationships (I call them *"Related Triggers"*) can affect you *personally* is an absolutely essential part of being able to craft your defenses against alcohol. That is why this Level consumes by far the largest single portion of this book—there are dozens of possible triggers to consider (and it is very likely there are many other trigger/trigger combinations that are not covered here). Believe me, it is time well worth spending, and again, absolutely critical to your success in the broader Conquer Program.

STARTING TO BUILD YOUR TRIGGER DEFENSES

As you go through each trigger analysis, look for each of the elements discussed below. They will help you in fully understanding the deeper aspects of the trigger, and—*if applicable*—help you identify and implement ways of defending against it.

- **Overview and description.** What the trigger *is* and *is not,* including signs it can be a significant or *major trigger* for you: that it makes you drink more often than not and that it can do so independently of any other triggers, and/or can set off other "related triggers" that can quickly increase your desire to drink.

Even if you do not think a trigger is applicable to you personally, I would encourage you to read the rest of each trigger's discussion thoroughly. Not only might you change your mind, the trigger may be "related" to another that *is* significant to you, and thus very important to include in selecting and building your defenses for some situations.

- **Views from other alcoholics.** Testimonials from other alcoholics (current and former) on how the trigger affected them; and sometimes ideas on how they coped with it. These are very important in that they not only bring to life how a trigger can really manifest itself in someone's life, but can help you think of similar situations/feelings in your own life to help you decide if a trigger is truly "significant."

- **Key facts and professional insights.** Most triggers include research from the medical and psychiatric professions that seem particularly insightful and useable. This research will help you understand the deeper causes of a particular trigger, and how it might have come to be one for you personally—e.g., help you identify the "root cause."

- **Tips for dealing with the trigger without alcohol.** Here is where we start the actual defense building. These are handy ideas for dealing with the trigger, based on the above data and other sources, sometimes including my own experience. View these as starting points to think about personal, *practical* coping and defense mechanisms.

- **"Related" Triggers.** As introduced in the previous section, this describes how this trigger can "activate" or "be activated by" other triggers. The ones listed for each trigger are by no means intended to be all-inclusive, but instead are ones—often in light of the above information—that have a high likelihood of occurring frequently.

- **Key Defense Levels.** This lists what other Levels in the Conquer Program can be of particular use in defending against the trigger. These Levels (and how you implement them) can be used along with the Tips to defend against the trigger, or in combination with other Levels of defense.

What Are the Differences Between Tips and Key Defense Levels?

Both have (in my opinion) high potential for helping you defend against the particular trigger attack. However, many of the Tips may not be applicable for your situation, general lifestyle, and/or personality. So you might not use many of them, or even any of them (I urge you to try to use at least one tip though).

In contrast, at least one Key Defense Level should be applicable for *all* of you in one form or another. As such, I list them separately and after Tips; you *have* to have *at least one* Defense Level in *any* defense progression; otherwise the progression will be very weak—it would go directly from a tip to your floor defenses. "Floor" Defenses are those that are there for most if not all of your triggers in one form or another and you can use when all other defenses fail. This defense will vary greatly by person and is used as a kind of last resort. Floor Defenses are discussed in much more detail in Level 13—Develop Your Defense Progressions.

Again, a key premise of The Conquer Program is that no one method/tip/ approach/defense will work all the time for all situations. In fact, many of them will weaken the alcohol attack, which will increase the odds of the next Tip/Level working for you.

Appendix B includes a number of checklists and templates that you can use in a variety of ways as you progress throughout this program. Before you read any further, I would strongly encourage you to review this appendix, and even make copies of the various lists and templates that you can fill out as you read the rest of this book.

The real power of the Conquer Program shows itself when you *combine* all these—the Tips that are applicable for each trigger, the Tips for their Related Triggers, and the Levels of Defense that support these trigger defenses and provide a broader structure for them.

The process of accumulating tips and defenses starts in this Level and continues throughout Levels 3 to 12. The final Level, Level 13 (Develop Your Defense Progressions), puts them all together in various combinations best *for you* to best defend against *your* personal triggers. Combining them is specifically for the purpose of trying to defend against *all* of the ways that alcohol can attack you *all* of the time. Alcohol only has to attack you successfully *once* for your life to get back on the road to destruction—you have to defend yourself *all* the time.

Not only are combining these tips and ideas from other Levels together very powerful, so can *the specific order in which you do them.* You might not want to call your best friend (part of Level 4—Engage Friends and Family) first thing every time you have an alcohol-related problem—that could get old after a while. Or you might try to do so but they are not available. So in those circumstances instead you might first want to work on a particular hobby (Level 9) to get your mind off the trigger. If that is not enough, you might choose to do something spiritual (Level 10) such as meditate or read certain literature. If that still is not enough, then going to an alcoholic community meeting (Level 6) might be just the ticket. Even if any given *individual* defense is not successful in itself, it *will* be helpful in weakening the triggering attack so your next defense is that much more likely to succeed.[2]

This kind of sequence of defenses is called a "progression," and you will build it to be unique to you, your circumstances, and the best defenses (Tips and Levels) available to you *at the time* you need them. In different circumstances (e.g., triggers and the particulars involving them) you might do a completely different progression. For example you might first call your therapist (Level 7), and/or eat something particularly pleasant (or unpleasant; see Level 12—Make Yourself Sick of Alcohol), then contemplate how drinking might cause you severe health problems (Level 3—Listen to Your Body!). Helping you develop these combinations and in what order is what Level 13—Develop Your Defense Progressions is all about.

All this might sound pretty damn complicated. From a certain perspective it can be, because like many complicated things in life there usually is not one, simple, "magic" solution (if only!) and that is certainly the case when it comes to your drinking in general and for dealing with your drinking triggers in particular.

But another way to look at it is very simple: something (trigger or triggers) makes you want to drink. You have to find something else to think about or do (the tips and levels of defense) so you *won't* drink.

DRINKING TRIGGERS FROM A TO Z

When I first started considering drinking triggers, my first approach was to focus on what I knew to be—through rehab, therapy and community meetings—my major triggers: Boredom, Escape, Insomnia, Times of Day, (Fear of) Quitting, and my eX were some of the biggies, plus a few others playing somewhat lesser roles. I was not able to articulate all of my personal specific triggers immediately, nor their root causes. It was only over the course of doing the research and writing this book that some of the less obvious ones became clear to me. Most importantly, I came to realize that over time my triggers changed in type, intensity, and priority.

Then I thought back to some of the acronyms taught in rehab to help in remembering triggers, such as HALT: **H**ungry (many people replace this with **H**orny), **A**ngry, **L**onely, **T**ired; and the RIDs: **R**estless, **I**rritable, and **D**iscontent. RID was fairly useful, HALT sometimes so. In total these two well bandied-about acronyms touched only a small portion of my triggers; all the other ones came up as one-offs. Even worse, little context nor broader association of one trigger with another was ever discussed in any level of detail in the rehab and therapy programs I went through.

The key point is that all those various treatment programs never had anything resembling a comprehensive list of triggers, in one place, easily referenced, and discussed in *useable,* helpful detail. Even worse, the information provided on *specific* triggers was fragmented—different sources saying different things on the same topic—and many triggers having little in the way of scientific research providing insight into the *why* it could be a trigger, *how* it might manifest itself, and not all that much on *what* I should do to deal with them beyond very general, not-trigger-specific "guidance" and step-program mantras.

These observations and experiences evolved into the alphabetical A to Z trigger list discussed below. Some letters were difficult to limit to one trigger, so some of them have two, three, or even four when I thought that had a strong chance of applying to many alcoholics. One or two (like the letter "Z") was a bit of a force fit I admit.

Again, this list is not intended to be all inclusive of all possible triggers let alone their potential interrelationships, but it does cover—in my opinion—the most likely ones for the majority of alcoholics. If your specific trigger or trigger interrelationship is not discussed in the following discussion, do not despair. Instead, apply the same analysis approach used below to the additional ones: 1) research its definition and underlying causes; 2) find others alcoholics who have similar feelings and experiences (through internet searches and community meetings); 3) understand its related triggers and if, how, and in what progression they occur for you, and 4) research things you might do ("tips") for dealing with that trigger/related triggers *without* alcohol.

To repeat, it is CRITICAL that you *accurately* **and** *comprehensively,* **and** *in as much detail as possible* **determine your triggers.** *It is ESSENTIAL for success.* In this program or any other.

The level of detail is critical, as you need to get as close to the root cause of the trigger as possible. Why? Because at the end of the day your triggers are *your* triggers—they impact you in ways personal and even unique to your personality, history, and circumstances. In addition, some triggers listed here, such as Money or Stress, can be caused by literally dozens of different reasons, and how you defend against them will depend on those specific reasons.

For example, while Money (the lack of) may be sufficient for some, for many others it may be too general. Worrying about paying the rent (but not your credit card) may be a specific "Money" trigger for you. Frustration with your spouse's spending habits, or eX's[3] alimony demands are other examples of how you need to "peel the onion" to get at the core triggers (and an example of how triggers can be closely related, as Frustration itself is a trigger in this example).

Getting underneath the covers on the reasons for your Stress is another example. Just saying you are "Stressed" will do **nothing** to help you de-stress without alcohol; you *have* to get to the underlying cause(s). Hopefully, you get the idea. The triggers are covered in alphabetical order, and I strongly encourage you to review all of them, even if you think you know your major ones, since others could well be significant related triggers.

ANGER

Anger happens to be first alphabetically in this discussion of triggers, but it is (arguably) the worst of all of them due to the *immediate, sometimes deadly* negative impact that it can have on a situation, relationship, or even a life.

There are two dimensions to Anger in the context of drinking: 1) How getting Angry makes you *want* to drink (e.g., a "true" trigger), and 2) How drinking makes you more prone to *becoming* angry. In true chicken-and-egg fashion, a too common scenario is where a person starts drinking because he or she is Angry—proceeds to get angrier due to the effects of the alcohol—which in turn results in him/her drinking even more, which results in . . . an extremely volatile progression and escalation of whatever caused the Anger in the first place.

We will focus on the "true" trigger aspects here; the escalation and results are a major issue of course and discussed in the Level 1—Are You An Alcoholic? chapter. But in truth it is a wholly separate, extremely complex topic outside the scope of this book.

Personally and in retrospect, while Anger did accompany my drinking on occasion, I'd be hard pressed to call it a personal major trigger. But, unfortunately, for many it is one.

> *"Stress and my inability to express unhappiness and anger lead to my recent relapse, I am now sharing more at meetings and it's helping a lot."*
>
> reptilewoman, alcoholism.about.com

Reptilewoman's sharing very likely has much more detail that she didn't post online. Since just being unhappy and Angry, at a high level, won't be of much use to anyone, it is clear that sharing in meetings (see Level 7—Join a Community) helped her articulate the detailed reasons for her unhappiness and Anger. *As with all triggers, you HAVE to get at the root cause of the underlying feelings and drivers of what is causing you to want to drink because of that trigger.*

> *Anger will trigger me big time. I have three responses to anger: run away, shut down or explode. I have been sober for one year. I used to drink away my anger. Now, I call my sponsor and/or go to a meeting. I also journal. That helps a lot!*
>
> qwriter, alcoholism.about.com

This testimonial starts to illustrate how a deeper understanding of your reaction to a trigger—in this case Anger—helps you articulate how you can and do react to certain situations. In the above testimonial, "gwriter" understands that he can either run away (which is a poor term for a good possible response), shut down (which is not necessarily good, depending on how he does it) or explode (which is likely not good in any situation). He found that talking to someone in his community (see Level 7) and journaling (a new hobby; see Level 9) could diffuse the Anger without drinking. This testimonial is also a basic example of him following his "progressions" for dealing with Anger—e.g., call his sponsor, and/or journal. How you develop progressions is the culmination of The Conquer Program and is discussed in Level 13. But you've got a lot to do before you are ready for that Level!

Everybody intuitively understands what Anger is and recognizes when they are Angry (at least they do when they are sober). But it doesn't have to be full-fledged Anger to make you want to drink; milder forms such as "irritated" or "annoyed" can be enough.

> *My biggest triggers seem to be when someone or something annoys me. Then I think it's ok to go and drink because I am annoyed. Like drinking the poison, hoping the other persons dies!*
>
> guest joni, alcoholism.about.com

Interestingly, while there is a ton of material and research about Anger (and its consequences) *caused* by drinking, there seems much less about Anger *causing* you to drink. *Alcoholrehab.com* has one of the best assessments about Anger and alcohol that I could find, excerpted below.

> For many alcoholics, the urge to drink can be directly linked to their level of anger. Some turn to alcohol to calm feelings of anger; others feel justified to relapse because a friend or a loved one has made them feel angry. In any case, **anger is both a catalyst and a byproduct of alcoholism.**

> **Since anger plays such a central role in the lives of so many alcoholics, learning to manage its effect is central to overcoming an addiction.** Experts at alcohol rehab centers are aware of this, and many incorporate anger management courses into their treatment programs.

> **It is important to consider the difference between anger as an emotional state versus a personality trait.** Chronic anger falls into the latter category, and this is the variety of interest to alcohol rehabilitation programs. A person prone to chronic anger will subconsciously seek out stimuli that activate anger and aggression. Anger can manifest without an immediate cause, and this tendency increases when alcohol is involved.

Another study found that **male-on-female physical abuse is eight times more likely when the man has been drinking.** This simple but profound statistic underscores the importance of working through anger and aggression while seeking alcohol rehabilitation. Given the positive link between intoxication and anger, dealing with one inadvertently addresses the other as well.

Anger Triggers Relapse—Anger plays a central role in poor decision making, which can lead to relapse for a recovering alcoholic. As avoiding relapse is one of the greatest challenges for recovering alcoholics, dealing with latent or unresolved anger is essential. Those who avoid engaging this relapse trigger limit their chances of success.

Anger and Alcohol Are Both Addictive—There are reasons beyond curbing the likelihood of relapse that prompt alcoholics to address unresolved anger. **Anger can actually become an addiction in itself** and can be treated alongside other addictive behaviors. Alcoholics receiving treatment and rehab services are in an ideal position to address an anger addiction as well.[4]

I was fascinated by the assertion that Anger could be an addiction in itself. Not at all to belittle that concept, but it might explain a lot of what you read in the tabloids.

In some cases, an alcoholic may not even understand how badly alcohol affects him or her, even when it comes to outbursts of Anger while drinking. These are truly unfortunate situations, particularly for the family, and often can only be "solved" by drastic measures:

> *My husband of 18 years has been a violent drunk—he's got a great job, wonderful kids and wife who love him, beautiful home, most would wish for, right? But alcohol has ruined his life and ours—we have over the years lost all trust in him, destroying the depth of love we had. Alcohol changes him into Jekyll & Hyde. He has been violent over the years where we have had to leave the home for protection. We had to force him out through authority.*

Guest Hope, alcoholism.about.com

Medical Contributors to Anger

One potentially significant contributor to Anger may be your physical Health, such as high blood pressure. Blood pressure refers to the pressure with which the blood flows in your arteries, used to measure and determine the cardiovascular health of a person. *High blood pressure* means higher tension in the arteries as the blood flows through them. Heavy alcohol intake, obesity, heredity, sedentary lifestyle, and poor diet are some of the factors that can lead to high blood pressure.[5]

In hindsight, before I realized I had high blood pressure and started taking medicine for it I was very quick to lose my temper. According to the Mayo Clinic[6], drinking too much alcohol can raise blood pressure to unhealthy levels. Having more than three drinks in one sitting increases your blood pressure temporarily and repeated binge drinking can lead to long-term increases. I think I easily qualified. I also no longer have high blood pressure since I've stopped drinking.

There are many other health factors—physical and mental—that can increase stress on your bodily systems and in turn how susceptible you can be to certain kinds of triggers, including Anger. This is a key reason for doing a comprehensive health assessment (in close consultation with your doctor) and is the third foundation Level in Phase 1. This is also covered in the Stress trigger discussion later in this Level.

Even if you do not drink much, or do not fit the definition of an alcoholic as defined earlier (particularly in the Conquer Quiz), but you DO get Angry often when you drink, you should strongly consider either a) abstaining, or b) drinking only by yourself, or with people with whom you *never* get angry. You, your friends, and particularly your loved ones will be *much* happier, without question.

Tips for Dealing with Anger without Alcohol

Some ideas common in numerous sources include:

• Remove yourself from the situation, e.g., get the hell away from whatever or whoever is pissing you off.

• Do something relaxing: listen to soft music, journal (e.g., write out your feelings), garden, talk to your pet.

• Talk to someone (a person) who is a good listener and not a gossip.

• Take a relaxing shower. The shower could be hot or cold, depending on many things.

• Talk to/make up with the person who "caused" the Anger. Do this after you have calmed down—it will go a long way to preventing the event from happening again. If making up is not an option, try—somehow—to make the best out of a bad situation, looking for *some* way to make lemonade out of lemons so to speak.

There are other, less conventional things you can do for immediate, convenient, and safe venting and draining of your anger. These can include:[7]

• Punch something—NOT someone (preferably soft, e.g., not a wall).

• Go for a fast walk or a run.

• Listen to angry music. Some ideas/examples: Alanis Morissette: *You Oughta Know*; Nirvana: *Smells Like Teen Spirit*; *many* kinds of heavy metal music such as Metallica's *And Justice for All*. A more recent addition: *Icona Pop—I Love It*.

• Scream. Not around someone who is likely to call 911.

• Engage in vigorous exercise (sit ups, push-ups, boxing a punching bag, etc.).

• Throw ice cubes against a shower wall or bathtub.

• Squeeze an ice cube tightly.

• Scrunch up some paper, unscrunch it and then rescrunch it again.

• Destroy something (of little or no value, e.g., a book or a toy).

• Stomp on empty cans (with shoes).

• Have a pillow fight with your wall.

• Rip up an old newspaper or a phone book.

• Get your hands on some Play-Doh or Plasticine[8]. Throw it. Smash it.

• Break sticks.

• Find something you want to tear (for example, let's say you go with the newspaper). Start off slowly and start ripping and saying why you are angry. Tell it why you are mad. Start ripping it faster. You may end up swearing, yelling, crying . . . it helps to vent.

Lemons into Lemonade Tip: Reflect on what your anger was about. Many times not *all* the reasons for your anger will be obvious, and others may be flat-out misinterpretations of the situation. Also, for some Anger-generating situations you may not be able to articulate precisely *why* you are angry. Figuring out why may help you in getting angry in similar situations again.

Overall Tip: If you feel that Anger is a major, frequent trigger for you, and *in particular* you frequently get overtly violent (e.g., often yelling, screaming, physically aggressive), I would encourage you to: A) see your medical doctor to see if there is an underlying contributor such as high blood pressure, and/or B) seek out anger management treatment, perhaps in coordination with a Rehab and Therapy program (if you are at that logical stage in the program). A search using the term "alcohol rehab anger management specialist" will start you in that direction.

Related Triggers: Many other triggers can cause Anger, notably Frustration, Job, Kids, Relationships, Stress, eX, and Yelling. Anger can activate triggers such as Anxiety, the desire to Escape, Health (such as elevated blood pressure), Stress, and Yelling.

Key Defense Levels: Engage Friends and Family, Rehab and Therapy (talk to a therapist), Join a Community (chill out in a neutral, understanding environment), Consider Spirituality

ANXIETY (INCLUDES WORRY)

Anxiety is another condition that can both *cause* drinking and *be caused* by drinking. As with many words or phrases associated with addiction, it is very important to have a clear and common definition before we get into a more detailed discussion:

> **Anxiety:** A displeasing feeling of fear and concern; or, a state of uneasiness and apprehension, particularly about the future.[9]

Everyone gets anxious at various points in their lives: before a big test; a public speech, flying on an airplane; meeting the future in-laws, etc. Generally it is not a big deal and passes quickly after the event has started or completed. It can even be motivational: studying hard for the test, repeatedly practicing the speech in front of a mirror, etc.

For some people this anxiety becomes far more insidious; occurring more often, in more situations, and in greater intensity. Actual anxiety disorders involve *"an excessive or inappropriate state of arousal characterized by feelings of apprehension, uncertainty, or fear."*[10]

●●●

Medical Categories of Anxiety

There are several types of Anxiety classified according to the severity and duration of their symptoms and specific behavioral characteristics. Categories include:

- Generalized anxiety disorder (GAD)

- Panic disorder

- Phobias

- Obsessive-compulsive disorder (OCD)

- Post-traumatic stress disorder (PTSD)

- Separation anxiety disorder (which is almost always seen in children)

GAD and panic disorder are the most common. Anxiety disorders are usually caused by a combination of psychological, physical, and genetic factors, and treatment is, in general, very effective.[11]

●●

The word is derived from the Latin, *angere,* which means to choke or strangle. The anxiety response is often not triggered by a real threat, but it can still paralyze the individual into inaction or withdrawal. It can become a very destructive force in their lives—impacting much of their mindset and thoughts of their daily lives. In some instances, the symptoms of anxiety will be what drove them to drink, in others drinking can make them anxious, and even cause *panic attacks*.[12]

> *I drink every day, 10 to 12 beers a day for years now, no shame here, I love it except for the anxiety (panic attacks) I suffer from time to time at work.*
> Guest Joe, alcoholism.about.com

Throughout this book, I use my experience in additional testimonials and ideas for dealing with a particular trigger such as the next one, Boredom. While I do not suffer from Anxiety as a general rule, I have experienced it in severe form, specifically panic attacks after I was hospitalized/confined to my home several times in less than a year.

During these attacks, I would have extreme claustrophobia. I couldn't sleep next to a wall so slept on the floor. I would stand in the hallway when I was visiting my doctor because being in a closed room freaked me out. In the dead of winter, I would stay outside until I nearly froze. I can now tell you from personal experience that when people say "What are you worried about?," or "Just calm down and relax" in response to severe Anxiety episodes that those people don't have a clue what they are talking about. A severe Anxiety-episode is *extremely* unpleasant—and I can't imagine going through life while dealing with clinical Anxiety much of the time. It is no surprise to me that sufferers are very tempted to self-medicate. In my case my doctor helped me through the episodes with counseling and medication until I could finally get up and out.

People who manage Anxiety successfully without alcohol can find that heavy drinking can actually make it worse, creatively called "alcohol-induced anxiety."

> *I am a 26-year-old female who started drinking once in a while when I was 18. Never really cared for it, until this past year when I found myself drinking almost every day if not every day just to function. I started to do it, to cope with my anxiety now to only find it is worse. I recently began shaking when I don't drink, extreme anxiety, sweating etc. and it is such a scary feeling. I fear seizures too if I completely quit and worry I may have liver damage.*
>
> guest seeking help, alcoholism.about.com

Alcohol can induce anxiety because of its chemical effects—a toxin causing havoc on your mind and body. Many anxious alcoholics drink because for them it has an *initial* calming effect, which increases the desire to drink every time an anxiety attack comes on, never mind that the effect goes away unless more drinking occurs, and builds up tolerance for future "calming" that requires ever increasing amounts to result in the same effect.

● ●

Anxiety Versus Worry

People with generalized anxiety disorder (GAD) are the worry experts. It's not uncommon for people with the disorder to assume that they are locked into daily uncontrollable worry. Untreated, these individuals learn to compensate in other ways, often settling for a lower quality of life; resigning themselves to physical and emotional discomfort.

This silent suffering can make diagnosing GAD difficult. It's also further complicated *because a certain amount of anxiety and worry are normal,* and other medical disorders can be involved as well.

If someone suspects they have GAD, it's very important for them to reflect on what situations cause anxious feelings, how long they have experienced these feelings and if the worry is reasonable. For example, someone in their 30s with no medical problems who has had two normal physical examinations in the past six months but spends the day worrying about their health may be experiencing GAD.

Most people with GAD describe themselves as constant worriers and acknowledge that this approach to situations is something they have done their entire lives. Often others describe them as "high strung," "nervous" or "tense."

But it's helpful to recognize this constant anxiety as a treatable disorder, not a quirk or an inherent character weakness. *Remember that heightened anxiety or worry has a purpose,* but for people with GAD, routine activities are perceived as risky, and this perception is strong and steadfast.

Excessive worry may change through the lifecycle in patients with GAD. For example, as children/students, the focus of distress might be grades, clothing or getting into the "right" school. These objects of concern can become so intense that studying becomes impossible.

In adulthood, different themes emerge. For example, concern over the health of the family might intensify to the point that it's impossible to allow a child to walk from the front door to a school bus without fearing for their safety. Anxiety over job security and/or promotion can reach the point that it interferes with performance because the worry interferes with the ability to concentrate on anything else.

For older people, end of life issues become the focus. Themes of catastrophic thinking may include who will take care of them if they become ill or what should they do with their money?

While the themes may vary with age and from person to person, the common thread is the same: chronic and exaggerated worry over situations and topics that can't be turned off at will. Whether it's an uncommon dread of missing appointments, worry about routine tasks, such as needing to change the car oil, or daily concern about finances despite being financially secure, the thoughts can interfere with daily life functions.

Regardless of the reason, once diagnosed, GAD is very treatable. Treatment methods include medication and cognitive-behavior therapy[13]. Having a diagnosis by a medical professional helps the person accept that this is a real disorder and treatment can be refocused on the underlying cause for physical and emotional pain.[14]

● ●

One major related trigger for Anxiety is significant Change in one's environment and associated circumstances. Here Anxiety is "activated" by that trigger and is also causing a *cascade* of other triggers that soon has the Anxiety-prone individual reaching for the bottle.

For example, major Change in one's surroundings and day-to-day activities can cause Depression, Insomnia, Loneliness, Relationship problems, and even Disorder (e.g., moving). It doesn't end there: Guilt (e.g., another upending of your children's lives), Mid-Life Crisis (last child out of the nest, menopause), and Powerlessness (feeling unable to control what is happening) can also come into play, many of which directly impact the anxiety disorders listed earlier. No small wonder that significant Change events can cause extreme Anxiety—the ripple effects are enormous!

As I discussed in the Phase 1 introduction, there are very distinct differences between women and men on how they view alcohol and react to alcohol. Certain triggers in particular—including Anxiety—and their related triggers seem to manifest themselves very differently in "methods" and frequency. Women are *twice* as susceptible to clinically defined Anxiety and Depression, and *twice* as likely as men to "deal with" them by using alcohol.[15] This increased susceptibility makes recognizing severe Anxiety and seeking professional help especially important.

Tips for Dealing with Anxiety without Alcohol

Treating Anxiety is a very specialized field, so if yours is so severe that you are seeing a therapist for it, I would *strongly* encourage you to open up to them about your drinking to see how they might adjust your treatment. If you do not see one, and you feel Anxiety is a major trigger for you, I would also strongly encourage you to seek out professional help. There are also a number of fairly straightforward tips for dealing with Anxiety that might be of good use in the context of avoiding drinking. These include:

• **Exercise.** Many studies have been carried out into the effects of exercise on anxiety levels. In one study, it was shown that a ten-week program of exercise by people suffering from panic disorder had the same impact on anxiety levels as a commonly prescribed anti-anxiety drug. Even as little as 30 minutes a day of aerobic exercise can help.

• **Meditation.** Meditation is a method of self-regulation of the mind practiced in various forms for thousands of years. Its goal is to slow down or still hyperactive thought processes. Studies have shown that meditation can cause a significant reduction in anxiety levels in people who are suffering from panic disorder or generalized anxiety disorder. More on this in Level 9.

• **Aromatherapy.** Aromatherapy uses the oils from certain plants, which are mixed with either oil or alcohol (obviously avoid the ones made with alcohol—it may activate the "Smell" trigger discussed later). These aromatic compounds are used to treat a variety of symptoms and can help to alter your mental state. They can either be applied directly to your skin when having a massage or a solution of them can be inhaled. Aromatherapy is probably best when used together with other anti-anxiety techniques, as a complementary therapy, since their effects are relatively mild. Common oils that are used to treat stress and anxiety include Bergamot, Ylang Ylang, Chamomile, Lavender and Geranium.

• **Diet.** The diet you eat can have a major effect on anxiety levels for some people. Studies have shown that people who eat a regular diet rich in vegetables, whole grains, fish, quality meat, and fruit are more than thirty percent less likely to suffer from anxiety and depression. Avoid a diet high in saturated fats and processed foods.

• **Avoid alcohol (of course) and coffee.** *Alcohol consumption can affect serotonin levels, and a drop in these the day after a drinking session can cause you to feel anxious and depressed.* It can also cause a drop in your blood sugar levels which can lead to feelings of nervousness, confusion, dizziness and shaking.

The caffeine in coffee is a powerful stimulant, which has been known to bring on panic attacks in people vulnerable to them. Caffeine can significantly increase the amount of adrenaline in your blood stream, which can make you feel jittery and increase your anxiety levels. If you like it, and have to have a cup of coffee, make sure it's decaffeinated. Be careful about drinking tea as well, this also contains caffeine, although not as much as coffee.

• **Practice Breathing Techniques.** Techniques such as *Qi Gong* combine the idea of exercise and meditation to produce a calm mental state by aligning your breathing with slow, stylized movement. It can be practiced by anyone, irrespective of age, and is a very relaxing activity that is good for your general health. More generally there are many sources of good breathing techniques for calming your mind and body and in turn reducing your anxiety levels.

• **Prayer.** There are many advocates of the utility of prayer in relieving Anxiety. Certainly there is much on the Internet; if you do a search for "Prayer and Anxiety" you get many hits. There seem to be numerous prayers for a number of triggers—including Anxiety—and even specific references to some triggers in various religious texts[16]. This book and program addresses spirituality and its possible role in helping to Conquer Alcoholism in Level 10—Consider Spirituality.

Since Change can be such a major related trigger in causing Anxiety or even panic attacks, try some relatively straight-forward activities to deal with the change (See also the Change trigger Tips section for additional ideas:

• Assuming Change is unavoidable, such as moving to a new house/city, look to re-establish as many normal activities as soon as you can, such as working out, grocery shopping, updating all your contact information so all your friends/family can quickly get in contact with you and vice versa.

• Try to hire help to deal with as much as you can, such as the actual packing, moving, and unpacking of your belongings. Yes, it might cost money for something you could have done yourself, but it may be money well spent.

• Be *particularly* on guard for the activation of related triggers discussed above. Very likely many of them *will* be triggered by the Change at some point. See the Tips in each of those trigger sections for additional ideas.

The article "A Better Way to Treat Anxiety," which appeared on May 28, 2012 in *The Wall Street Journal*[17] also provides some useful ideas for dealing with anxiety from a child-parent standpoint.

Lemons into Lemonade Tip: Try different, even highly unusual ideas for "managing" your Anxiety. Meditation is a great example. It is often talked about, but do you really know anyone who has tried this, let alone "practices" it often? Odds are against it, but it doesn't mean you should not try it yourself. It may help you not just with your Anxiety but with other triggers.

Overall Tip: As with Anger, if you feel that the above starts to describe you in significant detail, I would encourage you to seek out specialized professional treatment. If you do, be *totally* forthcoming about your alcohol consumption.

Related Triggers: Anxiety can be caused by many things, including Anger, Change, Depression, Frustration, Guilt, Health problems, Job, Kids, Mid-Life Crisis, Money, Peer Pressure, Powerlessness, (Fear of) Quitting, Relationships, Relatives, Sex, Social Situations, Victim, Weather, and Yelling. Anxiety can activate Depression, Extreme Emotions, Frustration, Insomnia, and Relationship issues.

Key Defense Levels: Engage Friends and Family, Listen to Your Body!, Rehab and Therapy, Consider Spirituality

BOREDOM

Boredom is a major issue both while drinking and when sober. In fact, in my view while it is one of those triggers that may be one of the most difficult to deal with while still drinking, it can become *much* worse after achieving sobriety. It doesn't take a genius to figure out why: when you are sober you are freeing up a lot of time, energy, and brain cycles that were consumed or destroyed when drinking. It is one of those triggers that need to be a very high priority in sobriety for that reason.

To me idleness directly breeds boredom, so I casually looked into the phrase "idle hands breed . . . " that I vaguely remembered from my childhood but couldn't remember the ending. Turns out there are an amazing amount of quotes on this in many languages, most having to do with the devil and vice. Apparently this is one of the universal truths that transcend borders—Boredom is Bad. For an entertainment break, I'm including a sampling here as a kind of alcoholic Rosetta Stone:

• *L'oisiveté est la mère de tous les vices* (Idleness is the mother of all vices)—French

• *Şeytan aylak ellere iş bulur* (The devil finds work for idle hands); *Tembellik tüm kötülüklerin* anasıdır* (Idleness is the mother of all vices)—Turkish

• *Cabeça vazia é oficina do diabo* (An empty head is the devil's workshop)—Portuguese

• نجسة البطّالة الإيد *el-eed el-baTTaala negsa* (The idle hand is impure)—Egyptian Arabic

- *Laiskuus on kaikkien paheiden äiti* (Laziness is the mother of all the vices)—Finnish

- *L'ozio è il padre dei vizi* (Idleness is the father of the vices)—Italian

- *Zahálka plodí neřest* (Idleness breeds vice); *Zahálka je matkou neřesti* (Idleness is the mother of vice)—Czech

- 小人閑居して不善をなす。(Piddling man, when idle, does evil)—Japanese supposedly based on a Chinese proverb.[18]

As you might infer, idleness/boredom was and is a huge trigger for me, and still one that has to be occasionally "reconquered" to prevent bad habits from forming. Not drinking per se, but others, such as over sleeping, eating, etc. I found *many* testimonials on this, with many coming from different angles but with the same result—Boredom as a major trigger, with several different types of bored alcoholics, including:

The Loner

As you'd suspect, The Loner is someone who vastly prefers drinking alone. It often mirrors the person's sober personality.

> *I've long recognized it's the boredom and loneliness that I'm drinking about. I'm not at all sure how I ended up a loner, I certainly don't want to be, that's just the way it worked out. I've tried many ways and times to connect with other people, but it seems there are very few if any that I can connect with. Past efforts got me used, ripped off, betrayed, and abandoned, so anymore I just keep to myself, and medicate myself out of boredom and loneliness with alcohol.*
>
> guyeva, socialanxietysupport.com

The Binger

The Binger often drinks until nothing is left to drink or passes out, whichever comes first.

> *Boredom is for me the main obvious conscious reason for binge drinking after a dull and boring week.*
>
> Anonymous

As a Habit or Routine

Drinking can become as much as a habit, routine, or even a ritual on a daily basis, even if there is no other reason, *or even desire,* to drink.

> *Personally and honestly, I feel these cravings are a result of boredom, or habit. I've never enjoyed the taste of alcohol and the effects of feeling buzzed are only fun for a short while during the fact . . . . I think it boils down to not liking not being in control of my day-to-day life.*
>
> Shrink, forums.macrumors.com

Loneliness and Boredom as Partners

I found many testimonials indicating Loneliness and Boredom go hand in hand:

> *OMG! Reading these posts I'm not alone! Just found this site, [I] don't normally write things about me, but I have to say, boredom in the evenings at the end of a stressful day, means I drink to cope with the loneliness and BOREDOM . . .*
>
> Rainbow1, socialanxietysupport.com

Simplicity at Its Finest

At the end of the day, the usual reason is the simplest:

> *I was a heavy drinker for years, if I was bored, I drank.*
>
> Anonymous

As you might imagine, boredom is frequently cited in studies as a key reason for why addicts relapse after a period away from addiction. In more scientific-speak, *"if life lacks meaningful activities the individual may yearn for the excitement that they associate with using alcohol or drugs."*[19]

For many people, it may have been feelings of boredom that encouraged the person to begin experimenting with mind-altering stuff in the first place.

There is a large amount of medical-related writing out there on this topic, a lot of it mind-numbing (re: boring). To avoid inflicting *that* on you, I focused on some key excerpts that I thought were meaningful:

• Substance abuse takes up a lot of time and energy and can even give life apparent meaning.

- Feelings of boredom are particularly dangerous in rehab because it can sap motivation.

- Isolation can further increase feelings of boredom. (Author's note: See? Medical science can prove things that are common sense to the rest of us!)

- Boredom is a form of depression. (Author's note: Not sure I agree with this, but it is intriguing. I'm sure that boredom can deepen depression, but is it the same thing?)

- **Boredom is the first step on the road to relapse in many cases.**

Without a doubt the last bullet is very, very common.

Tips for Dealing with Boredom without Alcohol

The good news is that there are, of course, many ways to theoretically alleviate boredom. The not-so-good news is that it can be very tough to figure out what works. Obviously, as I harp on continuously in this program, *finding new hobbies is absolutely key for alleviating boredom* that can stretch for hours, days, weeks, as well as help dealing with many other triggers.

> *The boredom should get better over time. I think lots of people's problem is not replacing your addiction with something else. I've heard of stories of people who smoked, and being obsessed with the internet or a sport has caused them to quit smoking or basically not give them time to smoke. Try to find something to replace drinking if you can.*
>
> Robot The Human, socialanxietysupport.com

One hobby frequently cited in the testimonials I found about how to combat Boredom was Exercise, which I address in Level 9—Develop New Hobbies. Meditation was also suggested as a means for dealing with Boredom and other negative feelings in general. Various meditation techniques can teach the individual to observe feelings like boredom in such a way as to make them more manageable, such as *Walking Meditation* (Meditation is covered in more detail later in Appendix A—Learning to Sleep in Early Sobriety).

Not all hobbies are created equally of course—particularly when it comes to avoiding drinking. Obviously you want to enjoy them, but equally—if not *more* important—are the following:

- **They need to be time-consuming.** This can mean eating up a bunch of time in one "session," such as an all-afternoon hiking excursion, or it can mean adding up to a lot of time, such as walking 45 minutes three times a week.

- **They need to be mentally occupying.** Doing only physical activities alone won't cut it; you need to keep yourself from dwelling on the particular triggers-of-the-day. Challenging games can do this—essentially focusing your attention on something else, and gradually slowing down your thought processes as you begin to tire from the challenge. Another (strange) way of doing this are *very* boring activities such as cleaning your house, balancing your checkbook, or even listening (in a vague way) to very boring music.

- **Admit—***and accept***—that sometimes you just want to be "numb."** One of the big reasons that people often want to drink/use drugs is the ability to literally "numb" their brains/bodies to the problems around them. This desire to numb yourself is discussed more in the Escape trigger and very extensively in Level 11—Make Yourself Sick of Alcohol. Bottom line is that if you can drain away the excess energy in your body (e.g., exercising, hiking, etc.) *and* mind, you will find it has a very similar effect to what you tried to do when you were drinking. You might even supplement it with a nice cup of tea (or other nonalcoholic beverage) that you can come to associate with this new—and far better way—of numbing yourself.

Don't limit the above tips to just "formal" hobbies—use the same concepts in other, more everyday activities such as running errands, playing with your children, or driving to/from work.[20]

● ●

Boredom Ideas in the Military

Go clean (weapon, work area or common areas), file, collate something or engage in some other meaningful activity. Submit work orders for broken items. Inventory and requisition needed supplies. Speak with your NCOIC about getting some more work.

If you can't find work, read manuals and/or learn something useful such as another language or how to conduct night operations or something. Do things that are productive instead of just trying to kill time . . . that's what liberty and leave are for.[21]

● ●

Other Ideas for Dealing with Boredom without Alcohol

• **TV Repeats!** If you are like me, you forgot many of the details of your favorite TV series or movies while you were drinking. Take another run at viewing them—it's almost like seeing them for the first time, with the added benefit of *knowing* you are going to like them (even if you don't remember exactly why). In this age of Netflix, Hulu, and DVDs sold everywhere there is practically nothing you can't find no matter how old or obscure.

• **"New" Shows!** You might also try viewing "new" shows that you never had time for while you were drinking. I recently started watching "Breaking Bad"—I had heard a lot about it while drinking but never got around to it because I had other things to do (e.g., serious drinking). This can also be helpful in a strange way if you think you have a bit of an addictive personality—you literally have *years* of episodes you can watch, and even if you try to cram them into a few weeks, it still can take up a bunch of time while being tons of fun!

• **Variety!** Pay attention to and seek out variety. While drinking, odds are you fell into at least one or two "ruts" of activities whether it was going to the same sushi restaurant or bowling in the same league on the same day with the same people. While this routine can be comforting in many ways, it can also be boring—particularly now that you have more mental "cycles" available to think about them. Try different restaurants; occasionally bowl at a different alley, and just in general mix things up a bit. It does not mean stop doing what you are used to; instead, it is just a new way of appreciating what, how, and why things entertain you and/or make you comfortable.

• **More Variety!** Indeed, you might consider trying to do nearly *everything* in your average day differently, at least for a while. Take a different route to and from work, go to different grocery stores, etc. If you like to take walks, don't just walk the same route around your house; go to various parks. No one of these, of course, is going to alleviate boredom all that much, but in total it might take a good part of the edge off it.

Lemons into Lemonade Tip: If you are *really* bored, use this "free time" to try something you would normally never be likely to do otherwise. No, I'm not talking about trying new recreational drugs, but I am talking about other new (to you) forms of recreational activities. Bowl or play squash if you have never done them before; go rent a convertible for the weekend; drive to a summer festival *way* out of your way; get some Indian or Korean food if you never have tried it, etc. Yes, some of these will undoubted not be terribly satisfying to you (or may even be genuinely awful), but don't consider them a waste of time; instead consider them broadening your horizons or some other way of viewing them positively. And if you do enough of them, you will be sure to find at least one that you enjoy so much you will want to do it again.

Overall Tip: In order to prevent relapse from Boredom, it is critical that the newly sober develop new interests *which is at the core of Level 9— Develop New Hobbies.*

Related Triggers: Boredom can come from many directions, but often from not having "Fun" as well as Loneliness. It can activate other triggers such as Depression, desire to Escape, Loneliness, and feeling Unfun/ Uninteresting.

Key Defense Levels: Engage Friends and Family, Join a Community, Develop New Hobbies

CHANGE

The words "change" and "alcoholism" in a search yields more results for alcoholics afraid of changing their life by not drinking than it does for Change, say a job Change, as a trigger for drinking. While the former may not technically seem to be a trigger, per se, it does get at the heart of what this concept is about—dealing with an alteration of circumstances and mindset—so I've included it later in its own (Fear of) Quitting trigger section. In this section, we address Change in terms of disruption to everyday life.

Change of course can be practically anything. Change that can materially affect people's mindsets can range from monumental (e.g., death, which is covered in more detail in Extreme Emotions) to the most trivial (e.g., clothes folded wrong, mold in the frig). Many of these changes such as death or moving to a new city are clearly major alterations in one's life and should be recognized as such. But as you move down the impact scale towards those more trivial ones, you would think that the reaction of those experiencing the change would decrease accordingly. *Not so.*

Change can set off *many* related triggers that are doozies in themselves, including Anxiety, Depression, Extreme Emotions, Frustration,

Guilt, Insomnia, Loneliness, Mid-Life Crisis, Powerlessness, and Stress. The inability to handle Change can also cause other problems that—while not technically triggers—can also have a major impact on your life, notably the inability to make decisions.

There were many sources about Change in general that did a good job boiling down why Change acts on us (humans) the way it does. These include (boiled down from several dozen articles):

• **Comfort and Predictability.** Most of us, even if we don't *like* where we are in life, get used to it, developing/falling into predictable, (relatively) comfortable patterns and life "rhythms" that get us through the day. We plan our day assuming those patterns and rhythms are going to be the same as they were in the days and weeks before. So when something happens to disrupt them, it can throw our life into chaos. This chaos can be big or small, depending on the Change, but even "mini-chaos" events can destroy the comfort we had "planned on" for that day.

• **Fear of the Unknown.** No matter how unhappy we are with our current life, there is always the fear that any significant change—planned or unplanned—will make it worse. We build our defenses (against any potential threat) around the certainties of our daily lives, with the goal of being safe against those threats, and changing those certainties will make us feel unsafe in the short term no matter how much they will improve our safety in the longer-term. This is at the heart of the (Fear of) Quitting trigger discussion later in this Level.

> *This process of change is a lot harder than I thought and is usually accompanied by fear. Even after overcoming the fear involved in living sober I still feel uncomfortable when there is a change in my life—even if I have instigated it.*[22]

• **Being overwhelmed.** Change in the form of new things to do fosters an "It's just too much" or "I don't have time for this" mentality. Very natural, as you have implicitly or explicitly planned your day or week around certain "certainties" that in effect we designed to make the most out of the available time that day/week. When new things happen, it's not just doing those new activities that cause you problems; it in effect has you scrambling your whole day, overwhelming you in the process that *everything* has to change to some degree to accommodate this new thing.

• **Feeling of being under personal attack or affront.** There is a saying, "bad things happen to good people" (and vice versa). A great deal of unplanned change (or one or two big changes close together) often causes the feeling of "Why Me?" instead of the more Zen-like feeling of "Shit Happens." That feeling of personal attack just magnifies the Anxiety, Frustration, and Powerlessness in your life, plus other feelings like being picked on (a Victim), "What did I do to deserve this (a Guilt trip)?" to a desire to lash out at the world (Anger).

As you probably surmised from all the related triggers listed above, the result for an alcoholic is very often a *strong* desire to drink in order to "deal with" this avalanche of triggers.

Even Change you can control and you *know* will be for the better can be extremely difficult for an alcoholic to handle:

> *As a practicing alcoholic for many years, I had no desire to try to better myself in any way, physically, mentally or spiritually. I frowned upon anyone else who might be trying to better themselves, people who went to the gym, people who studied hard, people who said they lived a spiritual life, people who were sober, people in general—the list went on ad nauseam. I know now that I was jealous of anyone who had their lives together and I dealt with that by putting them down. Even while I was looking up from the gutter, my alcoholic mind still told me I was better than the people standing on the sidewalk.*[23]

His contempt for people trying to better themselves arguably was another way of viewing Change with fear in addition to envy.

Tips for Dealing with Change without Alcohol

Some great ways of managing the chaos of Change include:

• **Pre-plan.** If there's a change coming in your life, get as much of your life in order as possible so you don't have to worry about those things also changing in the middle of everything else.

• **Monitor Yourself.** Watch your reactions to changes, and try to ask yourself at the time "Why am I (re)acting this way?" Just slowing down enough to ask yourself this question can help you relax and respond in a far better way than you might otherwise.

• **Seek Assistance.** Make sure you've got good support around you to give you good advice and moral support. Don't try to shoulder all the burden of major Change by yourself if you can avoid it.

• **Try to Be Philosophical.** Change is going to happen—there is no way to avoid it, even if you are the most orderly person and best planner in existence. Instead of going nuts about a something happening—*particularly* if it is something you can't control or could not have reasonably foreseen—*try* to take it in stride, try *not* to take it personally, *try* to make the best out of a bad situation, and overall *try to* take the philosophy that "Shit Happens" and roll with it from there.

Lemons into Lemonade Tip. Some of the most unpleasant and/or unexpected Changes in life can turn out to be good or even for the best in the long run. In my personal situation, these seemed to occur when I would encounter major Health problems. An extreme example is that I probably would not have gotten sober and written this book if I had not had very major health problems that came to a head all at once. *Extremely* unpleasant at the time. More generally, I believe if you look hard enough you can find ways to turn negative Changes into positive ones, sometimes even making the original changes feeling worth it. This attitude is also *very* helpful if you were responsible for the Change in the first place as it goes a long way in diminishing the Guilt that you might feel.

Overall Tip: No matter what your feelings about Alcoholics Anonymous (discussed in detail in Level 7—Join a Community), I have always liked how they end each meeting with The Serenity Prayer.[24] Try and use it whenever it makes sense—and it *often* makes sense.

> *God, grant me the serenity to accept the things I cannot change,*
> *The courage to change the things I can, ·*
> *And wisdom to know the difference.*

Related Triggers: Change as a drinking trigger can be caused by Job changes, a Mid-Life Crisis, Disorder, Money, (Fear of) Quitting, and Relationships/e(X) problems. Change in turn can cause Anxiety, Depression, desire to Escape, Extreme Emotions, Frustration, Guilt, Insomnia, Money problems, Disorder, Powerlessness, Relationship problems, even Zeal (Excitement).

Key Defense Levels: Engage Friends and Family, Join a Community (see how other alcoholics deal with Change), Therapy, Consider Spirituality

DEPRESSION

First and foremost, if you or your loved one feels that Depression could be a significant contributor to your alcoholism, **see a doctor** if you have not already done so. This section only touches on this very complex topic, and as I've reiterated I am not in any way a medical or psychological professional.

> **Depression** (noun): Severe despondency and dejection, accompanied by feelings of hopelessness and inadequacy. A condition of mental disturbance, typically with lack of energy and difficulty in maintaining concentration or interest in life.[25]

Of course there are various degrees of Depression, ranging from being slightly depressed over say a job setback to deep clinical Depression or thoughts of suicide. There are many types of depression.[26] This section touches on only the milder (and non-clinical) types of Depression, and only as it relates to alcohol. It also does not deal with what is called "*Dual Diagnosis*"—being both clinically depressed and an alcoholic.

> *I have now been sober for 7$^1/_2$ years. I would say that the only thing that makes me even think about drinking is depression. If I keep my depression and anxiety under control with talk therapy and medication, alcohol never even occurs to me as a solution to my problems. It took many years to get to that point though. And believe it or not I still have drinking dreams even after all this time.*
>
> Guest Trinity21204, alcoholism.about.com

There has been a great deal of research into the link between alcoholism and Depression. There are many reasons, issues, causes, concerns described in this research, but some of the more obvious/important observations include:

• Nearly one-third of people with *major depression* also have an alcohol problem. Conversely, alcohol abuse increases the risk for depression.[27] In many cases, depression may be the first to occur.

• Children who are depressed are more prone to develop alcohol problems once they reach adolescence. Teens who have had an episode of major depression are twice as likely as those who aren't depressed to start drinking alcohol.

- Depression may be a particularly significant trigger for alcohol use in *women, who are more than twice as likely to start drinking heavily* if they have a history of depression. Women are more likely than men to self-medicate with alcohol in general and twice as likely for this condition.

I think most of the above seems pretty intuitive, except the relationship/impact of depression on alcohol use for women. As I have researched this book (and noted in the Phase 1 introduction section) I was continually amazed at how much worse alcoholism seems to be for women than for men.

> *I've been sober since April 20 2011 and still feel mild depression at times. My health problem would be severe depression! It's gotten way better. But at times it's not a problem. So I'm guessing I just need more time to heal. I sometimes have headaches still, so hopefully I get back to normal.*
>
> Guest BritS, alcoholism.about.com

I'm not about to say anything close to saying that your depression will get better once you stop drinking. As the medical research above indicates, alcohol does nothing to help Depression, and potentially can make it much worse. All I can say is that I personally no longer have to take medication (Venlafaxine) for my depression now that I am sober.

Tips for Dealing with Depression without Alcohol

Depression is nothing to fool around with. Besides professional help, helpful ideas include:

- **To state the incredibly obvious: Don't drink alcohol!** It will not help your depression and will likely make it worse!

- **Build Supportive Relationships.** Level's 4 and 7 focus on building your support network. Use them for this trigger! Ask them to tell you when you are especially negative, as "negative thoughts" reinforce Depression[28].

- **Eat well-balanced meals, exercise, get good sleep, etc.** These are repeated over and over again in practically any self-help book, including those for Depression. Obviously the trick is 1) Remembering to do them, and 2) Finding the time, energy, and will-power to do so. Far easier said than done.

- **Light!** Turn on your lights. Get out into the sun. Paint your apartment/house with bright colors. Do little things that add brightness (literally) to your day. Buy a white/pink/yellow case for your phone. Light and brightness can be amazingly effective in lifting you out of a funk, particularly on dark days and long winter months.

- **Go to Bed Early.** One study recently linked going to bed consistently late (being a "night owl") with a higher rate of Depression.[29] Break that habit!

- **Draw on the Insights of other Levels.** As you can see from the list below, Depression has many additional defense levels that can be brought to bear. Use them!

Lemons into Lemonade Tip: Many people don't realize they have depression until their life has turned south in many ways and/or the symptoms are painfully obvious, e.g. excessive sleeping, lethargy, etc. Instead, if you even *suspect* you might have depression (regardless of whether you think it is a trigger or not), why not explore the possibility with your doctor? You can make it part of a broader health evaluation suggested in Level 3—Listen to Your Body!

Overall Tip: Seek professional help and/or support groups. Depression is an extremely complex medical/psychiatric area, and it is well worth the time and money to seek out professional help if you can. There are also literally dozens, if not hundreds of "amateur" support groups[30] out there that can also provide extremely useful tips for dealing with Depression, and the basic fact that they are out there can provide significant comfort to sufferers just by reading and/or posting on their various forums.

Related Triggers: Various possible causes include Anxiety, Boredom, Change, Guilt, Health problems, Kids (post-partum), Loneliness, Mid-Life Crisis, Money, Powerlessness, Relationship issues, Victim, and Weather (seasonal changes). Depression can cause Anxiety, desire to Escape, Insomnia, Loneliness, Disorder, Powerlessness, Relationship issues, and make you Tired.

Key Defense Levels: Listen to Your Body!, Engage Friends and Family, Join a Community, Rehab and Therapy, Break Bad Habits, Consider Spirituality

DISORDER

Disorder and chaos in one's day-to-day can, of course, be caused by an incredible number of factors. Many of them fall into what I call the Disorder trigger. I boil this trigger down into two "need" categories: the need for: 1) a clean living environment, and 2) good time management. The lack of either can be a major drinking trigger—ones that are very often overlooked (and never mentioned in rehab or therapy in my experience and research).

Living Environment

The need to have an ordered, clean living environment is one of the greatly underestimated parts of life for many people, including alcoholics. It can be soothing, relaxing, peaceful . . . pick your adjective. And the lack of such can be exactly the opposite: irritating, exasperating, stressful, and so on. Sometimes this aspect can be extremely negative on your mental well-being, depending on your personality and the rest of your broader living environment.

A disorganized, cluttered, dirty house was a major trigger for me, though unfortunately I did not recognize this until after I was sober. Much of my (drinking) working and married life was spent on the road as a management consultant. After working out of town all week, in alternately controlled/uncontrolled business chaos and often very high stress, living in hotel rooms, and plane travel (those two words cover many, many unpleasant things), what I really looked forward to (I realize now) once I got home for the weekend besides seeing my children was a calm, ordered home environment. Particularly after 4+ hours of plane and car travel to get there.

Instead what I too often found—particularly as my marriage deteriorated—was what I viewed as utter chaos. With children-related stuff that was generally ok, but often the house was a total mess, despite a stay-at-home spouse and money to hire periodic professional cleaning. There were dozens of other things I had to do in a very short period of time without having to clean before I had to hit the road again, but I did it anyway. The frequent arguments that resulted did not help with the chaos.

What I did not fully appreciate until I researched this topic was that this Disorder was a huge underlying cause/ related trigger to Relationship problems, Frustration, and even Anger for me. Those triggers, of course, were big-league ones by themselves that would help move my drinking along to even higher levels once I got home. Often instead of chilling and playing with the kids, I wound up vacuuming soon after I got home after traveling hell. Yes, even then I recognized this was anal, but then again it was productive and the noise prevented active arguments! Yet I often became more stressed, frustrated and alternatively depressed/angry in the process of cleaning, and of course drinking more and more to try to "deal" with those triggers.

My research indicated that the negative feelings I had resulting from the mess/disorder, and the great mix of positive feelings that resulted when that was not the case were by no means an anomaly:

> *A clean house can lift your spirits. When you come home at the end of a long day, the last thing you want to walk into is a messy, cluttered home. Being surrounded by clutter can cause you to feel stressed as you look around at all the stuff you still have left to do. Often, just looking at it can kill all of your energy, making it even harder to create the clean, clear environment that you crave. It's a vicious cycle. A messy house adds to feelings of stress, but the chore of cleaning can feel like added stress as well.*
>
> anonymous

After reading this, your first reaction might be "of course!" But who has the time? But the point is that this is an area where you definitely want to *make* time (see time management, next).

The state of your living area can be its own specialty area, with a host of focused tips and expertise such as Feng Shui taking it to great lengths beyond the obvious:

> The state of a person's home can often provide insight into the state of their overall well-being. Feng Shui teaches that clutter in the home causes depression and fatigue. Whether or not you believe in the art of Feng Shui,[31] there is absolutely a direct link between a messy home and depression.
>
> One factor of the link between a messy home and depression is that fatigue is a common symptom of depression. Those who are depressed may simply feel too tired and unmotivated to do the household chores, resulting in a buildup of clutter. Another symptom of depression is hopelessness. This symptom adds to

the problem, because the depressed person may think, "What's the point of cleaning, anyway?"[32]

In any event, it affirmed what I think a lot of us already know (particularly those with Obsessive Compulsive Disorder—OCD); that a messy environment can be detrimental to our moods, feelings, and even mental health, none of which we need as alcoholics! Having a clean, ordered environment can be a key factor in dealing with many other less-obvious related triggers, such as Change, Escape, and Times of Day.

Can *Order* Be a Trigger?

Anything can be a trigger, and that is no different here. A friend of mine told me about an alcoholic who seemed to have an OCD spouse as the main trigger. Whenever she would be particularly obsessive about order, like toothbrush or canned goods placement, he would go drink. I have no idea if this covered up larger issues, but certainly I've personally encountered stress in people's houses where they would freak out if you didn't take off your shoes in the foyer; use a coaster for drinks, etc. It is not far-fetched to think living with that kind of daily behavior could drive you nuts, but me thinks that might be symptoms of deeper issues and triggers than just Order.

Time Management

Time Management is a Disorder category that probably the vast majority of us are very conscious of, and do a crappy job of it. It is defined as: *"the act or process of planning and exercising conscious control over the amount of time spent on specific activities, especially to increase effectiveness, efficiency or productivity."*[33]

Right. Anyway, we obviously have only so many hours in the day, and for an alcoholic the number of productive hours can be in the *single* digits. We have serious drinking to get to! Of course, as a result, many important things do not get done, with the result that our daily lives get even more chaotic and stressful, in turn causing us to drink more! A vicious cycle if you ever needed one.

I believe you *will* find that the feeling of having had a well-managed and productive day greatly reduces your overall stress-levels, diminishes the burden of related triggers, and general feeling of being awash in a chaotic world, which greatly reduces your desire to drink.

Tips for Dealing with Disorder without Alcohol

Cleanliness and Timeliness! Both will do wonders for your feelings of Disorder:

Cleaning. If you can afford it *at all*, try to have a professional cleaner come in at least once a month. The rest of the time try to figure out the best "technique" that fits your style for daily picking and tidying up. A good article to read is *"Meet The Speed Cleaners"* (*The Wall Street Journal 7/3/13*). It lays out four types of cleaning styles to consider: Multi-tasking, Drive-By Swiping, Now and Later, and Dab A Little.

Time Management. Try to learn about various time management techniques and find one that fits your particular lifestyle and mindset. A good article on the topic (there are zillions of them), focusing on entrepreneurs is *"10 Time Management Tips that Work"* (*entrepreneur.com*). These include:

• Carry a schedule and record all your thoughts, conversations and activities for a week (this helps figure out just how chaotic your life actually is).

• Plan to spend at least 50 percent of your time engaged in the thoughts, activities and conversations that produce most of your results. This will undoubtedly take practice.

• Schedule time for interruptions. Plan time to be pulled away from what you're doing.

• Take the first 30 minutes of every day to plan your day. Don't start your day until you complete your time plan.

• Take five minutes before every call and task to decide what result you want to attain.

• Put up a "Do not disturb" sign when you absolutely have to get work done. (A consistent angry scowl will also work.)

• Practice *not* answering the phone just because it's ringing and e-mails just because they show up. I am amazed at how some people (like my mother) will pick up the phone when they *know* it is going to be a telemarketer. Human nature, I guess, made even worse in the age of texting and social media, where if you do not respond immediately to someone's message it is somehow interpreted as a "diss."

• Speaking of which, block out other distractions like Facebook and other forms of social media unless you use these tools to generate business, or at a minimum do not respond to personal messages until non-working hours.

• Remember that it's impossible to get everything done. Also remember that odds are good that 20 percent of your thoughts, conversations and activities produce 80 percent of your results. The 80–20 rule, so applicable for so many things in life.

• For personal, time-consuming, and particularly *new* activities, it can be very difficult to appropriately guess how long something is going to take. A great example is how long it took me to write this book. Even towards the end, when I was on the tail end of editing, it *always* took me longer to do than I estimated.[34] Consider doubling or tripling initial first-time estimate for these projects and plan accordingly; it is much more likely to be nearer reality.

Lemons into Lemonade Tip: Even if Disorder is not a major trigger for most people, I would suggest it is at least a *minor* trigger for many. After all, how can living in a pig-sty or anything close to it be good for your mental health? Take a few minutes every day to clean up, even if it is just one room or even a part of a room. You will very likely feel at least a bit more relaxed for your efforts.

Overall Tip: Do not discount how big a factor Disorder can be for your daily peace of mind.

Related Triggers: Disorder can be caused by Depression (not feeling like picking up after yourself or organizing your day), Kids, and (messy as in having slobs as your partner) Relationships. It can cause Anger, Change (as in nothing ever going as planned because of poor time management), desire to Escape, Frustration, poor Job performance, and physical Stress.

Key Defense Levels: Break Bad Habits, Develop New Hobbies (e.g., Feng Shui, learning Time Management techniques)

ENVY (INCLUDES JEALOUSY)

I think all of us who are now sober, or those still drinking in general who happen to be in a situation where they can't be seen drinking, fantasize about being like "everyone else" who seem to be able to have a few drinks without having to worry about their world crashing down on them. This is totally understandable and very common.

> *My problem I think is jealousy. Every time my fiancée drinks in front of me, I become incredibly jealous (to the point that after my last slip, she agreed to stop drinking in front of me). Will I ever stop being jealous of drinkers, or am I doomed to a life of envy and periodic relapse?*
>
> Actusreus, dailystrength.org

Unfortunately, there is no magic way of dealing with Envy/jealousy when it comes to alcohol. All of the testimonials I looked at in response said the same thing essentially: You just have to *accept* the reality that you will not be able to be like "them."

Certainly avoiding people drinking early in your sobriety is recommended, but not practical in the long term. Seeking out the fellowship of non-drinkers (applicable obviously to many triggers not just Envy) is highly recommended by many sources. One post had an interesting take that you categorize your envy of drinkers and being a part of that group as part of your fantasy life, kind of locking it away along with your dreams of being a star athlete or actress or . . . (I'm not going there—but you get the drift).

Tips for Dealing with Envy without Alcohol

Unless you are a saint (or equivalent), you will be hard pressed to not encounter this feeling occasionally. Hopefully, the feeling will be short-lived and not severe. When it is, consider:

• **Getting away from the source.** Physically, mentally, virtually, just remove yourself from the source of your Envy. If it is a generalized feeling of Envy, try to and find something *very* distracting to take your mind off it.

• **Practice accepting reality.** "Accept" the reality that you can't drink and most other people can. That's just the way it is and the way it always will be. Put it in the fantasy category of wanting to be a pro-football player, model, actress, etc. and forget about it. This will likely take time.

• **Try Psychology.** If there is a truism about the human race, it is that we want what we can't have. Not being able to drink yet wanting to do it—solely because you *can't*—is very consistent with this unfortunate way our brains are wired. The good news is that it is possible to change this particular way of thinking, even though it might take a great deal of practice reminding ourselves that wanting something just because we can't have it is logical and even stupid. But keep at it, and don't get discouraged. Eventually, your subconscious will stop thinking that way, and by doing so you will go a long way towards conquering the Envy trigger in the process.

Lemons into Lemonade Tip: I am sure I'm going to get a lot of grief for saying this, but there is *always* someone out there who is worse off than you (or put it the other way, you will always be better off than some people). That is just human nature, and the key reason people love to gossip, read tabloids, RSS TMZ[39], slow down to gawk at car wrecks, etc.

I think most of us feel somewhat embarrassed about making fun of others most of the time—which we kind of should particularly if we do it *a lot*—but it is perfectly fine in my opinion to do this if we are feeling particularly envious of others drinking that day/night. Otherwise silly/childish/stupid reactions to others drinking in front of you might be (from a male about a male) "What a wimp, bet he can't bench press what I do," or (for a female about a female) "What an atrocious outfit." You get the idea. Baldly stated, you are putting down others to make yourself feel better. That is ok (in my opinion) in moderation and if you keep it to yourself (this means NOT posting the feelings online). You might even consider praying for forgiveness (see Level 10—Consider Spirituality) afterwards.[40]

Overall Tip: You really can't do much about being envious of other people's ability to drink alcohol without its becoming a problem. "Practice" at "accepting" it as reality whenever you can, trying different means like talking with friends and family, going to meetings, and even spiritual means (all discussed in later levels).

Related Triggers: Envy can be caused by seeing others having drinking Fun, Peer Pressure, and Social Situations. Envy in turn can activate Overconfidence.

Key Defense Levels: Engage Friends and Family, Join a Community, Consider Spirituality

ESCAPE

Up to now I have not directly addressed what is a key underlying desire for many if not most people who drink—the desire for the alcohol to change our brain to feel different. We want to get "buzzed," to get a "rush," to feel "comfortably numb[35]." Or even get to the point where you want to completely "checkout"—where you feel nothing at all—up to and including the point where you pass out.

I think all of us who are now sober miss one or more of those feelings at one time or another (maybe a lot of the time). Many people who are contemplating getting sober (e.g., reading this book) wonder what life will be like without the ability to use those chemicals of alcohol to help us achieve it. I address this desire in *great* detail in Level 11—Make Yourself Sick of Alcohol. But the trigger of Escape is the first on our alphabetical list that hits the reality of this desire head on, so I provide a basic overview here.

In Level 11, I describe 4 "states" of desire for the chemical effect of alcohol, in order of increasing Blood Alcohol Content (BAC):

1. The desire for the initial "rush" of Euphoria[36] that comes with that first drink.

2. The desire for an ongoing "buzz" of Euphoria.

3. The desire to "numb" yourself so you don't have to think about things troubling you.

4. The desire to "checkout" of the world so to speak so you don't have to think about *anything*.

Collectively I refer to the 1 through 4 states of this rush/buzz/numb/checkout "continuum" as "buzz-rush" for short. The 3rd and 4th states described above describe the trigger Escape perfectly in my opinion. Arguably the desire to Escape lurks in the background of many other triggers—some more than others—but it is often one that leads the desire to drink for some alcoholics. It may well be related to one or more triggers on any given day, and indeed those triggers may "lead" to the desire to Escape, but other times the desire to numb yourself to your general troubles or even checkout from them or life in general completely is *the* main goal.

I've been drinking almost every day for the last few years. I drink alone and I just love the relaxed numb state it causes—I'm normally quite tense.

Recuser, socialanxietysupport.com

Escape was one of my personal major triggers. While any given day might find me worrying about Job issues, eX problems, and being Stressed in general, those triggers varied in intensity (as did my defenses) on a day-to-day basis. Usually the desire to Escape was always there to some degree, and often was the prime trigger for drinking that day. For some reason, Times of Day was a strong related trigger for me; even if the day had gone great, come 5:30 pm[37] I would be ready to numb myself for the remainder of the evening.

There is a strong drinking culture in the City—the pubs are packed on weeknights after work and (apart from Friday) quiet by about 9. Many don't even open Saturday or Sunday. Professionals in the City often work long hours and so want relief.

iStudentUK, forums.macrumors.com

Whether you call it Escape, relief or some other term, there is no doubt that many of us just want to numb ourselves to the world or even check-out completely from it on occasion—regardless of whether you are an alcoholic or not. But obviously (to me at least) if you *are* an alcoholic, you are much more likely to give in to this desire far more often than you should, in a way you shouldn't be doing at all.

Tips for "Escaping" without Alcohol

This trigger is very tricky: how to Escape without using alcohol or drugs. I focus here on alternative ideas for delivering an "Escape Effect," as it is unlikely (and even undesirable) to try to eliminate the desire; humans just aren't built that way.

Understand your root causes. First, I would encourage you to drill down on your desire to Escape to see if it is actually being caused by one of the other triggers discussed in this Level. Those triggers have more cus-tomized Tips for dealing with those particular trigger situations.

Escape without chemicals. If the general desire to Escape is your pri-mary trigger that day, there are many ways to do it without chemicals. This will vary *greatly* by individual. Some include:

- Massage. Done right it can be blissful escape.

- Learning to meditate. Tough to do right, but successful practitioners swear by it as a means of relaxation and various forms of mental escapism.

- Watching fantasy movies or TV series

- Reading historical-based novels, as well as fantasy-type ones, such as science fiction, comedy/paranormal romance, and apocalypse-themed novels, that take you far away from your current life (in your mind).

- Exercise. This takes the edge off of certain body stress dimensions and in turn can contribute to pleasurable and even "numb" feelings (more on this in Levels 9 and 11)

- Play (online) games. It is easy to lose yourself in (good) online games, e.g., checking out from the world.

When I say "chemicals" above I am referring to substance-abusing type chemicals such as alcohol and both prescription and non-prescription drugs[38]. There are many others that generally are not addictive such as various types of teas that have a long history of helping people relax (See Level 8—Break Bad Habits for a discussion of potentially relaxing teas and their ingredients).

If you can come to *associate* these types of non-addictive substances—generally in the form of beverages—with relaxation and even "Escape," you may eventually find that you feel a similar effect to the one you sought while drinking alcohol without, of course, all the incredible negatives/baggage that comes with doing so, and *with* the ability to control how/how much/when/where you actually drink it—unlikely with alcohol.

Find ways to *physically* Escape. This could be anything from taking a long hot relaxing shower or bath to taking *truly* relaxing vacations (e.g., don't go to Disneyworld where the waits and hassles make you more frazzled). Try new activities and hobbies that are in tranquil settings and are relaxing. Periodically take mini-vacations, doing a mix of the familiar and the brand new.

Use your Generic Defense Progression. Last but definitely not least is the use of the "Generic Defense Progression" described in Level 13—Develop Your Defense Progressions. See that Level for what this means and how to develop and customize it for your unique situation. It may allow you to *temporarily* Escape surprise situations without using alcohol.

Lemons into Lemonade Tip: Do *not* feel guilty, ashamed, or other similar feelings because you want to numb yourself and/or checkout from the world for a while. Everybody does at various points, and it is likely to *benefit* you in various ways—relaxing you, reducing physical stress and its toll on your body, taking your mind off a problem to allow time for a solution to present itself, etc. The trick, of course, is to do this without using alcohol and other potentially addictive substances. Experiment with non-addictive substances (e.g., tea) to see if you can transfer the association between alcohol and Escape to a new beverage.

Overall Tip: See Level 11—Make Yourself Sick of Alcohol, for a much deeper understanding of the effects of alcohol and in particular *why it really does not work well* for alcoholics in getting numb and/or checking out from the world.

Related Triggers: Many if not most of the other triggers in this Level could cause the desire to Escape. Ones that could be activated by the desire to Escape are Change, Insomnia, and in particular the desire for Fun via drinking.

Key Defense Levels: Engage Friends and Family, Join a Community, Break Bad Habits (e.g., substitute tea for alcohol), Develop New Hobbies, Make Yourself Sick of Alcohol (understand how and why alcohol has the effect on you as it does, and how transient it is).

EXTREME EMOTIONS (INCLUDES GRIEF)

Extreme sadness, hatred, grief—any strong or overwhelming emotion can trigger a relapse in even the strongest individual. These can be caused by many things, such as moving to a new city, starting a new job, or a child leaving the nest. I cover those kinds of events or situations in the Change section. Here though I focus on the kinds of change that cause the most extreme emotions—the threat of or reality of the loss of a loved one.

While a new job in a new city can be reasonably viewed as life-changing, it doesn't compare to death or the imminent threat of death as *life-altering*. As with Changes, alcohol provides escape from the extreme feeling of Grief associated with Death—and when these happen in early sobriety, it can result in a relapse.

> [My major trigger is] Funerals and loved ones becoming ill. I immediately want to go to my drug of choice to numb the pain. The guilt and sadness is too much to bear. I'm wondering if I should avoid funerals in the future.
>
> Guest Nommorelies, alcoholism.about.com

Dealing with Grief while dealing with an addiction is particularly problematic it appears, as illustrated by the above anecdote. The temptation by *anyone* to "deal with" Grief by using *drugs or alcohol is common, to try to forget about the death of someone and deny that they are feeling sad.*

The temptation will be even stronger for alcoholics. According to my research, there are two key danger points that are of particularly concern to alcoholics when it comes to grieving: watching out for related triggers and not isolating yourself during the grieving process.

• *Related Triggers.* When a person is grieving, they undergo many emotional changes that can be very serious, especially if they are trying to get or stay sober. These changes can activate many relating triggers, particularly Anger, (fear of) Change, Depression, Frustration, Guilt, Loneliness, and Powerlessness, to name a few of the more obvious triggers. Guilt may be particularly powerful as people may ask themselves "what-if" questions, putting into doubt their previous actions or taking on blame for the loss. Depression is also another common (and high-risk trigger) for people grieving. In addition, it is important to watch out for . . .

• *Loneliness.* There is no normal or right way for someone to grieve. Everybody reacts differently to the loss of someone. Obviously we as alcoholics may have our first temptation to turn to the bottle to ease our pain. Instead of doing that, professionals recommend spending time with family members, friends, attending professional counseling services, and exercising.[41]

Those are "good" ways to grieve, and they share one common element: you are not alone while grieving. While some counselors recommend having alone time as a coping mechanism in general, I do not believe that is the right approach for alcoholics. Far better for an alcoholic to be around someone than to be alone to dwell on the Grief and its related triggers.

Tips for Dealing with Grief without Alcohol

One of the best ways of dealing with Grief I believe is to remember that *your* future is dependent on staying sober and that *the person you have lost would want you to live your life the best way you can—starting with stopping drinking.*

Other, more short-term ways of coping include:

• Cry. Keeping the Grief inside will cause a lot of emotional havoc and tension. If you find it hard to cry, watch a sad movie.

• Do relaxing little activities when you can, such as taking a bath, lighting or some candles or incense.

• Journal. Write to someone about what you are feeling.

• Express your emotions musically. If you play an instrument, play it. If not, listen to music, even sad music.

• Spend time with your pet

• Meditate

• Sleep

• Hit stuff

• Let yourself feel and be in the moment. It's ok to be sad. That said . . .

• . . . find something to laugh about!

• Pray[42]

Lemons into Lemonade Tip: If the person you are grieving for was very close to you (and vice versa), it is very likely one of their last wishes would be for you to be happy and healthy—particularly if they knew of your addiction. Assume it was indeed one of their last wishes, and use it as additional motivation to get and stay sober in their memory, perhaps even using this last wish as "floor" defense (discussed in Level 13—Develop Your Progressions).[43]

Overall Tip: Remember time heals all wounds, including Grief. But in the meantime, do *not* hold the Grief inside; it will fester and quite possibly result in a relapse. Talk (and cry) with family and friends who knew the deceased as well as you did to help the healing process.

Related Triggers: Extreme Emotions can be caused by Change, Relationships, Relatives, and eX issues and loss. It can in turn activate Angry, Frustration, Guilt, Insomnia, and Yelling.

Key Defense Levels: Engage Friends and Family, Consider Spirituality

FRUSTRATION

Frustration is a trigger that most likely needs close personal examination, as there can be many underlying causes of it. In addition, it has a very close "cousin" trigger in the form of Anger, as it is frequently cited in scientific literature as being closely linked with Frustration, e.g., Frustration causing Anger, vice versa, or almost synonymous.

> *My biggest relapse trigger is anger and frustration at caregiving a relative. I have never endangered this relative but I have escaped to the bar and the home of a friend who always had liquor on hand.*
> Guest bobbys, alcoholism.about.com

My personal take, however, is one of common sense: people get frustrated over things they cannot control. In these situations people deal with the situation (or don't) in many different ways. The alcoholic's dealing of choice is to drink.

Frustration is a good example of a drinking trigger that may be better understood with some scientific background. I have tried to interpret some of the more dense explanations the best I could. I encourage you to do your own analysis if you are that interested—it is only helpful up to a point in my opinion.

One study (*Mental Health and Psychiatric Nursing: A Caring Approach*[44]) has Frustration rooted in what they call a Dependency-Independency conflict, which is the need for the alcoholic to be *dependent* (e.g., on alcohol) and *independent* (in *control) at the same time*. It asserts that many alcoholics are unable to confront or resolve this conflict, and as such need to repress one or the other. This conflict in turn increases the need for relief, e.g., alcohol.

I think I understand that, but it needs repeat reading. Put another way, the study asserts that the relationship between Frustration and dependency needs is very strong. In particular *it claims that many alcoholics have a low tolerance for Frustration,* which makes them more vulnerable to relapse. *That* I can understand.

The alcoholic becomes frustrated easily with even the most basic things. Something insignificant to most [people] can cause [me] to become extremely agitated and upset. Generally the frustration builds up and [I] will have minor or major outbursts to vent the gradually increasing pressure inside.

aa.activeboard.com

Frustration, Control, and Al-Anon

I have not been to nearly as many Al-Anon meetings as I have Alcoholics Anonymous (dozens versus hundreds of meetings). However, one of the biggest themes that come through for me in the Al-Anon discussions is the *Frustration* that nonalcoholics have with their inability to handle/deal with their alcoholic loved one. In particular it seems that their *inability to control* what alcohol is doing to their life is what frustrates them most. They can't control the alcoholic's drinking, how that drinking makes them think about themselves (e.g., is the drinking my fault), the inability to *not* feel responsible for the drinking, and their lack of control over how the drinking is damaging everyone's lives.

Hopefully, this book will help you—the nonalcoholic—understand the mindset of the alcoholic better, and in turn decrease the Frustration you feel. At the end of the day you *cannot* do much to help the alcoholic—the alcoholic *has* to do it for themselves. If you are the alcoholic, I encourage you to also try a few Al-Anon meetings[45] and/or go to their online discussion forum (*http://alanon.activeboard.com*). You may greatly benefit from it as well by getting a totally different perspective about the impact alcoholism is having on you and your loved ones.

Tips for Dealing with Frustration without Alcohol

Obviously since there are so many potential underlying causes of Frustration it would be impossible to champion any particular way of dealing with it. *However,* if you accept that a large number of underlying drivers relate to lack of control over a person/place/thing/situation—and a low tolerance for that lack of control—then I would assert that you have an excellent start on starting to deal with it.

There is a lot of advice out there for various *types* of Frustration, or at least when/where you happen to be when Frustration hits a peak, such as while and/or about working. Some of those tips include:

- **Stop and evaluate.** One of the best things to do is mentally stop and look at the situation. Ask yourself why you feel frustrated. Write it down, and be specific. Then think of one positive thing about the situation. For instance, if your boss is late for your meeting, then you have more time to prepare. Or, you use this time to relax.

- **Find something positive about the situation.** Thinking about a positive aspect of your situation often makes you look at things in a different way. This small change in your thinking can improve your mood. When it's people who are causing your frustration, they're probably not doing it deliberately to annoy you. And if it's a thing that's bothering you—well, it's certainly not personal! Don't get mad, just move on.

- **Remember the last time you felt frustrated.** The last time you were frustrated about something, the situation probably worked out just fine after a while, right? Your feelings of frustration or irritation probably didn't do much to solve the problem then, which means they're not doing anything for you right now.[46]

Sometimes seemingly stupid, silly things can be greatly blown out of proportion. One personal example for me is spam (the email variety). Despite doing everything I can to prevent it—security/spam/malware software, strict browsing controls, etc., and most of all flagging as spam the junk emails that make it past all that, I used to get extremely frustrated that despite all my "protection" junk made it through to irritate the hell out of me.[47]

Instead of getting and staying extremely frustrated, which is what I did for a long time, I finally decided to get even, not mad, even in little ways. I came to view my flagging as spam as soothing, not a time waster, knowing that every time I did it was having some impact by permanently disabling that source from ever being successful again, forcing them to spend at least a little time/money in figuring new ways of attacking me. It's now actually kind of fun, particularly when I don't get any more emails about that specific product/service. Take pleasure in the little victories like that instead of letting "them" win by getting boiling mad (or worse, clicking on a link that sends you even more spam if not a lot worse).

Overall, Frustration is often a very short-term trigger when it comes to alcohol, meaning it will often go away after a little while if you let it. Try to cool down any way you can even if it is only for a few minutes.

Take deep breaths, call someone (discussed in Level 4—Engage Friends and Family), or take some time to pray if so inclined (e.g., Level 10—Consider Spirituality).

If it is still sticking around after doing some of the above, there are others things you can do. As noted above, Frustration is closely related to Anger, and many of the tips in that chapter discussion can also be applied here. A subset of tips in the Anger chapter that seem particularly applicable for dealing with Frustration include:[48]

- Go for a fast walk or a run
- Listen to angry music
- Scream
- Vigorous exercise (sit ups, push-ups, etc.)
- Stomp on empty cans (with shoes)
- Have a pillow fight with your wall
- Break sticks
- Clean your room

Lemons into Lemonade Tip: Almost by definition "Frustration" is the inability to control/manage/influence a particular situation. Find things to do where you *can* control/manage/influence a situation that you have been putting off for one reason or another. You will likely find that doing so results in a sense of satisfaction of being able to *do* something, with the added benefit of taking your mind off the original frustration, giving you some time to cool off.

Overall Tip: Frustration will, usually, fade within a short time most of the time. In the *meantime, vent it if you have to but do it safely.*

Related Triggers: Frustration can be caused by your Job, Kids, Loneliness, Relationships issues, Powerlessness, and your eX, among others. In turn, it can activate Anger, Anxiety, Depression, Stress, and Yelling.

Key Defense Levels: Engage Friends and Family, Therapy, Consider Spirituality

FUN

I dealt extensively with "Fun" in Level 1, discussing how using alcohol while enjoying yourself can mutate into alcoholism. But this is only part of the perspective about fun and alcohol. Even well after we have descended into alcoholism, we are still yearning to have what I call "true fun." But many of us have lost sight of how to do it without alcohol involved. So let's step back and take a look at what we all think we know about fun and how we can do things without drinking being a part of it.

First, what is "fun?" Type in "definition of fun" in Google and this is what you get:

> **Noun**—Enjoyment, amusement, or lighthearted pleasure: "anyone who turns up can join in the fun."
>
> **Adjective**—Amusing, entertaining, or enjoyable: "it was a fun evening."
>
> **Verb**—Joke or tease: "no need to get sore; I was only funning"; they are just funning you."
>
> **Synonyms:** *noun.* Amusement; joke; sport; jest; lark; entertainment
> *verb.* Joke; jest : banter: jape: lark

This definition could mean practically anything and could involve practically anything. Since it's impossible to distill and summarize different things that can be fun into anything short of a few gigabytes, let's focus on some of the most obvious aspects of fun as it relates to alcohol. But first it might be helpful to talk about "types" of fun. An interesting guide to how these might be relevant to alcohol comes from *Canoeroots and Family Camping magazine*[49], and is adapted/mutated by me here.

Type I fun is the purest type of fun. It's fun while it's happening. It would be great if it never ended, and when it does end, it can't happen again too soon. It's bluebird days, skinny-dipping, long weekends, s'mores or ~~stopping for a cold beer and~~ a hamburger on the way home. (I struck out the beer, for obvious reasons.) It's the moments you hope for when planning your trip.

Type II fun is stuff that is "kind of fun." Or was fun *once*. You might be glad when it's over, getting home and saying to your partner "Gee, that was fun," kind of meaning it but hoping you don't have to do it again anytime soon. Certain kinds of parties might apply in general, and nearly ALL parties to alcoholics. This type of fun makes for great stories and provides inspiration towards planning your next similar activity, focused a lot on avoiding the same mistakes you made the first time. Camping may be a perfect example of this (sorry *Canoeroots* magazine).

For alcoholics, this may mean activities like going to a baseball game. Sure the game was fun, but being surrounded by tens of thousands of people drinking hundreds of thousands of pints of beer was decidedly *not*. Better to watch the damn thing on TV next time.

Type III fun isn't fun at all. Not while you're doing it, not afterwards. It can't be over fast enough, and you look forward to the day when you forget it ever happened. Examples of this one are limited only by the imagination.

In the article I found referencing this scale, the author related a Type III example: *"I've had my share of Type III moments. In fact, the guide that shared the Fun Scale with me did so as I was being evacuated from an Alaskan mountainside with a perforated lung."*

Unfortunately, there are many types of activities that are fun for the nonalcoholic that meet this Type III definition here for you and me. Parties and ballgames may or may not fit that description for you personally, but somewhere in the mix of other social activities and entertainment excursions you are bound to find an avalanche of Type III activities. Even passive activities like watching TV can fit this bill. Supposed comedies on TV can often be excruciating for the alcoholic, such as "Cougar Town," which has been called *"The most pro-alcohol show on TV."* One commentator says:

> It is more pro-wine than the Pinot Grigio lobby. Jules (Courtney Cox) and her gang of friends consume wine all of the time, often in the morning, with great joy, little embarrassment, and many uproarious drinking games. Just about every episode contains an extended bit about the group's drinking habits, delivered with zero judgment—no one's peeing themselves or losing their jobs here, just having a gay ol' time.[50]

And unfortunately one of the most critically acclaimed TV shows in recent years—Mad Men—is a close second. The commentator continues: *"For good reason,* Mad Men *is generally acknowledged to be the drunkest show on television, what with all the major characters heavily drinking from the time they wake until they go to bed at night."*

Even seemingly benign shows like *How I Met Your Mother* have at least half of their scenes set in a bar, discussing the story line while drinking. And of course the most innocent show can have a Dos Equis commercial with its extremely irritating "most interesting man in the world" theme. We as alcoholics do not need to watch or listen to this kind of crap in my opinion, no matter how well we think we've conquered our alcoholism.

So, when you are thinking about things to do for "true fun," make sure you bounce them off the above "Fun Scale"; it may make you rethink things a bit.

● ●

Fun and Being "Buzzed"

In the Escape trigger chapter, I introduced the Blood Alcohol Content (BAC)-based "desire states" of buzz, rush, numb, and checkout (buzz-rush for short). To me, the desire to have Fun with/by drinking falls right into State 2—the desire to be "buzzed." As discussed very extensively in Level 11—Make Yourself Sick of Alcohol, this state "occurs" at a BAC 0.04 to 0.09%. In this range "Euphoria"[51] is going full blast.[52]

The problem for alcoholics is that we have no control when it comes to drinking, which either means we can't stop drinking *at all* once we've started, or we can't *manage* our intake well enough to stay within our (BAC-driven) desired state. It would be (relatively) fine if we could manage our intake to know when we are starting to get into sloppy/impaired/loss of coordination/stupid behavior territory and stop *right there*. Effectively milking the buzz for all its worth.

But we can't! That's one of the most insidious effects of alcoholism as a disease—it destroys our ability to recognize that we have reached our "limit," which in this case means getting ready to pass into "numb" (where the negative dimensions of alcohol really kick in) and "checkout" (where the truly dangerous aspects come in) states. Or we recognize it and either don't want to stop, can't stop or don't care. Any way you look, it adds up to the same thing—we can't control alcohol. The "fun" part of alcohol—being "buzzed"—just doesn't last long before the shit really starts to hit the fan. So why bother?

● ●

Complicating the idea of "Fun" without alcohol is the fact that there are some very powerful related triggers that in turn can cause major obstacles to having true fun. These include Boredom, Escape, Holidays/ Special Occasions, and Peer Pressure (Friends). The perceived need to have Fun ripples throughout each one of these related triggers, and of course one of the common denominators is alcohol. See those trigger discussions for more details and tips on dealing with them without alcohol.

Tips for Having Fun without Alcohol

Defining whether you are having "fun" or not is not as simple as it sounds. There is a sliding scale from having great fun to not having fun at all—lots of tiny points in-between, not a yes/no answer. With that in mind, you might:

• **Test yourself.** First and foremost, give yourself a mini-test. Can you have fun (however you intuitively define it) without alcohol? Or put another way do you feel that alcohol *always* has to be involved for you to have any fun? If the answer to this second question is Yes, then I believe you have other triggers concealed by the Fun trigger. You may have underlying feelings of Anxiety, Depression, Escape, or Loneliness, for example, or the nature of your friends results in your feeling "Peer Pressure" to always drink when you are around them. You *have* to get at the root of this strong association of "Fun" and alcohol. Continue reading this Level, and reread it if you still are having problems getting at these underlying triggers.

• **Think outside the box.** Or in the box, if you are talking video games. There are many, many categories of *real* fun to consider that you had never thought of before, or dismissed them because they seemed boring or silly. It is very likely that you don't try many things *because* you have never done them before—a class Catch-22[53] situation. Excursions, games, many hobbies, certain types of media (Internet, music, radio, TV, etc.), reading, and sports are some of the most obvious ones. Find the ones that fit your personal tastes and fall into *Type I* fun as much as possible.

• **Laugh.** An area that provides great, true fun for me that I didn't really appreciate when I was drinking is humor writing. There are many authors such as Dave Berry, Janet Evanovich, Stephen King[54], Sophie Kinsella, Christopher Moore, and Terry Pratchett that I personally find hilarious, but it all depends on your taste. *The goal is to find someone or something that can make you laugh.* In the last few years there have also been a proliferation of goofy (intended or not) reality shows that can be very amusing, as well as websites such as *Cracked.com* whose sole purpose is finding as many things in life to make fun of as possible. Try them, try others, but find as many things as possible that will make you smile and laugh out loud (LOLROF, as they say, in texting land).

• **Develop new hobbies.** The need to find new ways of entertaining yourself—including having fun—is critically important for the newly sober, so much that it has its own level in this program: Level 9— Develop New Hobbies. When finally sober, one of the biggest challenges you will find is filling the time that was formerly occupied by your planning for, obtaining, consuming, and recovering from your alcohol consumption. We are talking *hours* a day here folks. One of the best ways to do this is developing a number of new hobbies that can fill the void and be true fun in the process.

• **Distinguish between types of fun.** The Types I, II, and III "fun" described earlier are a great way to classify new activities. Type I is obviously the goal, but you might think through beforehand new things to see if they are really Type II or in particular Type III activities and avoid them accordingly.

• **Watch out for new "addictions."** Perhaps a better term is watch out for new bad habits. Many "professionals" believe that alcoholics have what is called an "addictive personality"—that is, they are "predisposed" to addictive and/or obsessive behaviors—which in terms of non-alcohol fun could mean doing something *else* so frequently and intensely that they might seem like a kind of addiction. To help prevent that . . .

• **. . . Pursue variety.** I don't have a strong personal viewpoint about the prevalence of addictive personalities, but it does point towards a hazard when finding new fun activities—to overdo or repeat the activity until you are burned-out from, tired of, or bored with it. In short, you exhaust all the fun. The problem with this is that it forces you to find new activities to replace those you depleted of fun, which takes time, may not be quite as enjoyable, or may run into unforeseen related triggers. **So try to pace and mix up these new fun activities, so that they can provide enjoyment for many years to come.**

Lemons into Lemonade Tip: Take this opportunity to learn new, and more importantly much better ways to have *real* fun. Learn new ways to laugh, exert yourself, be excited, socialize, even love—those are opportunities that will start to come your way once you are sober. Believe it!

Overall Tip: The desire to have fun, of course, is not going to go away, nor should it—you can't live your life as some sort of Mr. Spock! You have to find new ways of having true fun, making sure you don't trip over other drinking triggers in the process.

Related Triggers: The desire to have Fun (via drinking) can in particular be caused by Boredom, a desire to Escape, Holidays/Special Occasions, Loneliness, Overconfidence, Peer Pressure, Social Situations, and in general feeling Unfun/Uninteresting, as well as a desire to feel Zeal (Excitement). Wanting to have Fun but not feeling that you can do so without alcohol can cause you to feel Boredom, Depression, Envy, a general desire to Escape, feeling Unfun/Uninteresting, and like a Victim (self-esteem issues, e.g., poor me poor me).

Key Defense Levels: Engage Friends and Family, Join a Community, Develop New Hobbies

GUILT (INCLUDES EMBARRASSMENT, REMORSE)

While I try to treat most triggers as relative equals in this program, there is no question that Guilt is an 800-pound gorilla in the alcohol trigger room. Nearly every alcoholic has done many things when they were drinking that they are profoundly ashamed about. Multiplying these misdeeds over the years resulted in broken lives, bodies, families, etc. that at the end of the day are almost impossible to ignore sober. Hence, we want to get drunk—to avoid and forget this Guilt. And of course this causes more misdeeds that result in more Guilt—on it goes in a never-ending cycle.

Guilt tends to kick in as a trigger in many alcoholic's life after several years of alcoholism, when at least a few instances of alcoholism's destruction have occurred (and we have begun to at least subconsciously acknowledge it), such as a lost job or strained marriage. For many of us, this Guilt doesn't stop or even slow our drinking. Perversely, we instead take the approach of "I've done so much damage that I can't undo, so fuck it." And continue, and even accelerate our drinking. It does not help *at all* that many of those closest to us are, usually, trying to Guilt-trip the hell out of us during this time.

In my very strong opinion, and as I indicate in several places in this book, Guilt should be left out of the sobriety equation until the alcoholic has a very significant degree of sobriety under their belt. In other words, **IGNORE GUILT.** But that is talking about dealing with Guilt *after* becoming sober. Dealing with it while trying to *get* sober is even harder. First, some definitions:

> According to *Webster's College Dictionary* guilt is defined as: *"the state of one who has committed an offense especially consciously."*

For sources that are supposedly dedicated to explaining a word they sure have some awkward phrasing . . .

> The *Dictionary of the Psychology* defines guilt as *"An emotional state produced by the knowledge that one has violated moral standards. Most authorities recognized an emotional state as guilt only when the individual has internalized the moral standards of the society; thus it is distinguished from simple fear of punishment from external source— **guilt is in a sense a self-administered punishment.**"*

The last nine words of this definition are the only ones that make any sense at all to me. Fortunately for us laymen, we know Guilt when we see (or feel it). As with the definitions of Addiction in Level 1, it seems like dictionary and medical sources are incapable of defining certain terms that make intuitive sense to the rest of us.

An alternative definition—off the top of my head—seems to get at the heart of it: *Guilt—Feeling bad due to things we have done or not done.* Catchy I know.

Guilt is a huge trigger for many people, both when drinking and after we get sober. While guilt can certainly be caused by many non-alcohol related reasons, it is the guilt for mistakes, misdeeds, lost opportunities and relationships, and the like directly or indirectly caused by alcohol that is the major driver behind Guilt as a drinking/relapse trigger.

> *I have only just realized what mental distress and torture I have put my lovely husband and two kids through. I have been progressively more aggressive towards my husband for at least 3 or 4 years as I can't pinpoint when it started. I am devastated now to the level of harm I have caused. I am now paying the price with the mental torture I am facing, coming to the realization of what I have done. I have devastated my family.*
>
> whathaveudoneclaire, alcoholism.about.com

The triggers of Relationships and (e)X wives et al. are very powerfully related when it comes to Guilt. After many years, I still try to avoid live telephone conversations with my eX because if there is any disagreement on any topic she inevitably brings out the Guilt card to try to bludgeon me with it. Very annoying to say the least. My solution? Do not talk to her live. Text and email instead! Numerous people in alcohol-related meetings I've attended (See Level 7—Join a Community) have brought up some variation of this problem and solution as well.

The medical profession agrees that Guilt is a major issue for alcoholics if you can wade through all of the overly complicated verbiage. To summarize a zillion pages of research, there are several possible reasons why alcoholics experience guilt, leading with:

- Things they did or said while under the influence of alcohol or drugs

- The impact of their addiction on family, friends, and work colleagues

- The damage to their health

- The damage to their finances

- The years wasted on addiction.

God knows how much money was spent on the studies that came up with those ground-breaking conclusions.

One of the biggest reasons in my view why Guilt is such a huge trigger is that it has such a large historical "weight" behind it, particularly compared to other triggers. Unlike say Proximity (being within physical sight of alcohol) or Boredom, which are relatively easy to deal with by avoidance or finding other things to do, Guilt is always there. You really can't avoid it, neutralize it, or walk away from it literally or figuratively. It's like a permanent philosophical hangover that you just can't cure.

Guilt requires a great deal of mental fortitude to deal with, frankly much more than many if not most of the other triggers. It is *way* too easy to let yourself essentially give up and say to yourself "Fuck it. I might as well keep drinking because I can't undo all the shit I've done."

Recognizing this truth is the main reason I emphasize **putting away your guilt.** Don't try to make amends *at this time;* don't try to rationalize; don't do *anything* that has to do with guilt. *Just forget about it, for now.* Plenty of time to make amends once you are once and for all sober and have truly conquered your alcoholism. Letting yourself feel guilty about the past before you are truly ready for it is just setting yourself up for a mega-relapse. And just forgetting about it is probably a good idea even if you *do* relapse.

Critical note: This advice is targeted specifically at the Guilt about the damage your alcoholism has caused your family and friends, as well as your personal life (e.g., impact on career, health, etc.). It is NOT intended for people who have done criminal acts or caused physical harm to others by drinking (e.g., drunk driving accidents, spouse beating and so forth), nor is it intended for far more complex issues such as Post-Traumatic Stress Disorder—PTSD in particular requiring specialized professional help. For criminal acts, you need to do the jail time, fines/fees, personal apologies, while still carrying that guilt the rest of your life (use that as a deterrent for any future possible driving while intoxicated temptations and a broader one to not drink at all). For spousal abuse, see if she/he will forgive you; if they won't then you will just have to deal with that (without drinking) as best you can, making as many amends as possible.

> *I was sober for many months and recently went on a 2 day binge. I don't feel guilty because it happened and it's over. I told a few friends in the program about what happened, however, I did not tell the whole group. I use to feel so guilty when I relapsed that I would stay drunk for months before sobering up.*
>
> anaconda22, soberrecovery.com

Here the alcoholic relapsed and went on a binge (obviously). He decided just to forget about it, plain and simple. If that happens to you it would also be my best advice, *but* I would closely examine the reasons (e.g., triggers) for the binge in the first place, particularly if you have been sober for some time as appears to be the case here.

Several sources coalesced around a few key common themes involving Guilt; all helpful when starting to think of ways to deal with it without alcohol. These include:

• *Many people turn to alcohol or drugs in the first place because they did not feel able to cope with their feelings of Guilt.* The classic chicken and egg: Guilt can cause drinking, as well as be *caused by* drinking. When Guilt is causing the drinking, dealing with it *before* becoming "fully sober" is a necessity. Otherwise relapses are almost guaranteed.

• *People can use Guilt as an excuse not to improve their life.* They may believe that they just do not deserve to be happy. There is a saying in therapy of "Poor, poor me—pour me another one." The person can become trapped in a cycle of self-pity (e.g. Victim-Mentality), Guilt, and non-stop drinking.

• *Feeling remorseful about bad actions can be a good thing.* It shows that you know right from wrong and wants to live a better life. However, *excessive guilt serves no useful purpose* for anyone involved. In that vein . . .

• *Some types of guilt will be more useful than others.* If people are feeling guilty about things they have no control over then this is just a waste of time. If there is something that *can* be done to remedy the situation, then guilt can be beneficial because it motivates action. The key: being aware of what type of guilt is present.

• *It is more productive to view guilt as a learning tool rather than a means of punishment.* Use it to *fix* the future, not destroy it.[55]

Tips on Dealing with Guilt without Alcohol

• **Put aside *ALL* Guilt.** Repeat: do NOT feel Guilty about what you have done while you were drinking. There is nothing you can/could/would/should do about it right now. Maybe later, after many moons of being sober have passed, and your defenses have been fully built, solidified, and tested. Right now all Guilt is a fast one-way ticket to relapse.

• **Do *something* positive.** If you are having a bad day, and/or Guilt is hovering around you waiting to pounce, do *something* positive. Help an old lady cross the street. Better yet, do something you do not *want* to do yet will have clear benefits, such as changing your bed sheets or cleaning your bathroom. In those little things can come a better feeling about yourself and your surroundings.

• **Volunteer.** For "broader" Guilt, consider volunteering. There are many, many volunteering opportunities, from animal shelters to book fairs to soup kitchens and so on. Note: you may have to try several to find the right one for you. You need to find some level of personal satisfaction in it or even enjoyment—it is not some exercise in self-flagellation. Combine it with Level 9—Develop New Hobbies, to potentially deal with other triggers as well.

• **Talk to someone close to you.** Talk to a family member/friend who is familiar with your reason(s) for Guilt and is a non-judgmental-type person. Talking can be greatly beneficial, particularly if you haven't shared your reasons for the Guilt with anyone to this point.

• **"Get" Spiritual.** If you are a spiritual person (or strongly considering it—see Level 10—Consider Spirituality), Guilt is "tailor-made" for it. I'm not being flippant when I say that Guilt (about sinning, etc.) is probably one of the top (if not the top) triggers that can be addressed by praying, asking for forgiveness, and associated acts (such as Communion for Catholics).

Lemons into Lemonade Tip: Retaining *some* Guilt *can* be an effective defense with the right mindset. Some trigger "liabilities" can be turned into assets in The Conquer Program, including Guilt. This is done by including it as part of your progressions (essentially a series of specific defenses for specific types of attacks) which we will be putting together in Level 13 (and building up all the component defenses in Levels 2 through 12).

If you can use your Guilt (or memories of embarrassing situations) as a *deterrent* defense in certain circumstances, such as thinking about how disappointed your youngest daughter will feel if she finds out you were drinking again, then it can be a very strong defense in situations where all your other defenses are breaking down for some reason. In other words, guilt is a kind of defense of last resort.

Overall Tip: If Guilt is not a major *cause* for your overall addiction, *put it aside* while you are getting sober and for a good period of time once achieved. If it IS a/the major cause of the drinking/addiction, and you can't put it aside for now, you may want to consider some professional help to talk through the issues.

An important side note on putting aside Guilt: It drives me a bit nuts when people ask me "when did you stop drinking?" They seem to expect an answer down to the # of days you have been in "recovery." To me, it somehow implies your life before sobriety (e.g., before AA) was a complete waste, which in turn is a subtle but real reminder about the Guilt you "should be" feeling. It also strongly implies that you should "reset" the clock if you have a relapse—that you are only as good as your latest attempt at sobriety. Maybe this is true for Alcoholics Anonymous, where after you relapse you are expected to go back to Step 1 (see Level 7 for more on AA's "12-Steps").

In contrast, The Conquer Program expects a continual building up of knowledge and progress as you work through each Level and program as a whole. Relapses, while regrettable and certainly not encouraged, are not necessarily all bad if you learn from them, specifically what triggers you did not defend against (at all or well enough) that caused you to relapse. Level 11 (Moderation, Relapses, and The Conquer Program) talks more about relapses and what to do if they occur.

Related Triggers: Guilt can be caused by Extreme Emotion (Grief), Kids (how your drinking affected them), Mid-Life Crisis (what did I do with my life), Reminders, damage you feel you did to your Relatives, Relationships, and/or your (e)X, and Victim (abuse you inflicted or feel you allowed). It can activate Anxiety, Depression, a desire to Escape, Loneliness (staying away from the people you hurt), and Victim (abuse and self-esteem issues), among others.

Key Level Defenses: Engage Friends and Family, Join a Community, Therapy, Break Bad Habits, Develop New Hobbies (e.g., volunteering), Consider Spirituality

HEALTH PROBLEMS (PARTICULARLY PAIN)

In Level 3—Listen to Your Body! I go into great detail on how alcohol can damage or even destroy your health. But in classic chicken-and-egg fashion, Health Problems can actually *cause* you to drink, in particular to relieve pain.

> *I had great success with diet and exercise until resulting health problems left me unable to and I find myself reaching for drink again to deal with the resulting stress and depression.*
>
> noscreenname, socialanxietysupport.com

Physical pain is, of course, one of the "best" reasons to seek medicinal-type relief; multi-billion dollar industries are built specifically around this premise. For an alcoholic one of the best "relievers" is of course to drink, and for the newly sober it is particularly difficult if they have a significant physical ailment.

A Google search on "pain and alcohol" yielded about 129 million hits. Interestingly the first hit was a site called *painaction.com.* It had some excellent excerpts, including:

> People have been using alcohol to cope with pain since the beginning of human history. Many people also use alcohol as a way to manage stress, and chronic pain is a significant stressor. Research studies have found that as many as 28% of people with chronic pain use alcohol as a pain management strategy. This research also indicates that men are more likely to have used alcohol as a pain management strategy than women. People with higher income

also may tend to use alcohol more. The use of alcohol to help control pain seems to be connected with the frequency of pain, as those with more frequent pain used more alcohol.

The use of alcohol was not related to how intense the pain was, or how long a person had been living with pain. It's the *regularity* of pain symptoms that seems most connected to the use of alcohol to relieve pain.[56]

I added italics above, since surprised me that drinking "because" of pain became a habit not so much due to how *much* pain the addict was in, but because of its *frequency*.

One interesting take on Pain is not the experiencing of it in the here and now so much as how easy it is to forget what it feels like—the consequences of drinking—be it physical or mental.

> *I am at 6 months and have been here before. I love being sober. It is so much easier to just not drink than to stop. It is when I am at the point where I forget how bad it is for me that I have the one beer. It doesn't start me into the full relapse right away. It is the first brick in the wall of denial. Days go by and then I do it again. Eventually, that will escalate to light to moderate drinking, then to daily and then 6 or more and wham! I'm Baaah Haaack! So, maybe the "trigger" is just poor memory of pain.*
>
> Guest [name withheld], alcoholism.about.com

Reminders of the downside of drinking are a critically important element of sobriety in my opinion, and one I have tried to incorporate into one of the later Levels in this program. It has been proven scientifically many times that the mind has no memory of pain in terms of being able to relive it consciously. This lack of reminders makes it easy to dismiss or diminish its importance when we come up with other triggers tempting us to relive our mistakes that originally led to the pain in the first place!

Tips for Dealing with Health Issues (e.g., Pain) without Alcohol

• **Consult your doctor.** The most obvious one is to consult with your doctor on the cause(s) of pain, and what you can do about it without alcohol—even if it means other kinds of pain killers[57].

• **Make it work for you as aversion therapy!** If you cannot avoid pain, or even if you can—make it *work* for you. The trick is not only to try to "burn" that pain into our conscious memory, but to also burn it into our emotions, sub-conscious memory, and body. Associate pain/discomfort and alcohol as much as you can, as often as you can, in as many circumstances as you can. Much more on this later in Level 11—Make Yourself Sick of Alcohol.

• **Consider alternative medicine.** I recently went to a chiropractor, after hearing very mixed signals about their effectiveness or even its validity as a medical practice. I learned a huge amount of how your skeletal health can impact the rest of your body, including organ health and most importantly pain. My treatments started reducing my pain (in lower back and hips) almost immediately, and longer-term therapy shows permanent correction promise for hip structure issues.

Acupuncture is another possibility for alternative pain management (which is also discussed as a possible alternative alcoholism treatment program in Level 6—Rehab and Therapy), though I have never personally tried it in either form.

Lemons into Lemonade Tip: If possible, try and use the pain as a motivator to exercise more. Many forms of pain can be relieved if the muscles around the affected areas can be strengthened, such as with arthritis.[58]

Overall Tip: When you do have pain, try as much as you can and as often as you can to associate it with alcohol. Even if it does not reflect reality, this constant association in your mind can eventually help you equate the two and help curtail and even eliminate the desire for alcohol (for this trigger at least) as you associate it with suffering and dis-associate it with pain relief.

Related Triggers: Arguably being in poor, painful Health affects nearly every aspect of your life, including most other drinking triggers. Notable ones are Anxiety and Depression, a desire to Escape, Money (paying for health problems) and Stress (causing or caused by health problems).

Key Defense Levels: Listen to Your Body! (in full consultation with your doctor), Consider Spirituality, Make Yourself Sick of Alcohol (only in consultation with your doctor), Develop New Hobbies (to make yourself stronger), Consider Spirituality

HOLIDAYS (INCLUDES SPECIAL OCCASIONS)

Holidays of various sorts can be a significant trigger for many people, particularly since they are unavoidable—there's no control over the calendar! Not all holidays are equal in terms of impact of course. Presidents Day is unlikely to have many people running for the bottle, whereas end-of-year holidays such as Thanksgiving, Christmas, and New Years can be much more of a problem.

There can be many underlying reasons for holidays to cause you to want to drink. Many, maybe even most of them are related to other triggers: the desire to really let go of yourself because everyone else is and you are supposed to be having "Fun" (a form of Peer Pressure); the getting together with Relatives and associated family issues; and Reminders of past holidays bringing back fond and not-so-fond memories are very common.

> *My biggest relapse trigger is coming up, Christmas! This will be my first one sober in many years. I used drinking and other things to cover up times like this and I've got to say that I'm scared to death. I'm going to my mom's for Christmas and going to be with 3 of my 4 kids and that is something I haven't done in years, because I was too busy doing something else. I'm blessed and fortunate to be able and allowed to go this year, but my addiction keeps telling me that I won't be able to handle everything without drinking or popping a pill. Anybody got any advice or words of wisdom? I sure could use it . . . thanks.*
>
> Guest Buffie, alcoholism.about.com

Holidays don't have to be the official ones where you get time off. Some of the more annoying ones fit this description, such as Valentine's Day and Mother's Day, where ads on TV and radio do an incredible job of trying to Guilt you into buying something. Special Occasions such as a friend's birthday, promotion, or baby shower are often just another name for getting together to drink. Even strange dates on the calendar such as Halloween can start a period of vulnerability.

> *I am able to get to $2^1/_2$ to $3^1/_2$ years clean, but I haven't made it to 4 years (yet). The holidays trigger me. I start getting depressed around Halloween, and the stress increases as the time nears for me to spend time with my family. Every year I say to myself, "not this year." Every year I do something*

different for the holidays to decrease the stress. Like last year I didn't put up outside lights and didn't put up my Dickens Village. And after 2¹/₂ years I had two glasses of wine. How crazy is that. Any suggestions for this holiday season are welcomed.

Barbara.jean, alcoholism.about.com

Some "special occasions" are so heavily skewed towards drinking that they are just an excuse to party:

I also remember that at Super Bowl parties and the like; I was struggling to not get too loaded. I would often argue with my date.

Anonymous

From a medical standpoint, there is even a heart-related condition related to holiday drinking, called "holiday heart syndrome," used to describe patients with *atrial fibrillation* who experienced a common and potentially dangerous form of heart palpitation after excessive drinking, which can be common during the winter holiday season. The symptoms, usually, went away when the revelers stopped drinking.[59]

Bottom line is that there are an incredible number of days of the year where you can be subject to a high temptation to drink. You need to be aware of them, particularly those that tempt you severely. Unfortunately most alcoholics are tempted on any day that ends in the letter "Y," so we need to be even more vigilant on these "special" dates.

Tips for Dealing with Holidays
and Special Occasions without Alcohol

• Clearly understand which Holidays and Special Occasions are *truly* issues for you, and which ones are just annoying, or a mild bother.

• Avoid "celebrating" them at all (which may be impossible I realize).

• Go to a community meeting. Trust me, if other alcoholics are attending a meeting on New Year's Eve, they are there for *exactly* the same reason you are.

• Be very conscious of the related triggers on this one. If the Fourth of July is a big one because of Proximity to beer, go to one of the smaller/local fireworks shows where they don't have a beer stand every 30 feet. For more personal occasions such as a friend's baby shower (e.g.,

Peer Pressure, Social Situations), send a gift instead of going to a get-together where you know practically everyone except the expectant mother will be fighting for the wine bottle.

• If your Relatives are a major trigger (or significant related trigger), see that discussion for additional tips you can use in all settings, including holidays.

Lemons into Lemonade Tip: Take the time to learn more about the roots of the holiday/special occasion in question. This new knowledge could be used to sympathize/tolerate the holiday/special occasion more, or at least provide interesting table talk.[60]

Overall Tip: If you can't avoid holiday gatherings, make time to go to a community meeting. There are *always* ones operating on holidays—particularly towards the end of the year—because that is a very vulnerable time for *many* alcoholics.

Related Triggers: The "need" to celebrate Holidays or Special Occasions is often caused by Guilt (if you didn't celebrate), desire to have Fun, Kids, Peer Pressure, Relationships, Relatives, and Social Situations. They can activate the Proximity, Relatives, Smell, Social Situations, and Zeal (excitement) triggers.

Key Defense Levels: Engage Friends and Family (ones that are also not drinking at the time), Join a Community (use often during the holidays), Break Bad Habits (e.g., don't "celebrate" out of Guilt).

HUNGRY (INCLUDES EATING DISORDERS)

Hungry is another area where my original thoughts on the topic were vastly different than what is discussed here. Hungry is the lead item in one of the most well-known trigger abbreviations in Rehab—HALT (Hungry, Angry, Lonely, Tired). For such a commonly used acronym in various therapy and treatment programs, there is surprisingly little research out there on the *direct* topic of Hunger as a drinking trigger. There are several theories however.

The most direct explanation of the "H" is that an increased desire for alcohol due to Hunger is when you have *low blood sugar*, also referred to as Hypoglycemia. Hypoglycemia can occur after a 'rush' of simple carbohydrates (sugar, processed wheat etc.), when blood sugar levels quickly increase, then decrease again just as sharply. It can also occur if you haven't eaten anything for a long time (unfortunately "long" is different by individual). This theory hypothesizes that alcohol craving comes about because *your body associates drinking alcohol with lots of quickly available carbohydrates, and that's what it asks from you.*[61] Low blood sugar is also common during withdrawal/detox

● ●

Hypoglycemia and Alcoholism—A link?

There are a number of proponents of a strong link between the two, notably Dr. Douglas M. Baird. His interest in the treatment of alcoholism dates back to the late 1970s, when he became intrigued by the withdrawal symptoms that many times accompany the cessation of drinking–tremors, weakness, sweating, increased reflexes, gastric symptoms and seizures. These symptoms, he said, often prevented alcoholics from quitting or caused them to replace alcohol with sugar, high carbohydrates, caffeine and/or tobacco.

Working on the premise that alcohol, like hypoglycemia, was related to faulty metabolism, Dr. Baird set out to design a program to meet the recovering alcoholic's needs. Preliminary physical and dietary evaluations are part of this, as well as blood and sugar testing. His goal was to bring back into alignment the chemical imbalance created by years of poor dietary habits [from alcoholism] via proper diet, vitamin therapy and lifestyle changes. He said his program worked because "it stabilize[d] the alcoholic's blood sugar and thus ma[de] it easier for the alcoholic to maintain abstinence."

Related opinions: According to Dr. James R. Milam, in his book, Under The influence, *"There is no question that a great majority of alcoholics suffer from chronic low blood sugar. When given a 5 hour glucose tolerance test, over 95% of both early and late-stage alcoholics experience a spike in blood sugar levels after intake of sugar and then a rapid plunge."*

In Dr. Atkins's *New Diet Revolution,* Dr. Atkins writes, "Experience shows that when an alcoholic succeeds in getting off alcohol, he usually substitutes sweets. This is because almost all alcoholics are hypoglycemic, and sugar provides the same temporary lift that alcohol once did." A number of other doctors echo this claim, saying things like: *"What is most important is the plethora of doctors and counselors who ignore the results of the research that prove that the alcoholic has a blood sugar problem,"* or *"To combat alcohol and other drug abuse, abstinence, proper diet, nutritional supplementation and education about abuse and hypoglycemia must be part of the program."*

In 1982, the concept was introduced. Then the aforementioned doctors wrote about it in the 1990s. Another proponent says: *"It is an absolute must that alcoholics change their diet to control their hypoglycemia or they will never get their alcohol under control . . . .It is very clear that the success rate in stabilizing alcoholism is shamelessly low because one of the main contributing factures, hypoglycemia, is not being addressed."*[62]

- -

The italicized premise (author's emphasis) in the above caption appears to be why this theory is not more prevalent (with little additional references other than the above), versus a much more prevalent view of alcoholism as a disease. But there are some people who have found it effective:

> *I decided to quit when I started losing everything that meant anything to me. The final straw was when I found myself in jail after a 3rd DUI and many years of struggling with alcohol.*
>
> *I used a nutritional approach—it works wonders to help stop alcoholism. I struggled for years trying all sorts of "programs" before I finally found out about the biochemical solution for alcoholism. For me, the physical cravings for alcohol were the problem, not the mental need to "escape" through drinking. What I discovered is common sense—I couldn't stop the physical craving with "talk therapy." I had to correct my biochemistry and change to an intense no sugar diet with several types of nutrients. When I took the sugar out of my diet, the physical cravings eventually went away because there is no "trigger" in the form of sugar or alcohol to start the vicious cycle.*
>
> *I know this all sounds crazy and does not fit what the mainstream media, doctors and pharmaceutical companies say about alcoholism (draw your own conclusions here . . .) But at the end of the day, nothing else worked.*
>
> *You don't have to always use mainstream techniques to stop alcohol. Investigate all options—especially those using a nutritional approach.*
>
> Shawn H., alcoholism.about.com

I have to agree wholeheartedly with the last two sentences—don't be afraid to add unconventional approaches to your defenses. More of these are discussed in Level 6 (Rehab and Therapy—Alternative/Unconventional Treatment Approaches).

● ●

That's All We Need—Drunkorxia!

There apparently is a new trend among college-age students called *Drunkorexia* that involves *not* consuming any calories *other than alcohol* to control weight. The name originated from *anorexia nervosa* [63] because this disorder has the same tendencies but with alcohol consumption. And apparently this is not just a girl thing either. Equal opportunity insanity!

The "key" to this idiocy is the restriction of calories, be it through over-exercising, controlling the diet or purging. People may limit their calorie intake or over-exercise during the day so that when they go out drinking they don't have to worry about gaining weight.[64]

I have to admit that in concept this is not that far from some alcoholics (including me) to eat less in the hours before and during their drinking, hoping for a quicker or longer-lasting buzz. But this seems to take it much further, making it a way of life. Hope they live long enough to enjoy it.

One of the less straightforward theories suggests that craving for alcohol is an *appetitive urge, similar to Hunger,* which varies in intensity and is characterized by withdrawal-like symptoms. The symptoms "are elicited by internal and external cues that evoke memory of the euphoric effects of alcohol and of the discomfort of withdrawal."[65]

Another possibility is a close association of being Hungry with other triggers, such as Taste, Times of Day, or Smell. A growling in your stomach may be what starts the desire to drink, but it may be these related triggers may be the real culprit.

Overall, my own opinion is that the most straightforward view is: A) you are Hungry; B) alcohol is filling; C) it also helps get you buzzed/numb and "deal with" other triggers; therefore D) Drink!

These theories seem to have some degree of common sense, but as I said there is surprisingly little research on the topic of Hunger as a trigger. I will go out on a limb and say that it is because Hunger as a specific, stand-alone drinking trigger is over-hyped due to its inclusion in the HALT acronym, and that it is not a *major, direct* trigger for most people. Certainly I never personally experienced it directly as far as I can tell. I also could not find testimonials for it like I could for nearly every other trigger.

That said, there are some very strong *indirect* drinking trigger elements associated with Hungry. As mentioned earlier, many alcoholics will often *avoid* eating (e.g., *go* Hungry) when planning on particularly serious drinking in the real or perceived view that if they don't eat they will get drunk faster. This was a favorite of mine. It is certainly true that you get drunk faster when you don't eat. It is also true that you will pay for it big-time later in the evening as you get sick or pass out, have an extra-atrocious morning hangover and as you deprive yourself long term of essential nutrients increasing the risk of damage to internal organs due to a more intense, undiluted poisoning of your body.

● ●

Eating Disorders and Bulimia

One eye-opening aspect I found in my later research was the connection between Bulimia and Alcoholism. Research suggests that nearly 50% of individuals with an eating disorder (ED) are also abusing drugs and/or alcohol; a rate 5 times greater than what is seen in the general population.[66]

Former Speaker of the New York City Council, Christine Quinn, was afflicted with both bulimia and alcoholism. According to an article on the topic, "the purging brought a momentary sense of relief to what seemed an out-of-control life. Ms. Quinn also said: *"For a brief moment, you've kind of expelled from your being the things that are making you feel bad."*[67]

Certainly many alcoholics can relate to the desire to "purge" or "numb" themselves to their triggers, even if they don't realize that is their goal in drinking. It is probably not surprising that Ms. Quinn also started drinking heavily at about the same time she started purging food (see the article), and both became regular habits even after her mother died. In her case, there was not a direct indication that one resulted in the other (though certainly the triggers appear similar), but there are others that do. Certainly more research is needed in this area.

Tips for Dealing with Hunger without Trigger

Consider the following:

• The most obvious one, of course, is to EAT. But the devil is in the details on this one, depending on what theory you think is applicable to you.

• If you subscribe to the blood-sugar theory, there is much research on what to do to detect, combat or prevent it (in general, not necessarily in relation to alcoholism). Symptoms can be found at numerous sources, including *www.mayoclinic.com/health/hypoglycemia/DS00198/DSECTION =symptoms.*

• If you believe you are susceptible to the desire to not eat because it will increase your "reaction" to other chemicals (including but not limited to alcohol), then this can be problematic to say the least. Specialized analysis and treatment are likely in order if you can't control those urges on your own. Examples might include downing large quantities of caffeine, smoking (e.g., nicotine), massive herbal supplements, and so on. In general, *regularly* consuming large amounts of practically anything on an empty stomach is not a good idea, and if you do, **tell** your doctor about it.

• If you suspect yourself of having bulimic-type symptoms (see *www.mayoclinic.com/health/bulimia/DS00607/DSECTION=symptoms*) **see your doctor.** There are also specialists who focus simultaneously on *both* eating disorders and alcoholism. If you think this applies to you, do more research and get professional help.

Lemons into Lemonade Tip: Since most people have a desire to lose weight (regardless of whether they need to or not), this trigger is tailor-made to "re-purpose," as in repurposing hunger from a reason to drink to an "enabler" for losing weight. When the desire to drink comes from the arrival of hunger pains, concentrate on re-associating that hunger to the prospective benefit of weight loss, and refrain from drinking (and even eating) *anything.* This is obviously not the best way to lose weight and is a short-term solution until other defenses can kick in (such as arriving at a meeting, where you can safely eat some cookies or drink some coffee).

Related Triggers: Hungry as a trigger can be influenced by Anxiety, Depression, a desire to Escape, Proximity (of alcohol or food), Sex (Body Image issues), Smell and Taste of alcohol/food), and Time of Day. It can activate Anxiety, Depression, Escape, Guilt, and being Tired.

Key Defense Levels: Listen to Your Body!, Break Bad Habits, Develop New Hobbies (particularly those requiring physical activity)

INSOMNIA

For many, many alcoholics, sleep-related difficulties are a major factor in when and how much they drink. For some, they just can't get to sleep without it or cannot stay asleep all night if they don't have enough alcohol in their system. Others (including me) feared going to sleep without (enough) alcohol because of the tremendously bad dreams they experience. Bad dreams are a common side effect of alcohol withdrawal, and discussed elsewhere in this book, particularly in Appendix A. We will hit each of these in turn, but first you need to understand the strange dual nature of alcohol as both a sedative and a stimulant.

Alcohol produces both stimulant and sedating effects in humans. These two seemingly opposite effects are central to the understanding of much of the literature on alcohol use and misuse. Drinking alcohol can significantly increase heart rate and aggression by causing Dopamine[68] release. But at its chemical core it is a depressant, significantly slowing down your brain and body functions.[69] As alcoholics well know, both the stimulant and depressant effects of alcohol are very often experienced in the same session of drinking. In fact, many of us want to get past the stimulant effects quickly—particularly as the night wears on—and drink more to get us to that depressant stage so we can get to sleep.

Getting to Sleep

This is tough! I can't sleep without alcohol. It's ruled my life for so long and has robbed me of the quality of it, which I regret the most.

bertistheword, alcoholism.about.com

The most commonly understood aspect of Insomnia, of course, is the inability to fall asleep. According to the Mayo Clinic, common causes of Insomnia include: Stress, Anxiety, Depression, medical conditions (Health), caffeine, nicotine, Change in your environment or work schedule, poor sleep habits, eating too much in the evening, and "learned" sleep habits. And of course, alcohol, particularly when it is in its "stimulant" stage.[70]

But once it passes (at least temporarily in this stage) many of us can fall asleep. Of course, there is a fine line between falling asleep and passing out . . .

Medical Fun Fact

Q: Why do people sometimes pass out from drinking too much alcohol?

A: A person may pass out from drinking too much alcohol when it reaches high levels in the *Reticular Activating System*, or RAS. The RAS is the part of the brainstem and midbrain that controls whether you are awake or asleep. Alcohol levels quickly reach equilibrium throughout the brain. Different brain regions have different levels of sensitivity to alcohol. Some are affected by very low levels of alcohol while others require **higher levels** of exposure.[71]

Higher levels indeed. And of course it doesn't help that the longer we drink the more we have to drink to achieve the same effect, e.g., the building up of tolerance—a critical element of alcoholism. This is true in general and also specifically in falling asleep.

Staying Asleep

Alcohol may help you fall asleep, but once the alcohol levels are reduced by the passage of time, normal sleeping patterns are disrupted.

After a night or two of very little sleep, I think that a few drinks will help. They do knock me out, but a few hours later I am in the same situation again. I remind myself that it is better to be tired in the morning than hungover, and there are natural remedies for insomnia.

guest Anne, alcoholism.about.com

According to the National Institute of Alcohol Abuse and Alcoholism (NIAAA), alcohol can affect sleep in multiple ways (bear with me in some pretty dense medical language below, but it is important).

First, many studies divide sleeping into two periods—the first half and the second half (they needed a doctorate for that?). The first period is the getting to sleep/early sleep period. In an assessment of various studies, the NIAAA found that (particularly at higher alcohol doses) increased wake periods occurred during the second half of the sleep period. This second-half disruption of sleep continuity is interpreted as a "rebound effect" once alcohol has been completely metabolized and eliminated from the body. But this is not a "good" rebound, as it causes major sleep disruption.

In addition to screwing up both halves in general, the studies found significant disruptions within each half. Most studies reported a dose-dependent (re: how much you scarfed down) suppression of *REM sleep* at least during the first half of the sleep period. Those studies that have demonstrated alcohol-induced REM suppression during the first half of the sleep period also have frequently found a REM rebound (i.e., longer-than-normal REM periods) during the second half of the night. Bottom Line: Alcohol screws up all stages of sleep.[72]

Fear of Nightmares

So, alcohol obviously screws up sleeping. But to add to the misery, many alcoholics experience *very* bad dreams, a.k.a. bitch nightmares, when we are sleeping. This fear is almost a trigger in itself—to drink and drink so much that you can blast past these nightmares.

This was one of my biggest personal sub-triggers for wanting or "needing" to drink to fall asleep (e.g., pass out). In other words, I wanted to avoid or ignore the nightmares I had when I did NOT drink, or drink enough. This in turn was a major factor in my related trigger—(Fear of) Quitting.

According to *WebMD.com,* nightmares are *"vividly realistic, disturbing dreams that rattle you awake from a deep sleep,"* which can also make your sleep so exhausting that you can wake up more tired than you were when you went to bed. They often set your heart pounding from fear. Nightmares tend to occur most often during rapid eye movement (REM) sleep, when most dreaming takes place. **Unsurprising and, unfortunately, withdrawal from medications and substances, including alcohol and tranquilizers, may trigger nightmares.**[73] Hence, my personal fear of going to bed sober, which was one of the biggest—if not THE biggest—post-drinking adjustments I had to make. Appendix A—Learning to Sleep in Early Sobriety, discusses some possibilities for helping you in getting to sleep without alcohol. But you may have to face the hard reality, as I did—*learning to sleep once you are sober can be a long, frustrating process.* But one you can get through, and be glad you did! It took me months to get to a point where I could get a good night's sleep, but it was worth it since my quality of life is far, far better than before, particularly in terms of energy levels and hours of productivity.

Tips for Dealing with Insomnia without Alcohol

For Tips dealing with Insomnia both while you are getting sober and afterwards, see Appendix A—Learning To Sleep in Early Sobriety.

Lemons into Lemonade Tip: Several people I know who are affected by insomnia are also some of the most productive. They use time in the middle of the night to accomplish many things such as furniture refinishing—activities that otherwise would never get done or take "normal" people far longer. The point: try and make the most of this extra time.

Related Triggers: Insomnia can be caused by many things, most notably Anxiety, Change, Depression, (Fear Of) Quitting, Stress, and being overly Tired. It can activate or make worse many other triggers, particularly the desire to Escape, Job issues, Fear of Quitting, physical Stress, and of course Tired.

Key Defense Levels: Break Bad Habits (that worsen insomnia, such as caffeine; drink relaxing non-addictive beverages), Develop New Hobbies (particularly physically strenuous ones), Consider Spirituality, Appendix A

JOB

Your Job is a leading nominee in the most-alcohol-consumed-because-of trigger category. There are so many sub-triggers it's hard to count them: having a lousy boss, bad pay, no chance for advancement, not being good at your job, being too good at your job, being in a boring business, being in a too dynamic business, lousy coworkers, too-good coworkers, difficult customers, administrative nightmares, and maybe above all: hating the work that you actually do because its dull, boring, too easy, too hard, or maybe all of the above.

Of course, to have any of the above feelings, you actually have to *have* a job. At the time of this writing (2013–2014), the economy has been in essentially a recession or a period of very slow growth mode for over six years, resulting in many, many unhappy, unemployed/underemployed alcoholics:

> *I've been unemployed for $2^1/_2$ yrs. now and drink heavily every day. I keep saying I will look for work "tomorrow." I know I'm digging my hole deeper every day. My sister who is also an alcoholic moved in with me due to certain circumstances. She's not in good health mostly due to her own alcohol consumption. My brother-in-law just recently died from alcohol. I feel totally lost and want help. I feel totally trapped.*
>
> Leslie114, alcoholism.about.com

Hopefully, you have at least some job, as unemployment brings on oodles of free time that is just begging for a drink, and of course other troubles like Frustration and Money troubles. But even if you do, odds are there are at least one or two dimensions of your job that you don't particularly like. "Fortunately" there are whole legions of psychiatrists and business gurus who make their living out of analyzing work and their impact on the individual. Many large companies even used to have in-house psychiatrists to "help" in the hiring, management, and firing of workers, believe it or not.[74] However, my experience is that these resources do not focus on alcohol-consuming *cause* dimensions of the workplace.

Instead, the research and material out there is focused on the *result* of alcohol in the workplace—not the potential causes of alcohol abuse *by* the workplace—including identifying substance abuse issues in workers (drinking right before or during working hours, and/or heavy drinking before causing hangovers during work), the results (accidents, lost productivity), dealing with it (legal and regulatory requirements[75]), statistics (injuries, frequency), as well as dimensions around substance abuse policies within company health benefit programs.

One interesting area I found was that certain industries are more prone to alcohol abuse than others. These include:

- Food service
- Construction
- Mining and Drilling
- Excavation
- Installation, maintenance and repair[76]

Construction and Mining have the highest percentage of alcohol abuse, with 1 in 7 having such problems.[77] Frustratingly, these studies do not get into meaningful analysis of *why* these industries have such high rates of alcohol abuse. One could make educated guesses such as the preponderance of males in those fields (males representing two-thirds of the alcoholic population in general, and probably 95% of those physically working those environments), a higher degree of physical risk, injuries, and/or medical problems, and so on—but there is no meaningful data to support such theories. And they don't begin to address other totally different industries such as food service, with its higher representation of women. As meaningful insight as it gets seems to be along the lines of "Employees with alcohol problems are not likely to leave those problems behind when they come to work."[78] No shit.

One theory that I strongly support is around the relationship between one's Job and their personal "identity"—who we think we are as a person, including how others perceive us positively or not. A job is not just the key to our income, nor just one of the single biggest things we do in our waking lives. It can be much more than that for many people—even representing the cornerstone of how we view ourselves—past, present, and future.

Many people, historically men but pretty much now an equal oppor-

● ●

A Note to Those in High Stress Industries

I'm not about to get into a debate about what constitutes a "high stress" industry. I do know I spent the first 15 years of my post-graduate employment in one—strategic management consulting. It routinely (and I mean far more often than not) required 60–80 workweeks, constant traveling, and bosses who gave exactly zero shits when it came to worrying about its impact on my personal life[79].

To make matters worse, it is (or at least was) a "work-hard, party-hard" environment to say the least. After a 12-hour workday, you were expected to go out with your project team for drinks, dinner, and more and more drinks, often to midnight or beyond, and then get up after 6 hours sleep and start the whole process again. That Job (via multiple firms) was (in hindsight) a major trigger for me, as I was a "Type B" person (e.g., low key) in a *very* "Type A" person (e.g., very aggressive) environment.

In retrospect, this "career" was my #1 trigger for many years. In addition, I am *convinced* that it laid one of the cornerstones for my alcoholism—Tolerance. You couldn't help but develop tolerance if you were drinking heavily 2–4 hours each night at least 2–3 nights a week while getting only 6 hours of sleep—particularly while traveling. Even when you weren't out with the project team, the nights and weekends you often had to work would "require" some alcoholic beverage almost every night just to "relax," the result being that rarely a day passed by when you didn't drink—a sure way to build tolerance.

If you see similarities above to your personal situation, be very concerned that this may be forming an alcoholism cornerstone for you in the future if it has not already. If you have already admitted you are an alcoholic in Level 1 or are starting to see signs of it, and you are in this kind of high stress job—*get out of it as soon as you can* is my unqualified advice. Period; no ifs, ands, or buts—do something else.

● ●

tunity misery maker for women, have a big part of their personal identity defined by what they do for a living: "I'm a lawyer"; "I'm a marketing manager"; "I'm a construction worker." In meeting a person for the first time in a social setting, after the usual small talk there is almost inevitably some form of the question, "What do you do?" And, even though people may mean well by the question, they may feel better about you or themselves, or even evaluate or think about you differently, based on your response.

There are, of course, many factors that go into determining our sense of self, e.g., defining the essence of who we are. Beyond innate personality, these include (in no particular order) appearance, family, ethnicity, socio-economic status (e.g., middle class), gender, sexual orientation, friends, dating/relationship "status," religion, and last but not least occupation.[80] Unsurprisingly, when one of those pillars of identity is attacked or damaged, we as an individual feel personally attacked or damaged.

> *After almost eleven years of work and twenty months sober, my employer let me go. I was hurt, confused although I know this is just an "at will" working state (CA) Any normal person would just move on. I felt like I'd gone through a painful breakup. This man had been at my wedding, met my family, I'd visited his family on the east coast.*
>
> Guest Donna B. alcoholism.about.com

More typically, however, people don't psychoanalyze themselves when it comes to their job, particularly when they are not dealing with extremes of unemployment, job loss, or extreme circumstances (e.g., sexual harassment) within the job. More typically it is "just" dissatisfaction with the general everyday circumstances of the day-to-day activities. These typically fall into one of the following categories (and are tailor-made for a Top Ten List[81]):

10 **You think the grass is greener someplace else.** If your friends (or much more likely friends of friends of friends) are having an amazing experience at another company, why wouldn't you be envious? This is periodically made worse by highly irritating media love-fests with twenty-something Facebook-type founders rolling in millions/billions of $. This kind of "what if" (what if I had done this instead of that) kind of "Guilt" (remorse) added to Envy can be significant related drinking triggers.

9 **Your values don't align with the company.** Dissatisfaction is bound to happen if your skills, priorities, and personality don't fit with those of your company. You may value creativity and collaboration, but your company wants robotic automatons, or vice versa. This dissatisfaction gets worse if the quest for the almighty buck totally obscures more personal feelings such as work-life balance, employee satisfaction, etc.

8 **You don't feel valued.** You never get positive feedback. You are constantly criticized. You feel you are making less for contributions compared to others around you. There are many forms this can take, cutting particularly close to your sense of identity. If you don't feel valued in your job, you may not feel valued as a person—hence making you want to drink to deal with the Depression and/or Escape from reality.

7 **Job insecurity.** It's easy to dislike your job when you're worried whether you will still have it a few months or a year from now. If your company is going through hard times, the instability may be taking a toll on you and everyone around you. Nothing like living in a climate of fear to make you want to Escape at the end of the day.

6 **There's no room for advancement.** A great reason for being Depressed. With no room to grow career-wise, you may feel that you have no room to improve as a person, e.g., your sense of identity starts to feel stalled, or at a dead end. This feeling can activate many other potential drinking triggers, such as Escape, Envy, and Frustration.

5 **You're unhappy with your pay.** A direct extension of #8 above, nothing extinguishes passion and generates feelings of unhappiness quite like the feeling of being paid less than you deserve.

4 **There's too much red tape.** While, hopefully, no one ever turned to a bottle specifically because of bureaucratic BS, there is no doubt this is an area that can cause a great deal of Frustration.

3 **You are not being challenged.** This has Boredom written all over it!

2 **The passion's gone.** There's a huge difference between living to work and working to live. The current job climate has led many people to take on jobs they don't love. Or don't like. Or hate hate hate. And makes you want to Escape Escape Escape. By drinking.

1 **Your boss sucks.** A bad boss is number 1 for a reason; more than any other factor having a good or bad boss can be by far the biggest single factor in happiness (or not) in your job. In my view a slightly boring, somewhat dead-end job is much more positive (for an alcoholic anyway) than a really good job with a horrendous boss.

So keep these kinds of root job dissatisfaction reasons in mind as you figure out if, and if so how, your Job may make you want to drink. Of course, you may think you may be stuck even if you know *exactly* why your Job sucks and makes you want to drink, but there are nearly always options—if not right at the moment then sometime relatively soon if you do a bit of planning ahead.

· ·

A Note on Women and Job Stress

According to the *Wall Street Journal*, women feel especially stuck and tense, with more women than men saying that their employers don't provide sufficient opportunities for internal advancement. Women are more likely to feel tense during a typical workday, reporting more often that their employer doesn't appreciate what they do.

The article states: "Emotional responses to [Job] stress often divide along gender lines, with men more likely to have a "fight or flight" reaction while women are more likely to have a "tend and befriend" response." It continues: "Women tend to 'internalize' [Job problems] which contributes to their stress . . . Many women [in Job situations] hesitate to speak up for themselves or challenge behavior they see as unfair."[82]

· ·

Tips for Dealing with Job Issues without Alcohol

Everyone's situation is going to be different, of course, with very significant constraints about and around the types of Jobs they can do based on training, education, technical skills, physical capabilities, etc. as well as obviously the economic conditions of the time, where they live, what industries are prevalent, etc. So offering Job tips is kind of pointless, and certainly outside the scope of this book. That said, there are some things you can do—and *not* do—to help reduce how much your Job may cause you to want to drink. These include:

• **Identify your sub-triggers.** This section started out with a bunch of different ways that your Job could really bug you. Instead of just saying "my job sucks," try to get underneath what *specifically* is causing you problems. It might be obvious (e.g., crappy boss), but then again maybe not (your job is starting to bore you but you don't consciously realize it). Then manage your day-to-day working life as best you can to minimize the stress and chaos that particular sub-trigger causes.

- **Avoid drinking situations.** Obvious yes, but not so easy to avoid, particularly if you don't want your co-workers to know about your situation (which is probably 99% of the time). Maybe you need to go to the company holiday party for political reasons, but that does *not* mean you have to go to the Friday happy hours after work. Make excuses (got errands to run), lie outright, whatever it takes—but do *not* give into real or perceived pressure to be in high-risk drinking environments.

- **Plan ahead.** This is not so much a drinking-specific tip as it is general career planning. You need to plan for a worst-case scenario, which is, usually, either A) job loss or B) the job from hell. Odds are it *will* happen to you at least once, and when it does it will be one of the most vulnerable times in your trying-to-stay-sober life. Getting a new job is *very* time-consuming, and in bad economic times can take one to two years if you are starting from scratch.

So make sure you will *not* be starting from scratch, and by that I mean always have your resume fresh; continue to build/maintain your network of contacts; post your resume on job boards; periodically apply to jobs to get the latest experience and see what other employers are looking for; continually look for opportunities to upgrade your skills, and so forth. Remember, you will have those "extra special" related triggers like Boredom or Money problems just waiting to jump on your trigger bandwagon. So a prolonged period of a bad or no Job will continue to magnify your desire to drink as time progresses.

Lemons into Lemonade Tip: Many happy jobs have been found due to *un*happy Jobs. Indeed, unless the employment situation becomes miserable, many people will not find the motivation to look for better opportunities. Try it!

Overall Tip: Reflect on the positive—before you go home at night, take a moment to savor the day's "wins." A recent research study from the *Academy of Management Journal* shows that workers reported lower stress levels in the evenings after spending a few minutes jotting down positive events at the end of the day, along with why those things made them feel good.[83]

Related Triggers: Triggers that can both influence and be influenced by Job issues and situations include Anger, Anxiety, Boredom, Change, Frustration, Money, Social Situations, and Stress.

Key Defense Levels: Listen to Your Body! (understanding the substance abuse benefits of your employer health plans), Engage Friends and Family (vent, discuss your Job and career)

KIDS (CHILDREN)

Children are our joy, blessing, reason for existing, etc., etc., etc. And no, I'm not being sarcastic; I have four children of my own and firmly believe that and more. However, no one who has children, particularly ones fairly close in age, can deny that there are times when they can drive you absolutely batshit with the crying, whining, screaming, fighting, drooling, barfing, poopy diapers, and destruction of, well, anything and everything. You don't have to be an alcoholic to let this chaos drive you to drink. A lot.

> *It was hard to look at my triggers, because the number one item on the list was my kids. Admitting my kids were my biggest trigger, and having safe people to talk to about it, was the turning point in my early recovery.*
>
> Anonymous

The related triggers associated with children can be very heavy on the senses, particularly for younger children when it comes to Noise, Disorder, and Smell. After hours of sensory overload, a parent can understandably want to take a load off and de-Stress, with alcohol often the easiest way to do so.

A *very interesting article on women and drinking*—particularly wine—came out recently (June 2013) in the *Wall Street Journal.* The following is one key excerpt regarding children:

> Alcohol and motherhood were intertwined, so much so that after I had my third daughter in the anxious autumn after 9/11, I received bottle after bottle of wine as baby gifts.
>
> The growing female predilection for wine seems at first glance like a harmless indulgence for harried mothers who deserve a break. There are T-shirts with a spilled wineglass that say, "Not so loud, I had book club last night." Nearly 650,000 women follow "Moms Who Need Wine" on Facebook and another 131,000 women are fans of the group called "OMG, I So Need a Glass of Wine or I'm Gonna Sell My Kids." The drinking mom has become

a cultural trope, from highbrow to pop: Jonathan Franzen's Patty Berglund wanders through the first half of "Freedom" with a ruddy complexion he calls the "Chardonnay Splotch." Wine is so linked to the women of "Real Housewives" that several cast members have introduced their own brands.[84]

And it doesn't necessarily get better as the children get older. Just different:

> *Well friends, I can't allow them [my kids] to pull me under the way I have in the past. Why is it that as parents, we love them unconditionally, yet they judge, belittle, don't even call, and they don't think that hurts. I have to be vigilant when it comes to letting them break my heart, [because] I will drink. It has happened before, but I won't let it happen again. They are 29, 26, 24 and an 8-year-old grandson, so their lives are a whirlwind and they keep me out of the loop since my divorce from their dad. The hurt can literally drop me to my knees sobbing. It has been 11 years since the split. I have learned to pay no bother to others, that are mean, why can't I deal with them the same way? I will not drink, I will not give in . . . .today.*
>
> Guest Kid-o, alcoholism.about.com

Several publications in psychological literature support the theory that children are a major source of Stress for their parents. Not surprisingly, parents of children with behavior problems—particularly children with attention deficit hyperactivity disorder (ADHD)—experience highly elevated levels of daily child-rearing stresses. Children with ADHD disregard parental requests, commands, and rules; fight with siblings; disturb neighbors and have frequent negative encounters with schoolteachers and principals. Although many investigations have dealt with parenting stress caused by disruptive children, only a handful of studies have addressed the question of how parents cope with this stress. Those studies strongly support the assumption that the deviant child behaviors that represent major chronic interpersonal stressors for parents of ADHD children *are associated with increased parental alcohol consumption.*

Studies also have demonstrated that *parenting hassles may result in increased alcohol consumption in parents of "normal" children.*[85]

So if you think you may be a "bad" parent because your children make you want to drink, or if you think you are a small minority to use alcohol to "cope" with the stress of parenting, you are not alone—not by a long stretch. Below are some ideas for doing something other than drinking to deal with or unwind after a long day of "child management." Many are just common sense ideas, but ones that tend to get lost in the daily chaos of child-rearing. These are just the tip of the iceberg—you will need to find your own, highly personalized way to deal with this particular trigger.

Tips for "de-Stressing" From Dealing with Children without Alcohol

• **Take a *good* time-out.** When your children are safely pre-occupied or sleeping, *don't* just veg-out. It is not all that stress-reducing and may well lead to the temptation to drink. Instead try to listen to music, meditate, or practice relaxation and/or stretching/yoga techniques.

• **Eat well-balanced meals.** An obvious one that is often first on the list of things we do NOT do. *Do not* skip any meals. Make the ones you have count for the most nutrition you can while still keeping them appetizing. *Do* keep healthful, energy-boosting snacks on hand. *Don't* eat foods with which you have a close association with drinking, particularly wine.

• **Avoid Smoking and other substances associated with drinking.** Many people closely associate drinking with smoking and vice versa. *Understand* what substances you do associate with drinking, and avoid them like the plague when you are de-stressing.

• **Limit caffeine.** Caffeine can also aggravate Anxiety and trigger panic attacks. Tough to do when you are operating on a few hours' sleep (see below); this makes having regular, well-balanced meals all the more important in terms of helping your energy levels.

• **Get enough sleep.** If only! But when stressed, your body needs additional sleep and rest. Try to work out an arrangement with your partner to take turns with the nighttime and morning routines so you can both get some solid sleep at least some of the time! Grogginess due to lack of sleep may well make you vulnerable to your other triggers.

• **Exercise daily.** Going to the gym might be a pipe-dream to many in terms of time and logistics. But it is essential in helping you feel good and maintain your health, in addition to "working off" stress. There are lots of opportunities for exercise when you have children: walking them in a stroller when they are young; strolling the sidelines during games when they are older; power-walking through the store or mall; playing with them on the playground instead of just sitting; doing stretching exercises when preparing meals. There are lots of opportunities if you look for them and *remind yourself to do them at the time;* because they are so easy to forget, despite best intentions.

• **Stretch.** I carved this out separately from Exercise because a) you can literally do it at almost any time and b) it is *greatly* underappreciated as a stress reliever. Stress does an amazing job of collecting in your muscles—neck, shoulders, back, even hands and feet. And it just sits there and festers, which hardly helps in resisting a desire to drink. While stretching is a huge part of Yoga, to realize its benefits you do *not* have to go to a class or sit at the feet of some yoga master. Once you've got the *basic stretches* down, you can do them almost anywhere, from taking a shower to eating to getting ready for bed.

• **Slow down your blood pressure.** During particularly challenging child caring periods (e.g., the baby has screamed non-stop for an hour) take deep breaths, inhale and exhale slowly. Count to 10 slowly. Repeat, and count to 20 if necessary. This activity can evolve into deeper meditation and relaxation techniques, but just doing these basic ones can help a great deal. The temptation to take a sedative (e.g., alcohol) can be particularly acute during these periods.

• **Control Disorder.** This related drinking trigger is often grossly underestimated by all alcoholics, and for parents in particular having a reasonably ordered, clean living environment can be a massive challenge. If you can at all afford the $ it takes to have a periodic professional cleaning, it is well worth it, even if it is only once a month.

In general, though, you need to think through the best times of the day for you to pick up after your children. Some may do it every time something drops on the ground, falls over, is left out of the toy bin, etc. This approach may indeed be the least stressing, but consider whether it might make more sense (from a stress perspective, not to mention your lower back) to do it all at once at the end of the day, or at set times such as when the kids are down for a nap or getting ready for bed.

Not to venture into parental advice territory (don't shoot me!), but if you can establish rules for your children about putting their toys away when done or (as they get older) putting their dirty clothes in the hamper, you will reap the benefits of such discipline for years to come when it comes to controlling disorder.

- **Strategically choose your personal leisure activities.** Make them *as far away* from drinking as you can, mentally and physically. This includes *not* going out with your friends that you know will be drinking. Or running an errand for your partner or friend that they are perfectly capable of doing for themselves. In other words, *be selfish.* Try to do something for yourself, such as a manicure or massage. I recommend a massage in particular; they are very enjoyable and even can be proven to release Stress. The Touch Research Institute at the University of Miami School of Medicine found in a 2005 study that just 30 minutes of massage lowered *cortisol (a stress hormone)* by a third.[86]

- **Do your best, and accept that you cannot control everything.** Instead of aiming for perfection and total control, which isn't possible, try to get as close as you can without stressing yourself out. *And don't feel you have to be perfect in all things with regards to your child.* Accepting this is one of the hardest lessons to learn as a new parent.

One of the more interesting stories my (eX) wife and I tell about having four children was how we reacted when his/her pacifier would fall to the ground when they were infants/toddlers. For child #1 we would rush to sterilize it with boiling water, wait for it to cool, and then stick it back into his mouth. For #2, we would rinse it off in a faucet, at first at least waiting for it to get hot, and then only waiting for it to get warm, then finally any temperature would do. For #3, we would just stick it in our mouth to clean it off. And for #4 we would just brush the pacifier off on our shirt to get rid of the visible stuff. Gross you say! Perhaps, but they all turned out fine, and none came down with any diseases from our practices. And it helped us stay a little bit more sane.

- **Find humor wherever you can.** A good laugh goes a long way to taking the edge off of stress. Instead of watching or reading depressing news, find something funny! Sometimes finding something that specifically recognizes the challenges of alcoholics—in a funny way—can be very relaxing, such as *www.cracked.com/article_18824_5-things-nobody-tells-you-about-quitting-drinking.html.*

- **Talk to someone.** This is last but certainly not least. Talking to friends or acquaintances that have children and/or are in similar personal circumstances can be very therapeutic as well as fun (obviously *don't* do this while meeting a drinking friend at a bar or similar environment). Maybe combine talking with some of the other tips, such as exercising/ walking. As we all know, multi-tasking is essential when it comes to having children!

Lemons into Lemonade Tip: Before you know if your children will be out of the nest, and if you don't prepare for it you may find the transition very jarring, even to the point of relapsing due to Boredom, etc. Use the time while they are at school wisely, perhaps even going back to school yourself, to prepare for essentially a new life once the children are gone.

Overall Tip: One of the toughest things to do when we are under various forms of high stress is to step back and reflect on the positive things in our life. While children can certainly bring very high (and unique) levels of stress in our life, they also can bring the greatest joy possible. Reflect on this fact whenever you can, and incorporate it as much as you can in your collection of defenses against alcohol when the daily stress of dealing with Kids seems overwhelming.

Related Triggers: Triggers that can aggravate children issues include Relationships, Relatives, and your eX. Kids can create Guilt (that your drinking has on them), Noise, Disorder, new Relationship issues, pushy Relatives, Smell, and Stress.

Key Levels of Defense: Engage Friends and Family, Join a Community (that can provide downtimes, other activities without alcohol), Break Bad Habits, Develop New Hobbies (e.g., without children)

LONELINESS

Loneliness is a strong trigger for many people, particularly those with few friends or family close by, or few or none at all. You may have many family members, but if you have been an alcoholic for a long time odds are you are estranged from many of them—either by their choice or yours.

Same deal with friends—once you think about it (when not drinking). You may realize you don't have many friends, and/or the ones you do have are "drinking" friends, which in *many* respects are not friends *at all* for people dealing with drinking problems. So the net result is that you feel all alone, even surrounded by people.

There are times when the lonely feelings creep back in. They make me feel like I am alone in a room full of people. They make me feel like I will be "single" for the rest of my life, with no one to share the goings on of busy life. They make me feel like I don't have a voice, that maybe I am not good enough at what I do.

NH, cryingoutnow.com

Loneliness has long been recognized as a major trigger of alcohol abuse, being enshrined in one of the most well-known acronyms used in rehab—H.A.L.T.—for **H**ungry, **A**ngry, **L**onely, and **T**ired. That's great on the surface, but in my experience most rehabs don't drill down that much on what "Loneliness" actually means; instead they assume that everyone knows the meaning. But this is *wrong*—Loneliness can mean *very* different things to different people. These people can range from "natural" loners to ones who supposedly have many strong relationships.

"Loners"

One way of defining a loner would be to say that it refers to people *who prefer to be alone,* especially one who *avoids the company of others.* This behavior of desiring to be alone has traditionally been viewed as odd or suspicious. The term lone wolf may be used to refer to such people because just like humans the wolf is considered to be a social animal. It is common to view loners as people who are missing out on the joy of life, but this is *not* always the case. There are people who just genuinely prefer their own company and are quite comfortable with solitude. This is how I view myself in general, and the specific "naturally introverted" and "shy" types described in the panel (depending on the circumstances).

● ●

Types of Loners

The word *loner* can be used to describe a number of different types of people including:

- *Naturally introverted.* Some people just prefer their own company, and they do not feel like they are missing out on anything by spending a great deal of their time alone.

- *The shy individual.* These people may not like being alone, but they just do not feel comfortable around other people. The fact of being a loner can make shy people feel miserable.

- *It's "Good."* Some people choose to become loners because they feel it will benefit their life in some way. An example of this would be the spiritual seekers who go live in a cave so they can meditate undisturbed, or those people who go live in the middle of nowhere so they can write a great novel.

- *Self-fulfillers.* Those are people who worry about what other people think—including with respect to alcohol—and may do all their drinking behind closed curtains, so they become more isolated. This isolation causes them to drink more, which . . .

- *Physical Health.* Some people just become isolated because of where they live or because their physical health has deteriorated so that they are house bound.[87]

● ●

There are no statistics that I'm aware of that indicate if, how, and to what degree these types of people are more susceptible to alcohol abuse than others. But it is safe to say that if you *do* have an alcohol problem, *and* you can admit to yourself that Loneliness is a major trigger for you, *and* you can articulate to yourself how it manifests itself in one of the above categories, then you are close to figuring out your underlying reasons for drinking (at least for this trigger and its related triggers).

> *I never get really drunk, I just get to the point where I don't feel the emotional emptiness and pain of being alone all the time. I really wish I had something better to do, but I don't know what it would be. I don't have a lot of options currently.*
>
> Guyeva, socialanxietysupport.com

But Loneliness is not the exclusive territory of the Loner. Even people who supposedly have many friends can feel that way. If you already have an alcohol problem, being married or having a long-term partner can make Loneliness *worse,* as the odds are also leaning towards your being estranged from them. Many such companions will have "nagged" you about your drinking for quite a while before you started to consider that you actually have a problem—let alone start to do something about it. So in all likelihood you have started to shut them out of your drinking life, which basically means most of your waking life. You feel you can't confide in them about what you are thinking and feeling, because if you do you either feel they are not listening or even worse use your words and feelings against you. It is a sick feeling; *one that can make you want to drink even more.*

To make matters worse, there are many related triggers for Loneliness, including Boredom, Depression, Escape, Peer Pressure, Relationships, and Social Situations. *Not* a good group of triggers to potentially cascade down upon you! My research indicates Boredom and Loneliness are particularly strongly linked. If you believe one of these is a strong trigger for you, then you should strongly consider the other as at least a related trigger.

From a medical/psychiatric standpoint, there are numerous risks from acute Loneliness, many of which feed into (or are fed by) alcohol abuse. These include:

• It can lead to depression.

• People who are lonely may struggle to get to sleep at night.

• A lack of social support likely means that the individual will struggle more with the challenges of life.

• **Many people will turn to substance abuse in order to deal with loneliness.**

• **It is a relapse trigger for people in addiction recovery.**

• **People who are lonely are far more likely to commit suicide.**

• **It causes increased levels of stress hormone that can cause high blood pressure.**[88]

Not good. Even if you are an introverted type, and believe you are much more comfortable and even happier in general being by yourself than with others, you need to recognize that Humans are social animals. We depend on each other for survival. Lack of interactions with others is not only a source of emotional discomfort, but has also been shown to have a damaging impact on both mental and physical health. Those who "escape" an addiction are at particular risk from Loneliness because it can lead eventually to relapse.

Tips for Dealing with Loneliness without Alcohol

Life continually throws a ton of crap at you. Indeed much of Level 2 is dedicated to figuring out how to deal with the various forms that this crap takes. When it comes to dealing with Loneliness, the "obvious answer" is to seek out interactions with others. But who are these "others" and what do "interactions" really mean?

The "who" is varied, depending on your personality and situation. It could be friends, family, work colleagues, and/or community members. BUT you may not have many—or *any*—of these, at least right now. *But you have to develop at least a few of these.* Without such support, it can be a lot more difficult for people to cope with life. This is because such a network of people provides four key functions:

1. Members of a support group can provide **physical assistance** to one another.

2. A social support group will **provide feedback** on the behavior of members. The reactions of other people allow the individual to evaluate his or her own behavior. If a member of the group makes a bad decision, then other members can point this out.

3. This group provides **emotional support** to the individual.
4. A social support network is a **resource for advice and information**.[89]

Those people who are dealing with loneliness will, usually, be lacking in social support. This lack of support means that they are at a great disadvantage when it comes to managing day-to-day living. With that said, there are numerous *specific* tips for dealing with Loneliness with alcohol, including:

• **Force yourself to interact.** The most obvious one is to try to get together, face-to-face or virtually, with family and friends who will not judge you and/or activate other related triggers. That may be impossible to do face-to-face, but easier online. In fact, if you are partially estranged from some of them, but have them included on Facebook, try to start communicating with them (starting with "Likes") on safe topics and build from there. But at the end of the day "virtual" interactions only can go so far in helping Loneliness in my opinion, particularly for the lonely alcoholic.

• **Join an alcoholic community.** Loneliness is a trigger area where Level 7—Join a Community can be a *huge* help. In all likelihood, most of the people you encounter at meetings are actively dealing with their own loneliness or have done so in the past. While I can't recall Loneliness ever being a formal topic in a meeting, and not often in open discussion (see Level 7 for a description of types of alcoholic community meetings), it is always there in the background to some degree. A big part of why people are there in the first place is to be around other people who are in the same boat, not just being an alcoholic but sharing common triggers—a big one of which is Loneliness.

• **Get a pet.** This can be *greatly* beneficial, even to the most naturally isolated types of persons. Pets are non-judgmental and—depending on the pet—can provide large amounts of unconditional affection that can be greatly mood altering. It doesn't even have to be a "sentient" pet—having a fish tank (with fish) can be very therapeutic by just knowing there are other living creatures around you.

• **Be on the lookout for bad times.** Be very careful of when "lonely-times" are coming at you, such as your spouse going out of town. Plan ahead about what you will be doing while they are gone.

> *I drank quite regularly for nearly 5 years and finally realized and admitted to myself that I had a problem. I've been completely sober for 110 days now, but now find myself alone while my wife is away for the weekend. I have had an ongoing dilemma in my mind from the moment she left—"should I use this opportunity to drink while she's gone or not?"*
>
> Guest Mountain Guest, alcoholism.about.com

• **Use everyday interactions (Part 1).** Try to incorporate as much human interaction in your day-to-day activities as you can (stand). At your Job is one obvious area, but you may be limited in that depending on the work you actually do, who you do it with (and if you can stand them or not), politics, etc. And going with them for drinks after work is obviously not a good idea that can limit informal interactions.

If you are self-employed in an area such as writing or research (e.g., ones that don't require a lot of face-to-face interactions), try to do those activities in an environment where there is a bit of bustle of human activity. You can take your computer to a Starbucks, McDonalds, or another place with free Wi-Fi. You will be surprised at the positive effect just being around other people can have on your mood, even if you don't actually interact with them. This is even true in sedate places like your local library.

• **Use everyday interactions (Part 2).** Beyond the job, try to make your non-job activities and errands have as much positive personal interaction as possible. Personal interaction can be as simple as having a polite conversation with the cashier at the grocery store. Yes you may think it is stupid, and you have nothing in common with them except the transaction you are trying to complete, but it can add positivity into something that would otherwise be purely a chore. Those "little bits" can add up and make a real impact.

Through the tips discussions of other triggers in this section, I frequently reference the need to "strategically" choose personal activities that specifically help deal with those triggers. Loneliness can leverage these, such as going to get a pedicure, massage, or even a haircut. Instead of being stonily silent while you are having these done, be open to engaging in a conversation with your provider. In a way they are a captive (and paid) audience, and are great for getting things off your chest in a safe environment. It can also ease your sense of Loneliness.

• **Consider Spirituality.** If you are a spiritual person (or considering trying to become one, see Level 10—Consider Spirituality) there are many opportunities for getting together with like-minded people. One caveat: if you trying to incorporate spirituality into your life for the purposes of this program, go *slowly,* as you may have to try different approaches to find the best way of incorporating spirituality into your daily life and dealings with alcohol attacks. This includes being careful with what types of spiritual groups you become associated with as many of those participants can seem overly aggressive at this stage of your sobriety and turn you off to the whole experience. My first experiences with AA were much like this (See Level 7—Join a Community Alcoholics Anonymous analysis).

• **Volunteer.** Other activities such as volunteering are a good way to get out of your house and yourself, meet people in safe environments, and feel good about what you are doing all at the same time!

• **Utilize Online Resources.** Websites that *can*[90] be helpful for this trigger include:
  - Facebook and Twitter (search alcohol-related groups)
  - Daily Strength.org—*www.dailystrength.org/c/Loneliness/support-group*
  - Loneliness Support Groups—*http://loneliness.supportgroups.com/*
  - Loners Club—*www.loners-club.com/*
  - Meetup.com—*www.Meetup.com*
  - Sober Recovery.com—*www.soberrecovery.com/forums/*
  - Social Anxiety Support—*www.socialanxietysupport.com*

Lemons into Lemonade Tip: As strange as it sounds, it is often not a large leap from being introverted to becoming extraverted, even being a social animal. Often all it takes is a bit of practice saying out loud (to other people) many of the things you say to yourself inside your head. Try it!

Overall Tip: You are not alone in your loneliness, as strange as that might sound. Remembering that can make you feel not so alone (as strange at *that* might sound). There are many things you can do to ease loneliness and do so in safe/comfortable settings. As you progress in your sobriety, people around you will begin to sense you are becoming a better/nicer/more approachable/less nasty person, and they will become more willing to engage with you and (re)establish relationships. So in a very real way sobriety will be a kind of cure for Loneliness!

Related Triggers: Loneliness can be caused or made worse by Boredom, Depression, Peer Pressure, Relationship problems, Social Situations, feeling Unfun/Uninteresting, and Victim (low self-esteem). It can cause or aggravate Boredom, Depression, desire for Escape, and Victim (low self-esteem).

Key Level Defenses: Engage Friends and Family, Join a Community, Develop New Hobbies (e.g., Pets, Volunteering), Consider Spirituality

MEDIA

For many years, the media has been blamed for a wide variety of ills including everything from an increase in violence to a decrease in the doing of homework. TV shows and movies have led the way in receiving this criticism, as they have the ads that support them. Testimonials abound describing this negative impact, and alcohol relapse is no different when describing the media as a trigger:

> *I am 2 weeks and 2 days sober (this is my 3rd weekend, YAY!). What kills me is how the media portrays alcohol. It's on almost every show. It is glorified and made to seem "the norm." No, you don't have to drink a glass (or in my case, bottle) of wine to be classy.*
>
> Finallyhit_rockbottom, alcoholism.about.com

> *In early sobriety and for a couple of years after I quit drinking . . . those billboards with the icy cold beer made me froth at the mouth, especially on a hot summer day . . . those advertisements on TV kicked in my stinking thinking (boy, wouldn't it be nice . . .) and I had to turn the channel, and it*

seemed like every movie I watched people were just pouring down the alcohol . . . couldn't watch them either.

Jane, alcoholism.about.com

When faced with the image or smell of alcohol I would run off to a meeting . . . call other alcoholics . . . turn the channel . . . walk down a different street . . . find something else to do (crossword puzzles, crocheting) . . . stopped watching TV or listening to certain kinds of music and began to play games with my kids, play cards, walk around the block, bicycle across town, meet other people for coffee or lunch. These avoidance tactics were the only control for my obsession with alcohol. And they worked!

Rhonda W., alcoholism.about.com

While I don't think anyone can reasonably and logically blame the media as being the main reason for their being a drunk, *it sure as hell does not help.* Before I got sober, I was immune to alcohol in the media, both in general and as a trigger. I had many more important triggers to focus on after all! I became much more aware of it once I became sober. It seems like it is everywhere! Every TV show and movie seems to have alcohol as either a major presence within the plot line or at a minimum in multiple scenes as a backdrop. Consider the following analysis from *vulture.com* of some of the top TV shows today (2012–2013 season):

For good reason, *Mad Men* is generally acknowledged to be the drunkest show on television, what with all the major characters heavily drinking from the time they wake until they go to bed at night. HBO's new *Boardwalk Empire,* about Atlantic City bootleggers, seems poised to give *Mad Men* a run for its alcohol poisoning . . . But there is one show on TV where drinking seems to be all sweetness and light: *Cougar Town.*

It continues: To get a sense of the show's pro-drinking vibe, consider last season's eighteenth episode, "Turn This Car Around." In it, Jules decided to prove she can quit drinking for an entire month. Just days into the experiment, her friends stage an intervention so that she'll start drinking again. Without alcohol she's become uptight and boring. "Mom, you need to start drinking again," says her son. "Nothing could ever make me stop loving you, except you not drinking," says her best friend. "Twelve steps, shmelve steps. Alcohol makes people fun."

Hilarious. Though extreme, the above examples are indicative of the mentality that Hollywood has towards drinking. Sure there is the occasional drunk making an idiot of themselves, but the vast majority of the time alcohol is glorified or at a minimum is portrayed to be a natural, welcome part of everyday life. Never mind the legions of actors and actresses checking in and out of rehab so often they deserve their own parking space.

The portrayal of the linkage between Sex, "Fun," and alcohol in the media is another huge problem for many including me. I totally understand the business reason for doing this—Sex *does* sell—but that doesn't mean I have to like it. Beer commercials are by far the worst offender of this in my opinion; nearly *every* beer commercial seems to be selling the association between their product, being cool, and getting the girl. Those that don't, usually, have a cute dog and/or some portrayal of having a great time on the beach or another exotic locale.

The beer commercials are almost universally targeted at men. For women, it is the wine makers that are their nemesis. For decades, wine makers have had women as their strategic #1 priority. In Gabrielle Glaser's book *Her Best Kept Secret,* she provides an extensive overview about how American winemakers very successfully targeted women as their key growth engine, starting with American housewives. "We used to joke that if we could get a bottle of sherry into the kitchen, we'd be better off," said an early marketer.[91] Funny, not. Of course since then wine advertising has become far more "sophisticated," but ads are still targeted primarily towards women.

As a capper, most of these commercials are tapped off with a tiny whisper at the end of "please drink responsibly." What a joke.

"So What?" you say? While it is true that the presence of alcohol is no more than a minor irritant for me[92], even before I became permanently sober, it was a significant trigger. I suspect it becomes less of a trigger for most alcoholics the older you get (that is just my opinion—I could be totally wrong).

Perhaps "minor" irritant is putting it too mildly. I spend a significant amount of time in my car, and generally listen to the radio news channels. Unfortunately it seems my favorite stations are ad magnets for alcohol. Not just straightforward alcohol ads either. It seems that ads for products and services that have nothing to do with alcohol somehow manage to wedge it in. My favorite (not) was an ad for a senior citizen dancing class. Nothing could be safer right? No, they put in: "not only we dance for fun, we party hard too!" I couldn't believe it. Sure, let's exhaust a bunch of seniors with dancing, ply them with drinks, and then shove them back on the road to get home. Public Service ad!

Anonymous

However, for alcoholics in their early years, e.g., 20's and even worse teenagers in their development years, it is a different story. You are thinking: that's just my opinion—there is no proof. Wrong!
One study analyzed nearly 2.7 million product advertisements placed by alcohol companies from 2001 to 2009, purchased at an estimated cost of more than $8 billion. Key findings included (source: *www.camy.org*):

• The average annual number of alcohol ads seen by youth (12 to 20 years old) watching television increased from 217 in 2001 to 366 in 2009, *approximately one alcohol ad per day.*

• On cable television, the majority of youth exposure (to alcohol advertising) came from advertising more likely to be seen by youth per capita than by adults ages 21 and above.

• From 2001 to 2009, youth were 22 times more likely to see an alcohol product ad than an alcohol company-sponsored "responsibility" ad whose primary message warned against underage drinking and/or alcohol-impaired driving.

"So What?" you say again, perhaps a little less forcefully. Well, in January 2013 the results of a study were published in the medical journal *Pediatrics* (Source: *http://thechart.blogs.cnn.com/2013/01/29/tv-ads-may-be-driving-children-to-drink/*). It found that seventh-graders who are exposed to alcohol ads on television—and who say they like the ads—may experience more severe problems related to drinking alcohol later in their adolescence. "Exposure to advertising was found to have a significant correlation with alcohol use, particularly among girls," the study concluded. "Liking the ads was connected with alcohol-related problems (defined as not being able to do homework, getting into fights, neglecting responsibilities, or causing someone shame or embarrassment), particularly in boys. *For both boys and girls, the more they were exposed to the ads and liked them, the more their alcohol use grew from seventh to 10th grade.*" That, of course, leads to a greater potential for alcohol-related problems later on.

Tips for Dealing with the Media without Alcohol

How to deal with Media as a major trigger obviously depends on the specific mediums that you watch—e.g., TV shows, movies, ads—and to a lesser extent the platforms you watch them on—television, theatres, computers, handhelds, etc. But the simple, obvious answer is the best one: Don't watch, listen to, or click on the fucking things! If you can't, here are some additional ideas:

• **Get Even (kind of).** Normally I try to avoid petty, pointless ideas of things to do in this book, but I'm making an exception here. There will be a natural reaction to get irritable, mad, or even personally insulted when you encounter what seems to be a gratuitous reference to alcohol in a TV show or an extremely obnoxious ad for it. Don't get mad—get even! Send emails to the producers of shows; boycott products that associate themselves with alcohol; even post vicious rants (anonymously) against actors/TV characters who seem to glorify alcohol. Yes, these are petty actions, and very unlikely to make even the slightest difference to those people. BUT it may make you feel better, and that's what counts when it comes to this trigger.

• **Filter Content.** That said, if you do have children at home, you might want to take a much more vocal action against the shows/ads that glorify alcohol. Again it may make little/no difference, but it will make you feel better. Possible action includes trying to screen out material (particularly for young children) that seems to exceptionally play up alcohol, which *can* make a difference![93]

Lemons into Lemonade Tip: There is no law that says you have to watch the crap that is on TV, or in a movie theater, or listen to the crap that passes as music today. Radically change your viewing/listening habits if some form of Media is a trigger for you, or cut the cord completely and discover the world of books!

However, if you have to watch TV, I would recommend watching the show *Intervention* (available online at *www.aetv.com/intervention/video,* on Amazon Prime, and on your cable provider).[94] While in general I hate Reality TV, this is by far the best in my opinion. While it delivers very mixed signals on the effectiveness of doing interventions, it nonetheless provides a stark reminder to all addicts of what we were once like, and what we could be again. I highly recommend it if you must watch some TV.

Overall Tip: At the end of the day, media is the most controllable, and in particular avoidable, of triggers—even if alcohol seems to be everywhere you look. If it does, don't look, even if you have to change your viewing habits radically. It will be worth it!

Related Triggers: Media as a trigger can activate a desire for "Fun," as well as the Music, Reminders, and Sex triggers. It is also very annoying when it comes to Holidays and Special Occasions.

Key Defense Levels: Break Bad Habits (stop watching and listening to stuff that remind you of alcohol), Develop New Hobbies (do fun stuff that avoids alcohol ads and the like)

MIDLIFE CRISIS (INCLUDES ELDERLY DRINKING)

Midlife crisis is a term coined in 1965 by Elliott Jaques[95] stating it's a time where adults come to realize their own mortality and how much time is left in their life—usually when they realize that life may be more than halfway over. It happens between the ages of 40 and 60. It can be caused by many things: children leaving home, a parent's death, menopause, hitting a Zero mark (40, 50), a job crisis, or many other things.

This time is one of great sensitivity and vulnerability when it comes to alcohol. For tried-and-true alcoholics, it is one more major trigger to add to their already lengthy list. Past problem drinkers—even those who had slowed down or even stopped in earlier years—may find their desire to drink coming back with a vengeance.

> *I believe my father is going through a mid-life crisis. Although he was always an alcoholic, his habits have become even more destructive and his words more harsh and cold. Or maybe it's just his addiction getting worse, I can't say for sure. All I know is that the problem has escalated and turned into a monster that cannot be controlled. I fear he'll drink himself to death, which he's already started doing.*
>
> anonymous, Guystuffcounseling.com

> *I am in the midst of a mid-life crisis. I am abusing alcohol, and find no pleasure in any aspect of my life and my life has lost all meaning and purpose. I don't live anymore, I just exist. I used to be fun and happy. Now, I am a miserable SOB.*
>
> LG, Guystuffcounseling.com

Psychiatrists have begun to notice a disturbing increase in drinking in mid-life. According to a recent study, there has been a significant increase in over-50 binge drinking in the last few years.[96] To cap it off, suicide rates have also started to rise, particularly for 45–54-year-old males.[97]

What explains these increases? No one knows for sure. And data on happiness in midlife is confusing; while suicide is increasing, so are

Top 10 Common Signs of a Midlife Crisis[100]

1. A growing sense of regret over unattained goals.

2. New feelings of self-consciousness around more successful colleagues.

3. A new emphasis on remaining youthful when the effort previously seemed unimportant.

4. A desire to spend more time alone or with certain peers who could be characterized as "youthful" or "comfortable in their own skin."

5. **A newfound tendency to abuse alcohol.**

6. Placing import on acquiring unusual or expensive items when such purchases could previously have been described as frivolous or impulsive.

7. A sharp increase in self-criticism with a correlating decline in self-compassion.

8. Obsessing over one's physical appearance when similar attention was previously unpaid.

9. Placing unusual amounts of pressure and stress on one's children to excel in a variety of fields.

10. Entering relationships with younger partners.

Besides the obvious indicator at #5, the above screams of related triggers. #1 is Guilt (remorse); #2—Job (dead-end career); #3, #8, and #10—Sex (Body Image in particular, but also concerns about diminishing libido and/or differences between you and your partner); #4—Peer Pressure (being around other people in crisis if those people are also drinking heavily); #7—Victim (self-esteem issues); and #9—Kids (adding more pressure on yourself than is already there from day-to-day child rearing).

Yikes! But once you have "got over" your mid-life crisis, you shouldn't have problems with alcohol, right? Wrong.

reports of happiness and wellness in middle age. Of course, some of the same pressures that apply to all baby boomers could apply here: Difficulty in dealing with aging parents, seeing what is ahead of them in terms of a long and protracted life, but without much quality of life. These experiences seem to be creating a kind of stress that has been unknown to previous generations. So perhaps the suicide rates among middle-aged men are, in part, related to the ease of obtaining prescription drugs and the prevalence of substance use. [98]

While men seem to be most affected by the above, women have also started to increase the abuse of alcohol in their mid-life years. One alcohol abuse treatment center states: *"Most of our female clients slip into harmful drinking in their 40s and 50s, masking the discomfort of fluctuating hormones, the adjustment to an empty nest, the death of parents and other role losses."*[99]

Alcohol Abuse among the Elderly

Although alcohol and substance abuse is statistically at epidemic proportions among the elderly, it remains for the most part unreported, undiagnosed, or ignored. Why? Most have to do with the fact they are no longer active in mainstream society, and there is simply no one around to notice. They are less likely to get in trouble with the law—stopped for driving under the influence, having a traffic accident, or causing problems in the community. Therefore, they have little contact with the police or the criminal justice system. Since many are retired, there is very little chance their drinking will cause them to lose a job or career.

Basically, nobody notices.

> *He stops by the club and has only a couple of drinks with his buddies and catches up on the news. But when he goes home he doesn't stop, he drinks more, a lot more. It wasn't always like this. When he was younger he was an occasional "social" drinker, but life changed. He was forced to retire early from his life-long career, and his wife left him. He was lonely, frustrated, and scared. To ease the pain, he turned to the bottle.*
>
> anonymous

Of 86 percent of elderly patients who end up getting treatment for a history of binge drinking, *76 percent began drinking heavily in mid or late life,* according to a Canadian study. Women are even more likely to start heavy drinking later in life.[101]

He stumbles while carrying out the trash, falls down the stairs, and breaks an arm. At the Emergency Room the doctor asks about his alcohol use. He says he only has a couple with the boys at Happy Hour every afternoon. He lies about the drinking he does alone because he doesn't want to give it up. It has become a friend to him now, the only friend he can count on to be there.

Anonymous

Tips for Dealing with Midlife Crisis without Alcohol

There are many, many sources and ideas for dealing with a mid-life crisis. Below are some of the ones I believe most applicable to helping an alcoholic:

• **Don't believe in the myth of a happy youth.** And, by extension, an *un*happy last half of your life. *"From many points of view, midlife permits many of us to feel on top of the world, in control of our lives,"* says one study. Researchers surmised that while stresses about money and children are at a peak, so are competence and a sense of mastery.

More to the point: Your youth may not have been all that great. Researchers say the most Anxiety-ridden years are the 20s and early 30s. Even adolescence and childhood tend to have more critical moments than midlife does.[102]

• **Don't have an affair.** Yes, Sex is a huge issue at many points of our lives, and midlife is certainly a biggie. Men in particular may be very tempted to have an affair, but women, of course, may not be far behind, dealing with menopause, children leaving the nest and aging in general. Either way, if alcoholism hasn't broken up your marriage by now, then it obviously has great things going for it—DON'T fuck it up by having an affair.

• **Practice Schadenfreude (wisely and sparingly).** Schadenfreude—the pleasure derived from the misfortunes of others—can be a handy therapeutic tool if used right. Making fun of snooty people who think they know wine is one of my favorites, which has the added benefit of working for the Envy trigger as well.

• **Don't take it out on your kids.** They've had enough to deal with your alcohol problems. Don't add this to it.

- **Don't go buying midlife toys.** Besides making it obvious to the whole world of your midlife crisis, you don't need to add another trigger (Money issues) to your trigger portfolio.

- **Make time to go out.** You may be tempted to stay inside and sulk. And get Depressed. And drink. Don't—instead get out of the house and do things you haven't done before,[103] a kind of a fresh start in the hobby department.

- **Get more information!** There are an increasing number of sources about drinking later in life as this issue becomes more prevalent and widely known. One excellent source is insurance carriers, which other than wanting to avoid high cost treatments, generally can be counted on to provide objective information. One such source is Cigna's *Coping With Substance Abuse* web series, such as *The Complexity and Diagnosis: Hidden Epidemic of Older Adults with Addiction Disorders* (materials at *www.cigna .com/assets/docs/behavioral-health-series/substance-abuse/2013/june-drug-and-alcohol-seminar.pdf*, and MP3 file at: *www.cigna.com/assets/media/audio/ behavioral-health-series/substance-abuse/2013/drug-and-alcohol-seminar-replay.mp3*).

Lemons into Lemonade Tip: The phrase "Life begins at (pick a number)" is not a cliché. For many people, and very much in particular for alcoholics, mid-life can be a chance to make a completely new start on life. Use the experiences of the first part of your life—even lousy ones—to make the next part that much more rewarding, even if it "only" helps you avoid making the same mistakes again. Even better, counsel younger people so that they don't make the same mistakes you did. In that way, you will be creating and passing on a legacy that will make even that first (horrible) part of your life very valuable to others and yourself.

Overall Tip: You have made it this far despite your alcohol problems. Thank (pick your deity or object) that despite everything you have done to yourself and others that you (and they) are alive to tell the tale. You've been given a gift—use it to make the most of the rest of your life happy for you and your loved ones. Ideally by not drinking, but at a minimum *not* using a midlife crisis as another reason to drink.

Related Triggers: A Mid-Life Crisis can be activated or heavily influenced by Change, Extreme Emotions (Grief over death of parent), Health (pain issues, feeling of getting old), Kids (leaving the nest), Job (career stagnation), Peer Pressure (see others progress around you), and Sex (reduced Libido, body image issues). It can activate or aggravate triggers such as Anxiety, (need for radical) Change, Depression, Relationships/Sex issues, and Victim (self-esteem) issues.

Key Defense Levels: Listen to Your Body! (risks of drinking heavily as you age), Engage Friends and Family, Therapy, Develop New Hobbies, Consider Spirituality

MONEY

Next to various generators of Stress (and a major cause of it too), Money problems are probably one of the biggest triggers around, at least in terms of it being such a common problem for *so* many people. Like Stress, Money problems can be caused by seemingly countless and never ending reasons: overspending, car payments and repairs, medical bills, cost of insurance, rent/mortgage payment due, cost of food, legal bills, children's education, taxes, more taxes, and on and on.

> *Stress, plain and simple money problems, boyfriend's little white lies, bad memories. I am new to recovery, and am just looking at this tough road ahead seems insurmountable. But it must happen. I've done so many things I regret and hurt people that I love dearly. I have got to get past this slimy pit of self-loathing in my belly, the shaking hands, the house of cards barely holding around me.*
>
> carrienations, alcoholism.about.com

For those particularly low on disposable income, the temporary freedom that comes with getting paid can be a significant trigger.

> *Money in my pocket, it is like I start thinking of where and what I am going to drink. And then comes the thoughts of using my other drug of choice, cocaine and I'm out seeking it as well. I realize that there are other factors to consider for my usage but the facts are this is my biggest trigger.*
>
> anonymous

I did not bother researching any medical analysis of the link between Money problems and alcohol/alcoholism. Anybody who paid money to fund such studies deserves to lose all *their* money. It's easy—no money, then big problems are at your doorstep ready to stomp you down. Desired state: not to worry about it right now. Solution? Drink.[104]

Money is one of those triggers that requires *detailed* reflection as to what specifically is the problem causing you the most concern and desire to drink and their implications. No rent money? Probably spikes as a trigger near the end of the month—watch out then. Spouse spends like a drunken sailor at a mall? Spikes when she/he calls from work saying she/he's going to go "browse" a bit. And so on and so forth. The point being is that the vast majority of us (not just alcoholics) frequently have money problems. So we (alcoholics) need to manage the desire to drink that may come with it accordingly, and that means extra caution and guard when those *specific* problems hit their peak.

Tips for Dealing with Money Problems without Alcohol

Ah, to not worry about Money! I spent nearly all of my adult life worrying about it, and did not truly "appreciate" how much Money problems contributed to my overall drinking until I wrote this book. Of course, nearly everyone encounters severe Money-troubles in their lifetime, but drinking only makes them worse. Some ideas on helping your troubles include:

• **Do. Not. Drink.** To state the obvious, don't drink! What is much less obvious is *how much* money alcoholics spend on alcohol. The problem is that most alcoholics view this in a day-at-a-time context—$10–$20 a day for your booze. No biggie, right? That might not seem a lot, but putting it in month-at-a-time terms it is $300 to $600! Put it in yearly terms if that is more effective—$3,600 to $7,200. Obviously anyone can do that math if they want to, but most do not want to! Force yourself to think in total amounts over long periods of time, and get as far away from day-to-day amounts as you can.

• **Restructure your debts.** Odds are you've racked up some tremendous debts while you were drinking. If so, you might want to consider declaring bankruptcy. Bankruptcy is harder than it used to be but still doable. It has some major downsides in that it costs money and shows up on your credit report for 10 years—which almost guarantees that you will have major problems getting a major loan or even a credit card during that time. But if Money is a major trigger for you it may well be worth doing to get that monkey off your back.

- **Carefully manage your bank account.** Helpful in general of course, but more to the point *avoid overdraft charges!* Whenever I would get an overdraft charge, I would go ballistic. It rained related triggers—Anger, Anxiety (what else was going to bounce), Depression (how would I ever get the spending under control), Escape (I just wanted to checkout completely), Frustration, Relationship stress. Even an acute feeling of Disorder; was there not anything that could be simple, clean, predictable?

- **Avoid surprises.** To this last point, try to make your expenditures as predictable as possible. Assuming you have the funds, try to set up automatic monthly payments to key accounts, so you don't have to worry about them. Key accounts include credit card payments (at least the minimum), car loan, utilities (they have budget programs so it is the same amount every month), and so on. This can provide great peace-of-mind and a bit of simplicity to your life. *Sub-Tips:* Get overdraft protection for your checking account and alerts sent to your cell phone when a payment is coming due, or you are nearing your credit limit. These steps help you avoid late charges, overdraft fees, or the embarrassment of being rejected when trying to buy something.

Lemons into Lemonade Tip: Use the "look how much money I saved by not drinking" mantra as often as you can. It is a great deterrent, and will make you feel even better about yourself. You didn't drink, saving money that will hopefully take the edge off some of your Money-related worries.

Overall Tip: At the end of the day, this is one of the most controllable triggers—do not use it as an excuse to drink!

Related Triggers: Money as a drinking trigger can be caused by many things, notably Health problems (that cost big $), Job (or lack thereof), Kids (expenses), and Relationships/eX costs. It can cause or aggravate Anxiety, desire to Escape, Frustration, Health, Insomnia, Relationships issues, and Stress.

Key Defense Levels: Break Bad Habits (stop thinking about alcohol purchase totals on a daily basis), Develop New Hobbies (learn how to manage money), Consider Spirituality

MUSIC

I never thought much about Music as a trigger before I started writing this book. However, I became very aware that it was a trigger for me even though I didn't realize it while I was drinking, and that there are many who view it as a very significant one overall. As best as I can tell, triggers fall into two categories: 1) specific words elicit desire to drink and 2) songs elicit specific memories that cause the desire to drink, e.g., tightly linked with the trigger Reminders.

> *I avoided going down the aisle in the grocery store where "the alcohol" was shelved. Listening to those "cryin' in your beer, country music songs" got me started, too. Early on, just the smell of alcohol was enough to start my stinking thinking, so the actual image of it wreaked more havoc within my sick brain.*
>
> Rhonda W., alcoholism.about.com

> *When I would see an ad or hear ole' Jimmy Buffet sing a tune and thoughts of the old days would cross my mind . . . just for a few seconds . . . then I would remember my last drunk.*
>
> Magic, alcoholism.about.com

> *Well I use to think I didn't have any triggers, I was wrong! When I first got sober I found them and had to deal with them. One was music, I love music, all kinds. I didn't know what to do then a friend suggested that I eat some candy, it helped. I've since have learned why that trigger hit me and when I started to accept it for what it was I can say now I enjoy all kinds music again.*
>
> anonymous

This last testimonial obviously didn't explain why music was a trigger, or how he was able to get back to enjoying it. Obviously he conquered this trigger somehow. Maybe it was the candy . . .

Tips for Dealing with Music as a Trigger without Alcohol

There are some relatively easy ways to avoid the specific songs that bother you. The key is in your control of what is being blasted at you. These include:

- **Avoid traditional radio.** The most uncontrollable source of music is advertising-based radio. There is no predicting what songs will be next. If your worst songs are of a specific genre (e.g., country, 70s/80s/90s rock), then do not listen to those stations.

- **Try different music.** Try something completely different. If you are a rock person, for example, try a classical music station, or some instrumental music CDs. Besides being completely different, these genres in particular can be very relaxing.

- **Use pay music channels.** Since there are many ways of controlling exactly what music you can listen to, e.g., iTunes, Pandora, Spotify, etc., use those methods for music instead. For some reason if this is not possible, switch to something that you know won't play those songs, like classical music or NPR. If you say "bleh" to those, consider XM Sirius radio that seems more narrowly focused on specific genres (e.g., only 70s music) so you can more easily avoid something that gets you worked up.

Lemons into Lemonade Tip: As an "old" guy, I find much of the music made today as so much crap—particularly the lyrics. Try and write your own music. It may not amount to anything, but you will never know until you try, and at least you won't be wasting time reminiscing about old painful songs.

Overall Tip: Music is unusual for being able to have both major negative and positive emotional effects on you. Your challenge is reversing/eliminating all negative aspects to ones of benefit—going from a trigger to a method of relaxation, even Escape. Since nearly all people have some affinity for music, the challenge is finding what type of music has a soothing effect on you (e.g. a new genre) and the best conditions to hear it (e.g. without a bunch of annoying ads). Above all, as with Media in general, Music is one of the most controllable triggers—do not use it as an excuse to drink!

Related Triggers: Music as a trigger can influence or be influenced by Fun, Media, Noise, and particularly Reminders.

Key Defense Levels: Develop New Hobbies, Break Bad Habits (break the alcohol associations)

NOISE

Sound can be a significant trigger as indicated in the Music trigger just discussed. However, sounds of any type can also be triggers and often underlie others such as Frustration. Particular sounds like a dog barking, a baby crying, or an irritating tone of voice (think *Fran Drescher*) can set people of all types off, both alcoholics and nonalcoholics. But with alcoholics, being "set off" generally means wanting to reach for a drink.

> *I found that I have a very low tolerance for noise levels (loud noise in particular) and also for when "multiple stimuli" (many voices or sounds) come at me all at once. As an alcoholic, I believe I tend to tire more easily of certain stimuli such as noise, because I walked around for so long dulled with a "veil" of drunkenness hampering my ability to accurately sense the world around me. I remember first getting sober after many years of daily drinking and using, where everything seemed so loud and bright. I was exhausted quickly as my brain attempted to process all this new "information" that was coming my way now that the "paper bag over my head" that alcohol put there was no longer in place.*
>
> jonijoni1, aa.activeboard.com

It doesn't have to be a particular sound. It can be a lot of different sounds at once, high volume, or high frequency of more benign sounds like non-stop talking that can cause a large amount of sensory stimulation which can be triggers.

Personally I had a very low tolerance for anyone talking in small, confined spaces. I also find I have far less tolerance for loud talkers in general (which particularly irritates the hell out of me to this day), and certain (not all) frequencies at which small children cry.

Medical Fun Fact

Several studies have shown that sudden, jarring noises and constant, irritating noises have negative health effects. A 2010 study in *Noise Health* (yes, I couldn't believe such a resource existed either) revealed that workers with the greatest exposure to noise also had the highest levels of *cortisol* (a stress hormone) in their saliva at the end of the day.

To make matters worse, certain medical conditions like Tinnitus can be frustrating as well and a danger to alcoholics. Tinnitus is not an actual disease, but instead a symptom with many possible causes. It is experienced as a noise in the ear or head. This noise can be something like a swishing, humming, or ringing sound. The pitch of this noise can be quite low or very high. Tinnitus is often a subjective experience of sound. **This means that nobody else will be able to hear it.**

There is debate about whether or not alcohol directly causes tinnitus, but it almost certainly can exacerbate the problem. Many of those who abuse alcohol will need to deal with the symptoms of this condition. Some individuals attempt to self-medicate with alcohol, to deal with tinnitus, and this can lead to hazardous drinking.[105]

Tips for Dealing with Noise without Alcohol

Of course you cannot avoid sound unless you are the proverbial monk in a cave. Consciously discovering exactly what sounds, types of sounds, situations of sounds, etc. are particularly irritating/distressing/annoying/frustrating will be a great help. Plan your activities accordingly to avoid or minimize their impact. Some other ideas:

• Have a "Quiet" room in your home where you can go to relax and avoid the daily noises around you.

• For those with young children, perhaps consider a quiet period of the day for them to go their rooms and play or read.

• When traveling, do your best to minimize the inevitable low roar that accompanies you, by bringing earplugs, sitting in the Quiet car on Amtrak, or traveling early in the morning/late at night where the environmental noise is significantly less.

• Invest and use some comfortable, high-quality headsets to listen to relaxing music, audio books, and videos. These headsets will both improve the quality of your experience by blocking out extraneous noise and reduce the noise "pollution" of your "noise" on others.

• There are numerous white noise machines and services that can be used to block out annoying background noise. You can buy dedicated machines—portable and usually very small—or (my personal favorite) air filters that effectively clean air and block out most background noise. You can also download various apps, ranging from pure static to sounds of rain falling or oceans moving to "mood music"—practically anything that makes you relax and block out other noise—that you can play in a continuous loop on your computer or even cell phone.

Lemons into Lemonade Tip: Set aside 15 minutes a day to have as your "quiet time." Use your quiet room or other place where you won't be bothered by anyone else. Meditate, read, or just zone-out, but make sure the end goal is to "reset" yourself from the pressures that you've accumulated that day and get ready for the rest of it.

Overall Tip: Consider having a hearing test if Noise is a major trigger for you. It is possible you have Tinnitus or some other hearing issue that makes you particularly sensitive to certain kinds of noises.

Related Triggers: There are many potential related triggers to Noise. The most common ones are those that generate noise, of course, such as Kids, Music, and Yelling. Others are more indirect such as on-the-Job noises. Noise can aggravate Insomnia/being Tired, or causing you to feel physical Stress.

Key Defense Levels: Listen to Your Body! (noise-susceptibility problems such as Tinnitus), Break Bad Habits (that generate Noise), Develop New Hobbies (quiet ones)

OVERCONFIDENCE (INCLUDES EGO, "PINK CLOUD")

Anyone who has made even a half-assed attempt at sobriety has probably felt at some point "Hey, I can do this! I can drink like normal people!" Right. This feeling comes in fits and starts, often early in sobriety during in-between times of feelings of unhappiness, sickness, etc.

> *I began my journey into "recovery" starting in 1995. During the span of years to date, I have managed to stay sober twice for two years straight, six times for a year stretch, and many staggered months in between my relapses. I swore I would never drink again, only to be sober for three, maybe four, sometimes more and then I get blindsided. You start feeling just a little "TOO" good, and wham!!! There you are again, drunk.*
>
> Name redacted, alcoholism.about.com

This is one example of Overconfidence, where feeling good has you thinking you can indeed drink like "normal" people, or, forgetting about all the pain and unpleasantness that happens when you drink. As you increase your sobriety so to speak, particularly in your early sobriety, this relative "high" becomes more frequent and with it an increased danger of Overconfidence. This kind of "feeling really good" is also referred to as the "Pink Cloud."

Early recovery is often referred to as a rollercoaster ride because it involves a mixture of great highs and great lows. Emotions that have been anesthetized with alcohol and drugs suddenly awaken, and feelings can be particularly intense. As the body and mind adjusts to this new life, there can be rapid changes in mood. **There will, usually, come a time when the individual hits a smooth patch. Life will feel wonderful and the future exceptionally bright. Staying free of addiction now feels effortless and the individual may wonder what all the fuss was about** (Author's emphasis). The concept of *pink cloud syndrome* in addiction recovery was first described by Alcoholics Anonymous.

It might seem odd to claim that there would be any disadvantages to feeling good. The addict may have spent decades battling their problem so it seems reasonable and even "fair" that they should get to feel great now. While it is true that life in sobriety should be about enjoying life, there can be problems if people become too confident and complacent. They may conclude that their problems are over and that there is no need to do anything more to maintain their sobriety. There is also a risk that when the pink cloud period ends, it will lead to huge disappointment.

In short, don't get too big for your early sobriety britches . . .

If an individual experiences a particularly pleasant period in early sobriety, then it can be disappointing when it ends. Life is full of ups and downs, and nobody can stay up forever. Emotions eventually settle down as the body adjusts to life without alcohol, and the highs and lows become less intense. The individual can respond to the end of the pink cloud by assuming that they have done something wrong. They can begin to lose faith in those tools that have been keeping them away from alcohol and drugs. They may even start to question if sobriety is that worthwhile after all. People can feel "cheated" when the super highs of early sobriety are replaced by more modest emotions.[106]

One of the best testimonials I came across in my research and certainly the best on this topic is below.

> *People have redefined the early-recovery phenomenon of "pink cloud" to mean different things—things which in and of themselves are all valid. They're just not the 'pink clouds' of AA/NA as passed down through the generations.*

Well first and foremost, a pink cloud takes place in early recovery, mak-
ing it by definition transient; a phase. A pink cloud is called "pink" because
you feel this tremendous revitalization of both mind and body in those first
magical weeks once you begin to really hit your old stride again with no
drugs or drink onboard. A pink cloud is called a "cloud" because it is not a
down-to-Earth, stabilized sobriety that can last on its own.

The pink-cloud period itself is usually not a perilous time. People in
groups warn you of it because they know that eventually, you have to come
down and continue relearning how to live life in the real world, with its
ups and the downs.

In fact, it is that interim during which you are transitioning from the
giddiness of your "pink cloud" period back to a more down-to-Earth
mood in which you are actually more vulnerable to a relapse. (Author's
emphasis)

Ever heard of the term "90-day wonder"? That's the newcomer who
keeps relapsing, either right after picking up their 90-day chip, or when
they were just about to. In our area, that chip is red—red to signify danger.
(Author's note: I checked this and the AA chips 90 day chips seem to be a
variety of colors, so I'm not sure of his "area"—but it is a great idea).

Well, both the "pink-cloud" and "90 day wonder" phenomena are very
much related. Typically, that initial "pink cloud" that newcomers ride will
begin to dissipate after several weeks to a few months, giving way to the
more sober aspects of . . . well, sobriety.

For many people, this is the perilous time—that time when the pink
cloud begins to wear off. People may become more complacent. They may
become less passionate about working whatever program they have been
working for the last few months. They may quit going to meetings every
single day, if they were previously committed to 90 N 90.

Add to that going back to old playgrounds and to old playmates, and
young sobriety hasn't a chance.

So there you are [name]. Hope this lil' recount helps you to understand
more of that magical, short period which many know as . . . the pink
cloud.[107]

The best way to deal with this potential trigger is education. You need
to recognize it for what it is and prepare for the highs and then a return
to earth without *using either* as a reason to drink.

Tips for Dealing with Overconfidence Regarding Alcohol

The key here is to make yourself remember, at every opportunity, the hell you went through while drinking and what you had to do to get sober. And also to remember that you are not cured—*there IS no fucking cure.* No matter how good you feel, *you* will *always* have the four corner-stones of alcoholism ready to crash down on your head: no control to stop drinking once you take a drink; a never-ending-once-you-start-drinking-again craving to use alcohol as a way of "dealing" with your problems; and the high physical tolerance that will require ever increas-ing amounts of booze to make you feel like you want and the associated physical dependency that comes with it. I personally don't like tattoos but if that's what it takes, tattoo it on your forehead, so you remind your-self every time you look in the mirror.

To reinforce the above, use whatever means necessary to "humble" yourself and remind you of the damage alcohol did to you and your life before you got sober: lost jobs and marriages, broken homes, financial destruction, angry children, horrible health—whatever it takes. This is one area where using Guilt can be very effective as a way to *defend* against another trigger. If you have to, use it.

Level 11—Make Yourself Sick of Alcohol can be a very important level of defense against Overconfidence. If all the above fails, making yourself physically sick to the smell, taste, and/or effect of alcohol can be a very effective deterrent of last resort *in my opinion.* Again, this Level is optional. Level 10—Consider Spirituality can also be effective in "humbling" the Overconfidence in some people.

Lemons into Lemonade Tip: Having a lot of confidence in yourself is not at all a bad thing, if channeled correctly. Certainly overcoming alco-holism justifies a great deal of pride and satisfaction in conquering such a major life obstacle. Instead of gloating, or worse falling into the trap that you can drink like a normal person, use this confidence to attack other problems in your life, or strive to accomplish new things such as opening a business or achieving a major life goal.

Overall Tip: Sooner or later your happiness in sobriety will tempt you to think you "can drink like a normal person." *You cannot, so don't try.* If you find yourself thinking this way, use it as a prompt to come back to this book and remind yourself why you decided to conquer alcohol in the first place.

Related Triggers: Overconfidence can be influenced by Envy and im-provement in your Health (from not drinking), and resurrect the (grossly wrong) belief that you can return to drinking Fun.

Key Defense Levels: Listen to Your Body! (never forget the damage alcohol can do to it), Consider Spirituality (practice humility), Make Yourself Sick of Alcohol

PEER PRESSURE ("FRIENDS")

Peer Pressure is a form of social *pressure* by a group for one to take action in order to be accepted. As a major drinking trigger it generally comes in two time ranges in alcoholics: first, during our youth years (particularly high school); and second, during certain stretches later in life where we find ourselves with few commitments and otherwise alone with alcohol-intensive "friends" as our primary connection with the outside world.

Youth Peer Pressure

Our younger years—generally from early teens to early/mid-twenties—are when we have the largest amount of Peer Pressure. This is not just pressure to drink or use drugs, but to look the same, act the same, even talk the same as our "peers."[108] Obviously the "selection" of one's peers is a critical element—there *is* a reason your parents were concerned with whom you hung out.

> *I heard the same things from my new friends at middle school nearly every day. "Yo, Charlene, let's not go to school today. Let's go smoke and get some alcohol."[109]*

Peer Pressure is probably the worst for very young drinkers. As a teenager, there are likely to be many times when you feel pressure to drink alcohol. It may be that all your friends are doing it, and they seem to be having a good time. Or it may be that you simply do not want to be left out at the parties and social gatherings you attend that increasingly seem to revolve around drinking.

For many teenagers, getting involved with alcohol is simply part of growing up, but for others, it can quickly become a serious problem. While there are a number of factors why youths start drinking in the first place,[110] Peer Pressure is likely at the top of the list. You want to be "cool," to "fit in" or "have fun," or at least not stand out as an oddity—a cardinal sin when it comes to teenage social standing and associated bullying.

Later Stage Peer Pressure

Peer Pressure for older heavy drinkers/alcoholics is likely more intense in period(s) of their lives when there aren't many other commitments (e.g., marriage, children, and career) and their "friends" are the most important aspect of their lives when it comes to human interactions. These "friends" are likely heavy drinkers, as heavy drinkers will tend to associate with other heavy drinkers. Within this social group, using alcohol to excess will not be viewed as bad behavior—in fact it may be the non-drinker who is considered the bad or deviant one. Such a group can provide a feeling of acceptance and great comfort in general.

Heavy drinkers are less likely to confront others about their drinking. Instead, they will encourage it because they also like to consume alcohol. The alcoholic might seek out such a group of people, or they may already belong to such a group.

> *I was sober and largely happy for 18 months after a near fatal bout of alcoholic pneumonia. I had a friend who was a drinker and said I could probably cope. I have been a saint and still get treated badly at work and by others. I thought, "what's the point of being good when others are bad and life is good to them?"*
>
> Anonymous

Other Forms of Peer Pressure

The vast majority of people who drink, of course, are not "bad" persons. They may or may not have some sort of drinking problem, and they are certainly unlikely to mean you harm by pushing or even benignly influencing you to drink with them. That makes separating yourself from them that much harder.

Social Situations is where this kind of weak Peer Pressure may be a huge related trigger. Whether it is a party, a family get-together or a general outing with the girls/boys, the pressure to drink can be intense— *even if it is self-inflicted.* In these kinds of more casual encounters, with people you know, that's what the pressure you may feel actually is— self-inflicted. Most of those people will not notice if you are drinking anything—regardless of whether or not it includes alcohol!

That said, Peer Tolerance can be nearly as big a trigger as Peer Pressure, and is something to watch out for. Hanging out with people who use drugs and drink, tolerate addictive behaviors in you, or are in any way neutral or non-supportive of your sobriety is a kind of social vacuum that can suck you in. It's far easier to pick up a drink when you are around people who aren't going to hold you accountable for your actions.

Tips for Dealing with Peer Pressure without Alcohol

For younger drinkers:

Don't be fooled: the real reason everyone wants you to drink is because they're insecure. They don't want to be around anyone sober who might notice what sloppy drunks they're being.

You might think you're the only person who isn't drinking—particularly at parties—but that's probably not true. Other people might be sober but are choosing not to draw attention to themselves. Identify and stick with them, and you're sure to have a fun time. Other ideas include:

• **Clue in a friend or two.** If you tell your BFF before the party that you plan on staying sober, you'll be more likely to stick to your word than if you keep it to yourself.

• **Plan to be the designated driver** (only if you have a license, of course). That way, you'll have an easy, non-negotiable excuse for not drinking. Plus, your friends will totally owe you one.

• If someone tries to hand you a drink, **say you have to be somewhere later**. To them, it'll sound like you're saying, "This party might be cool enough for *you,* but I've got bigger and better places to go."

• **Carry around a cup** filled with soda or water. People will assume you're drinking booze, and there's no reason you have to set the record straight for them.

• If people keep bothering you to take a drink, **say you're having enough fun without it**. It'll probably make them wonder why *they* aren't secure enough to have fun without being wasted. (Besides, you'll be telling the truth).

• If you're *still* not comfortable, **leave the friggin' party**. People who don't know how to party without drinking—and without forcing everyone around them to drink—aren't worth partying with.[111]

For older drinkers:

A big trigger to drink for many is the old drinking buddies. Just being with them can be enough for a relapse, even if they are not drinking! If you want to get and stay sober, *consider your old drinking buddies as enemies.* Sever all their contacts, and most importantly get as many new friends as you can who don't drink, because losing your old friends will make you lonely and will act as a trigger. Other ideas include:

• **Avoid bars and other drinking establishments** as much as possible. Perhaps obvious, but something that many newly sober people insist on doing, like it is a "test." Until you are fully confident in your alcohol defenses, don't tempt fate.

• **Surround yourself with people who know what you're doing and are supportive.** Your friends and family are key here (see Level 4— Engage Friends and Family), as are your friends and acquaintances in other support groups (see Level 7—Join a Community).

• **Make sure that you remain in positive environments**—if possible, free of alcohol and drugs. This is a combination of the previous two bullet points, but more generalized. Many environments can be downers even if they have nothing to do with alcohol—dark rooms, sparse surroundings, dirty rooms. Being in positive environments will help you just-say-no easier even when faced with heavy Peer Pressure.

Lemons into Lemonade Tip: Unfortunately by the time you finally realize you have a serious drinking problem, you likely will have few friends left. Those still around will likely be "drinking buddies" that likely have a long list of their own issues to deal with. They are typically not people who will be friends with you once you get sober, nor will you *want* them to be your friends after that happens. In other words, since your "friends" via their Peer Pressure are a major cause of your drinking who will not want to be around after you get sober, why not dump them right now? Consider this a social house cleaning for your new life and the start of building a new set of real friends for your new, sober life.

Overall Tip: Friends who encourage you to drink, particularly when they know you don't want to, ***are not friends!*** Dump them if possible; avoid them if not, but do not be around them!

Related Triggers: The feeling of being pressured by your "Peers" is most often caused by their desire to have drinking "Fun." Being in Social Situations where alcohol is right there (e.g., Proximity) and everyone around you is drinking can make this much worse, and not drinking can make you feel Unfun/Uninteresting and even Lonely. It can also cause feelings of Powerlessness (e.g., you cannot control the situations). An extremely dangerous and difficult to defend collection of triggers.

Key Defense Levels: Engage Friends and Family (non-drinking and drugging friends), Join a Community (where alcohol is not central to their activities), Break Bad Habits (don't hang around in areas where alcohol is likely to be), Develop New Hobbies (that are unlikely to include alcohol), and Consider Spirituality (to give you strength in very difficult pressure environments).

POWERLESSNESS (INCLUDING BEING CONTROLLED)

Powerlessness can be tricky to define. At its simplest it refers to a lack of control over key dimensions of your life, such as your job, relationships, and marriage. It becomes more complex when it starts to include other confusing and uncomfortable dimensions of one's life, particularly physical changes (puberty, sexual awareness and identity, and Mid-Life Crisis) and the related triggers that come pouring in on top such as Anxiety and Depression.

This trigger appears to be particularly acute for females. Males (in my experience) will rarely admit to anyone including themselves that they don't have the power do *something* about something—until things really go to hell. Their ego won't allow it—to them it is a sign of weakness. It goes hand-in-hand with not admitting that they are lost and asking for directions. In fact, one can argue that some males drink alcohol precisely because it helps them "deal" with feelings of powerlessness since alcohol increases aggression levels (see the Anger trigger discussion in particular).

For women, powerlessness in any form is not a good thing. As the author of *Why She Drinks: Women and Alcohol Abuse* (*Wall Street Journal*, June 2013) put it:

> "It doesn't take an advanced degree in gender studies to realize that this approach (AA and powerlessness[112])—which has worked well for millions of people—may not be perfect for **women whose biggest problem is not an excess of ego but a lack of it** (author's emphasis). Women are twice as likely to suffer from depression

and anxiety as men—and are far more likely to medicate those conditions with alcohol. [113]

It goes on to say that many women who drink heavily are also the victims of sexual abuse and have had eating disorders. These are covered in other trigger discussions,[114] but it starts to give you a perspective on just how complex these issues can be—and the importance of related triggers.

A Note to Nonalcoholics on Being Controlling

As noted in the Frustration trigger section, I've been to dozens of Al-Anon meetings, looking to gain insight into the perception of alcoholism by the nonalcoholic. There are two key themes I've observed that come up in open discussion—Frustration, and about being controlling. Nonalcoholics—very understandably—want their alcoholic loved one to stop drinking. The temptation to try to dictate and control the alcoholic about their drinking is overwhelming, as is their Frustration with their inability to do so. A big theme in Al-Anon is helping people let go of this controlling nature, so they can start to get some balance and happiness back in their lives. This is a good thing.

Why? Because *the alcoholic does not want to be controlled, and trying to do so is often counter-productive.* He or she is already frustrated with their inability to control their drinking, and the last thing they want is to have someone hounding them and trying to manage their every move. Like a child, they will react to someone telling what not to do by making sure they *do* it—even when they don't want to! As strange as it sounds, it is a way for an alcoholic to exhibit some control over a topic that they are otherwise powerless—by rebelling against your demands to stop!

The article continues with the idea that being powerless can underscore a woman's sense of vulnerability. *"Women need to feel powerful, not like victims of something beyond their control,"* a doctor says in the article. *"It gives women power to feel they themselves can change."*

Tips for Dealing with Powerlessness without Alcohol

There are numerous psychological opinions, media pundits, and people next door who have tons of advice on this topic. Some of this advice—culled from numerous sources—that seem to have the most relevance to alcoholics include:

- **Stop giving away your power.** Becoming powerless doesn't happen in a single dramatic stroke, as the barbarian hordes are breaking down your door and burning your house. It's a process, and for most people, the process is so gradual that they don't notice it. They are more than happy, in fact, to give away their power by degrees. Why? Because being powerless seems to be an easy way to be popular, accepted, and protected. *Author's Note:* The process described of "giving away your power"—being so gradual that you don't even notice it—is a process very similar to the one that made us alcoholics. We didn't start out that way but, usually, became one over a large amount of time. Recognizing and "rebooting" your life to how it was before your slide into powerlessness/ alcoholism may be a way of killing two birds with one stone!

- **Watch out for the slide into being a Victim.** Powerlessness can make you start chipping away at your self-worth, a key aspect of the Victim trigger described later in this Level. You do not want to have these two major triggers egging you on to drink! Having given away too much of themselves, the first step for victims is to realize that their role is voluntary. They are not trapped by fate, destiny, or the will of God. Their role is a personal choice, and they can choose differently.

- **Trust in a power that transcends everyday reality.** The "Higher Power" concept in AA, Al-Anon, and other programs can be extremely useful. It does not require any religion or even any reference to God.[115]

- **Accept yourself as you are, without criticism or harsh judgment.** But at the same time look for opportunities to assert yourself more often. A great place to start is in developing your strength of defenses against alcohol.

- **Learn to recognize bullies, and avoid or even confront them.** Some people are "natural" bullies who pick on people because it makes them feel more powerful. Bullies do not like people who standup to them, and will go and pick easier targets.

- **Just say No when you are unable to do something.** This is a version of taking back some control. Saying No to drinking opportunities is obviously a huge start. Do not feel Guilty when you do so!

- **Do something when you are feeling stuck in a certain powerless situation.** Ideally do something productive or fun, or even better, do something you are good at to boost your ego.

- **Learn from your experiences, and praise and reward yourself when you do well.** Do this particularly when successfully avoiding drinking situations where in the past you might have indulged.[116]

Lemons into Lemonade Tip: People who feel and act powerless are also often very kind and gentle. There are many careers that can benefit from this character trait, such a taking care of small children, the elderly, or animals in shelters, etc.

You can also do many things to change the perception of you by others from a weak person to a strong (or at least stronger) personality. It doesn't have to be a wholesale change. Instead, just start to ask a few forceful questions in meetings, or push back strong when someone tries to get you to doing something you don't want to. After a few of these you will not be perceived as "weak," or powerless, at least externally (indeed even a small response will seem large to others given your "normal" behavior), and it may even help internally (in your own self-perception) as well.

Overall Tip: Be on the constant lookout for opportunities for making lemonade when life delivers its lemons to you. Try to figure out at least one good thing you can make out of each bad or powerless-feeling situation you encounter.

Related Triggers: Powerlessness can be caused or aggravated by Frustration, Guilt, a Mid-Life Crisis, Peer Pressure, Relationship and Sexual issues, and Victim (abuse, low self-esteem issues). It can activate Anxiety, Depression, a desire to Escape, Frustration, Guilt, Loneliness, and Victim (low Self-Esteem).

Key Defense Levels: Engage Friends and Family, Join a Community (Women-only groups, Al-Anon), Rehab and Therapy, Develop New Hobbies (self-assertiveness classes), Consider Spirituality (particularly the concept of a "Higher Power")

PROXIMITY

The Proximity to alcohol is one of the easiest triggers to understand, and one of the hardest to deal with on a practical day-to-day basis. Physically staying away from alcohol, e.g., being within sight or smelling distance, can be a major drinking trigger for many of us, particularly in early sobriety. The temptation is great—it is right there! No one is around to see if I pick it up, open it up, taste it . . .

To a significant degree it depends on your specific environment and even geography. It depends on if there is alcohol in the house, what types of stores are allowed to sell alcohol in the state you live in (including store hours), whether the restaurants you frequent serve alcohol, and to what degree they emphasize it (e.g., bar and grill), even whether such stores/restaurants are on your route to/from home or work. These are just a few examples of where temptation can strike.

> *I have always known that alcohol is something that I have a difficult time controlling and that it sometimes takes over my life in a flash. It's just so weird how one minute you are going to the gym regularly and not even thinking about the wine store when you walk past it on your way home and the next minute you haven't been to the gym in months because you have been passing it up to go home and sit in front of the TV.*
>
> Guest Lily, alcoholism.about.com

If Proximity to alcohol is a strong trigger, just trying to avoid being near it will not be enough. You just can't avoid it, not if you don't want to change your lifestyle radically. Dealing with this kind of trigger is one of the areas I address in Level 11—Make Yourself Sick of Alcohol (an optional Level). Part of that Level is training your mind to make your body physically sick with respect to alcohol. Not just from drinking it but also in actually seeing it, smelling it, tasting something like it, or even reading words that describe it. Eventually, you can change that self-induced distaste into a non-craving including getting rid of the desire that being near alcohol can cause.

> *I miss the taste of drinking some good ol' wine. After meeting a psychiatrist, I found out that I'm not supposed to be drinking any wine at all because with the medication I'm taking. And it is boring not being able to drink alcohol, especially during holiday season. I'd see all the wine bottles and beer, and I'd be craving for it. But it's so hard to restrain myself.*
>
> Marielabete, socialanxietysupport.com

The above testimonial is another illustration of the importance of Level 3—Listen to Your Body!, particularly in consulting with your doctor about your alcohol problems and being very aware of any dangerous side effects of combining alcohol with your medication. It also illustrates how certain Social Situations and/or Holidays can be powerful related triggers.

Tips for Dealing with Proximity to Alcohol

How often you are physically near alcohol will depend on many factors, particularly your lifestyle and even other factors such as relationships,[117] friends, family, job, even where you live[118]. Ways to deal include:

• **Avoid it!** First and most obvious, try to limit your exposure to places and situations where alcohol is easy to get, particularly early in sobriety. Avoidance may be easy—such as turning down invitations to parties— or damn near impossible, such as living in a state where alcohol seems to be everywhere except vending machines! But this is easier to do than you might think with a bit of planning, so you should . . .

• **. . . Plan ahead.** This is particularly true for Holiday family get-togethers and Social Situations. See those trigger discussions for more detailed ideas.

• **Get the booze out of your house.** While you may think having some there is a good "test" of your defenses, it is a needless one—why tempt fate? Hopefully, your spouse/partner/roommate will go along with this approach. If they don't for whatever reasons, there are a number of possibilities. One excellent compromise is having a place where they can lock up the booze with only them having the key (you should be unaware of where this place is for your own protection).

If for some reason alcohol has to be visible in your residence (or if you think you can handle it), try to make it at least a *little* difficult to get if you happen to be tempted. Recent research showed how having wrappers on candy was an effective way to lose weight.[119] You can extend that logic to alcohol—make sure that any alcohol on the premises *has not been opened yet.* You might be amazed how such a little thing can be an effective deterrent, particularly if you know someone will notice it.[120]

• **Consider Smell and Taste.** Many of the tips for dealing with the Smell and Taste of alcohol are applicable here. Indeed, there is a separate chapter dedicated to the combination of Proximity, Smell, and Taste in Level 11—Make Yourself Sick of Alcohol. That discussion provides more radical ideas for dealing with those triggers.

• **Don't let your guard down, and don't give in to temptation.** I thought I had Proximity nailed, but alcohol is always looking for a chink in your defenses. After a very long winter, my neighborhood recently had a spring festival that featured specials on margaritas, complete with a working machine outside on the boardwalk. Boy was I tempted! But I remembered: for us, one is never enough. Even if you only did *one* that day, the next time will be "hey I had one no problem, why not *two?*" And before you know it you will be on a very slippery slope back to hell.

Lemons into Lemonade Tip: Use the proximity to alcohol as a way of reinforcing your aversion to it. Aversion is discussed in great detail in Level 11—Make Yourself Sick of Alcohol. I do this every so often. When I am with a good friend who has ordered a drink, I will deliberately use the nearness to alcohol to pick it up and remember all the pain it has brought me in the past. It reinforces the sense of nausea that I developed through the techniques described in Level 11.

Overall Tip: Make sure you are not caught unaware about places and situations that may have alcohol on-hand; this may put a crack in your defenses for which you were not prepared. See Level 13—Develop Your Defense Progressions, particularly on how to develop a "generic" progression, for dealing with circumstances like these.

Related Triggers: Proximity can be activated in almost any situation at any time, but particularly during many types of "Fun," Holidays/Special Occasions, with Peer Pressure (being with friends who often drink), Relationships (with people who often drink), Smell (even if you don't see it), Social Situations, Taste (of something similar—even kissing someone who has been drinking!). It can activate other triggers as well, notably Envy, Overconfidence, and Smell and Taste.

Key Defense Levels: Listen to Your Body! (medication side effects), Detox (break the association between pleasure and alcohol), Make Yourself Sick of Alcohol, The Last Detox

QUITTING (FEAR OF)

I can't tell you how many people in rehab, AA, or elsewhere told me that just before they entered those programs, usually the day or days before, they drank heavily. I did this as well just prior to previous attempts to stop drinking. Some would say it was a desire to "get it out of their system" or to get so drunk that their hangover would cause them to go into rehab, detox, etc. with open arms.

Maybe. But the *real* general consensus was that it wasn't a desire to have some last "fun" or even "soften themselves up for detox," but instead driven by a deep fear of what life would be like without alcohol. This concept was introduced in the "Change" section earlier and might seem strange to those nonalcoholics reading this.

Consider: life for the alcoholic has revolved heavily around alcohol for years, even decades, and has become as much a part of him or her as an arm or leg, eating or sleeping. Maybe that seems melodramatic, but it's the truth. Many alcoholics can't imagine or remember a life without alcohol, and if they can it probably scares them to death. They *know* a life with alcohol (even if it sucks); they *don't know* life without it. The unknown creates fear—**Big Time.**

My fears about quitting drinking were so numerous that they kept me from quitting drinking for over 22 years past when I knew I was an alcoholic.

anonymous

Outside of work, I drank in the evenings and weekends, and I couldn't think of what I would do with myself without drinking. When I tried to cut back or stop on my own, I was fearful about everything and had panic attacks.

I was fearful of being alone without drinking and facing my feelings, since I always drank when I was alone. I thought I might go crazy. And I was scared to death of trying to quit drinking in a program and failing, because that would mean I was really hopeless.

sarahtroy, mdjunction.com

My main fear was how I was going to live without it. I had been drinking for 15 years, 10 of them daily. It was all I knew since I began in my teens. I had no clue as to what life would look like without booze. I was terrified of the idea of trying to live without having a drink. What would I do? How could I function without it? I realized I had no concept of the kind of normalcy that non-drinkers or social drinkers had. My normalcy was hanging out with those who drank a lot, too. It was all normal to me.

uppitywoman, mdjunction.com

Fear of Quitting is actually one of the "simpler" triggers in my opinion. It is also one of the most onerous ones because there are not many "tips" for "dealing" with it—you just have to *do* it.

That said, I believe you will find that this fear diminishes as you *really* start to understand your other triggers for drinking. Boredom for example:

> *My fears about quitting, hmmm? . . . I guess I don't want to be bored. As lame as that sounds it's true. I actually fear boredom. That's the same reason I pack my days and life full of one activity after another, my kids school activities and homework, kids' sports and other lessons, my own school work, church stuff, and my substance of choice . . .*
>
> Anonymous, mdjunction.com

Or unfortunately it can be many, many things:

> *Fears: having to just "be" in my head, or with my head; Fear in social situations without it; be lonely without it; not at least every once in a while getting "that feeling"; I'll have to pay attention to the pain and hurt; I'll miss the little drinking "rituals" I have; not being able to handle my husband; the need to smoke more weed; the cravings; the nightmares, the physical detox symptoms; and that I CAN'T . . .*
>
> bfly, mdjunction.com

A very big part of your fear is likely to be related to the trigger of Change. If you have been drinking for many years, it has likely been embedded into almost every aspect of your personal and professional life. Not drinking anymore is going to require many big adjustments in so many areas that may well scare you to death! These adjustments, probably more than anything, is why it was a major trigger for me for so many years.

> *I believe it is the enormity of what lies ahead for most people that scares them. It is far easier to return to drinking than face the reality of what may need to change in your life. This may include what you do, where you go, who you socialize with even excluding certain people from your life if necessary.*
>
> Jacobs, alcoholism.about.com

Tips for Dealing with Fear of Quitting

Fear of Quitting is one of those triggers that *masks* the true root causes of drinking. You are not afraid of quitting per se. What you *really* are afraid of is the Anxiety you will be forced to feel. The Boredom you think you will experience. The Escape you will no longer be able to do on demand. The Fun you think you will never have again. The Guilt you know is lurking behind you waiting to strike when you sober up. The Insomnia you know will be coming, and on and on and on. Triggers that hardly ever make an appearance in your regular daily life will suddenly become part of this fear, such as "how will I deal with the Holidays?" Issues that you thought were stable and relatively comfortable, such as your Sex life, can become great unknowns. No wonder you are scared to death! Do the following to break and calm this fear:

• **Understand your underlying triggers.** This is by far the most important thing you can do. Is not knowing what to do with your time (e.g., Boredom) the biggie? Is no longer being able to Escape whenever you want to? Horrendous Guilt? Having to revisit your entire Relationship(s) because of underlying (but up to now hidden) Sexual issues? Prioritize these as to which generates the biggest fear individually. Understanding these underlying triggers are what you *really* need to get to the heart of—once you do, the general fear of quitting *will* start to disappear, I promise.

• **Identify some obvious alternatives to drinking.** You will very likely have a combination of several major and minor triggers. Do a quick reading of the tips and defenses of those underlying triggers, and pick out the ones that first leap to mind. These will likely be ones that will have the most impact, and the fact that they exist as an alternative to drinking should help calm some of your overall fear.

• **Pick out a Floor Defense.** This is one that you can use either as a deterrent, a motivation, a goal or in combination. This process is described more in Level 13; mine are my Health and my children.

• **Understand the Process.** Once you think you've got a handle on what those are, then you have to get tactical. How do you Quit? What will Detox be like? (What to expect in Detox is discussed in Level 5). Do you go to a Rehab place, and if so what kind and which one? Do you need Therapy? (Different kinds of Rehab and Therapy are discussed in Level 6). What is the best approach for you? Make out a plan—do your research and figure out the best place for you to go to start the process. Knowing the process *in detail* will take away much of the fear of the unknown.

- **Avoid last-minute hiccups.** One big danger you may face is the desire to do a "last" binge as a kind of going away present to yourself, make yourself more "ready" for detox, or some other rationalization. However, it could well cause you to not follow through with your determination to start detoxing, going into rehab, or whatever method you plan on using to clean out your body. Thus, a critical Tip: Do NOT do a "last" binge before you detox/try to begin a path of sobriety. It doesn't have any real, *lasting*[121] impact in my opinion, and just *makes the detox process that much more uncomfortable and longer lasting.*

- **Just do it!** Don't overthink it once you have the above in place—pull the trigger (pun intended) and start the process of stopping drinking!

Lemons into Lemonade Tip: Once you stop drinking, you can use the Fear of Quitting trigger as a *positive.* Using Reminders of how unpleasant life was *before* you stopped drinking as an effective deterrent to starting up again. Remind yourself of the positives that have occurred now that you are sober. In particular try to remember the unpleasantness of your Detox's, and how fucked up your life was in general while you were drinking. Do you really want to go back to that royally fucked-up state? NO.

This is also a trigger where using another trigger as a defense can be helpful—specifically Guilt. As I have discussed before, I view one of the best ways to deal with Guilt—at least early in sobriety—is to not feel Guilty. Put it away and don't think about it for now.

If, however, you are thinking about going back to drinking (in effect trying to put your fear of quitting behind you), OR you have a relapse, use Guilt as a tool to bring you back to sober thinking. Do you really want a *new* reason to feel Guilty? Again, **NO.** It will probably not be as easy to put this new Guilt behind you like the old Guilt, so why go down that path again?

Overall Tip: Like many fears, it is better to talk about them than keep them inside. You may well feel ashamed, or a "coward," or just uncomfortable with talking about this fear with someone else. My advice: *Do it anyway.* You will feel much better, particularly if you can start to articulate some of the true underlying fears such as Boredom, etc.

Related Triggers: Fear of Quitting can be caused or influenced by many factors, with Anxiety, Boredom, Change, Guilt, and Insomnia being some of the more common ones. It can influence nearly every other trigger in this Level. *Overall it is the fear of the unknown—how massively your life will change without alcohol—plus the collective fears of how you are going to deal with all the other triggers in your life that makes Fear of Quitting so scary.*

Key Defense Levels: Know Your Triggers (understanding *completely* all your other triggers), Listen to Your Body! (how not drinking will improve your health), Engage Friends and Family, Detox (understand what is coming at you), Join a Community, Rehab and Therapy, Break Bad Habits (how quitting drinking will improve your personality), Develop New Hobbies (how you can fill your new free time), Consider Spirituality, Make Yourself Sick of Alcohol (how you can deal with the combined triggers of Proximity, Smell, and Taste), The Last Detox (if "regular" detox did not work for you before)

RELATIONSHIPS

For the purposes of this trigger section, I define a Relationship as another person with whom you:

A. Have or had a romantic connection to (which may or may not have included sex)

B. With whom you are/were monogamous—or otherwise some real or inferred commitment—such as not dating other people and/or only having sexual relations with

C. A and B have lasted/did last at least several months.

The reason for this definition is that there are, of course, many types of general "relationships" possible as well as their duration. In my view those other types (except eX's, discussed shortly) are probably unlikely to be considered a "true" potential drinking trigger by most people, even if they end badly.[122]

> *I have drank on and off since my teens. I had a handle on it, but after going through several breaks ups, disappointments, family problems, you name it I have turned to alcohol to deal with my emotions. I black out every time. I can't sleep without it. I am almost numb inside; I have horrible anger; diarrhea every morning. I've woken up sick at night and stumbled into the bathroom sweaty and sick.*
>
> Guest guest, alcoholism.about.com

As you can see from the above, the person has lumped several potential triggers together, including something possibly resembling our definition of a Relationship, but also "disappointments" (e.g., perhaps some kind of Depression), Relatives, Insomnia, Anger, and Health problems. Who knows the real triggers involved here that ramped up his/her drinking, let alone their relative priorities?

The Difference Between a Former Relationship and an "eX"

It is important to note a *critical* distinction between the definition of a Relationship that is over and an "eX."

An eX has all the definition components of a Relationship, plus: 1) is likely to have lasted longer, several years, not just months; and most importantly 2) Resulted in having to have some sort of ongoing interaction with after the relationship is over, whether you want to or not. This ongoing interaction, usually, is related to Money (e.g., alimony), and children—"things" that you have to interact with each other fairly often such as a few times a year. The Tips for dealing with an eX without drinking are similar on the surface yet distinctly different in detail and are discussed in the e(X) trigger section.

For active Relationships it is critical to get underneath the other issues that are truly driving the problems (likely to include a number of other triggers), not just some generalized "my boyfriend is really stressing me out."

> *My biggest relapse triggers are definitely stress [related]. And unneeded stress cause by others. An example of this is my boyfriend. I have to step back and calm myself down and remember that it will only affect me in a negative way if I relapse. He doesn't get it.*
>
> anonymous

Thinking About Starting a New Relationship Once Recently Sober? Think Again

One of the pieces of strong advice given by Alcoholics Anonymous is to *not* enter into a new relationship within one year of becoming sober. I *strongly* agree with this advice.

Why? The freshly sober or actively trying to get sober person is in very vulnerable period of their life. They are, usually, pretty unhappy, perhaps physically weak, and often in a poor state of mind to make sound life decisions as they struggle with giving up alcohol. Alternatively, they can be on a "pink cloud" (see Overconfidence), where they think all is right with the world and in bursts of euphoria start seeing someone they would normally view as incompatible. They may invest so much of themselves emotionally that if and when the new Relationship ends (for whatever reason) they are so distraught that they relapse. All are good reasons to avoid entering into new romances during this period.

But once you get past this stage, you may well find that you are looking at possible new relationships in a way you had never done before. I am far from a relationship expert, but it is not a big leap to suggest that you might seek out those who are *not* likely to push your triggers. For example, if Boredom is a trigger, you might look for someone very dynamic, even unpredictable. On the other hand, if Change is a trigger, then you might look for someone almost the opposite—someone very even keeled and predictable. If Disorder is a trigger, do not link up with someone who is a slob; sooner or later it is bound to get to you. And so on; it will be an interesting experience, I assure you!

● ●

Relationship problems will have many obvious related triggers, such as Frustration, Money, and Sex, as well as some other (very numerous), yet less clear reasons could of course be what are driving you to want to drink, including:

• Fear of commitment (which could also be a more general fear of Change, which can be a trigger in itself)

• Compatibility problems

• Differing priorities, now and in the future

• Past(s) coming back to haunt you

• (Physical) living situations (e.g., wanting/not wanting to live together)

How you address these issues may have a material impact on the short-term and long-term success (or not) of your Relationship. Using alcohol to somehow "deal with" them will not help and may well make them worse—much worse.

When The Spouse is an "Enabler"

"Enabler" is one of those (too) often used, much misunderstood terms when it comes to addiction. It is commonly used to describe someone who "helps" a person perpetuate their addiction, such as a wife who buys her alcoholic husband's booze (and sometimes complains about it: see *www.miamiherald.com/2013/07/23/3516105/ dear-abby-wife-of-alcoholic-should.html*).

While admittedly extreme, it's that kind of behavior that certainly does not help an alcoholic's struggles, particularly if he or she is trying to deal with their problems. A spouse that often drinks around the alcoholic, insists on dragging them to parties, or ignores the drinking alcoholic can legitimately be called an enabler. On the other hand, a spouse that constantly harps on the drinking often does more harm than good since it can "activate" all sorts of related reasons for drinking, such as Anger, Depression, Guilt, and even Noise, resulting in a desire to drown them figuratively or even literally. A little "harping" is good, a lot is not.

However, the existence of enablers as defined above is not going to make much difference in the alcoholic's drinking—it is the underlying triggers that will. For that reason, it is critical to distinguish between a (often well-meaning or sometimes oblivious or even stupid) spousal enabler like the above and a Relationship that is a core part of the alcoholic's trigger portfolio. If a spouse is truly "harping"—nagging, irritating, and constant—then it is likely an indication of deeper problems with the Relationship, perhaps even qualifying as an actual drinking trigger.

Tips for Dealing with Relationship Issues without Alcohol

For Relationships that are still "active," but going through tough times, deteriorating, or even ending, I'd encourage you to try to break those problems down into other individual related triggers. If you think there are other issues underlying your Relationship issues, I'd encourage you to do some research on your own. There are *many* sites/people out there willing and wanting to give you relationship advice.[123] If issues are particularly severe, such as Fear of Commitment, you may want to seek out professional help to talk through the underlying reasons for that fear/uncertainty.

The below tips are focused on *former* Relationships, and include:

• **Create new Boundaries.** Your best defense after a breakup? Immediately create new boundaries with your former boyfriend/girlfriend/ partner/lover/roommate[124]. That means *no* phone calls, *no* e-mails, *no* texting, and definitely *no* late-night visits. Your Former is just that—*former*. That means it's time to remove him or her from your life, and take the wanting-to-make-you-drink issues with them.

• **Avoid Being Each Other's Crutch.** You loved. You lost. You are now in mourning. A word of warning when you're in post-breakup mourning: DO NOT seek comfort in the arms of your former lover. That's a huge recovery[125] no-no! You may well want to show your former girlfriend/boyfriend that you are now a new (wo)man in not drinking, which may lead to one thing leading to another, and back you are together again—at least for a few hours. But if it doesn't last, the breakup may wind up being a huge potential relapse trigger. Why put yourself through that? Better to move on to a new life.

• **Be Careful of Your Friends.** If you shared many of the same friends while you were together, be careful of who you associate with/tell intimate things to after you break up. This includes your plans/activities for dealing with alcohol.

Instead, recruit a support system from your inner circle of friends, preferably friends who have your best interests at heart and won't report back to your Former on your progress and setbacks. Having a support system is one of the single most important steps you can follow during your breakup recovery. To heal and move on, you're going to need help. That help should NOT come in the form of the reason for it! The same is true for you. If he/she calls, emails, texts, or stops by seeking comfort for his/her broken heart? Don't open your arms. Instead, kindly but firmly let the Former know that you are no longer his go-to support system. Then shut the door on any and all opportunities to help each other heal following the breakup.

• **No Online Ex-Bashing.** After a breakup, it's only natural to feel some residual anger, resentment, bitterness, etc. And in the era of social networking sites and YouTube, it's all too easy to go online and spew in front of millions of readers/viewers.[126] Don't do it! By going online and bashing that person on your blog, via video diary, or to everyone in your social network, you are inviting bad breakup karma into your life. And you know what they say—what comes around goes around. If you were the alcoholic in the Relationship, and you start bashing her online, then she has the ammunition to do *far* more harm to you online than you do to her. Like telling all your friends and coworkers that you drink too much . . .

- **Handle the Dreaded Run-in with Class.** While it would be fabulous if your Former could be automatically ejected from the planet following the breakup, such technology has yet to be invented. Depending on the size of the city you live in, a post-breakup run-in with your Former is not only possible, it's probable. Rather than become a shut-in out of fear of encountering your Former, embrace the possibility and plan for it. First, imagine the absolute worst-case scenario: You haven't showered in days. Your clothes are wrinkled and smelly. Your hair is a mess. THEN you happen to run into your Former on a date with the most gorgeous girl you've ever seen. In fact, they're engaged as evidenced by the huge shiny rock on her left hand. [127] Can you see it in your mind? Pretty painful, right?

Chances are that's not going to happen. In fact, your Former encounter will probably be a lot less dramatic than this scenario. However, the pain may still be there. In bumping into your Former, you may be reminded of what you loved about him or her. It may even reignite those familiar feelings of love, lust, or just plain loneliness. Do not use the run-in as an excuse to reconnect. What's done is done. Your Former is now your *former*. Bumping into him does not mean that the two of you are meant to be together. Instead, summon that inner strength, smile politely, and extricate yourself from the situation as soon as is possible without being rude.

- **Follow the Six-Month Rule.** After a breakup, the best rule of thumb is to avoid all contact with your Former for at least six months.[128] Think about what you can do in six months—train for a marathon, plan and take a well-deserved vacation, buy property, change jobs, heal and move on. In giving yourself a six-month cushion, you greatly increase your chances of getting over your Former. In the throes of post-breakup angst, you may not like the sound of that. Like it or not, it's what's best for you. Rather than fight what you know is right for you, give yourself permission to put the six-month rule into practice.[129]

Lemons into Lemonade Tip: To paraphrase Einstein, the definition of stupidity is to do the same thing over and over again and expect different results. If alcohol (and other personal characteristics) destroyed a past relationship, why not do things differently next time around? I can tell you from personal experience that trying to correct past mistakes (and telling your new partner about them) goes a long way of making that next relationship work that much better.

Overall Tip: Not to get all Oprah-like or Dr. Phil-ish, but the number-one skill I've learned (far too late to save my first marriage) is to listen. Next up is to let loose about your feelings. Just the two of those can go a long way towards resolving Relationship conflicts and issues.

Related Triggers: Relationships as a trigger can be caused or influenced by various forms of major Change, Frustration, Guilt, Loneliness, Peer Pressure (mutual friends), Reminders, Sex, Social Situations (mutual friends/acquaintances). It can activate Anger, Anxiety, Depression, desire to Escape, Frustration, Kids complications, Loneliness, Money problems, a sense of Powerlessness, Relatives issues, Stress, eX complications, and Yelling.

Key Defense Levels: Engage Friends and Family, Therapy (couples therapy), Break Bad Habits (stop (re)acting in negative ways), Develop New Hobbies (ones that can spice up an active relationship, or you did not do with your Former).

RELATIVES

They say you can choose your friends, but you can't choose your family. For an alcoholic, this truism can cause significant strain on an alcoholic. For the most part, the degree of difficulty in dealing with difficult relatives is a function of closeness, both genetically and geographically. Mother-In-Law living downstairs = Very Not Good. Drunk Uncle Paul living in Stockholm = I Can Deal With.

> *I have found family and friends to be one of the largest triggers—especially when I am returning from rehab.*[130]
>
> anonymous

People may joke about how hard it is to spend time with family, but for many families this is very true. Even anticipating a family get-together can drive some people to drink, because of the stress and dysfunction this time can bring. Other people wait until they are at a family gathering and then negative interactions with family members can cause them to drink.

Unfortunately, the Relatives that seem to cause much of the difficulties (at least as perceived by the alcoholic) are the parents. I don't have any statistics to prove it, but it seems like the mother is often the one to cause the most mental distress in children:

My mom makes me feel like I'm useless and stupid. And if that wasn't enough she loves my younger and older sister. All through high school she would get upset if I wasn't getting an A, even an A–, she would talk to the teacher about bring my grade up. I graduated at age 17 and graduated college at age 19.

Mila, answers.yahoo.com (family relationships)

I'm obviously not a psychiatrist, but the above illustrates a number of possible related triggers: feelings of Powerlessness, Frustration, Victim (self-esteem), and even sibling rivalry (a form of Envy). These may or may not be justified—after all, the mother might be motivated by her seeing great potential in that person and wants to drive her to make the most of it (while perhaps recognizing the sister didn't have that potential and was easier on her as result). Who knows?

I've heard in many meetings about how a person's mother (or mother-in-law, which can be worse) are driving them crazy and making them want to drink. Clearly unfortunate, and requires exceptional mental strength to overcome.

As you might imagine, this trigger can be closely linked with Holidays, as these are the times where your presence is required, and you are forced to interact with your relative nemesis.

Tips for Dealing with Relatives without Alcohol

Dealing with drive-you-so-crazy-that-you-need-to-drink-Relatives is doable, but it may take some significant changes in how you interact with them.

• **Learning to face critical Relatives.** The key is to *expect* these comments/criticisms ahead of time. Wishing they won't be critical is just wasting your time. Instead, mentally compile a checklist of the things that relative disapproves of and prepare a matter-of-fact response to expected criticisms so you won't be taken off guard. If a question is embarrassing, respond with another question to avoid the pain of answering with an insult to yourself. You can also seek out those who are critical of you and approach them with friendly conversation before they have a chance to take you off guard.

• **Develop new strategies to survive difficult In-Laws.** Have a frank discussion prior to the in-laws' visit if they present difficulty for one partner. Partners should also create a "rescue signal" to let the other know when they've hit the limit. If you are having trouble dealing with in-laws, it might help to use humor, and keep your perspective that this is only one day out of the year. If one person grinds your nerves, stay away from them and focus on those people at the gathering that make you feel good.

• **Learn to "manage" Family Gatherings (particularly during holidays).** Holidays give people license to drink excessively. Ideally the person(s) hosting will know about your alcoholism (even if others do not) and be sensitive to it, particularly if there is another person who drinks a lot in these settings (even if they are not an alcoholic). Even if there is not, try to get your host to do a number of things, like:

  • Limiting the amount of alcohol that is out in plain view

  • Pour wine by the glass instead of having open bottles sitting on the table

  • Serve other drinks without alcohol as well and clear away alcohol after the meal, going for coffee and dessert and skipping after-dinner drinks.[131]

Lemons into Lemonade Tip: Your family is your family, and with a few exceptions are prepared to forgive anything. If you have had an estranged relationship with a relative in the past, use your new sobriety as a (very) good excuse to "reboot" the relationship. Odds are they have been aware of your alcoholism problems and will be very receptive to a fresh start.

Overall Tip: You may find that "historical" grievances are much less significant once you can think more clearly about them. If they are still big once you are sober, you will likely be able to ignore or diminish them much more easily—and possibly even resolve them!

Relative Triggers: Relatives as a trigger can be caused or influenced by Extreme Emotions (death of a loved one), Guilt, Holidays, Proximity (to drinking relatives), Relationships (the in-laws), and Reminders. It can activate Anxiety, desire for Escape, Extreme Emotions, Frustration, Guilt, Powerlessness, Reminders, and Victim (abuse or self-esteem issues).

Key Defense Levels: Engage Friends and Family (non-triggering Relatives), Break Bad Habits (how you react historically to difficult Relatives)

REMINDERS

Reminders can be a minor trigger, or they can be a *huge* trigger, depending on the person and the specific reminder. For some alcoholics it may be no more than an irritant like coming across an old photo of a happy vacation with your eX and remembering good times on the beach with a Piña Colada in your hand. That same type of Reminder could be far more impactful in terms of being a strong drinking trigger to others.

Or it can be much worse. It may seem like everything you see (like old photos of your kids) or hear (like sad country songs) reminds you of a good time or *bad* time that occurred while you were drinking. For whatever reason, you *closely* associate memories of these times with drinking.

If you fall into its-a-huge-trigger-for-me category, don't be discouraged. It is totally understandable, as it potentially has many related triggers. In fact, many of the other triggers in this section can be a related trigger, such as "Fun," Holidays, Job (drinking after work), and Social Situations (when you could drink without someone noticing you). Music (and the Media in general) may be particularly hard. Certain songs (or ads, shows, etc.) can remind you of particularly good times (where you were drinking), or songs that you somehow associate with a past Relationship or an eX which in turn activates all of *their* related triggers. It can even be the strangest things:

> With me, the first "shock" I received after coming home was opening the cabinet and seeing "THE GLASS" that I always used to pour the whiskey just so-so. I got rid of it. Why do we alcoholics take such a chance? So, I just don't tease the tiger.
>
> Ray S., alcoholism.about.com

Tips for Dealing with Reminders without Alcohol

Almost by definition, Reminders as a trigger are *associated* with alcohol, more so than any other trigger discussed in this Level. That can make it incredibly difficult to deal with, but deal with it you must—short of a lobotomy they are not going away by themselves.

> When the drinking stopped, all of the scary things came flooding back. The things I started drinking to suppress. Memories, feelings, thoughts.
>
> Anonymous, cryingoutloud.com

The first thing you need to do is understand what *specific* reminders hit you the hardest, and why. Is it something relatively straightforward like "THE GLASS" above? Get rid of the fucking thing. Easy. Unfortunately, getting rid of most reminders won't be so easy.

Others may be because of the underlying related triggers. So the next thing to do is determine what those are (through completing this Level) and see which ones are most likely to continue to throw various reminders at you after you stop drinking. The tips in each of those trigger sections that help you deal with those *specific* triggers may help you with the reminders associated with them, such as Music or your eX. Do those first.

If those don't work or work well enough or often enough, you have to find additional ways of dealing with them. There are three possible ways of doing so: *avoiding* the reminder, *ignoring* the reminder, and *breaking the association* between the reminder and alcohol.

Avoiding the Reminder is an obvious step, with "The Glass" being a good example. Get rid of the damn things that have an obvious, strong relationship with alcohol. This, of course, includes any remaining alcohol bottles/cans around your house, but you'd be surprised at how many alcoholics trying to become/stay sober don't get rid of it. There are various rationalizations, such as them being "proof" of their sobriety; their spouse still drinks, etc. But until you are confident you won't relapse, get rid of all alcohol in your house. It's a temptation you don't need right now.

> *Remember it's all about what you connect with while you drank. When I am angry with a loved one or I hear a blender, I flash to drinking. I remind myself that a thought is just a thought. It doesn't mean I'm still that sick. It only means that alcoholics will think like that and it's normal.*
>
> Guest hacha, alcoholsm.about.com

Avoiding something useful like a blender might be a bit more difficult. This may be something that you have to eventually train yourself to ignore (discussed next). Perhaps you can even "avoid" by throwing out that specific appliance and getting one that does the same function, but doesn't look anything like the old one.

If Music is a particular Reminder, there are some relatively easy ways to avoid the specific songs that bother you. These tips are discussed in that section, such as changing what stations/types of stations you listen to, or how you listen to music in general.

●●

A Note on Reminders and Memory

As you'll see in more detail in a section about Memory Problems (Level 3—Listen to Your Body!), alcoholism can cause severe difficulties in remembering past events and information, perhaps some even permanently. This, of course, is so ironic that it is literally dripping with irony that I'm discussing it in this trigger section.

Yes, many of the linkages that your brain uses to *reach* memories[132] may have been destroyed by alcohol, but time and other "reminders of those reminders" may recreate them. As a result, as time goes by once you are sober you will likely remember more and more Reminders (as strange as that may sound). An old song may cause you to remember an event or situation that happened years ago, that makes you think of great relationship at the time, that causes you to remember why you broke up, which unleashes other memories and so on.

So the bottom line is that Reminders may (and probably will) get worse the longer you are sober, so be prepared with the tips below!

●●

If you can't avoid the Reminder, *ignore* it if you can. Some will undoubtedly be easier to do than others, particularly if they are short in duration. Driving past liquor stores is a great example. Look at or think about something else if you can. The next time, try to pre-program your brain to look at the left side of the road (if the store is on the right) when you are in the area.

The hardest Reminders to deal with are those that you can't avoid, can't ignore, occur without any warning, and for some reason your "generic defense" (discussed in the overall tip) doesn't work all the time. For those Reminders, try to *break* them by "re" associating them with something else. This reminder could be good (discussed next), but it also could be bad/unpleasant.

For example, I spent a lot of time trying (and ultimately being successful) at making the word "Liquor" literally make me queasy. This was helpful since it seemed to tempt me often, and I live in an area where Liquor Stores seem to be fucking everywhere. How I did this is discussed in Level 11—Make Yourself Sick of Alcohol section. But more generally the best way to break a bad association is somehow associating it with an even worse association (that stops your wanting to do it in its tracks), *or* re-associating it with something good.

Lemons into Lemonade Tip: When you are breaking the association for some Reminders, try to replace them with something far more positive. For example, a photo of your children when they were young may bring along a great deal of sadness/unhappiness because it reminds you of the good times you did have, or could have had, when they were young and you were not drinking or drinking as much, and/or were happier times with your eX.[133] Turn that around and think only about the happy memories of them (just the children—ignore the eX) now, and how happy they are/will be that you are no longer drinking. Then call them up and see how they are doing. If estranged from them, start the process of making things better, including (if you are ready to tell them) that you are finally doing something to stop drinking.

● ●

A Note on Using Reminders for Positive Purposes

As discussed in Level 3 (Listen to Your Body!), memory problems are a common result of long-term drinking. Odds are all of you will have many problems remembering things/events, etc. even after you get sober, particularly in the first few months. In fact, it is likely that some of those memories from when you were drinking are gone for good[134]. But it is likely that *most* of your memories are still there; you've just wiped out your connection to them. But you can "regrow"[135] these connections by using methods such as looking at old photos, talking to old friends and family members, and similar activities that will help you reconnect to these memories.

● ●

Overall Tip: Quite possibly the hardest Reminders to deal with are the ones you are not prepared for at all. So you want to minimize them if at all possible, and most importantly put together a set of defenses that can be used in many different situations.

In Level 13 (Develop Your Progressions), you will create what is called a "generic progression" of defense. These are a variety of tips and defenses—in a specific order—which you will use when you are unprepared for an alcohol attack. After all, there is no way you can be prepared for *all* the myriad of ways that alcohol can attack—you'd go nuts. Generally it's used for triggers that, usually, are not a problem, but for some reason at that time/place/situation/circumstance it is hitting you particularly hard. Use this generic progression when you encounter Reminders that you did not prepare for via the earlier tips.

Related Triggers: There are potentially many, and they will vary greatly by the individual. Some of the more likely ones to cause or influence this trigger are Fun (times you had when drinking), Guilt, Holidays, Kids, Media, Mid-Life Crisis, Music, Proximity (to visual cues), Smell, Social Situations, and an eX. It can cause Depression, activate Guilt and influence active Relationships.

Key Defense Levels: Listen to Your Body! (memory issues), Engage Friends and Family, Break Bad Habits (breaking associations with alcohol)

SEX

This section will *not* be what you are expecting, at least if you are a male. My initial draft of this was written from the prototypical male perspective: in general we always want sex, and when we drink we want more.[136] This has to do with the stimulating, more "powerful" feeling that alcohol has on males. The flip side is that after enough drinks, and/or if you are older, you start to *forget* about sex (particularly if none is available) as the depressant side of alcohol kicks in. Probably the best summary statement (for males) is: *"Alcohol increases sexual desire but inhibits sexual performance."* I'll go out on a limb and say this is pretty obvious to most of us.

But in my research and talking with women's groups (particularly Women For Sobriety), I found that sex is *far* more complicated for females. This is what I focus on in this section. In particular, there appears to be several sub-dimensions and associated triggers for Sex as it relates to alcohol. At the risk of driving researchers crazy, I categorize them as follows:

- Body Image
- Sexual Abuse
- Sexual Discovery and Identity
- Sex and Post-Sobriety

I cover sexual abuse in the Victim section and eating disorders in the Hungry section.

Body Image

Whoever said, "Don't judge a book by its cover" was right yet totally full of shit when it came to understanding the human psyche. From the time we hit puberty[137], we are continually bombarded with images about what the "ideal" state of our body should look like. Historically it has varied *greatly*, particularly for women. Consider that:

• In the 1600s, during Elizabethan times, the fashionable female body shape was like a bell: a huge lower half, small waist and flat chest.

• In the 1700s, corsets became more like the corsets we recognize today. Petticoat hoops and rolls fell out of favor giving the lower half of the body a more natural shape. Later in the 1700's skirts were hooped again but the hoops were flat at the front and back to make a wide shape from side to side.

• In the early 1800s, a more flowing and forgiving Greek-style silhouette was in fashion. This style did not last long though and in Victorian times women pursued the ultimate hourglass shape. In the mid-1800's, the crinoline went out of fashion, and the 'Gibson girl' image came into style. A bustle in the back of the skirt was used to make a woman's hips and buttocks look bigger.

• In the early 1900s, Edwardian corsetry was less harsh and with the introduction of the so-called 'health corset' ladies no longer restricted a woman's movements and breathing but a small waist was still the ideal.

Then body image went nuts. In a relatively short space of 50 years around the turn of the 1900's, there was a massive change in the way people expected a woman's body to look. Over this time, with more participation in sports, women started to become more active and athletic.

• The slim ideal was central in the 1920s, when fashionable women known as "flappers" struggled for a thin, boyish figure with few or no curves.

• In the 1930s, women sought a slightly curvier figure with a bigger bust but still wanted slim hips. Women of the 1930s brought the corset back, then called a 'girdle,' which, usually, came with a bra and attached garters.

• In the late 1940s with the return to a wealthier lifestyle after the war, curves were back in fashion! The return of the hourglass figure for women was influenced by a new girdle. In the 1950s, women's undergarments began to emphasize the breasts instead of the waist. Bra cup sizing finally caught on in Britain.

• In the 1960s, everything changed yet again. The mini-skirt took the fashion world by storm that meant the end of full fifties petticoats and the curves that went them. Because the mini-skirt was so 'mini' stockings could no longer be worn and were replaced by tights or bare legs.

• In the 1970s, a slightly more natural shape came in as petticoats and girdles became completely outdated, and the 'hippy' lifestyle came into fashion. However, for mainstream society the look made fashionable for women was small hips and waist, but large breasts—meaning a good bra was essential.

> [We] came of age in the late 1960s and early 1970s. The picture of female sexuality came from movies and TV, a little Marilyn Monroe here, a little Mary Tyler Moore there. Sex bomb; good girl. Those were really the only two options.[138]

• In the 1980s, it became popular for people to sculpt their bodies through "working out." The 80's was the "power" decade when women were expected to diet and exercise to become thin and more muscular but still with curves in the 'right places'. Madonna's cone-shaped bra, the ultimate 'power' underwear, gained a place in lingerie history!

• Weight loss became a huge industry in the 1990s. Model Kate Moss epitomizes the tall, skinny "waif" look. The other prevailing ideal is for women to be tall and slim but also with big boobs, a very rare body shape to occur naturally and extremely difficult to achieve.

• In this early part of the 21st century, for many women today, thinness is the ultimate body shape goal. Women resort to extreme and expensive measures including plastic surgery, gastric reductions and radical diets in their struggle to get skinny.[139]

Perhaps this is impossible for many men to truly understand, but for better or worse this is the reality that women have been living for centuries. So it shouldn't be a surprise that dissatisfaction with one's body image—particularly female—can result in potentially great unhappiness. This dissatisfaction starts in the teenage years and for all practical purposes *never* stops. Thus, early unhappiness with one's body can lay the later seeds to self-medicate.

Sexual Discovery and Identity

These are two related but distinct triggers. Sexual discovery is about how alcohol can play a key role in initially learning and experiencing sex—and continuing to play a major role that can last long into middle age. The second is about how "differences" in traditional societies' views regarding sexual orientation can be a major drinking trigger for some people as they struggle to understand a same-sex orientation or other variation (e.g., transgender). I'm not going to get into this second dimension in detail as it probably warrants a whole book in itself. I do not have personal experience with it beyond a number of people telling me the struggle and process of becoming comfortable with their sexual orientation that was a very significant factor in their drinking.

When it comes to sexual discovery, particularly the first few times, alcohol can, of course, play a very, very significant role. By the time you hit your teenage years, you have been soaked in Sex—it is everywhere, seemingly at the top of every ad, show, song, posting, and discussion with your friends. It seems like the world's last great mystery. But it can be incredibly scary for many people, as well as feeling that they "are not ready" whether they admit it or not. For both of those, alcohol is ready to "help" in terms of suppressing scary feelings and lowering inhibitions.

> Meg was scared of her own body, and she was scared of men's bodies, and so most of the time she'd just lie there with her drunkenness and her doubts. So she drank and the drink loosened her up enough to act sexual. Meg felt mute, objectified, frightened—and alcohol took all that away.[140]

The problem is when drinking and Sex become closely intertwined with each other, to the point of not being able to "enjoy" one without the other. Since the "need" to have sex (for relationships, procreation, and bodily urges) often far outlives the actual *desire* for sex, alcohol over time starts to play the dominant role in the sex-alcohol partnership.

That can spell big-time (and *very* complicated) problems, depending on many factors including gender, age, strength of the relationship(s), body image, medical issues, etc. If your "solution" to dealing with them is counting on alcohol to sweep them away so you can actually have/enjoy sex, then it becomes a debilitating association and one of the scarier ones to face once you get sober.

Sex and Post-Sobriety

As you might infer from the above discussion but made very clear here is that sex for many people is very complicated. This seems to be true particularly for alcoholic women in sobriety. Many don't want to do it at all. Indeed, one of the major factors in the success of women-only programs such as Women For Sobriety (WFS) is their understanding of Sex as an issue in alcohol abuse, particularly the fear of what sex is going to be like post-sobriety. One example is from *A Women's Guide to Sex and Recovery*[141]:

> *"I had one big fear when I was in treatment for my alcoholism,"* said Barbara, an attractive brunette in her late thirties. *"I dreaded going home and sleeping with my husband, Mike."*

Though she loved Mike, Barbara had buried a great deal of resentments while she was drinking. She *"detested the thought of having sex with him,"* thinking that *"for 12 years I'd taken care of his needs, burying my resentments in a bottle. Now that I was sober, I couldn't bear the thought of meeting his demands."*

Wow. I don't think it is much of a stretch to say that such an attitude would be incomprehensible to most males,[142] but *very* understandable to many females. Talk about a Mars and Venus issue!

Jean Kirkpatrick, founder of WFS, believed that sexuality is one of the rawest areas of a new-to-sobriety woman's shredded self-esteem and that for many of them drug and drinking problems are sexual problems in disguise.[143]

Tips for Dealing with Sexual Issues without Alcohol

I am not about to provide specific ideas on how this perspective can be addressed—it can be *very* complex and is an area for specialized expertise. The Women for Sobriety (*www.womenforsobriety.org*) support group addresses this as a major trigger and ways of dealing with it both pre and post-sobriety.

As seen below in the Related Trigger list, there are also *many* other triggers that can come along for the ride. Getting to the bottom of these issues may take quite some time. That said, according to many sources difficulties in this area are rooted in sexual fears and insecurities, as well as childhood sexual abuse (discussed in the Victim trigger section). Thus,

I would encourage you to fully read the sources referenced here and those listed elsewhere in this book. The bottom line (to me) is that this is one more (and extremely important) example of how critical it is to get to the *root* of your drinking triggers, otherwise sobriety may be very fleeting.

Lemons into Lemonade Tip: Sex can generate so many types of issues it is hard to know where to start. The best I can come up with is that if you had sexual hang-ups in the past, use your new sobriety as a kind of a brand new life, including a brand new *sex* life. Try things you never did before, put away past guilt/issues, etc., and enjoy sex with your partner to the fullest extent possible. It may even become a new, improved hobby again!

Overall Tip: Seek professional help if you believe sexual issues are a major cause of your alcoholism, particularly if they are bound up with other major triggers such as Depression, Relationships, and Victim history.

Related Triggers: Sex as a trigger (as defined in this section) can be caused or influenced by Anger (resentment), Anxiety, Depression, a general desire for Fun, Guilt, Health, Mid-Life Crisis, Powerlessness, Reminders, Relationships, Social Situations, being Tired, and past Victim issues. It can activate or influence Anxiety, Depression, a desire for Escape, Guilt, a sense of Powerlessness, and Victim issues.

Key Defense Levels: Listen to Your Body!, Therapy, Join a Community

SMELL

It's probably obvious that most of our five senses can turn against us in the form of triggers. Taste is particularly apparent, while Touch probably the least so. Sight is also obvious, which I've categorized separately under "Media" and "Proximity." Sound is covered under Music and Noise. Taste is covered in its own section (and as we will see is closely related to Smell). That leaves Smell.

Smell seemed to be a large, frequently cited trigger. For me personally, Smell is an excellent example of turning what was a negative into a positive. I taught myself to make my body get grossed out by the smell of wine, for example, which was no mean trick as I drank wine exclusively for several years. It was my first indication that I could teach my mind and body to get be repulsed by the smell (and even thought) of alcohol. Unfortunately, it didn't cover ALL kinds of alcohol—just those that smelled strong. I turned to Vodka specifically because it didn't, and was many more years figuring out how to deal with it (e.g., this program).

> *My relapse triggers can be anything. They can be music on the radio or billboards on the highway with alcohol on them. Another is people drinking in restaurants around me, especially wine. The smell of wine is very strong. I never drank wine but it still sets me off.*
>
> Guest Kimberly, alcoholism.about.com

To make it worse, Smell as a trigger does not even have to be the smell of alcohol. It can be *anything:*

> *After 8 months of sobriety, I went up north to go snowmobiling w some friends (Who are non-drinkers). When I used to drink I always was snow-mobiling. So low and behold the smell of the exhaust from a snowmobile (the 2 cycle oil burning smell) triggered me to tell the guys while we were all around the bonfire and cooking burgers, that I had to gas up my sled cause it was almost empty. I went to the liquor store and bought a fifth and pounded it down and washed it back with a soda. Now to this day I am aware that that smell will trigger a craving in me and I am ready for it.[144]*
>
> Guest Terry, alcoholism.about.com

The best way to deal with Smell as a trigger is to turn it against itself. Meaning instead of it making you to want to drink, you "retrain" your nose and mind for it to make you sick, hopefully in turn dragging other triggers into the nausea equation such Holidays and in particular Taste. More on this in the Taste section. Both smell and taste are the main emphasis behind a whole separate (and optional) Level in this program, Level 11—Make Yourself Sick of Alcohol.

Tips for Dealing with Smell without Alcohol

The intensity of Smell as a trigger greatly varies by individual of course, and their preferred type of alcohol. Ways to deal with it include:

• Try to train yourself to make the particular smells that directly and indirectly cause a desire to drink as unpleasant as possible. See Level 11—Make Yourself Sick of Alcohol for ideas.

- To state the obvious, try to avoid the Smell that is "bothering" you. Some tricks that are not so obvious depend on the situation. If you can, get outside where the air/wind will "dilute" the smell. Move to a different room, or change the people you are talking with. Try to "distract" the Smell with others Smells and Taste, by eating whatever is available in the circumstance (the more powerful smell, the better).[145]

- There are numerous oils and other substances that can effectively mask all sorts of smells, including alcohol. Take some time to research these, including *Aromatherapy*, which looks to induce positive feelings and even pleasure by various smells.

Lemons into Lemonade Tip: As with the Proximity trigger, use the presence of alcohol as a way of reinforcing your aversion to it. This is discussed in great detail in Level 11—Make Yourself Sick of Alcohol. I do this every so often; when I am with a good friend who has ordered a drink, I will deliberately pick it up and smell it (almost sticking my nose in it). It will immediately activate a sense of nausea that I developed thought the techniques described in Level 11.

Overall Tip: Since Smell and Taste are so closely intertwined, see the Taste section for additional ideas, and their combination along with Proximity as "the axis of evil" in Level 11—Make Yourself Sick of Alcohol. That Level provides a more radical approach for dealing with the Proximity, Smell, and Taste triggers.

Related Triggers: The Smell of alcohol is most likely to occur in Proximity to alcohol, including Holidays, Peer Pressure situations, Relationships (if they are drinking), Social Situations, and Taste. It can activate Reminders and even Taste.

Key Defense Levels: Detox (try to associate the Smell of Alcohol with Detox unpleasantness), Make Yourself Sick of Alcohol, The LAST Detox

SOCIAL SITUATIONS

Many people feel uncomfortable or even anxious in social situations, such as talking with strangers (or even friends) or speaking in front of a group of people. Many alcoholics use alcohol as a way of "dealing with" this discomfort, anxiety, or even outright fear—to make themselves looser, more relaxed, or more talkative.

I tend to drink very little mid-week coz of me job. But at weekends and holidays I totally over-do it. I use it as a crutch to get me through social situations and lessen the SA (social anxiety).

Dub16, socialanxietysupport.com

I had this problem at various parts of my life, even before I became an alcoholic. I had a pretty severe stutter and difficulty in pronouncing the letter "r" in my youth. My sisters would delight in having me say, "dirty purple bird," which came out "durrrty poopple buurd." Even to this day I have to be very careful in enunciating that letter. Even though I eventually got over this, I believe it was a significant factor later in my adult life—causing nervousness in meeting new people, particularly first dates. In retrospect, I drank a lot in those situations.

In the general population, this kind of "social anxiety" exists on a continuum from mild to severe, even getting to the point of being clinically defined as "social anxiety disorder."

What Is Social Anxiety Disorder?

A clinical diagnosis of social anxiety disorder, also referred to as social phobia, is assigned only when the social anxiety results in significant fear when faced with the situation, impairment of performance, or avoidance of anxiety–provoking situations. Eating or speaking in public are common examples of this problem.

This condition affects many more people than you might think; estimates range from 2 to 13 percent of the U.S. population. Many sufferers self-medicate, with about one–fifth of patients with social anxiety disorder also suffering from alcohol abuse or dependence.

One theory to explain the comorbidity between social anxiety disorder and AUDs is the tension reduction theory, which posits that people with social anxiety use alcohol to alleviate their fears[146]. This expectation that alcohol reduces anxiety may motivate alcohol consumption even if pharmacological studies do not support that assumption. Social anxiety disorder is treatable with both pharmacotherapy and psychotherapy.[147]

Tips for Dealing with Social Situations without Alcohol

Parties are generally the worst Social Situations. But instead of dreading them like the plague, try to use them as a learning opportunity, from new ideas to gossip to stock tips. You might "use" drunk people at the party to remind you how stupid you must have seemed, using them to reinforce your defenses (e.g. making sure you never do those kinds of things again). Other tips include:

• If people don't know you have an alcohol problem (very likely), and you don't want to be questioned about what you are drinking, get a beverage that looks like an alcoholic drink, e.g., club soda with lime (a gin and tonic), a soft drink with ice in it (looks like any sort of mixer). Do *not* get a "non"-alcoholic beer—most have some alcohol. Besides anyone who knows beer can tell!

• If you don't want to bother with the pretense, and want say a bottled water—do it! If someone is so rude as to ask you why you are not drinking (alcohol), just say it doesn't agree with your medicine, you have a headache and don't want to make it worse, etc. If they continue to pry, then mentally tell them to fuck off and go talk to someone else . . .

• Smaller social situations can be easier, or harder, depending on the circumstances. For people who have this as a significant trigger, smaller situations where you do not know or know well the people you are interacting with can be very difficult. I've recently started dating again after a long hiatus, and have found that having a beverage in hand to be very helpful in pauses between gaps in conversation. So far none of the dates have commented on my ordering tea as my conversation drink, even meeting at wine bars!

• For both large and small settings, one "trick" for dealing with them comes courtesy of mobile technology. Amazingly, looking at your phone, texting, surfing the Internet, or even placing/taking a call in a social gathering is not only considered *not* rude, it is not even commented on. It can even be seen by some (particularly people under 25) as a perverse status symbol (See? I'm so cool I have to interact with my fans even during this not-quite-so-cool function). [148]

There are a significant number of online support groups and information forums focused on social anxiety. A few of these include:

• Social Anxiety Disorder and Social Phobia Support (*www.socialanxiety support.com*)

• Shyness & Social Anxiety Meetup Groups (*www.shyness.meetup.com*)

- Social Phobics Anonymous, Social Anxiety, Support Groups for Help ... (*www.healsocialanxiety.com*)

- List of Social Anxiety Support Groups—*Social Anxiety Disorder* (http://socialanxietydisorder.about.com/od/supportgroups/tp/supportgroups.htm)

Lemons into Lemonade Tip: An aversion to social situations can be turned on its head, making what had been a weakness into a strength. I was so determined to break my panic about public speaking that I sought out every class and opportunity to try and improve. Eventually (or suddenly) you will see a dramatic improvement, and may even begin to actively seek speaking opportunities, believe it or not. But it takes effort; few people are born public speakers, the rest of us have to put a lot of work into it.

Overall Tip: You may have been drinking so long that you haven't had a social situation experience without alcohol in years, if not decades. Give your new sober self an opportunity to experience these situations; with a bit of practice, you will likely be very surprised at how well you do.

Related Triggers: Social Situations as a trigger can be caused by or influenced by broader Anxiety issues, the desire for Fun (including parties), Holidays, a Job (social events), the Proximity to Alcohol, Relationships and Relatives outings, the Smell at outings, and feeling Unfun/Uninteresting. It can activate broader Anxiety and a desire to Escape.

Key Level Defenses: Engage Friends and Family (go to an event with someone you know), Join a Community (practice public speaking), Develop New Hobbies (e.g., take public speaking courses, other activities that require social interaction in relatively safe settings)

STRESS (PHYSICAL STRESS)

As noted many times before, it is essential that you break down drinking triggers into as much detail as possible for this (or any) program to be successful. That is especially important here, as Stress at a high level is probably the largest single trigger in the entire list in this Level.

> *Some people eat, others smoke when they get stressed. When I get stressed alcohol is all I can think about. We sold our business, made some money but had HUGE debts to begin with (stress), my husband is semi-retired at 64 and is discouraged he can't find even a part time job (stress) I had a*

three year contract and lost it, I was also relapsing with the stress (I didn't really understand the job with technology) so I lost the job after my 3 month review (stress). Stopped eating, ended up in detox, good care nice people, but who really wants to be there than your own bed.

Guest itsgottatakesoon!, alcoholism.about.com

But just saying you are "Stressed" and leaving it there is probably not going to do a lot of good. Is it primarily caused by professional life, e.g., your Job or Money? Or is it in your personal life; your Kids, your Relatives, your Relationships, or something else? Just lumping all together in one big pile and calling it "Stress" is not going to do you much good.

All of these are primarily mental stress-related triggers; odds are you can pinpoint it (or at least narrow it down) if you focus on the discussions in each one of those related triggers. It may well be more than one, but at least you'll start getting to the roots of your overall stress.

So in this section we focus on the *physical* aspects of Stress, caused by those related triggers and/or other factors that physically are taking a toll on your body.

● ●

What Is Physical Stress?

Stress is a normal physical response to events that make you feel threatened or upset your balance in some way. When you sense danger—whether it's real or imagined—the body's defenses kick into high gear in a rapid, automatic process known as the "fight-or-flight" reaction or the stress response.

The stress response is the body's way of protecting you. When working properly, it helps you stay focused, energetic, and alert. In emergency situations, stress can save your life—giving you extra strength to defend yourself, for example, or spurring you to slam on the brakes to avoid an accident.

The stress response also helps you rise to meet challenges. Stress is what keeps you on your toes during a presentation at work, sharpens your concentration when you're attempting the game-winning free throw, or drives you to study for an exam when you'd rather be watching TV.[149]

● ●

It is important to distinguish physical Stress discussed here versus physical pain discussed earlier in the Health trigger section. The primary distinction between the two is that physical pain/Health issues discussed earlier mostly revolve around the need for some sort of active pain relief due to some underlying physical medical condition (typically under the care of a physician). In contrast, physical Stress discussed in this section is primarily caused by various forms of *mental* issues and typically does not require attention of a medical doctor except in extreme cases.

That said, beyond a certain point physical Stress stops being helpful and starts causing major damage to your health, your mood, your productivity, your relationships, and your quality of life.

At a detailed physical level, the body responds to stress by secreting hormones into the bloodstream that spur accelerated heart rate and breathing and tensing of muscles. People who experience Stress as a positive often have increased blood flow to the brain, muscles and limbs, similar to the effects of aerobic exercise.[150] Those who feel frightened or threatened, however, often have an erratic heart rate and constricting blood vessels. Their blood pressure rises and hands and feet may grow cold. They may become agitated, speak more loudly or experience lapses in judgment.[151]

• •

Effects of Chronic Stress

The body doesn't distinguish between physical and psychological threats. When you're stressed over a busy schedule, an argument with a friend, a traffic jam, or a mountain of bills, your body reacts just as strongly as if you were facing a life-or-death situation. If you have a lot of responsibilities and worries, your emergency stress response may be "on" most of the time. The more your body's stress system is activated, the harder it is to shut off.

Long-term exposure to stress can lead to serious health problems. Chronic stress disrupts nearly every system in your body. It can raise blood pressure, suppress the immune system, increase the risk of heart attack and stroke, contribute to infertility, cause digestive and sleep problems, and speed up the aging process. Long-term stress can even rewire the brain, leaving you more vulnerable to anxiety and depression.[152]

• •

It's important to learn how to recognize when your stress levels are out of control. The most dangerous thing about stress is how easily it can creep up on you. You get used to it. It starts to feels familiar even normal. You don't notice how much it's affecting you, even as it takes a heavy toll.

The signs and symptoms of stress overload can be almost anything. Stress affects the mind, body, and behavior in many ways, and everyone experiences stress differently.

Physical symptoms of Stress include:

- Aches and pains
- Diarrhea or constipation
- Nausea, dizziness
- Chest pain, rapid heartbeat
- Loss of sex drive
- Frequent colds
- Eating more or less
- Sleeping too much or too little
- Isolating yourself from others
- Procrastinating or neglecting responsibilities
- Nervous habits (e.g., nail biting, pacing).[153]

Physical Stress, even in positive situations, can cause many people (not just alcoholics) to want to reach for a drink; to "chill out," "take a load off," or in general relax. The challenge for us, of course, is how to do it without alcohol.

Tips for Dealing with Stress without Alcohol

Most physical Stress—at least for alcoholics—will come from the mental stress from other related triggers, many of which were mentioned above. The first and absolutely most important thing to do is get to the root(s) of that stress, be it your Job, Money, Relationships, etc. See those related triggers discussion for ways to identify those detailed triggers and tips for dealing with them without alcohol.

More generally, try to learn *and incorporate into your everyday life* the following:

- **Learn how to manage stress.** You may feel like the stress in your life is out of your control, but you can always control the way you respond. Managing stress is all about taking charge: taking charge of your thoughts, your emotions, your schedule, your environment, and the way you deal with problems. *Stress management*[154] involves changing the stressful situation when you can, changing your reaction when you can't, taking care of yourself, and making time for rest and relaxation.

• **Learn how to relax.** You can't completely eliminate stress from your life, but you can control how much it affects you. *Relaxation techniques*[155] such as yoga, meditation, and deep breathing activate the body's relaxation response, the state of restfulness that is the opposite of the stress response. When regularly practiced, these activities lead to a reduction in your everyday stress levels and a boost in your feelings of joy and serenity. They also increase your ability to stay calm and collected under pressure.

• **Learn quick stress relief.** Everybody has the power to reduce the impact of stress as it's happening in that moment. With practice, you can learn to spot stressors and stay in control when the pressure builds. *Sensory stress-busting techniques*[156] give you a powerful tool for staying clear-headed and in control in the middle of stressful situations. They give you the confidence to face challenges, knowing that you can rapidly bring yourself back into balance.[157]

• **Consider alternative medicine.** Despite many attempts to dismiss them as nonscientific, Acupuncture and *Chiropractic* are considered by many to be very effective, so you may want to give them a try—unless your doctor expressly forbids it. I have tried Chiropractic and found it to be very effective in helping with some lower back and hip pain. It even fixed my tennis elbow![158] Acupuncture is covered more in Level 6, under Alternative/ Unconventional Treatment Approaches.

Chinese medicine has made some huge strides into the mainstream in recent years as evidenced by this article in the *Wall Street Journal:* "A Top Hospital Opens Up To Chinese Herbs As Medicines."[159]

Lemons into Lemonade Tip: As with Health (Pain), use physical Stress as a motivator, particularly when it comes to exercise. *Nothing* will relieve physical stress on your body like exercise, and improve many other physical and mental strains as well. Note however not all exercise is the same; consult your doctor before beginning any exercise program.

Overall Tip: Again, seek out the underlying mental triggers for your physical stress. In addition, particularly for older alcoholics who have been drinking for many years, pay attention to any and all signs of physical stress and quickly seek out medical attention if you experience any kind of physical pain or unusual functions.

Related Triggers: Some of the more common causes of physical Stress can be caused by Anger, Anxiety, Health, Insomnia, Job, Kids, Money, Noise, and Relationships. It can cause a desire to Escape, aggravate Health problems and Insomnia, and to be Tired.

Key Defense Levels: Listen to Your Body!, Break Bad Habits, Develop New Hobbies

TASTE

I miss the taste of drinking some good ol' wine.

Marielabete, socialanxietysupport.com

No question, many of us love the taste of our favorite alcoholic beverage. For some of us it was an acquired taste, for others it seems like we were born for the beverage. Or we migrated from one type of drink to another after our taste buds for one got a bit fried from overuse.

Dealing with this trigger is challenging for at least two reasons. First, there are beverages out there that are a close facsimile to the "real thing." Nonalcoholic beers (most of which have a trace of alcohol by the way) and wines are the most obvious examples. "Virgin" cocktails such as piña coladas and margaritas are other examples. Some may view these "substitutes" as a great thing (assuming the taste is not that different). It may well be. But for others it may be too much of a reminder of what they are missing versus the "real thing," and be driven even more so to want to drink because of it.

The second is that even if we refrain from tasting anything that resembles our former favorite beverage, the Smell is always there to jump on us as a trigger. It is very difficult to disassociate the Smell and Taste of alcohol from each other.

The Relationship Between Taste and Smell

Taste and smell are separate senses with their own receptor organs, yet they are intimately entwined. Tastants, chemicals in foods, are detected by taste buds, which consist of special sensory cells. When stimulated, these cells send signals to specific areas of the brain, which make us conscious of the perception of taste. Similarly, specialized cells in the nose pick up odorants, airborne odor molecules. Odorants stimulate receptor proteins found on hair-like cilia at the tips of the sensory cells, a process that initiates a neural response. Ultimately, messages about taste and smell converge, allowing us to detect the flavors of food.[160]

• •

Tips for Dealing with the Taste Trigger without Alcohol

As with Smell, the severity of Taste as a trigger will vary hugely by individual and their beverage of choice. Ways to deal include:

• Do not drink nonalcoholic wine or beer, or "virgin" drinks, if you *at all* think this might make you want the "real thing," as opposed to somehow "disarming" that trigger and your desire for the real McCoy.

• Avoid (if possible) situations where the Smell of your favorite beverage will be there in abundance. An unfortunate but perfect example is pro baseball games, where the seats, floors, and even bathrooms smell like beer (and you *know* why).

• Try different ideas for making yourself dislike the Taste and Smell of your most vulnerable alcoholic beverages (See Level 11—Make Yourself Sick of Alcohol).

• In extreme circumstances, you can deliberately try to screw up your smelling system by putting other substance under your nostrils, like Vicks Vapor Rub. Medical examiners and law enforcement do something similar in the presence of a rotting corpse. (And if that comparison seems weirdly symbolic to our situation then so be it.)

Lemons into Lemonade Tip: You will be surprised as to how much you begin to taste other foods and beverages after you have been sober for a while—it is actually quite an experience. So use that as one more motivator (particularly when dining out, surrounded by people with alcoholic beverages) to be glad you are no longer drinking.

Overall Tip: If Taste is a major trigger for you, make sure you read in detail all aspects of the Smell trigger, as they are so intertwined. These triggers, plus Proximity, have their own special section in Level 11—Make Yourself Sick of Alcohol.

Related Triggers: The Taste trigger can be caused by the Proximity and Smell of alcohol, as well as Taste-related Reminders (like past pairings of food and wine). It can activate the desire for Escape or to have drinking Fun.

Key Defense Levels: Detox (try to associate the Taste of Alcohol with Detox unpleasantness), Make Yourself Sick of Alcohol, The LAST Detox

TIMES OF DAY

Time of Day (TOD) is an interesting trigger in many respects, most notably that it does not have any obvious negative aspect to it like many other triggers do. Perhaps it is rooted in the role that "The Cocktail Hour" (the generic term) or "Happy Hour" (the marketing term) plays in our society. I'm obviously guessing here, but I thought it deserved some research, and found the following (source: *Wikipedia.org*):

> One possible origin of the term is from the United States Navy. In the 1920s, "Happy Hour" was slang for a scheduled entertainment period on board a ship during which boxing and wrestling bouts took place; this was a valuable opportunity for sailors to relieve the stress accumulated during the long periods at sea.
>
> The idea of drinking before dinner has its roots in the Prohibition era. When the 18th Amendment and the Volstead Act were passed banning alcohol consumption, citizens would host "cocktail hours," also known as "happy hours," at a speakeasy (an illegal drinking establishment) before eating at restaurants where alcohol could not be served. Cocktail lounges continued the trend of drinking before dinner.
>
> "Happy hour" entered civilian use around 1960, especially after a *Saturday Evening Post* article on military life in 1959.

Most references to it agree it generally refers to the time between 4 pm and 8 pm. So there you go: you can blame the military, Prohibition, or the Saturday Evening Post. Since this was one of my major triggers (generally between 5:30 pm and 8 pm) and I had no idea of this history, I guess I have to pin it on some other unknown source. Even when I didn't have a watch or clock, my body (or mind) seemed to know when that Time of Day had arrived.

I looked at my triggers and could see there were times of day, situations and feelings that always made me want to drink . . . The toughest time of day was late afternoon and early evening, and I spent the first couple of months white-knuckling it, muddling through, until I followed the advice to change my patterns. During the tough hours I would talk to another recovering alcoholic on the phone, go for a walk or lose myself in video games or mindless movies.

I had two small kids at home, so I couldn't just escape any time I wanted to, but I would pile them into the car and head to the playground at 5:30pm if I had to. I walked in a different door of my house for a while. I rearranged furniture and I cleaned like a maniac. It didn't matter what I did, really, as long as it helped me get out of my head for a little while . . . [This was an] important part of my early recovery—breaking patterns.[161]

I found this testimonial to be particularly insightful, particularly about the need to change up your daily activities. It seems to go hand-in-glove with breaking/changing your overall daily patterns (see Break Bad Habits and Develop New Hobbies Levels). A pattern, such as simply walking in the same door every day, is, of course, by no means a bad habit. But if it can in any way help break a bad habit, like heading for the bar at 5:30, then changing that pattern may well do a lot of good.

A nonalcoholic friend of mine has the view that Times of Day, at least for her, is about shifting gears from one phase of the day to another, such as from work to after-work relaxation. I believe this has much merit, particularly if one's routine is very predictable with respect to days of the week and the time of day when this gear shifting occurs.

As a side note, I found myself getting irritable during my vulnerable times of day long after I got sober. It gradually went away particularly after I became aware of it. BUT it was replaced by a desire to eat food or candy during that time—all the time—which was strange. Once I became aware of *that*, I was able to cut back, but it remains a mild craving.

Tips for Dealing with Times of Day Issues without Alcohol

This is one of the toughest remaining triggers for me, and I continue to experiment with new ways of coping with it. Successful methods so far include:

• **Identify your most vulnerable periods.** First and foremost, try to specifically identify those times or time ranges where you find yourself thinking about alcohol. Perhaps it is a big range, say 5pm to 9pm. Perhaps it is lunch or dinnertime.

If it is a specific range of time, try to reduce/narrow down the range at the outer ends, such as pushing it to 5:30 to 8:30—a kind of whittling down process. You can do this by planning each day with very specific mind and/or body-intensive things for that 30 to 60 minutes on each end, such as regular exercise classes or watching the History channel—anything that makes you forget what time it is. As you see the vulnerable time range start to narrow, then add other activities to take the next 30–60 minute chunk out of your vulnerable period.

If it is a *specific* time, such as 5:30pm ("happy" hour), or dinnertime, then you have a *very specific* association that you need to break. For something like a happy hour vulnerability, make sure you *always* have something planned for 30 minutes on either side, such as the exercise class or TV show just discussed. If it is an unavoidable time period, like dinnertime, then that will be trickier. You might substitute something like tea as a dinnertime beverage, or even nonalcoholic wine. If your dinnertime has always been at a set time, such as 6pm, then shift it an hour earlier or later and see what impact that has on your desire. It may require some experimentation, but the key is somehow to break the association of that specific time with the consumption (including the Smell and Proximity) of alcohol.

• **Modify your ritual.** This is particularly important if you believe the shifting gears mindset is applicable to your lifestyle. If sitting down with a glass of wine (the first of many) is a key element of your gear shifting routine, seek an alternative. Replace the wine with a cup of hot tea for instance; that way you are not disrupting an otherwise healthy and enjoyable ritual.

• **Talk. Talk some more.** Be around and/or talk with other people during particularly vulnerable times, particularly those that can relate to your situation. Select people who are not likely to activate another trigger and who won't suggest you meet up for a drink.

• **Break your patterns.** As noted in the earlier testimonial—*break your patterns.* A huge part of Times of Day being a trigger is its very close association with alcohol, e.g., happy hour. Get in a new habit of doing something else during specific times, such as playing with your children before dinner, walking immediately after dinner, and so forth. Do little things differently too during those time periods—where you walk in the door, how you park the car, clean—just as long you didn't do these things before while you were drinking.

• **Exercise.** This has a number of benefits, most notably 1) it is an environment almost guaranteed not to have alcohol (e.g., a gym, walking in a park); and 2) it takes the edge of possible related triggers, particularly Stress in various forms (e.g., Job, Kids, Noise).

• **Calibrate new activities.** Do new activities, paying particular attention to days and times. This includes new hobbies that are better done in certain periods of time than others, such as outdoor sports (e.g., requiring daylight) or league types of activities that require you to be a certain place at a certain day and time, such as bowling leagues.

• **Do "old" activities at new times—particularly errands.** Change how, where, and particularly *when* you do your errands, "repositioning" them to your vulnerable Times of Day. You may wind up bunching several of them together to fill up a great deal of time on one day, or spreading them out to fill "holes" in your "schedule" on other days.

• **Use an "anchor time."** You might consider doing some of the above in combination with one "anchor time," which is one time of the day, every day, when you know *exactly* what you will be doing. That does not mean doing the *same* thing every day; instead, you are making a point of setting up and knowing what you will be doing at a specific time on any given day. Maybe it is a regular status meeting at work; a once a week massage; your bowling night, etc. It also doesn't mean you can't try different things *during* the activity—you are just anchoring the overall timeframe for the activity. Doing so can be calming, particularly when the rest of your day or night is unpredictable.

• **Meditate.** Level 6 (Alternative/Unconventional Treatment Approaches) and Appendix A—Learning To Sleep In Early Sobriety, describe various forms of meditation that might be particularly helpful for certain Times of Day. If your Time of Day is just before sleeping, the "Sleep Meditation" technique described in Appendix A may greatly help. If time of day is early evening (or anytime you can carve out time), try to do 15–30 minutes of one of the meditations described in Level 6 to both fill out that specific time period and also possibly have a positive carryover effect into the time afterwards.

Lemons into Lemonade Tip: There may be other bad habits (not the drinking kind) that you have that have some time of day element to them. For me it was eating late night snacks, which is not a good idea in general and particularly if you have intestinal issues like I have. I use some of the tips above (and the overall tip below) to deter myself when I crave a late snack, and have, in fact, (mostly) succeeded in stopping any form of eating after 7 pm.[162]

Overall Tip: Try to make your vulnerable Times of Day a time where you get a lot of things done—cleaning, exercising, playing with your kids, catching up on past chores, etc. You will get a sense of satisfaction from doing productive things (versus a sense of Guilt or other sensations), while distracting you from that time period. Eventually, Times of Day will diminish and even disappear with enough practice and "time."

Related Triggers: Times of Day as a trigger can be influenced by Boredom, Change (of time zones), Insomnia, physical Stress, and being Tired. It can activate the desire for Escape or drinking Fun, and influence Insomnia.

Key Defense Levels: Join a Community, Break Bad Habits, Develop New Hobbies

TIRED

Another part of HALT (Hungry, Angry, Lonely, Tired), the Tired part, is one that may mystify some people on the surface. Won't drinking when Tired just make me want to pass out? For some people that is exactly the point. If you are Tired, it will make it that much easier to get to the numb/checkout part of the rush/buzz/numb/checkout continuum.

However, for others alcohol can act as a stimulant, providing extra energy:

> *I was just wondering . . . . . I quit drinking 3 months ago . . . . . I used to drink daily, then I cut down to just the weekends. I never woke up and started drinking, but I would drink heavily most of the time when I did drink. Back then, when I was not drinking, I was tired, and then I would drink and wake up.*
>
> PennyLane, medhelp.org

Both the stimulus and depressant effects, while seemingly opposite, have a scientific basis. At lower Blood Alcohol Content Levels (a few drinks) alcohol can instill a sense of Euphoria, which also can serve as a form of stimulant, but at higher BAC levels its true chemical effect of being a depressant kicks in. Thus, it will give you an initial burst of stimulated energy, and then wipe you out!

Alcohol also has a lot of refined white sugar in it. Even long after stopping your drinking for the evening, these residues of sugar remain until flushed out of your body completely. This is why many people make it a point (even if they don't realize why) of drinking a lot of water before they go to bed after a long night of drinking—besides diluting the alcohol and increasing the need to pass urine, it is also flushing out the refined sugar.

In general my opinion of the Tired trigger is mainly one of it being a Bad Habit. You've got into the habit of a drink (turning into many drinks) during or after dinner, or a supposed nightcap that goes on for hours, or something similar. If you are truly tired and need energy, then something with caffeine will work much more effectively. If you are Tired and want to "numb" yourself, well—you are already halfway there!

Tips for Dealing with Being Tired without Alcohol

Ways of dealing with this situation include:

• **Swap out your stimulating (or relaxing) beverage.** If you're tired, drink a caffeinated drink—with sugar if you can. If you are looking for a faster "numbing" effect, drink a relaxing *hot* (non-caffeinated) beverage. There is a variety of teas that include herbs that have relaxation properties,[163] but any warm beverage may work just as well. Get in the new habit of doing this at the time and circumstances that you formerly drank while you were Tired.

• **Take a shower or bath.** Depending on your goal—to wake up (cold shower), or relax (warm or hot), this works on the same principle—either stimulating your brain and muscles or relaxing them.

• **Get your diet in order. Exercise.** Your energy levels are most impacted by diet and exercise. While this is unlikely to be a shock to anyone, it becomes a bit more complicated when being Tired is a drinking trigger. You may have to do some experimentation to figure out what diet has the best impact on your energy levels—when you want to be energetic, and when you do not. Similarly, exercise can be both a stimulant (getting your metabolism up) and a relaxation mechanism (draining excess energy). You may have to try different combinations of exercise types (e.g., walking vs. going to the gym) and times (doing it in the morning vs. the evening) to get it right.

Lemons into Lemonade Tip: If you are Tired, try and use it to your advantage. Go to sleep (obviously) if you can, but if not use it to do some other mental relaxation techniques such as meditation, or just plain zone-out for a little while. You may be surprised at how doing either can give you a substance-free pick-me-up, at least for a little while.

Overall Tip: If it is a stimulating effect you want, you are far better off with caffeinated beverages. But be careful not to have them too close to bedtime, as it will make it that much harder to sleep (see Appendix A— Learning to Sleep in Early Sobriety).

Related Triggers: Being Tired, of course, can be caused by numerous things, notably Insomnia, your Job, Kids, Stress, and Times of Day. It can activate the desire to Escape, Insomnia (being overly Tired), and physical Stress.

Key Defense Levels: Listen to Your Body!, Break Bad Habits, Develop New Hobbies, Appendix A (ways to improve your sleep habits)

UNFUN/UNINTERESTING

This is one of the more interesting triggers given it is completely and totally a matter of perception—some by others, but mostly by you the alcoholic. It was also one of the most cited when I was researching trigger testimonials.

> *I believe that I drink a lot when I'm out with friends, or when my husband and I go out on a super rare occasion, because being drunk feels good and makes me feel like a more interesting, outgoing person to be around. That is, except when the night devolves in to me being in a drunken stupor, falling off my chair, having someone pour me back into my house later that night. Me, not remembering the second half of so many nights.*
>
> Ariel, cryingoutloud.com

Social Situations is probably the most impactful related trigger. Why is it discussed separately from Unfun/Uninteresting (the "Un's")? Primarily because feelings of being the "Un's" can be totally distinct and unrelated from fear of being in public, social settings. Indeed they can show up in situations far from those situations, such as in the privacy of the bedroom:

> *I asked my husband what makes him want to drink. He agrees with Unfun—that he is not interesting and doesn't have fun unless he is drinking or drunk. I gave him examples of when I thought we had fun when he was sober. His answer surprised me. He said he only agreed to do the "sober" things because he thought there would be sex at the end. To him that's having fun—he equates sex as the only fun worth having and drinking as the way to getting it. I believe that brain of his is definitely having some problems even without the alcohol.*
>
> ImmortalAlkysWife, alcoholism.about.com

In early sobriety these "Un" feelings can be particularly pronounced:

> *I am 213 days sober. I just feel uninteresting, Unfun and boring without drinking. Not sure why I am all of a sudden worrying about relapsing. First summer sober and trying to learn how to feel comfortable with myself sober and have fun at the same time. Thinking about going to AA meetings. Never attended and been doing this with help of friends and exercise. Thinking I might need that extra help of support of others that have experienced the same feelings. Guess it couldn't hurt?*
>
> soberdutchess1, alcoholism.about.com

Besides highlighting three kinds of defenses Levels[164], the above testimonial illustrates how feeling the Un's by themselves can be a relapse trigger. Unfun can be a generalized feeling like the above, or brought on by specific events:

> *I am on the tail of a three day trip to hell. I am dealing with the withdrawals, guilt, remorse, and the absolute terror of having a relapse after months of alcohol free bliss. My trigger was going out on a first date, and the thought entered my mind to become this relaxed, fun and charming date. Well I got lost, never got to my date's home, was abused with a nasty text. I just felt it would [be] more fun with a few drinks along the way.*
>
> Hopeful member, alcoholism.about.com

I attribute these kinds of feelings to two factors. First, you may well *be* Uninteresting and/or Unfun in early sobriety. The first several months are notable in that it is a rebuilding period for your brain. It is still healing from your alcohol over-use, and this makes it harder for you to experience strong positive emotions. For the first several months of sobriety,

I felt like my head was stuffed with cotton, making it very hard to engage in general polite conversation. I just preferred to listen and try to process what I was hearing.

Second and most importantly, what you perceived as being "Fun" and "Interesting" while you were drinking was very noticeably *not* that to everyone around you (at least the ones that were sober[165]). As you will experience once you are comfortable enough in your defenses to be in situations where others are drinking heavily, these people are NOT funny, nor interesting for the most part. At best some are mildly amusing, but most others will run the gamut from boorish to downright pathetic.

> *My cousin binge drinks once a week. She has diabetes 2. Not surprised. That aside, I don't drink and God help me if I happen to be with her when she drinks. She becomes grandiose, ever so intelligent, theatrical, insightful, deep thinking, and desperately laments losing her perceived beauty. Sad and pathetic. The alcohol will make you feel good for an evening but the lasting effects will make you sick and you'll look end up looking like an old booze hag . . . with missing limbs. Is it worth it?*
>
> Evin4, alcoholism.about.com

The actress Helen Mirren, during the remake of *Arthur* in 2010, commented on her experience with alcoholics: "I just didn't think a film about a drunken small guy was remotely funny. The reality about alcoholics is that they're boring and tedious, and I'd spent enough nights in pubs with drunken boys to know it was not something I'd ever want to be caught up in. And I particularly objected to the way women were depicted—which was something I felt about most movies I saw back then—as kind of slave-enablers."[166]

● ●
Why Isn't Unhappiness a Trigger?

I thought about this a great deal. Arguably it is one of the biggest "things" that make us drink. But it has two issues: 1) It is so general, so commonplace, that it literally begs to be broken down into more detail; and 2) Almost all examples I could think of and research could be very directly and easily broken down into other triggers. Unhappy at work? See the Job discussion. Relationship going sour? See Relationships. Car problems getting you down? Probably Money, or maybe Frustration. And so on. Even "general" unhappiness could be addressed by Anxiety and/or Depression. So if you got to "U" hoping to find a trigger discussion, I strongly encourage you to go back through the A-T triggers (and of course the V-Z ones). Odds are very strong what ails you is in there somewhere.

● ●

Tips for Feeling Unfun/Uninteresting without Alcohol

Key things to consider about this trigger include:

• **You ARE Unfun when you are drinking.** The first and best overall tip is to recognize that for the vast majority of you, the vast majority of the time, you are *NOT* Fun and Interesting when you are drinking. You just aren't. Period. I suspect nearly all of you will, after a few months of non-drinking, start to get comments (particularly from those who know you are an alcoholic) like "Gee Jack/Jill, you seem much more pleasant to be around," or, "You are much nicer now," or "Boy, you were an unpleasant son-of-a-bitch to be around before, but you are great now!"

• **Be patient. Your best qualities will shine when sober.** In my opinion and experience, introverted alcoholics are particularly likely to feel that they are more "interesting" and "fun" when they've had a few. To address this in sobriety, the best advice I can give is to recognize that the "pleasant" personality characteristics that you thought you saw while you were drinking are indeed there within you while sober, and will come out once you stop drinking, with the added benefit that they are not distorted or obscured by the other unpleasant personality changes that come to all of us while drinking.

• **Get out of your shell.** To fully make these come out, you just need to get out of your shell in other ways—new hobbies, more (sober) experience in social settings, and so on. Like so many things in life, it will get better with practice.

Lemons into Lemonade Tip: In experimenting with new hobbies, try to do a very difficult one/one that you've always dreamed about but thought you never had any talent for it, like playing the guitar. Even if it is true you are no good at it, it will give you an appreciation for what is needed to become proficient, as well as "picking up the lingo." Who knows when this might be of value in making you look more "interesting."

Overall Tip: Once you are secure enough in your overall defenses, make a point to go out to situations where people are likely to be drinking heavily: a bar during a big game, parties where you know heavy drinkers will be, etc. You will be shocked at how their behavior—once seemingly cool, funny, etc., is now the opposite.

Related Triggers: Feeling Unfun/Uninteresting can be caused by Boredom, Depression, (seeing other people having) Fun, Holidays, Loneliness, Peer Pressure, and Social Situations. It can activate Boredom, Depression, Escape, (desire for drinking) Fun, and Loneliness.

Key Defense Levels: Engage Friends and Family, Join a Community, Develop New Hobbies

VICTIM-MENTALITY (INCLUDES CHILD AND SEXUAL ABUSE, LOW SELF-ESTEEM)

"When I was five years old I was molested. I remember feeling, literally, right before it happened, I just could not believe that this person was going to do this to me. That thing followed me all my life. The shame of thinking my molestation was my fault. It led me to believe I wasn't worth anything."[167]

Wanting to drink because of feelings and experiences of being victimized is a common trigger for many alcoholics. This Victim-Mentality can come in many forms, and vary by person, environment, and demographics—particularly gender. Some of these forms can come from the feeling that you are racing against the world and time and losing; that nothing you can do will make a difference (very similar to Powerlessness); or that no one appreciates all you have to offer. All of these are a form of self-esteem issues. Others can be blocked for years in the sub-conscious, and/or have a major impact on many dimensions of your life. Very specific instances of trauma in your past—particularly abuse (physical or sexual) as a child or young teenager—is a powerful reason for turning to alcohol.

Child and Sexual Abuse

According to research estimates, each year more than 1 million children in the United States experience some form of abuse or neglect.

The experience of being abused as a child may significantly increase a person's risk for alcohol-related problems as an adult.[168]

● ●

Types of Child Abuse

Child abuse manifests in various forms, including physical abuse, sexual abuse, neglect, and emotional or psychological abuse. *Physical abuse* refers to all types of maltreatment that result in physical injuries, such as bruises, welts, burns, abrasions, lacerations, cuts, or fractures. *Sexual abuse* also can encompass a variety of abusive behaviors, ranging from fondling or touching to sodomy, incest, or rape. *Neglect* is defined as any situation in which a child receives no care by a parent or other primary caregiver or receives care that is below acceptable community or professional standards (e.g., fails to provide adequate food, clothing, shelter, or medical attention). *Emotional and psychological abuse,* which may occur in conjunction with the other types of abuse previously mentioned, also can have profound long-term consequences for the child.

● ●

While some types of abuse (general neglect, emotional and psychological abuse) have indeterminate findings with respect to alcohol use, there *are* conclusive research findings concerning the relationship between childhood victimization—particularly childhood abuse and neglect among women—and subsequent adult alcohol abuse.[169]

Researchers at the National Institute on Drug Abuse conducted a survey on inpatients being treated for alcohol and drug dependence. Almost 25% of men and 33% of women reported a history of childhood physical abuse, while rates of sexual abuse were 12% for men and 49% for women.[170]

Several factors most likely contribute to or influence this relationship, including coping skills; antisocial behavior; and psychological problems, such as post-traumatic stress disorder. But these obvious (to others) behaviors are not "required" to spot such trauma; some people respond by trying to hide behind "very good" behavior:

When I was a young child I was sexually abused. I dealt with it by never telling anyone, and eventually forgetting it myself. After high school I was date raped, and again I dealt by keeping it a secret. Throughout high school and college, I strived to make sure people only saw perfection in me—I was an Honor student, sports captain, hung out with the "good" crowd. But hidden away where no one else could see, there was shame, fear, and guilt. I coped with these feelings by running away from home, abusing drugs and alcohol, sleeping too much or not at all, and engaging in self-injury.

Cadence, pandys.org

Of course, while sexual abuse is inflicted statistically most on females, it is not limited to them:

To the outside world, I was a "normal" guy, but, I held a terrible secret. I was abused [by his football coach] for two years from the age of 11 to 13. The very first incident of sexual abuse was everything to me. This meant that I was a BAD person. Somehow, I had determined that I "gave in," that I was to blame. This devastated my self-esteem for years . . . To me, it was imperative that no one found out my secret. I withstood repeated abuse to avoid discovery. This secret dominated my life for 25 years. I spent 22 of the 25 years as an advancing alcoholic, along with other self-destructive behaviors. It is very difficult for me to convey to you the overwhelming fear that I had of being discovered. All of this happened and was allowed to happen right under my parents' noses.[171]

While the above testimonial does not detail the specifics of the parental situation, research suggests that parental alcohol abuse may leave children more *vulnerable* to sexual abuse by others.[172]

In total such abuse leads to many related triggers as well, including Anxiety, Depression, Guilt[173], Powerlessness, and Sexual issues. They also can contribute very significantly to self-esteem issues, though abuse is not a "requirement" for such issues of course.

Some Causes of Low Self-Esteem

As you might imagine, there are dozens if not hundreds of causes for low self-esteem, such as dead-end career (Job), deteriorating or lack of Relationships, clinical Depression, and of course various forms of abuse. Some psychological definitions in themselves can be useful in helping gain insight into how we can wind up coming to have a low opinion of ourselves:

Self Esteem: How humans evaluate themselves overall in relation to self-worth. It can be described as the confidence and satisfaction that the individual has with their own life. The terms self-esteem and self-worth tend to be used interchangeably; although feelings of self-esteem tend to be more fluid than self-worth.[174]

It is useful noting how the above definition notes the "fluidity" of self-esteem, versus a more general and less changing view of self-worth. It is my view that the most likely time people with Victim-Mentality (and hence a low level of self-worth) might relapse is when they have a serious dip in their self-esteem due to a particularly bad day, episode, etc.

Self-pity is another variation of both low self-esteem and low self-worth and is formally defined as:

> **Self-pity** A psychological state of mind of an individual in perceived adverse situations who has not accepted the situation and does not have the confidence nor ability to cope with it.[175]

Coping skills, or lack thereof, is what is key here. Drinking to "cope" is not coping in the slightest. As with triggers in general, it is key to get to the underlying cause(s) of the low self-esteem. In addition to child sexual abuse, these can include:

• **Parental neglect.** If parents fail to make their child feel valued and important, then this can later lead to poor self-esteem. If young people feel that they have failed to live up to their parent's standards, it can mean they find it difficult to value themselves.

• **Excessive criticism.** Receiving too much criticism when growing up can leave behind mental scars. People who are always being told that they are a failure will start to believe it. This includes consistent negative feedback from peers.

• **Personal identity issues.** When people feel that they do not fit in anywhere, it will change the way they view themselves. Being a victim of racism or sexual preference prejudice can also change the way people view themselves. As seen in the Sex trigger discussion, "Guilt" (conceived and enforced by society) can be a significant related trigger to add to self-esteem issues.

• **Personal appearance issues.** Those individuals who have issues around their physical appearance can easily develop feelings of low self-worth. The Sex trigger section also discusses this as a related trigger, in the context of one's body image.

There are multiple effects from low self-esteem, none of them good, particularly for alcoholics. These include:

- **Not taking care of yourself.** People with low self-esteem may not see the point of putting much effort into your body and/or mind, translating into poor physical and mental health. Since alcohol is abusing your body to begin with, this can be particularly devastating. You may also find yourself in a vicious circle, where you drink more because of your poor physical condition, which worsens your physical condition, which makes you want to drink more, which . . . you get the idea.

- **Limiting your potential.** You may not be willing to put the necessary effort in to achieve your dreams, believing it won't bring results. Such people may be convinced that mediocrity is all they deserve. This is another area where a vicious cycle might result.

- **Abusive or highly insecure relationships.** You might feel inwardly like such relationships are all you deserve. This puts increased pressure on top of already strained Relationships caused by alcoholism.

- **Bowing to Peer Pressure.** There is much evidence that many individuals who end up in dangerous cults suffer from low self-esteem. You don't have to be "cultish" however to let low self-esteem make you vulnerable to "going with the crowd," particularly when it calls for drinking. You may also be vulnerable to bullying. Hence, Peer Pressure is a major related trigger.

- **Difficulty in trusting other people.** You may believe that anyone who is trying to help has a hidden agenda. You can also go to the other extreme where you trust unworthy individuals too much, such as the cult example above. Either way, you set yourself up for either a) having no relationships, resulting in Loneliness, or b) getting into Relationships that are destined for destruction. Either is a potential related trigger making you want to drink.

As in the abuse section above, a person who has major self-esteem issues may not be obvious to the outside world:

> *I have been a highly performing alcoholic for more than 20 years. I have a very low self-esteem and am always doing something and everything for everyone else and don't have time to look after myself. Since my dad committed suicide 12 years ago I went away for a while and met another alcoholic and we married. We are now cohabitation Alcoholics. No one*

would know. We are the most social and entertaining people most of our friends know. We work hard and make good money but we drink every single night—at least 3 bottles of champagne plus several beers. Always ok in the morning.[176] Well most of the time. But well hidden.

Guest DeeDee, alcoholism.about.com

Overall, self-esteem and self-pity issues and feelings can lead people back to drinking, even after long-periods of sobriety. Indeed, self-pity has inspired a number of philosophical-type quotes to reflect this:

"Self-pity is easily the most destructive of the non-pharmaceutical narcotics; it is addictive, gives momentary pleasure and separates the victim from reality."

—JOHN GARDNER

"Take a drink because you pity yourself, and then the drink pities you and has a drink, and then two good drinks get together and that calls for drinks all around."

—H. BEAM PIPER, LITTLE FUZZY

In Alcoholics Anonymous (original source unknown), there is a much repeated saying: "Poor me, poor me, pour me a drink." It provides justification for a relapse because it means the individual can blame other people, their circumstances, or their luck for the decision.

Tips for Dealing with Victim Experiences/Feelings without Alcohol (Child and Sexual Abuse)

This is a hugely complex area, defying any sort of quick fix. That said consider the following:

General Tips

• **Professional Help.** First and foremost, seek out professional help if you have not done so already. There are numerous professionals and therapy programs that treat both abuse and alcoholism.

• **Online Support Groups and Forums.** There are also numerous online support groups and forums for this. Women for Sobriety (WFS—*www.womenforsobriety.org*, discussed in Level 6), deals with women-specific alcoholism issues, including abuse, as does Do It Now (*www.doit now.org*). There are numerous other such programs/groups that deal with sexual abuse more generally, such as Pandora's Project (*www.pandys.org*), Vera House (*www.verahouse.org*), and The Rape, Abuse, and Incest National Network (*www.rainn.org*).

Self-Esteem Tips

Persons with major self-esteem issues should also seek professional help and the aid of support groups, bearing in mind that there are differences in treatment and support approaches depending on whether or not you have also been the victim of abuse. These include Women for Sobriety (WFS—*www.womenforsobriety.org*), which in addition to abuse focuses extensively on self-esteem issues for female alcoholics. Other more general self-esteem forums include *www.socialanxietysupport.com,* Women SelfEsteem.com (*http:// women selfesteem.proboards.com/index.cgi*), and PsychCentral.com (provides links to various support groups at (*http://psychcentral.com/resources/Self_Esteem_and_Shyness/Support_Groups/*).[177]

However, the best overall tip for low self-esteem is to:

Stop drinking! It will have a major impact on your self-esteem. Alcohol works as a depressant, which of course will not help at all with low self-esteem issues. Conversely, recognize that beating addiction is absolutely one of the hardest things anyone can do, which should provide a major boost to you.

For self-pity in particular, there are a number of everyday things you can do to help you feel better, including:

- Do something kind for someone . . . anonymously.

- Clean your house.

- Exercise.

- Volunteer at a local mission.

- Make a decision to think positive thoughts about yourself today.

- Take donuts to your co-workers.

- When you notice negative thoughts, stop and remind yourself you have a choice.

- Send a card instead of an email.

- Plant some flowers.

- Make your bed.[178]

Lemons into Lemonade Tip: Always remember: *you are not alone.* In watching dozens of episodes of *Intervention*, I would estimate about half of the subjects were victims of childhood sexual or physical/mental abuse. Take advantage of the many online forums to meet new people, and possibly even meet some in person. Nothing will help like talking about your experiences with someone who has been there.

Overall Tip: The concept of different stages of sobriety was introduced earlier (and is discussed in detail in Level 13), which describes how certain triggers can follow you in life no matter how long you are sober in the Ongoing Sobriety stage. The nature of your Victim-Mentality history may be such that it will always be a major trigger for you. Thus, you will *always* have to be ready with defenses even if it is years after you become sober.

Also as a general rule you should seek professional help if this trigger is a major one for you, particularly if you are a victim of childhood sexual abuse.

Related Triggers: Feeling like a Victim/Victimized can be caused by Anger, Guilt, Loneliness, Powerlessness, Reminders, Relationships, Sex, and Yelling. It can activate Anxiety, Depression, Escape, Guilt, and Powerlessness.

Key Defense Levels: Engage Friends and Family, Join a Community (women-only, specialized support groups), Rehab and Therapy

WEATHER (INCLUDES SEASONS)

I first became aware of this trigger in one of my AA meetings, where an elderly gentleman described how his biggest triggers were violent (rain) storms as well as snowstorms. He never offered any details as to why these were such major triggers. While I can make some guesses (fear of lightning or tornados, being snowed in and helpless, etc.) the more general point is that you never know what can cause people to want to drink. This is why it is important to be as specific as possible in your identification of triggers. Weather is also an excellent example of a trigger that is impossible to avoid, and the need to have a ready means for dealing with it in a non-drinking way. In the elderly gentleman's case it was to go to as many meetings as possible, though I never did find out how he coped when he was snowed in . . .

Interestingly I could not find any anecdotes or scientific research views on Weather as an explicit trigger for drinking. Even more interesting I did not find studies on the *direct* impact of seasons and overall climate on drinking. One would hypothesize that in geographies with harsh winters, there was a higher potential for alcohol abuse—particularly *during* the winter—than those geographies with less harsh ones. A circumstantial case can be made that many northern countries, particularly in Eastern Europe, have higher alcoholism rates based on volume per capita as profiled in an article by *The Wall Street Journal*.[179] This article has countries with a reputation for alcoholism and a northern climate ·such as Russia high on the per capita consumption list. However, there are other northern countries with harsh climates such as Canada and Norway that have relatively low consumption per capita.

An extension of this hypothesis is that the potential for abuse worsens in geographies where latitudes had darkness prevail for most of the day, such as in the Pacific Northwest, Alaska, large parts of Russia, etc. However as I said I could not find any such *direct* research.

However, there is a substantial body of research regarding *related* triggers and such climates. One such "condition" is called seasonal affective disorder (SAD), which is characterized as:

> **Seasonal Affective Disorder (SAD)** A type of depression that occurs at the same time every year. If you're like most people with seasonal affective disorder, your symptoms start in the fall and may continue into the winter months, sapping your energy and making you feel moody. Less often, seasonal affective disorder causes depression in the spring or early summer.[180]

If you live in a northern region, where skies are normally gray from October to March, it's not uncommon for a lack of sunshine to make you feel depressed. Research has proved that brain chemistry is affected by bright light, although the exact process is not clear. Less than 1% of the population in sunny Florida report symptoms of SAD, yet about 10% of Alaskans report severe winter depression. It is a real illness that affects as many as 6 out of 100 people in the U.S. Even 10 to 20% more people may experience a milder form of SAD. It's more common in women and usually first appears in one's 20s. People with SAD typically feel better when spring comes, and then experience symptoms again in the late fall.[181]

Symptoms of SAD vary, but include (for winter-related SAD) outright Depression, feelings of hopelessness (e.g., Powerlessness), Anxiety, loss of energy, social withdrawal, oversleeping, and appetite changes/weight gain. Spring/Summer SAD is less common and differs somewhat, including Insomnia, agitation, weight loss, poor appetite, and increased Sex drive (words that are capitalized denote drinking-specific triggers discussed elsewhere in this Level).[182]

Treatment for seasonal affective disorder includes light therapy (phototherapy), psychotherapy and medications (e.g., anti-depressants).

Tips for Dealing with Weather/Seasonal Issues without Alcohol

Besides the above types of therapy, other possibilities include:

• First and foremost, do not brush off that yearly feeling as simply a case of the "winter blues" or a seasonal funk that you have to tough out on your own. Proactively take steps to keep your mood and motivation steady throughout the year, including:

• Exercising more frequently

• Spending more time outdoors

• Opening blinds and turning on more lights. Technology is improving options for light therapy, such as described in one recent *article*[183] on Health and Wellness.

• Making sure you don't gradually withdrawal into yourself, e.g., reach out to friends and family

• Limiting sugar and refined foods

• Weather-specific problems are different and most likely dependent upon the *specific* type of feelings caused, such as Anxiety (about being snowed in, fear of tornados) and Zeal (excitement of a beautiful day after a long period of crappy weather). Consult those trigger discussions for ideas on how to deal with them, but, of course, try first to understand *why* those weather events cause such issues in you in as much detail as you can. My (total) guess is that many of them are related to early childhood experiences.[184]

Lemons into Lemonade Tip: If weather/seasons is indeed a major trigger for you, along with strong related triggers, then you need to consider moving to a different area of the country. If you live in Seattle and get depressed about rain and darkness, then Seattle is not the place for you! Changing regions of the country is, of course, a major step, but it may ultimately be for the best for you and your family. It may also resolve other major triggers if done with proper planning.[185]

Overall Tip: Go to a community meeting (in person if possible) when weather/seasonal changes are getting to you. Speak up about your feelings. I guarantee that at least one or two others in the room are feeling the same way.

Related Triggers: Weather or Seasonal issues do not have any obvious causes (beyond the actual weather and seasonal changes). It can activate Anxiety, Boredom, Change, Depression, need to Escape, desire for Fun, Loneliness, Tired, and Zeal (unused energy).

Key Defense Levels: Engage Friends and Family, Join a Community, Develop New Hobbies (different hobbies for different seasons; both indoor and outdoor hobbies)

XS—EX-SPOUSE/EX-PARTNER

An "X" has nearly all the components of a former Relationship (please see that section earlier in this Level or refer to the endnote),[186] plus it: 1) is likely to have lasted longer—years, not just months; and most importantly 2) resulted in having to have some sort of ongoing interaction after the relationship is over, whether you want to or not. This, usually, is Money (e.g., alimony), and/or Kids/children—"things" about which you have to interact with each other fairly often, say at least a few times a year.

It is likely that a number of the issues that caused your breakup/divorce will carry over in why and how your eX continues to be a drinking trigger, even long after the parting of ways. In fact, it can be argued that becoming an "Ex" is just the end result of several other unsuccessfully dealt with marriage-related triggers, such as Anger, Anxiety, Frustration, Guilt, Money problems, Powerlessness, Sex issues, or overall Stress just to name some of the more obvious ones.

You will need to face the likely fact that your drinking quite possibly contributed to many of these problems, and in fact may have been the primary reason for the breakup.[187]

● ●

The Seven-Year Itch and Alcohol?

A huge number of testimonials referenced how alcohol destroyed marriages. Unfortunately, many marriages do not need such "help." It is common knowledge that roughly half of marriages end in divorce today. But these divorces do not occur consistently across time. When J. Lo and Marc Anthony called it quits after seven years, thoughts of the infamous *"seven-year itch"* surfaced. But in reality, 10 percent of first marriages end in divorce in the first five years.

According to a National Institutes of Health study on relationships, it's between the 3.5 and 5-year range where you're most likely to experience a significant drop in marital quality and most likely to get divorced. The honeymoon effect has worn off, and romance is trumped by problems like money worries and family drama. Stress levels peak at the three-year mark. What once was a minor irritation, like poor table manners, shifts to majorly annoying. This time slot is coined the *"three-year glitch."*[188]

The study indicates there's smooth sailing once again until around 10 years, and then it gets rocky again between 16 and 20 years. If you make it past 20, you've pretty much achieved a level of satisfaction and companionship.[189]

● ●

Sobriety through this program or others may—or may not—lessen these related triggers. In fact, you may likely find that these eX related triggers disappear entirely the longer you are sober (more on this in Level 13). It might even tempt you to get back together, thinking your problems are now behind you. Beware however of the consequences if this does not work out:

> *Well, [to me] a healthy, self-worth, and happy lifestyle is everything [and] the big reason behind sobriety. A dream so to speak, whether it is a loved one, maybe a job—basically something or someone that keeps you hopeful; your "drive" for success. My relapse was when it shattered. A female I held dear to my heart, my dream, my purpose for a future told me she didn't care what happened to me. She didn't care! After 5 to 6 years; I wanted nothing more than to spend my life in her life. My reason to stay clean was gone. Then, so too was I gone on drugs. I felt hopeless, unloved, and alone; isolated from the world. [Drugs and alcohol] eased the pain. It stopped me from feeling.*

Anonymous

It is also very easy to blame the eX as the root of all your drinking problems, as seen here:

> *[I] was problem drinker for a very long time, then I married the wrong person. Marriage went under after a few years—with divorce soon. I don't blame drinking for ruining my marriage. I blame alcohol—in part—for contributing to the very bad decision of marrying her in the first place. Let's just say she had a hidden agenda (until the day after our nuptials that is), I didn't know her and she didn't know me (and the me not knowing her part was something she wanted and ensured, until the day after we said "I do"). My way of coping with my mistake was to escape by drinking, not to deal with the problem, and life got worse and worse. My drinking got worse too, but not as quickly as my life did, with her taking money from me in various ways, ruining my reputation, etc. I made a lot of bad choices, and not doing the smart thing at various points (divorce) was because I drank instead of facing reality.*
>
> *Your ex doesn't necessarily have to be a trigger for you drinking, but it can be a very complicating factor in your life after you are sober, and one more reason not to drink, because you can do things that you will regret long afterwards, even if they should have been perceive as innocent.*

Guest F'd up dude, alcoholism.about.com

So if you think your eX is a major reason behind your drinking, you need to get to the bottom of why you think that is so.

A big part of the problem—maybe the biggest—with an eX is that they very likely know what buttons to push to most upset you. This means he/she can hit all of your *other* triggers instinctively and with ease. It may be done deliberately, or accidently, but they do it often and with major results. They lay a Guilt-trip on you with no effort (often having to do with alcohol); make you Angry and Frustrated with unreasonable (to you) demands and/or faulty logic; and generally just do an unparalleled job of pissing you off. And *that* is not a good thing *at all* for the alcoholic looking to get/stay sober.

As seen later (Level 13), it turned out that my eX is no longer a trigger, let alone my #1 trigger, yet she was a major trigger for me for many years prior to getting sober and for several months thereafter. The point is that it is very important to clearly understand how, why, and with what impact your eX is still a trigger in your life—*in detail*—so you can find ways to successfully extricate yourself from them and move on.[190]

How to Deal with Your eX without Alcohol

Note: Some of the following tips were introduced in the Relationships trigger section, as they are equally applicable to a current relationship or a past one. In this section, I also emphasize/add certain points as they pertain only to eX situations.

There were a surprising (to me at least) amount of ideas out there to deal with issues with your eX, and to avoid him or her all together. These include:

• **Create new Boundaries.** Your best defense after a breakup? Immediately create new boundaries with your eX. That means a minimal number of phone calls, e-mails, and texting, and no face-to-face interactions if you can avoid them. Your eX is now your *eX*. That means it's time to "eX-tricate" him or her from your life. *It is no longer your "job" to make him or her happy.*[191]

What if you can't completely cut off contact because you have children together, run a business together, or work together? This is obviously more challenging, but it's not impossible. You just have to create special new boundaries, *only dealing with and talking to your eX when absolutely necessary* about your common interests, i.e., the children, business, work. If your eX wants to know how you're handling the breakup? Shut him or her down. If he's curious whether you're dating again? Tell him it's none of his business. The same is true for you. Don't pry into your eX's post-breakup recovery. Just as you deserve to heal and move on, so does your eX. Give him/her the space and time to do so.

• **Avoid Being Each Other's Crutch.** You loved; you lost, and you are now in mourning. A word of warning when you're in post-breakup mourning (or any other kind of mourning): DO NOT seek comfort in the arms of your eX. That's a huge recovery[192] no-no!

Instead, lean on your inner circle of friends and family (discussed in Level 4—Engage Friends and Family), preferably those who have your best interests at heart (and knowledge of your alcoholism) and *won't* report back to your eX on your progress and setbacks. Support is one of the single most important steps you can follow during your breakup/divorce. To heal and move on, you're going to need help. That help should NOT come in the form of your eX. The same is true for you. If your eX calls, emails, texts, or stops by seeking comfort for his broken heart? Don't open your arms. Instead, kindly but firmly let him/her know that you are no longer his/her go-to support system. Then shut the door on any and all opportunities to help each other heal following the breakup (or for any other circumstances where they need help short of legal/moral obligations).

• **No Online Ex-Bashing.** After a breakup, it's only natural to feel some residual anger, resentment, bitterness, etc. And in the era of social networking sites and YouTube, it's all too easy to go online and spew in front of millions of readers/viewers. Don't do it! By going online and bashing your eX on your blog, via video diary, or to everyone in your social network, you are inviting bad breakup karma into your life.[193] And you know what they say—what comes around goes around. When it comes around? Ouch!

• **Handle Face-to-Face Interactions with Class.** While it would be fabulous if your eX could be automatically ejected from the planet following the breakup/divorce, this technology has yet to be invented. Depending on the size of the city you live in, a post-breakup run-in with your eX is not only possible, it's probable. Rather than become a shut-in out of fear of your eX encounter, embrace the possibility and plan for it.

Chances are that's not going to happen. Your eX encounters will probably be a lot less dramatic than you expect and will diminish over time. However, the pain may still be there. In having to face your eX for some reason, you may be reminded of what you loved about him or her. It may even reignite those familiar feelings of love, lust, or just plain Loneliness. Do *not* use the run-in as an excuse to reconnect. What's done is done. Your eX is now your eX. Instead, summon that inner strength, smile politely, and extricate yourself from the interaction (or get it over with quickly, depending on the circumstance) as soon as is possible without being rude.[194]

The above has some good ideas, though it seems mostly from the perspective of your eX being the person that initiated the breakup. To supplement them, I would add that understanding as fully as possible your Related Triggers with respect to your e(X) is extremely important in my opinion. Understanding his/her primary motivation in "wanting" to interact with you in the first place tops the list, with Money and/or Kids probably up there. Figure out how to deal with those "must" interactions, *then avoid/ignore all the other ones.* You'll be happier, and he/she may well be happier as well—maybe, but maybe not. But regardless, always remember: *It is not your job to make them happy anymore—so forget about the "old" stuff and move on.* This may take a *long* time to incorporate fully into your new life and ways of thinking, and will take lots of practice.

Obviously eX is one of the most personal of all triggers, but I can offer some additional ideas that worked for me, and may for you. Despite her divorcing me, my eX would (and does) contact me far more often than the other way around. A great way I found to deal with that is rooted in the idea of control: control when I "talked" to her, about what, and *how.* This is a variation of the "Create New Boundaries" tip in that trigger discussion.

I started with the how. As we had both very painfully experienced before the divorce and certainly after, we could not have a phone or face-to-face conversation on practically any topic without it degenerating into a full-blown argument in less than a minute.

Once the divorce was fully settled and I moved away, the phone discussion problems did not get better—they actually got worse. I think 20 seconds was the record from a pleasant hello to a hang up. I decided I would take advantage of the tools I had available—cell phone and computer—and resolved *only* to use text messaging, supplemented with emails for longer stuff. I did not answer her calls, and did not even check the voice messages, as they would inevitably contain (in my very sensitive state, I admit) accusations, guilt trips, demands for money, or just unpleasant tones. I fully recognize that some might feel this approach is cowardly;[195] if so, then so be it. One thing that was certain in her communications was that they were never good news for me, so why not minimize the stress, aggravation, and other emotions by looking at clean, minimally abusive text?

Lemons into Lemonade Tip: As with the Relationships trigger, the "lemonade" is not repeating the mistakes you made with your eX (before she was an eX) in any new relationship. With an eX there are more mistakes to be avoided, or put positively more opportunities to learn from your past mistakes. These opportunities could range from better money management to improved raising/relationships with children to better handling of in-laws. Make the past (even if it was lousy) count for a better future!

Overall Tip: Odds are very high that your eX will become less of a trigger the longer you are sober, particularly once you incorporate and practice some of the above tips.

Related Triggers: Issues with your eX can be caused by (among others) Anger, Change, Frustration, Guilt, Kids, Money, Powerlessness, Relationships (issue carry-over from before the breakup), and Reminders. It can activate Anger, Change, Depression, Loneliness, (carry over into) Relationships, Stress, and Yelling.

Key Defense Levels: Engage Friends and Family, Therapy, Break Bad Habits (stop (re)acting like you did when you were together), Develop New Hobbies (ones that you did not do with before with your eX)

YELLING (INCLUDES ARGUMENTS, CONFLICT, CONFRONTATION)

Yelling is distinct from Anger, in that Yelling, arguments, or even confrontations do not necessarily have a hostile, potentially violent aspect to them. Nonetheless, I heard many times in various drinking-related forums those who had a very hard time with others raising their voices in any context, making them want to withdraw, Escape, and yes—drink.

Drinking, of course, even in an attempt to withdraw, often has the opposite effect of escalating minor arguments into Anger and major conflict. It doesn't help that most alcoholics—particularly those that have not admitted their addiction—feel very defensive or "put upon" in general (not to mention comments about their drinking) leading to fast creations of mountains out of molehills.

Yelling can also be done for theoretically positive purposes, such as yelling at a teenager "for their own good"[196], and Yelling for "its own sake"—as a kind of stress release (the trick for the latter is doing it in private, *not* at the person causing the stress).

However, much of Yelling as a drinking trigger lies in wanting to escape or avoid conflict, a kind of a fear of Yelling. Wanting to avoid conflict appears to be particularly common to many alcoholics who are children of alcoholics:

> "Many alcoholics can become mean and abusive when they are drinking. Consequently, their children sometimes grow up being frightened of angry people. They can become scared of any kind

of conflict or confrontation, always concerned the situation will explode into violence."[197]

Regardless of the source, fear of conflict can ripple through many dimensions of your life. It can impact how and how well you do your Job; evolution and success of Relationships, even your Health as you internalize issues instead of expressing/venting them. It may lead to low self-esteem (Victim), and in general color how you deal with everyday life.

> There was never any physical abuse toward me or my two siblings, but there was verbal abuse. My dad would both physically and mentally abuse my mom. I hated the yelling and screaming and to this day cannot handle loud talking or yelling.
>
> Learning, about.alcoholism.com

Handling conflict/Yelling can be particularly difficult in early sobriety. An addiction, alcohol, usually, focuses people on their own desires. They can carry this self-obsession with these needs into sobriety and continue to put their needs above everyone else's.

When alcoholics put their needs first, it can make life difficult for family and friends who have their own needs. Family and friends may still be recovering from the damage caused by your alcoholism. Emotions can still be raw, and it can be easy to open up old wounds—leading to arguments, Yelling and in turn the desire to drink.[198]

Tips on Dealing with Yelling (Conflict) without Alcohol

You obviously can't avoid all Yelling, but you can greatly reduce it in your life by using some solid commons sense ideas, including:

• **Figure out the root of your Yelling trigger.** In keeping with the philosophy of the Conquer Program, try to get to the heart of why Yelling/fear of conflict works on you as it does. Talking with trusted friends and family may help greatly here, particularly ones who have known you for a long time. Therapy (discussed in Level 6) may be needed to get to the underlying issues.

• **Watch out for its impact on your self-esteem.** Fear of conflict may well have led over time to significant self-esteem issues. Try and figure out if conflict leads to this related trigger (e.g. Victim Mentality) and consider using the tips in that section. Therapy may well help you here as well.

• **Improve your communications.** This is particularly important with your significant other, Kids, and your boss/coworkers. These are likely the people you talk to most and have the most areas of possible conflict. Look for ways to improve communications with those with whom you have frequent conflicts. One of the best approaches is to identify and clear up any misunderstandings before they become an issue by asking questions and seeking clarification. Those with low self-esteem and difficulty speaking your mind may hold back and not do this, resulting in problems growing, festering, and finally exploding into conflict. You might also seek out opportunities to practice your communications in safe settings, such as public speaking classes.

• **Detect personality clashes.** Recognize that personality clashes are another common contributor to conflict. Sometimes the characteristics of one person will not mix very well with those of another. At least *trying* to understand where the person is coming from is worthwhile. But it may well be that mixing with some people is like mixing oil and vinegar—no matter how hard or long you shake the bottle they will always separate. In such cases avoid those people, or if not possible, seek out intermediaries to help you resolve the conflict.

• **Get out of yourself.** Spend time thinking about the needs of other people. Loved ones may become resentful when they feel that their needs are being ignored, perhaps even more so once you are sober. Eventually, this boils over into open conflict. Taking other people for granted leads to trouble down the road.

• **Avoid office politics.** I have met only a few people who like office politics, and they were extremely unpleasant excuses for human beings. Avoid office politics as much as possible. For the vast majority of us, the costs (stress, blood pressure levels, general unhappiness) far outweigh the benefits.

• **Be willing to listen.** This can be crucial in avoiding later problems. Just allowing the other person to express their feelings can be a way to defuse the situation before it snowballs into something much larger.

• **Pick your battles.** It is not necessary for people to get their way all the time. Even when you are clearly in the right, there may be times when it is wise just to leave things unmentioned. A wise general knows which battles to choose and which to ignore.

Lemons into Lemonade Tip: At some point in your life you are going to have to be able to tolerate, if not outright manage and forcefully respond to yelling and conflict. The good news is that there are many education programs to learn to do this, such as *www.helpguide.org/mental/eq8_conflict_resolution.htm*, which coaches on how to turn conflicts into opportunities. So there is no reason not to reach for the stars, and turn your fear of conflict into a positive!

Overall Tip: You may well find that your ability to deal with confrontation, rude behavior, and other similar situations will *greatly* improve with sobriety. The ability to react coolly and logically will also be a deterrent to others who in the past (pre-sobriety) thought you were a "soft touch" or one to present off-the-wall arguments that were easily defeated.

Related Triggers: Yelling (including fear of confrontation) can be caused by Anger, Frustration, Noise, Relationships, and Stress. It can activate triggers such as Anger, desire to Escape, Victim (self-esteem issues) and Zeal (High Energy and Excitement)

Key Defense Levels: Engage Friends and Family, Join a Community, Therapy, Develop New Hobbies, Consider Spirituality

ZEAL (INCLUDES EXCITEMENT, HIGH ENERGY)

Zeal (*Noun*)
1. Great energy or enthusiasm in pursuit of a cause or an objective.
"His zeal for his team"
Synonyms: passion, ardor, love, fervor, fire, avidity, **excitement,** *keenness, appetite, devotion, relish, gusto, vigor,* **energy,** *intensity*

Yes, this is an example of where I was reaching to come up with a trigger that started with Z. Nonetheless, Zeal—particularly the Excitement synonym—is a *very* real and dangerous trigger for some. There are at least three reasons Excitement can make you want to drink—to *enhance* or "spike" the feeling, to *extend* the feeling, or to *diminish* the feeling.

Zeal/Excitement is a different trigger that is mostly a *good* thing, in contrast with the vast majority of triggers that are mostly or fully negative (e.g., Boredom, Loneliness, Guilt, etc.). Other triggers can be a decided mix, with some such as your Job being good (e.g., landing a Job, a promotion, a big increase in pay), not just "bad" (Job-related stress). Life, even for the alcoholic, isn't throwing bean balls at our head *all* the time; sometimes we get a nice fat pitch down the middle of the plate and we hit it good. Unfortunately for some of us Excitement makes us want to prolong/extend/enhance the feeling via alcohol.

As discussed before, the first drink of alcohol creates an initial period of excitement (the "rush" in the rush/buzz/numb/checkout continuum).[199] The 'rush" is a feeling of general pleasure (euphoria[200]) that lasts (through the rush/buzz blood alcohol content levels) for a short time before it crosses over into dysphoria[201]. Many people want to drink to enhance the feeling of Excitement in a kind of piggy-backing; others do so in an (ultimately futile) attempt to prolong or intensify the initial rush/buzz. For some people a major reason behind their Fear of Quitting is that they will not be able to feel these kinds of "improved" Excitement sensations or even have "Fun" anymore since it has become so closely associated with the rush and buzz that comes from alcohol.

Reasons Behind Feeling "Blahs" in Early Sobriety

• Your brain is still healing from your alcohol overuse, and this makes it harder for you to experience strong positive emotions.

• Many people run into something that's known as 'the wall' between 2 and 4 months into sobriety, as the early glow of success fades and the harsher business of reality settles in (more on this in Overconfidence trigger discussion).

• You may feel that your sober life probably isn't as "exciting" as your using or drinking life. This really is a very good thing (because most substance abuse excitement is the kind you really don't want). Nevertheless, you'll still miss those regular moments of what you thought of as 'Fun' excitement that using or drinking provided.[202]

Interestingly, some alcoholics drink to *dampen* the Excitement, feeling perhaps that being too excited will have negative repercussions, such as getting their hopes up too high (only to see them dashed), or even to more quickly reach the "numb" phase of the continuum where they might better enjoy the event causing the Excitement.[203] This latter feeling/driver was a personal trigger to me—I did not want to get too excited lest I get tremendously disappointed (e.g., Depressed) if my team lost.

Gambling problems can offer a different take on Excitement and addiction. Studies have shown that in "pathological gamblers" dopamine release (which causes euphoria) appears to be associated with increased excitement levels. It is possible that similar cause and effects can be found in other forms of addiction, including alcoholism.[204]

● ●

Compulsive Gambling and Attention Deficit Disorder (ADD)[205]

Gambling can be an addiction just like drugs or alcohol. In particular it can provide a different form and intensity of excitement. Gambling addiction is considered an impulse-control disorder where *a person cannot control the impulse* to gamble. Although these persons know that gambling may hurt them and their loved ones, they still do it. They would want to gamble no matter what the consequences might be.

So what does this have to do with ADD? Recent studies showed that there is a strong link between ADD and gambling. The most basic definition of ADD is someone who has a "neurobehavioral" developmental disorder—being impulsive, overactive, easily agitated, unable to concentrate and other similar symptoms. *The thought of winning serves as their stimulation*—which is why experts have found a strong link between the two.

● ●

I've encountered a number of extremely intelligent people (e.g., near genius-level) who wound up being addicts. My theory is that they use drugs and/or alcohol to *slow down* their brain, so they don't have to think at such an intense rate—to be "normal" in other words. They wind up wanting to be at this "slower" rate so much that they wind up becoming addicted to the substances. Boredom is a major related trigger for these kinds of people; in fact some occasionally go the opposite route and get addicted to Excitement and even danger, such as getting into drug dealing.

Tips for Dealing with Excitement without Alcohol

As with many of the triggers discussed in this Level, it is very important to figure out exactly *why* being excited makes you want to drink. Is it a desire to prolong the fun that you are having? To somehow capitalize on the extra energy you feel in certain exciting situations? A way of forgetting a natural state of Depression, or to Escape in general? A way of calming yourself, so you don't get *over*-excited? The possibilities go on and on. Think long and hard on this if it seems to be a major trigger for you; Therapy may well help if it is not clear.

Obviously you don't want to become a Mr. Spock with no emotions; Excitement is a key component to positive mental health and stimulation after all, not to mention real fun. So the goal of any tip should be in stripping the negative (drinking) aspects of Excitement but leaving the core of it intact.

One interesting concept I came across in my research for this trigger is called "Islands of Excitement."[206] It centers on the premise that we all need things to look forward to—things that make all the tough and mundane moments worthwhile. It breaks it down into two components:

• We need to look forward to small moments of fun or excitement on a very regular basis.

• We need to have bigger things to look forward to for every once in a while.
Examples of Excitement Islands (both large and small) include:

• Going away for a weekend with friends or family members (particularly with those who know about your alcohol issues)

• Going out to try a new nice restaurant (perhaps using the money you used to spend on alcohol or drugs)

• Going to a matinee movie (it's cheaper, but any movie will do)

• Going for coffee with an old friend (beware of caffeine-related issues, discussed below)

• Going to a ball game[207] or a play

• Getting a massage or spa treatment

• Taking the day off work

• Going camping

If you are the type of person that doesn't like to be excited, or wants to be careful on when this happens, there are a number of ways to relax without alcohol. These include:

• **Exercise.** Excitement often gives you extra energy, which in turn can generate extra excitement. If you can burn some of the energy off, you may succeed in lowering your excitement levels and in turn increasing your chances of relaxation. While this might not be possible in some venues (such as a professional sports event), it may be possible in more informal ones, such as walking the sideline during one of your kid's soccer events.

• **Avoid caffeine.** If you know you will be in for some excitement (e.g., going to a sports event, anticipating a big performance review), do not ingest caffeine that day. It can raise your blood pressure, particularly if you already have high blood pressure[208], making it that much harder to relax.

• **Practice Breathing Techniques.** Taking several slow, deep breaths or other more formal breathing techniques can do much to relax and lower your excitement levels. This has the added advantage of being able to be done in practically any situation and without anyone noticing.

• **Meditation and Prayer.** If you have the luxury of time in whatever is causing your Excitement, consider meditation or prayer. There are many advocates about the utility of prayer for achieving many benefits, including relaxation and tranquility. This concept is addressed in Level 10—Consider Spirituality.

• **Avoid the Cause.** For me, I would become exceptionally excited during close games of my favorite sports teams. My solution was to tape/DVR the games. Sometimes I would try to avoid knowing what the outcome was (and being able to check the final score at any point during the playback). Other times I would only watch if they won (which was actually very relaxing to watch, knowing they did win).

Lemons into Lemonade Tip: Since high energy levels often go hand in hand with Excitement, try to use it to your advantage. Take on chores and errands that require more than normal energy and strength that you have been putting off. You will feel the satisfaction of getting those things out of the way while bringing those energy levels back to normal.

Overall Tip: Additional tips in the Boredom trigger discussion may also be very helpful.

Related Triggers: Zeal (both High Energy and Excitement) can be caused by a number of factors including Fun, Holidays, Music, Sex, and Weather. It can activate triggers such as Escape (desire to slow down), Fun, Overconfidence, Sex, and Yelling.

Key Defense Levels: Listen to Your Body! (high blood pressure/hypertension), Break Bad Habits (ways to calm yourself down without alcohol), Develop New Hobbies (same rationale), Consider Spirituality

So you have got through Level 2—Congratulations! I know that was some tough reading, particularly as you recognized some of the major triggers in your life and identified with some of the testimonials of other alcoholics struggling with triggers perhaps in ways very similar to your own. So what do you do next?

Answer: you *reread* Level 2, this time focusing in *much* more detail on those triggers you think are your likely major triggers. There is a large amount of information to process in this Level, and more importantly it may require you to do some deep, introspective thinking about yourself, your personality, your motivations, and how you think in general. Use the forms in Appendix B to help you. The first one (labeled Level 2—Drinking Triggers Checklist) is a checklist that will help you simplify the trigger identification process. Each trigger described has a column to check whether you believe it is a major trigger. To refresh, a major trigger is a circumstance, situation, event, or state of mind that drives you to want to drink more often than not and can do so independently of any other triggers. A major trigger is also one that can set off or "activate" other "related triggers" that it combination can quickly increase your desire to drink.

The checklist also has a column to capture possible related triggers, as well as space to write down additional information specifics about your trigger as well as tips and defenses that caught your attention.

Before you start your reread, take a stab at filing out the form based on your recollection of what you read the first time. Then, as you reread Level 2, adjust and expand on your first impressions. By the end of the reread, you should have a very good idea of what your major triggers are, your key related triggers for each major trigger, and a good selection of tips and defenses that you think will be helpful.

You might also try and fill out the second form for Level 2 in the Appendix: Level 2—Drinking Triggers History and Projection. This form is intended to help you think about how your major triggers have evolved over time. Doing so may help you get to their roots, and will be useful when you get to Level 13 (Develop Your Defense Progressions) and start to think about how you can diminish or eliminate your major triggers over time.[209]

The remainder of the Levels 3 through 13 are all to some degree built and depend upon what you learned about yourself in Level 2, specifically what triggers make you most want to drink and why. These Levels describe specific types of defenses that you can use to protect against these triggers.

The next Level, Level 3, is the final foundation-building Level in the Conquer Program. It is foundational in that it may be very important for you to understand how much damage alcohol has already done to your body, and what medical steps (in addition to not drinking) you may need to do to stop or reverse that damage as you embark on the remainder of the program. Even if you are lucky enough to not have incurred serious damage yet, it will describe in detail what damage *is* awaiting you if you don't stop drinking.

LEVEL 3

Listen to Your Body!

Death by alcohol. Could it happen to you, or someone you know?

> *One phone call you never want to receive is one from your mother, scream-*
> *ing that she has found her first-born child (my brother) dead from the*
> *effects of alcoholism. Believe me, she was never the same. To her last days*
> *this year, she was unable to talk about him at all. My brother was 48—we*
> *were only 11 months apart. My heart will always ache for him.*
>
> Guest Susan W., alcoholism.about.com

Even if you consider the above unlikely, there is no question that alcohol is *not* good for you in general, and certainly not in excessive quantities. While a lucky few may never experience alcohol-related health
problems, it is safe to say nearly all alcoholics *will* experience problems.
Some small at first . . .

> *Why do we all think Alcohol is harmless? Even the press says "2 glasses of*
> *red wine are good for you." The health benefits are actually found in the*
> *grapes, so if you're looking to be healthy, eat healthy—don't drink poison. I*
> *turned to alcohol to ease the stresses of the day, and found myself using*
> *more of it, more often. I have acid reflux now, after 10 years of drinking 2–3*
> *nights a week.*
>
> Guest ruth, alcoholism.about.com

. . . and getting progressively worse . . .

> *I have alcohol gastritis. I have been sober 3 weeks, but I am going to crack. I*
> *just cry in agony. I need a drink, but I know it's over if I do.*
>
> Guest Tomish, alcoholism.about.com

. . . and worse.

> *My mother is the alcoholic. She has everything going for her—2 kids (my brother 23 and myself 21), two wonderful grandchildren from my brother, a loving boyfriend, family support and a beautiful home. I question why she drinks, every time she relapses especially since she has pancreatitis and the doctors told her she's going to die if she keeps it up, even one beer a day, which is never the case. Why?*
> Guest daughter, alcoholism.about.com

Here are some sobering statistics to supplement the stories above: The World Health Organization estimates that up to **4 percent** of all deaths worldwide are alcohol-related. Alcohol deaths account for **2.5 million deaths** annually, with over 300,000 between the ages of 15 and 29— almost **9 percent** of the total. Alcohol is a factor in up to **60 different diseases** and injuries including cirrhosis, poisonings, violence, cancer and heart disease. It is reportedly the world's **third-largest** risk factor for disease burden.

Yikes!

Unfortunately, as Joseph Stalin once said, "One death is a tragedy, a million deaths is a statistic." As much as I hope Old Joe is rotting in the worst part of hell right next to his buddy Adolf, he had a point: we pay far more attention to the details of one person's individual agony than we do to the anonymous pain of many. No one is ever going to stop drinking because of the above statistics, but they may well do so because of the individual stories that preceded it and are used throughout this book. Let's take a closer look at how those stories are even possible.

ALCOHOL-RELATED HEALTH PROBLEMS FROM A TO Z

No question, alcoholism can be *very* detrimental to your health. It can impact many dimensions of your body and mind, including very negative impacts to your liver, nervous system, heart, skin stomach/intestines, and of course your brain. But this is not all, not by a long shot.

Alcohol abuse and addiction also produce other medical side effects. Alcoholics frequently attribute these complications to other health conditions, as they attempt to avoid ownership of the consequences of their drinking. Common medical side effects include high blood pressure, sexual problems, stomach problems, osteoporosis in women, even cancer. Skin disorders are also a common and major side effect of chronic excessive alcohol abuse, with pleasant sounding names such as *urticarial* (hives), *porphyria cutanea tarda, cutaneous stigmata of cirrhosis, psoriasis, pruritus* (itching), *seborrheic dermatitis* and *rosacea*. Look these up—they are *not* pretty or fun.

Not enough for you? Even as I personally dealt with skin aliments[1] and several other alcohol-related health issues over the years—whether I acknowledged them or not at the time—I had no idea how many dimensions of our health alcohol could affect until I was researching this book.

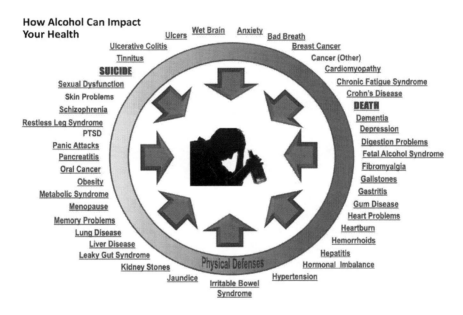

Figure 12: Alcohol-Related Diseases from A to Z

A good quick reference on the effects of alcoholism on health comes from *http://alcoholrehab.com/alcohol-rehab*, where it has succinct overviews of a cornucopia of health issues alcohol can cause or impact, many of which are in Table 1 below. Scared the hell out of me when I came across this list! I had no idea about many of the ways alcohol can screw you up. I wish I had known about these earlier, since I wound up with several of them (though I frankly doubt that would have impacted my drinking, but wishful thinking is free).

TABLE 1: HOW ALCOHOL CAN DESTROY YOUR HEALTH FROM A TO Z

Anxiety (Alcohol Induced)	Gum Disease	Obesity
Bad Breath	Heart Problems	Oral Cancer
Breast Cancer	Heartburn	Pancreatitis
Cancer (Other)	Hemorrhoids	Panic Attacks (Alcohol Induced)
Cardiomyopathy	Hepatitis	
Chronic Fatigue Syndrome	Hormonal Imbalance	Post-Traumatic Stress Disorder
Crohn's Disease	Hypertension	
DEATH	Jaundice	Restless Leg Syndrome
Dementia (Alcohol Induced)	Irritable Bowel Syndrome	Schizophrenia
Depression (Alcohol Induced)	Kidney Stones	Sexual Dysfunction
	Leaky Gut Syndrome	Skin Problems
Digestive Problems	Liver Disease	SUICIDE
Fetal Alcohol Syndrome	Lung Disease	Tinnitus
Fibromyalgia	Memory Problems	Ulcerative Colitis
Gallstones	Menopause Problems	Ulcers
Gastritis	Metabolic Syndrome	Wet Brain

My body wanted to flee for the exits after my mind saw this list . . . Made me want to run around knocking people's drinks from their hands screaming, "Don't you have any idea what this can do to you?"

I had *no* idea that alcohol could cause or worsen so many dimensions of my mind and body, and I bet 99% of alcoholics have no idea either.

For women, the news is even worse. According to numerous studies, women develop long-term health complications of alcohol dependence more rapidly than do men. Alcohol abuse increases the risk of breast cancer. And over time it has been found to have a negative effect on reproductive functioning in women, resulting in anovulation, decreased ovarian mass, problems or irregularity of the menstrual cycle and early menopause. The final indignity: women have a higher mortality rate from alcoholism than men (more on women and alcohol later in this Level).

My mother was an everyday drinker for the 10 years prior to her illness, she drank wine. She started to show signs of minor swelling in her legs (edema) and after I had to convince her, she went to the doctor. Her doc told her that she had cirrhosis of the Liver and Hepatitis C. She quit drinking on that day! For the next 3 years that she lived with this disease she went through bouts of Ascites, Edema, and hepatic encephalopathy. My mother was a very petite woman, and when she could not control her swelling she looked and felt like she was 9 months pregnant. She would have to get her stomach drained of the fluid and even then she would constantly get asked when she was due. She lived for almost a year with her stomach like that until she was able to get some control over it.

But just as one symptom subsided another would show up. It was in the last 6 months of her life that on a routine scan of her liver they found a "mass" on her liver. It was just before Christmas that the doctors confirmed that it was Cancer. Now because I did a lot of research on the progression of the disease, I knew that there was a great possibility of cancer with cirrhosis and with hepatitis too. She went to have chemotherapy done on Jan of 2008. Chemo left her very weak and almost unable to care for herself, not to mention that she reacted to the meds and had to stay across the state alone for a week. When she came home it was constant doctors' appointments. Her hepatic encephalopathy became much worse and it brought her to the hospital on several occasions with ammonia levels off the chart. She lost all her hair as a result of the chemo.

It was two weeks prior to her passing that I found her semi-conscious in her apartment; I knew it was her ammonia levels. My brother had been to see her early that day and she said that she was not feeling well, but he made sure that she took her meds. It was 8 at night that I found her, her meds were not working. While in the hospital we became aware of her kidneys not functioning properly. Her sodium levels were too high, so she couldn't take her meds to keep the swelling down, and to top it all off she lost all control over her bowels and had to use diapers. She was also unable to walk, so she couldn't get to the bathroom anyway!

My mother left the hospital on a Friday, and was transferred to a hospice center. It was Easter Sunday that I walked into her room to see her semi-conscious and gasping for air. She looked at me and said that she was scared to die . . . these were her last words. She died early on Tuesday morning. My mother was 55 years old. Her death was not something that was easy, she struggled for 2 days to breath. The pain that she went through prior to her death was not easy either.[2]

I've included the full post above to show how you can go from minor symptoms of alcohol-related problems to death in a just a few years. Men or women, it all stinks. Nonalcoholics can scratch their heads and say, "How can they do that to themselves?" It is obvious *to them* that "any normal person" should have stopped well before things got so awful (even though in this case she stopped pretty quickly once *major* problems were diagnosed). Yes, it is true that alcoholics are not normal—at least in terms of being able to defend against alcohol. The better answer is that the vast majority of the time alcohol-related health problems evolve over time, often too slowly or just not quite severe enough to really get our attention. Or in our drunken stupor or next day hangover we just blew them off. Just as "Fun" devolved into alcoholism over a great deal of time (as discussed in Level 1), so do many of our physical health problems come at us gradually (this is true for nonalcoholics as well). *By the time we get to the point where our physical problems are severe enough to make us want to quit drinking—a kind of physical bottoming out—it is often too late.*

THE JOINT PROGRESSION OF DISEASE AND ALCOHOLISM—AGE DOESN'T MATTER!

Most people don't think something bad can happen to them. This disbelief is not a sign of arrogance or stupidity—it is just human nature. Alcoholics are certainly not exempt from this trait. It doesn't help that like alcoholism the damage to your health can sneak up on you. Or there can be obvious progressive downward signs (that you ignore) towards pain and death. Or it can be sudden—out of the blue. Meaning? *Damage from alcohol is totally unpredictable* in what and when and how. **But what IS predictable is that it WILL happen to you** if you drink large amounts long enough and it will *always be awful* when it does. Not if—but *when.* **And it can happen at any age.** The following testimonials show how alcohol and health problems can occur/progress as we age.[3]

The Experimental Teens and Roaring Twenties

Health problems at an early age from alcohol, while unusual, is certainly possible:

> *I'm 17 and have been drinking since I was 12. Getting drunk was my only objective. I drank so much that the past few months I had to drink an entire*

handle of 80 proof vodka to get drunk. And I could still drink more. I never threw up, only blacked out. I would drink more even when I was blacked out until I would eventually drop. A week ago I started having blackouts while I was sober. But I figured it was just after effects from the nights before, until 2 days ago I drank 2 handles of McCormick's and several mixed drinks. I blacked out, I have no recollection of the night, but there are videos. Two days ago I was not the life of the party, I saw myself on video, drinking on the bathroom floor alone. That made me want to change. Yesterday morning I woke up and threw up blood. So I know things need to change.

anonymous

The tolerance levels needed to get to (a satisfactory level of) being drunk vary widely by person, by age, and by how long (and how intense) they have been drinking, among other factors. Usually, it is a gradual progression, which makes it easier for your drinking volume to increase unnoticed or ignored by you. He fast tracked this one.

I have been drinking since I moved away from my hometown. I am starting to get worried about my health. I haven't had any health problems yet, but a 40 oz. vodka doesn't last me 3 days. I'm really getting worried but I do not want to upset my family I'm 19, and I have already lost my driver's license, due to drinking and my car I am still paying for. I owe so much money due to that one mistake, but I can't stop, and the sad part is I want to stop when I'm drinking, but when I'm sober I get mad when someone tells me I need help . . .

Guest Rylan, alcoholism.about.com

The Conquer Quiz in Level 1 focuses on the behavior and end results caused by drinking to determine if a person is an alcoholic. Unfortunately, for a very young drinker, they really haven't had enough time to "royally fuck up their life" in multiple ways. Thus, they may score much lower than they might say five years later. But the man who posted the testimonial above certainly got a fast start with respect to a DUI, financial problems, and now health.

I started drinking at the age of 17. Before then I had never had a drink. I started off with a bang and then eased into casual drinking until about 19 when I started binge drinking every day 12–24 beers a day or half a fifth to a fifth depending on what was around. I continued to drink like this for a few years. After I hit 21 I slowed down a bit for about a year. At that point I started drinking like a fish 5 days a week (I didn't drink on the weekends much). At this point I started seeing health problems. I got an ulcer, I ate less than I already did. I weigh about 108 pounds, probably less now. I also started having memory problems to the point that when I drank I couldn't remember anything that happen. My eyes started to twitch, and I was mildly depressed. I never had DTs or felt that I really needed a drink to the point that I would go out of my way to get one but if it was there I would drink it. I'm 23 now and have been sober for about 3 days.

anonymous[4]

I can't tell if the writer of this testimonial is male or female; I believe male. I'm guessing (hoping) that the 108 pounds was a typo. Otherwise, he is far, far worse off than he describes. I give kudos to him for recognizing how his drinking was progressing and recognizing the downward spiral at such an early age. This brings up an interesting idea for research: determining the differences in what type of alcohol and how much of it is drunk by gender and age. Hopefully, I'm not being sexist here by assuming that this is a male drinking a case of beer and a fifth of booze (More on women and alcohol later in this level).

I'm a 24-year-old male I went to my Dr. because I was suffering with heart palpitations which were getting worse and I had other side effects on top like chest pain sweating pain in my left arm. He asked how much I drank? 30 units a day every day. I have vomited blood as well which made me go. Anyway he diagnosed me with severe alcoholism as I've drank that amount for 5yrs and refused to do any test on my heart, blood pressure etc. because the amount I was drinking. He told me everything is to do with the amount of alcohol I've consumed. The chest pains etc. is anxiety related which leads to panic attacks. I'm getting help with drinking problem now but anxiety levels are through the roof palpitations and more frequent panic attacks not sure if that's a good sign or bad sign all I know it worries me to death that I'm dying which makes everything 10 times worse it's a horrible circle.

anonymous

How in hell this doctor "diagnosed" severe alcoholism is beyond me. Maybe he felt that this kind of pronouncement would be the only way of getting through to this young drinking maniac, though the not doing additional tests sounds very suspicious. But it sounds like both the drinking monster and his doctor both intuitively understood the main cause, even if the drinker was incredibly naïve, and the physician wanted to play psychologist instead of a medical doctor. Kudos also to this young man for admitting how much he actually drank—something that many, many older and supposedly wiser drinkers do NOT do, to their medical health sorrow.

> *I'm 25 years old and I'm from Norway and in the last 5 years I've spent roughly $100,000 on partying. My big problem is that I do not get hangovers. Because I do not get hangovers I can go on benders 3 to 4 nights in a row each week. Now my memory is failing, my joints are painful, I've lost my flexibility, I get massive stomach aches after I've been drinking and I'm just sick and tired of being sick and tired.*
>
> Guest 25 and a drinker, alcoholism.about.com

Besides illustrating the danger of being young and vulnerable with a lot of money (I'm being very polite here—I wanted to say something much more caustic), this testimonial illustrates a factor in alcoholism that should be researched extensively by some blue-ribbon team of doctors—the role of the Hangover in preventing alcohol abuse and alcoholism, particularly early in a budding alcoholic's career. There is some subset of alcoholics—I have no idea how big, but I know it included me—that hardly *ever* get hangovers when drinking heavily. Hangovers are probably the first line of defense when it comes to excessive drinking:

> **Hangover** pron.: is the experience of various unpleasant physiological effects following heavy consumption of alcoholic beverages. The most commonly reported characteristics of a hangover include headache, nausea, sensitivity to light and noise, lethargy, dysphoria, diarrhea and thirst, typically after the intoxicating effect of the alcohol begin to wear off. While a hangover can be experienced at any time, generally a hangover is experienced the morning after a night of heavy drinking. In addition to the physical symptoms, a hangover may also induce psychological symptoms including heightened feelings of depression and anxiety. *Source: Wikipedia.org*

A hangover is your body and mind telling you in no uncertain terms that what you did to it was bad, very Bad. For "normal people," and probably some unknown % of alcoholics, this first line of defense is, usually, enough to deter drinking again for some period ranging from days to weeks. But if you wake up and feel few if any of the effects described in the above definition, then obviously that line of defense is a total failure in inhibiting your drinking—one more step on the gas on your road to alcoholism. More on this in Level 11—Make Yourself Sick of Alcohol.

> *I'm 29, and have been worried lately that I may have a problem. I quit my job and broke up with my girlfriend about 6 months ago. I felt like my life had hit rock bottom and started drinking maybe a 6 pack 4/5 nights per week to deal with the depression. This increased until I was drinking 8–10 beers or half a bottle of liquor almost every night. My mind isn't sharp, I get anxious, feel depressed, lazy, and I'm packing on the pounds even though I regularly exercise. That's why I'm leaving my stamp here. I'm going to stop. We'll see how this turns out.*
>
> Guest kc, alcoholism.about.com

The above shows how alcohol damage can start to sneak up on you, starting with mental issues and maybe some extra weight. The damage is just starting to appear. But you are *never* too young to start having *major* physical problems . . .

> *I am a 29-year-old girl with 10 months sober. I decided it was time to get clean and sober after I had a $1/3$ of my liver removed at 17 and had pancreatitis 3 times. The last time I had pancreatitis I was 24 and it is the most painful thing I had ever gone through. Usually when you have alcohol-induced pancreatitis you are given morphine so I was then addicted to morphine I was given to take home. This almost gave me two addictions I couldn't shake! I knew it was time to stop. It took me two more years to finally do it.*
>
> Guest Kimberly, alcoholism.about.com

Pancreatitis was the second-most cited disease cited in my testimonial research. A separate discussion of it follows later in this Level.

The "Progressive" Thirties

Assuming you have been drinking heavily for a few years by the age of 30, odds are you will start to experience some significant health issues in that timeframe.

I have been drinking bourbon specifically Wild Turkey 101 since I was 18. It started off as a mixed drink while just relaxing after work. I am now 30 and since then my alcohol consumption has significantly increased. On average, I drink a pint 3–4 days a week starting around 6–7 pm. When I stop drinking by the 2nd night around dinner time I am a bit irritable, my lower back hurts, extremely tired. Around bedtime, I get headache, night sweats and I can't sleep.

Guest Angies, alcoholism.about.com

I don't have any statistics to prove it, but around age 30 seems to me to be an age where you arrive at a fork in the road when it comes to drinking. It either: A) stays about where it is, settling into the normal background of daily life with *relatively* few episodes of heavy drinking, or B) you really start to snowball in your drinking behavior, progressively upping your frequency and volume of alcohol intake, veering decidedly towards the path to alcoholism (or much more likely where the disease of alcoholism—lack of control and high tolerance in particular—*really* starts to manifest itself).

I'm in my 30's, I regularly go out with my mates and we drink socially, I have noticed a change recently in my drinking habits. I now drink alcohol like its water, and at a certain point I can't control the need for more, I then usually forget what I'm doing, and regularly put myself at risk by walking home. The next day I will wake up and be sick every 30 minutes or so for about 6 or 7 hours. Disabling myself for the whole day.

Guest Zoe, alcoholism.about.com

As best as I can tell, my alcoholism started about this age, both intuitively (in hindsight) as well as when I think I met the threshold of alcoholism as defined in The Conquer Quiz in Level 1.

I started drinking at age 13 and LOVED it. I drank whenever possible, didn't care. As I got older it got easier. Benders every weekend. I am an alcoholic, but still achieved a college degree while working and am a somewhat successful 30-year-old female. But I started to drink far too much and it caught up with me. Physically I was sick, mentally my brain was getting damaged, and therefore sad. I knew I had to quit. After 4 months sober I slipped and it was bad. I cannot drink because I AM an alcoholic, and really wish I wasn't.

anonymous

While many of the testimonials I found in my research referenced starting to drink heavily in their teens, it doesn't mean you can't get a late start on it.[5] If you factor genetics in, it means no age is safe to start drinking, as indicated next and discussed in more detail later in this Level.

> *I started drinking less than a year ago. I lost my mom at 44 to cirrhosis and my sister at 24 to cirrhosis. I'm 35 and now have hepatitis C and am an alcoholic, less than 12 months after starting. I'd drink a pint or more of vodka daily, blacking out every time. I have had gastric bypass surgery and have an ulcer on top of it. I'm terrified of dying of this illness. I have lost temporary custody of my daughters, ages 7 and 4. I have been sober less than a week and have been in outpatient treatment for 11 weeks already. I am trying to numb my pain. I don't want to die.*
>
> Guest Amy, alcoholism.about.com

The above testimonial is a very frightening example of how genetics can play a *major* role when it comes to your health and alcohol. If you have heavy drinking/alcoholism in your immediately family, you MUST add Relatives to your list of health concerns and in particular to your list of triggers (e.g., being around your alcoholic Relatives) to avoid.

> *I started drinking at the age of 13 and haven't stopped since. I am now 37 and have to drink 2–3 bottles of wine a day to achieve a "normal" state. The irony is, my cousin died a horrible death from cirrhosis and kidney failure (ascites, bacterial peritonitis, you name it) and I WAS THERE when she died—after that, I have had no control over my drinking, I just drink and drink and drink. My life is a complete wasteland. My health is terrible— can't eat solid food anymore, so I just drink and smoke all day. I pass out every night and wake up with the shakes, last about 2 hours before I have to drink again. So to say that my health has been affected is an understatement—my life has gone down the drain and my body is giving up.*
>
> Guest anna, alcoholism.about.com

The mid to late thirties seems to be an age range where our drinking volumes have become way out of control, setting us up for the bigger health problems coming our way.

> *My sister who is 39 was just hospitalized her kidneys and liver had stopped working and her potassium level was so low they said she could have a heart attack at any moment . . . Her kidneys are working now her liver is*

working 25 percent she's very jaundice her belly looks like she's having triplets I think she dying but I don't know the hospital says that he liver could get back to 75 percent she has cirrhosis they said her liver is bigger than they ever seen is she going to die?

anonymous

The Deteriorating Forties

By the age of 40, many alcoholics may have a decade or two of heavy drinking under their belts. Unsurprisingly, this is when major problems start to appear if they haven't already.

I'm 41, I've had a drinking problem since I was 16. I packed up drinking just seven weeks ago and the change has been enormous. Previously I weighed in at 290 lbs, had serious trouble with digestion, my short term memory was terrible, My legs would swell up like balloons and were covered in sores. My mid-section was swollen to the point where I had breathing difficulty. I decided enough was enough after I watched a friend die slowly and horribly through cirrhosis of the liver and pancreatitis. In seven weeks I've lost 22 lbs, my legs are back to normal, the swelling has gone down and I can eat (and poo!) properly again, and I'm exercising daily. Everyone tells me I'm looking younger and my recall is certainly much sharper. I'm suffering from tremors and mood swings, but the good far outweighs the bad.

Guest Hedgey Hogg, alcoholism.about.com

Starting drinking at an early age certainly cannot be a good thing, and studies indicate that the earlier you drink, the higher risk you are for mental development problems. Memory problems can also seem to start in the 40s[6], and obviously alcohol problems won't help. More on this later in this Level.

Really started as a casual drinker, then because this disease is so sneaky and aggressive, I became a raging alcoholic. The physical problems started 5 years ago (I'm now 45). I paid no attention and kept drinking. Finally went to rehab and AA with a bad attitude so, of course, I relapsed. Finally got so sick with end stage liver disease I had to quit. By some miracle I was placed on a transplant list and received my transplant within 6 weeks! I had been sober for well over 6 months before being added to list, but the damage was done. Both mentally and physically. My memory problems have improved slightly since transplant and the new lease on life my donor has given me is beyond description. However, the damage I did to others may never go away. My husband has stayed by my side, but he/we will never be the same. My parents almost lost a child, my son almost lost his mother. I did this! I would do anything to never have had a drink. I'm an alcoholic and always will be sorry.

Guest thhout, alcoholism.about.com

It seems to me that age 40–45 is when major health problems really start to become obvious/ snowball for many alcoholics—another great topic for formal research.

My husband is so deep in denial, he's even convinced his own children, my step-children. However, my children and I (yes, blended family) see it. In fact, his oldest son (19) is probably following his footsteps, same as my husband followed his father's. Our home is like solitary confinement, each person hides in their rooms to avoid the arguments, the heat, the highs and lows of one individual's happiness which dictates the mood and activity of the day. I can't tap my toothbrush in the morning (it's too loud); we keep the lights off in the house and pull the shades; we dare not make noise or create commotion. Other people's happiness is sarcastically envied by my husband. I envy their peace. His Lies rule my relationships w/ my in-laws who enable, they need to protect their brother. Instead, they're killing him too. Time to move on?

Guest For better or worse???, alcoholism.about.com

This testimonial brings up the topic of how and when alcohol plays into divorce. It is common knowledge that roughly half of marriages end in divorce today. But these divorces do not occur consistently across time. As mentioned earlier, there is some evidence supporting a "7-year itch." But in reality, 10 percent of first marriages end in divorce in the first five years. According to a National Institutes of Health study on relationships, it's between the 3.5 and 5-year range where you're most likely to experience a significant drop in marital quality and most likely to get divorced. The honeymoon effect has worn off, and romance is trumped by problems like money worries and family drama. Stress levels peak at the three-year mark. What once was a minor irritation, like poor table manners, shifts to majorly annoying. This time slot is coined the "three-year glitch."[7]

The study indicates there's smooth sailing once again until around 10 years, and then it gets rocky again between 16 and 20 years. If you make it past 20, you've pretty much achieved a level of satisfaction and companionship. The 30-year benchmark can bring on some surprises like a Tipper and Al Gore split.

That study did not assess specific factors that caused the divorce. It likely assumed that the unique factors in any one divorce would average out to be about the same when it comes to an analysis of a large number of divorces. HOWEVER, I would hypothesize that when alcoholism comes into play during one of these "rocky" cycles—particularly in the 16–20 years of marriage range—is when many marriages with an alcoholic break up. Another research topic!

> *I am 48 years old and have been to an outpatient rehab which didn't work. I have 4 granddaughters and one that was born with $\frac{1}{2}$ a heart and during my stay in Denver with her and 2 open heart surgeries, I came home to nothing , my spouse left me for a girl 2 years older than his daughter! It's been so hard and really I can't find anyone that can help . . . now my health is in danger. I've contacted in house treatment centers and I've been denied, unless I have a court order, DWI, vehicular homicide etc. I am willing and need help . . . where's it at?*
>
> anonymous

Among all the other worries that you have as you get older, a BIG one is (lack of) health insurance, which I'm inferring is the issue here (besides the jerk spouse). I have no idea how Obamacare/Affordable Care Act is going to impact someone like this lady. Why she had to actually commit a crime to get treatment, I have no idea.

The Fifties—Make or Break Time

If you've continued to drink heavily over the last couple of decades+, you have been begging for some major problems. The fifties are when they really hit, really hard.

> *Day one and this is probably the 50th time I've tried to stop. My health sucks, most of my old friends don't talk to me anymore, and my oldest son hasn't spoken to me in two years. My wife and daughter and my grandkids live with me now. I don't want to screw up the grandpa thing. Nobody really thinks I can do it. I've done AA and rehab. My wife even had me*

locked in one time in a mental ward. I work, pay my bills, but I'm 52 now
and down to quit or die. I don't seem to be able to do either one.

anonymous

When I found this testimonial, I was struck by his comment that it was now "down to quit or die." I'm going to hypothesize that it is around age 50 where the make or break point comes in terms of health. If you can quit by then, there may well be time to get back to good health. If you don't, then you're on the express track to an early death.[8] Another great research topic for the medical community. The testimonials from here on out get progressively grimmer.

I am 50 yrs. old and drinking alcohol for the past 20 years about average
400 ML of alcohol and now I have high levels of Triglycerides (293) and
High blood pressure 100/130 after medication.

anonymous

Chronic drinking has a major impact on blood pressure for some people, including me. I have not had to take any medicine for it since a few weeks after I stopped drinking.[9]

I care for my brother, who has been an alcoholic since he was a teen. He's
52 now and in poor health. He developed pancreatitis from the drinking
and had surgery to remove part of his pancreas. He was told then that he
also had cirrhosis and needed to stop drinking. He managed to get a C-Diff
infection and it went untreated, resulting in the removal of most of his intes-
tines. He had an open incision for over a year in addition to the ileostomy.
It was a nightmare. He continued drinking hard liquor. Then his intestines
ruptured. Now, after yet another surgery to repair the intestines and close
the incision, he drinks more than ever. Lately, he has been having severe
leg and hand cramps, which I discovered often happens to people suffering
from final stages of liver disease. I can't believe anyone could stay in denial
after all he's been through.

Guest CareGiver, alcoholism.about.com

I can tell you from personal experience having severe long-term intestinal pain is extremely uncomfortable and painful. The problem for alcoholics with medical issues is that the mind holds no memory of pain. So, many people like the above go right back after the booze after the miracle of modern science has fixed their current agony. Trying to leverage this pain so it *can* be used in a positive fashion is the key foundation underlying Level 11—Make Yourself Sick of Alcohol, and Level 12—The LAST Detox.

> *My brother Bob drank steady from the time he woke to the time he went to sleep each night until it finally took his life! Great funny bubbly personality! Everyone loved him! He died this past Wednesday as he drove himself to the Emergency room and was admitted in critical care coughing up blood. That night he was on life support. Just had his 52nd birthday.*
>
> Guest JoAnn, alcoholism.about.com

Too often the "funny, bubbly" personality is used to distract people from how much you are drinking. Beware the funny drunk!

> *I'm 53 now [date of this posting unknown]. I started Christmas Eve 2008 internal bleeding been coughing up blood all night, day before was sick on oxtail soup which I hadn't eaten prior to that. No warning signs. Always been heavy drinker since age 14 like kids do with no concern for your 50's. I'm alive now due to ambulance that morning taking me to the right hospital. My kids, my friend Di and willpower. I have cirrhosis but a 2nd chance. I am checked constantly by hospital I am proof it can be done. Saying that another mate of mine was cremated today. Liver, alcohol, female, 50's another statistic for the books.*
>
> Guest Yes, alcoholism.about.com

And so the deaths start mounting . . . but there are also forms of living death.

> *I have been sober for 22 years and five years ago I was diagnosed with Alzheimer's and the doctors have linked the early onset to my drinking and drugging for over 25 years. I started at age 11 and quit at age 35. I am now a 57-year-old female who was addicted to alcohol and drugs for the entire time I used. I wrote a book about my story with input from my family called "Alive." Alzheimer's has taken my life away.[10]*
>
> Guest Eileen, alcoholism.about.com

Alcohol Dementia is one of the diseases we started this Level with in our A to Z list, and is similar to Alzheimer's[11]. You can find out more at *http://en.wikipedia.org/wiki/Alcohol_dementia*.

I am a social worker. I daily work with men and women who have to be hospitalized due to end stage liver disease which is a result of risky sexual behavior while drinking and do drugs. Depending on the physical stamina of the person it usually ends in death. A slow painful death that is very lonely. The stomach region swells with fluid retention called ascites. Ammonia may build up in the brain causing comas. The body systems such as heart and lungs and brain are also affected. The person gets alcoholic induced dementia with severe memory loss and inability to function independently. The lungs fail. The kidneys fail. The person may get congestive heart failure with edema or swelling of extremities. They can get jaundice. I have a 61-year-old man who is dying slowly of chronic homelessness and alcoholism. I have a mother in her mid-fifties who is dying with the ammonia build ups. I have another mother in her mid-fifties who is dying of the end stage liver disease. Alcohol kills.

Guest yes sir, alcoholism.about.com

A "perfect" lead-in to our next decade.

The Sick Sixties+

The title says it all:

I have seen first-hand the health effects of excessive alcohol consumption. My dad passed away at the age of 60 from acute kidney and liver failure as a result of cirrhosis. I witnessed the seizures, the withdrawal shakes, swelling ankles and stomach, jaundice, confusion, coma and death. These images will forever be instilled in me. My dad was a loving and wonderful individual.

Guest summer1985, alcoholism.about.com

I'm 64 yrs. old. Had first drink at 14yrs. old and have never stopped, except for 4 detoxes and rehabs. Tried AA and counseling, which would help for periods of time, but I would for some reason I'd relapse. I've had triple bypass surgery 7stents and carotid surgery. Got divorced after 28 years of marriage. Lost my job at age 63. Thru all my 2 girls and friends have been supportive but stopped enabling me. But for some reason the devil comes back. I know booze is the worst thing I could but I still do it. I am 3 days sober and have an appt. in 2 days with an AA counselor and try again to get sober for good. I must have a trigger but I don't know what. Hopefully counseling can help. I have 3 grandchildren & 2 daughters whom I adore &want to see grow in life. I've been lucky and blessed to still be alive and have another chance. I pray it will work. FOR ANY ONE STRUGGLING KEEP ON TRYING, THERE IS ALWAYS A CHANCE WE MIGHT GET IT! GOD BLESS.

anonymous

So many places in this book I could use this testimonial. Some are good, starting with the fact that he is still alive and trying. But it obviously goes downhill from there. My personal recommendation is to use this kind of emotion and desire as a form of "floor defense": something that can motivate you to not drink in almost any circumstance. Much more on Floor Defenses in Level 13—Develop Your Progressions.

I am 44 years old and I have been cheated from having a mother all my life due to her heavy drinking. I have tried many times to help her, but she is in denial. Now she has grandchildren, and it is history repeating itself. I cope with it through anger. I know that is wrong. My father says he has done all to get her help, but I disagree. She comes from a family that is full of addiction. The funny thing is when they need help. She got it for them. I don't know where to turn anymore. My father protects her rather than helping her. My mother is also on all kinds of meds for stroke level high blood pressure. To sit back and watch her drink herself to death is killing me. My mother used to be a very loving and happy person. Now she is nasty and unemotional. To not only watch her fall apart, but a whole family as well. I am not a person to give up, I want to see my mother smile and be loving as she once was.

Guest gloria, alcoholism.about.com

The fact that these persons are alive in their 60s and 70s after the abuse they inflicted on themselves (and their families) is definitely the exception and not the rule. Depending on the study you believe, **alcoholics can expect a reduction of 10–12 years from what their life expectancy would have been**. Some put it as high as 30 years. It is impossible to tell, which is one of the key reasons I used so many testimonials in this chapter to show that disease, agony, and death from alcohol can happen at ANY age.

My interpretation (sure to cause great agony to health professionals) of the above and other observations results in the following rules of thumb of what might constitute the "typical" progression of your alcoholism as you stumble through your alcoholic life:

● ●

A Prototype for Drinking Over Your Lifetime

- *13–20 years old:* Start drinking significantly.

- *Mid-20s:* Drinking patterns (what, when, how much, where) start to develop. Volumes start to increase materially as does the frequency of drinking.

- *Early 30s:* The "tipping point," when you effectively "decide" to become an alcoholic or not. Or put another way: when the disease is successful (or not) in determining your life's path.

- *Mid-30s:* Hard core drinking accelerates. Health problems start to develop; many "under the radar" (e.g., not noticeable in your stupor or you ignore the symptoms). Drinking becomes a major source of marital friction, increasing physical and mental stress (and desire to drink).

- *Early 40s:* Significant health problems become apparent. You can't ignore them anymore.

- *Mid-40s:* Functional Addicts find their functioning starting to deteriorate. Marriages reach the point of no return and divorce.

- *Early 50s:* Reach "stop or die" point when it comes to drinking.

- *Age 60:* Dead by then, or will be soon. Death; very ugly and painful.

● ●

I'm sure you can poke a million holes in the above conjecture, but like I said it is a rule of thumb. Of course, any similar conjecture is going to depend on dozens or hundreds of variables that can't be quantified.

A rare few are "lucky" enough to live past sixty with no health problems. There are always those who seem to have no ill effects from massively abusing something, whether it is alcohol, tobacco, other drugs, etc. These are extremely unusual cases, and unfortunately, they serve no purpose to society other than make others think what they are putting in their bodies won't harm them either. If you are striving to be one of these "lucky" elders, here is a sample of what you can look forward to:

> *I have been dating someone for over 2 years. When I met him, he told people in front of me that he had stopped drinking—I had no idea he was an alcoholic who really drank constantly every single day. He hid it from me until I started spending more time with him. A beer with breakfast, then wine and sometimes a Martini in between. Now he adds something to his coffee.*

I have discussed this with him, and he knows he has a problem, but his retired life is centered around alcohol. His grown kids apparently ignore it [or have given up]. I do not know what to do—I have separated from him and gone back but now I realize I don't want [to be with] an [emotional] invalid.

Getrea, alcoholism.about.com

THE ROLE OF GENETICS IN ALCOHOLISM

Genetics *does* play a significant role in alcoholism, but . . . how and how much is open to tremendous debate. Alcoholism often seems to run in families, and there are many efforts underway in search of and to understand the concept of an "alcoholism gene"—potentially even leading to treatment (one day, but not now). Genetics certainly can influence our likelihood of developing alcoholism, but the devil is in the details on this one, and those aren't clear yet.

Genetic factors may account for about half of the total risk for alcoholism. Looked at another way, *genes alone do not determine whether someone will become an alcoholic.* Environmental factors, as well as gene and environment interactions, account for the remainder of the risk.

The role that genetics plays in alcoholism is complex, and it is likely that many different genes are involved. Research suggests that alcohol dependence and other substance addictions may be associated with genetic variations in 51 different chromosomal regions. There are genes that increase a person's risk, as well as those that may decrease that risk, directly or indirectly.[12]

Evidence for a genetic component in the susceptibility to alcoholism has been increasing over the past three decades. American Indians in particular are thought to be genetically pre-deposed to higher alcohol consumption, where Asians are thought to be almost the opposite. Why? Research has identified differences among population groups in the enzyme systems that regulate alcohol metabolism; those differences are thought to account for some cultural differences in drinking patterns.

For instance, some people of Asian descent carry a gene variant that alters their rate of alcohol metabolism, causing them to have symptoms like flushing, nausea, and rapid heartbeat when they drink. Many people who experience these effects avoid alcohol, which helps protect them from developing alcoholism. For example, the "flushing response" is an unpleasant reddening or flushing of the skin, sometimes accompanied by nausea, causing discomfort which in turn is credited with fostering lower levels of alcohol abuse for those with that reaction to alcohol[13]. (Note: This plays into the discussion in Level 11—Make Yourself Sick of Alcohol).

Outside ethnicity, many scientific studies, including research conducted among twins and children of alcoholics have shown that genetic factors influence alcoholism[14]. These findings show that **children of alcoholics are about four times more likely than the general population to develop alcohol problems**. Children of alcoholics also have a higher risk for many other behavioral and emotional problems. But alcoholism is not determined only by the genes you inherit from your parents. In fact, **more than one–half of all children of alcoholics do not become alcoholic**. Research shows that many factors influence your risk of developing alcoholism. Some factors raise the risk while others lower it.

One very interesting dimension of genetics and alcohol is the apparent linkage to tolerance to alcohol.

● ●

Tolerance and the Predisposition to Alcoholism

Animal studies indicate that *some aspects of tolerance are genetically determined.* Tolerance development was analyzed in rats that were bred to prefer or not prefer alcohol over water. The alcohol-preferring rats developed acute tolerance to some alcohol effects more rapidly and/or to a greater extent than the non-preferring rats. In addition, only the alcohol-preferring rats developed tolerance to alcohol's effects when tested over several drinking sessions. These differences suggest that the potential to develop tolerance is genetically determined and may contribute to increased alcohol consumption.

In humans, genetically determined differences in tolerance that may affect drinking behavior were investigated by comparing sons of alcoholic fathers (SOA's) with sons of nonalcoholic fathers (SONA's). Several studies found that SOA's were less impaired by alcohol than SONA's. Other studies found that, compared with SONA's, SOA's were affected more strongly by alcohol early in the drinking session but developed more tolerance later in the drinking session. These studies suggest that at the start of drinking, when alcohol's pleasurable effects prevail, SOA's experience these strongly. Later in the drinking session, when impairing effects prevail, SOA's do not experience these as strongly because they have developed tolerance. *This predisposition could contribute to increased drinking and the risk for alcoholism in SOA's.* [15]

● ●

Genes are not the only things children inherit from their parents of course. How parents act and how they treat each other and their children, has an influence on children growing up in the family. These aspects of family life also affect the risk for alcoholism. Researchers believe a person's risk increases if he or she is in a family where an alcoholic parent is depressed or has other psychological problems; both parents abuse alcohol and other drugs; the parents' alcohol abuse is severe; and/or conflicts lead to aggression and violence in the family.[16]

Genetic risk factors don't act alone and simply having them does not at all mean that someone will become an alcoholic. But you should be extra cautious if very heavy drinking seems to run in your family. *If alcohol abuse runs in your family, use it as one more defense against alcohol, e.g., one more reason NOT to drink, not as an excuse TO drink.* More on this in Level 13—Develop Your Defense Progressions.

HOW ALCOHOL CAN DESTROY YOUR BODY—A SAMPLING

In the A-to-Z list, I highlighted over two dozen illnesses that can be directly caused by or greatly aggravated by alcohol abuse. In this section, I'll go into more detail on a subset of those, which I've selected because of their prevalence and/or familiarity to most people concerned with drinking. These include liver disease, memory problems, pancreatitis, and skin problems. To repeat a key disclaimer, what is discussed here (and this Level overall) is for informational purposes only. Again, I am not a medical doctor, and before acting on any health issue discussed here, please consult your doctor.

Liver Disease

Liver disease is a disease with a justifiably close association with alcohol abuse, and an extremely unpleasant disease overall, as the below image illustrates:

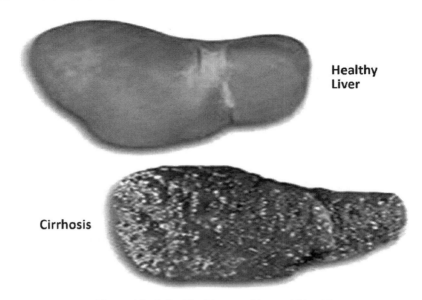

Figure 13: A Healthy Liver vs. Diseased Liver[1]

First, some key facts.

Alcohol remains one of the most common causes of liver disease in the United States, causing up to 50% of cases of end-stage liver disease according to the Center for Disease Control. It is the third leading preventable cause of death in the United States. The mortality from alcoholic cirrhosis is higher than that of nonalcoholic cirrhosis with a survival rate at 5 and 10 years of only 23% and 7%, respectively. Given these grim statistics, the mortality from liver disease is more than that of many major forms of cancer, such as breast, colon and prostate. **Once alcoholic liver disease is established in the body, abstinence from alcohol use is the only accepted treatment outside of a liver transplant, which many facilities are reluctant to perform for active or high relapse risk alcoholics.**[18]

> *My husband is an alcoholic, he has alcoholic liver disease. He has been told he has maximum of 5 years to live. He won't quit. He has yellow eyes, recently developed a swollen stomach, and sleeps every two hours for 2–4 hours at a time. He is on lactulose, is very angry and nasty towards our children, then nice as pie. No one will tell me how long this will go on, why this is going on or how bad this will get, what to expect? Can anyone help?*
>
> Guest wifeofdrinker, alcoholism.about.com

Alcohol is toxic to liver cells (known as hepatocytes) and causes inflammation. The effect of drinking on hepatocytes is immediate, but in most healthy nonalcoholics the body repairs itself. Unsurprisingly, it is the *repeated* levels of exposure to alcohol that causes chronic and continuing inflammation to the liver, resulting in scarring of the liver. This scarring is the beginning of alcoholic liver disease.

The symptoms of this disease include:

- Painful stomach cramps

- Jaundice

- Chest pain

- Headaches and light-headedness

- Nausea and vomiting

- Significant weight change

- Blood or dark bowel movements

- Mood changes including agitation and confusion

- Nosebleeds

- Reddening of the hands and feet

It can cause you to lose the ability to clot blood, which allows *easy bruising* and *can be extremely dangerous as even minor cuts will bleed excessively.*

> *I am too an alcoholic. I'm a 38-year-old female, starting to consume many bruises on my body due to drinking, I can no longer go out. It's a hard illness to fight. We are all human and people are so easy to judge if they don't understand what alcoholics go thru. It's discouraging to look for help when people just judge us.*
>
> Anonymous

To add to the fun, there is even a genetic component. It is believed that when you drink, certain genes trigger an immune reaction that causes liver damage. For those with the gene present, your body will begin to attack itself and cause serious and even life-threatening damage to the liver including cirrhosis. **Once you have cirrhosis, you have a 50 percent chance of being dead in two years or less.**

There are three main stages of liver disease:

• *Fatty Liver Disease*—This is a precursor to alcoholic liver disease, and will not progress further if you stop drinking. It causes the body to accumulate fat instead of healthy liver tissue, resulting in an enlarged and inflamed liver. Symptoms include fatigue, nausea and vomiting, confusion, abdominal discomfort, weight loss, and jaundice.

• *Alcoholic Hepatitis*—This is caused by untreated Fatty Liver Disease (e.g., you did not stop drinking). This is where serious tissue damage occurs to the liver, including cirrhosis. Hepatitis causes many problems including cholesterol and protein metabolizing, processing of fats and sugars, hormone regulating, and impaired immune functions. If and when the liver is severely damaged by alcoholic hepatitis, these functions can be interfered with to the point that the liver is unable to function. The disease has progressed to cirrhosis.[19]

> *Good luck. I know how difficult it is to deal with a bullheaded husband. Mine ignored his hepatitis C diagnosis for years. He ignored the diagnosis of fatty liver for about 4 years and then he found himself in the hospital this past February with Hepatic Encephalopathy. Very nasty symptom of liver failure. The man truly thought he could dodge this bullet (HepC and fatty liver) but he was sadly mistaken. He goes for a liver biopsy in 3 weeks to find out the exact status of his liver.*
>
> *I'm afraid he has damaged it to the point that the only thing that will help him is a liver transplant and he can't get that until he has achieved one year of sobriety and is determined to be sick enough to be placed on the list. He has type O blood so he can only get a transplant from another person who is Type O. Our doctor says that could take quite some time. He may very likely die while waiting. I have a hard time wrapping my mind around all of that some days. Other days I just feel shell shocked. I knew this day would come . . . I just didn't think it would come without more warning. One day doing fine and the next almost in coma from increased ammonia. Scary.*
>
> Grace724, medhelp.org

• *Cirrhosis*—When a person develops cirrhosis, their liver is so scarred that it is no longer able to repair itself. Cirrhosis is a very serious condition that contributes to the development of liver cancer and death. **Death for 50 percent within two years.** *The only "treatment" for cirrhosis is an organ replacement.*

I lost everything, career and family. This only gave me more reason to continue. At 45 years old I was told I needed a transplant or I would die. I've been through it all, throwing up blood (five times) that required transfusions and ascites. The symptoms of cirrhosis are horrific. I had a transplant two years ago and was doing well until I began to reject recently. I just got out of the hospital after a 23 day stay and was told things could go either way.

Zippy, alcoholism.about.com

My father is in the hospital now he has been in for 3 days today is March 7 2012. He has the yellowing, liver is dead, kidneys are failing to work they have him on meds but we won't know if they are working till tomorrow. He is really bad we don't know what to do anymore I guess just wait and be prepared for the worst. My dad has been in AA for 10 years and he just had a relapse just 2 months ago and this is when he started to get sick now it's too late. To all that have a family member or friend please help them this is no joke or to say I'll quit tomorrow because that tomorrow will never come.

(Name redacted), alcoholism.about.com

Memory Problems

Alcohol also can do severe damage to your brain, which becomes more evident the older you become:

The brain of a normal person

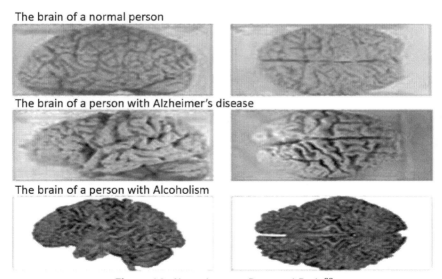

The brain of a person with Alzheimer's disease

The brain of a person with Alcoholism

Figure 14: Normal versus Damaged Brain[20]

Difficulty walking, blurred vision, slurred speech, slowed reaction times, impaired memory: Clearly, alcohol affects the brain. Some of these impairments are detectable after only one or two drinks and quickly resolve when drinking stops. On the other hand, a person who drinks heavily over a long period may have brain deficits that persist well after he or she achieves sobriety. Exactly how alcohol affects the brain and the likelihood of reversing the impact of heavy drinking on the brain remain hot topics in alcohol research today.

We do know that heavy drinking may have extensive and far–reaching effects on the brain, ranging from simple "slips" in memory to permanent and debilitating conditions that require lifetime custodial care. And even moderate drinking leads to short–term impairment as shown by extensive research on the impact of drinking on driving.

A number of factors influence how and to what extent alcohol affects the brain, including:

- How much and how often a person drinks;

- The age at which he or she first began drinking, and how long he or she has been drinking;

- A person's age, level of education, gender, genetic background, and family history of alcoholism;

- Whether he or she is at risk as a result of prenatal alcohol exposure; and

- His or her general health status.[21]

Blackouts and Memory Lapses

Alcohol can produce detectable impairments in memory after only a few drinks and, as the amount of alcohol increases, so does the degree of impairment. Large quantities of alcohol, especially when consumed quickly and on an empty stomach, can produce a blackout, or an interval of time for which the intoxicated person cannot recall key details of events, or even entire events.

I have a good career, a loving partner, glamorous friends, and a glamorous life. The problem is that I am also a hard-core alcoholic. I drink "moderately"Wednesday to Thursday (by my standards). On the weekends, however, I can easily finish off a magnum or more of wine on my

own. A pint of vodka is nothing. Two bottles of wine in one night is noth-
ing. Whenever I have one drink, my only concern is where I will get the
next. My drinking ends only when I lose consciousness. Behavior during
blackouts has led to more embarrassment, shame, and guilt than I can
carry, or admit to myself.

NYSoc57, alcoholism.about.com

Blackouts are much more common among social drinkers than previously assumed and should be viewed as a potential consequence of acute intoxication regardless of age or whether the drinker is clinically dependent on alcohol. A survey of college undergraduates about their experiences with blackouts asked, "Have you ever awoken after a night of drinking not able to remember things that you did or places that you went?" Of the students who had ever consumed alcohol, 51 percent reported blacking out at some point in their lives, and 40 percent reported experiencing a blackout in the year before the survey. The students reported learning later that they had participated in a wide range of potentially dangerous events they could not remember, including vandalism, unprotected sex, and driving.[22]

Research has shown that heavy alcohol use clearly damages retrospective memory; that is, the learning, retention and retrieval of previously presented materials. Less is known about the effects of alcohol on *day-to-day* memory function, specifically, prospective memory, remembering to do things at some future point in time, and everyday memory, remembering to complete daily activities. Obviously we all forget things from time to time; however, heavy users of alcohol make noticeably more of these mistakes than either non- or low-users of alcohol.

● ●
Reminders as a Trigger and a Tool
for Memory Problems

When I first got sober (for real), for several months my head felt like it was stuffed with cotton. One of the many issues I had post-sobriety (particularly a variety of sleeping problems; see Appendix A) was a *great* deal of difficulty with remembering even simple things. I would forget things I did an hour before, and for some strange reason I would forget where I would put down my glasses and wallet,[23] even literally 30 seconds after I put them down somewhere.

There seemed to be high variability in my memory loss in those months. Some topics/categories of info were "readily accessed" (particularly work-related info), while others were total blanks (particularly personal history). Over time I gradually "regrew[24]" the linkages[25] to most memories, naturally or by various reminders (both the trigger and non-trigger variety).

Reminders in the form of a drinking trigger are discussed in Level 2. Most triggers in most forms tend to be negative—that's why they are drinking triggers! But not all triggers are negative (Zeal or Excitement), for example, and most aspects of raising Kids). While the discussion on Reminders was mostly negative, it can be a very real (and positive) tool for re-growing your "access" to many of your memories. One way to do this is to talk to family, take out old photos, look at old emails, etc., to get your brain to *recognize* what it did/said/saw. When it does that it is in effect creating new linkages to replace the ones you wiped out with drinking.[26]

• •

Drinkers who experience blackouts typically drink too much and too quickly, which causes their blood alcohol levels to rise very rapidly. College students may be at particular risk for experiencing a blackout as an alarming number of college students engage in binge drinking. Binge drinking, for a typical adult, is defined as consuming five or more drinks in about 2 hours for men, or four or more drinks for women.

Equal numbers of men and women reported experiencing blackouts, despite the fact that the men drank significantly more often and more heavily than the women. This outcome suggests that regardless of the amount of alcohol consumed, females—a group infrequently studied in the literature on blackouts—are at greater risk than males for experiencing blackouts. **A woman's tendency to black out more easily** probably results from differences in how men and women metabolize alcohol. **Females also may be more susceptible than males to milder forms of alcohol-induced memory impairments**, even when men and women consume comparable amounts of alcohol.

As illustrated by my own testimonial above, memory problems will vary greatly by individual, particularly in duration and categories of memory affected:

My memory has been affected from alcohol abuse- short term mainly and also organizational skills . . . I start something and then get easily distracted and change what I meant to be doing, I never used to be like this, I was a really good teacher, now I am flat out not remembering what day it is! and I am only 42. Drinking has definitely made me more vague and seriously forgetful, hang on what was I saying before . . . and yes, bad at organization and forgetful, did I just say that??? (Note: Poster is female)

Anonymous

While not a doctor, I would say that is never too late to get your memory back, even after decades of abuse. That said, it would be prudent to expect some permanent loss if there is no change at all after a long (e.g. over 2 years) period of sobriety.

I worry still about health. Although sober almost two years, my short term memory is shot. I have not seen my sponsor in a while. Life in general has been too busy. I am going to meetings but am scared of a relapse. I don't want to ever have a seizure or those anxious feelings again. What happens when one has a seizure? Can someone tell me? I am curious. Alcohol causes so many health issues. I don't, at age 56, want to see health problems. I need to be alive for my children.

Guest susan7, alcoholism.about.com

But the most likely outcome is that your memory *will* come back, but not equally in all areas of the brain, and at the same time:

After two long years of drinking my body had begun feeling the effects of alcohol. I quit at age 44 and it took my brain two years to recover. My memory is better, but not fully functioning as before. I still have trouble remembering words. Quit before it is too late. A grateful recovering alcoholic.

Guest Jacklyn S., alcoholism.about.com

Alcoholic Dementia

One of the most heart-breaking results of chronic alcohol abuse is *alcoholic dementia*. It is similar to Alzheimer's disease as it impacts memory and cognitive ability. Once an individual has progressed to this state, there may be little that can be done to reverse it. This type of dementia can develop in people of any age. Alcoholic dementia is comprised of two separate conditions known as Wernicke's encephalopathy and Korsakoff psychosis. This type of dementia can also be referred to as Wernicke-Korsakoff Syndrome or the extremely unpleasant sounding *wet brain*.

Symptoms include:

- Mental confusion
- Agitation and paranoia
- Lack of muscle coordination
- Eye problems
- The inability to create new memories
- False memories
- The loss of memories
- Hallucinations[27]

> *Anyone out there have any experience with alcoholic dementia? My husband, who has drank for years, has been exhibiting new and bizarre behavior. He is having big lapses in memory, forgets whole conversations (doesn't even remember talking to the person), repeats himself over and over (even when sober), one night told me that he had been talking to dead people and another time came crying to me about something that happened in Viet Nam (which I know didn't happen).*
>
> *He doesn't even remember telling me the story. The last was him picking a fight with my 18-year-old for no reason. It was so bad that I had to call the cops. I told him the next time he acts like that I am going to have him committed. The cop even told me it would be the thing to do. He has gotten scared over this (although I don't think he has stopped drinking) and has made an appointment with a therapist and doctor. But I know that there is a physical reason for the dementia, right?*

Selaine, alcoholism.about.com

Pancreatitis

Pancreatitis is inflammation of the pancreas. The pancreas is a large gland behind the stomach and close to the duodenum—the first part of the small intestine. The pancreas secretes digestive juices, or enzymes, into the duodenum through a tube called the pancreatic duct. Pancreatic enzymes join with bile—a liquid produced in the liver and stored in the gallbladder—to digest food. The pancreas also releases the hormones insulin and glucagon into the bloodstream. These hormones help the body regulate the glucose it takes from food for energy.

Normally, digestive enzymes secreted by the pancreas do not become active until they reach the small intestine. But when the pancreas is inflamed, the enzymes inside it attack and damage the tissues that produce them.

Pancreatitis can be acute or chronic. Either form is serious and can lead to complications. In severe cases, bleeding, infection, and permanent tissue damage may occur. Both forms of pancreatitis occur more often in men than women.[28]

Chronic, heavy use of alcohol is a common cause of pancreatitis. Over 200,000 people a year are admitted to the hospital with acute pancreatitis. It can be life threatening and is nearly always extremely painful.

I was hospitalized for acute pancreatitis, the next drink could kill me, but I can't stop. Constant pain in my guts.

Guest Danny, alcoholism.about.com

Pancreatic Cancer

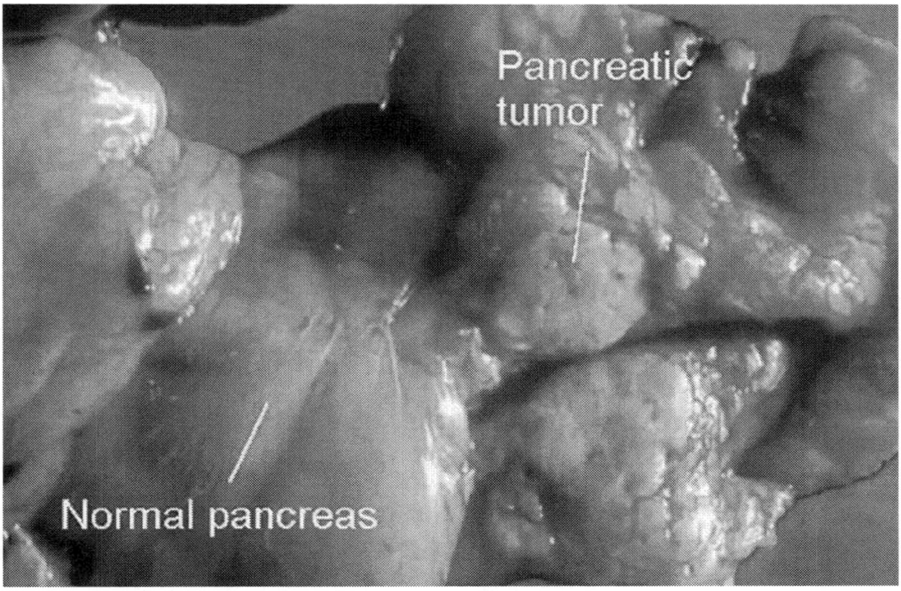

Figure 15: Pancreatic Cancer[29]

There are several different types of pancreatic cancer. The most common type is ductal adenocarcinoma, which starts from cells in the lining of the pancreatic ducts. Ninety-five percent of pancreatic cancers are ductal adenocarcinomas. Other, less common, types of pancreatic cancer include:

• *Cystic tumors*—these are fluid-filled sacs in the pancreas, some of which are cancerous

• *Acinar cell carcinomas*—these start from the cells that make pancreatic juice

• *Neuroendocrine tumors*—these begin in the endocrine cells where insulin and other hormones are made

• *Lymphoma*—this is a cancer of the lymphatic tissue in the pancreas.[30]

There is also some evidence of a higher risk for pancreatic cancer in people with alcoholism, although this higher risk may occur only in people who are also smokers.

Symptoms of pancreatitis may include:

• Acute upper abdominal pain that may spread to the upper back

• Vomiting

• Jaundice

• High or low blood pressure

• Fever

• Abdominal tenderness

• Weight loss

• Nausea

> *I did not believe people could die of drinking. But it just happened to my ex-fiancé—dead at 41 of alcoholic pancreatitis. He was very good at hiding his drinking and I have just realized now that so many things that happened to him, health-wise when we were together, were the result of his heavy drinking. If you are reading this and you feel like you may be drinking too much, or others have told you that you drink too much, please get help. Your drinking can and will kill you. Pancreatitis, cirrhosis, kidney failure, etc. And the slow death from alcoholism is not a good death. Please get help, before it's too late and all anyone can do is mourn you.*
>
> Anonymous

> *I was recently diagnosed with acute pancreatitis due to alcohol—despite*

the fact that my drinking habits are not over the top and certainly had not been just prior to developing stomach pain. But my Dr. says that the only thing I can do now to prevent pancreatic damage/possible other awful complications (including death) is to abstain completely from alcohol for the rest of my life. I'm 31.

Alaskagrl, city-data.com

Note: this is an *extremely* painful disease.

Skin Problems

You've seen the ruddy skin, the broken veins, the W.C. Fields nose. They are stereotypical, yet often accurate signs of alcohol abuse. Skin problems due to alcohol are the most visible indicators of abuse to the outside world. While you may be a functional alcohol and hide in all other respects, to a large extent the skin doesn't lie. It can be an excellent motivator in helping you quit drinking because ugly skin problems *can* go away if you do. They certainly did with me.

Alcohol has the impact it does on the skin because of the way it impacts your intake and usage of water. The water you drink serves as a type of internal moisturizer for your skin. Staying properly hydrated has all sorts of positive benefits for the skin, from smoothing out wrinkles to having a healthy glow. Alcohol, along with caffeinated drinks like coffee and soda, has the opposite effect. A drink will dehydrate you and deplete vital skin nutrients, making your skin appear dull. Dehydration directly explains the phenomena of "cotton mouth," where you wake up after a night of drinking with your tongue glued to your teeth and feeling like you camped out in the Sahara Desert. It also explains why, at least for some people, drinking a lot of water before going drinking can have beneficial effects the next day. Doctors have also found that those who drink heavily tend to have less healthy diets, which can deprive the skin of necessary nutrients that keep it looking healthy and young.

Drinking alcohol also causes facial blood vessels to dilate, and *repeated overindulgence can cause the vessels to dilate permanently,* causing red, spidery veins. And if you have a pre-existing skin condition, excessive alcohol use can worsen it. According to the American Academy of Dermatology, alcohol consumption may exacerbate flare-ups of rosacea and psoriasis, and dermatologists recommend minimizing your intake to avoid these issues.[31]

I'm a married mother of two and also work full time. I feel stuck in a rut! I drink 1–2 bottles of wine 3–4 nights a week! My skin is a mess and I look and feel awful! I don't seem to know when I've had too much!

Figure 16: The Effects of Alcohol with Skin Disease[32]

Common alcohol-induced skin conditions include:

• *Acne*—Your body's hormone levels may play a significant role in the hormonal disorder known as acne, which is signified by the development and recurrence of blackheads, whiteheads or cysts in the skin. Dozens of medical studies have demonstrated alcohol's significant role in creating hormonal imbalances and fluctuations in both men and women, which may contribute to the acne skin disorder.

• *Skin Problems from Cirrhosis*—Excessive consumption of alcohol can lead to a liver condition known as cirrhosis. Cirrhosis may negatively affect your skin, as well as general bodily functions like digestion. If you have cirrhosis, your skin may turn yellow and become marked with thin blood vessels visible on the surface.

• *Psoriasis*—Psoriasis is a chronic inflammatory disease that affects the skin by causing increased thickness of the skin due to its cells dividing more than they should normally. Alcohol abuse increases the possibility of aggravating or producing psoriasis.

• *Poisoning*—Acute alcohol poisoning may lead to your skin turning blue as blood flow to the surface decreases. The skin may also become moist to the touch and feel cold. This is a very dangerous condition and needs immediate medical attention.

• *Skin Aging*- Alcohol can make your skin look prematurely old. Common signs include wrinkles and skin discoloration. This may be because alcohol consumption lowers your consumption of healthy substances that could otherwise help repair and maintain the skin's appearance, and it may also release free radicals that damage the skin cells.

• *Bloating*—Drinking alcohol three hours or less before going to bed can make your facial skin look bloated and sag. This is because alcohol boosts the risk of your blood capillaries leaking. Over time, this can lead to wrinkles and poor facial skin tone.

But these are only part of the story; there are a number of other direct and indirect changes of alcohol on the skin. Alcoholic liver abnormality disturbs the estrogen and bile salt metabolism with peculiar signs of inflammation and redness on the skin. **In male alcoholics, there is an increase in the female hormone called estrogen and a decrease in the male hormone testosterone.** A rise in estrogen with a decrease in testosterone causes a feminizing effect such as development of breasts, feminine pattern of body and pubic hair and redistribution of body fat. Liver cirrhosis and portal hypertension account for the distinctive skin condition around the belly button called *caput medusae* or distended veins.

Alcoholics tend to have an increase in systemic and superficial skin problems with bacterial and fungal infections. This is because of alcohol-induced nutritional deficiency and impaired absorption of zinc and vitamins from the intestines, which results in decreased immunity. The deficiencies of zinc, vitamin C and trace elements cause a weakening of mucosal barriers, poor wound healing and a tendency for infections.

Other abnormalities of the skin include fissuring in the corners of the lips, pinpoint bleeds due to vitamin B deficiency (called pellagra), development of red and purple hemorrhagic spots on the skin and a tendency for bruising easily.

Alcohol, by acting on various enzymes, results in a flare up of porphyria cutanea tarda causing skin blisters and eruptions in sun-exposed areas that heal with scarring and milia (tiny white bumps in the skin). Alcohol is also responsible for disturbing the center of the brain that controls the tone of blood vessels. Alcohol causes dilation of skin vessels that increases the blood supply to the skin and gives the skin its distinctive redness and flushing. A genetic deficiency of an alcohol metabolic enzyme is also responsible for facial redness and erythema.[33]

> *I have chronic psoriasis and psoriatic arthritis and both conditions flare up when I drink too much. Also the medication I am on is strong and doesn't mix well with alcohol at all. So yes it is affecting my health. Plus I hate the short term effects such as vomiting loose stools headaches depression anxiety blackouts*
>
> Anonymous

Note: I had a variety of skin problems while I was drinking, including scab-like abrasions that would never heal. When I stopped drinking for good, they dried up and went away, though I had had them so long they left white patches on my skin.

Tip: If you have visible veins on your face (including your nose), there are various types of laser treatments that can greatly reduce them or even make them disappear.

SUICIDE AND PAINFUL DEATH BY ALCOHOL

Unfortunately, this giant health guillotine blade hanging over most alcoholics' necks is not enough to deter them from drinking. Some of that is likely to be "logic," as in "Well that won't happen to me," or "If it hasn't happened yet it won't" and the like. Even when an alcoholic has been told in no uncertain terms that another drink could kill him or her *specifically,* it usually is still not enough to prevent those next drinks, as illustrated over and over again in this chapter. And even if it is enough, without further help for their enforced sobriety their quality of life will likely suck, or worse. But what many people don't appreciate is how some of us are deliberately using it to commit suicide. Or using it not caring if we live or die. Or committing suicide while we are intoxicated. I'm not sure which is worse.

Suicide and Alcohol

In the United States, suicide is the 11th most common cause of death. According the NCBI, *over fifty percent of all suicides are associated with alcohol and drug dependence and at least 25% of alcoholics and drug addicts commit suicide.*[34] *Almost a quarter of ALL of the people who commit suicide will be intoxicated at the time.* And the overall trend towards suicide as a whole is increasing—the CDC announced in 2013 that suicides now outnumber automobile accidents for the first time!

Those who kill themselves will often do so impulsively. The individual is so overwhelmed by stress, specific issues or life in general that they are unable to comprehend what they are doing or the consequences of their actions fully. Of course, suicide is not a rational decision, which is where alcohol comes in. Alcohol interferes with rational thought, making the decision making far worse, and it makes people act impulsively and very short term in nature.[35]

> *I started dating my fiancé 2 years ago. I noticed then that he drank quite a bit. Over the past 2 years I have witnessed him falling down in the middle of the night, always having the flu, not going to work. It was always something. Six weeks ago, he decided he was hopeless and shot himself in the heart. I found him and life hasn't been the same since. After going through his bills and receipts I have come to found out he was drinking a case a day from 3:30 to 1:00 in the morning, vodka, bottles of wine, anything really. I had no idea this man was consuming all this alcohol. It would explain the yellow in his eyes and the funny smell that I had noticed in the last two weeks before he passed. This man had everything, I mean everything. Beautiful house, Harley, trucks, antiques, pond, farm and he worked for [the state DOT]. He had it all! Yet the alcohol is what killed him. Yet I feel like he was lying to me for 2 years. He loved me to death, but just couldn't stop. What a hold this drug must have!*
>
> anonymous

More specifically, there are a number of reasons why alcohol can increase the risk of suicide, including:

• Alcohol is a depressant. Considering that many alcoholics have depressive symptoms to start with (up to 40 percent[36]), you have an unpleasant multiplier effect. And those who are depressed are far more likely to kill themselves.

322   How to Conquer Your Alcoholism

• As noted, alcohol makes people act impulsively, and suicide is often an impulsive act

• Alcohol also increases levels of aggression, which is also closely associated with suicide (or behavior that would be considered suicidal to a sober person, like driving over 100 miles an hour on a two lane twisting road, etc.).

More broadly, alcoholism leads to deterioration in the life of the individual—losing family, friends, employment, possessions, and, of course, health. This deterioration will greatly increase the amount of stress they deal with in life, and suicide is the ultimate stress avoider (for them, NOT their loved ones).

But in addition to the horror of deliberate, sudden suicide aided by alcohol, there is another, much more insidious variation on alcohol and suicide—wanting to drink yourself to death.

The phone rang mid-morning on Sunday. My husband and I did our usual routine of looking at the caller ID, you know . . . the "It's for you, you pick it up" routine. It read "Private Number," so I decided to answer. On the other end was a strange woman's voice asking "Is this Wendi? May I please speak with Larry?" As I handed the phone to him I was immediately overcome with a sinking feeling in my heart . . . without a word coming out of his mouth yet, I already knew that this was the call we had been anticipating for quite some time.

You see, since I met Larry (which was almost seven years ago) he had been complaining about his brother's heavy drinking. I heard many stories about the kind of drinking he did, and was unfortunate enough to actually witness it when we all vacationed together for a week. Although he was drinking daily during the vacation, he didn't seem to be drinking nearly as much I had envisioned.

[T]hat was five years ago, and last Sunday my brother-in-law was found dead in his house. He drank himself to death!

We knew he had been hitting the bottle very heavily, and steadily, for quite some time. He would either call our house plastered, or not call for a few days in a row . . . meaning he was in his "black out" binge drinking mode. Three weeks ago he showed up at our door step, with the intention of going hunting with my husband. He literally could not walk. He had to be carried up the stairs. It is inconceivable to me how the man managed to make it out of his driveway, never mind the 390 mile drive from his house to ours. I had never seen anyone shake as badly as he did for the three days that he was here. We basically watched the man detox on our living room couch, then hop into his truck to make the six hour trip back home and proceed with his slow, and painful, suicide.

After receiving the phone call, we decided it would best to wait until early Monday morning to make the trip up there. While preparing for our trip we received three separate phone calls, warning us about how messy the place was. One call came from the State Trooper who was there for the removal of the body (and also had the foresight to remove the multiple "loaded" guns that were lying around the house,) and two more calls came from the neighbors who found the body. We were warned . . . but by no means could we have been prepared.

The instant my husband opened the door to that house I began to gag. The odor was beyond anything I could have ever imagined . . . and we were only at the entrance of the laundry room. There were clothes (both clean and extremely soiled) piled over the entire room, I could barely make out the washer and dryer underneath it all. We proceeded to the kitchen, where I almost lost my breakfast. There wasn't a single unsoiled dish, or clean spot in that room. The only way I can describe what I was smelling (and what I still can't get out of my head) was a combination of spoiled food, alcohol, dead animals, and feces combined. The farther we made our way into the house, the more powerful the odor became.

I completely broke down. I could no longer handle it. I have spent my entire life surrounded by the disease of "Alcoholism." My father died of an aneurysm at the age of 65, but his health had been failing for years due to his very heavy drinking and smoking. My younger sister had spent several nightmarish years in the depth of addiction before finding her footing 15 years ago. And I spent almost 30 years of my life trying to drink myself to death . . . although not quite as viciously as this man did. So when I saw what had become of him, and how badly his disease had progressed, I could not process what had happened at all . . . I still can't.[37]

So there you have it: suicide "induced" by alcohol via a bullet or pills or a bridge that might not have happened otherwise, or a *slow but deliberate* path to death by drinking.

Finally, there are other variations such as those who could not stand to live without alcohol, literally:

I had an uncle who was told that one more beer would kill him because of what it was doing to his body, and he very reluctantly stopped. However he did not get any additional help, and within a year committed suicide. There was no note, but his ex-wife (my aunt) strongly feels that his not being able to drink very significantly contributed to his decision to commit suicide. He simply could not cope, refused help, and never learned another way of living, so he chose death. Leaving behind four beautiful children.

anonymous

So even if you can or are forced to stop drinking, you must address the broader issue of alcoholism in your life and what is behind it, or you are likely to still have a very unpleasant—and perhaps short—one.

Suicide by alcohol using one of these forms is going to get worse. The CDC study noted two extremely alarming statistics: 1) that middle-aged suicides (age 35–64) have risen over 30% in the last decade, and 2) the number of men in this age range who commit suicide outnumber women by 4 to 1! This is very, VERY bad news. I strongly suspect that this "trend" is going to be overly represented by middle-aged alcoholics and others—particularly male—who kill themselves while, by, or because of drinking.

Painful Death by Alcohol

If all of the above still does not flip that switch in your head that alcohol is bad for you, and death by alcohol is *still* an abstract concept, think about it differently. Maybe yes, you readily concede that you shouldn't be drinking. But everyone dies, right? "Might as well go out doing something I love to do" you might say to yourself. Fine, everyone is going to die, of course. You may even be trying to commit a slow suicide in the back of your mind, but you should ask yourself a question—*do you want to die in agonizing pain?*

My father had cirrhosis. He never seemed like a drunk, and even held down a big job. But on his down time could drink through two or three bottles of red wine. He lied to us all about his diagnosis, saying he was fine, preferring instead to drink. Of course this caught up with him. The liver produces the coagulants that stop you from bleeding. When your liver starts failing, you start bleeding. In your stomach, from your mouth, through your ears, nose everywhere. My little sisters and I watched my 53-year-old father drown on his own blood over a 3 week period in hospital while, despite being classified as being in a 'stage 4 coma' was still aware enough to scream my name once and communicate through blinking that he needed

pain killers. He was on the transplant list but it was too late. Trapped in
your own body, drowning on your own blood is the future that awaits you.
And kids that will always remember you didn't love them enough to even
try and live.

mizmoo76, alcoholism.about.com

[My Husband] tried AA, treatment, therapy, Ativan, and Campal and he
just couldn't quit. He passed away of liver failure on July 13, 2012. [It was]
the most heart wrenching death to watch. I believe that if some alcoholics
would quit drinking if they had to watch the pain an alcoholic suffers when
they are dying. It is pure hell to see a loved on suffer and die like this.

Guest widow, alcoholism.about.com

If anything, I have learned that I don't want to die an alcoholic death. A
few years ago, I was confronted with the cold reality of untreated alco-
holism. Someone close to me began drinking heavily in part to silence the
punishing voice of their conscience. They had only used alcohol in modera-
tion up to the last few years, and had been given a clean bill of health just
months prior to a sudden decline. Being an alcoholic myself, I saw the pro-
gression from occasional use to excess on a daily basis. But I was unpre-
pared for what was to come.

I received a phone call informing me of this person's admission to the
SICU of a local hospital. He was suffering from severe abdominal pain,
and the doctors couldn't figure out why. When I saw them, it was obvious
to me that he was also experiencing symptoms of acute alcohol withdrawal.
Our brief conversation on that day would turn out to be our last.

As the next days passed, the pain became so intense that a morphine
induced sleep was the only way to keep him stable at all. But after a week,
organ failure became the paramount concern. As the sickness progressed,
kidney failure and a cardiac arrest prompted an emergency exploratory sur-
gery. Inside, the surgeon found a mass of infection where the now liquefied
pancreas used to reside. These septic remains had spread throughout the
body, propagating organ failure. The surgeon cleaned as much away as he
could and predicted a dismal outcome.

Two weeks after that first phone call, I was forced to make a decision as
to resuscitation efforts to be utilized when the next inevitable crash
occurred. [His] survival would be precarious and very limited at best, with
complications such as diabetes, constant pain, having to relearn how to
write and speak again, and an overall quality of life that would be a mere

shadow of their former self. That was in addition to the breaking of ribs and other agony that heroic measures would entail.

I tried to put myself in the same position as best as I could and made the choice. For the next three hours I stood beside holding the hand of someone who had always been there for me, and watched the monitors display the heart rate decrease to an unchanging horizontal streak. The last moment consisted of a sudden strong squeeze of my hand and a mix of blood and other fluids from the mouth and nose. It was finished.[38]

I got the call on a Wednesday night around seven telling me to get to the hospital. Since we had for years been expecting this, I thought that it would not affect me the way it did. I arrived at the hospital just as they were bringing [my uncle] in. I stood with my aunt and cousins waiting for them to come and tell us that he had not survived the trip. That did not happen. Instead they came out and said they would come and get us when they had him settled in the emergency room. After that it was us endlessly taking turns going back to see him and telling him goodbye.

What I saw that night was not my uncle the way I had known him. Instead there was this very yellow man whose stomach was so swollen that I thought at any minute it could burst. He was so yellow that the only way I can describe it, was that he was the color of a banana skin. This included his eyes, and even his lips and tongue.

Somehow, and I don't know how, he was still awake and talking to me like it was just another day. From seven pm to three am, this endless visiting went on. He eventually started coughing up blood and after a while they had to suction it out, but yet he still lay there talking. You could tell he was getting weaker by the minute, but it seemed as if he had so much he still needed to say.

We all said our I love yous and we went out to wait until they said we could go up. At three thirty they let us go up to see him. I remember his two grandsons going in the room as we were walking towards it, and they just walked in and came right out sobbing. My mom who was a former nurse went in to see him and then came back out and told his daughters they needed to get in there. As we all went in the room together, there he lay, no longer awake and talking but he had slipped into the coma in that thirty minutes while they were moving him.

We watch as his breathing got slower and slower, and then it stopped.[39]

Lest I end this section on such a horrible note, below is a post I found on one of the forums:

> *I'm only 16 I've never drank before. I came to this site because I had to write a report on alcohol and its effects. After reading some of these stories I'm convinced that I'm not going to take the risk and get into heavy drinking. And for all of you out there suffering there is light at the end of the tunnel, don't give up.*
>
> Guest Joe, alcoholism.about.com

THE CONQUER PROGRAM HEALTH ASSESSMENT GUIDE

Hopefully, the overview of the major health problems associated with alcoholism just scared the living shit out of you. That was the goal. If it resulted in a kind of alcoholism *Scared Straight* result, and you are determined to stop drinking now just to avoid the health nightmare—fantastic! But if it only served to sensitize you to the real unpleasantness coming at you, that will be sufficient for now.

The checklist at the end of this section is an easy way to tally the *specific* health problems OR symptoms that you have. Assessing how "bad" a health problem or symptom can be incredibly subjective. But there is medical precedent for trying to gauge the severity of such subjective problems, notably for pain:[40]

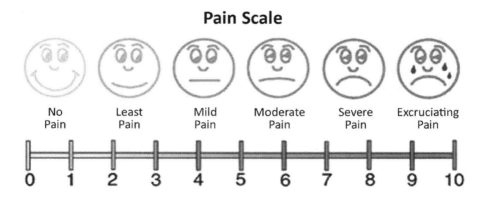

Figure 17: Commonly Used Pain Scale

This scale is simple, understandable, and standardized in the medical profession. It is also a great example of trying to quantify something that is unavoidably subjective. In addition, for certain types of diseases the medical profession has developed "Stage" definitions to articulate the seriousness, with cancer being the most notable:

Stage 0: This is an early form of cancer that is defined by the absence of invasion of tumor cells into the surrounding tissue. It is considered a precursor or incipient form of cancer.

Stage I: cancers are localized to one part of the body. Stage I cancer can be surgically removed if small enough.

Stage II: cancers are locally advanced. Stage II cancer can be treated by chemo, radiation, or surgery.

Stage III: cancers are also locally advanced. Whether the cancer is designated as Stage II or Stage III can depend on the specific type of cancer.

Stage IV: cancers have often metastasized, or spread to other organs or throughout the body. Stage IV cancer can be treated be chemo, radiation, surgery, or clinical trials.

I've used the concepts of scales and stages to take a crack below at something similar for assessing the severity of an alcohol-related health problem. I'm sure the headaches it causes in health professionals will soar to a 10 on the above pain scale, but it at least will give you a place to start. *Your doctor should be the one to do this assessment,* but doing it yourself is better than nothing, particularly if it forces you to get off your butt and see one.

● ●

The Conquer Program Alcoholic Health Problem Severity Scale

0–1 No symptoms at all; mild problem in your family history.

1–3 A discernible problem in your immediate family; Occasional episodes (once every 2–3 months); doctor comments that it is something to "watch out for." Alcohol is mentioned as a possible contributor.

3–5 More frequent episodes—once a month at least. Doctor indicates that it is a chronic condition, e.g.; it is not going away no matter what you do (exception: stop drinking). Medication is prescribed for that condition.

5–7 You have had to go to the emergency room or be admitted to the hospital at least once in the past year. Surgery for the condition is being considered. You have been told clearly that you need to dramatically cut down or eliminate drinking.

7–9 You have had to go to the emergency room or be admitted to the hospital 2 or more times in the past year. You have had surgery for the condition. Your doctor has issued a "Quit or Die" ultimatum regarding alcohol.

9–10 Condition requires MAJOR surgery (e.g., liver transplant). You have been diagnosed as terminal or in the last state of the condition. One drink may well kill you.

The purpose of assigning a severity and filling out the checklist in general is to make you think about how alcohol is affecting your health problem-by-problem, symptom-by-symptom. This analysis will, hopefully, force you to consider the effects of drinking on your health *in total.* Too often we tend to consider our health problems in isolation from each other, which is, usually, not unreasonable. For example, digestion problems are *typically* not connected to heart problems that are not connected to poison ivy.

But the word "typically" is not applicable when it comes to alcoholism; drinking could well be one of the root causes of all those aliments. As we've seen, alcohol can very negatively impact nearly all parts of the body and mind. *So if you have multiple health issues, you have to strongly consider the possibility that alcohol is at the bottom of many of your medical problems.*

Before you go any further in executing The Conquer Program, I strongly urge you to consult your doctor about these problems. Bring the scorecard with you as a consultation starter if you want, particularly if you haven't seen a doctor in quite a while, OR you have been lying to him or her about how much you drink. You will be glad you did, and *it may save your life.*[41]

TABLE 2: THE CONQUER PROGRAM HEALTH CHECKLIST

Condition/ Disease	Year Started	Severity (1–10)	Your Symptoms	Defense Action Taken/ Doctor's Comments
Alcoholism—Family History (at least 2 generations)				
Anxiety (e.g., GAD)				
Bad Breath (chronic)				
Breast Cancer (incl. Family History)				
Cancer—Other (incl. Family History)				
Cardiomyopathy				
Chronic Fatigue Syndrome				
Crohn's Disease				
Dementia (incl. Family History)				
Depression (incl. Family History)				

Condition/ Disease	Year Started	Severity (1–10)	Your Symptoms	Defense Action Taken/ Doctor's Comments
Digestive Problems				
Fetal Alcohol Syndrome [1]				
Fibromyalgia				
Gallstones				
Gastritis				
Gum Disease				
Heart Problems (incl. Family History)				
Heartburn (chronic)				
Hemorrhoids				
Hormonal Imbalance				
Hypertension				

Condition/ Disease	Year Started	Severity (1–10)	Your Symptoms	Defense Action Taken/ Doctor's Comments
Jaundice				
Irritable Bowel Syndrome				
Liver Disease				
Lung Disease				
Memory Problems				
Menopause Problems				
Metabolic Syndrome				
Oral Cancer				
Pancreatitis				
Panic Attacks				
Post Traumatic SD (PTSD)				

Condition/ Disease	Year Started	Severity (1–10)	Your Symptoms	Defense Action Taken/ Doctor's Comments
Restless Leg Syndrome				
Schizophrenia				
Sexual Dysfunction				
Skin Problems				
Suicidal Thoughts				
Tinnitus				
Ulcerative Colitis				
Ulcers				
Wet Brain				
Other				

⌧   ⌧   ⌧

This completes Phase 1 of the Conquer Program. Hopefully, you have achieved its three main goals:

1. Truly understanding and admitting you are an alcoholic,

2. Identifying all your major drinking triggers and their related triggers. You have identified which tips and Key Defense Levels you think will be particularly helpful in successfully defending you against those trigger-based alcohol attacks, and

3. Determined what, if any, damage alcohol has done and is doing to your body. In consultation with your doctor, develop a broader plan for limiting or correcting that damage, in sync with your broader efforts to stop drinking via the Conquer Program.

If you do not feel that you have accomplished the above, start over again, this time with much more attention to detail. If there were a quick, simple fix for alcoholism, it would have appeared long ago! You have to put some *real* effort into it. (Recognizing this, I've tried to make the Program and book overall as interesting and entertaining as possible, so it all doesn't feel like work).

Phase 1 should take you as little as a few days to perhaps a few weeks, depending on how fast you read and embrace the Conquer Program, how easy it was to identify your triggers and new ways of dealing with them without alcohol, and how fast your doctor can do an alcohol-focused analysis of your medical situation (if one had not been done already). However, if you zipped through it in just a couple of hours (for example, you went into it knowing you were an alcoholic and the specific damage it has done to your body). I would still encourage you to go back and reread it, particularly Level 2—Know Your Triggers. It is *absolutely essential* that you get that Level right, and your triggers may be far subtler or nuanced than you thought at first reading.

We now move into Phase 2, where your defense building begins in earnest.

PHASE 2

BUILD YOUR NEW DEFENSES

As noted in the introduction, much of this book and particularly this phase is in many aspects a revisiting of existing ways of dealing with alcoholism. It discusses "traditional" methods such as rehab, therapy, AA meetings and the like, delves into such "basics" as developing new hobbies, and touches on sensitive topics such as the role of religion in dealing with alcoholism.

That said, what I have tried to do is portray many of these topics in a different and *much* more practical light than I experienced when I first went through these traditional methods. As I've noted before and will continue to emphasize, one of my biggest complaints was how little of the traditional methods were *practical and useful* on a daily basis in combating my alcoholism. Much of it was general—"ear candy" that sounded good at the time but was a distant memory within days if not hours—and mostly useless when it came to helping me change my thinking or actions.

I've tried to enhance what I "learned" and experienced in this set of chapters and indeed the whole program and book as a whole. I hope that a new, much more practical take on these methods will make them much more impactful for you, the alcoholic and even you the alcoholic's family member or friend. At the end of Phase 2, if you believe you have gained a new appreciation for how you can conquer alcoholism based on the traditional methods, wonderful! If not, then at a minimum hopefully you will have a much more open mind with which to take on the Levels in Phase 3. Figure 13 below shows the six Levels in Phase 2:

Phase 2—Build New Defenses

Figure 18: The Six Levels of Phase 2

LEVEL 4—*Engage Friends and Family* starts the building of your support network, by engaging trusted friends and family with your admission of alcoholism and the other first steps you've taken towards sobriety. Engagement is universally preached, but unevenly applied in most treatment programs. We focus on who to engage (you *really* don't want *all* your friends and family involved with this), what they should expect, and how and when you should engage them.

LEVEL 5—*Detox* looks to inform you about the details of detoxification, separating the hype from the reality. The goal here is to learn how to make the most out of what will likely be a pretty unpleasant process.

LEVEL 6—*Rehab and Therapy* comes next, areas that most people are aware of in concept and woefully ignorant in practice, particularly when it comes to alcoholism. We dive into the details of the benefits and trade-offs of inpatient vs. outpatient rehabilitation, and discuss the myriad of potential therapy options that may or may not work for you and why.

With much of the "hard" stuff now under your belt, it's time to start the rebuilding of your life and accelerate the continuing building of your defenses against alcohol.

LEVEL 7—*Join a Community* builds on Level 4 by having you join an "alcoholic" community, such as Alcoholics Anonymous or Women For Sobriety (there are many to choose from). We do an in-depth analysis and critique of AA, since that is the 800 pound gorilla in the alcoholism treatment room.

You might even do more than one, or try variations with a given community. The important thing is to get out and link up with others who can understand what you have been through and what you face in the future. Along with your friends and family, this community support is critical for your defenses—*you can't do this alone!*

The balance of Phase 2 is focused on "retraining" what you do in your day-to-day life. Do not think of this as a burden—quite the contrary it is a key part of building a happy new life and actually a lot of fun! Since you are shaking up so much of your day-to-day by eliminating drinking, why not use it to break old habits and do fun new things? It is time worth spending—and you will have time to spend now that alcohol isn't consuming so much of your daily life!

LEVEL 8—*Break Bad Habits* focuses on identifying and eliminating unpleasant habits that may have been caused by or made worse by drinking. Whether it is cutting down on swearing or leaving your house clean each day, changes in your habits can have a major impact on your overall living environment, how others relate to you, and your overall attitude towards daily life.

LEVEL 9—*Develop New Hobbies* focuses on identifying new hobbies (or rediscovering old ones) that will allow you to enjoy that newly freed leisure time. Hobbies will offer some level of predictability to that freed up time that will prevent you from wandering back towards a drinking state of mind. These hobbies are not just meant to be fun, but to be key, active contributors to defenses against the triggers you identified in Level 2.

Since there are literally thousands of hobbies, this chapter helps you identify the things you should look for as you consider possible hobbies beyond just being fun, but also how they can counteract, minimize, soothe, or even eliminate particular types of trigger attacks. Remember, drinking took up a *huge* part of your former "leisure time." It is *essential* that you replace it with other purposeful and/or entertaining activities—ones that help you defend against alcohol in the process.

LEVEL 4

Engage Friends and Family

This level is the first full defense building level in the Conquer Program. The three Levels in Phase 1 were primarily foundational in nature, meaning they were intended to help you learn about yourself—why you drink and how it has left you defenseless and vulnerable to an ever-worsening life of alcoholism. In addition, Level 2 provided you with a great number of Tips that you can use to deal with those particular triggers that attack you the most, *without* alcohol. It also identified Key Defense Levels that will supplement, complement, enhance and join with these Tips to develop new and progressively stronger defenses, Level by Level.

Each of these new Levels offers additional ways, methods, techniques, and ideas for defense that can be used *on a practical, day-to-day basis* to successfully defend against alcohol attacks.

Again, where the real power of The Conquer Program shows itself is in *how* you combine all these—the tips that are applicable for each trigger (alone or in combination with the tips for their related triggers), and the Levels of Defense that support these tips and provide a broader structure for them. This combination is specifically for the purpose of trying to defend against *all* of the ways that alcohol can attack you *all* of the time. Alcohol only has to successfully attack you *once* for your life to get back on the road to destruction—you have to defend yourself *all* the time.

To do this *takes* time and is often difficult to do. But there are ways to make it easier, starting with engaging friends and family in your quest to Conquer Alcoholism, since:

YOU CAN'T DO IT ALONE

If there is one simple truth in trying to recover from or conquer alcoholism, it is that while *you* have to do it *for yourself,* you *can't do it alone.* Engaging friends and family early in the process of any program is a must in my opinion. And while it seems simple in words, there is no doubt that it can be tough to do. Pride and shame are the main reasons.

If you are like me, you tried to hide your alcoholism for as long as you could, even after admitting it to yourself. Who wants to seem "weak," "deficient," "powerless"—pick your adjective—even if none of those words are true? This is a frigging disease, but even after many years of becoming "mainstream" many people still have outdated (and very unpleasant) perceptions of alcoholics. Many of us—particularly older ones (say over the age of 35)—still consider it a particularly shameful condition whether we admit it or not.

Of course, your friends and family were likely to have seen your addiction long before you admitted it, Indeed *many of them probably did their best to make your life a living hell, under the totally misguided notion that they could "guilt" you into stopping drinking.* I emphasize this point for you nonalcoholics reading this book. In my opinion "Guilting" does not help the vast majority of alcoholics, and may well make things much worse (see the Guilt section of "Know Your Triggers" earlier in this book).

Even once you admitted you were an alcoholic and resigned yourself to having your friends and family know, it is still a far cry from asking them to help you out. Frankly, it is far easier to engage a stranger with the same problem than to ask someone you know (without the problem) for help. *But you need to do it.*

WHO AND HOW TO ASK FOR HELP

When I recommend engaging friends and family, I do not mean engaging *all* of them, nor even a large subset of them without some significant vetting. By vetting, I mean finding friend(s) and family member(s) (one minimum of each) who:

- Are not judgmental and can be objective
- Have a basic understanding of alcoholism as a disease
- Are fairly patient

- Are not gossips

- Are decent listeners

- Are willing to dedicate a reasonable amount of free time for you

- Will be there in an emergency

- Can deal with pressure and responsibility.

Hopefully, your first reaction is not: "Right! Like that is going to happen in my family!" It will probably be tougher to find family members who meet these criteria than it will be friends, but it is important to find at least one family member, as they are more likely to be willing to see you through the toughest times than friends who have their own family obligations. Of course, the best single person (in theory) can be your spouse/partner (if applicable):

> [Responding to a post by an alcoholic] *You are already on the right track. You know your drinking is a problem and it sounds like you are fed up with it. You have a support system behind you in your husband, who knows you have a problem but hasn't pushed you to confront it until you're ready.*
>
> Malvern Institute, cryingoutnow.com

Unfortunately, your spouse or partner may not fit all the criteria listed above, but it is hardly likely you can embark on this journey without his or her having become aware of it. This is *not* the time to treat getting sober as a surprise birthday present!

The person(s) you select (and agrees to help you) will be particularly important as you go through some of the tasks associated with parts of the program such as Detox (Levels 5 and 12) and Level 11—Make Yourself Sick of Alcohol (an optional Level). Indeed you may have to live with one of them for part of it. They will continue to be very important once you have achieved sobriety, as a key Level of defense in the circumstances where familiar, friendly, intimate faces are the best option in certain vulnerable situations.

For the most part, however, it is the moral support that family and friends can provide that is the most important reason for engaging them. While fellow alcoholics can provide a unique degree of support that (nonalcoholic) friends and family cannot, at the end of the day they are strangers who can only provide certain degrees and types of support, and can't be counted on to help you when things get really ugly, which they are likely to do at some point.

> *I woke my husband up at 5am this morning and told him that I wanted to stop drinking, and I needed his help. He held me and said how pleased he was that I had made this decision—and what did we need to do to make this possible.*

Anonymous, cryingoutnow.com

One exception to not being able to depend on strangers for support is if you attend Alcoholics Anonymous meetings and you get a sponsor as part of that program (both discussed in great detail in Level 7—Join a Community). An AA sponsor can be a great type of person to have in your court when you are struggling for sobriety. However, since AA is not for everyone, and in particular since sharing your deepest feelings and problems with a complete stranger (at first) makes many people very uncomfortable, a sponsor may not work for you.

So the bottom line here is: swallow your pride, put aside any "shame" you might feel, and ask for the support of (some) of your friends and family. **Besides being an essential Level for defense in this program, you will find that just asking for support (and in the process maybe admitting your alcoholism to them for the first time) will be very cathartic[1] by itself.**

Ways to Get Started

By now you, hopefully, have recognized the potential benefits of engaging others to help you in your Conquer quest. The criteria for selecting these trusted few have been laid out, so there is no uncertainty there. What may still be very uncertain is how you bring up the topic and request support in the first place.

Obviously how you do this will depend very significantly on whether that person knows about your excessive drinking or not. This is more likely a to-what-degree question; if they are close to you in any way they would have to be blind not to know you are a heavy drinker. But even so that is not the same thing as knowing you are an alcoholic.

The challenge might be compounded if you tried to stop before and failed. In this case you will need to introduce them to the Conquer Program (a good idea in any scenario). Get their opinions on how you scored on the Conquer Quiz and your initial take on what your major drinking triggers are. Not only will that help convince them that you are really serious, you will undoubtedly get great feedback, such as perhaps highlighting a trigger that you missed, or (as detailed later on) helping you figure out which are the highest priority for you.

If the person does not realize you are an alcoholic or even have a serious drinking problem (meaning you were great at hiding it), then you may need to open up a conversation something like this:

> *"Hey [insert name here], you may have noticed that I seem to be drinking a lot lately. Well, I've been doing that a long time, a lot more than you many realize, and I think I have a big problem. I am going to try a program that I think will help. Part of the program strongly suggests having a close (friend, family member) involved in various parts of the program. Since I consider you a very close (friend, family member), I was wondering if you would be up to being involved in it."*

If they say yes, one of the first things they will ask is what is involved on their end. Besides suggesting they skim through this book, you might also say something like:

> *"It depends on where I am in the Program. It has 13 levels, most of which will not require much, if any, effort on your part."*

At this point what else you say will depend on where you think they can really help. If you have it mapped out, fine, but odds are you haven't fully thought through it at this point in reading this book. You can say something like:

> *"I'm not 100% sure. I would like someone to call while I am in Detox. You might also go through the trigger list with me to see if I've left any off, or you think I should prioritize some higher than others. And for some of those triggers, you may be very high on how I cope with them without drinking. It might add up to a few hours a week."*

Odds are they will be flattered and honored at your request, particularly as they learn more about it. You might ask them to go through the Conquer Quiz with you, both to confirm your initial answers (or add more points to it), as well as using it as a basis of discussion and opening up about your problem, which can only help both of you to start interacting (and even bonding) about the experience. You could also ask them for help in identifying your bad habits (discussed in Level 8—Break Bad Habits), which are often very hard for someone to see for themselves. They likely will find great fun in pointing out your bad habits! If so you should not take it personally; instead, view it as a kind of a partial "makeover" of your personality that will only result in good things.

The above should be a reasonable list for a close friend or family member to accept. Make sure though that you have gone through the vetting process described above to make certain they are a good fit. Once you ask it may be difficult to "un-ask." You might prepare for a rejection— some people may not have the time or even freak out about the whole thing. If so don't take it personally, just say you understand and ask them to keep it to themselves.

Asking someone to help however takes a different tone if you decide you are going to detox yourself, and you want his or her help. As discussed in Level 5—Detox, detoxing under medical supervision is *strongly* recommended. However, there are situations (mostly due to time and money) where you feel you can't go the medically supervised route and that you can detox "on your own." But on your own should *not* mean by yourself—you need someone near you as much as possible to help you deal with possible problems. You will need to make that someone understand that it is a serious commitment you are asking, one that requires them to be checking up on you pretty frequently and possibly even living with you part of the time or vice versa. They may even need to be ready to take you to the ER if the detox becomes particularly worrisome. This kind of commitment is a game changer in terms of commitment, and they may be reluctant to do so.

USING FRIENDS AND FAMILY AS AN ALCOHOL DEFENSE

You will find that you will use this Level very often for triggers that require some degree of relaxation or activity in a social interaction, such as Anger, Kids, and Loneliness among many others. You will also particularly need them in circumstances where their knowledge of what you are trying to do and intimate knowledge of your history will be of particular value, such as Change, Mid-Life Crisis, Relationships, and Relatives.

Engaging friends and family will be of special importance as you go through the physical Levels of this program: Level 5—Detox, Level 11— Make Yourself Sick of Alcohol (optional), and Level 12—The LAST Detox. Even if you do medically-supervised detox, there is nothing like physical unpleasantness to really make you want to have a caring shoulder to cry on, bitch at, or even help you clean up from.

While fairly intense face-to-face interactions with friends and family will sometimes be needed as you go through this program, for many talking on the phone or casual face-to-face get- togethers will often do the job, depending on the trigger(s) and the particular circumstances you are facing that day. Do them in environments that exclude other possible triggers to the extent possible. This means no bars, not at their house if they have screaming kids (if Kids or Noise is one of your triggers), etc. Also do them when you both have enough time to deal with the circumstance you are dealing with. If a 15-minute phone conversation will do it—great, if more time is required, make sure you find a way to do it so your conversation is not cut short.

In today's world, of course, there are many other ways of getting together with friends and family other than face-to-face or a phone call. Email is one, though the time lag can defeat the purpose. Texting is better but is inherently limited on how much you can say. But it can work well in many situations. Both email and texting, and of course phone calls and in person conversations have the added advantage of being private, which can be extremely important when you are talking about alcoholism and alcoholism treatment.

Notes on Using Online Resources

Online social media—Facebook in particular—is great for venting your feelings and in general connecting with people you might otherwise rarely do so via phone or person. *However,* be *very* aware that these online forums, and in particular those where you can*not* be anonymous, are NOT private—not anywhere close to it. *Everything* you post on Facebook and Twitter is monitored by people other than your "Friends"—total strangers looking for objectionable content, by legions of advertisers, and often by total strangers just looking to snoop.[2]

The general rule of thumb is "if you don't want the world to see it, don't post it on the Internet." This rule of thumb is approaching a near certainty as everyone tries to make money off of what everybody else on the Internet is doing or saying. *SO, if you do not want the world to know you are an alcoholic, do NOT post anything related to your problems with alcohol on Facebook or any forum that can be personally linked with your identity.*

That said, using some sort of Internet resource still can be a great way of being (or at least seeming) connected with the outside world when phone, face-to-face, texting or email isn't an option at the time and you just want to post/share your (non-alcohol-related) feelings with your "friends."

But if sharing alcohol-related feelings is what you need to do at the moment—and online is the only option—there are FAR better options to do so. Alcohol-specific sites such as *www.alcoholism.about.com* and *www.cryingoutnow.com,* as well as other community sites sponsored by specific programs such as Women For Sobriety (*www.womenforsobriety-online.com/*) provide relatively safe, anonymous outlets for your issues with alcoholism. Other sites such as *www.socialanxietysupport.com* provide trigger-specific outlets and idea-sharing forums. Sites such as these are discussed in Level 7—Join a Community (for alcohol-specific forums) and in the Tips section for many of the triggers discussed in Level 2.

Additional Ideas and Concerns on This Level

Asking for the kind of help discussed above can put a lot of pressure on a person, so again be sure in your vetting process that they are both willing and able to take it. Not everyone can, even a parent or sibling. Recognize that they have their own lives, and this is going to draw down on some of it.

Additional pressure will be felt from all sides if this is not the first time you have tried to get sober. They may be extremely skeptical. In those cases strongly urge them to read this book in its entirety to have them fully understand how it is different. Them reading the intro or doing a 15-minute skim is not going to be enough. Sitting down with them to discuss each of the Levels may help greatly even if they are reluctant to read the book.

Now that you have at least one friend and/or family member ready to assist you, let's turn to what many alcoholics fear the most: detoxification.

LEVEL 5

Detox

Detoxification is not exactly about *building* defenses—unlike most of the Levels in this program—as it is *clearing the debris* from your mind and body from its past battles with alcohol. To continue the analogy, this will allow you to continue building your broader defenses on a clear(er) field, instead of trying to do so upon the rubble of your active drinking. If you haven't stopped drinking by the time you reach this Level (which is very likely), well, *now* is the time. Dependence on alcohol gets worse with time in every way—mentally, emotionally, and physically. Detox follows a similar path; the more and longer you drink, the more difficult the detoxification process.

INTRO TO DETOXIFICATION

Type in "what is detoxification" in Google, and you get:

- *The process of removing toxic substances or qualities.*

- *Medical treatment of an alcoholic or drug addict involving abstention from drink or drugs until the bloodstream is free of toxins.*[1]

Detox's overall goal is to get rid of the physical dependence your body and mind has on alcohol, a dependence that has developed due to the drinking of large amounts over an extended period of time. Let's explore what this means in detail:

Physical Dependence on Alcohol

Dependence on alcohol has two main components. One is mental/psychological, where you have come to *associate* alcohol as a way to "relieve" or "deal with" various life issues such as Boredom or Guilt. These were discussed *extensively* in Level 2—Know Your Triggers.

The second is *physical* dependence, where your mind and body have become so chemically acclimated to the presence of alcohol in your system that its absence starts to have a material, visible effect on you. In other words, you experience physical *withdrawal* from alcohol when it is out of your system for too long. Signs of this happening when you go without a drink for too long include:

- Getting sweaty

- Tremors or shakes

- Feeling sick or vomiting, and/or

- Feeling panicky, anxious and agitated.[2]

The Role of Tolerance in Alcohol Dependency

While physical dependency occurs when you drink large amounts over a long period of time (how much/how long is discussed shortly), it is nearly always preceded in the alcoholic by a building up of your "tolerance" to alcohol, essentially meaning having to drink ever-larger amounts of alcohol to achieve the same effect.

There are different types of alcohol tolerance. It is possible to have more than one of these. Knowing which one(s) are applicable can be very helpful to the alcoholic in understanding how he or she got to be one in the first place. These include:

- Functional Tolerance

- Acute Tolerance

- Environment-Dependent Tolerance

- Learned Tolerance

- Metabolic Tolerance

● ●

Types of Alcohol Tolerance

Functional tolerance. People develop a tolerance when their brain functions adapt to compensate for the disruption caused by alcohol in both their behavior and their bodily functions, known as functional tolerance. *Chronic heavy drinkers display func-*

tional tolerance when they show few obvious signs of intoxication even at high blood alcohol concentrations (BAC's), which in others would be incapacitating or even fatal. *Because the drinker does not experience significant behavioral impairment as a result of drinking, tolerance may help the consumption of ever increasing amounts of alcohol. This can result in physical dependence and alcohol-related organ damage. Author's note: This type of tolerance is consistent with people who seem to be able to "hold their liquor." This allows them to continue drinking long after "normal" people would have stopped (or had others stop them).*

Development of tolerance to different alcohol effects at different rates also can influence how much a person drinks. Rapid development of tolerance to unpleasant, but not to pleasurable, alcohol effects could promote increased alcohol consumption. Author's note: This last sentence is huge, in that you can "tolerate" hangovers as a necessary "cost" of the pleasurable effects of alcohol.

Acute tolerance. Although tolerance to most alcohol effects develops over time and several drinking sessions, it also has been observed within a single drinking session. This phenomenon is called acute tolerance. *It means that the alcohol-induced impairment is greater when measured soon after beginning alcohol consumption[3] than when* measured later in the drinking session, even if the BAC is the same at both times. *Author's note: this is consistent with the "rush" right after you begin drinking. More on this in Level 11.*

Environment-dependent tolerance. The development of tolerance to alcohol's effects over several drinking sessions is accelerated *if alcohol is always administered in the same environment or is accompanied by the same cues,* called environment-dependent tolerance. This develops in particular for "social" drinkers in response to alcohol-associated cues. *This suggests that for many people, a bar contains cues that are associated with alcohol consumption and promote environment-dependent tolerance. Author's Note: This means that drinking in the same place or situation, like a bar or after-work hangout, is not a good thing. It could even apply to other repeat environments such as sitting in your favorite chair during a football game, making you crave a beer when you otherwise would not want one. It is one more reason to avoid bars, parties, and other types of environments where booze is always one of if not the leading part of the environmental setting.*

Metabolic Tolerance. Tolerance that results from a more rapid elimination of alcohol from the body is called metabolic tolerance. It is associated with a specific group of liver enzymes that metabolize alcohol and that are activated after chronic drinking. *Enzyme activation increases alcohol degradation and reduces the time during which alcohol is active in the body,* thereby reducing the duration of alcohol's intoxicating effects. *Author's Note: On the surface you might think this is a good thing, but it is not,* *particular the day after. I believe I personally had/have this "ability," as I practically never got hangovers. All that did was eliminate the typical 1–3 day period where severely hung-over people don't drink ("Never again!" they say). Until the following weekend. The mind does not remember pain for better or worse—worse in my opinion when it comes to drinking. So I had no residual pain and agony to keep me from drinking the very next day, which of course I did.*

Learned tolerance. The development of tolerance also can be accelerated by practicing a task while under the influence of alcohol, called behaviorally augmented (i.e., learned) tolerance. *Humans can develop a tolerance more rapidly and at lower alcohol doses if they practice a task while under the influence of alcohol.*

Learned and environment-dependent tolerance has important consequences for situations such as drinking and driving. Repeated practice of a task while under the influence of low levels of alcohol, such as driving a particular route, could lead to the development of tolerance, possibly reducing impairment. However, *the tolerance acquired for a specific situation is not readily transferable to new conditions. A driver encountering an unexpected situation could instantly lose any previously acquired tolerance to alcohol's impairing effects on driving performance.*[4] *Author's note: This means that you may think you can drive home ok after you've been drinking, because you know the route so well. But any unexpected deviations could destroy this "knowledge," making your driving much more dangerous almost instantly.*

The bottom line is that increased tolerance—in whatever form—causes the alcoholic to drink more to achieve the same effect, which progressively increases the chemical changes in your mind and body and ultimately causes a physical addiction to alcohol. **Managing the taking away of this chemical dependence—safely and effectively—is what Detox is all about.**

How Much/How Long Does It Take to Get Physically Dependent?

The "simple" answer is however much you drink for however long it takes before you start having the signs of physical dependence described earlier. Since those signs of physical dependence will manifest themselves in as little as a few hours to as long as 2 days, it is relatively safe to say if you haven't had any signs after 2 days of not drinking that you are not yet physically dependent.

However, that "answer" doesn't really provide much guidance on *getting* dependent, and is more complicated since physical dependency depends on many things, including gender, body weight, "tolerance" of alcohol, diet, and exercise. However, a good rule of thumb for how much you need to drink to "achieve" physical dependence is the following:

- Men who have 15 or more drinks[5] a week

- Women who have 12 or more drinks a week

- Anyone who has five or more drinks per occasion at least once a week[6]

How *long* drinking these amounts is another question, even less easily answered. It could be as little as a few weeks to as many as several months of the amounts above. Consistency of that drinking is certainly a factor. If you average 15 drinks a week over 3 months for a total of 180 drinks, its impact could be very different from if you drank 20 drinks for 3 weeks, stopped completely for a week, and then repeated the same thing for the next two months. While it's the same number of total drinks, in effect you were giving your body some "off time" to do mini-withdrawals that may or may not be visible.

The point is *not* that you can "game" your body to avoid the most severe symptoms of physical dependence and withdrawal. The point *is* that you *will* become physically dependent on alcohol relatively quickly no matter how many stops[7] you have along the way, and you will need to deal with it through detoxification.

THE POSSIBLE SIDE EFFECTS OF DETOX

This section is not to scare the bejezzus out of you, but to make you aware of the *possible* serious side effects of the process. While these effects are statistically unlikely, in my opinion the more you know of the possibilities (and probabilities), the more relaxed you will be throughout the process. Trust me on this: so much of the process will be unknown to you, you need to grab hold of all the knowledge you can get before hand—the key point of this Level!

The first time you go through a *serious*[8] effort at stopping drinking is a scary one. You don't know what to expect; you've heard a ton of horror stories, and bottom line you are probably scared shitless about facing the world without alcohol. How you got to the point of being willing to go through detoxification is important and interesting in the abstract. Now that you are here—facing the prospect of life without the alcohol— the "why" can seem like a distant memory. Don't let that happen! *Keep refreshing your mind about why you are here!* It will give you the strength to get through detox. And detox does require strength—there is no way around it.

> *The first three days were living hell. I slept a total of five hours in three days. Went through withdrawals, tremors, etc. Blood pressure went through the roof. I truly believed I thought I was going to have a heart attack. Anxiety set in bad. Now it's been five days and I feel much better. I still feel a little funky, but much better.*
>
> Fishman, alcoholism.about.com

The first and most important rule about Detox, particularly your first time, is *DO NOT DETOX ALONE, AND IF AT ALL POSSIBLE DO IT UNDER TRAINED MEDICAL SUPERVISION.* Detoxification can be extremely dangerous as the body reacts to the absence of the substance it has become accustomed to, often over a period of years if not decades. *Burningtree.com* provides the following synopsis:

● ●

Major Symptoms of Alcohol Detoxification

Mental and Neurological Reactions

Within six to forty-eight hours of the last drink, mental and neurological changes may suddenly develop in individuals undergoing alcohol detoxification. Symptoms such as visual, auditory, or olfactory hallucinations may occur in which the heightened effect of images, sounds, or even smells in any type of environmental situation may induce extreme flight or fight responses. Seizures are often brought on by delirium tremens (DTs), and may range in severity from mild to grand mal. The profound impact of alcohol withdrawal on the brain is so intense that even a mild seizure can lead to respiratory distress and heart failure if untreated. Other mental reactions to alcohol withdrawal include confusion, disorientation, difficulty talking, and temporary loss of short-term memory.

Heart Attack, Stroke, and Death

Chronic alcohol abusers are at the greatest risk for experiencing the most dangerous withdrawal symptoms from alcohol. As mentioned previously, seizures are commonly associated with delirium tremens and manifest the primary neurological impact of alcohol withdrawal on the brain. Seizures and DT's often create irregular cardiac activity such as palpitations, heart arrhythmias, tachycardia, and abnormal spikes in blood pressure that increase the potential risk of succumbing to cardiovascular injury or death.[9]

• •

Clearly this is NOT something to mess around with. DTs in particular are something to be worried about. Though I never experienced them personally, in rehab (my first detox) I "roomed" with someone who had the DTs, and let me tell you he was not a happy camper. They were coming to check on him every 10 minutes it seemed. They apparently were waiting on a free room in their dedicated DT area or equivalent, as he was moved in a few hours. It was NOT a fun few hours I can tell you, with his constant moaning and groaning punctuated by occasional yells.

• •

More on Delirium Tremens

Latin for "shaking frenzy," —also referred to as The DTs, "the horrors," or "the shakes."— Delirium Tremens is an acute episode of delirium (severe confusion) that is, usually, caused by withdrawal from alcohol. While withdrawal from other substances can cause DTs, withdrawal reactions as a result of physical dependence on alcohol is the most dangerous and *can be fatal*. It often creates a full-blown effect, which is physically evident through shivering, palpitations, sweating and in some cases, convulsions and death, if not treated.

In the U.S., fewer than about 50% to 60% of alcoholics will develop any significant withdrawal symptoms upon cessation of alcohol intake, and of these, only 5% of cases of acute alcohol withdrawal progress to DT. Mortality was as high as 35% before the advent of intensive care and advanced pharmacotherapy; in the modern era of medicine, death rates range from 5–15%.

The main symptoms of DTs are nightmares, agitation, global confusion, disorientation, visual and auditory hallucinations, fevers, hypertension, diaphoresis, and other signs of autonomic hyperactivity (tachycardia and hypertension). These symptoms may appear suddenly but can develop 2–3 days after cessation of drinking heavily with its highest intensity on the fourth or fifth day. Also, these "symptoms are characteristically worse at night."

In general, *DTs are considered as the most severe manifestation of alcohol with-drawal,* which occurs 3–10 days following the last drink. Other symptoms include intense perceptual disturbance such as visions of insects, snakes, or rats. These may be hallucinations, or illusions related to the environment, e.g., patterns on the wallpaper or in the peripheral vision that the patient falsely perceives as a resemblance to the morphology of an insect, and are also associated with tactile hallucinations such as sensations of something crawling on the subject. DTs usually include intense feelings of "impending doom," as well as severe anxiety and feelings of imminent death.

DT should be distinguished from alcoholic hallucinosis, which develops about 12 to 24 hours after drinking stops and involves auditory and visual hallucinations, most commonly accusatory or threatening voices. This condition is distinct from DTs since it develops and resolves rapidly, involves a limited set of hallucinations and has no other physical symptoms. *Alcoholic hallucinosis occurs in approximately 20% of hospitalized alcoholics and does not carry a significant mortality.* In contrast, DT occurs in 5–10% of alcoholics and carries up to 15% mortality with treatment and up to 35% mortality without treatment.[10]

• •

Like alcoholics need one more thing to worry about when facing sobriety, but it is a sad truth. The good news is that you have a relatively small statistical chance of enduring an acute detox such as described above, *but you won't know until you've done it. It is best to have your Detox done under clinical/medical supervision if you can possibly swing it. If you can't, do it with someone else who is in a position to call 911 if things start to seem bad. This may require you living with them (or vice versa) for the entire detox period.*

TYPES OF MEDICALLY SUPERVISED DETOX

Many rehabilitation programs, particularly ones done in hospitals or hospital-like[11] facilities, offer medically supervised detoxification periods and services as part of a much broader set of addiction services. These services are a natural extension of their broader Rehab programs, as all require you to be detoxed before entering the main body of their treatment.

There are five levels of detoxification care, according to the American Society of Addiction Medicine (ASAM).[12]

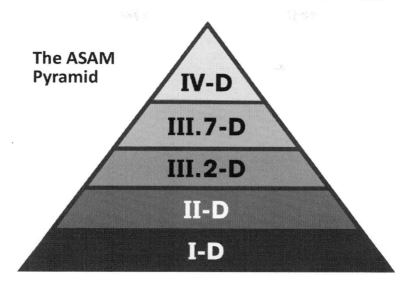

The ASAM Pyramid

IV-D

III.7-D

III.2-D

II-D

I-D

Figure 19: ASAM Five Levels of Detoxification Care

In order of increasing severity and medical intensity, these are:

Level I-D—Ambulatory Detoxification without Extended On-Site Monitoring

Elements include:

• Organized outpatient service.

• May be delivered in an office setting, healthcare or addiction treatment facility or a patient's home.

• Trained clinicians provide medically supervised evaluation, detoxification and referral services in regularly scheduled sessions.

• Services should be delivered under a defined set of policies and procedures or medical protocols.

Level II-D—Ambulatory Detoxification with Extended On-Site Monitoring

Elements include:

• Organized outpatient service.

• May be delivered in an office setting or healthcare or addiction treatment facility.

- Trained clinicians provide medically supervised evaluation, detoxification, and referral services in regularly scheduled sessions.

- Essential to this level of care is the availability of appropriately credentialed and licensed nurses (RN, LPN) who monitor patients over a period of several hours each day of service.

Level III-D—Residential/Inpatient Detoxification

There are two different parts within this level, depending on the setting. The first is Level III-D, or Residential/Inpatient Detoxification. Criteria are provided for two types of Level III detoxification programs:

- The *"residential"* level has in the past been synonymous with rehabilitation services.

- Detoxification services and the *"inpatient"* level of care have been synonymous with acute inpatient hospital care.

Level III.2-D—Clinically Managed Residential Detoxification

- Sometimes referred to as "social setting" detoxification.

- Organized service that may be delivered by *appropriately trained staff* that provide 24-hour supervision, observation, and support for patients who are intoxicated or are experiencing withdrawal.

- Characterized by emphasis on peer and social support.

Level III.7-D—Medically Monitored Inpatient Detoxification

The second part of this level is Level III.7-D, defined by the following characteristics:

- Organized service delivered by *medical and nursing professionals*, which provides for 24-hour medically supervised evaluation and withdrawal management.

- A permanent facility with inpatient beds and services that are delivered under a defined set of physician-approved policies and physician-monitored procedures or clinical protocols.

- 24-hour observation, monitoring, and treatment are available.

- Relies on established clinical protocols to identify patients who are in need of medical services beyond the capacity of the facility in order to transfer such patients to the appropriate level of care.

• Provides care to patients whose withdrawal signs and symptoms are sufficiently severe to require 24-hour inpatient care.

• Sometimes provided by overlapping with Level IV-D services (as a "step down" service) in a specialty unit of an acute general or psychiatric hospital.

• Full resources of an acute general hospital or a medically managed intensive inpatient treatment program are not necessary.

Level IV-D—Medically Managed Intensive Inpatient Detoxification

The mother of all detoxes, it includes:

• Organized service delivered by medical and nursing professionals, which provides for 24-hour medically directed evaluation and withdrawal management in an acute care inpatient setting.

• Provides care to patients whose withdrawal signs and symptoms are sufficiently severe to require primary medical and nursing care services.

• 24-hour observation, monitoring, and treatment are available.

• Specially designed for *acute* medical detoxification.

There are no statistics that I could find that break out Detox by level of care, though most planned (as opposed to emergency) supervised detoxes appear to take place at Level III.[13] If you choose to Detox in a clinical/medical professional care setting, make sure you understand which Level(s) the facility and staff is licensed to provide. Such licenses are issued at a state level, and may or may not specifically follow the ASAM designations above, so be sure to get into *specific* detail about the services the facility does and does not provide.

WHAT TO EXPECT STEP BY STEP

While each facility (and intensity level) will have its own structure, you can generally expect the following:

Selecting the Treatment Facility

The "easy" way to do this is to have your medical doctor or psychiatrist (whoever is treating your alcoholism) select the facility for you. The selection may be based on their experience and relationships with the facility staff. It may also greatly depend on your commitment for a full

Rehabilitation stay beyond the initial Detox; many facilities that offer Rehab services require you to be detoxed before arriving, thereby excluding those facilities. Many hospitals offer Detox-only services that may be your best choice if Rehab is not in your plans. It also may be a simple matter of what and who your insurance covers.[14]

If you are doing this yourself, with no professional guidance, and/or you still have many options open to you, selecting a facility can be more difficult. The Website Resources section at the end of this book may help, as will general web searching. I particularly recommend getting testimonials about particular programs directly from former patients if possible. Also, depending on the state you live in (or want to Detox in), there may be a state-run department specifically for substance abuse, such as the New York State OASAS (Office of Alcoholism and Substance Abuse Services): *www.oasas.ny.gov/pio/needhlp.cfm*. A general index of treatment centers, that may (or may not) include detoxification services, can be found at *www.theagapecenter.com/Treatment-Centers/index.htm*.

Making Arrangements

Once you've selected your facility, you will likely have to make a reservation, just like a hotel, though some facilities allow walk-ins. There may be a waiting list to get in (known as an "available bed"), so it might be as long as a couple weeks between making the call to the center and actually being admitted. This delay can obviously create problems about what to do in the meantime. Many people understandably get cold feet and back out if they cannot get in within a couple days of making the decision to detox.

This shows the importance of having one of your key friends or family members step in. He or she can keep you committed to the detox process and make/handle the reservation process for you so you won't obsess about it—a kind of detox travel agent (and chauffeur to take you when a slot opens up). You generally won't want to take a car (even if you happen to be sober at time). You may not even be allowed to have a car on the premises in order to prevent you from going "off-campus" to get alcohol. This is particularly true if you are also doing broader rehabilitation, discussed in Level 6—Rehab and Therapy.

Generally 2–5 days is the normal time to get alcohol completely out of your system, depending on your drinking history, how recently you drank (and how much) and personal physical characteristics.

Preparation and Check-In

Preparation—What to Bring (and Not Bring)

You should be very aware that all of the possessions you bring to any medically supervised Detox will be examined, and possibly rejected or held for the duration of your stay. You should contact the facility about what you can take with you. You may or may not be allowed to smoke on the grounds, but they may give you a nicotine patch if smoking is not allowed.

See if you are allowed to bring some books to read, and you may have to leave your laptop/iPad, etc. at home. They want you focused on your Detox (and if applicable) your broader Rehab. You can bring your phone, but it may be held and you probably won't be able to use it often (it is possible that you may have to use an old-fashioned pay phone, so plan accordingly, e.g., bring your contact numbers and lots of quarters for the pay phone). People visiting you *cannot* bring you food or drink.

Check to see if they will provide cosmetics (e.g., shampoo); some of these can contain alcohol and as such prohibited.[15] In general, they will be very paranoid about anything that can be used to hide booze or drugs, particularly if you or other patients have been forced to be there in the first place. You may be required to bring comfortable clothing that does not have any slogans on it, or have drawstrings, including sneakers with laces.[16]

You will be required to hand over all normal medications that you take upon admission, which they will hand out at the time and in the amount you need them. They may even prescribe and source the medications themselves. Depending on how you are handling detox (e.g., shakes, DTs), they may also prescribe medications to help during the worst of it (this is much more common with drug withdrawal than alcohol withdrawal however).

Check-In

Do not drive yourself to the facility; it is highly unlikely they will allow it (to prevent going offsite to obtain alcohol). Upon arrival, you will need to answer numerous questions during check-in as a broader effort to compile a complete profile of your addiction. Most of these will be about your medical and drinking history (including past detoxes), as well as what/how much/when you have been drinking over the last several days and weeks. They may also ask about your home life, such as if you are depressed, what your home life is like, and other intensely personal questions. Answer *honestly*. They will also want to know your post-detox plans (if you have not already committed to post-detox rehab or other treatment).

After Check-In

You will be assigned a room—either one or two person rooms, depending on the facility, preferences, availability, type of detox, and insurance. You will likely have an exam soon after check-in to take basic vitals. How extensive the exam is will vary, likely including a urine or other test to determine Blood Alcohol Content (BAC) levels, as well as blood pressure, weight, and other typical exam elements. More extensive ones may be done, particularly in acute cases.

Once you have settled into your room, you may be given a tour of the facilities, as well as a schedule of daily activities (discussed next). You may be allowed to wear your own clothes, or given a patient gown, depending on what kind of condition you are in. Meals will also depend on your condition, and are generally strictly scheduled and controlled. In general, by the time you are finally in your room that first evening you will be exhausted by the day's events, not to mention the beginnings of your detoxification.

Day One, Two

Unless you have a severe withdrawal, you will not just be lying in a bed for 2–5 days. Generally 2–5 days is the normal time to get alcohol *completely* out of your system, depending on your drinking history, how recently you drank (and how much) and personal physical characteristics. But the first couple of days is the most important.

What happens in that first day or two? It very much depends on the individual and the severity of the withdrawal. A "normal" withdrawal will be one of the shakes and sweats, perhaps some nausea and headaches—nothing to freak out about, but still benefiting from periodic oversight by professional staff. How "periodic" will depend on your entry diagnosis, day of detox, and time of day. For your first full day, at least, you will essentially be confined to bed (and glad for it). You will be checked on as little as every couple of hours, continuously, or somewhere in between. Depending on the severity of your condition it is possible that you may be allowed to leave your room for meals and obtain any prescriptions, but in general you should assume staying in your room all day.

Day Two+

After the first day or two you will likely be up and around for meals, meetings, and even socializing. Odds are that you'll be in a unit where you are going to be around others who are detoxing from various substances (not just alcohol), and lots of different personalities—many whom may be *very* unpleasant in their current state.

● ●

Other People You May Encounter

During your stay at a detox/rehab facility I strongly recommend you try to keep to yourself, as you have enough to deal with without getting involved in other people's problems. However, there may be a person or two who may try to befriend you, which may or may not be ok depending on the person. There are addicts (not just alcoholics) who may want to just be friendly so they're not going through it alone (certainly a very worthy motivation), but others may have more sinister purposes, such as making new contacts or even to assist in smuggling substances into the facility (particularly drugs). This may sound crazy, but it happens sometimes—often enough not to risk it.

The balance of your stay in Detox will be highly structured. A prototypical daily routine is described below.[17]

● ●

The Daily Routine (once ambulatory)

7:00 am: Wake Up (they may even wake you up earlier to take your blood pressure and/or do other tests. In the first day these tests may be done every few hours, including the middle of the night).

7:30 am: Breakfast (this may be brought to you at first, then later you may go to a cafeteria-type area). You may shower during this time as well. Possibly a little free time to clear your head so to speak; rehabs are not done with a military mindset.

8:45 am: Take medications

9:00–11 am: Morning Meetings/Counseling session(s) (snacks may be available)

11–11:45 am: Free time

**11:45 am–
12:30 pm:**   Lunch

12:30–1 pm: Medical checkup, meds

1–2 pm: Free time

2–4 pm: Group and/or personal counseling sessions

4–6 pm: Free time (phone and computer access, exercise)[18]

6–8 pm: Dinner and Free time

8–9 pm: Alcoholics Anonymous or similar group meeting

9 pm+:   Free time until bedtime, which may be dictated, such as 11 pm.

Throughout the day, social workers and drug counselors and other people will pull you to the side to talk to you. The nurses will take your vitals to make sure you're alright, and they'll medicate you if one of your symptoms starts getting bad.

The number and types of meetings (if any) you will attend will depend on where you are in your detox process, the facility, and whether you will also be staying at the facility post-detox. Assuming you will be staying at the facility as part of a broader rehab, there will be progressively more meetings as the focus shifts from your immediate physical health to your longer-term mental health and sobriety.

These meetings and other sessions may be boring to some, but it's better to go—and participate—even if you don't want to or still feel unwell. They can be very helpful, both educationally and in getting you out of your head and the misery you are going through. They are often mandatory, so you won't be able to vegetate in your room anyway if you are physically able to attend. *Author's Personal Note: If you skip these meetings anyway and are generally uncooperative they are well within their rights to kick you out. And they will—I've seen it done.*

Checkout and the Next Few Days

Once you complete your program, you will be checked out in a manner very similar to a regular hospital, including returning your belongings, signing forms, completing surveys, etc. If you are continuing in a formal Rehab program at the same facility after your Detox, there should not be any discharge/readmission. In fact, not much will change except you will likely be transferred to a room in a non-detox housing unit, and you will attend more/different meetings and counseling sessions.

The above (including the example schedule) may be very similar to what you can experience in Rehab, discussed next. *I strongly urge you to combine the Detox and Rehab processes if you can.* At a bare minimum it provides a protected and controlled environment post-detox, and more importantly provides excellent education and an overall solid level of defense in the Conquer Program. Try to avoid any time gap between Detox and Rehab, as it breaks your "momentum" and adds to the risk of an early relapse.

If you do have to have a gap (for work considerations, scheduling issues, etc.), try to spend the first few days after release/check-out with a trusted family member or friend (again, the importance of Level 4 is demonstrated). They can help you deal with any lingering feelings of unease and doubt, and protect against any temptations—meaning triggers. I strongly urge you to read and re-read this book throughout the process if you can, and particularly during the time immediately after your release from Detox or Detox/Rehab, as it can be a very vulnerable time for many newly clean alcoholics.

LEVEL 6

Rehab and Therapy

I have grouped the discussions of rehabilitation programs and the types of therapy together in Level 6 since many alcoholics initially encounter them in combination. Various types of psychological/psychiatric counseling are usually part of rehab experiences. In other cases, a therapist may recommend that a patient enter rehab with a plan to continue therapy sessions once the program is complete. You may find that Level 5 (Detox), Level 6 (Rehab and Therapy), and Level 7 (Join a Community) do not have to occur in that specific order, and can even be interwoven with each other as a practical matter.[1]

Regardless of timing, rehab and therapy have a similar purpose: to get the alcoholic to understand more about him or herself, their disease of alcoholism, and the alternatives to a life of drinking. Depending on the specific rehab and/or therapeutic approach—and, more important, the attitude of the person undergoing the treatment—the result can be very effective. Both are highly recommended for the newly confessed alcoholic.

That said, while rehab and/or therapy can be sufficient to help an alcoholic get sober, their benefits are *often not long lasting* once the rehab or therapy is over. This comment is not meant to be an indictment of those approaches. Rather, once an alcoholic is back out on his or her own without the professional handholding, the pressures and temptation to relapse is much greater. That is the reason this Level is just one of many Levels in this program. You will likely need *all* of them to defend against alcohol attacks *all* of the time.

Rehab and therapy are best (in my personal experience) at helping you to better understand the bigger picture of the disease of alcoholism, as well as helping you identify and explore deep, or even hidden, reasons for drinking (e.g. triggers) that you may be unable to unearth without therapeutic help.

REHABILITATION TREATMENT PROGRAMS

Overcoming a dependency as invasive in nature as alcoholism can be tough to manage without help and, in some people's view (including mine), almost impossible. This difficulty is why many people advocate some type of formal rehabilitation treatment program. However, before you go down that road, you might consider talking to your general practitioner. Besides being aware of the current condition of your body (and hopefully *aware of your alcoholism and the specifics of how much you drink*), he or she might be able to refer you to an alcohol-related program in your local hospital. Many hospitals have addiction programs/departments that can help, potentially at much lower cost than a dedicated rehabilitation clinic. These types of hospital programs often require a doctor's referral, and there may be a wait time of days or weeks, which, of course, may sap your motivation to go. If this is the case, do as many positive things as you can (including rereading this book), and talk often with the family member(s) and friend(s) selected in Level 4 to keep your spirits and motivation levels up.

● ●

Is Rehab Even Effective? Well . . .

Every day it seems there is news about some celebrity going "back" into rehab. I find it odd that hardly ever is there any questioning of the effectiveness of rehab such that it requires return visits. Somehow rehab is supposed to wipe the record clean, and you are a new person? So much so that it's ok to do it again and again and again? According to the Substance Abuse and Mental Health Services Administration, **six people out of every ten admitted were going back for repeat treatments** in 2010. In other words, they had been to treatment before but relapsed after they got out.[2] The percentage of relapses is likely far higher since it doesn't account for people who gave up on rehab after the initial stint.

I was a bit surprised on learning the number was that high, but not *that* surprised. Rehab is not a *bad* process; in fact, it can be quite excellent in terms of getting you initially sober and arming you with some basic facts about the disease you are facing. However, the positive effects cannot be reasonably expected to last forever; the disease is just too powerful, and there are too many ways one can succumb. The relapse rate just reinforces the importance of the multi-level approach of the Conquer Program.

● ●

There are two types of rehab programs: *Inpatient*, where the addict checks into a hospital or hospital-like setting and goes through a set of programs in a controlled environment, and *Outpatient*, where the addict goes through a similar set of rehabilitation activities but without the degree of control and oversight present in inpatient programs—essentially doing it part-time a few hours a week.

There are hundreds if not thousands of rehab treatment programs in the United States. How to find the right one for you is discussed later in this Level.

Inpatient Rehab

Inpatient rehab programs are usually *highly* controlled—strictly dictating patient activities and their do's and don'ts, often with the underlying philosophy that patients will attempt to evade significant portions of the treatment program and indulge in their abused substance if given the chance. At a minimum, inpatient programs are intended to fully consume a patient's time and attention, from the time they wake up until "lights out" time.

Specifically, going into an inpatient treatment program involves entering a structured and restricted form of living. The rules and expectations will differ from rehab to rehab but will, usually, include:

• Patients will need to remain *completely* abstinent of alcohol during their stay. They will very likely kick your ass out (no money refunded, the court notified, etc.) if they catch you drinking. I saw some very creative ways of people trying to get their fix (both alcohol and drugs) while I was in rehab. As far as I know nearly all were caught.

• Patients will be expected to take part in the prescribed/scheduled activities. If you are medically able to, you *will* be expected to go to these things; there is no sitting around on your ass just because you want to or don't feel "good." Each day will, usually, be highly structured, and you will need to adapt to this, or many facilities will kick you out as uncooperative.

• There will be rules to ensure that individuals maintain a high level of civility to each other. Patients may experience a lot of anger, but this will need to be managed effectively without causing too much disruption. Physical violence will very likely get you kicked out.[3]

- There will be restrictions on where you can go. You will, usually, not be allowed to leave the treatment facility; they may prohibit you parking your car on campus to help avoid the temptation.

- Contact with the outside world is usually limited. It might only be permissible to contact family members at certain times, including visitation, which are often done on select days of the week, often around dinner time.

- You will be expected to attend groups where you will be asked to share personal information about yourself. Some group meetings will be Alcoholics Anonymous-type meetings.[4]

- Therapists and other clients may challenge the behavior of the individual (meaning get in your face).

- There are expectations that you will be completely honest. I *strongly* encourage you to do so; not doing so will diminish the possibility of success, and everyone can see you lying anyway.

- If the rehab is not gender-specific, there will be rules discouraging any romantic/sexual encounters. In my experience, I saw/was told of a significant amount of such encounters. New sobriety plus daily/hourly contact with someone you are attracted to and have a lot in common with often equals strong sexual attraction. For this reason, housing is usually not coed.

The advantages of an Inpatient treatment program include:

- *Safety.* Believe it or not, protecting you from yourself and others is a key benefit of inpatient rehab. It reduces temptation, addresses if not soothes stress, and most of all helps protect you from the stresses and strains that would normally provide an excuse to drink, meaning that triggers can be avoided or carefully controlled. Inpatient programs also have medical staff on hand at all times to deal with everything from emergencies to daily medication needs.

- *Focus.* Individuals are expected to and driven to devote themselves fully to overcoming their addiction. For this reason, taking sick time or a leave of absence from work is best,[5] otherwise use vacation time or other personal time.

- *Knowledge and Resources.* This includes training and educating the addict on how to deal with their alcoholism, as well as providing advice for how to handle challenges that will arise when they return to normal living. To me this is the #1 benefit of rehab programs.

- *Planning for the future.* These types of programs provide you time and encouragement to reflect on your life up to now and make plans for the future. My experience is that this is a worthy goal, rarely accomplished, but definitely worth trying.

- *Support.* This not only comes from the professionals but also from other patients, 24/7.[6]

There are some disadvantages associated with rehab that need to be considered including:

- *Transition.* The transition from rehab back to home can be a treacherous time, with a high risk of relapse. It can come as a shock to move from such a protective and supportive environment back to the real world.

> *I did 28 days in a treatment center, and that was good while I was in there. But when I left the center, I was back in my own environment. The center actually gave me a false sense of security. I was safe there, when I got out I wasn't so safe.*
>
> Tracy, alcoholism.about.com

- Publically funded rehabs can be overcrowded and may not provide enough individualized attention for clients. There can also be a long wait to get into public inpatient treatment programs.

- Entering rehab means devoting much time to recovery. It can be difficult for people to walk away from their responsibilities for this length of time.

A lot of the above may seem scary, even onerous. But everything is relative. It's not so bad when compared to Russia, where drug and alcohol abuse is seen as a personal failing, and the health care system and law enforcement place sole blame on the individual for not succeeding at kicking their habit.

Russian treatment centers do not handcuff addicts to their beds anymore. But caged together on double-decker bunks with no way out, they have no choice but to endure the agonies of withdrawal, the first step in a harsh, coercive approach to drug treatment that has gained wide support in Russia.

A thick silence fills [a] little room crammed with tall metal beds, obscuring the fact that there are 37 men lying shoulder to shoulder, each lost in a personal world of misery. Outside the chamber, known as the quarantine room, 60 men who have emerged—after as long as a month with only bread and water or gruel—work at menial jobs, lift weights, or cook in a regimen of continued isolation from the world that staff members said usually takes a year.[7]

Much, much more than scary. Comparing rehab (in the U.S.) to something like this (or death) is one very effective way of looking at rehab—there are *far* worse things out there.

Outpatient Treatment Programs

Having done both Inpatient and Outpatient Programs, my view is that Inpatient programs are more likely to get you sober and on the *initial* path for continuing sobriety. This is obvious in most respects: you are in a dedicated environment, strictly controlled, monitored, and kept away—forcibly—from indulging in your habit. Good, if in a big brother sort of way.

It is also obvious as to why many people don't "do" inpatient. Despite the Russian example making our programs seem relatively comfortable, giving up this kind of control over one's life can be very disconcerting. And there is a practical side: the addict can't afford to be away from their job and other life responsibilities for 30 to 90 days or longer. Cost is another key concern; even with insurance there can still be a hefty out-of-pocket. Here outpatient help can be key:

I entered an 18 week outpatient program and committed myself to changing how I viewed myself and the world around me. This was key to my successful recovery to date. There was no "graduation" from the program. I was provided an invaluable education in what tools and resources are necessary and available to begin the second half of my life, sober.

Boo, alcoholism.about.com

The decision was made for me. Once it was made clear to me that I was an alcoholic, and the consequences of the path I was on were dire, I committed to change. I went into an outpatient rehab program. I was fortunate. I committed to change and gave up fighting, and submitted to my higher power. Find a good outpatient program, they are around. Health insurance may cover the cost. City / county assistance may be available. Stick to it.

anonymous, alcoholism.about.com

There is also a concern regarding the perception as it is hard to hide a weeks-long absence from your coworkers and friends without them guessing at the reason. Outpatient programs have certain advantages in that regard, including:

• Ability for the patient to stay in school or continue with employment while attending outpatient rehab.

• Easier to deal with the transition from rehab to home. The patient continues to live at home!

• It is a lot easier to keep attendance at an outpatient program a secret.

• An outpatient program will, usually, be a lot cheaper than an inpatient program.

• The individual will still be able to go home every night while attending the program. Of course, this may not necessarily be an advantage if the home life is chaotic and home to many triggers.

Outpatient programs will vary greatly, but they tend to include the following requirements:

• The expectation to remain completely abstinent from alcohol or recreational drugs.

• An agreement to attend a certain number of therapy sessions each week, as well as seminars and activities.

• Rules governing the behavior of the individual while they attend the rehab. Ejection is a possibility for rules violation.

• There may be a need to modify the treatment plan if it is proving to be ineffective.

• An expectation to divulge personal information in one-on-one sessions and in group with other patients.

Outpatient rehab is not for everyone. The disadvantages roughly are the opposite of inpatient advantages, and include:

• Many more opportunities for temptation than those staying in inpatient rehab and much greater potential for acting on them.

• Far less support for addicts versus inpatient programs. The staff leading outpatient programs tend to be less well trained than inpatient resources, and they certainly are not as accessible as inpatient resources. This latter is my opinion based on my experiences, but could be totally off base.

• Far more distractions. This is far from trivial, and it can be difficult for people to build a new life if they have too many distractions at this early stage of sobriety.

• Little avoidance of triggers, except during actual program attendance.

In short, both Inpatient and Outpatient programs can be very beneficial to the newly admitted or newly relapsed alcoholic. In my experience and opinion, Inpatient is much more effective for achieving initial sobriety (not surprising given the degree of control). Outpatient is better—particularly from a practical standpoint—for "refreshing" inpatient lessons and helping maintain already achieved sobriety.

The huge problem, of course, is that both cost money. Even if you have insurance, it will only cover certain types of treatments, restrict your facility choice, possibly cap the amount of coverage in terms of money or days,[8] and still have a hefty co-pay/deductible. Those with no insurance (or unaffordable deductibles) are much more limited in terms of options, of course, but there are some public funded programs that may be available depending on the state you live in and your financial situation.

So even if formal treatment programs seem to work for you initially, they have a natural "expiration date" after which you are on your own. **This is one more example of why you have to have a "multiple layers of defense" strategy in building a sober life. Just going to rehab and expecting that to have miraculously "cured" you for all time no matter how successful it was is naïve at best and vastly stupid at worst.**

❂ ❂ ❂

The availability of both inpatient and outpatient rehabilitation services are of course highly dependent upon an alcoholic's insurance coverage. In addition, for employed alcoholics a major concern is how they practically obtain full-time or near full-time treatment without jeopardizing their job. Regulatory protections are in place to help address both of these concerns.

Key Legal and Regulatory Protections

As if trying to figure out how to overcome alcoholism wasn't challenging enough, doing so in a cost effective way can be even more challenging, as can making sure that you don't put your job in jeopardy while you are off at a rehab facility. There are three laws that help in this regard: the *Affordable Care Act* (ACA), the *Family and Medical Leave Act* (FMLA), and the *American with Disabilities Act* (ADA).

Affordable Care Act

The Affordable Care Act (also known as Obamacare) required starting in 2014 that every adult American have health insurance or pay a penalty. The ACA defined a set of ten Essential Health Benefits (EHB) that most small Group (insured) and individual policies must cover. Large Group (insured and Administered Services Only-ASO) and all grandfathered plans are not required to cover EHB.

The ten EHBs are: ambulatory patient services; emergency services; hospitalization; maternity and newborn care; *mental health and substance use disorder services, including behavioral health treatment;* prescription drugs; rehabilitative and habilitative services and devices; laboratory services; preventive and wellness services and chronic disease management; and pediatric services, including oral and vision care.[9] These are the basics on EHB, but as the law continues being implemented, changes are in process even as we enter 2015. For example, each state can make determinations on what is considered an EHB.

Substance abuse being one of the ten dimensions of EHB coverage is important in two respects for the average alcoholic: 1) *many alcoholics who may not have had insurance (and hence no access to substance abuse services) now may obtain it through the individual or the small group insurance markets,* with their associated EHB coverage; and 2) the degree to which such plans offer such substance abuse services have to be *at parity* with other medical services. At parity means that *mental health and substance use disorder coverage that is comparable to their general medical and surgical coverage.* No longer can a plan offer comprehensive medical and surgical coverage yet offer paltry substance abuse coverage. There are also fewer limitations on annual and lifetime benefits under the ACA.[10] More information on the ACA EHBs can be found at *www.cigna.com/health-care-reform/essential-health-benefits.*

While the ACA offers previously uninsured (and often currently jobless) people the ability to obtain some level of substance abuse treatment, it does not offer any protections against job *loss* due to substance abuse and seeking substance abuse treatment. The Family Medical Leave Act and Americans with Disabilities Act both help in those respects.

Family Medical Leave Act (FMLA)

The ability to protect you from losing your job while you are trying to overcome alcoholism is an important yet often overlooked (until too late) part of getting sober. According to a 2011 National Survey on Drug Use and Health, approximately 65% of all illegal drug addicts are employed full or part time, a percentage likely to be similar or higher for alcoholism.[11] Few people have the luxury of having several weeks of vacation and/or sick leave that they can use to take time off for treatment. Even worse is the harsh reality that many employers have historically discriminated against those with mental illnesses and/or a substance abuse problem, often terminating them under the slightest pretense or no pretense at all. The FMLA was passed with both these circumstances in mind. However, as with most things governmental, the devil is in the details.

The Family and Medical Leave Act ("FMLA") provides certain employees with up to 12 work weeks (or 26 weeks if the family member is a military service member) of *unpaid, job-protected leave a year, and requires group health benefits to be maintained* during the leave as if employees continued to work instead of taking leave. It requires the employer to return employees taking FMLA leave to the same position or an equivalent position with equivalent pay.

FMLA applies to all:

• Public agencies, including State, local and Federal employers, and local education agencies (schools); and,

• Private sector employers who employ 50 or more employees for at least 20 workweeks in the current or preceding calendar year—including joint employers and successors of covered employers.

To be eligible for FMLA leave, *an employee must work for a covered employer and:*

- Have worked for that employer for at least 12 months; and

- Have worked at least 1,250 hours during the 12 months prior to the start of the FMLA leave; and,

- Work at a location where at least 50 employees are employed at the location or within 75 miles of the location.

A covered employer must grant an eligible employee up to a total of *12 work weeks of unpaid leave* (or 26 weeks if the family member is a military service member) in a 12 month period for certain situations concerning children, as well as:

- For the birth of a son or daughter, and to care for the newborn child;

- For the placement with the employee of a child for adoption or foster care, and to care for the newly placed child;

- *To care for an immediate family member (spouse, child, or parent—but not a parent "in-law") with a serious health condition; and*

- *When the employee is unable to work because of a serious health condition.*

These last two italicized points are the critical ones for alcoholics, particularly the last one. Specifically, a "serious health condition" means an illness, injury, impairment, or physical or mental condition that involves:

- *Any period of incapacity or treatment connected with inpatient care (i.e., an overnight stay) in a hospital, hospice, or residential medical care facility;* or

- *A period of incapacity requiring absence of more than three calendar days from work,* school, or other regular daily activities *that also involves continuing treatment by (or under the supervision of) a health care provider;*

- Any period of incapacity due to pregnancy, or for prenatal care; or

- Any period of incapacity (or treatment therefore) due to a chronic serious health condition (e.g., asthma, diabetes, epilepsy, etc.); or

- A period of incapacity that is permanent or long-term due to a condition for which treatment may not be effective (e.g., Alzheimer's, stroke, terminal diseases, etc.); or,

• Any absences to receive multiple treatments (including any period of recovery therefrom) by, or on referral by, a health care provider for a condition that likely would result in incapacity of more than three consecutive days if left untreated (e.g., chemotherapy, physical therapy, dialysis, etc.).[12]

Thus, Inpatient care for the treatment of alcoholism *can be* covered under the FMLA. Specifically, FLMA regulations state that "leave may . . . be taken for treatment for substance abuse by a health care provider." *However,* the exact wording of the Act on this topic is critical, the key excerpt being the following:

The Family and Medical Leave Act—Section §825.119
Leave for treatment of substance abuse.
(a) Substance abuse may be a serious health condition if the conditions of §§825.113 through 825.115 are met (*§825.113 Serious health condition. §825.114 Inpatient care. §825.115 Continuing treatment.*). However, *FMLA leave may only be taken for treatment for substance abuse by a health care provider or by a provider of health care services on referral by a health care provider. On the other hand, absence because of the employee's use of the substance, rather than for treatment, does not qualify for FMLA leave.*
(b) *Treatment for substance abuse does not prevent an employer from taking employment action against an employee.* The employer may not take action against the employee because the employee has exercised his or her right to take FMLA leave for treatment. However, if the employer has an established policy, applied in a non-discriminatory manner that has been communicated to all employees, *that provides under certain circumstances an employee may be terminated for substance abuse, pursuant to that policy the employee may be terminated whether or not the employee is presently taking FMLA leave.*
    An employee may also take FMLA leave to care for a covered family member who is receiving treatment for substance abuse. The employer *may not* take action against an employee who is providing care for a covered family member receiving treatment for substance abuse.[13]

While most of the above is good news (particularly regarding a family member taking leave to care for someone in treatment), it is greatly tempered by the regulations that states that "absence because of the employee's *use* of the substance, rather than for *treatment,* does not qualify for FMLA leave." ***The distinction between treatment and use is critical,*** and has resulted in extensive litigation that supports an employer's right to terminate a substance abuser under certain conditions.

The bottom line is that if you are to take leave under FLMA you need to: make sure you are under a doctor's care and you have been *referred to, accepted by,* and *admitted to* an inpatient alcoholism treatment center *before* you notify your company that you are taking FLMA leave. Informing the employer *before* you begin treatment may make you vulnerable to termination under other company policies regarding substance abuse and the legal precedents allowing that termination.

While the above precaution may not be necessary, depending on your specific company's policies and your history and relationship with it, *you should assume the worst* and anticipate that the company will try to terminate you once they find out about your substance abuse. To do otherwise is an unnecessary risk, in my opinion.

As noted earlier in Level 1 (Interventions), planning an intervention is very difficult. The timing is particularly difficult, as you are trying to time the intervention with the near immediate start of treatment. If the alcoholic is employed, then the family members planning the intervention may want to use the FMLA provisions to protect the alcoholic's job while they are in treatment. But this *may require not informing the alcoholic's employer until after the person is already in treatment.* While this might seem unfair to the company (particularly if the employee has been there for many years and has a close relationship with co-workers), that is *not* relevant, and you cannot risk the alcoholic's job by telling the company prematurely. However, you should tell the employer immediately (as in the next work day) about the situation, to avoid any claims of absenteeism by the company. Again, note that only companies of a certain size, and an employee of certain longevity, are eligible for FLMA's protections. Companies that do not meet these criteria (particularly small companies) are not subject to FLMA.

Key links for additional information on FLMA include:

- The Employee's Guide to The Family and Medical Leave Act: *www.dol.gov/whd/fmla/employeeguide.pdf.*

- U.S. Department of Labor FMLA Compliance Guide: *www.dol.gov/whd/regs/compliance/1421.htm.*

- The Family and Medical Leave Act full text: *www.ecfr.gov/cgi-bin/text-idx?c=ecfr&sid=abbd92cdff37c5d32de741cc5ccc1e81&rgn=div5&view=text&node=29:3.1.1.3.54&idno=29.*

Americans with Disabilities Act (ADA)

The ADA has broader coverage than the FMLA. For example, the ADA covers employers with 15 or more employees versus the FMLA's 50 employees and other restrictions. The ADA also draws harder distinctions between alcoholism and addiction to illegal drugs, with the latter having more restrictions on applicability and eligibility.

The ADA specifically protects alcoholics from the following discrimination: *"an individual with a current alcohol dependence problem who can perform the essential function of the job sought or held and does not present a direct threat to the health or safety of other individuals in the work place. (42.U.S.C. §§ 12114(b), 1211(8) and 12113(a)and (b.).)"*[14]

Key provisions for employers and employees include:

- *An individual who is currently engaging in the illegal use of drugs is not an "individual with a disability" when the employer acts on the basis of such use.*

- *An employer may not discriminate against a person who has a* history *of drug addiction but who is not currently using drugs and who has been rehabilitated.*

- An employer may prohibit the illegal use of drugs and the use of alcohol at the workplace.

- *It is not a violation of the ADA for an employer to give tests for the illegal use of drugs.*

- *An employer may discharge or deny employment to persons who currently engage in the illegal use of drugs.*

- Employees who use drugs or alcohol may be required to meet the same standards of performance and conduct that are set for other employees.

- *Employees may be required to follow the Drug-Free Workplace Act of 1988 and rules set by federal agencies pertaining to drug and alcohol use in the workplace.*[15]

In addition, courts routinely hold that employees cannot blame misconduct on alcoholism. In short, you cannot drink on the job, nor do you have any "right" to perform the job in a different (e.g. worse) way than non-alcoholics.[16] *Employees can still be disciplined for work-related issues stemming from their alcoholism without running afoul of the ADA, so long as they are treated the same as other employees.*

Generally, alcoholism is considered to be a disability under the ADA. *Individuals who abuse alcohol may be considered disabled under the ADA if "the person is an alcoholic or a recovering alcoholic." Courts have supported the notion that alcoholism is a covered disability, and that employers must provide a "reasonable accommodation."*

Reasonable Accommodation for Alcoholics

The duty to provide reasonable accommodations to qualified individuals with disabilities is considered one of the most important statutory requirements of the ADA. *Reasonable accommodation for an alcoholic would generally involve a modified work schedule so the employee could attend Alcoholics Anonymous meetings, or a leave of absence so the employee could seek treatment. In Schmidt v. Safeway, Inc.,* for example, the court held that the employer must provide a leave of absence so the employee could obtain medical treatment for alcoholism.

The ADA *does not require an employer to provide an alcohol rehabilitation program or to offer rehabilitation in lieu of disciplining an employee for alcohol-related misconduct or performance problems.*

An employer is generally not required to provide leave to an alcoholic employee if the treatment would appear to be futile. For example, in *Schmidt v. Safeway, Inc.,* the court said an employer would not be required "to provide repeated leaves of absence (or perhaps even a single leave of absence) for an alcoholic employee with a poor prognosis for recovery." And in *Fuller v. Frank,* the court held that the *employer was not required to give an alcoholic employee another leave of absence when alcohol treatment had repeatedly failed in the past.*

Finally, an employer generally has no duty to provide an accommodation to an employee who has not asked for an accommodation and who denies having a disability.[17]

Because of these protections, when an employee informs his or her employer that she/he is an alcoholic, it is advisable that the employer begin working with the employee to determine whether there is an accommodation that would be appropriate and reasonable under the circumstances. *An employee's entitlement to a reasonable accommodation does not preclude an employer from also taking whatever action is deemed appropriate to address work or performance-related issues.*

According to the *EEOC Technical Assistance Manual: Title I of the ADA* , "[a] person who currently uses alcohol is not automatically denied protection simply because of the alcohol use. An alcoholic is a person with a disability under the ADA and may be entitled to consideration of accommodation, if s/he is qualified to perform the essential functions of a job. *However, a[n] employer may discipline, discharge or deny employment to an alcoholic whose use of alcohol adversely affects job performance or conduct to the extent that s/he is not "qualified."*[18]

Unlike the FMLA, the ADA does not prescribe specific leave timeframes. In fact, a qualified employee with a disability may be entitled under the ADA to leave with job protection *beyond* what the FMLA requires. The EEOC has taken the position that "no fault" policies that provide for automatic termination after a specified amount of time off work are inconsistent with the *"individualized analysis"* requirement of the ADA, even if the length of time to automatic termination is very generous (as much as a year with pay, in one situation challenged by the EEOC).

Accordingly, to avoid risk of an ADA challenge, some employers allow employees who have exhausted FMLA leave but need additional time off work due to a condition that may qualify as a disability the opportunity to request additional leave as a reasonable accommodation. In evaluating whether additional leave is reasonable, courts have looked to factors such as how much more time the employee likely needs; the nature of the job and organization; whether the employee is expected to be able to perform all essential job functions with or without reasonable accommodation upon the return to work; whether the expected return date is reliable or uncertain (which may be evidenced by a pattern of previous extensions); and whether the employee is likely to have ongoing unplanned absences.[19] Thus while the ADA potentially enables significant benefits, it can also potentially limit those benefits—depending on the individual circumstances involved. Court rulings have not looked favorably on those with a history of repeated problems with alcohol and unsuccessful treatments, ruling against them due to in part of their high potential for relapse.

Bottom line: the protections against discrimination for recovering drug addicts and for alcoholics are real, but somewhat limited, undefined, and dependent on individual circumstances. The term "reasonable accommodation" is vague and can be open to interpretation in borderline cases. As such, while those still drinking have some protection, active use can make them more vulnerable to rejection, particularly with respect to job performance, if the issues were to come up in a court dispute regarding "reasonable accommodation."

For additional information on the ADA, key links include:

• The U.S. Commission on Civil Rights: *www.usccr.gov/pubs/ada/ch4.htm.*

• The Americans with Disabilities Act: A Summary of Alcohol and Drugs and AIDS Provisions: *http://lac.org/doc_library/lac/publications/ada.pdf.*

• Americans with Disabilities Act (Electronic Code of Federal Regulations): *www.ecfr.gov/cgi-bin/text-idx?tpl=/ecfrbrowse/Title29/29cfr1630_main_02.tpl.*

• ADAAA Final Regulations: Frequently Asked Questions: *www.faegrebd.com/14146.*

How Do I Select a Facility and Program?

The good news/bad news here is that *you* may not be able to select it—your insurance carrier will. That will most likely be the case for inpatient treatment and possibly less so for outpatient.

If you do have a choice, there are several considerations beyond cost (if you have that luxury). There are several commercial online sources to help such as Recovery.org (*www.recovery.org/topics/find-the-best-residential-inpatient-rehab-center/*), The Agape Center (*www.theagapecenter.com/Treatment-Centers/index.htm*), and Rehabs.com (*www.rehabs.com/about/alcohol-rehab/*), which like all such sites obviously have a profit motive and hence possibly bias. Non-profit sources include the Substance Abuse and Mental Health Services Administration's (SAMSHA) Substance Abuse Facility Locator at *www.samhsa.gov/Treatment/*, and various state-specific organizations that can be found at *http://findtreatment.samhsa.gov/TreatmentLocator/faces/abuseAgencies.jspx* or by doing a search on state government websites, finding ones such as New York State's OASIS Department (Office of Alcoholism and Substance Abuse Services) at *www.oasas.ny.gov/pio/needhlp.cfm.*

If you do have options, there are several criteria you should look for besides inpatient versus outpatient, coverage, and overall cost (make sure you pay close attention to how your deductible works). These include:

• **Variety of programs.** Types of supervised programs are covered in Level 5, and should be primarily determined by your doctor and possibly the facility itself, depending on your condition at the time of entry.

• **Family Involvement.** Some (inpatient) centers allow frequent interaction with family members. This interaction may or may not be desirable; you will have to decide that for yourself. For some, it can be an integral part of engaging key family and friends (e.g. Level 4), while others may not want any reminders of the outside world. There is no right or wrong decision here, just what is best for *you.*

• **Certifications and Licenses.** All quality facilities should have competent counselors certified in treating chemical dependency, such as *American Society of Addiction Medicine (ASAM) certification.*[20] Ask. Check to see if the facility is licensed as a hospital by the state (such requirements may vary greatly by state).

• **Transition help.** Is there a transitional program to help individuals move from inpatient or residential treatment back into community life? Or do they kind of show you the door and forget about you? This can include:

   Follow-up and support services. These could include Internet webcam consultations and follow-up by a physician. A relatively new twist in the treatment world that can be effective.

• **Experience.** I love it when counselors are former addicts. Conversely, I don't have a great deal of faith in people who do not have personal experience in addiction, either themselves or with a loved one. They are just ivory tower academics, in my view, no matter how many "studies" they have under their belt.[21]

• **12 Step programs.** Despite my criticisms of Alcoholics Anonymous (next, in Level 7) there is much good that can come from such programs, particularly in introducing you to the concept of an alcoholic community.

- **Attitude on drugs.** This can be an interesting one, in that some facilities may support the use of various drugs to help with your treatment. These drugs are discussed in detail in Level 11. I have a personal bias against using any drugs in getting sober (particularly if those drugs can be addictive), but certainly for some people in some circumstances some drugs may well play a positive role in a broader treatment plan.[22]

- **Convenience.**

This last item—convenience—is a tricky one, as the best programs for you may well not be the closest to you. This is particularly true if you want the "best" (as in most well-known at least) such as Hazelden (*www.hazelden.org/*) with multiple locations skewed towards the west half of the country, or The Betty Ford Clinic (*www.bettyfordcenter.org/ index.php*) in California. You will likely have to expect pretty large out-of-pocket costs regardless of insurance for these kinds of programs.

For outpatient programs, convenience leaps to the top of the list next to the cost. Since you are trying to live the rest of your life at the same time (e.g. work, school, kids), convenience may trump everything else, so you might expect some great variability in quality. That is my personal experience, though all seemed to cover the basics well.[23]

TRADITIONAL THERAPY

During the time I was in therapy—off and on over two years not counting rehab-based therapy sessions—I had no idea and less interest in the different types of therapy that were possible. To this day I have no idea what kind of approaches my two psychiatrists/psychologists (one of each) took in treating me. I was pushed into treatment by my then-spouse, and to say I was an unwilling participant would be a gross understatement. At the time, it was primarily for Depression, though concerns about my drinking were growing rapidly by her and others. It was amusing to find the below testimonial in my research; it was an exact replica of my thinking and experience.

> *If you are like me, you view or viewed going to a shrink as so much bullshit and a waste of time and money. In my case it was the first thing my wife was able to convince me to do as she became increasingly concerned regarding my alcohol intake.*
>
> Anonymous

However, since I was paying for it, I tried to get some value out of it, along two dimensions. The first was to vent about all the things that were wrong with my life and the injustices and indignities that were being done to me by others. In this respect, it was fairly satisfying (if somewhat childish), and I suspect it was helpful in lowering my blood pressure. I certainly felt calmer afterward, if annoyed at the money I just spent.

The second was much more deep rooted. I was convinced that there were some (at least one) deep rooted, buried experience(s) in my past that were contributing to my Depression and overall alcohol intake. In retrospect, I was right—they were my Triggers![24] Unfortunately, my sessions with both therapists did not help me that much, probably because I didn't want to be there nor did I believe at the time that I was truly an alcoholic. Even with that failure, I believe if done "right," therapy can be of significant help to many alcoholics.

> *Your journey sounds a lot like what I'm going through right now, too. I've been struggling with maintaining continuous sobriety over the last few months—it's a battle, but one I know will be worth it. I just started seeing a therapist again—being truthful for the first time in therapy was a huge step—and feel blessed to have gotten to the place where I'm finally ready to be kind to myself. My yoga practice and community help, too.*
>
> Anonymous, cryingoutloud.com

The key, I believe, is to find the right doctor with the right type of therapy and demeanor for you, and for the appropriate amount of time. It seemed my first therapist said practically nothing during our sessions; even the ones on TV seemed at least to ask a fair amount of "Why" and "How" questions. A great discussion of therapist styles can be found at *http://alcoholrehab.com/alcohol-rehab/rehab-therapist-styles/*. The second asked more questions but were all over the map with no discernible approach as discussed next.

One interesting opinion (I learned there are no "facts" in Therapy) I came across is that the "right" amount of time in therapy is 12 to 16 sessions. Seems reasonable on the surface; not enough sessions do not allow you to develop a rapport and "peel the onion" to get at your core issues. More sessions are probably a waste of time and money—if you haven't figured out the issues after 4 months of sessions it is probably not going to happen.

As noted before, I am *not* a medical professional in any way shape or form. All I can do is provide an overview and an addict's superficial opinion on a sampling of the different types of therapies available to alcoholics. There are of course others; I've listed a couple of sources in the Website Resources at the end of this book that can help you explore these areas. The below are some of the more well-known ones; I offer color commentary on a few.

Behavioral Couples Therapy

Alcohol behavioral couple therapy (ABCT) is an outpatient treatment for individuals with alcohol use disorders and their intimate partners. ABCT is based on two assumptions: Intimate partner behaviors and couple interactions can be triggers for drinking, and a positive intimate relationship is a key source of motivation to change drinking behavior. Using cognitive-behavioral therapy (discussed next), ABCT aims to identify and decrease the partner's behaviors that cue or reinforce the client's drinking; strengthen the partner's support of the client's efforts to change; increase positive couple interactions by improving interpersonal communication and problem-solving skills as a couple; and improve the client's coping skills and relapse prevention techniques to achieve and maintain abstinence.

The treatment program consists of 2–3 hours of assessment for treatment planning, followed by 12–20 weekly, 90-minute therapy sessions for the client with his or her partner. The number of treatment sessions may be increased if sessions of less than 90 minutes are desired. Treatment follows cognitive-behavioral principles applied to couples therapy and specific therapeutic interventions for alcohol use disorders. The optimal implementation of ABCT occurs in the context of an existing clinic or private practice with certified/licensed mental health or addictions professionals who have a background in treating alcohol use disorders and knowledge of cognitive-behavioral therapy.[25]

Another description: "ABCT combines a focus on alcoholism recovery with efforts to repair and improve relationships. For the therapy to be effective, both partners must be committed to the relationship and want to strengthen it. Only one spouse should be alcohol dependent for the therapy to have an impact. If both couples are alcoholics, different strategies need to be deployed, so couples are less likely to relapse together.

Therapy includes providing the non-dependent partner with training on communication and support strategies that facilitate the advancement of treatment and sobriety. An integral component of couple's therapy involves developing a "contract" agreeing that:

- The alcoholic-dependent partner will commit to abstinence

- The non-dependent partner will offer continual support and reinforcement

- Neither partner will discuss past addictive behavior and its consequences

- Neither partner will discuss the future and misuse outside of the therapy sessions."[26]

Author's Note: This certainly sounds like a powerful way of addressing alcoholism and marital problems at the same time. But (to my cynical eyes) it would require a great deal of self-discipline on both parties to adhere to the last two bullets.

Cognitive-Behavioral Therapy

Cognitive behavior therapy is mostly used to treat depression, anxiety disorders, phobias, and other mental disorders, but it has also been shown to be valuable in treating alcoholism and drug addiction, especially as part of an overall program of recovery.

Cognitive-behavioral coping skills treatment is a short-term, focused therapeutic approach to helping drug-dependent people become abstinent by using the same learning processes the person used to develop alcohol and drug dependence initially.

Cognitive behavior therapy is based on the idea that feelings and behaviors are caused by a person's thoughts, not on outside stimuli like people, situations, and events. People may not be able to change their circumstances, but they can change how they think about them and therefore change how they feel and behave, according to cognitive-behavior therapists.

In the treatment for alcohol and drug dependence, *the goal of cognitive behavioral therapy is to teach the person to recognize situations where they are most likely to drink or use drugs, avoid these circumstances if possible, and cope with other problems and behaviors which may lead to their substance abuse.*

According to the National Association of Cognitive-Behavioral Therapists, there are several approaches to cognitive-behavioral therapy, or CBT as it is called. These therapies include *Rational Emotive Behavior Therapy*, Rational Behavior Therapy, Rational Living Therapy, Cognitive Therapy, and *Dialectic Behavior Therapy*.[27]

A simpler description of CBT is: "Cognitive behavior therapy helps alcohol-dependent people acquire skills to recognize, cope and change problem-drinking behaviors. *By understanding what needs are filled by drinking,* the therapist can work with an alcoholic patient to find new ways to address needs that don't include drinking—and modify psychological dependence on the drug. During therapy sessions, patients are taught essential coping skills to:

- *Recognize what triggers the urge to drink*

- Manage negative moods and emotional vulnerabilities

- Change social outlets and friendships to focus on something other than drinking."[28]

Supposedly there are a number of studies that tout CBT as one of the most effective ways of dealing with addiction. But there are also studies that failed to identify specific CBT components that could account for the treatment's effectiveness. Huh? It works, but we don't know why? Thanks for that.

I would think the answer is obvious: the CBT approaches that focus extensively on triggers as a cause for alcohol abuse are more likely to be successful, in my opinion. Or another way of looking at it is making sure that if you go to a CBT therapist that the one you select adheres strongly and explicitly to the notion of drinking triggers (the simpler description above), and not the weaker, more vague approach (the first description).

In addition, other studies suggested that CBT's effectiveness was limited to specific treatment contexts, particularly that it needed to be delivered as part of a comprehensive treatment program, and to patients with very severe alcohol dependence (I have no idea how they measured that). They also said that CBT worked best when combined with other methods such as group therapy.[29] I interpret this to mean that CBT by itself is not enough for many people: that it needs to be combined with other approaches and methods. Which is exactly the philosophy of The Conquer Program.

Motivational Enhancement Therapy

Motivational Enhancement Therapy (MET) is based on principles of motivational psychology and is designed to produce rapid, internally motivated change. *This treatment strategy does not attempt to guide and train the client, step by step, through recovery, but instead employs motivational strategies to mobilize the client's resources.* MET consists of four carefully planned and individualized treatment sessions. The first two sessions focus on structured feedback from the initial assessment, future plans, and motivation for change. The final two sessions at the midpoint and end of treatment provide opportunities for the therapist to reinforce progress, encourage reassessment, and provide an objective perspective on the process of change.[30]

The above description from the NIAAA seems reasonable if a bit vague. Another description I found states: *"These [Motivational Enhancement] Programs are designed to raise drinkers' awareness of the impact alcohol has on their lives, as well as the lives of family, co-workers and society. They are encouraged to accept responsibility for past actions and make a commitment to change future behavior."*[31] This sounds like they try to Guilt the hell out of you.

Step Facilitation Therapy

This peer-support approach encourages people to become involved with a 12-step or similar program that complements professionally supervised therapy, e.g., go to AA but come to my couch as well. Seems like this could work if the therapy tries to capitalize on and extend what the addict learned in the group meetings.

AA and its 12 steps are covered in Level 7—Join a Community.

Time Perspective Therapy

Time Perspective Therapy tries to figure out what kind of person you are, and use that as a basis for treatment. "Figuring out" involves classifying you into one of six different outlooks. These outlooks, along with my interpretation of how triggers might be applicable for them, include:

• *Past-positive.* Here you love the past, which can be good (you have less baggage) or not so good (you live in the past, like an aging high school football quarterback). These people are likely to want to Escape (to the past, from unmet potential, etc.).

- *Past-negative.* Here *you have regrets and bad things happened in your past*—or things that you now exaggerate as bad. This type of personality has Guilt as one of their top triggers, no question.

- *Present hedonism and/or fatalism.* You enjoy the present and like to reward yourself. In additional (or alternatively), you take a fatalistic view on life, e.g. *you feel that events are beyond your control,* so why bother? Powerlessness and possibly Victim-Mentality may be involved here. Alternatively, you feel a desire to have Fun (still in the drinking equals Fun stage), Escape and/or feel Excitement (Zeal) and want to enhance it with alcohol.

- *Goal-oriented future.* You are a plan-ahead type thinker who weighs the costs and benefits of any decision. This may cause generalized Anxiety, as well as specific types of stress-inducing feelings like Job anxiety (worrying about the state of your career) and Money stress (how will you make rent? Get ready for retirements?)

- *Transcendental futurist.* You live a good life because you believe the reward is a heaven after death. I suspect that not many alcoholics are in this mental place. The ones that do might have Anxiety or Depression, or possibly bouts of Powerlessness, but this is conjecture on my part as I don't think there will be many of you falling into this category.

The best profile to have, one doctor says, is a blend of a high level of past-positive, a moderately high level of future orientation and a moderate level of selected present hedonism. In other words, you like your past, work for the future—but not so hard that you become a workaholic—and choose when to seek pleasure in the present. I doubt that many alcoholics are in this happy hybrid state.

The worst time-perspective profile to have is a high level of past-negative coupled with a high level of present fatalism. "These people are living in a negative past and think nothing they do can change it," says Dr. Zimbardo, co-author of the book *"The Time Cure."* They also score low on present hedonism and have a low future orientation. People who are clinically depressed or have Post-Traumatic Stress Disorder typically have this profile.

The good news, says Dr. Zimbardo, is that *people can change their time perspective.* A person can raise a *past-positive* score, for example, by focusing on the *good* in your past: create photo albums, write letters of gratitude to people who inspired you, start an oral history of your family. Nearly all alcoholics have done good things in the past. The challenge is to a) remember them, and b) get them to rise to the front of your consciousness without all the other Reminder baggage the memories may bring with it.

To lower your *past-negative* scores you can work to silence your pessimistic inner critic by meditating or keeping an ongoing list of all the good things in your life right now. The idea is to think about what's good in your life now, rather than what was bad in your life in your drinking past. This will be difficult to do, and require much practice.

You can increase your *present hedonism* (feeling good about the present—without alcohol) by doing something to balance your moods, such as exercise or a nature walk. Also, reward your hard work with an activity you enjoy: dinner with a friend, a massage, an afternoon playing your favorite sport, and so on.

And you can reduce your *future fatalistic* perspective by learning a new skill or hobby that allows you to see your change. Doing it with a partner is less isolating since the other person can give you positive feedback.

Your future orientation can also get a boost by organizing your calendar or planning a family vacation, actions that get you to envision and plan for a positive future. Volunteering or becoming a mentor can help you see that your actions can have a positive impact. These ideas are highlighted in particular for the Disorder and Guilt triggers, respectively.[32]

Important Note: I came across this type of therapy for the first time shortly before publishing this book. As such, I have no personal experience, but on the surface it seems like it might be a highly effective approach for many alcoholics. *However, I must point out that the article above is based on says nothing about alcoholism.*

Overall Author's Note: I know the above brief therapy assessments are simplistic, but at least they introduce you to the concept that there are many different "flavors" of therapy for alcoholism. You should take the time to understand which approaches are open to you, particularly when considering the skills and training of specific Therapists.

How Do I Select a Therapist?

There is similar good news/bad news as with a Rehab facility, in that you may not have much choice since your insurance carrier will likely determine the treatment options available to you. However, you will have some choice in theory. The big problem today for people seeking therapy is that many, even most therapists are not accepting new patients. They are booked solid. Good news if you are a therapist, not at all good if you are looking for a therapist with somewhat scarce skills in addiction therapy.

Assuming you do have a choice, I would encourage you to look for two things: specialty and style. Let's take "style" first.

Therapists have a style like anyone else. Some will ask you specific questions (Did you drink at all this week?). Some will be generalists (How did your week go?). Some will be even *more* general (How do you feel? What do you want to talk about?). And some will just sit there and listen to you and say hardly anything. You have to figure out which style works for you, which is not easy, and what a potential doctor's styles *is*—very tough to do before seeing them. There are not exactly Yelp reviews for psychologists and psychiatrists, and asking a friend for a recommendation is not exactly in the cards here. But do your best. I have a personal bias towards ones that focus on asking progressively detailed questions that help you get to the heart of whatever matter you are discussing, but it is just that—a personal bias. The style has to work for *you*.

What specialty they have is more important. While you may want them specifically to have addiction counseling experience, this experience may come at a cost of being resistant to new treatment approaches, e.g. this program. But in general experience is better than no experience.

What you will want to do is make sure their specialty (and style) aligns with your goals in going to them in the first place. In the context of the Conquer Program, you may have one or multiple goals. You may want help in identifying your triggers; in exploring a trigger in detail; figuring out defenses to suit your personality; or in general when you just want to bounce ideas regarding your alcoholism off someone impartial and sympathetic.

Keeping these goal(s) in mind, you will want to know what kind of approach they used. Several were discussed earlier in this section, such as Cognitive Behavior Therapy and Motivational Enhancement Therapy. In fact, all mentioned have been used specifically for alcoholism therapy;

it's just that CBT and MET come closest to a focus on triggers in my opinion.

Like for rehab facilities, there are a number of websites that help you find therapists. Note that as I use the word therapist, it covers both psychologists and psychiatrists. Some equate the term with only psychologists or even including "psychotherapists" and "counselors," that while trained are not degreed like psychologists and psychiatrists.[33] While all are trained professionals, only psychiatrists are Medical Doctors (M.D.); thus, they are the only ones that can prescribe medications. However, that does not necessarily mean one is better than another; both require many years of training and education. In the end, it may be the intangibles such as style that make the most difference in your therapy, not the number of diplomas on the wall.

There are two online sources for therapists from Psychology Today, a respected industry publication. One for psychologists is at *http://therapists.psychologytoday.com/rms/prof_search.php*. They also have a similar site for psychiatrists at *http://psychiatrists.psychologytoday.com/rms/prof_search.php*. The problem with these sites is that they key off your zip code only, so you then have to search individual doctors for their specialty. However, each doctor describes their approach at least a little, which may give you some indications in terms of specialty area and the elusive "style." There are also other commercial specialty (for addiction) sites that may be helpful, including one from The Association For Addiction Professionals at *www.naadac.org/sap-directory*. At the end though it may come down to what providers are covered under your insurance plan, *and* who is accepting new patients.

ALTERNATIVE/UNCONVENTIONAL TREATMENT APPROACHES

The programs described earlier are ones that are well known and/or follow roughly the same philosophies in trying to help an addict become sober. The following describe methods or treatments that are not as well known or are utilized much less frequently. For the record I have never tried any of the following programs so cannot offer an opinion as to the experience,[34] so the below references only medical and other literature available on the Internet. However, all of the programs/treatments have been around at least a few years, and have persons who swear by (or at) them, so you still might consider at least investigating them as a possible defense in your quest for sobriety.

Acupuncture

Western medicine has proved to be highly effective in the treatment of many diseases and conditions. However, sometimes of course it is not always effective or only partially so. Thus, people will often turn to complementary treatment approaches for a solution. Acupuncture is one such treatment approach and probably the most widely used.

Acupuncture is said to be effective in preventing and curing many physical, as well as mental conditions. It has been used for at least 2,000 years in China and other parts of Asia. This makes it one of the oldest surviving healing practices in existence. In my view anything that has been around for millennia is not something to be easily dismissed, no matter what doctors (including my own) say.

Acupuncture is based on the idea that physical and mental symptoms are caused by imbalances within the body. Chinese medicine views such imbalances as leading to blockages of *Qi*. The ability of Qi to move unimpeded is important because this is the life force. When this force gets trapped, it leads to mental or physical symptoms. There are 14 major energy paths in the body, and these are called *meridians*. Along these meridian paths are hundreds of acupuncture points.

Acupuncture uses tiny needles to promote the flow of Qi. These needles are placed in specific acupuncture points depending on the problem.

Acupuncture has been used in the treatment of addiction since at least the early 1970s. It is not viewed as a complete treatment for withdrawals, but it has proved to reduce the strength of some of the more unpleasant symptoms. Acupuncture is believed to be beneficial in the treatment of addiction because it promotes:

- Less severe withdrawal symptoms

- Reduced experiences of craving

- Improved ability to sleep at night

- Reduced anxiety and depression.

The primary benefit appears to be in helping with the withdrawals process, *particularly as a complementary therapy*. Many rehabs now offer such treatments to clients. A good unbiased source of information can be found at *www.webmd.com/fibromyalgia/tc/acupuncture-topic-overview*.

Aversion Therapy

Aversion Therapy is considered by some as a non-traditional, even fringe-type of therapy, and it probably is frankly. At its heart, it is a program that looks to make you physically sick when you drink alcohol. This concept plays a key part in Level 11—Make Yourself Sick of Alcohol (with major modifications and enhancements), but I introduce it here to expose alcoholics to a significantly different concept in trying to get sober than other stand-alone programs, such as Alcoholics Anonymous.

At the core of aversion therapy is the concept of breaking the association between alcohol and pleasure, and establishing a new association between alcohol and pain and misery.

You may have heard little or nothing about aversion therapy. There is a good reason for this: there are relatively few hospitals/clinics that offer this treatment, and they are all expensive—generally well into the five-digit territory. While they profess to take insurance, the bald fact is that insurance, usually, will not take *them.* Typical insurance plans nearly universally cover only traditional types of outpatient/inpatient substance abuse help.

So what is Aversion Therapy? It is a form of psychological treatment in which the patient is exposed to a stimulus while simultaneously being subjected to some form of discomfort. The primary goal of aversion therapies is to produce an *aversive reaction* to alcohol by establishing a conditioned response to cues associated with drinking. The conditioning can be accomplished by using electric shock, apneic paralysis, chemical agents such as Disulfiram/Antabuse (discussed shortly), or negative image-based[35] techniques.[36]

This conditioning is intended to cause the patient to associate a stimulus with unpleasant sensations in order to stop the specific behavior. In other words, *give you something to make you sick while you are doing something you want to do, but are not supposed to be doing.*

The *premise* of aversion therapy with respect to alcoholism assumes the brain has, over time, directly "learned" that drinking alcohol equals some very positive physiological benefits, such as relaxation, reduced stress, and pleasure in general. We alcoholics thus come to rely on drinking for these benefits; to the point that we feel we cannot achieve them *without* alcohol. Thus, there is a need under this premise to unlearn or "break" this association and consequential behavior (drinking), *essentially by punishing you.* The main way of doing this in a clinical session is combining certain drugs with drinking, often with a drug called Disulfiram.

● ●

How Disulfiram (Antabuse) Works In Aversion Therapy?

Disulfiram changes the way your body breaks down (metabolizes) alcohol. If you drink alcohol while you are taking disulfiram, you will experience uncomfortable symptoms, including severe nausea, vomiting, and headache. These symptoms discourage you from drinking alcohol by making it unpleasant.

The effectiveness of disulfiram varies. When taken as directed, it can help you completely stop drinking by increasing the number of days you go without a drink. It works best if you are motivated to stop drinking and you take the medicine as directed.

The effects from disulfiram are *intentionally unpleasant* to help encourage you to remain sober. Disulfiram causes the following effects when you drink alcohol, with effects lasting from 30 minutes to 2 hours.

- Face and body flushing
- Throbbing in your head and neck, severe headache
- Blurred vision
- Fast heartbeat
- Sweating
- Dry mouth

- Nausea, vomiting
- Dizziness
- Weakness
- Breathing difficulty
- Severe low blood pressure
- Confusion

When you take disulfiram and do not drink, the main effect is drowsiness. Use caution when you drive or operate machinery while taking this medicine.[37]

● ●

Disulfiram is by no means a miracle drug for alcoholism; indeed no such drug exists (See Level 11 for more information on drugs for alcoholism). The typical benefit achieved is a short-term stoppage of drinking, which combined with other mechanisms (like this program) may help build the momentum for long-term sobriety.

> *I used Antabuse and it worked well for me when I first started strictly as a deterrent. It also gave my family some comfort at a time when they really needed at least to feel a little more secure after I had blown them out of the water with my drunkenness. All it did for me was help me to get some time under my belt while I went to meetings. When I stopped taking Antabuse I did relapse, one of several relapses I had.[38]*

Many individuals who take Antabuse describe feelings of being liberated when taking this medication as it makes the option of drinking not a pleasant one. However, **if you stop and the root causes of drinking have not been addressed, you are essentially right back where you started.**

There are some other drug treatments for alcoholism. One is acamprosate (Campral) that is a type of opiate receptor blocker that supposedly reduces cravings and urges to drink in those who have been through detox and are medically stable. A similar one is Naltrexone, which works by blocking in the brain the "high" that people experience when they drink alcohol or take opioids like heroin and cocaine. More on all these drugs in Level 11—Make Yourself Sick of Alcohol. *Author's Opinion: Again, these drugs may help in the short-term, but not in the long-term unless the underlying drinking triggers are addressed.*

When researching aversion therapy it reminded me of a short story I read by Stephen King titled *Quitters, Inc.*[39] If aversion therapy appeals to you in the slightest, I highly recommend reading it. It has the same underlying principles as real-world aversion therapy, albeit a bit more severe in its punishment methods. Hilarious, disturbing, and thought provoking all at the same time—it makes electric shock look like it is for wussies.

One of the most well-known Aversion Therapy clinics, at least in the western U.S., is Schick Shadel Hospital, based in Seattle (*www.schickshadel.com*). Having lived in Seattle for a few years, I became very familiar with their ads, and those seemed to have some (locally) well known endorsements. I attempted to use them, but my insurance would not cover it, and to pay it myself was approximately $15,000 (this was in 2009).

Problems with Aversion Therapy

While aversion therapy proponents claim it is a relatively successful method for dealing with alcohol addiction, there are a number of issues associated with it. First, long-term compliance is needed as an individual may be expected to take nausea-inducing drugs for *many years.* Also, alcoholics can just quit Antabuse or a similar drug if they wish to return to their addiction. There are high dropout rates. It may only be effective for a specific type of alcohol, not alcohol in general. It accentuates the negative with no positive reinforcement.

While in its traditional form, aversion therapy does little to address the underlying craving for alcohol and its associated triggers for the individual alcoholic. BUT, as I utilize it in Level 11—Make Yourself Sick of Alcohol, I modify its target purpose for specifically dealing with the triggers of Proximity, Smell, and Taste. I have personally found it to be extremely effective for those triggers, but as the process for making so can be physically risky, Level 11 is optional.

Hypnosis

Hypnosis, also known as hypnotherapy, as an addiction treatment is gaining some credibility in the medical and psychiatric communities. It can be of help for those who have gone through the initial stages of rehabilitation to cope with cravings and stave off relapse. Before attempting hypnosis, the alcoholic has to detoxify his or her system completely. (The need for complete detoxification before attempting hypnotherapy is repeatedly emphasized in every source I researched.)

A medical professional offering hypnosis as a treatment for addiction is a *hypnotherapist*. This person guides the recovering alcoholic into a trance-like mental state in which the person is more susceptible to ideas and suggestions. In this state, those being hypnotized can become more imaginative and better at problem solving. In short, they're in prime position to sort out strategies for conquering their own addictive behaviors.

● ●

What Does Hypnosis Really Feel Like?

The experience of a *hypnotic trance* is not so unusual or strange. To the contrary, it feels vaguely familiar to countless other moments in your life where you were absorbed in a zone, lost in thought, enthralled by bliss, or perhaps simply meditating. Meditation is the closest you can come to a state of trance without being guided there as you would experience in hypnosis.[40]

● ●

However, *the only way that hypnosis can be effective as a treatment for addiction is if the person being hypnotized wants to give up their destructive habits and behaviors.* The treatment does not change minds or induce new outlooks. Instead, it helps to hone and refine a preexisting mindset.

It's important to understand that hypnosis is not a cure-all for addiction, but it can serve a *complementary* role in the treatment. It's considered particularly useful in helping recovered alcoholics stay on the right track, e.g., as a kind of maintenance therapy.

During this relaxed state, the person being hypnotized is more open to exploring the mechanics of their addiction to alcohol. This openness allows them to explore the ebb and flow of their cravings—with the goal of putting together strategies to overcome them—without any stress or feelings of guilt getting in the way. Author's Note: The "mechanics" to me sound very much like the underlying causes of drinking, e.g. your triggers.

In some cases, the hypnotherapist may also train their patients to practice self-hypnosis in their daily lives. Going into a lightly hypnotic state is an excellent way to overcome a craving in real time.[41]

Meditation

When the word *meditation* is mentioned, most people will get a mental image of somebody sitting cross-legged with their eyes closed humming some sort of mantra nonsense. While it is true that this is how some meditators practice, it is certainly not by any means the full story. It is possible to meditate in a number of positions including sitting, standing, and lying down. It is even possible to meditate when doing everyday movements such as driving a car, and even doing physical activities such as walking and running, even karate! And you don't have to chant. Great, you say! But what the hell does it have to do with addiction treatment? First, some background.

● ●

What is Meditation?

Meditation is a practice often associated with Eastern traditions but is present in almost every world culture in some form. Traditionally a part of spiritual practices in India, China, Japan, and other Eastern cultures, Western versions of meditation are often more focused on relaxation and stress reduction.

There are *thousands* of specific meditation practices. Some practices focus on quieting and clearing the mind to experience a deep sense of presence in silence and connection to the spiritual world. Others bring the mind's focus to a single, specific thought or intention. The practice is, usually, self-guided and can involve the use of music, chant, breathing techniques, specific postures, or focus on a visuali-zation or external image.[42]

In essence, it is a way of clearing and/or relaxing one's mind, helping to discard troubles of the day and helping put you "in a better place," mentally, for a period of time ranging from many minutes to as long as several hours, and possibly even days.

● ●

Meditation for Addiction

A small but growing body of research is lending support to meditation's effectiveness in treating addiction, either alone or in combination with other more conventional treatments.

Some of these studies have shown meditation's effectiveness at decreas-ing substance use and relapse in several settings. The changes in thought processes and brain function that accompany meditation also have con-tributed to scientists understanding of the biological addiction process.

● ●

Studies Supporting Meditation in Addiction Treatment

• A 2011 peer-reviewed study established the effects of prayer and meditation on dopamine levels, servicing the mind and body by creating contentedness and calm through the brain's pathways—an effect formerly produced by drug use.[43]

• Alternative and Eastern-based meditative practices incorporated into individual alcoholism and drug abuse treatment plans seem to garner some of the most encouraging results, according to emerging research. In 2010, the use of the *qi gong* meditative practice (a type of "moving meditation" within mindfulness meditation, discussed later) was studied among nearly 250 substance abusers. Practicing qi gong increasing addiction recovery completion by 14 percent for those in this study. Those who participated in qi gong also experienced reduced cravings, lowered anx-iety levels and fewer withdrawal symptoms.[44]

• A 2009 study of 168 alcoholic individuals by the *University of Washington Depart-ment of Psychology* found that those who participated in *mindfulness-based* relapse prevention therapy had lower [alcohol] relapse rates in the four months after inpa-tient or outpatient graduation than those who experienced traditional treatment alone. Those who participated in mindfulness treatment also experienced reduced cravings, and exhibited higher levels of awareness and acceptance than their tradi-tionally treated counterparts.[45]

• A 2008 study published in the *Journal of Addiction Medicine* also established the positive physical effects of meditation on those in addiction treatment. Of individuals in recovery who combined the daily habit of meditative practices with guided meditation experienced *increased mindfulness,* lowered depression and reduced anxiety levels. In fact, positive physical ramifications were also found in those who practiced meditation, including a decrease in cortisol stress hormone levels and an increase in interlukin-6—a protein associated with strengthened immunity.[46]

• One 2007 study showed that individuals who participated in meditative practices during recovery gained higher levels of coping skills, as well as an heightened awareness of substance abuse triggers that aided addiction recovery.[47]

• A *2006 study of addicted and incarcerated individuals* found that *Vipassana meditation* (a form of mindfulness meditation) reduced rates of alcohol, marijuana and crack cocaine abuse in released prisoners who learned the meditative technique. In fact, Vipassana participants also exhibited fewer alcohol-related setbacks, fewer mental health conditions and more positive social experiences.[48]

• A 2003 study of 550 intravenous drug users conducted by the *University of Maryland Center for Integrative Medicine* found that those who participated in complementary alternative therapies, such as stress-reduction techniques and meditation, perceived the mind-body techniques aided their recovery.[49]

The point of the above is not to assert in any way that meditation by itself can overcome alcoholism. However, there is enough evidence to justify considering doing meditation as *an additional tool* to add to your overall Conquer Program defenses. The results—if any—will vary greatly by individual, as well as type of meditation, discussed next.

Types of Meditation

There are many different types of meditation, *which all work to slow down the chatter of the mind and promote relaxation and mental clarity.* The different types of meditation techniques that have evolved from Hinduism, Christianity, and Buddhism can be classified under five categories: Concentration, Reflective, Heart-Centered, Creative, and Mindfulness Meditation.[50]

While Mindfulness seems to have the highest potential specifically for addiction, that view is based on a small body of research (e.g. the studies cited earlier), thus I cover all the main types of meditation below (though

I focus most on Mindfulness meditation). It is my view that for *any* meditation to be effective as a Conquer Program defense, you have to:

a. Give the concept the benefit of the doubt (meaning don't bother trying it if you think it is a joke)

b. Find a meditation type that works for your personality type. There is a ton of different ones that use different methods, so don't try to force fit yourself into something that feels silly or awkward for you—try a different one.

c. Fully understand your triggers and if/how one or more might benefit from meditation, and

d. Actually give it a meaningful try in terms of attempts, time, and attitude (meaning don't do it half-assed—it won't work).

Item c is, of course, the trickiest part of using meditation of any kind to help alcoholism, at least in the context of the Conquer Program. My view is that while most triggers could theoretically benefit from meditation, it is the ones that cause physical stress, such as a jump in blood pressure, which could benefit the most. These include Anger, Anxiety, Extreme Emotions, Frustration, Noise, Stress (Pain), Yelling, and Zeal (Excitement). These are ones where it seems common sense to take a step back to try and calm down, and meditation seems a great way to do so. Insomnia and being Tired could also benefit as well (Meditation as a sleep aid is discussed in Appendix A).

Note: In the below discussions I provide a variety of links to various sub-categories of meditation. I am not at all an expert on any of these forms, so I chose sources that seemed to be easily understood and had some elements of how-to in them. If you are interested in any of these forms of meditation, I encourage you to do additional research. Ask friends and visit online forums, as relying solely on Internet material comes with an uneven range of quality, ease of learning, and profit motive (particularly with respect to Transcendental Meditation).[51]

Concentration Meditation

Concentration is at the heart of all the types of meditation, but in some techniques, focus is predominantly on *building* concentration. Why is concentration so important? Because in order to benefit from meditation, you need to train the mind to concentrate and focus on an object or nothingness, that is to *cut all distractions*. This concentration allows your mind to be calm and awaken beyond thought elaboration and even beyond your sense of self. Once you hold this view of awareness, you can use it for your wellness and the greater good. It is more correct to say that it affects positively all the beings; yourself included. A good quick step guide can be found at *www.wikihow.com/Do-Concentration-Meditation*.

There are five types Concentration Meditation: *Zen, Transcendental, Om, Samadhi,* and *Chakra.*

Reflective Meditation

Also known as analytical meditation and refers to *disciplined thinking.* In order to successfully practice reflective meditation, you will need to choose a question, theme, or topic and focus your analysis or reflection upon it. Initially, your thoughts may wander to other topics but then you need to train your mind to come back to the topic in question.

In order to do this, you need to learn concentration meditation first. Example questions or themes include: Who am I? What is the true purpose of my life? What is my role in this universe? How can I help remove the sufferings of others? There are numerous sources for additional information, but for a quick video overview watch *www.youtube.com/watch?v =0Tk6_FA0Cek*.

Heart-Centered Meditation.

Heart-centered meditation will help you release all your fears and sadness and bathe in the radiance of loving kindness and compassion. It is also known as the heart chakra meditation. Practicing this meditation over a period of time will help you to heal your heart and that of others.

This meditation technique helps in opening the *heart chakra* and removes any negative energy that exists. In order to practice this meditation technique, choose a quiet place, set the right posture and focus on the heart area while inhaling and exhaling slowly but smoothly. You can also connect your heart to the heart of a teacher or a person you feel that is compassionate. A video on how to do this can be found at *www.youtube.com/watch?v=6iKz1Qz24TQ*.

Creative Meditation.

A different type of meditation technique, *Creative Meditation* will enable you to consciously cultivate as well as strengthen different qualities of your mind. It focuses on strengthening qualities, such as appreciation, joy, compassion, patience, empathy, love, gratitude, compassion, humility, fearlessness, and tenderness, among others. More specifically, its goal is to use the mind to build positive pictures and give them life and direction with the thought energy of the mind (such as a visualization for healing).

A video on how to do this can be found at *www.youtube.com/watch?v =MCwX_zjgcdw.*

Mindfulness Meditation

Mindfulness meditation is considered one the most powerful and alternative meditation techniques, which emphasizes cultivating a highly receptive mindful attention toward any action or objects within your sphere of influence. It emphasizes a simple thing: to pay attention or be "mindful." This type of meditation is known to provide pain relief and help for those suffering from anxiety and depression.[52] It is also considered to be the most successful category of meditation in helping addiction—to the extent it can and does help.

One of the studies on meditation cited earlier, regarding the prison population support, showed that decreased alcohol use was demonstrated in inmates who incorporated Vipassana meditation, a mindfulness form of meditation *that focuses on acceptance of unwanted thoughts.*

There are several different types of Mindfulness Meditation techniques, including:

• *Vipassana meditation.* Vipassana is a way of self-transformation through self-observation. It focuses on the deep interconnection between mind and body, which can be experienced directly by disciplined attention to the physical sensations that form the life of the body, and that continuously interconnect and condition the life of the mind. It is this observation-based, self-exploratory journey to the common root of mind and body that dissolves mental impurity, resulting in a balanced mind full of love and compassion.[53]

In Vipassana meditation, one does not try to deny or ignore thoughts related to addiction. Rather, when a thought or craving to use arises, it teaches one to observe and accept the presence of the thought while not over-identifying with it. In this way, one can acknowledge the reality of such thoughts while learning to refocus energy and intention elsewhere.

This type of meditation is appealing to some because it avoids blame and stigmatization related to the addictive thought process while also acknowledging its reality.[54]

• *Movement meditation.* This is usually yoga, *t'ai chi, qi gong* or another physical mind-body exercise. This type of meditation involves focusing on your bodily sensations, breathing and mindfully watching and perhaps letting go of whatever thoughts and emotions arise as you practice. Slow *walking meditation* is another possibility.

• *Breathing meditation.* Many meditations involve focusing on the breath. Two variations of breathing meditation techniques include Breath Awareness meditation and Stillness in the Breath meditation; the second builds on success with the first. Both are what they sound like, but take a bit of practice; you can find step-by-step instructions at *www.meditationoasis.com/how-to-meditate/simple-meditations/breathing-meditations/*. A video showing a third variation—deep breathing meditation—can be found at *www.youtube.com/watch?v=hD2eGsGTldc*. Another variation is Breathing Space meditation.

• *Body scan meditation.* Often done lying down, but you can use any posture you like. This meditation involves becoming aware of your bodily sensations in a mindful way, step by step. You can start from the top of your head and move downwards, or at your toes and move upwards, or even from your heart outwards in a spiral. You will begin to discover how easily your attention wanders off to other thoughts and how to be kind to yourself rather than self-critical when this happens.

• *Visualization meditation.* Visualization techniques work well for those who find it difficult to focus on a mantra or a particular topic, and/or for people who mostly imagine negative things instead of positive (e.g. alcoholics). It involves generating an image or idea in your mind, such as love or joy or a positive, then building a visual image of what that might mean. With each inhale, you feel your body expand with potential, and exhale your positive thought into your world.[55] Visualization meditation can also be done in groups, with each member adding to the previous person's description of their images.

Two main visual meditations include:

• *Mountain meditation.* This meditation helps you to cultivate stability and groundedness and feel more centered.

• *Lake meditation.* This meditation is about exploring the beauty of accepting and allowing experiences to be just as they are.

A good overall description of visualization meditation can be found at *www.project-meditation.org/a_mt4/meditation_visualization_techniques.html.* A good YouTube video (that is nothing but verbal narrative) can be found at *www.youtube.com/watch?v=wVt_WmUHSNQ.*

• *Gardening Meditation (also known as "Hoeing" Meditation).* I think I invented this, and it is my favorite. This involves having a gardening spot where you just go to hoe the earth with a spade. I have a small 10 x 10 community garden spot where I live. While working in the garden, I came to realize that the continuous, rhythmic, motion of hoeing a garden puts me in an almost trancelike state, after which I find myself very relaxed. Perfect for the avid (alcoholic) gardener or even those of you who are not but have to weed the flower beds, etc. Turning it into a relaxing exercise, instead of a chore, with an added cardiovascular benefit is win-win all around in my book.

• *Expanding Awareness Meditation.* This is usually called sitting meditation, but it can be practiced in any position. The meditation involves focusing (often in the following order) on your breath, body, sounds, thoughts and feelings, and finally developing an open awareness where you're choicelessly aware of whatever is most predominant in your consciousness.

You can break down Expanding Awareness Meditation into separate meditations, each powerful and transformative in themselves:

• *Mindfulness of breath meditation.* Focusing your attention on the feeling of your in-breath and out-breath. Each time your mind wanders, bring your attention back non-judgmentally.

• *Mindfulness of body meditation.* Feeling the physical sensation in your body from moment to moment. You can also practice this together with the awareness of breathing.

• *Mindfulness of sounds meditation.* Being aware of sounds as they arise and pass away. If no ambient sounds exist, you can simply listen to the silence and notice what effect doing so has on you.

• *Mindfulness of thoughts meditation.* Being aware of your thoughts arising and passing through your mind, creating a sense of distance between yourself and your thoughts. You allow the thoughts to come and go as they please, without judging or attaching to them.

• *Mindfulness of feelings meditation.* Noticing whatever feelings arise for you. In particular, you notice where you feel the emotion in your body and bring a quality of acceptance and curiosity to your emotions.

• *Open awareness meditation.* Sometimes called choiceless awareness, because you become aware of whatever's most predominant in your awareness without choosing. You may be aware of any of the above meditation experiences as well.[56]

As you can see, there are literally dozens of different meditation types to choose from, and it only takes one to possibly help. All of the above meditation types could provide potential benefits to alcoholics seeking a great sense of tranquility and relaxation, though again there is no definitive proof of such benefits. Like so many things in life, the benefits you receive will be in direct proportion to the effort you make.

Salvation Army Rehab

The Salvation Army (SA) is a charitable organization operating in 126 countries known for a variety of charitable works and its charity stores. It operates with a quasi-military structure (e.g., "Army" is no accident in the name). It is characterized as a Christian organization, primarily Methodist in its beliefs, although distinct in government and practice. Its objectives include "the advancement of the Christian religion . . . of education, the relief of poverty . . . beneficial to society or the community of mankind as a whole."

Sobriety and abstinence from alcohol is an important cornerstone of SA's beliefs and activities. *It does not believe alcohol has any positive effect in any society.* As part of this philosophy, the SA has established its Adult Rehabilitation Centers (ARC), which is in large part focused on combating substance abuse but also in providing work therapy; life skills training; and individual, group and family counseling.

Each person considered for admittance into the Salvation Army Adult Rehabilitation Center must:

• Admit the need for rehabilitation to overcome problems

- Be in good physical health

- Be willing to participate in the entire program

- *Commit to a six-month period of rehabilitation (inpatient in nearly all respects)*

- Be free of intoxicating drugs, including alcohol, upon admission

- Express a desire to rebuild a lifestyle free of chemical dependency

During the stay, each man (not usually women)[57] is offered counseling, group therapy, spiritual guidance, educational programs, work therapy, chemical dependency classes, Christian living classes (practical application of Christian ethics), Bible study, literacy education, medical screening, and help with anger management and relapse prevention.

Work therapy is a major part of the program. When possible, men are placed in an assignment compatible with past work experience and abilities. In many work therapy areas, fundamental training is provided to prepare men for entering the job market. Chemical dependency classes have guest lecturers and film viewing sessions showing all aspects of addiction including many classic symptoms and emotional phases through which the disease progresses.

SA provides access to other support groups including Alcoholics Anonymous and Narcotics Anonymous.[58]

Author's Note: As you might imagine, this program is probably best suited for men who have hit complete bottom, are very open to incorporating religion into their daily regimen, and in general need a completely new start in nearly every aspect of their life. I almost did this once, but the six-month commitment was too much for me at the time, as I was still somewhat functional and was still making some money.

As you can tell by now, anyone who suggests you "need therapy" or should "go to rehab" without any education or experience into what is involved, doesn't know what the hell they are talking about. But that shouldn't dissuade you from trying them; you just need to go into the process educated on what they are about and with the right set of expectations.

What is the right set of expectations? For rehab (particularly inpatient), it is an expectation that you are entering a "safe harbor" that will protect you—for a time—from the temptations of alcohol while you get your head wrapped around a future without it. If you are doing it while reading this book, it will give you time and an opportunity to explore your triggers and possible new defenses without worrying about an unexpected attack.[59] In addition, any rehab program will provide a certain level of "baseline" education on the nature of alcoholism and how you can combat it, which can only help.

The discussion on therapy also shows how just throwing around the term "go to therapy" or "see a shrink" is insufficient. You need to investigate possible therapists thoroughly; in particular examining what kind of therapy they practice and how much experience they have in treating alcoholics.

Finally, recognize that even with the best rehab and/or therapy, _**they will not be enough to keep you sober longer-term.**_ Eventually the defenses they provide you will begin to weaken, or attacks will come from other areas where rehab/therapy did not provide much in the way of defenses to begin with. If you expect this reality, and treat rehab/therapy as just two levels of defense in a much bigger fortress of protection, then you will make the most out them and they will serve as a valuable part of your long-term defense. If you expect that either will be sufficient by themselves long term or will provide some sort of "cure," you are *completely* deluding yourself.

Therapy and in particular Rehab is where many alcoholics are introduced to the concept of an alcoholic "community," discussed next.

LEVEL 7

Join a Community

From a timing standpoint, whether you first do rehab and therapy, and then join one of the support communities discussed here such as AA or Women For Sobriety (WFS), or you join a community first and then do rehab and therapy, really doesn't matter. The key is to join *at least one* community that you can turn to as part of your overall defense building efforts and support structure.

There are numerous support organizations that have been established over the years to help alcoholics achieve and maintain sobriety. Many of these were established to support specific recovery/rehabilitation programs, often formulated by the organization's founder(s). The most well-known is Alcoholics Anonymous (AA), but there are others with various focuses (e.g., Women-only) and/or philosophies (with or without religion/spirituality, viewing or not viewing alcoholism as a disease), etc. Some of the more well-known ones are listed here in alphabetical order: I strongly encourage you to do a thorough research for *alcoholic* communities to join at least one.

Why?

We introduced the concept and importance of building a support network in Level 4—Engage Friends and Family. This Level is the next logical extension of this concept. Now that you have Detoxed, and perhaps been introduced to the concepts of support programs in Rehab, Therapy or during your Detox, you are ready to extend your support network to a new group of people—other alcoholics looking to become sober or who are already sober.

A *critical aspect to recognize is that most if not all of these programs view themselves as* stand-alone *treatment/support programs, e.g., that your sobriety begins and ends, succeeds or fails,* with them. *That is NOT a view that this program endorses. Not because it is not a worthy goal; rather it is because* **few of these programs work on a stand-alone basis for most of their participants.** *Stats vary depending on the program and the effectiveness methodology, but* none *of these programs has anything approaching a double-digit success rate.*

● ●

Calculating Treatment Program "Success" Rates

Measuring the success rates of addiction treatment programs can be very complex and incredibly subjective. It mainly depends on three factors:

1. When a person is considered to have "entered" the program;

2. How long after that he or she is "measured"; and

3. The definition of "success" (and by implication "failure").

For example, if a person has entered a program and is still there a year later, is that a "success?" Would they still be a success if they drank or relapsed during that time but kept coming to meetings? How often or consistently would they have to come to be considered to still be "in the program?" Would or should they have to complete a certain number of steps (or some specific steps) to be considered to have "tried" the program? It can get pretty muddled pretty quickly when you get into the details.

The *vast* majority of people in programs such as AA drop out within a year (95% according to AA!),[1] with "dropping out" apparently just meaning they don't go to meetings anymore (there is no additional detail). So the assumption is those who have been there at least a year have been successful at stopping their drinking (does it also presume they have "completed" all the steps in that time? Still use their sponsor?). If you *only* measure people who have "been in the program" (however that is defined) for at least a year, you are going to have *far* higher "success rates" than if you counted ALL people starting from Day 1 (more on AA success rates and issues later in the broader AA analysis section).

From a layman's perspective (including mine), most objective observers would focus on the latter. Anybody and everybody who has tried AA (at least for a couple meetings) should be counted. If they drop out (e.g., don't come to meetings anymore for at least a couple of months) they should count towards the "failure rate." Using that as a premise you are going to see the success rate after say a year drop to low single digits, and *that* presumes that those remaining still don't drink at all, which is likely a stretch. So discount those remaining by 20%—another guess. Similar logic could apply to all treatment programs (potentially including this one).

In general, after taking all these factors into account a rough consensus (and the math), **_there seems to be that a 3–5% "success rate" applies to AA and similar programs._** How the Conquer Program's success rate will be objectively calculated is to be determined. However, in my (obviously biased) opinion it should only include people who have read the entire book, _and_ tried Levels 1 through 9 (e.g., Phases 1 and 2). Nor would I include people who relapsed as a "failure" as long as they learned from it and continued refining their program defenses. You can see how this gets pretty complicated pretty quickly.

For you executing the Conquer Program, you should view these other programs more broadly—_as a Community extension of your support network._ These programs are there to help you defend against alcohol when other methods are not working well on that day for that particular trigger or circumstance. In those situations, calling a fellow community member or going to a meeting may be just the ticket you need, not necessarily to hear about step 4 in the AA 12 step list, but to hear and be around others who know about the daily struggles with alcoholism.

· ·

WHAT TO LOOK FOR IN A COMMUNITY

There are four key things to look for in an alcoholism community: Relatability, Demographics, Convenience, and Variety.

"Relatability"

The most important thing you want in your community is what I call Relatability, which is your ability to "relate" to the persons attending the same meetings as you. Also known as "identifying," this refers to the degree that you see some of yourself and your background in them. This is important because if you think a person has nothing in common with you about how they became an alcoholic, what their triggers are (even if they do not call them that), what their daily life is like, etc., then frankly you will not listen to them let alone feel like they are people with whom you feel comfortable sharing your own stories.

You don't want them to be exactly like you by any means; you just want them to be enough like you to have common background elements. These elements include their personalities, their "back stories" (history), and their general attitudes towards getting and staying sober, both individually and how they express themselves as a group. As you might guess, these can vary widely between groups. Some groups are informal and very outgoing, while others can be strictly business, with a specific agenda and process. While some of the surface demographics will give some indication of relatability, e.g., demeanor, dress, gender, age, you have to spend time with the group (at least a couple meetings) to get a sense of the nature of the group and the people who attend.

Demographics

Don't discount the importance of demographics. It can be extremely important, particularly when it comes to *gender* and *age*. As noted before, many women have issues with certain aspects of some types of alcoholic communities, so ones that offer women-only groups/meetings may be attractive. Same for age—youth is often greatly underrepresented in many groups and meetings and several youths have told me that they feel very uncomfortable in them. Many groups also can have a large proportion of blue-collar persons (e.g., vs. professional/white collar) which may be important for some, and certainly as it relates to Job-related issues.

Convenience

Some communities, particularly AA, seem to have meetings everywhere, all the time. This availability can be of enormous help, because for many people if a meeting is at all *in*convenient then that is an easy excuse not to go! Some are moving towards online meetings to address the convenience issue (it also helps anonymity), but you should recognize there is *no* substitute for face-to-face interaction when it comes to Community for the purposes of *this* program. You want someone you have gotten to know face-to-face to be able to help you or just to talk to when you are in a pinch regarding some crisis or tough situation.

Variety

There is no denying it: some meetings can be incredibly boring, particularly if they cover the same topic in the same style every time, like "Big Book" readings, with the same people talking about the same things after the readings. I fully recognize my reaction may just be because of my personality. Some people likely find great comfort in that predictability and routine, but for me I just need more variety. That's one of the reasons

I like speaker-type meetings so much. You never know what the story is going to be for these individuals; some are extremely fascinating in what they went through during their drinking and how they clawed their way out if it. There is no right way, just what fits your personality and even mood at the time.

* *
# Combining Other Community Program Teachings With The Conquer Program

For some of you, the teachings, steps, or other parts of programs advocated by an individual community may *alone* be enough to get you sober. If that is the case, great! Recognize that you will be one of the relatively small percentage for which this is so, making it even more important to adhere and diligently practice over time the concepts and steps contained in that particular program.

However, I would strongly encourage you to *also* continue following the Conquer Program. Not only does it not preclude or conflict with any other treatment programs that I am aware of, its very nature can make it very complementary to those programs, such as discussions of triggers (whether they are called that or not) and the use of spirituality.

There are always exceptions of course. Some programs take a very strong stand against spirituality, or refuse to treat alcoholism as a disease, or negatively view the use of rehabs, therapy, or other medical practices in alcoholism treatment. My view is that these programs are few and generally operate at the fringes of accepted medical practice. Even so, much of the Conquer Program can be done in coexistence with these programs, and at a minimum can serve as a backup in case your individual program of choice fails for some reason some day.

* *

COMMUNITY EXAMPLES

The following provides an overview of some Communities to consider for this Level. It is by no means an exhaustive list, but they are some of the more well-known ones. I lead with Alcoholics Anonymous, not just because it is first alphabetically but because it is by far the most well-known and convenient alcoholism Community available.

For that reason, I spend a large amount of time here not just providing an overview of what it is, but also in analyzing its philosophy, approach and issues. I do recommend that you try at least a few AA meetings to get a feeling for what the seemingly big deal of AA is, but for many different reasons it may not be for you. Frankly I don't care which Community you join, but you *need* to join at least one—to provide that extended part of your support network defense if and when you need it to combat particular alcohol-related situations that your other defenses cannot do that day. Or just to have a safe place to relax knowing you are in a completely alcohol-free environment.

Alcoholics Anonymous—The Gorilla in the Support Room

Alcoholics Anonymous (AA) is the most well-known program in the world for addressing alcoholism. It is the "big kahuna;" the 800-pound gorilla in the alcoholic treatment/support program world. Why? Perhaps because it was one of the first such programs, founded in 1935. But there can be no doubt that it has successfully kept sober many individuals over the years. Every alcoholic seeking sobriety should try it—at least by attending a few meetings. That said, AA has several aspects that can be problematic for many people. *And, its success rate is FAR lower than generally believed.*

What is AA?

First, some basic info: AA was founded in 1935 by a couple of men frustrated by their inability to stay sober. They formulated a "12-Step" program, and over time developed a variety of teachings and other guidance captured in what has come to be called *"The Big Book."* These steps and readings from *The Big Book* form the basis of most AA meetings.

AA as an organization views the thousands of meetings that take place each day as the work of autonomous groups, responsible for supervising themselves.[2] While there is no actual count, one AA chapter estimate has overall AA "membership" in the US at approximately 2 million people in almost 100,000 Groups. Groups are local chapters that coordinate and conduct their own set of meetings.

For example, a self-named "New Life" group may organize Monday 7:30 pm, Wednesday 7:30 pm and Friday 8 pm evening meetings at the local Baptist church. Another group with a different name may organize its own meetings on Monday evenings at 6 pm, Wednesday afternoons at noon, and Saturday mornings at 8 am in another venue a few miles down the road. The only coordination involved is passing organizational info to regional AA organizations that maintain a master list of all groups and meeting times/types for publication on websites and other forums.

There is NO data captured on the individual identities or other personal information of members/attendees. The whole program is based on anonymity.

● ●

What Are AA Meetings Like?

AA is based on anonymity, with "members" (really, anyone who shows up) identifying themselves only with their first name, so there is absolutely no reason to think you have to attend one meeting over another. That said; there are "specialized" meetings, such as women/men-only, Open (alcoholics and nonalcoholics invited), and Closed (only alcoholics) being some of the most common variations. There are no statistics available about the demographics of AA participants. My observation is that it is skewed towards older men, but that is just my personal experience (based on several hundred meetings across about 50 groups in half a dozen states). Participation, without exception, was majority male in every single meeting I attended (exception: those meetings I went to while in Inpatient Rehab were predominantly female, which is weird in retrospect). It is a safe bet that with the exception of Women-only meetings the majority of participants (in "outside" meetings) will be male most of the time.

Meetings generally start with a quick overview of what AA is about (often called the "preamble"), including its anonymous nature. Then the meeting focuses on a particular topic, usually a particular Step in AA's 12-Step program and/or reading from a chapter from *The Big Book,* which is in effect a much more detailed discussion of a particular alcoholism issue or step. Some meetings are "speaker" meetings, where a specific person (usually not a regular member of the group, and often a total stranger to the attendees) talks about his or her experiences with alcohol. Personal note: speaker meetings were my favorite, since they allowed me to relate to someone else's situation in great detail, and were often very interesting in general.

After the readings or speakers, the remainder of the meeting is "open discussion," where anybody who wants to can talk about his or her thoughts on the particular topic or what is bugging them that day in general. Cross-talk, e.g., more than one person at a time talking is not allowed. At the end of the meeting (usually 1 hour) the meeting is often closed with *The Serenity Prayer.*

Tip: when trying out AA for the first time, try a few different groups and/or meeting times, not just the one closest to you at the most convenient time. While it can be hard to precisely define, different groups and different meetings can have different "personalities" in total and of course in the individuals who attend, even in the same geographical area.

● ●

Finding a group that you are comfortable with and decide to attend regularly is the most important decision in pursuing AA—at least as it applies to the Conquer Program. The reason is that the Community nature of this Level is not just having warm bodies around you—it is getting to know at least some of the other attendees (even if you never find out their last name!). There may be ones you can call in a crisis and maybe even ones who you feel comfortable asking to be a sponsor if you decide you want to try the AA program to its fullest.

● ●

What Is an AA Sponsor?

Newcomers to AA are encouraged to find an experienced fellow alcoholic, called a sponsor, to help them understand and follow the AA program. The sponsor should preferably have experience in all twelve of the steps, be the same gender as the sponsored person and refrain from imposing personal views on the sponsored person.[3] There is no "qualification" or certification of any kind required to be a sponsor; anyone can show up and offer to be one.

● ●

This group can (it does not have to) become your "home group," which really only means that you can (not must) put your name (just your first name and initial of your last name) on a roster list and indicate whether or not you are willing to sponsor other alcoholics. You can get emails about announcements as well, e.g., a meeting postponed, an upcoming treasurer meeting, a member death, etc. (you do NOT get on any sort of spam list, and you do not get emailed about trivial matters). Nothing prevents you from selecting multiple groups as your "home" group, or from selecting any group as one at all. It is just a label for a group whose meetings are the ones you go to the most.

Groups are self-supporting, generally on a shoe-string. During the meeting, a basket is passed around for those who want to put one dollar in—there is no obligation. This money is used to buy supplies (e.g., coffee, cookies) and pay rent (meetings are often held in local churches, either for free or at a very low rate).

If you are not comfortable with one group of people, then try another. However, all the ones in my experience were/are universally friendly, supportive, and very open to helping new members.

Is AA Effective?

Certainly one can convincingly argue that AA has helped hundreds of thousands of people become and stay sober since its founding in 1935. Testimonials abound:

> *It has been 6 years, 2 months since my last drink. So, how did I get to the point where the compulsion to drink has been removed? Early on, I went to at least one meeting daily. I got a sponsor and worked the steps. I studied the big book and the 12 x 12 and got into service very early on. And today, I am in service, have a sponsor and attend 3–5 meetings per week.*
>
> guest andrew, alcoholism.about.com

From my research, I would say the AA testimonials were roughly 50/50 between those that credited the program "secularly" and those where references to God and/or a higher power took center stage. The sometimes intense nature of AA with respect to God/religion/spirituality is discussed shortly.

> *I am sober in AA for 25 years, not bragging or complaining. It always is just for today. I could not stop drinking. If I am afraid of a trigger, it means the gun is still loaded. I need to continue with thorough inventory and disposing of what is not worth having and cultivating what is desirable. We all look for fulfillment, ecstasy, instead of looking in a bottle, look for love, for God, self, others. Do not despair. Rest when you must, but never quit. May God richly bless all who seek the peace and fulfillment they desire.*
>
> Guest1985, alcoholism.about.com

A simple search on Google will easily find hundreds of testimonials like the ones above. If you haven't tried AA, I strongly encourage you to do so—it is in many ways "simpler" than this program and has proven it works *sometimes.* But relying *solely* on AA frankly seems to work over the long-term for *only for a small percentage* of alcoholics.

How effective is AA from a broader statistical viewpoint? The numbers can be all over the map, depending on who is doing the "reporting" and what they are measuring. Did they measure anyone who tried AA even once? Kept at it for a year? Five years? Did starting AA in a rehab program influence the numbers? Did one relapse count, or did it have to be back to full-time drinking to be considered a "failure?" Who would even know if you were drinking or not? And on and on.

One of the simplest measures for AA specifically (not so much for other communities that have far fewer meetings but other tools) is how long people keep coming to AA meetings. And by its own account the statistics are damning. A piece of an actual memo from the Alcoholics Anonymous GSO (General Services Office) based on an analysis of a survey period that ran for 12 years stated:

> **"After just one month in the Fellowship, 81% of the new members have already dropped out. After three months, 90% have left, and 95% have discontinued attendance inside one year."** (Kolenda, 2003, Golden Text Publishing Company).[4]

This memo strongly implies, at best, that AA effectively has a 5 *percent success rate*, maximum! This contrasts with the general populace perception that perceives a *far* higher success rate for AA than reality. Any discussion about alcohol treatment in the media seems to reference AA and/or rehab when someone in the news admits an alcohol problem. Courts (in the U.S.) regularly dictate AA meetings for DUI offenders or juveniles with alcohol-related charges.[5]

What is far less known is that many people (including me) *do* try AA and *cannot* get it to work despite their best efforts. Here are some examples:

> *What the hell am I supposed to do? I am not an AA person. I've been to at least 100 different meetings and I just don't connect with anyone. After rehab I tried meetings, but I guess when it comes to my own problems I just don't like telling people my secrets. So I stayed sober and lonely for a while, but eventually it got easier until money problems came into effect and now I picked it up again—not every day, but I started sneaking a shot or two. I think because I don't have anybody to talk to. Help, I'm not AA material.*
>
> Guest can't tell u, alcoholism.about.com

> *Boy I wish it had worked for me, but it didn't. But in all honesty I really didn't give it a try. I got a sponsor but didn't meet with or call him. I went to meetings but mostly zoned off, except for the stories.[6]*
>
> anonymous

The 12 Steps

At the core of AA are its 12 Steps. The steps provide a kind of progressive roadmap for alcoholics to follow to ultimately reach and maintain sobriety. There are various versions and adaptations of the steps, but the below is from the official AA website:[7]

The 12 Steps of Alcoholics Anonymous

1. We admitted we were powerless over alcohol—that our lives had become unmanageable.

2. Came to believe that a Power greater than ourselves could restore us to sanity.

3. Made a decision to turn our will and our lives over to the care of God as we understood Him.

4. Made a searching and fearless moral inventory of ourselves.

5. Admitted to God, to ourselves, and to another human being the exact nature of our wrongs.

6. Were entirely ready to have God remove all these defects of character.

7. Humbly asked Him to remove our shortcomings.

8. Made a list of all persons we had harmed, and became willing to make amends to them all.

9. Made direct amends to such people wherever possible, except when to do so would injure them or others.

10. Continued to take personal inventory and when we were wrong promptly admitted it.

11. Sought through prayer and meditation to improve our conscious contact with God, as we understood Him, praying only for knowledge of His will for us and the power to carry that out.

12. Having had a spiritual awakening as the result of these Steps, we tried to carry this message to alcoholics, and to practice these principles in all our affairs.

Certainly these steps seem fairly reasonable on the surface and can be effective for some. But since it appears that only a small percentage of alcoholics can get and stay sober solely using AA, it is obvious that there are some major issues. I have tried to identify the most obvious and common to those for whom AA did not work.

AA Issues, Analysis, and Critique

Before I get into my personal step-by-step analysis of AA's 12-Steps, I need to address some other issues that have been widely publicized recently about AA. The first is called "The 13th Step" which is *not* an official part of the AA program. It occurs when somebody who is an AA "veteran," e.g. been in AA for several months or much longer and feels like they know the ropes (even to the point of being a sponsor), tries to start up a sexual relationship with somebody who is new to AA and/or recovery. There is no doubt that the *potential* for this to happen is high; persons just getting sober are often confused and are looking to AA to provide guidance in their screwed-up life. Meeting and spending time with someone who seems "wise" in comparison, has common interests (e.g. alcohol recovery), and other factors such as a reawaking sexual desire[8] is tailor-made for such liaisons. AA recognizes this potential and *strongly* discourages having a sponsor of the opposite sex (and even goes further by discouraging anyone new to sobriety from forming any new sexual relationship for at least a year after getting sober). But that doesn't mean sponsor/AA-newcomer sexual relationships don't happen. While I have personally never witnessed such activity, and most AA participants generally view it negatively, sometimes it happens.

In 2013 there were a bit of a rash of negative writings about AA, particularly on the topic of AA and its (un)suitability for women, notably from a major article in *The Wall Street Journal* titled "Why She Drinks: Women and Alcohol Abuse."[9] The 13th step is discussed and harshly criticized in this article in general as well as referencing its potential danger for women from sexual predators who apparently deliberately target AA meetings. However, it should be noted that several (women) readers pushed back harshly on this portrayal of AA as some sort of unsafe prowling ground for unsavory characters. I certainly have never personally observed anything remotely resembling inappropriate sexual advances, but the fact that there is a commonly known phrase as "The 13th Step" is disturbing in itself.

Beyond the sexual vulnerability issue, the WSJ article and other recent books, such as Gabrielle Glaser's *Her Best Kept Secret,* take strong issue with how the lessons of powerlessness and humility are at odds with what many women need when it comes to dealing with their addiction. The article states that *"It doesn't take an advanced degree in gender studies to realize that this approach—which has worked well for millions of people—may not be perfect for women whose biggest problem is not an excess of ego but a lack of it. Women are twice as likely to suffer from depression and anxiety as men—and are far more likely to medicate those conditions with alcohol."*[10]

It goes on to say *"Many women who drink heavily are also the victims of sexual abuse and have had eating disorders. The idea of being powerless can underscore a woman's sense of vulnerability, researchers say. 'Women need to feel powerful, not like victims of something beyond their control,' says [a doctor being referenced in the article]. 'It gives women power to feel they themselves can change.'"*

Powerlessness as a trigger is explored in significant detail in Level 2—Know Your Triggers, as is Anxiety and Depression.

A Critique of the AA 12 Steps

While the AA 12-steps seem reasonable on the surface and seemingly effective for many (despite the concerns quoted in the article), they were not for me because of issues I found with the steps themselves, itemized below. I also include in the step-by-step analysis below how the 12-steps mesh (or do not) with The Conquer Program.

Let's take these one at a time and the reasons I viewed them as problematic. Most boiled down to the large prevalence of God/religion in them, which is fine if you are ready for God/religion/spirituality to be part of becoming and staying sober.[11] I was not.

Step 1 (Admitting that you are "powerless" over alcohol)—This one was an easy, logical step to accept and adopt, given that I had already admitted to myself I was an alcoholic, though at that point I had a great deal of trouble admitting it out loud to others. There is a reason this is the first step. If you can't admit that you are *out of control* when it comes to drinking, then the rest of the steps are pointless, and you are wasting your and everyone else's time. That is the very reason getting yourself to admit you are an alcoholic is the goal of the first Level of this program.

Despite what I feel is a fairly obvious and reasonable step, some people apparently have a great deal of difficulties with it. As implied by the below testimonial, it may be a function of it being perceived as a sign of weakness, refusal to take responsibility, or inability to accept a major imperfection in one's self. Those are just guesses—it will depend on the person. But in retrospect I can see where my delay in accepting my addiction could have been aggravated by my subconsciously equating it with weakness or major imperfection.

> *My biggest trigger, for years, was the inability to truly own the 1st Step. Taking accountability that I was powerless (doesn't matter why) over alcohol and my life had become unmanageable.*
>
> guest john m, alcoholism.about.com

> *I am currently a daily drinker. I have tried AA and have family members in the program. I personally have seen how it works, but I do not agree that anybody is powerless over anything. I think it stems from boredom and habit. People need to figure out the root of their problem, including me.*
>
> Anonymous, cryingoutnow.com

While I wasn't ready to stop drinking when I started attending AA, and drank on several occasions immediately before and after meetings when this step was discussed, it was obvious to me the criticality of embracing the concept of being powerless over alcohol. It turned out I couldn't embrace most of the remaining ones. From a Conquer Program standpoint, it is perfectly consistent with the central theme of *lack of control* equals *powerless.*

Step 2 (*Power greater than ourselves*)—During the first times I was in AA,[12] I was not sure I wanted to stop drinking, and certainly had not done so. But I *did* want someone or something to help me to get to the state of *wanting* to stop drinking. I knew I couldn't do it myself, nor did I think any human could get me there as well, so I was open to the "something else."

However, I was an agnostic—I believed in God, but that was about it. I was not ready to put my faith, such as it was, in a God I was unsure about on many different levels. However, I did like the concept of a Higher Power, particularly as the AA program leaders during the step 1 discussions I attended emphasized that the Higher Power could be anything—real or imagined, live or not.

At the time, I hadn't looked at the steps further down the line to fully appreciate how quickly the concept of a generic "higher power" was replaced with very specific references to God, so I accepted the explanation at face value. Since I was not ready to commit to God as my higher power, I chose my dog Mollie, who had recently passed away. This choice was by no means a trivializing of the higher power concept; my marriage was deteriorating rapidly and I felt extremely lonely, and Mollie was my constant companion until she literally died in my arms. I missed her terribly and felt I would do my best with her constantly in my thoughts during this process. Alas, it was not enough.

I wish the AA step writers had stuck to the higher power concept throughout instead of essentially stopping here so early in the program. As my thinking on God, faith, and other spiritual issues evolved over the years, I continued to believe in the concept of a higher power. I believe this is one of the early highlights of the AA program and frankly a missed opportunity to engage people who—like me at that point—did not view God as essential to stopping drinking, felt uncomfortable incorporating religion into their alcoholism, or only reluctantly considered spirituality as a key element in their quest for sobriety.

Step 3 (Made a decision to turn to . . . the care of God)—Here, as an agnostic, is where the 12 steps started to lose me with the phrase *"God, as we understood Him."* To me, cynic that I was, the "as we understood Him" sounded almost like an afterthought. It was as if a subset of the writers of the steps were fighting a losing battle to keep specific God references to a relative minimum versus the concept of a higher power. Indeed, references to a Higher Power or even any similar qualifier to God appear nowhere after this step (except Step 11 with an "as we understood him" reference, which again seemed like a grudging afterthought). It is pretty much God and God only from here on out.

Step 4 (Make a "moral inventory")—While I had no problem with this step in concept (though doing it wasn't a lot of fun), I quit pretty early in the process. I was never quite clear on what a "moral" inventory was. I asked, but never got a satisfactory answer. Whose "morals?" My morals? I don't think so—that maybe was a factor in why I was an alcoholic to begin with. Other people's morals? I didn't see any reason to think their morals were any better than mine for the purposes of this step. The key purpose of this step (along with Steps 8 and 9) is to expunge the guilt of the past. So in this regard it is a cousin to identifying triggers discussed in this book, such as Anger and particularly Guilt.

Besides, how was I expected to accept a human's perception on what was "moral" when so many of the steps were predicated on having God (as I "understood him") help me? How was I to judge what He thought was moral? The Bible? Besides the Ten Commandments, laymen—particularly those who never read the Bible, such as me—sometimes have a difficult time determining what He clearly thought was right or wrong in the scriptures (besides obvious things like killing people, though there sure is a bunch of that going on), at least as far as *everyday* living is concerned.

Step 5 (Admitted to God . . .)—Frankly this is where I stopped cold in the steps. There wasn't anything objectionable or unreasonable in this step, *if* you were willing to fully drop the pretense of a higher power and invest totally in the concept of God as your partner in this journey. I was not.

Since I stopped at Step 5, my comments on the remainder are based solely on my looking back on those remaining steps as they were discussed in meetings.

Steps 6 and 7 (Ready to have God . . . /Humbly asked Him . . .)—These steps seem to place the full burden of fixing yourself on God, almost seeming like a faith-healing exercise. As I was faltering in Steps 4 and 5 and looking towards Step 6, this was just too much. While I didn't want personal accountability, I wasn't naïve (or drunk) enough not to recognize that I had to do much of this in my own head and with my own efforts, versus wishing for divine intervention to do it for me.

Steps 8 and 9 (Make a list of all I had harmed; make amends to them)—Besides scaring the hell out of me, even sober I'm not at all convinced about the need to make amends to *all* the people I harmed by my drinking. Making amends to family, of course, and key friends and even some past co-workers, but not *everyone* by any stretch. You have to consider that you had to be in the right in *some* of the disputes and that alcohol did not play a part in *every* interaction you had that did not turnout well.

Also, I continue to question in general the philosophy of this step and its timing. Everyone I have ever encountered in treatment programs has stressed that I had to get sober "for myself;" that the future was what mattered; that no one else mattered in my objective to get sober; and I had to focus on making the rest of my life worthwhile.

Yet here Steps 8 and 9 were focused on apologizing for or "fixing" what I had done to others in the past! In addition, presumably by the time one reached Steps 8 and 9 the alcoholic would have only been sober for a short time—perhaps only a few weeks. Suddenly going back and scraping open old wounds seems like a high-risk activity for potential relapse. These steps are also at odds with other very specific teachings in AA, particularly about "not regretting the past."[13]

Step 10 (Continually reassessing yourself; admit when you are wrong)— I have no problem in continually (re)assessing yourself (in a general way if not a "moral" way). In fact, I would strongly encourage it no matter how you get sober as a way to nip problems in the bud before they can fester.[14] Level 8—Break Bad Habits is one way to help you here.

Step 11 (Prayer, connection with God, et.al.)—All pretenses about not being overtly God-focused were given up by this step.

Step 12 (Carry message to other alcoholics)—I wholeheartedly agree with this step, and it really is the bottom line in my view. You went through hell to get sober, so why not try to help others do the same? It's the ultimate in volunteer work—using your tragedy to help others out with theirs. It will also *help you maintain your sobriety*, in my opinion, though the step doesn't specifically say so.[15]

While there are many worthwhile elements in the 12 Steps individually and AA in general, much of it seemed very evangelistic to me (and unfortunately still does), and I was not ready for it. Many would counter that while the 12 Steps might seem religious on the surface, they are often taught/discussed in an almost secular manner, depending on the AA group and the step/topic being discussed. Having attended many different AA groups I am very willing to concede that point. Certainly different groups have different approaches and tones when it comes to discussing the 12 Steps.

However, to those who say that it is wrong to view the steps as religious to begin with I would point them to various AA history discussions, such as *http://silkworth.net/dickb/12stephistory5.html*.[16] One excerpt:

Dr. Bob said he didn't write the Twelve Steps or have anything to do with the writing of them. He said the basic ideas came from the pioneers' study of the Bible. He specifically pointed to three Bible segments he said old timers considered "absolutely essential" (See DR. BOB and the Good Oldtimers; and Dick B., The Good Book and The Big Book; Why Early A.A. Succeeded: The Good Book in A.A. Yesterday and Today). The three Bible segments were Jesus's sermon on the mount (Matthew, Chapters Five to Seven), the entire Book of James, and 1 Corinthians 13.

The bottom line here is that if you are not ready for, open to, or at least able to tolerate a very God-oriented approach to getting sober, AA will probably not be right for you. If you have concerns about the makeup of the types of people who might be attending and how they might take advantage of you, AA might also not be right for you (though you can deal with this problem by being only part of certain types of groups, e.g., Women-only meetings).

In addition, some feel that participation in AA is a never-ending process. Others view it as "a lifelong preoccupation," or "forever recovering." Unfortunately, I agree with these phrases, and the desire to avoid that same fate is a core tenet of The Conquer Program.

> *Dear Prudie, My husband and I will celebrate our seventh anniversary this year. We have two children, 4 years and six months old. About a year and a half ago, after the threat of divorce, my husband joined AA and has been sober since. In my opinion, AA has taken over his life, to the point I see him less now that he is sober than when he was drunk. He goes to meetings once to twice daily, and several times on the weekends. We both work full time, and I pick up the kids make dinner, get them ready for bed and get the kitchen cleaned by the time he walks in the door at night (about 8 p.m.). I feel horrible when I say anything, since I complained when he was drunk, and now I am complaining when he was sober, but I am exhausted!*
>
> AA Wife[17]

Put another way: *If* you **do** enter the program with an open affinity and willingness towards religion or at least spirituality, *and* you **are** willing to have God become a key part of your life going forward, *and* if you **are** willing to set aside a good chunk of your longer-term life going to weekly or even daily meetings, AA stands a decent chance of working for you—even on a standalone basis.

But for most of you, **joining something like AA, Women For Sobriety (discussed shortly), or similar step programs will be mostly helpful in broadening your support network and filling key defense needs in vulnerable times**. You may also find that many of their topic discussions mesh well with various parts of this program, such as certain triggers. Always bear in mind that the Conquer Program is a multi-level program, and joining a Community such as AA is just one of thirteen.

Remember: There *will* be circumstances and triggers where going to a meeting or calling Community friends may be at the top of your list for best dealing with a bad situation, so you want to have those defenses ready to go when needed.

The balance of this Level discussion provides an overview of some other types of Community programs you might want to consider. Some take an AA-type approach, while others are expressly anti-AA. I encourage you to consider them and any others of which you might become aware. Frankly it does not matter too much which one you select—but you need to select at least one, so you have this kind of alcoholic Community defense ready if and when you really need it.

Rational Recovery

While most alcohol support programs, including Alcoholics Anonymous, focus on providing a softer approach to battling addiction. Rational Recovery takes a no-nonsense, hard-core attitude that an individual must quit their excessive drinking or be forced to lose everything. It is also one of the most vocal anti-AA groups out there. Key dimensions include:

• Rational Recovery does not regard alcoholism as a disease, but rather a voluntary behavior.

• Rational Recovery discourages adoption of the forever "recovering" drunk persona.

• There are no Rational Recovery support groups (although meetings were held throughout the country during the 1990s).

• Great emphasis is placed on self-efficacy (e.g., one's own ability to reach goals or complete tasks).

- There are no discrete steps and no consideration of religious matters.

At the core of Rational Recovery (RR) is its *Addictive Voice Recognition Technique* (AVRT). The program is offered for free via the Internet and through books, videos, and lectures. The Rational Recovery program is based on the premise that the addict *both desires and is capable of permanent, planned abstinence.* However, the Rational Recovery program recognizes that, paradoxically, the addict also wants to *continue* using. This paradox is because of his belief in the power of a substance to quell his anxiety; an anxiety that is itself partially substance-induced, as well as greatly enhanced, *by* the substance. This ambivalence is the Rational Recovery definition of addiction.

According to this [approach], the primary force driving an addict's predicament is what [the founder] calls the "addictive voice," which can physiologically be understood as being related to the parts of the human brain that control our core survival functions such as hunger, sex, and bowel control. Consequently, when the desires of this "voice" are not satiated, the addict experiences anxiety, depression, restlessness, irritability, and *anhedonia* (inability to feel pleasure). In essence, the RR method is to first make a commitment to planned, permanent abstinence from the undesirable substance or behavior, and then equip oneself with the mental tools to stick to that commitment. Most important to recovering addicts is the recognition of this addictive voice, and determination to remain abstinent by constantly reminding themselves of the rational basis of their decision to quit. As time progresses, the recovering addict begins to see the benefits of separating themselves and their rational minds from a bodily impulse that has no regard for responsibility, success, delayed gratification, or moral obligation.

[Overall] The RR program is based on recognizing and defeating what the program refers to as the "addictive voice" (internal thoughts that support self-intoxication) and *dissociation* from addictive impulses. The specific techniques of Addictive Voice Recognition Technique (AVRT) are concerned with demonstrating to the practitioner that the practitioner is in control of the addictive voice, not the other way around.[18]

The AVRT approach is not inconsistent with that of the Conquer Program, with the "addictive voice" being not that different from our drinking triggers, though on a much more limited and general basis. Its emphasis on dissociation is also consistent; the Conquer Program spends a great deal of time in breaking old, destructive associations and building new, more positive ones.

Attitude Towards AA

To say Rational Recovery is very anti-AA is to put it mildly. The program is founded on the belief that programs, such as AA, and more clinical treatment methods, such as rehab centers are both scientifically and spiritually "incorrect." It goes further with AA, stridently opposing several of its core dimensions such as its heavy reliance on God, attitude towards relapses, and often forced nature of attending AA meetings. Consider this quote from their website (*https://rational.org*):

> *AVRT-based recovery fits well with any religion except the 12-step program of Alcoholics Anonymous. In fact, AVRT does not advance any general philosophy or system of values; it merely rests upon universal family values such as family loyalty, honesty, privacy, individual responsibility, and self-restraint. Instead of setting forth new beliefs and values, AVRT directs one back to his or her original family values, especially the concepts of resisting temptation and choosing right over wrong, ideas that are acquired in the family and well-understood by age five.*
>
> *We object to the practice of requiring addicted people to seize upon a newfound "understanding" of God, and then depend upon that self-made entity for strength, wisdom and guidance. Addicted people cannot conceive of any benevolent entity that would condemn the act of self-intoxication. Indeed, the "God" of AA is a one-dimensional, loving God, infinitely tolerant of "relapses." Many groupers discover that, in spite of God's loving tolerance of "relapses," the cost of self-intoxication is still a painful death. To anyone versed in AVRT, AA's God-as-you-understand-him is none other than the Beast of addiction itself, and the 12-step program is the doctrinal form of the Addictive Voice.[19]*

Rational Recovery also strenuously objects to the regular habit of our (the U.S.) court system in mandating participation in AA. I have some sympathy with this view because the courts seem to have a greatly exaggerated sense of AA's effectiveness. As a general observation, Rational Recovery will not suit those searching for a more friendly approach to dealing with addiction and *certainly* not those who believe it is a disease or want to include some spiritual element in their getting sober. In fact, RR tends to view alcoholism as an indulgent behavior that can only be made worse by programs such as AA or clinical rehabilitation. As you might expect, RR has a narrow appeal in general and practically no appeal to established institutions like religious groups and our judicial system (it has sued, unsuccessfully as far as I can tell, to protest rulings making individuals attend AA).

As you might guess, I'm not going on record as recommending this program. However, I did not want to limit the possibilities to consider, and RR certainly gives you a perspective on the range of options to consider when considering Community programs. All have a worthy end goal but sometimes radically different approaches to try and achieve it.

Secular Organizations for Sobriety (SOS)

Secular Organizations for Sobriety (SOS) (*www.sossobriety.org/*), also known as Save Our Selves, is a non-profit network of autonomous addiction recovery groups. It emphasizes rational decision-making and is not religious or spiritual in nature, specifically avoiding spiritually-based addiction recovery programs philosophies. At its core are a number of guiding principles:

• SOS is not a spin-off of any religious or secular group. There is no hidden agenda, as SOS is concerned with achieving and maintaining sobriety (abstinence).

• SOS seeks only to promote sobriety amongst those who suffer from addictions.

• As a group, SOS has no opinion on outside matters and does not wish to become entangled in outside controversy.

• Although sobriety is an individual responsibility, life does not have to be faced alone. The support of other alcoholics and addicts is a vital adjunct to recovery.

• In SOS, members share experiences, insights, information, strength, and encouragement in friendly, honest, anonymous, and supportive group meetings.

- To avoid unnecessary entanglements, each SOS group is self-supporting through contributions from its members and refuses outside support.

- Sobriety is the number one priority in a recovering person's life.

- As such, he or she must abstain from all drugs or alcohol.

- Honest, clear, and direct communication of feelings, thoughts, and knowledge aids in recovery and in choosing nondestructive, non-delusional, and rational approaches to living sober and rewarding lives.

- As knowledge of addiction might cause a person harm or embarrassment in the outside world, SOS guards the anonymity of its membership and the contents of its discussions from those not within the group.

- SOS encourages the scientific study of addiction in all its aspects. SOS does not limit its outlook to one area of knowledge or theory of addiction.[20]

SOS recognizes genetic and environmental factors contributing to addiction, but allows each member to decide *whether or not alcoholism is a disease*. SOS holds the view that alcoholics can recover (addictive behaviors can be arrested) but that ultimately it is *never* cured, and relapse is always possible. SOS does not endorse sponsor/sponsored relationships.

Their guidelines seem a bit like "eye candy"—they sound good but how do I use them? However, I never tried SOS (and did not even know it existed until I was researching this book) and can't vouch for it personally, so perhaps the details within the program are much better. I do not like that they do not take a stand about alcoholism as a disease, which is a bit strange given their stated emphasis on pursuing addiction science.

SMART Recovery

Standing for *Self-Management and Recovery Training*, SMART Recovery focuses on empowering participants to abstain from drinking and create a more positive lifestyle. It is more science-based than other programs and looks at addiction as both a physical and a mental disorder and condones the use of the appropriate medication and psychological treatments. The following is from the website *www.smartrecovery.org*:

Our participants learn tools for addiction recovery based on the latest scientific research and participate in a world-wide community which includes free, self-empowering, science-based mutual help groups.

The SMART Recovery 4-Point Program® helps people recover from all types of addiction and addictive behaviors, including: drug abuse, drug addiction, substance abuse, alcohol abuse, gambling addiction, cocaine addiction, prescription drug abuse, and problem addiction to other substances and activities. SMART Recovery sponsors face-to-face meetings around the world, and daily online meetings. In addition, our online message board and 24/7 chat room are excellent forums to learn about SMART Recovery and obtain addiction recovery support.

SMART is built around a 4 Point Program that offers tools and techniques for each program point:

1. Building and Maintaining Motivation

2. Coping with Urges

3. Managing Thoughts, Feelings and Behaviors

4. Living a Balanced Life.

Like many non-AA programs, Smart Recovery tries to distinguish itself clearly from that program. They consider their differences to be summed up by the following:

• SMART Recovery is not an ideology but focuses on rational analysis and action.

• It does not consider that all addicts are alike. Thus, no one "solution" fits all.

• It does not claim that it is the best program for everyone with addiction problems, and in fact encourages trying other programs if it does not work.

• It emphasizes personal choice and responsibility for one's actions, versus being "powerless."

• It does not view religious and spiritual beliefs as essential in solving the problems of addiction.

• It does not consider "alcoholism" a life-long preoccupation.

- There is no single "alcoholic personality" type or profile.

- SMART Recovery meetings are self-help groups, not support groups.

- There is no definitive and incontrovertible text, such as AA's *Big Book.*

I confess I like a lot of the above. While their 4 Point Program is extremely general, a lot of the underlying details are well articulated, and I can see how that can translate into usable help. I also never tried it so I can't vouch for it personally. The fact that it says its program can work on *all* addictive behaviors is a bit concerning, despite saying elsewhere that all addicts are not alike, and no one solutions fits all. This implies to me a lack of focus on the nuances of alcohol addiction specifically.

Women for Sobriety (WFS)

Women for Sobriety (*http://womenforsobriety.org*)is the USA's first national program specifically designed for women alcoholics, founded in 1975. It aims to deal with the many issues that women have when it comes to excessive drinking or a dependency on alcohol, and was influenced by a mix of medical and feminist principles. It asserts that alcohol dependent women have fundamentally different needs in recovery than do men. *Author Note: This viewpoint has become increasingly visible and vocal as indicated in the AA discussion earlier.*

While still premised on alcoholism as a disease and using the Self-Help support group model, WFS has some major differences from Alcoholics Anonymous (though it positions itself as more of a complement to AA than an alternative). It never mentions God or a "Higher Power." Instead, women are helped to determine why they became so dependent—an approach very consistent with the Conquer Program. Participants are assisted to become self-empowered and to change their thinking.

Lapses are more tolerated in WFS, with no need to begin at day one of sobriety again, and openly talking to other members during meetings is allowed (unlike in AA that have no cross-talk rules). Another difference is the greeting; instead of announcing and labeling oneself as an alcoholic, members introduce themselves by stating, "Hi, I'm [name], and I'm a competent woman." There's no concern about being egotistical or the need to be humble (like AA emphasizes). Instead, WFS asserts that for most women with an alcohol problem there is a need to emphasize empowerment and increasing self-worth.

WFS has 13 affirmations in its New Life Acceptance Program. They are:

1. I have a life-threatening problem that once had me.
I now take charge of my life and my disease. I accept the responsibility.

2. Negative thoughts destroy only myself.
My first conscious sober act must be to remove negativity from my life.

3. Happiness is a habit I will develop.
Happiness is created, not waited for.

4. Problems bother me only to the degree I permit them to.
I now better understand my problems and do not permit problems to overwhelm me.

5. I am what I think.
I am a capable, competent, caring, compassionate woman.

6. Life can be ordinary or it can be great.
Greatness is mine by a conscious effort.

7. Love can change the course of my world.
Caring becomes all important.

8. The fundamental object of life is emotional and spiritual growth.
Daily I put my life into a proper order, knowing which are the priorities.

9. The past is gone forever.
No longer will I be victimized by the past. I am a new person.

10. All love given returns.
I will learn to know that others love me.

11. Enthusiasm is my daily exercise.
I treasure all moments of my new life.

12. I am a competent woman and have much to give life.
This is what I am and I shall know it always.

13. I am responsible for myself and for my actions.
I am in charge of my mind, my thoughts, and my life.

To make the Program effective for you, arise each morning fifteen minutes earlier than usual and go over the Thirteen Affirmations. Then begin to think about each one by itself. Take one Statement and use it consciously all day. At the end of the day review the use of it and what effects it had that day for you and your actions.[21]

From my research I found Women for Sobriety has more testimonials than any other group except for AA, both positive and negative. They do not appear to have a critical mass of in-person meetings like AA does, relying more on online forums. I had an opportunity to talk with one of the officers of WFS, who gave me some valuable insight into female-specific alcoholism issues as well as pointing me to additional material that I reference throughout this book. They did not let me join WFS, however, being very strict on it being women-only.

From my research, it is certainly true that alcoholism hits women in substantially different ways than men, from the triggers involved to medical issues. WFS takes this viewpoint even further, saying that women need their own program to successfully overcome the female-specific issues that come with alcoholism.

Online Communities

All of the above communities have various types of online forums for supporting their members. Some, like AA, do not focus much on electronic information. Whereas others (particularly those with relatively few or no face-to-face meetings), rely very heavily on online tools and forums to supplement their literature and other support capabilities.

In addition, there are online-only resources that can be of great help, such *www.alcoholism.about.com*. An excellent overview of support groups can also be found at *www.cigna.com/healthwellness/behavioral-awareness-series/coping-with-substance-abuse* (specifically the MP3 webinar recording at *www.cigna.com/assets/media/audio/behavioral-health-series/substance-abuse/2014/march2014-substance-abuse-replay.mp3*, and the supporting materials at *www.cigna.com/assets/docs/behavioral-health-series/substance-abuse/2014/maintaining-sobriety-march2014.pdf*).

Throughout this book, there are many other online sources that provide elements of support in various dimensions and perspectives of alcoholism. See the Resources section at the end of this book for those links.

Hopefully, this section has provided insight into what types of alcoholic communities are out there. It is very important that you give at least one of these a try. Even if the tenets of a specific program are not successful by themselves (which is likely), remember that *the* goal here is to get to know other alcoholics looking to become and stay sober. Those alcoholics and the meetings they attend can really help you out in certain situations where your defenses are otherwise vulnerable.

LEVEL 8

Break Bad Habits

As I've made plain already in several Levels of this book, developing or adopting new hobbies is an *essential* part of your new life of sobriety. To reiterate, becoming sober means you are freeing up an *immense* amount of time that you formerly spent obtaining, using, and recovering from alcohol. But before we get to hobbies, let's talk about habits, particularly *bad* habits. In my view, adopting a new hobby—particularly one that involves interacting with others—while still carrying around a bunch of bad habit baggage is a recipe for trouble in reaching and happily maintaining your sobriety. Bad habits can cause conflict and turmoil in your head and everyday life that you just don't need. Odds are that you either developed or made far worse some bad habits while you were drinking that made life uncomfortable, if not downright unpleasant, for many people around you.

First, let's look at some practical definitions. Like a lot of words used when discussing alcoholism, the word "habit" is familiar without necessarily meaning the same thing to different people. Hence, definition(s) are in order. *Thefreedictionary.com* defines a habit as:

> A recurrent, often unconscious pattern of behavior that is acquired through frequent repetition; An established disposition of the mind or character; A customary manner or practice.

Habits, of course, can be good or bad, or just *there*. Your routine before you go to bed is an example of one that is just there, with some positive overtones: you make sure the doors are locked, dishes are washed, kids are asleep, lights are out, brush your teeth, read a book, go to sleep. You may be thinking about other things that have nothing to do with those activities; they just happen.

While locking the doors, checking on the kids, and brushing our teeth can easily be viewed as "good," most of our habits are likely skewed more toward the Dark Side of habits. Unfortunately, bad habits—ones that have a detrimental impact on you and/or others—seem to be developed much easier than good ones (in my opinion) and are usually very hard to break (in nearly everybody's opinion). Most importantly, they can lurk in the background and make our lives and the lives of the people around us unpleasant. An unpleasant environment is *not* good for the newly sober; we are very fragile and vulnerable, and any negative may throw us back into the abyss.

Of course, many "bad" habits are minor, and many may be totally irrelevant to a sobriety discussion. Examples include chewing with your mouth open, belching (without saying excuse me), cracking your knuckles, fidgeting, and chewing your fingernails. But others are not so trivial.

ALCOHOL-RELATED BAD HABITS

Examples of bad habits that, in my experience, can have a negative impact on sobriety due to their potential for creating a negative or hostile environment by or around the alcoholic include:

- (Deliberately or unconsciously) alienating others
- Attention-seeking behavior (Look at me! Look at me!)
- Chronic lateness, procrastination
- Constantly complaining, being argumentative
- (Excessive) cursing
- Eavesdropping
- Freeloading
- Gossiping
- Impulsive behavior to the point of recklessness
- Interrupting
- Lying, exaggerating
- Monopolizing the conversation
- Nitpicking, being critical and controlling

- (Deliberate and excessive) non-conformity, often for its own sake

- Reacting quickly and often without thinking to various things, often with bad consequences

- (Not) smiling when the situation clearly calls for it

- Smoking

- Whining

It may well be that you developed or worsened these bad habits while, and in part because, you were drinking. It is also very possible to resurrect long dormant bad habits or even develop them from scratch once you get sober. That certainly happened to me with respect to nit-picking!

So as you enter this new and wonderful phase of life, it is worthwhile to step back and do an honest assessment of what kind of bad habits you've had. You can then make a very conscious effort to stop, eliminate, or reduce them as best as you can. This is one area where *engaging your friends and family* can have an early payoff by getting them to point out to you when you are "indulging" in the habit, since much of the time you are probably not even aware of it. You and everyone around you will be much happier, and you will find it that much easier to stay sober!

IDEAS FOR BREAKING BAD HABITS POST-SOBRIETY

I'm not going to cover all the bad habits listed above. I've listed websites for each in the resources section (Break Bad Habits subsection) at the end of this book that may help. Here, I am going to address those I think are likely caused or severely aggravated by drinking, *and* not likely to immediately disappear or diminish in severity once you stop drinking. These are based purely on my personal experience.

Deliberately (or Unconsciously) Alienating Others

For me, this was a deliberate strategy when I was drinking, though I wasn't fully cognizant that I did it until people starting telling me about what I was like "before." I apparently was one mean son-of-a-bitch when I was drinking. Not necessarily while I was drunk and certainly not violent, but unpleasant nonetheless. I don't remember much about it either because a) those memories were wiped out by drinking (or never regis-

tered to begin with) or b) I'm repressing them because of Guilt. It probably will be years before I regain them—and that's okay (see Tips for
avoiding the Guilt trigger in Level 2).

In any event, one thing you will want to find out once you are sober is
how you behaved before you got sober both when you were drunk or
before you had started that day. If you were a happy and relaxed drunk,
great; you don't have to worry about this a bit. But if you were a mean,
obnoxious person to your friends, family, coworkers, grocery store
cashiers, people who bumped into you (you get the idea)—even when
you were not drinking—this is a habit you need to break. It may not
immediately end when you stop drinking, because being sober doesn't
automatically make you feel good all the time mentally and physically,
particularly early on.

At the very least, you will have a major perception problem on your
hands if people a) didn't know you were an alcoholic or b) don't believe
that you have really stopped drinking.

So the first thing to do is to find out *what* kind of drunk personality
you were, and *who* you took out that behavior on the most and in what
forms. Asking family and friends who know about your alcoholism *and*
know you are committing to a new life of sobriety is the first step.
Beyond that, it is up to you on how you try to repair those relationships
based on the specifics of your interactions. This is a distant cousin to the
"making amends" step in Alcoholics Anonymous, but with a key difference: you are not necessarily making apologizes for your drinking or
even acknowledging what you did to those people. You are just behaving
a lot better towards them: friendlier, politer, or more sensitive, more
helpful. They may immediately recognize this new behavior and wonder
what is up (particularly if they don't know about your alcoholism), but
too bad for them. You don't have to explain yourself if you don't want
to. Eventually, they will accept it as a new (and much happier) norm.

Chronic Lateness, Procrastination

Personally I found myself going to bed later and later, getting up later
and later (when I could get away with it), and having less-and-less
energy to get things done as my drinking progressed. All of which contributed to a very unproductive lifestyle of lateness and procrastination.
If this sounds like you, recognize that these habits are not going to go
away immediately after you stop drinking for good. It takes a lot of time.

For me, I had several months of feeling that my head was stuffed full of cotton, which made me both lethargic at times and forgetful a lot of the time. I found that making and keeping lists of things to do and places to be was very helpful, as I could no longer rely on my memory (that had been deteriorating anyway). The good news was that this "cotton head" feeling eventually went away as did my lethargy. My memory also (slowly) improved. I started getting up earlier in the morning and got stuff done before noon, which frankly continues to be a weird experience. But a good one!

Constantly Complaining, Being Critical, Argumentative, Interrupting, and Nitpicking

One of the "downsides" of being sober is that much more of your brain is active as are your senses, enabling you to see much more of the world around you than you did before. Unfortunately, you may not like a lot of what you see and want to make others aware of it, sometimes mid-sentence when the other person is talking. Complaining, being critical, arguing, interrupting and nitpicking are cousins to alienating others above, and are often hard to realize you are doing it a lot of the time. Asking your friends and family to point out this behavior *at the time you are doing it* is another area where your friends and family can help. You will be able to make the "real-time" adjustments that over time will help eliminate this habit.

Lying and Exaggeration

One of the biggest and worst habits to break that was perfected while drinking is lying. You were probably less than honest about whether you were drinking, and about where, what, how much you drank. In addition, you probably lied about when or how long you had stopped drinking, or the "fact" that you could stop anytime you want to . . .

Unfortunately, for many lying was not restricted to drinking—it became a part of everyday life; as natural as talking. Some therapists even go so far to say that lying is the number one negative aspect of alcoholism, and even a cause of alcoholism. While I don't believe that lying can *directly* cause alcoholism, a case can be made for it indirectly *contributing* to it. Lying helps a person hide increasing alcohol consumption for so long that the person becomes physically dependent before anyone else notices and calls them out on it. Certainly lying is one of the very negative dimensions that comes hand-in-hand with alcohol abuse.

There are many resources such as Wikihow (*www.wikihow.com/Stop-Lying*) for good mini-steps and tips for dealing with lying. In reality, the first step in dealing with lying is understanding about what, when and how you lied when you were drinking—*on topics other than drinking*. This knowledge will show you the extent of the problem and what areas are particular ones to focus on remedying. Here again is when friends and family are invaluable, by them telling you in *real-time* when they think you are full of shit either in terms of exaggeration or out-right lies. In fact, you can even make a game out of it. There is a card game called "Bullshit" (*www.wikihow.com/Play-Bullshit*) that you modify into a reality game where you get a point every time someone calls you a liar and you prove you were not. Dinner is on them if you reach 5 points in a month, but on you if you were caught five times. A possible new hobby!

Reacting Without Thinking

As noted above, this type of behavior can often result (particularly for alcoholics while drinking at the time or hung-over) in unpleasant consequences—no surprise there. But it can continue even after you are sober (short-term or long-term); this was the case with my ex-wife. Even long after we were divorced I found myself "instinctively" reacting to her jibes and irritations. The best response I found was actually a two-parter. First, I would ignore them. One way I did this was eventually not talking with her live if at all possible (more on this in the eX trigger discussion in Level 2). If she would text me or email me with what I thought of as silly, stupid, or irrelevant topics I would ignore them completely. Second, if it were a topic I could not ignore (but not an emergency), I would (and do) wait a day. I found my later response was often different (and better) than the one that first came to mind, and even that some of the topics "went away" in that delayed time frame.

If one of your bad habits is not one specifically listed above, do some research—it seems like there are plenty of people with ideas on even the most obscure habits.[1] Another, perhaps general, approach to bad habits is to associate them with something unpleasant—in other words really *break* them. I talk about this kind of approach in Level 11—Make Yourself Sick of Alcohol. Making yourself physically ill is probably the most extreme example, though there are variations (I actually was able to associate the word "liquor" with being nauseated for example). But the more general (and less queasy) approach is to try to think of something unpleasant/sick/gross when you find yourself doing something you know is a bad habit. I'll leave it to you for what meets that definition. If you do this often enough, you may well find it very effective in stopping you from doing a bad habit, or at least doing it less often.

The bottom line here-always treat the process of becoming sober as an opportunity to build a better future, NOT as something to dread. By breaking bad habits, you make yourself far more attractive to others than you have been while you were drinking, which in turn can have only positive benefits on how you enjoy your new life.

Smoking

I recently started dating (or more accurately, looking for people to date). In the brave new world of Match.com, eHarmony.com, and countless others, nearly all have a profile section where you detail your personal characteristics. Most of them have a section about smoking and drinking. They do not ask just Yes/No, but give a variety of possible answers and often an option to make your own answer. One amusing aspect is that as many people seem to answer "Yes, but only when drinking," as "Yes, but trying to quit."

I originally thought this was a phenomenon restricted to my parents' generation, but clearly it is not. It seems *many* people only smoke while they drink, or nearly so. So if you are one of those, there is *no better time* to quit smoking than when you are trying to get sober! The key is to associate *both* with pain and misery, and break the physical association in the process.

Of course, if you are a smoke-only-when-drinking alcoholic then that may—but not necessarily—mean you also smoked a great deal, to the degree that there is a physical addiction. But if you believe that drinking was a trigger for smoking, and there is no physical addiction, there is no reason you can't quit both at the same time in my opinion.

Of course, if smoking is not just a habit but an *independent and physical* addiction, then it is a *much* different story. I've watched otherwise very capable (and controlled) people try to kick the smoking habit and fail miserably. The physical addiction part appears to be even worse than for alcohol addiction, and as hard to kick as an illegal drug habit. I make no assertion at all that this program will work for nicotine addiction. However, it is still worth trying to quit smoking and drinking at the same time, through the approach of re-associating them with pain and misery. Level 12—The Last Detox, where you detox while you have a significant illness, is modeled along similar lines.

However, this brings up a much-underestimated problem associated with breaking alcohol (and smoking) addiction: What do I do with my hands and mouth? That is not a joke. A solution is needed, such as key "hand hobbies" such as gardening or knitting, but also anytime activities such as having a beverage that you can have many times a day. Tea is one such beverage.

TEA—A POSSIBLE SUBSTITUTE FOR ALCOHOL?

It may well be that one of your Bad Habits is associating alcohol with sitting down and "relaxing" with a cold beer, glass of wine, or a cocktail. If you are an alcoholic of course, you can't just have 1 or 2—it goes way beyond that nearly every time. But that doesn't mean you can't essentially do the same thing (the initial sitting down and relaxing with a beverage) with something else. I have found that some decaffeinated hot herbal teas do something similar. It turns out that some of these teas do have ingredients that have some (at least theoretical) level of real effect on getting your mind and body to relax.[2]

I am not claiming that any of these might be effective for you. I do think they make an effective substitute for alcohol in certain conditions, depending on your mindset and attitude. Other beverages, particularly hot ones, like hot chocolate may be as equally effective. I have tried several teas with a number of the ingredients discussed below. I found them relaxing, even making them part of my Escape trigger defenses. Whether they do so because of their chemical properties or because I just want to associate relaxation with a nice beverage, is open for debate. What matters is that it works for me, and may for you.

A popular product class is a "sleepy time" tea. These are the teas which purport to help you unwind from a rough day, relax in the midst of chaos, and in general "chill out." The key is in the ingredients, which can include:

Kava Kava

Kava is a crop grown in the South Pacific. Traditionally, its roots were chewed fresh (with the resultant liquid often spit into communal bowl . . .Yum!), pounded to release the moisture, or sun-dried, ground, and steeped in water to make an intoxicating, relaxing mild sedative. Nowadays, the active *kavalactones* are also extracted and pressed into capsules.

Kava Kava is supposed to reduce anxiety, induce calmness, cause sedation without mental impairment, and chill a person out. There is some scientific evidence that it is effective against anxiety and has no significant negative effects on cognition. Kava Kava root itself is non-habit forming and does not appear to impair driving ability.[3] Kava Kava can be found in various places in various forms including Amazon.com and Walmart. One brand to look for is the Yogi Tea Stress Release, which has a very good website showing ingredients for all their teas—which are more than discussed in this section—at *www.yogiproducts.com/ingredients/A/*.

● ●

What About Non-Alcoholic Beers and Wines?

These beverages are certainly an option. There are two issues: 1) Few of these are *completely* alcohol-free. They typically have about 0.5% alcohol content. However, I don't personally view that as much of an issue as you would probably have to drown yourself in them to actually get drunk.

The big issue is that these guys do not taste exactly like the real thing, in addition to not working like the real thing. They can get close however on the tasting and smell fronts. The problem will start if the faux beer/wine[4] starts stimulating Reminders in your head via its Smell and/or Taste and starts making you want the real thing. In my opinion, the risk is not worth whatever temporary gratification you may gain.

● ●

L-Theanine

L-theanine is an amino acid found in tea leaves, especially green tea. It has supposedly been used ever since people have been harvesting and brewing tea. However, it wasn't until 1949 that L-theanine was isolated and identified by Japanese scientists who proceeded to stick it into a variety of different products.

L-theanine is promoted as a stress-relieving compound that binds to GABA receptors and induces changes in brain waves indicative of relaxation. Some research shows that it reduces anxiety and reduces the rise in blood pressure, can improve sleep quality, provide some relief from anxiety, induce drowsiness, and increase *GABA levels* and *dopamine*.[5] It can be found in certain types of green tea, with *matcha* appearing to have the highest L-theanine content.

Chamomile

Chamomile is a flowering plant similar to the daisy that can be infused in hot water to produce a relaxing, calming tea. The use of chamomile as a medicinal herb dates back at least to the ancient Egyptians. It acts as a mild sedative and anti-anxiety agent. Some research shows that Chamomile extracts can reduce anxiety levels among some people. *Apigenin,* a component of chamomile, possesses anxiolytic and sedative effects. Chamomile tea, being one of the more common varieties, is easy to find in practically any store stocking a decent variety of teas.

Valerian Root

Valerian Root is a root (obviously) whose dried powder is used in teas and other applications. The plant itself has flowers and leaves that resemble ferns. Ayurvedic, Chinese, and classical Hellenic medical systems employed valerian as an anti-insomnia and anti-anxiety medicine. It supposedly acts as a mild but effective sedative, anxiolytic, and sleep aid, akin to the benzodiazepine class of drugs without the side effects.

Research trying to prove its effects is mixed. Valerian extract shows signs of an anxiolytic effect on the "psychic symptoms of anxiety," on obsessive-compulsive disorder, in improving "sleep efficiency" and in reducing morning grogginess. It can be found in certain grocery store teas, health food stores or online, in tea form or the root itself. I take it occasionally in the form of a capsule, but be warned—it smells!

Rhodiola Rosea

This plant is also known as rose root or arctic root, and originally hails from Siberia and pretty much everywhere else that is cold—the Arctic, the Rockies, Northern Europe, the mountains of central Asia. Rhodiola Rosea possesses a root with interesting characteristics. Ancient Greeks, Viking raiders, Central Asian horsemen, Chinese emperors, etc. viewed *rhodiola rosea* as an anti-fatigue, anti-stress medicinal herb. It acts as an *adaptogen*[6], a compound that supposedly improves your ability to adapt to physiological stressors without compromising your body's normal ability to function once removed.

There is research showing that the bioactive compounds in Rhodiola Rosea are effective against depression, anxiety, fatigue, and stress. It can be found online or in specialty tea stores.

Magnolia Bark

Magnolia bark is the lay name for magnolia officinalis, a deciduous tree whose bark is prized in traditional Chinese medicine. It supposedly can act as a sedative with strong anti-anxiety and anti-stress effects. Components of magnolia bark have been shown to *enhance the activity of GABA receptors*[7] in the brain, offering an explanation for its anti-anxiety, calming effects. It may also reduce anxiety and stress levels in certain conditions, and even help weight loss. Magnolia bark can be found online.

Some teas blend some or all of these (and other) ingredients, so not only are you getting the active compounds found in the herbs or roots describe here, but potentially dozens of others. Some common additional ones are *Ashwagandha*, *Eleutherococcus*, *Hawthorne*, and *Passionflower*.[8] Since one ingredient might enhance, inhibit, or otherwise modify the action of another ingredient, it is difficult to exactly predict what you'll be getting out of a blend.

I am not trying to portray tea as some wonder replacement for alcohol. What I am suggesting is using it when you need to occupy your hands and/or mouth (when you would have drank alcohol previously), as well as introducing a new way to associate drinking with relaxation. You should consider using (tea) ingredients that are chemically relaxing, but not addictive. Surely hundreds of years of English history (and many more in China) can't be wrong when they say, "there is nothing like a nice cup of tea!"

Hopefully, you are now fully convinced of the importance of ridding yourself of bad habits as an essential part of having a very positive new life of sobriety. I hope you feel armed with a number of ways to do so. We now move to the Hobbies Level. It is not necessary to complete the Bad Habits Level before starting Level 9. In fact, you can work on this and all the remaining Levels in parallel, but at least get a start on bad habits now. Breaking them is likely to take some time, and a great deal of practice, so the sooner you start the better!

LEVEL 9

Develop New Hobbies

Okay, we are finally here at the Hobbies chapter. To repeat for the twenty-third time, you have *got* to find new hobbies to enjoyably fill the *gigantic* time hole in your life that *not* drinking frees up.

WHY DEVELOPING NEW HOBBIES IS SO IMPORTANT

My best estimate is that I spent somewhere between 4–8 hours a day, *every* day, planning, obtaining, using, and recovering from alcohol (or recovering in the morning from the night before). My actual drinking was done over 3 to 6 hours. Recovering the next day enough to function, took at least an hour of extra prep time in the morning and caused productivity issues for the first portion of the workday.

Of course, I was not drinking continuously during that 3–6 hours, but *every* activity was centered around it; a glass or bottle was never far from hand during that time. Planning would be involved if I were in an unfamiliar city.[1] If I was in my normal grazing area (e.g. home), I spent a lot of time rotating my alcohol purchases across different stores (so they wouldn't think I drank too much)[2]. This liquor store hopping was further complicated by the fact that I usually bought my alcohol the day I drank it, in the belief it would help limit my consumption. To a certain degree it did, as I never bought more than I planned on drinking (e.g., a quart of vodka towards the end), because if I did I would probably drink that as well. Buying on a real-time basis as it were probably tacked on at least 30 minutes a day to my total.

Good. Hopefully, you are convinced that you spend huge amounts of your daily life with booze in one way, or another, and need ways to refill that with sober activities. So what hobbies might make sense? Some might be obvious—ones you had and enjoyed before you became an alcoholic—such as bowling, gardening, reading, walking, etc., while others may be ones you have only idly thought of at various points. I suggest you try as many as you can as your tastes and interests may have evolved over the time while you were drinking, and you were not even aware of it! While there obviously hundreds and hundreds of potential hobbies, you should look for ones that have several (not necessarily all for any one hobby) of the following attributes:

- Mind occupying
- Physically challenging
- Not depressing (Exception: Volunteer work)
- NOT boring
- Requires creativity
- New to you and/or has a high learning component
- High social interaction
- High laughter component
- Relaxing
- Relatively low financial commitment.

In addition, if you have a what-do-I-do-with-my-hands problem described in the previous Level, add a "high usage of hands" component to the above list.

POTENTIAL HOBBIES FROM A TO Z

Examples of hobbies that address many of these attributes include:
AA (e.g., attending meetings)

Antiques	Beadwork/Beading	Bug Hunting (finding computer programming errors)
Art/Arts and Crafts	Biking	
Astrology	Bird watching	
Astronomy	Bowling	Camping
Ballet/Ballroom/ Belly Dancing	Bumper Stickers (creating)	Candle Making

Carpentry

Cave Exploration

Clubs and Lodges (join and be active)

Coaching

Collecting (e.g., coins, stamps, autographs, etc.)

Cooking

Crocheting

Dancing (many sub examples)

Driving

Dog Training

Drawing/Sketching

Embroidery

Engraving

Exercise (many sub examples)

Fantasy Sports

Fashion Designing

Feng Shui

Fishing

Floral Arrangements

Foreign Language (learning one)

Games (Computer/ non-Computer— many sub examples; can be combined with others, such as Clubs)

Gardening

Genealogy

Glass Etching

Golfing

Hiking

Horse Riding

Hunting

Ice Skating

Internet (Surfing)

Irish Dancing

Jamming/Jarring

Jewelry Making

Journaling

Judo

Karate

Kayaking

Kickboxing

Knitting

Latin Dances

Leatherworking

Loitering (includes People Watching)

Martial Arts (many sub examples)

Magic (learning and performing)

Meditation

Meetings

Models (building, displaying)

Movies (going to, making)

Music (many sub examples)

Nail Polishing

Needlepointing

Numismatics (Coin and Currency Collecting)

Online Hobbies (Blogging, Chatting, Dating, Games, Music, Social Networking)

Organize (Filing, Closets, etc.)

Origami

Painting

Paper Crafts

Pets (many sub examples)

Photography

Piano (learning, playing)

Pool (e.g., Billiards)

Quilting

Racing (many sub examples)

Radio (Ham)

Reading

Recipe Collecting

Renovations

Rock/Mountain Climbing

Sailing/Boating

Sand Art

School (Go back to)

Scale Modeling

Scrapbooking

Sculpting

Sewing

Skating

Skiing

Singing

Soap Making

Sudoku

Sports (many sub
examples)

Stained Glass
(making)

Swimming

Teaching

Toy Making

Traveling

Trekking

Tutoring

Unicycling

Video Creation
(e.g., YouTube)

Volunteer Work
(many sub examples)

Website (creating,
editing, learning
how to do)

Wood Carving/
Woodworking

Writing (many sub
examples)

Xylophone (learning
to play)

Yoga

Yo-Yo tricks
(learning, doing)

Zoos (visiting,
volunteering)

A convenient reference for many of these hobbies can be found at *www.buzzle.com/articles/list-types-of-hobbies/*. For some really unusual ones go to *www.thehobbyfiles.com/static_html/sitemap.htm#HL.* An excellent resource for finding and coordinating with others with similar interests is *www.Meetup.com.*

Not all hobbies are created equal of course, and for newly sober alcoholics the choice of hobbies can be very important in terms of time and emotional investment and return. In my view the most important factor in choosing one or more hobbies—besides having a natural interest—is that you can do them often, and they last for substantial periods of time, each time. Bowling is an example; with multiple people and at least three games it can last for 2–3 hours. It is also relatively cheap.

You need to align your triggers with your hobbies. If one of your major triggers is Times of Day (say early evening hours), and you are on a limited budget (e.g. Money is an issue), bowling in a league (for Social Situations) might be an excellent choice. Note, most bowling alleys have a bar, and many league bowlers seem to be beer drinkers (particularly men-only leagues), so it might not be a smart choice for those affected by Proximity and Smell triggers. These little details can make a big difference. The Level 9 checklist in Appendix B has a specific column for aligning possible hobbies with your triggers.

"EXTRA-SPECIAL" HOBBIES

From my research there are three hobbies—really hobby categories—that have the highest potential both in terms of return and of widest degree of interest across alcoholic demographics: Exercise, Pets, and Volunteer work. Each has many sub-categories and permutations, but all have many benefits.

Exercise

A large part of the appeal of exercise in sobriety is that of the physical exertion—even *exhaustion*—involved. It can significantly dampen or drain the energy that your mind would otherwise spend thinking about alcohol. It can also possibly (for certain types of exercise) even mimic its effects. Either way is a plus.

Getting started can be difficult, so best to start off slow and build up to more active levels. *Aerobics* and Yoga[3] are both recommended for this reason as both have very specific warm-up and cool-down periods. Stretching is also important and is generally part of both of these exercise sub-categories and any significant physical exercise such as walking, playing pick-up basketball, doing the treadmill, etc.

It is fairly safe to say that many alcoholics tend to be in poor physical shape (though a surprising number of active alcoholics frequently exercise). The longer the alcohol abuse, the worse shape you become, with advancing age not helping in the slightest. Even people who have abused alcohol for only a relatively short period will likely still have a low tolerance for physical activity at first.

It is important that newly sober alcoholics consult their doctor before embarking on a serious exercise program. Besides alcoholics being in generally poor shape, there may be other specific ailments (alcohol related or not) that need to be taken into account, such as high blood pressure. There is no doubt getting into shape for most alcoholics will be tough, but the benefits can be great, not just in general but in terms of dealing with specific triggers.

Also recognize that for some people, particularly younger alcoholics, exercise may not be enough to fully take the edge off like . . . .

I'm a 22-year-old, first-year-student in the UK but boredom is the main thing that keeps me drinking. I've tried to keep myself occupied with the gym (I go for at least an hour a day, to keep myself occupied) but I still spend the rest of my day watching films to stave of the urge to drink.

Funny, socialanxietysupport.com

Level 13—Develop Your Defense Progressions presents examples of how you can build exercise into a broader set of defenses. Helping you make the most out of whatever exercise you can do may somewhat alleviate various triggers, such as Boredom and Escape.

Benefits of exercise for those recovering from alcohol addiction can be far-reaching. In addition to basic health improvements, which are obtainable by anyone who regularly exercises, there will also be benefits that are of particular advantage to alcoholics. These include:

- Improved brain function and decision making

- Improved sleeping habits and patterns

- Stress reduction, particularly stress that has manifested itself in the muscles

- More positive demeanor (at least for a few hours after exercising).

Endorphins and Exercise and Alcohol

Endorphins are released from the body after a great workout and can result in feelings of great pleasure. Indeed there is even a term for it—the "runners high."[4] One theory on alcohol abuse has Endorphins playing a major role,[5] which in turn may explain why some people can supposedly get "addicted" to exercise. But it also explains why exercise can be a great *substitute* for drinking.

While there is likely not much reason to worry about too much exercise in the newly sober, there are some causes for concern. Too much exercise can lead to injury, burnout, and possibly even long-term health problems. There is more on these kinds of "mini-addictions" shortly.

Exercise does *not* equal having to go to the gym or other "work-like" activities. Practically anything that gets your butt off your couch and moving around qualifies. Walking the dog, gardening, even (actual store) shopping and playing some video games[6] qualify! Your list of hobbies *must* include at least one or two that give you some significant physical movement, particularly every day in early sobriety. It helps *greatly* to wear yourself out physically as much as you practically can.

Exercise is also excellent in that it can be applied to most drinking triggers, at least in some form. The trick, of course, is matching the exercise type with the trigger and the specific situation. Angry? Go outside for a walk if it's a cool night and literally chill out. Bored? Go play an outdoor sport. Depressed? Play with a pet by throwing a ball or playing tug-of-war with them. Noise? Go for a quiet viewing in a museum. Indeed, you can turn anything that does not involve sitting on the couch into some form of exercise. And there are hundreds of types of exercise; how you apply them to your triggers is limited only by your imagination.

Exercise both takes your mind off of alcohol—particularly your triggers—and sometimes also replicates the "buzz" you felt while drinking. What more incentive do you need?

Pets

While most people think of massage, meditation, and yoga as natural, healthy stress relievers, there's another option that's fluffier and more loveable: getting a pet. Not only do pets help relieve stress, but they can also improve your mood, control your blood pressure, reduce loneliness, and provide social support. All of these are important to the health and well-being of alcoholics in particular to help avoid or relieve stress and depression that can lead to relapse.

Animals (at least dogs and cats) are usually relatively consistent in their behaviors (locations and times of eating, sleeping, and cuddling, etc.), which provides a stable and predictable (and thus less stressful) aspect in the alcoholic's life. Their unconditional love is also extremely comforting—pets greet you with excitement when you come home, they can usually tell when you're upset, and most pets will cuddle up next to you, providing soothing contact.

In fact, a study suggests that spending time with a pet can be even more beneficial in reducing stress than talking to a loved one! In the 2002 study, researchers at the State University of New York at Buffalo showed that people experienced less stress during stressful tasks when their pets were with them than when a spouse or close friend was with them. Pet owners also had significantly lower baseline heart rates and blood pressure than the participants who did not have pets. Those with pets also had lower "reactivity" to the stress tests and returned to baseline levels more quickly.[7] Other tests such as some with AIDS patient show similar results. So here is a great way to deal with the trigger (physical) Stress!

Owning a pet can certainly decrease Loneliness and even Depression. Pet owners tend to feel less lonely and isolated, and caring for a pet often results in a sense of satisfaction and fulfillment. In addition, owning a dog increases the likelihood of going outside and interacting with others, providing safe opportunities for practicing with the trigger Social Situations. A dog park where you can let them off the leash is a particularly great way to do this, since talking about your dogs is one of the safest topics I can imagine.

One interesting take on getting a pet is how it might relieve Guilt as a trigger, particularly if you adopt a homeless animal from a shelter or the like. The added responsibility in doing so might also help alleviate triggers ranging from Anxiety to your eX. It can even help Times of Day, where you plan some of your walks around your vulnerable times. As I write this paragraph, I am in the library where pet owners have come in to let children read to the dogs. As with exercise, you are only limited by your imagination!

Of course, pets do come with additional responsibilities of the (possibly) not so good kind, which can raise stress levels for some people. *If you are a recovering alcoholic and struggle with high levels of overall stress, you should research different pets to see which types, breeds, personalities, and ages seem like a good match for you.* For instance, if having to potty train a puppy sounds stressful to you, look into getting a dog that is already trained. Small dogs are much different to deal with than big dogs, particularly if you live in a small space and/or big city. Different breeds have their own individual issues, and some bark more than others—an issue if Noise is a problem for you (or is Yelling from your neighbors). If you are away from home often, or are just more limited in time, a more self-sufficient animal like a cat might be a better choice.

If you suffer from the Disorder trigger, a dog or cat might not be right for you however. Fish can be very relaxing and are pretty low maintenance once you get setup. However, fish can be costly pushing $500 or more for a good tank, filters, and supplies, not to mention the actual fish. The ongoing cost is very low, much lower than pretty much all other pets. Some other ideas include crabs and snakes and even specially-bred hedgehogs and pigs! See *www.apartmentlist.com/blog/cool-apartment-pets/* for more info on these guys.

The annual cost of a dog or cat ranges from about $500 to $1000/year, not including the cost of acquisition and assuming no serious illness (major health problems in pets are major bucks). Even rabbits, guinea pigs, and birds cost about that much annually. Again, fish are much lower once you get past the initial setup and acquisition, under $100/year. More info on these can be found at *http://visualeconomics.cred-itloan.com/how-much-our-pets-cost-in-a-lifetime/*.

Don't underestimate the negatives that pets might generate. Besides costing Money, most pets will contribute some amount of Disorder and even different types of Stress, such as additional time you need to take to walk the dog, take the pet to the vet, arrange someone to care for them while you are traveling, etc. Indeed, if you travel a fair amount, or you cannot predict your home time with any reliability, a pet (except maybe fish) is probably not for you. And the addition of responsibility into your early sober life may not be a good idea if you are not *ready* for that responsibility, whether it is a dog or some fish. Nor might it be a good idea if you have some version of the Extreme Emotions trigger where a death of a pet would activate it. Also, be aware that once you commit, you cannot un-commit, otherwise you will likely add more burden on triggers such as Guilt.

All that said, the bottom line is there's nothing quite like having a warm ball of fur curl up next to you or being greeted by an excitedly thumping tail. It's even more satisfying to know that these furry friends are helping to improve our lives (and help deal with many of our triggers without alcohol). Or the relaxation that can come from just zoning out in the dark in front of a (lighted) fish tank. Or just having a hamster or bird that reacts to your presence, so you don't come home to an empty, Lonely space. With alcoholism, even these little lives can make a big difference in your sense of happiness.

Volunteer Work

Despite my various criticisms of AA in this book, the 12th Step, about "carry[ing] this message to [other] alcoholics," resonates strongly because it recognizes the importance of helping others for both their longer-term benefit as well as the newly sober.

In AA we call it "being of service." We sponsor (e.g., mentor) other individuals, take commitments to help with the various parts of meetings (from making coffee to clean up to being the secretary of a meeting). There is also what is called H&I—which is hospitals and institutions, where we basically run a meeting at a hospital, jail, or treatment center. Even if AA isn't your thing, you can help other alcoholics by sharing your experience, strength, and hope.

NewMe11109, soberrecovery.com

Unlike AA, which includes helping other alcoholics as a formal step in its process, this program views volunteering as more of a "hobby"— not because it is not important, but recognizing that many people do not have the luxury of time and/or money to volunteer as much as they might otherwise.

Helping others really helps me to get out of my own head—it was a refreshing perspective after 20 years of alcoholism . . . .it feels good to do something constructive, and not expect rewards—although it is rewarding to me personally to actually give something back.

Dee74, soberrecovery.com

Also, it is a "hobby" because it is important that you, the alcoholic doing the volunteering, have a strong, personal interest so you have the drive and energy to continue doing it long-term.

I can tell you that in the past I got a lot out of my volunteer work at a shelter for battered women. It fills a real need. It can be frustrating to watch people return to abusive situations, but you learn that just as in quitting drinking, it takes many people several "practice" attempts to change their situation before lasting change is possible.

LexieCat, soberrecovery.com

One of the benefits of volunteering is an opportunity to learn from others; staying sober in many respects is a constant learning experience:

At no cost I've been conducting a dual-diagnosis treatment information class at an adult care facility for some time. The reward has been both rewarding and educational. I learn as much as I impart. I cannot believe how much this experience alters ones perspectives . . . mine and theirs.

Zencat, soberrecovery.com

You may even find a volunteering experience to be a spark in your spiritual life:

The same week I began recovering I 'fell' into a volunteer situation that changed my life. I got involved in a Women's Drop In Centre in the downtown core of a major city. It was a place where women who lived on the street or in poverty could spend the day. These women could come in and greet us with a smile, even though they had no home, no family, no money at all. Very quickly, my problems with recovery were put in perspective. I volunteered there for 8 years and it was truly one of the best experiences of my life, [making] me absolutely sure that the Universe has a plan for me.

Anna, soberrecovery.com

There are so many opportunities, ranging from the *Red Cross, United Way, The Salvation Army, Ronald McDonald House,* and *Habitat for Humanity,* to homeless and abuse shelters, to your church, to no-kill animal organizations, to search and rescue—the possibilities are endless.

You might even volunteer at an area alcoholism treatment program clinic or center! Be careful that doing so won't activate some key triggers of your own, such as Reminders. But my view (and indeed a key premise of this book) is there is *nothing* like getting help when you are in rehab (for example) from someone who knows *first-hand* the experience you are going through. If you think this might be for you, AND you believe your defenses and sobriety are rock solid, I would encourage you to contact some of your local treatment centers. I am sure you will find one eager for your help!

POTENTIAL FOR ADDICTION TO NEW ACTIVITIES

There seems to be a belief in the treatment world that if you can be addicted to something—particularly substances like alcohol—you will also have an *"addictive personality"* making you more susceptible to other addictions, like drugs. Specifically, an addictive personality *"refers to a particular set of personality traits that make an individual predisposed to addictions."*[8] While not unreasonable on the surface (and a commonly held view), I surprisingly did not find much medical evidence to support this as it specifically relates to alcoholism except there are many people with joint drug-alcohol addictions.[9]

There is a very specific mental illness called *"Addiction Personality Disorder"* (APD) which does characterize a broader psychological disorder about addictions beyond alcoholism or drug addiction. According to a study prepared for the National Academy of Sciences, APD is the result of a set of personality traits that predispose certain people toward addiction. In simple terms, someone with APD is more likely, depending on the severity of the condition, to develop an addiction—to anything.[10] But there is no commonly agreed to set of personality factors that characterize the condition, no insight into the more common sets of addictions (e.g. drugs and alcohol, sex and gambling, etc.), nor credible research that I could find on underlying causes.

In fact, the idea of an addictive personality is not universally accepted by everyone in the psychological world. Critics point out that a personality just refers to *a way of acting and thinking* at a certain time. Personality is not a static thing but instead changes as people pass through their life. Labeling people as having an addictive personality may do more harm than good. The fact that *researchers are unable to agree completely on the traits of an addictive personality* further suggests that it may not exist at all.[11]

I do not subscribe to the most-alcoholics-will-get-addicted-to-other-stuff theory. Since the scientific understanding of even dual addictions is very limited, it is my view until proven otherwise that APD, if it exists, is very much the exception and not the rule when it comes to alcoholism. Much more research is needed, not just on APD but in other very specific possible addiction disorders. For example, it would be very beneficial to understand the *specific* links between mental illnesses such as bipolar and the propensity for multiple substance abuse addictions, since some sufferers may use a variety of methods (drugs, alcohol, etc.) to mask or cope with their symptoms. If so, this would support the hypothesis that untreated mental illness is a major contributor to alcoholism, drug addiction, and/or addictive personality disorder in general.

Unfortunately, no such research has been done, and as noted the concept of addictive personality disorder in itself is in dispute. As a precaution, however, I strongly urge you to not do any drugs not prescribed by your doctor while in early sobriety, e.g. illegal drugs and over-the-counter mind-altering drugs such as sleep-aids.[12]

With all that in mind, there *is* a danger that as you move into the sober phase of your life, you have the potential to become obsessed with other "things," particularly for those people with certain triggers like Boredom where you have many sober hours to fill.[13] While it is possible that other substances are a risk—particularly if you have easy access to drugs—it is more likely to manifest itself in more mundane things, such as eating or shopping, particularly early in sobriety when your defenses are still in flux and you have time on your hands. Some "addictions"[14] can actually be good, such as exercise, or harmless, like wanting to Feng Shui everyone's house. The good news is if you have any of these (except for other addictive substances) they are likely to be of short duration as you solidify and tune your overall defenses. But they still can be a cause for concern.

> *My primary addiction is alcohol from which I have been sober for almost 2 years. I was also at one point addicted to work. Here's the problem. I have replaced the alcohol with abusing prescription meds. I quit that then became addicted to exercise. I moderated that then over-ate. I got that under control then I started getting involved in addictive relationships e.g., had an affair with my psychiatrist. I ended that so for a few months now I have had no addictions plaguing my life. I even quit cigarettes recently. But what's next and how can I prevent picking up another addiction in order to satisfy the craving for a high?*
>
> Anonymous

I have experienced a few "mini-addictions," particularly eating candy, drinking tea, shopping, and exercising. These varied in intensity and duration: candy was very intense for several months, while a strangely intense desire to shop went away after I explored all the stores in my area. I drank a great deal of (non-caffeinated) tea, which is harmless and (arguably) even beneficial, but abruptly subsided for no apparent reason.[15] The candy mini-addiction was the worst to overcome; I wound up using a quick version of the Conquer Program (reexamining my triggers in particular, then adjusting my hobbies) to beat it. The need to exercise continues to this day, though not at the obsessive levels I had for a few months (if this ever qualified as an "addiction," it's one I am happy to deal with).

The lessons of my above experience are multifaceted, and can be summed up by three rules of thumb:

• Expect some "mini-addictions"

• Most of them will pass in time or at least decrease in intensity—particularly as you solidify and tune your overall defenses

• Even if one or two remain, if they are not harmful to you and others, then who cares—particularly if they are beneficial?

The last bullet is particularly applicable to new hobbies—if you find something in the list earlier (or something else) that you want to make a new obsession, then why not? Assuming you don't injure yourself, exercise seems to be a popular obsession for some former alcoholics:

> *I exercise 1–2 hours a day for triathlons. The warm fuzzy feeling from endorphins when exercising is exactly as I feel when drinking so the temptation is to extend the feeling. Eventually I get frustrated with the effect on my training but after a few weeks when I have recovered the temptation reoccurs.*
>
> Guest cyclist, alcoholism.about.com

As with practically anything in life, however, doing something too much can eventually turn against you. Exercise can fall into this category, particularly since some alcoholics turn to it with a vengeance by their motivation of *"being sick and tired of being sick and tired."* With this as a primary motivation to get sober, it is no surprise that some turn to exercise with a vengeance. Some people adopt every stray cat in their county, and so on. It is *not* likely to happen to you.

● ●
But What If I Do Get A Mini-Addiction?

If you do think a mini-addiction[16] is happening, then apply a mini-Conquer Program to deal with it. This would be:

Level 1—Recognize that you are developing a mini-addiction/bad habit. If a friend comments on how much you are doing something (eating candy, gambling, whatever) take this as a possible warning sign. If you are doing it several times a week that is also a possible warning sign. This is the mini-equivalent of Level 1.

Level 2—Figure out why and when you are doing it, e.g. what are your "mini-triggers." I found myself going too often (once a week, sometimes twice) to a local casino. Even though, I wasn't gambling a lot or losing a lot I realized that this could be a bad thing. I figured out that it wasn't the actual gambling that was the attraction for me; it was to be around a large number of active people. In other words, it was a version of Loneliness.

Multiple Levels—Modify your defenses/figure out alternatives. I reviewed the Loneliness trigger tips section (historically Loneliness wasn't that major a trigger for me). In my case I had to figure out new social environments whenever I felt the urge to go to a casino. I go to outside malls on very nice days, and any festivals or group gatherings I can find, even if the purpose is not that interesting. I also go to brand-new AA meetings to see new people, which is a variation on Level 7. Even if I don't meet new people just being around them was beneficial for me.

Another possibility in general is doing a kind of mini-aversion therapy. This concept was introduced in Level 6 and will be discussed much more in Level 11. Basically, you try and make yourself sick of something (alcohol) by doing too much of it in a short time. It is risky and perhaps not high probability. But it worked for me for alcohol (see Level 11) and it worked again for gambling. I went three times in five days (two of those days I had no desire to go), and finally found myself getting bored—bored of the drive, bored of the cheesy decorations, bored at losing, and bored at seeing the same types of people.[17] Since Boredom is my #1 trigger, the fact that I made gambling in essence boring dramatically reduced the desire for any casino trips.

Again, this aversion therapy approach might work, but at the risk of not working and truly getting yourself into some psychological dependency on the activity.

● ●

For most of us, the general guideline is to just not overdo any one thing. While there is always the chance to get "addicted," even if it is not harmful, *the greater danger is that you will get bored by overuse*—thereby removing a useful activity/hobby from your box of defenses. Do *not* get burnt out on a new fun thing!

We have now reached the end of Phase 2. For some of you, Phases 1 and 2 may be enough. They provide the essential foundation for understanding alcoholism in general and how it is impacting *your* life *specifically* (Phase 1). You will have a great set of starter tools and tips to draw on and guide you using the best that existing treatment methods have to offer (Phase 2). I would encourage you to re-read these first two phases, and in particular Level 2, to make sure you are getting *everything* you can out of what is described there. There is a huge amount of material, and it may be hard to digest all of it in one go.

But I suspect that for most of you reading this book Phases 1 and 2 will *not* be enough. You need something *really* new. Hence, Phase 3 that describes new ways of approaching "old" ideas like spirituality and aversion therapy. You will also find some completely new stuff—particularly Level 13, where you learn how to integrate all of the tips, tools, defenses, and other ideas of the previous twelve Levels, making them *much* stronger than the sum of their individual parts.

Phase 3 may take some time to digest and may require re-reading as well. But again, I have tried to stuff as many interesting and fun items as I can into it, so your attention and energy builds and by the end you are *excited* about what is coming up in your life. Enjoy!

PHASE 3

COMPLETE YOUR FORTIFICATIONS

I f the Levels in Phase 2 worked for you, meaning you either quit drinking or believe you truly have a handle on it and are dramatically reducing your consumption, but are reading the rest of this for further insights or even entertainment purposes—congrats! However, if you met the criteria for being an alcoholic as determined by the Conquer Quiz, and are *still* drinking—even at a reduced level—it is still a great cause for concern. I *strongly* encourage you to continue to Phase 3. Even if you did not score high on the quiz, e.g. you were in problem drinker territory, which is now hopefully no longer a problem, please continue reading to get some additional ideas to solidify your control. As noted before, Phase 2 is essentially a "best-of" synthesis of alcoholism treatment methods that have been around for years and in some cases decades. Those *individual* methods may work well for many alcoholics, but for others they may not work well or only for a short time.

So, if Phase 2 did not *quite* work for you (e.g. you were unable to stop drinking completely), *but you saw signs of potential improvement*, then there is still great hope. Perhaps you were able to deal successfully with *some* of your major triggers, or your volumes and frequency of alcohol consumption decreased significantly, or you see how this program could help you complete your path to sobriety. If so, then my first best recommendation is to go back through Phases 1 and 2 again, and in particular Level 2. There is a great deal of material covered there. You will likely find additional insights into why you drink, and hone the tips and defenses to add to those you found there the first time, again using the best of "traditional" methods.

But "traditional" methods, no matter how well scrubbed and organized, may not provide *all* the defenses you need to successfully defend against alcohol *all* of the time. Some extra Levels may be needed to complete your fortifications against alcohol.

Phase 3—Complete Your Fortifications

LEVEL 13	DEVELOP YOUR PROGRESSIONS	*Combine Your Defenses*
LEVEL 12	THE LAST DETOX	*Add New Wrinkles*
LEVEL 11	MAKE YOURSELF SICK	*Build Specialized Defenses (Optional)*
LEVEL 10	CONSIDER SPIRTUALITY	*Consider a Spiritual Core*

Figure 20: The Four Levels of Phase 3

Phase 3 takes an unorthodox approach in these additional defenses, both in what they are and how you build them.

* *

Are You Tempted to Skip to Phase 3 without 1 and 2? DON'T!

Some people may be tempted to skip to the last few Levels of this program or Phase, without doing the first two phases, or doing some part of them previously with mixed or no results. My advice is as follows: **DO NOT.**

The Conquer Program is centered on a "multiple layers of defense" and "build up your fortifications" strategy. This assumes no *one* treatment method or defense against alcohol will work all the time in all circumstances, so this methodical, systematic building and layering of defenses is essential. Also, you really don't want to "use" some of the Levels in Phase 3 if you don't have to—particularly the physical elements (Parts of Levels 11 and 12). They are kind of a last resort and physically risky (and therefore totally optional and at your own risk). *Most importantly,* ALL of the Levels and actions in Phase 3 are critically dependent on the ability for your mind and body to draw on the learnings from *all* the earlier Levels.

Thus, even if you have done alcohol treatment programs in the past—do NOT assume you have covered the content as it is laid out in the steps of Phases 1 and 2. It is **essential** you revisit those Levels as much as practical (except perhaps rehab and therapy if you have completed before and do not believe repeating them will help, or cannot afford to).[18] Revisiting those lessons will refresh in your mind, and your support structure, as you embark on the final phase.

For those of you new to alcoholic treatment programs, it is *essential* that you go through the progression of Levels described here and invest as much time and effort as you can in understanding and applying the teachings they offer. Needless to say, but I'll say it anyway, if you try to jump to Phase 3 without going through Phase 1 and 2, *you will likely fail.* If there were successful short cuts, then there would be far, far more sober people than there are today. Invest the time and energy; you will be so glad that you did!

* *

The first Level within Phase 3—Consider Spirituality—while long emphasized by various quarters as an effective means of combating addiction, has been very uneven in how it is applied. Probably you have experienced very little in some places, or have been beaten over the head in others—a kind of all or nothing approach.

LEVEL 10—*Consider Spirituality* looks to find a middle ground of getting *some* degree of Spirituality into your life and describes ways that you can "learn" to do it, at least a little. Why is this important?

Because developing some level of spiritual foundation with respect to sobriety can be *very* helpful for some people to achieve sobriety.

The Conquer Program does not take a strong opinion on spirituality. Indeed, spirituality and religion are both *deliberately avoided* in Phases 1 and 2, since for some people not only is it not needed, but it can actually be a deterrent to embracing a program. At its most basic, spirituality is just about expanding your contacts and community—just in a different way! *And you cannot do this by yourself.* If Levels 4 and 7—which were designed to build your support network—do not seem to work as well as you feel you need, then adding spirituality to your "network" may be just the thing to complete this type of defense.

LEVEL 11—*Make Yourself Sick of Alcohol.* With the exception of traditional detox, Phases 1 and 2 and the VAST majority of other treatment programs focus almost exclusively on modifying how your *mind* thinks about alcohol. What they seem to forget is that the *body* has a huge role in your drinking, and not just as a receptacle for it. Phase 3 places a great deal of emphasis on using your body as a defense against alcohol.

Since the "helpful hints" your body has been providing you as described in the Level 3—Listen to Your Body! have not been sufficient for you to stop abusing it, Level 11 draws on the lessons of Aversion Therapy **to club you over the head.** It is specifically targeted at the triggers of Proximity, Smell and Taste of alcohol—triggers for which other defenses may just not work for you. THIS LEVEL IS OPTIONAL, as it can be physically risky.

LEVEL 12—*The Last Detox.* There are many alcoholics who are unable to successfully detox, meaning that they either bailed on the treatment approach (e.g. during medically supervised or home-based detoxes) or very quickly went back to drinking sometime soon after the detox, such as a few days or weeks. This could be an indication of many things, such as not really wanting to stop in the first place, being in that vulnerable time afterwards where it seems all it would take is a drop of the hat in the wrong circumstances to drink, or that the tips and defenses you built in earlier Levels were not complete or well structured. You may well be afraid to go back and try a traditional detox again, and instead are searching for a different way of going about it.

A different way of detoxing is the purpose of this Level, which suggests you detox while you are *ill with something else,* potentially achieving several benefits while doing a kind of "killing two birds with one stone," and/or wanting to try something completely different. Other unusual ideas are also discussed in this Level. This level is completely optional, as it is physically risky, and should only be done in consultation with your doctor.

LEVEL 13—*Develop Your Defense Progressions.* This is a new concept in alcoholism treatment. This is where all the individual defenses you have built during the previous Levels combine to create a powerful integration of defenses that, *in total,* will be able to successfully defend against *all* alcohol attacks *all* of the time. If one defense fails in a circumstance, you have others ready to come to your aid. Don't consider that first defense a failure—it will have weakened the attack so that your subsequent defenses have an even stronger chance of succeeding than they would have by themselves.

The end result of The Conquer Program is a new way of being able to think and act towards alcohol—so that it no longer dominates your life in ANY way. It may well be that you will essentially be able to *ignore* alcohol in any situation, being at most a minor nuisance, instead of something that is all-consuming in your daily activities.

LEVEL 10

Consider Spirituality

Considering Spirituality was a very tricky chapter to write for many reasons, but two in particular. First, I've tried to take as much emotion out of the Levels of The Conquer Program as I could, to appeal to logic and reason when understanding why you drink and how you can stop.

Trying to apply *logic* to the question of spirituality or religion is problematic at best and impossible at worst. Spirituality almost by definition relies on emotion, and the faith that certain beliefs are true—beliefs that may have little or no factual evidence to back them up.

Second, I strongly believe that it is *very* possible to become and stay sober without spirituality even coming into the discussion. Phases 1 and 2 reflect that belief, as well as the fear that imposing or encouraging any sort of spiritual practice *too soon* or *needlessly* into an alcoholism treatment program can be very counter-productive by scaring off persons who otherwise would be very interested in the program. I speak from personal experience. I was an agnostic when I first tried Alcoholics Anonymous. It's very heavy emphasis on God deterred me from embracing its overarching messages and eventually led to my abandoning the program (sees Level 7 for a more detailed analysis of AA).

But let's face facts. If you went through Phases 1 and 2 without much success (e.g. you are still drinking and have not cut down much in frequency and volume), you should strongly consider opening yourself up to the need for spirituality in your life and quest for sobriety. It is not something to be feared or anxious about—at its most basic spirituality is about expanding your contacts and community, just in a different way! *And you cannot do this by yourself,* even if that means expanding your definition of what "support" actually includes. At the end of the day not only can spirituality not hurt, you may be very surprised as how it adds an extra layer of defense and support in resisting the temptations of alcohol. There are many ways to adopt and practice some form of spirituality, and doing so is not by any means an "all or nothing" proposition. There are many ways to do Spirituality Lite!

But let's start with the spirituality "heavy"—Organized Religion. This refers to specific, formal organizations and belief systems that have institutional elements such as structures, texts, teachings, and leaders, and have existed for dozens, hundreds, and even thousands of years. Before we get to the broader concept of Spirituality and Alcoholism, it is very useful to see how Organized Religion and Alcoholism come together in useful (or destructive) ways.

ORGANIZED RELIGION AND ALCOHOLISM

First, a high-level (no pun intended) synopsis on the relationship between Alcohol and Religion:

● ●

The Relationship between Religion and Alcohol

The world's religions have had differing relationships with alcohol. Many religions forbid alcoholic consumption or see it as sinful or negative. Others have allocated a specific place for it, as in the Christian practice of drinking Communion wine, which either symbolically represents or is believed to transubstantiate into the blood of Jesus Christ. Other indicators of acceptance abound, such as monastic communities having brewed beer and made wine for many centuries.

Alcoholic beverages appear in the Bible though drunkenness is condemned (by the stories of Noah and Lot). Some Christians including Pentecostals and Methodists today believe one ought to abstain from alcohol. Alcohol consumption is also prohibited by Mormonism's "Word of Wisdom." The Temperance and Prohibitionist movements that led to prohibition in the United States had religious elements starting in the Methodists and Christian movements.

Islam considers consumption of fermented drinks sinful under Islamic dietary laws. Buddhists typically avoid consuming alcohol, as it violates the basic Buddhist code of ethics and can disrupt mindfulness. In Hinduism, wines are sometimes used as medicine.[1]

● ●

In other words, *alcohol is all over the map when it comes to how it is viewed (and even used) by organized religion.* It can be useful, something to be avoided, or outright banned, depending on the *specific* religion or denomination. All seem to recognize that there is a danger in drinking too much alcohol and have incorporated it into their teachings in one form or another.

While religious institutions have differing perspectives on alcohol use, the good news is that it appears to some degree all have universal teachings against alcohol abuse. There is even some research that shows people who are active in their faith are less likely to have problems with alcohol.[2] However, the research also indicates that for others it is especially difficult to seek help, particularly from groups that emphasize alcoholism as a problem of human "sinfulness" that can be overcome by "free will." Religious groups that are more understanding of genetic and social factors that contribute to the disease seem to be more open in confronting alcoholism. While others consider succumbing to the power of addiction as an obvious manifestation of weakness or even the work of the devil.

Dealing with alcoholism can even extend to family members of alcoholics, who can isolate themselves out of fear of what other people will think, gradually disappearing from the social arena of community and church. Yet research indicates being part of caring communities can help alcoholics come to terms with their addiction and provide family members and friends with critical support.[3]

So religious communities can be of significant help, or hindrance, when it comes to your alcoholism, depending on the specifics of your religion, denomination, and local community. If you believe your particular religion and its community falls into the "helpful" category, seek support there to add to what you developed in Level 4—Engage Friends and Family and Level 7—Join a Community.

As we move from an organized religion discussion to a broader spirituality one, it is worth noting two organizations that fall into what I call "Quasi-Religious" organizations—ones that focus specifically on alcoholism/addiction and include a heavy emphasis on God in their treatment. These are Alcoholics Anonymous and The Salvation Army. AA is covered extensively in Level 7—Join a Community, and The Salvation Army is covered in Level 6 as an alternative/unconventional treatment approach.[4]

While AA and SA are the most well-known of these quasi-religious alcoholism programs, there are numerous others. These are what I call "specialty" organizations—mostly Christian based—that combine elements of organized religion and alcoholism treatment. Organizations such as *Addictions Victorious, Alcoholics for Christ, Celebrate Recovery, Christians in Recovery,* and *Strawberry Ministries,* to name a few—there are many of them. I have no specific opinion on the capabilities or structure of such organizations/programs,[5] but if you want to try to merge your beliefs (in Christianity) with alcoholism treatment, it might be worth investigating.

THE CONCEPT OF A "HIGHER POWER"

In my research, I found many testimonials about how a "higher power" helped alcoholics—often desperate ones—attain sobriety. Many, but not all, of these were described in the context of Alcoholics Anonymous. AA is by far the most visible treatment program that encourages the use of a higher power, via its Step 2: *"Came to believe that a power greater than ourselves could restore us to sanity."*[6]

> *I was drinking every day. I got sick so many times it wasn't funny. Finally I did a 2nd step; I found a higher power. I trusted alcohol so much it hurt me so much that I decided to trust a higher power. Alcohol was my God but no more. I did a 3rd step and felt so much peace. My higher power removed all that hurt buried in my subconscious. It was a miracle. I felt so much peace. That is what I was looking for in alcohol, but alcohol is a deceiver. I will stick with my higher power.*
>
> rudy41063, alcoholism.about.com

The concept of a Higher Power can be very helpful, in my opinion, for people who want to embrace spirituality, but are uncomfortable with Organized Religion or opposed to explicitly naming God as that source of spirituality. There are many reasons why a person might do so, and they are very specific to the individual.

In my personal case, I was an agnostic, which (to me) meant that I believed in God, but that was as far as it went. I did not believe strongly enough that I was willing to turn my will and life over to God (a key tenet of AA, even if they qualify it with "as we understood him"). I certainly did not think He would care about me personally and/or in enough "detail" to become involved in my alcoholism.

However, the concept of a Higher Power—one that I could use to mean anything—was very appealing to me when I tried AA.[7] But you don't have to be in AA to use it—and it can be made part of your everyday life.

> *I have found something better and much safer in my higher power. Alcoholism is a living hell and more is gone in my life. I appreciate just getting up in the morning not sick and needing a drink.*
>
> anonymous

The main benefit of using the words *higher power* is that it cannot be easily defined. This means that people can interpret the concept as they wish. It makes it possible for a Christian to follow the steps alongside a Buddhist or even an atheist. Most people interpret *higher power* as meaning "a" deity, but it does not have to be interpreted this way. It is left up to the individual to decide how they wish to define it. There are no rules except that this power has to be greater than the individual.

The Potential Benefits of a Higher Power

A higher power can help in a myriad of ways, mentally and even physically. These include:

• **More forms of support.** Trying to escape alcoholism can feel absolutely overwhelming, if not impossible. As stated numerous times in this book, *you cannot do this alone.* Help does not have to be in the form of a person; in the AA program they rely on a *power greater than themselves* to give them the strength they need. Whether this power is perceived or real strength does not matter.

• **More empathy.** Many people who believe in a higher power will, usually, find it easier to forgive other people who have wronged them. It also becomes easier to let go of resentments, which is an integral part of AA steps around taking inventory of one's self and making amends.

• **A source of comfort.** Like many forms of spirituality, a higher power can be a great source of comfort to believe in—one that is providing help in *some* form. In the Conquer Program's view, this is good news, and really another form of support, not much different from that support you built in Level 4—Engage Friends and Family and Level 7—Join a Community.

- **Relief.** If the addiction becomes too much to handle, the person can *hand it over* to their higher power which can be like lifting a great weight off their shoulders.[8] In AA, they encourage members to learn how to *let go*. This means adopting a completely new approach to life, which may heavily involve spirituality of some form, e.g. a higher power. One key philosophy from this is the belief that if you do the right things (e.g. not drinking, making amends, etc.), then good things will happen to you (their *"Promises"*). This belief can provide peace of mind and a great deal of positive reinforcement.

One of the biggest potential benefits of incorporating a higher power into a newly sober life is that it can provide a new or renewed sense of purpose. This new approach to life—a kind of clean slate approach—can strengthen a person and reduce the risk of relapse. Those who follow a spiritual path claim that it brings a great deal of happiness to their life. It can also have related benefits such as introducing the person to a new set of activities (e.g. attending spiritual group meetings, volunteer efforts) that can provide key defenses for specific triggers such as Boredom.[9]

Higher Power and Atheism in AA

People who have difficulty with the concept of God or reject it entirely can struggle with the concept of a higher power in Alcoholics Anonymous. While in the AA Big Book there is a whole chapter called *We Agnostics,* encouraging those who lack religion to work the 12 Steps, my personal view is that it can be very difficult to pull off in practice.[10]

However, in theory it is possible because there is absolutely no obligation to divulge the nature of one's higher power.[11] Atheists in particular can view it as the power of the group, or as an impersonal force in nature. *All that is required is that they believe that this power is greater than they are and that they can benefit from it.*[12]

WAYS TO "GET SPIRITUAL"

I fully recognize that some people may think this section may be complete BS—either you are spiritual or you are not, right? I disagree; I think you can convince yourself—even *teach* yourself—to gain some degree of spirituality.

● ●

What Is Spirituality?

Some possible definitions:

OED: *The quality or condition of being spiritual; attachment to or regard for things of the spirit as opposed to material or worldly interests.*

Wiktionary: *The concern for that which is unseen and intangible, as opposed to physical or mundane. Also: Appreciation for religion values.*

National Cancer Institute: *Having to do with deep, often religious, feelings and beliefs, including a person's sense of peace, purpose, connection to others, and beliefs about the meaning of life.*

Nursing: *[Spirituality] is that which gives meaning to one's life and draws one to transcend oneself. Spirituality is a broader concept than religion, although that is one expression of spirituality. Other expressions include prayer, meditation, interactions with others or nature, and relationship with God or a higher power."*

Neurobehavioral: *Spirituality means any experience that is thought to bring the experience into contact with the divine (in other words, not just any experience that feels meaningful).*

● ●

The above definitions are okay, but I like the following the best:

> Spirituality refers to the beliefs and practices by which people live. These beliefs are varied and may include the presence of a divine being, a higher power or other spiritual beings. Spirituality plays an important role in guiding people and bringing inner peace, self-awareness and a purpose in life.[13]

For the sake of simplicity I believe there are four main ways that people become spiritual per the above definition, at least ones that are potentially relevant to the alcoholic. These are:

• *Religious Upbringing and Community* (Covered in earlier Organized Religion and Alcoholism discussion)

• *Religious/spiritual literature, teaching and testimonials* (includes Higher Power)

• *A Spiritual "Event" or Epiphany* (includes rock bottom and near death experiences)

• *Preponderance of the evidence.*

Religious Literature, Teaching, and Testimonials

One way to "get" spirituality, or specifically religion, is in the study of it. Of course there are a *huge* amount of texts, teachings, and stories of a spiritual or religious nature dating back centuries and even millennia, including the Bible (Christianity), the Tanakh (Judaism), and the Koran (Islam) to name a few of the over 20 major religions in the world.

I'm not about to go into a detailed study of the role of alcohol in individual religious practices, but as you can guess there are tomes on the topic. To summarize (a very dangerous practice when it comes to religion), it is safe to say that religion's viewpoint on alcohol ranges from embracing it to equating it with the worst of evils, with most wandering in between, even *within* a religion. So unless your religion explicitly teaches that it is wrong to drink alcohol (AND you believe and accept that), it may be hard to find clear guidance on dealing with your alcoholism, even if you were brought up with and practice the religion. If this latter applies to you, I would strongly encourage you to speak with leaders of your church or equivalent about your problems with alcohol and see what kind of *specific* guidance the religion can offer. Even if you don't believe your religious leaders will be able to provide specific, useable-on-a-daily-basis help for your situation, you may find moral/ spiritual support as you do it yourself.

Even if your religion does not provide specific guidance on how to deal with alcohol problems, it may still have provided you with an excellent grounding in how spirituality can play a role in your life. You presumably believe in some form of higher power (God, angels, and the like)—now is the time to use it. It is *your* task to apply those teachings and beliefs to bear specifically to *your* alcoholism.

Here is an excellent place to bring in what you found out about yourself in the foundation building Levels 1 through 3. Level 2—Know Your Triggers is particularly important. Since you specifically and in great detail determined what causes or tempts you to drink, you can look to your religion's literature and leadership for help and teachings on those specific topics. Odds are there is a great deal that has been written or taught on each one of your triggers and how to deal with them. However, you may have to "translate" the triggers of this program into the "language" of your religion, with some triggers being harder than others (Change, Job[14], and Sex immediately come to mind). Specific teachings on your triggers may make much more of an impact on you and your drinking than any broader teachings on alcohol. However, it may require consulting with your minister or equivalent, who *should* be able to help point you to specific texts and passages.

Fortunately, there are many religious/spiritual texts to choose from if you want to go the route of reading/teaching yourself. *Unfortunately, there are many religious/spiritual texts to choose from if you want to go the route of reading/teaching yourself. I had no idea of the number before I researched this section: there are hundreds if not thousands to choose from!*

First you have to select your religious denomination or spiritual approach. There are dozens to choose from, including:

TABLE 3: RELIGIOUS AND SPIRITUAL APPROACHES FROM A TO Z

Adi Dam	Ancient Greece	Science of Mind
Ásatrú	Hermeticism	Scientology
Atenism	Hinduism	Shinto
Ayyavazhi	Islam	Sikhism
Bahá'í Faith	Jainism	Spiritism
Bön	Judaism	Sumerian
Buddhism	LaVeyan Satanism	Swedenborgianism
Cheondoism	Mandaeanism	Taoism
Christianity	Manichaeism	Tenrikyo
Confucianism	Meher Baba	Thelema
Discordianism	Native American Church	Unification Church
Druidism	New Age religions	Urantianism
Druze	Orphism	Wicca
Ancient Egyptian religion	Raëlism	Yârsân
Eternal Divine Path, Mission of Maitreya	Rastafari movement	Yazidi
	Ravidassia	Yorùbá
Etruscan religion	Samaritanism	Zoroastrianism

Source: Wikipedia. "Religious Text." Accessed August 28, 2014.
http://en.wikipedia.org/wiki/Religious_text.

Yikes! For each of these, there is at least one and, more likely, several individual texts. Some cover different topics, while others are different versions of the same thing![15]

Take the Bible for instance. There is not just one Bible, nor are they just used for Christianity. According to Wikipedia, the **Bible** is a canonical collection of texts considered sacred in *Judaism* as well as in *Christianity*. The term Bible is shared between the two religions, although the contents of each of their collections of canonical texts are not the same. Different religious groups include different books within their canons, in different orders, and sometimes divide or combine books, or incorporate additional material into canonical books.

Ok. When it comes to individual texts, the Bible texts appear divided into two types—the *Old Testament* and *New Testament*—totaling over a hundred versions according to Wikipedia, including:

• For *Protestantism*, this is the 66-book canon—the *Jewish Tanakh* of 24 books divided differently (into 39 books) and the universal 27-book *New Testament*.

• For *Catholicism*, this includes seven *deuterocanonical books* in the Old Testament for a total of 73 books, called the *Canon of Trent* (in versions of the Latin Vulgate, *3 Esdras* and *4 Esdras* are included in an appendix, but considered non-canonical).

• For the *Eastern Orthodox Church*, this includes the *anagignoskomena*, which consist of the Catholic Deuterocanon, plus *3 Maccabees*, *Psalm 151*, the *Prayer of Manasseh*, and 3 Esdras. *4 Maccabees* is considered to be canonical by the *Georgian Orthodox Church*.[16]

• The *Ethiopian Orthodox Tewahedo Church* (and its offspring, the *Eritrean Orthodox Church*) adds various books depending on the specific enumeration of the canon (see *Ethiopian Biblical canon*), but always includes 4 Esdras, the *Book of Jubilees*, *1 Enoch*, *4 Baruch*, and *1, 2, and 3 Meqabyan* (no relation to the Books of Maccabees).

• Some *Syriac churches* accept the *Letter of Baruch* as scripture.

Where to start? Probably the easiest way is starting with those texts you are using today (if at all) or those with which you were brought up. You may not have read them much, but even if you have, you did not with a specific eye towards alcoholism and/or triggers. You also might try some religious/spiritual-based addiction programs (generally Christian, discussed earlier in this Level) to see what texts they use. If you have no preference, you might try to do a side-by-side comparison of all the different types out there; a good starting point might be *www.religionfacts.com/big_religion_chart.htm*).[17]

Spiritual "Event" or Epiphany (includes rock bottom)

I call this Spirituality by being Scared To Death.

Many of us—particularly older humans (not necessarily alcoholics)—have encountered life-threatening situations. Maybe a severe illness, a car accident, or a near disaster that left us physically unscarred but mentally traumatized, at least for a while. In those situations, you may have said to yourself "If I get out of this I'll be a better person" or some similar variation, even a vow to become more religious. A common phrase for this is "there are no atheists in foxholes."[18]

The same source for the definition of spirituality also provided this perception of a Spiritual Event:

A spiritual experience can be described as an event or moment where a feeling of a purpose, a defined moment of clarity, or even of seeing angels, ghosts or spiritual beings occurs. It is believed that this experience changes a person's direction in life and has been linked to individuals giving up a life of abusing alcohol or drugs. Some individuals use this experience to find a new sober path in their life.

The challenge, of course, is that many people forget this event, or the pain or trauma "wears off" so we forget the vow or the determination to do things in our life differently. My view is this is often because many of these promises are often too vague or general, difficult to put into action on a day-to-day basis. Instead, if/when these occur, you should very specifically use the situation to focus on your alcoholism, and even on a specific person you want to prove your new resolve to:

I ended up in hospital in serious condition from drinking and, of course, not eating. I was a total physical, emotional and spiritual wreck. I hated myself so much that the only thing to do seemed to be drinking to oblivion. A doctor came by my bed twice a day to tell me I was a drunk and only I could change that. I found out much later this doctor was a godsend to many alcoholics. I was so angry with him I thought, I'll show him I can quit.

Louise, alcoholism.about.com

I finally hit rock bottom! I have been in and out of AA, in and out of institutions, rehabs and got really sick and tired of myself playing games to my mind. I blamed people, I blamed my family, most of all I blamed God for all of my wrong doings. I had a traumatic brain injury due to my chosen sport, this was the time to learn about me, a chance to get myself clean and sober. I have a purpose in living and knowing what's true, right and correct.

Anonymous4, examiner.com

Many of these experiences happen at the same time—or are caused by, depending on your perspective—as a feeling of having hit "rock bottom." Also called "bottoming out," it is a feeling that—except for death—your life can't get any worse. For some people it is a failed marriage, lost job, or another traumatic event that finally convinces them that they *have* to get help.

You don't have to be in physical danger to feel this way of course. It may be some other peril that causes you to think about life in a different way. This is often called an "epiphany"[19] or an "a-ha" moment, when something that has been lurking in your brain that you have been unable to articulate suddenly becomes clear—sometimes called "a moment of clarity."

I decided to stop drinking after I was charged with a DWI in Missouri. This was the "a-ha" life altering moment for me. I realized I needed to stop before I hurt myself, or more importantly, my family. Although the DWI charge had the potential to be much more life altering than it was, this was still the low point for me.

Rocky L., alcoholism.about.com

For some, it may be that in the back of your mind you "knew" the end of your drinking was coming, but you just needed a kick-in-the-head to get you over the hump:

It became clear to me that I needed to quit when I was in the holding cell at the jail, which was almost 3 years ago. I had never been to jail in my life, and that scared the hell out of me. I was court ordered to participate in outpatient therapy. And, I was ready to quit because I knew it would happen that way. So I took it seriously, I showed up for every session, and soon I started really believing that I was an alcoholic. I always knew I was, but I didn't fully accept it until I was forced to!

nomorerebelling, alcoholism.about.com

As you may have noticed, many of the testimonials above are not overtly spiritual, but they do have some elements of "feeling a bit" spiritual, particularly from the definition earlier. Spirituality does not need to have God or some form of deity, nor even a higher power—it just needs to result in some *inner peace, self-awareness and a purpose in life*. I call this "Spirituality Lite." It's good and good for you, if organized religion is not working for you at the moment.

A bit more unorthodox—but possibly effective—way of becoming at least a little spiritual is a listen-to-your-dreams approach, such as described at *http://home.intekom.com/jly2/ttmtoldstop.htm*. Many entities such as *Scientific American* have put forth theories on the meaning of dreams. Read that article[20] if you are interested. My opinion is that if you have several experiences of the same, *very specific* dream, it *might* be that "something" —God, an angel, or just your subconscious trying to tell you something. One test is whether you remember the dream in detail—to me that speaks of something beyond the ordinary.

It doesn't even have to be a specific experience or situation that causes you to have an a-ha/kick-in-the-head moment. Even a bit of self-reflection on what alcohol is doing to your soul may do the job:

> *It wasn't being homeless, or losing my family or even my career of choice, a professional golfer. None of that mattered, and I later learned why, but what changed one day, having tried to drink myself into oblivion, even death, was how empty my soul felt and how completely alienated from life, from myself and from anything that mattered.*
>
> nick K., alcoholism.about.com

Some people cannot dissociate spirituality from religion—which, of course, is absolutely fine. Some even approach it very aggressively, in deciding to view alcohol and your alcoholism as evil, and the way to deal with it is from the other side of the coin—God.

> *Alcohol I hate you! U are destroying me! I am blind to see the truth! But I see it now! God please break this evil yoke! Upon my life! Jesus u paid for my future healings and sins I accept your deliverance today! Forgive my sin to drink and let it destroy me slowly! Help me to live anew life thru your help! Change me make me anew person thru you lord, I'm weak but you are strong! Give me total control and power to overcome this addiction! In Jesus name I pray, father amen! Then renounce alcohol.*
>
> Guest Ask for Gods Help, alcoholism.about.com

There are many, many variations on this. You may feel at some time that God is speaking to you while you are actually awake and aware. Why not?

> *I believe God spoke to me in a pub at 3 o'clock one morning, after 3 days of drinking. On the 21st of May 1981, I was sitting in a 24 hour pub in Sydney, it was the early hours of the morning around 3 am. When I had just ordered a double scotch ice with a shot of coke, because if you mixed it with coke you couldn't be an alcoholic, as I thought.*
>
> *Anyway I was chucking this stuff down my throat at a rate of knots but it was not working. It was at this point I heard an audible voice say to me "Mug" and that's what I was a Mug. The voice said "Mug, somebody could be cutting your wife and your children's throats, you would be none the wiser." Then I did something foreign I told the barmaid I did not need to drink any more.*
>
> *I left the bar and went home to find my wife sitting in the lounge When I looked at her I started to cry. In her eyes I saw confusion, is this the man I married some years earlier? Also in her eyes I could see the pain which I had put her and the kids through. For once I realized the problems I had caused, I told her I was sick and needed help.*

(name redacted), alcoholism.about.com

The main point of all of the above testimonials is that there are *many* ways you can introduce spirituality in your life, and a significant event in your life is a great way to start the process. Be on the lookout for such situations or events, and figure out the best way *for you* to get a bit of spirituality to help with your other defenses in conquering your alcoholism.

Preponderance of the Evidence

Do a search on "scientific evidence of God." You will get some amazingly smart-ass links, such as rationalwiki.org's compilation of *all scientific evidence for the existence of a deity* (2 tumbleweeds chasing each on screen) and godlessgeeks.com's *hundreds of proofs of gods existence* (designed to be completely asinine).[21] A more detailed reading of the search results will come up with many articles about "evidence," including some fairly well thought out pieces ranging from intelligent design, the creation and expansion of the universe, to dissecting Albert Einstein's theory of relativity. But—for better or worse—there is no definitive evidence that screams out—yes there is a god! You have to take a different approach when it comes to evidence-building.

● ●

A Note on Spirituality and Death

As discussed in Level 3, there are some alcoholics who drink because they have an active suicide wish. But there are likely many more who don't care one way or another (as strange as that sounds). Particularly those individuals who have active health problems and know that drinking is a very bad idea—but they do it anyway. There are even some who drink *because* they have a fear of death, particularly the elderly. But if these alcoholics can introduce spirituality into their lives in some form, odds are that it will help in some form and to some degree. Try it!

● ●

Probably one of the simplest, even easiest ways of believing that there is something beyond your life is the evidence before your own eyes: *you are still on this earth, even when by all logic you should be dead from your drinking.*

> *The physical withdrawals got worse and worse after shorter and shorter binges. It came to the point where only a 3-day binge would put me in the ER to detox from withdrawals. Whereas before, it would take 2 weeks, and before that, 2 months. Over 50 ER visits in 12 years? I'm lucky. By the grace of my HP.*
>
> 1hourataT9, alcoholism.about.com

Extending this type of evidence—to near-death stories from hundreds of individuals—can provide in total a powerful argument for life after death, and by inference—a power greater than ourselves. One of the best overall descriptions of the afterlife I found was in a *Newsweek* article titled "Proof of Heaven: A Doctor's experience with the Afterlife" by Dr. Eben Alexander. Dr. Alexander looks to prove from a medical/scientific perspective based on his own near-death experience that heaven exists.[22]

There are many similar stories and many sources for such stories. One good source is the Chicken Soup for the Soul series (visit *www.chicken-soup.com* for a list of titles). Depending on the specific title and category, the Chicken Soup books can offer many testimonials about the impact of spirituality in some form on their lives, including various miracle-type and near-death/after-life experiences. Individually, they might be easy to dismiss, but collectively they get you thinking.[23]

There is no reason not to combine some or all of the four categories of ways to get spiritual together—in fact, together they may be far more powerful. That is my personal experience.

In the end, it is up to you to determine what, if any, role a deity and/or other ways of looking beyond your life, play in conquering your addiction and your life in general. I'm not here to proselytize one way, or another. My only suggestion is that you keep an open mind and consider it—it could provide a formidable set of additional defenses against alcohol for you!

LEVEL 11

Make Yourself Sick of Alcohol

Warning: *This Level poses a potential health risk. Be sure to consult your doctor before utilizing.* This level is optional.[1] Why? Because depending on how you do it, it can be physically risky (as you probably guessed by the title). So why even consider doing it? The bottom line for me was I found some of the potential defenses for some triggers—particularly Smell, Taste, and Proximity (alcohol being *right there* within reach)— discussed in Level 2, were just not complete enough for me. In particular, I didn't just want to avoid those triggers—which is almost impossible anyway—I also wanted to function *completely* in those aromatic, tasty, buzz-beaconing, just-an-arm's-reach-away environments without having to worry about relapsing.

MODERATION, RELAPSES, AND THE CONQUER PROGRAM

Before we get into a discussion of why we might want to make ourselves literally sick of alcohol, let's talk about the temptation to try and use this program to "moderate" our drinking. I am not so naïve as to think some of you won't be tempted; after all, nearly all of us have tried to "cut down" in the past. If you are an alcoholic as we defined it in Level 1, this almost *never* lasts, starting with the definition of "a few less drinks."

For alcoholics "moderation" is a relative term. If you usually have 12 beers a day, "cutting down" may mean you now have 8 or 10. You had 6 glasses of wine a day before? Now it is 3 or 4. And so on. In relative terms, it looks like significant progress, but in absolute terms it is hardly *moderate* drinking. But say you can get it down to a "reasonable" amount, say 3 or 4 beers or 2 or 3 glasses of wine a day. Besides still being a lot—after all, you are doing it *every* day—the likelihood of you maintaining this "low" level of drinking is practically zero. Sooner or later you will slowly but surely add to your total: the average becomes 4 or 5 beers instead of 3 or 4, then 5 or 6, then 6 or 7. Soon you are right back where you started. But I don't believe this "moderation" is possible for the *vast* majority of alcoholics. You need *complete* sobriety, because alcoholics *cannot* control alcohol in general and certainly not in the long term.

Ok, you say, no moderation. But what happens if I relapse?

The good news is that unlike many programs, the Conquer Program does *not* consider you a "failure" if you have a relapse, nor that you need to restart your attempt at sobriety as if you had never tried before. In other words, you are not thrown back to 1st Grade, you Don't Pass "Go" without collecting $200,[2] or go back to Step 1 in AA, etc.

What is *does* mean, however, is that you did not do well enough earlier at a) identifying your major drinking triggers (and their related ones), and/or b) identifying an effective set of defenses against the trigger(s) that caused your relapse. So you may well need to go back to Level 2 and reread those sections to help yourself fully understand the reasons for your relapse.

However, it may be that you believe you *did* identify your triggers correctly, and devised a set of defenses that you thought *were* adequate, but obviously were not. It is in these circumstances where the full power of the Conquer Program can help, specifically in Level 13—Develop Your Defense Progressions, discussed shortly.

But it may instead be that the defenses identified earlier for certain triggers were just not enough to work for you in *any* circumstances. The triggers by far the most likely to cause this are Proximity, Smell, and/or Taste, as well as the overall rush/buzz/numb/checkout effects that come along with it. That is what *this* Level is about—offering more radical ways of defending against these triggers, through *literally making yourself sick of alcohol*. But to do this successfully you may need a lot more insight into what you are dealing with.

PROXIMITY, SMELL AND TASTE—THE AXIS OF EVIL?

These three triggers in combination can be one of the biggest problem situations for a person struggling to get and stay sober. For that reason, one of the biggest tips for all three is to stay away from alcohol if at all possible—particularly early in sobriety as you are building and tuning your defenses.

For many of us, the best-laid plans—not having alcohol in the house, staying away from situations and people where alcohol is likely to be—are just not practical, particularly in the long term. So if we cannot find a set of defenses that will allow us to function in environments and situations where alcohol is around, we've got a major practical life issue. The solution? To make ourselves sick—figuratively and possibly literally—at the sight, smell, and taste of alcohol.

The Desire for the Effect of Alcohol

Closely coupled with these "evil" triggers is a recognition of the *extreme* importance of the *effect* of alcohol to many if not most alcoholics, including me. Whether it is the initial *"rush"* that comes with the first drink, to the *"buzz"* after a few, to being "comfortably *numb*" after several, to the complete *"checking out* from the world" that comes after many (I call this rush/buzz/numb/checkout continuum, "buzz-rush" for short), the desire for one or more of those effects are intertwined with many of the triggers that underlie our desire to drink.

Why haven't I mentioned these rather obvious desires before, particularly in the triggers discussions in Level 2?[3] Primarily for three reasons:

1. Understanding your triggers and designing your defenses to them are complicated enough without including things like "tips to avoid the desire to be numb when you are depressed";

2. Addressing buzz-rush could completely overshadow its overall impact for many people, since it is often almost a minor by-product of the desire to avoid/rebut/escape from the trigger (particularly as you get older and move past the Fun trigger as a big reason for drinking); and

3. Since the desire for buzz-rush can underlie numerous triggers, it made more sense to cover it in a completely separate section—this one.

No substitute substance (that does not have the potential for addiction) will be able to create the same buzz-rush feelings that alcohol does. However, you can develop ways to make yourself actually not like these feelings as much, and even *dislike* them. Alternatively, there are some non-addictive substances that can replicate *some* of these feelings to *some* extent. Some scientific background is needed first before we get into these methods and alternative substances.

WHAT'S THE BUZZ—WHAT IT IS AND WHY WE WANT IT

As discussed above and initially in the Escape trigger section, the first drink of alcohol creates an initial period of excitement (the "rush" of pleasure in the rush/buzz/numb/checkout continuum) lasting for a short time. As we continue to drink, we progress through the states of being "buzzed," then if we drink enough getting to the point of being "numb," and eventually checking out (e.g., passing out).

It is *essential* to understanding why alcohol has this impact on us if we want to combat the desire to have it in the first place. I break this down into two parts: 1) understanding how different amounts of alcohol impact us in different ways and 2) understanding the underlying physiological/chemical impact factors on the human brain and body. Both will provide insight into how we can teach ourselves to *want to avoid* alcohol though making the smell, taste, and even sight and effect of it nauseating to us and, if necessary, consume alternative beverages that can help us relax in safe, non-addictive ways.

The desire for the buzz/rush/numb/checkout feelings that alcohol can provide either lurks in the background of many triggers, or it is front and center for others—particularly "Fun"—but also others like Escape (numb/checkout), Extreme Emotions (checkout), Guilt (numb), Insomnia (checkout), Peer Pressure (buzz/rush), Powerlessness (numb, checkout), and Zest/Zeal (rush).

In my research I found little referring to the terms "buzz," "rush," "numb[4]," and "checkout." Indeed most of what I found about the effects of alcohol dived immediately into medical terms such as "blood-ethanol concentration," "brain electroencephalographic activity," "GABA receptors," "serotonin concentration," "dopamine circuits," and "production of endorphins." Arrrggghhh! To say there is a *gigantic* disconnect between how the medical profession looks at alcohol and how you and I do is an understatement to say the least. Let's see if we can bridge that gap because it is *very* important to understand how the chemicals of alcohol interact with your brain and body to understand why it has an impact on us.

The best medical research and analysis I found that starts to bridge this gap was from Office of Drug and Alcohol Education at the University of Notre Dame.[5] It lays out a table of what to expect mentally and physically as you progress through different blood alcohol content levels. *Blood Alcohol Content* (BAC) is the amount of alcohol in one's system based on weight, number of drinks, and the period during which alcohol is consumed. Notre Dame makes a very specific point that BAC it *totally unrelated* to your *tolerance* of alcohol (Level 5—Detox provided a detailed discussion of the nature of tolerance). Meaning that the same BAC in two people could result in *far* different effects in their behavior and mental and body reactions, regardless of how similar they are in terms of weight, gender, age, etc.

In particular, Notre Dame uses the term "Euphoria." Notably it does not actually define that term, instead includes it in the same sentence as "positive" and "relaxed." But let's give it a definition.

Wikipedia.org defines Euphoria as:

> A mental and emotional condition in which a person experiences intense feelings of well-being, elation, happiness, excitement, and joy.[6]

I believe this is an excellent definition for the "rush" and "buzz" portions of our rush-buzz-numb-checkout continuum.

The Notre Dame website has an excellent continuum of its own related to Blood Alcohol Content (BAC) levels:

TABLE 4: BAC LEVEL GENERALIZED DOSE SPECIFIC EFFECTS

BAC Level	Effect of Alcohol
BAC = 0.02 to 0.03%	No loss of coordination, **slight euphoria** and loss of shyness. Depressant effects are not apparent.
BAC = 0.04 to 0.06%	Feeling of well-being, relaxation, lower inhibitions, and sensation of warmth. **Euphoria.** Some minor impairment of reasoning and memory, lowering of caution.
BAC = 0.07 to 0.09%	Slight impairment of balance, speech, vision, reaction time, and hearing. **Euphoria.** Reduced judgment and self-control. Impaired reasoning, memory, and sense of cautiousness.
BAC = 0.10–0.125%	Significant impairment of motor coordination and loss of good judgment. Speech may be slurred; balance, vision, reaction time, and hearing will be impaired.

BAC Level	Effect of Alcohol
BAC = 0.13–0.15%	Gross motor impairment and lack of physical control. Blurred vision and major loss of balance. **Euphoria is reducing and dysphoria[7] is beginning to appear.**
BAC = 0.16–0.20%	**Dysphoria predominates,** nausea may appear. The drinker has the appearance of a "sloppy drunk." May vomit.
BAC = 0.25%	**Needs assistance in walking; total mental confusion. Dysphoria with nausea and some vomiting. Death has occurred at this level, and it is considered a medical emergency.**
BAC = 0.30%	**Loss of consciousness.**
BAC = 0.40% +	**Onset of coma, possible death due to respiratory arrest.**

Source: Notre Dame Office of Alcohol and Drug Education. "What is Intoxication?" Accessed March 2, 2014. http://oade.nd.edu/educate-yourself-alcohol/what-is-intoxication/.

This is a fascinating table on many levels. First it demystifies why we act and feel the way we do relative to how much we have been drinking.[8] The table describes the results in terms that laymen can understand—not ones that glorify it (e.g., "I'm so High right now," or "Boy am I pissed"[9]) or put in medical terms that make your eyes glaze over.

Next, it illustrates to me is how temporary the "rush" (the slight euphoria of BAC 0.02 to 0.03%)[10] and the "buzz" (euphoria of BAC 0.04 to 0.09%)[11] are before degenerating into numb (BAC 0.10–0.125%) and "checkout" (BAC 0.13+)[12] territories.

Third, it shows the "transition point" **where the "positive" reaction to the alcohol turns negative.** Notre Dame says, *"When a BAC of .056 is exceeded, the negative, depressant effects of alcohol take place."* The 0.06% level is about where the positives (in terms of rush and buzz) are outweighed by the negatives (impaired judgment, inappropriate behavior, impaired coordination, slurred speech, talkative, intensified emotions, lowered inhibitions, *diminished senses, slowed mental processing, cannot listen well, follow conversations well, or understand what others are saying*).

I underlined these last phrases, as these define "numb" to me. Yes, that may be your objective from the start. But even that "state" doesn't last long; as you pass the 0.10% level, you start to enter the "checkout" level. Even if *that* is your goal (say for Insomnia or to wipe out a bad day), it is a very dangerous BAC level. A few variations in your drinking (how much, how fast, how much you ate, how tired you are, etc.), can mean *life-altering* differences. Legal drunk driving of course starts at a much lower level (0.08% in most states), but your "technical" drunk driving (how well you can actually do it) will likely very quickly deteriorate even more once you get once you get past the 0.10% level. And once you get past the 0.20% level, you are talking about grave risks to your health and life, even if you are sitting at home "safe."

You are probably gnashing your teeth by now asking "Yes, but how many drinks does it take to get me to BAC (insert number)?" The below tables (one for men and one for women)[13] provide that answer—but you'll need a calculator and an honest assessment of how much you drank/drink and how fast. It is time well spent—you will likely be surprised at your personal results.

TABLE 5: BLOOD ALCOHOL COUNT CALCULATION (MEN)

Drinks in one hour	Pure Alcohol Fluid Oz.	100lbs	120lbs	140lbs	160lbs	180lbs	200lbs	220lbs	240lbs	260lbs
		BAC CALCULATION FOR MEN								
0	0	.00%	.00%	.00%	.00%	.00%	.00%	.00%	.00%	.00%
1	½	.04	.03	.03	.02	.02	.02	.02	.02	.01
2	1	.07	.06	.05	.05	.04	.04	.03	.03	.03
3	1 ½	.11	.09	.08	.07	.06	.06	.05	.05	.04
4	2	.15	.12	.11	.09	.08	.07	.07	.06	.06
5	2 ½	.19	.16	.13	.12	.10	.09	.08	.08	.07
6	3	.22	.19	.16	.14	.12	.11	.10	.09	.09
7	3 ½	.26	.22	.19	.16	.15	.13	.12	.11	.10
8	4	.30	.25	.21	.20	.17	.15	.14	.12	.11

Source: Steven F. Groce, Attorney at Law. "How Much Can You Drink and Still Be Legal?" Accessed March 2, 2014. http://attorneydwi.com/bacperdrink.html.

To calculate BAC over time, subtract .01% for each 40 minutes after the first drink. One 12 Oz. beer, or 5 Oz. of wine, or 1 1/4 Oz. of 80 proof spirits, contains approximately 1/2 Oz. of pure ethyl alcohol.

TABLE 6: BLOOD ALCOHOL COUNT CALCULATION (WOMEN)

BAC CALCULATION FOR WOMEN									
Drinks in one hour	Pure Alcohol Fluid Oz.	100 lbs.	120 lbs.	140 lbs.	160 lbs.	180 lbs.	200 lbs.	220 lbs.	240 lbs.
0	0	.00%	.00%	.00%	.00%	.00%	.00%	.00%	.00%
1	½	.05	.04	.03	.03	.03	.02	.02	.02
2	1	.09	.08	.06	.06	.05	.05	.04	.04
3	1 1/2	.14	.11	.10	.09	.08	.07	.06	.06
4	2	.18	.15	.13	.11	.10	.09	.08	.08
5	2 1/2	.23	.19	.16	.14	.13	.11	.10	.09
6	3	.27	.23	.19	.17	.15	.14	.12	.11
7	3 1/2	.32	.27	.23	.20	.18	.16	.14	.13
8	4	.30	.25	.26	.23	.20	.18	.17	.15

Source: Steven F. Groce, Attorney at Law. "How Much Can You Drink and Still Be Legal?" Accessed March 2, 2014. http://attorneydwi.com/bacperdrink.html.

To calculate BAC over time, subtract .01% for each 40 minutes after the first drink. One 12 Oz. beer, or 5 Oz. of wine, or 1 1/4 Oz. of 80 proof spirits, contains approximately 1/2 Oz. of pure ethyl alcohol.[14]

Probably the biggest use of this is that this information can be used to help *anyone* stop or at least reduce their drinking—after a few drinks or not to bother in the first place. How?

Takeaway #1—You will NEVER replicate that initial feeling—the "rush"—after the first drink of the day/evening. No matter how much more you drink that day/night! So if that is your one and only goal, one (1) drink is all you "need," and *more won't prolong or repeat the feeling.* I would have *loved* to have known this many years ago.[15]

Takeaway #2—The "buzzed" feeling only works within a narrow BAC—e.g., only for a certain # of drinks in a certain period of time (you'll have to do your own calculation). One you go past that level (about 0.06%

BAC discussed above), the positive buzz starts to give way to the negative "buzz kill"[16] effect of alcohol.

Takeaway #3—If "numb" is your goal, it is also likely to not last long, because as an alcoholic you are very unlikely to stop drinking, entering "checkout" territory shortly afterwards. If you *can* usually stop, then it would seem that you do have some strong level of control left. However, this is highly unlikely in most if not all alcoholics as the inability to control drinking is a core part of our definition of alcoholism and the key distinction between a "problem drinker" and an alcoholic.

Takeaway #4—If "checkout" is your goal, be aware (if you are not already) that you are playing in *very* dangerous territory. For every Jason Bonham[17] and Amy Winehouse[18] there are hundreds if not thousands of others who wind up dead of alcohol poisoning, not to mention the tens of thousands of people killed by drunk driving every year.

Regardless of your "goals" with respect to the above, what I takeaway overall is that the effect you are looking for is either very short term, quickly surpassed or very dangerous. So if—like the vast majority of alcoholics—you can't stop[19] once you start, why bother to drink at all?

HOW AND WHY ALCOHOL AFFECTS YOUR BRAIN AND BODY

Prepare yourself for some deep medical/scientific terminology, but it does help get at the root of why alcohol hits us like it does:[20]

There are many kinds of *alcohol* in the chemical world, but the one we drink the most is *ethanol*. It's the particular shape of an ethanol molecule that gives a glass of beer or a shot of the hard stuff its specific effects on the human brain. The molecule is very tiny, made up of just two carbon atoms, six hydrogen atoms, and one oxygen atom. Ethanol is water soluble, which means it enters the blood stream readily; there to be carried quickly to all parts of the body (most notably the liver and the brain). It's also fat soluble; like an all-access pass through various cell membranes and other places that are normally off limits.

A certain portion of the ethanol you drink passes through your stomach to your small intestine, and is absorbed into your bloodstream and carried to your brain. Specifically, after swallowing, it is absorbed into the blood via small blood vessels in the stomach and intestines.[21] On an empty stomach, about 20 percent of the alcohol is absorbed by the stomach, and 80 percent by the intestines and the alcohol reaches its peak in about an hour. Alcohol consumed with a meal is absorbed much more slowly and reaches its peak in two hours.[22]

That's what we're concerned with. Research has *not* conclusively determined exactly how ethanol accomplishes all of its various effects in the brain, but there are some well-supported *theories.*

One key study has the slow reactions, slurred speech and memory loss from heavy drinking *probably* being caused by ethanol attaching to *glutamate receptors* in your brain's neural circuitry. These receptors normally receive chemical signals from other parts of the brain, but instead they get an ethanol molecule. This molecule disrupts the flow of signals and generally slows the whole brain down.

A similar theory has ethanol binding to *GABA (gamma-aminobutyric acid) receptors,* which normally serve to slow down brain activity. Unlike glutamate receptors, ethanol makes GABA receptors more receptive, causing the brain to slow down even more. But alcohol isn't simply a depressant, because it also stimulates the production of *dopamine* and *endorphins*, chemicals that produce feelings of pleasure. Research hasn't yet revealed the exact mechanism involved, but it may be similar to the way ethanol stimulates the GABA receptors.[23]

This may explain why and how alcohol can act as both as a stimulant and depressant.

Potential Reasons for the Individual Rush/Buzz/Numb/ Checkout "States" from Alcohol Consumption[24]

Euphoria, the feeling of well-being, has been reported during the early (10–15 minutes) phase of alcohol consumption (the time blood-ethanol concentration rises, e.g., the "Rush" and subsequent "Buzzed" states), and can be connected to changes in the brain *electroencephalographic* activity. The neurochemical basis of euphoria, in general, and that induced by alcohol in particular *remains unclear.* At least four neuronal mechanisms have so far been implicated, namely those involving the *dopaminergic, gamma-aminobutyric (GABA)-ergic, opioidergic,* and *serotonergic systems.*

●　●

Serotonin—The Key To Alcoholism?

As discussed in Level 1, a Lack of Control is one of the four "cornerstones" of alcoholism. In my opinion, this Lack of Control is THE biggest contributor to alcoholism overall by far. I will even go so far to say that someone cannot become an alcoholic if they *do* have control over alcohol (they can certainly be a problem drinker however). Unfortunately, this is just a theory, along with many other theories about the nature of and contributors to the disease.

That said, according to the *Cold Spring Harbor Laboratory-DNA Learning Center.* "*The Serotonegic System*"[25] serotonin is very much involved in impulsivity; that is to say, behavior occurring without foresight. Research with rats shows that if rats have low serotonin, they simply can't restrain themselves from responding when they shouldn't. If proven in humans (such tests are not underway as far as I could tell), this may be key to unlocking why alcohol affects alcoholics differently than other people, and in turn possibly generate specific drug research to boost/modify serotonin levels to help alcoholic's better control their alcohol consumption.

There have been other medical studies on the Lack of Control element, such as *www.ncbi.nlm.nih.gov/pubmed/10843306,*   and *http://pubs.niaaa.nih.gov/publications/arh21–2/114.pdf.* This latter report describes "Serotonin receptor subtypes and their potential roles in the development of alcohol abuse," describing one that "may control consummatory behavior, including alcohol consumption," and one that "may regulate alcohol consumption." [26]

Unfortunately, much more research is needed that focuses specifically and extensively on serotonin's impact on alcoholics' lack of control.

●　●

One generally accepted theory is that once in the bloodstream alcohol heads for the *nucleus accumbens,* an area of the brain associated with pleasure, gratification, hunger, thirst, stress reduction and sex. Once there, it has been suggested that ethanol[27] disturbs levels of *glutamate,* which cause neurons to fire and produces the initial alcohol high (the Rush and Buzzed states), as well as activating *GABA receptors,* which reduce neuron firing and is what makes many drinkers relax (e.g., Numb) and even sleepy (e.g., on their way to "Checkout").

A related theory is that euphoria may be caused by the release/increased production of *dopamine* and other pleasure-inducing chemicals including *serotonin* and *endorphins,* the brain's natural *opioids* (psychoactive chemicals that resemble morphine). It should be noted that in relation to alcohol consumption, it is difficult to consider whether euphoria is a mood state, an expression of drug reward, or both.[28]

Additional Note: While the above provides some compelling evidence on why alcohol affects us like it does (you may have to read it several times), the various sources make it clear that it does not provide conclusive evidence.

There are other theories as well, particularly with respect to the production of Endorphins:

● ●

Alcohol and Endorphins

A study[29] from the Ernest Gallo[30] Clinic and Research Centre at the University of California in 2012 marked the first time that endorphins have been directly observed in humans being released in two regions of the brain (the nucleus accumbens and orbitofrontal cortex) in response to drinking alcohol. The study provides the first direct evidence of how alcohol makes people feel good. It also shows how this may play a factor in why heavy drinkers continue to drink.

The researchers used PET imaging (positron emission tomography) to observe the immediate effects of alcohol in the brains of 13 heavy drinkers and 12 matched 'control' subjects who were not heavy drinkers. Drinking led to a release of endorphins in all those taking part. The more endorphins released in the nucleus accumbens, the greater the feelings of pleasure reported by each drinker. However, as levels of endorphins released in the orbitofrontal cortex went up, heavy drinkers felt more intoxicated—but not those in the control group.

[A doctor involved with the study] said "This indicates that the brains of heavy or problem drinkers are changed in a way that makes them more likely to find alcohol pleasant, and *may be a clue to how problem drinking develops in the first place . . .* That greater feeling of reward might cause them to drink too much . . . If we better understand how endorphins control drinking, we will have a better chance of creating more targeted therapies for substance addiction."[31]

● ●

Great! you say; obviously there is a ton of research that has been done, and new efforts are continuing to build on this all the time. A "cure" or miracle drug must be right around the corner, right? *Wrong.*

DRUGS TO "TREAT" ALCOHOLISM

There are currently only three medications approved by the U.S. Food and Drug Administration for the treatment of alcohol abuse and alcohol dependence. These are:

- Acamprosate
- Naltrexone
- Disulfiram

None of these drugs approach anything resembling a "cure" for alcoholism, and none of these medications are prescribed to people who are still drinking alcohol.[32] *These drugs only address certain, relatively limited facets of alcohol use or are effective only in early sobriety.*

Acamprosate

Campral, the brand name for *Acamprosate*, is the most recent medication approved for the treatment of alcohol dependence or alcoholism in the United States. It works by reducing the physical distress and emotional discomfort people usually experience when they quit drinking, including reducing sweating, anxiety and sleep disturbances that many experience during the early stages of alcohol abstinence. *How it does this is not completely understood.*

Acamprosate is *thought* to stabilize the chemical balance in the brain that would otherwise be disrupted by alcoholism, possibly by *antagonizing* glutamatergic *N-methyl-D-aspartate receptors* and *agonizing gamma-aminobutyric acid* (GABA) *type A receptors.*[33]

Bottom Line: Acamprosate helps you with some difficulties in the post-detox/early sobriety stages. It *cannot* be used while you are drinking (hence it cannot help you stop drinking). It does *not* help you with the actual detox process. It does *absolutely nothing* to prevent or inhibit you from relapsing.

Naltexone

Naltrexone is sold under the brand names Revia and Depade. An extended-release form of naltrexone is marketed under the trade name Vivitrol. It works by blocking in the brain the "high" that people experience when they drink alcohol or take opioids like heroin and cocaine.

For people who have stopped drinking, Naltrexone "reduces the craving" for alcohol that many alcohol dependent people experience when they quit drinking. *It is not fully understood how Naltrexone works* to reduce the craving for alcohol, but some scientists believe it works by affecting the neural pathways in the brain where the neurotransmitter *dopamine* is found.

Bottom Line: Naltrexone tries to stop you from feeling "pleasure" when you drink. The presumed reason for this, essentially blocking the production of dopamine, which is consistent with an earlier theory of how alcohol affects us. However, the definition of "craving" is very open to interpretation. In the Conquer Program "craving" is a general term for the desire to drink due to any number of other, *much more specific* reasons—your triggers. Drinking for "pleasure" means that you still associate drinking with having "Fun," which is a trigger in and of itself.

Disulfiram

Disulfiram, also known as Antabuse, was the first medicine approved for the treatment of alcohol abuse and alcohol dependence. It works by causing a severe adverse reaction when someone taking the medication consumes alcohol. Translation—it makes you sick, particularly in coordination with alcohol. It does this by increasing the concentration of acetaldehyde in your body, *which essentially causes the equivalent of a severe hangover.* This drug is discussed in more detail in the broader Aversion Therapy discussion in Level 6.

Bottom Line: Disulfiram-only based treatment *may* help you in initially getting you sober and shortly thereafter. If the treatment only focuses on the physical inducement of nausea—and not on re-associating that nausea with your underlying triggers—it is unlikely to work by itself in the long-term, and certainly not after you stop taking it. But the concept can be extremely valuable and is adapted for this program in the next section of this Level.

There you go. All this research and we have three drugs. One (Disulfiram/Antabuse) that makes you sick if you drink. Another, (Naltrexone) that blocks the "high" (the rush/buzz) when you drink. The third drug (Acamprosate) helps with early sobriety. It is my opinion that one or more of these drugs *may* help *some* alcoholics with *some* portion of the getting sober process for *some* period of time. I will defer to medical professionals on whether they might work for you. Note that all have potentially serious side effects, *and effectiveness wears off after treatment stops* (one possible exception: behavior changes that may result from aversion therapy).

None of them *specifically* address what I believe is the underlying issue behind our alcoholism—our lack of control—nor *comprehensively* what makes alcoholics want to drink most of the time—our triggers.

How Can These Drugs Be Used Within The Conquer Program?

While not even close to being miracle drugs, they can "nibble around the edges" of *some* of our triggers. Acamprosate may help with the Fear of Quitting trigger (particularly the Anxiety and Insomnia related triggers). Naltrexone looks like it might help the "Fun" and possibly "Escape" triggers. Disulfiram/Antabuse may help with the Smell, Taste, and (possibly) the Proximity triggers through its underlying make-you-sick theme. I will explore this shortly in much more detail as it is the overall point of this Level.

Again, *none* of these medications can "cure" alcoholism—or even come remotely close. Indeed they require you *to stop drinking before you start taking the drug.* When combined with the dismal record of psychological-based treatment programs, unfortunately, we alcoholics have to fix alcoholism mostly ourselves. Drugs or individual "traditional" or even older unconventional programs won't do much of it for us.[34]

AVERSION THERAPY REVISITED—
WHAT IT IS AND HOW IT MIGHT HELP

Aversion Therapy was introduced in Level 6 as an alternative treatment approach. Why do I revisit and emphasize it here? Because at its heart is the *philosophy* of *breaking the association* between alcohol and pleasure, and *re-associating* it with pain and misery. Aversion therapy as it has typically and historically been applied has had only limited success. However, I believe that if done somewhat *differently,* it can be done more *effectively* and not necessarily only in the setting of a formal alcoholism treatment facility.

A refresher:

Aversion Therapy Definition

Aversion therapy is a form of addiction treatment that uses behavioral principles to *eliminate unwanted behavior.* In this therapeutic method, the unwanted stimulus is repeatedly paired with discomfort. The goal of the conditioning process is to make the individual associate the stimulus with unpleasant or uncomfortable sensations.

During aversion therapy, the person may be asked to think of or engage in the behavior they enjoy while at the same time being exposed to something unpleasant such as a bad taste, a foul smell or even mild electric shocks. Once the unpleasant feelings become associated with the behavior, the hope is that the unwanted behaviors or actions will begin to decrease in frequency or stop entirely.

The Effectiveness of Aversion Therapy

The overall effectiveness of aversion therapy can depend upon a number of factors, including the methods used and whether or not the client continues to practice relapse prevention after treatment is concluded. In some instances, the client may return to previous patterns of behavior once they are out of treatment and no longer exposed to the deterrent.

I could not find any statistics on the effectiveness of aversion therapy. This is no doubt because of its scarcity of use and because it would require a controlled study environment to minimize the independent variables to draw statistically valid conclusions scientifically. Anecdotally my research indicated something along a 50–50 break for and against it in testimonials, but those are hardly enough to draw any scientific conclusions. But if commercial hospitals like Seattle's *Schick Shadel* hospital can last for several decades (and claim 60,000 successes), then that is least a small indicator of its potential for success.

Problems With Aversion Therapy

In addition to the lack of rigorous scientific evidence demonstrating aversion therapy's effectiveness, ethical issues over the use of punishments in therapy are also a major point of concern. Many people have a problem with the use of physical punishment no matter how desirable the result.[35]

Practitioners have also found that in some cases aversion therapy can increase anxiety, interfering with the treatment process. In other instances, some patients have also experienced anger and hostility during therapy; hardly "wanted" behavior.

Another problem is that there are relatively few clinics that specialize in aversion therapy, for the reasons cited above and probably as important, most insurance programs do not cover it.[36] So that leaves it to the individual to determine if they want to do a version of it themselves. The question is how.

The Importance of Pavlov's Dog

Part of the philosophy behind aversion therapy lies in "Pavlov's Dog," which many of us learned in high school. A refresher:

● ●

Who Was Ivan Pavlov?

Ivan Petrovich Pavlov was a famous Russian physiologist. The concept for which Pavlov is famous is the "conditioned reflex" he developed jointly with an assistant in 1901. He came to learn this concept of conditioned reflex when examining the rates of salivations among dogs.

Pavlov discovered that when a bell was rung in subsequent time with food being presented to the dog in consecutive sequences, the dog would initially salivate when presented with food. The dog will later **come to associate** the ringing of the bell with the presentation of the food and salivate upon the ringing of the bell. His writings also record the use of a wide variety of other stimuli, including electric shocks, whistles, metronomes, tuning forks, and a range of visual stimuli.[37]

● ●

At the risk of giving scores of academics, psychologists, psychiatrists and the like heart attacks or having them storming my home armed with sharpened pens and frothing like rabid dogs, my much broader extrapolation and takeaway from this and related research is as follows:

The mind can dictate the body's workings; the body can dictate the mind's thinking, and both can work (and communicate) together to the benefit, or detriment, of both.[38]

It is this philosophy that is at the core of possible approaches that follow. More specifically, they are intended to *break* the association of "the pleasure" of alcohol with the triggers of Proximity, Smell and Taste, as well as provide an excellent backup to your defenses against other triggers, particularly Escape and Fun.

Proximity Trigger Aversion Therapy

Let's start with the Proximity trigger. Is there a way to make the mere *sight* of alcohol (or anything visually related to it), make you feel unwell? The answer is maybe; I was able to do it, and some variation of it might work for you.

The possibility of sight-based "aversion therapy" first started to click with me as a result of colon problems I'd suffered for many years, and unfortunately in a negative way. Without getting too graphic, problem colons can be very sensitive to a variety of factors and in turn cause unpleasantness, or at least emergency trips to the bathroom. While I had experienced various instances of this over the (30!) years, they were for the most part manageable and controllable. It wasn't until after recovering from colon surgery that I realized this sensitivity wasn't just limited to what I ate or did with my body, but also to what I thought and sensed—sight in particular.

I could be perfectly fine colon-wise, even recently gone to the bathroom. However, I still found that the mere thought of going to the bathroom or even random thoughts on my intestinal health would cause a great uptick in the urgency to go again. I even found that if I was in a store—feeling perfectly fine—and saw a sign for "Restrooms" that I would have a sudden and urgent need to get there. Fast. And needed to be faster as I got physically closer and closer to said restroom.

This urge had happened to me before but never so insidiously. After thinking about it for a while (enjoyably lying in my hospital bed after surgery), I came to the conclusion (read: Hope) that this kind of mind-body connection could be created for *positive* purposes, namely my alcoholism. Once I was released, I started trying to think negative thoughts *every* time I saw the word "Liquor" on a store front or sign, and especially every time I saw a bottle of vodka (my long-time drink of choice and horrible nemesis).

In particular, each time I saw these I would think of how hideous I felt in the lead-up to my going to the hospital, and *try to actively associate these bad feelings with the sight of alcohol.*[39]

To my amazement it worked. After a couple of weeks of doing this (with probably about 100 "sightings") I would start to feel queasy whenever I happened across the word Liquor or sight of a vodka bottle. I was even able to extend the feelings to other types of alcohol. I felt I had broken (or at least seriously bent) the Proximity trigger! No longer did the sight of alcohol make my mind weaken and my mouth water! This feeling still lingers today (as a Reminder). While I no longer start to get physically sick at the sights, I have absolutely no temptation to go near anything that resembles alcohol in any form.[40]

Next—how was I to better defend against the Smell and Taste of alcohol?

Smell and Taste Aversion Therapy

Here is where aversion therapy gets even trickier, and (again) is totally optional and at your own risk.

Odds are there is some food or beverage that during some point in your past made you violently ill. Maybe you choked on popcorn once and can't bear the smell let alone taste of it. Maybe you have an allergic reaction to onions or nuts. Maybe there is some food that just tastes hideous to you (like lima beans—the most hideous vegetable ever created). You might even think back when your mom put something gross on your thumb to make you stop sucking it. Or maybe even some alcoholic beverage that you had such a horrible experience with that you vowed never to drink it again—and stuck to it![41] That is what we are trying to replicate here (at your own risk). In my case it was drinking *purely* for the purpose of getting sick, combined with a food that I was allergic to (red onions) to aid in the process.

Foods That Can Cause an Allergic Reaction

According to mayoclinic.com[42], there are eight foods included in food allergy labeling, accounting for an estimated 90 percent of allergic reactions. These eight foods are: Milk, Eggs, Peanuts, Tree Nuts (such as almonds, cashews, walnuts), Fish (such as bass, cod, flounder), Shellfish (such as crab, lobster, shrimp), Soy, and Wheat.

Other specific sources of reactions include Avocados, Bananas, Caffeine, Cheeses (aged in particular), Legumes (beans and peanuts), MSG, Onions, Peanut Butter, Pickled products, Pizza, Processed Meats, Yeast-based products, and Yogurt. Hopefully, it is obvious, but I'll state it here: **If you have a serious allergic reaction to anything here (such peanuts), do NOT use them if you attempt the approach described shortly.** The assumption is that you have a mild reaction to them, or that they regularly cause some indigestion.

First, the prerequisites. These are absolute requirements:

- Be at home or staying with a friend or family member

- Have that friend or family member with you at all times while you are drinking

- Do NOT drive under *any* circumstances

- You are *not* partying, socializing, or having a good time while you are drinking—*you are trying to make yourself sick.* That doesn't mean you can't watch TV, read a book, surf the internet, or other mildly entertaining activities. However, the focus is on making yourself vomit, break out in a hideous rash, or something similarly unpleasant (but not life threatening).

Some suggestions/recommendations are good if you can swing them, including:

• Write about your experiences, including amounts and times in a log, blog, or another forum.

• Try to plan on doing this when you can minimize personal and professional commitments. This will be difficult to do, since this can be a multi-week process, but do your best.

• Take some "selfies," before and after in the bathroom mirror, at various points in your drinking each night. Since you will likely be drunk and pass out, you might not remember what you looked like if you break out in a rash or become heavily flushed.

Last, run this approach by your doctor. If her or she says no, *don't do it.*

● ●

The Author's Extreme Approach to Making Myself Sick

• Five days/nights drinking for the *sole* purpose of drinking (vodka in my case, which by this time in my drinking "career" was pretty much the only thing I drank in volume). *No* fun, entertainment, parties, or socializing involved. **I was drinking *only* to try to make myself sick.** I included introducing my allergic-reaction inducing food (onions) into the mix, eating them right before I started drinking.

• Five days/nights NOT drinking. I didn't do anything special during these days besides not drink. And yes I essentially went through detox. I then repeated the process (including the associated detoxes[43]), with shorter time intervals:

— Four days/nights drinking

— Four days/nights NOT drinking

— Three days/nights drinking

— Three days/nights NOT drinking

— Two days/nights drinking.

By this point, I was sick of drinking and had no desire to do more. Also, I did not experience much in the way detox symptoms after the last round of drinking besides a few shakes that first subsequent day of not drinking. I kept on thinking my desire to drink would come back, but it didn't. I finally decided to do one final drinking session as a final "test," about 2 weeks after my previous drink, using a different type of alcohol (Margaritas). I felt nauseous after one drink, and two was enough to make me vomit.

I make absolutely no guarantee or warranty that this will work for anyone else. I do not recommend trying it, particularly if you can find some other way of defending against the Smell and Taste triggers.[44]

• •

As I "progressed" in the above approach my reactions to alcohol changed. While the "rush" was still ok (only lasting a few minutes), the "buzz" period got progressively shorter before I reached the "numb" state, which is when I started to experience queasiness and finally vomiting. Note that I *wanted* to vomit—and did *nothing* to prevent it, and even *encouraged* it when I was borderline. I was even able to "progress" to having a facial then full body rash break-out towards the end—I looked like I had the chicken pox a couple of times. I also passed out ("checked-out") drinking less and less the volume that I had always consumed before. After my final "test" drinks, which I forced, *I have had no desire to smell or taste alcohol since, and when I do, it does not bother me, other than occasional light nausea* (which is a good thing).

This process also increased my aversion to the sight of alcohol as well, using a variation of the visual aversion process described earlier. Last, but not least, I came to *dislike* the *effect* of alcohol. Instead of the "pleasure" of a rush/buzz/numb/checkout, drinking was now associated with being woozy, light-headed (not in a good way), nauseous, puking my guts out, gross rashes, and overall feeling of "yuk."[45]

Over time, the physical nausea when I came near alcohol went away, but the *indifference* remained—*I can ignore the presence or smell of alcohol* in any circumstance, often with a degree of disgust when I smell it up close. While I have not actually *tasted* alcohol since I did this process, the smell of it no longer has my mouth watering like it used to, which is more than enough to make me totally uninterested in it.[46] I have continued to "test" myself in many ways (though *not* with any actually drinking) in many forums, such as packed bars during the NCAA tournament, dozens of drunken students in college graduation parties (including even buying booze for someone else, and smelling the drinks), and walking down the liquor aisles when I go grocery shopping, and I am not tempted by it *at all*.

I have no idea if my specific approach is replicable or not, other than various "formal" medical-clinic aversion therapy testimonials, which frankly are kind of a mixed bag.[47] But that doesn't mean you can't find your *own* way to accomplish the same thing:

> *What I have to do for myself if a fleeting drinking thought comes to mind is to make it a point to "think the drink through" to its logical conclusion. These days it is HIGHLY unlikely that stopping off at a bar and drinking would net me any young, compliant, ego-stroking young women, but it likely WOULD net me yet another opportunity to try on some ill-fitting orange clothing. . . . The thought of wearing ill-fitting orange clothing and the attendant humiliation and loss of personal liberty goes a LONG way toward quelling the "euphoric recall." For others who do not have the advantage of having experienced a stay in the local drunk tank, their own personal version of hell will, no doubt, do nicely*
>
> Frank, eborg2.com

You don't have to go through what I did, nor go to prison to make yourself sick of alcohol. At the end of the day, it really is all about reminding yourself of your own personal version of hell and *continually associating* it with alcohol. Make its Smell, its Taste, its nearness (Proximity), its effect (rush/buzz/numb/checkout/Fun/Escape) equal to pain, misery, sickness, even death. With practice, you may be very pleased with the results and will have added another major defense in Conquering Your Alcoholism!

LEVEL 12

The Last Detox

Hopefully, you have successfully detoxed by the time you reach Phase 3, using the knowledge gained in Level 5, or have become heartily sick of alcohol using the aversion therapy-type approach described in Level 11. But odds are there is a significant percentage of you for which this is not the case. Perhaps you are scared to make an attempt (perfectly understandable), or perhaps you did try your best, and it just did not take hold for you. That is what this Level is about: to give you additional ideas to make this Detox the LAST one you ever do.

In particular, this Level is relevant for you if:

• You skipped Level 11—Make Yourself Sick of Alcohol, and you are still drinking; or

• You did parts of Level 11, but did not include actions to physically make you averse to the smell, taste, sight, and the effect of alcohol; or

• You did do Level 11 completely, but it did not work for you sufficiently such that you are still drinking.[1]

Regardless of the above, this Level is *only* for people who have tried to detox in some form in the past, e.g., during Level 5 or during some other program.[2] Assuming this is the case (and if not then go back to Level 5 in Phase 2), you've got some idea of what is coming at you. Maybe you are dreading it like the plague, or perhaps you are looking at it with trepidation or resignation, but also a large amount of skepticism that nothing is going to change. Regardless, with *this* detox, things are, hopefully, going to be different.

THE TRICK: DO IT WHILE YOU'RE SICK

The essence of this Level is to *do the detox process while you are sick with something else*. **This is completely optional and at your own risk.** The core idea is to combine the misery of detox with the pain and unpleasantness of your other aliment and blame *both* on alcohol. You are attempting to obliterate any association between alcohol and pleasure, and *replace it* with an association of misery, pain, and even agony.

In my personal experience, the sicker you do this the "better"—even being sick enough with your illness to be in the hospital. No, I'm not nuts. This was my situation, and it helped greatly believe it or not. I was in the hospital for what turned out to be a hole in my colon, with the symptoms being intense abdominal pain. This situation had several "advantages," including:

• Considering the pain I was in before deciding I needed to get to the hospital, I had already not been drinking for a couple of days—a running start as it were.

• With the pain I continued to suffer in the hospital, the last thing on my mind was getting a drink (except for water, which they wouldn't give me).

• There was absolutely no liquor around anyway.

• It was a very tightly controlled environment, even to the point of dictating my every movement. Kind of comforting in a strange way, knowing there was nothing I could do about my situation including obtaining alcohol.

• Having made absolutely sure they knew I was a raving alcoholic (my words to them), the doctors and staff were *very* conscious of how they prescribed medicines and were very sensitive to monitoring my vital signs for any potential detox complications.

• As such, I was killing two birds with one stone in terms of hospital admission: intestinal problems and alcohol detoxification. Helped with time and cost, no question.[3]

As mentioned numerous times before, lack of control over alcohol is one of the four cornerstones of alcoholism. Being (bed-ridden) ill in a strange way provides you a degree of safe control over alcohol—at least until you are well (and particularly if you are in the hospital). My theory is that one of the big reasons inpatient rehabs (including ones with detox-ification services) are so attractive and successful (*in the short term*), is that the alcoholic has no control over their drinking situation—*other peo-ple do.* In my hospital situation, it was strangely beneficial knowing that there was *nothing* I could do to obtain and drink alcohol, which after the initial panic and worst of the withdrawal turned out to be very comfort-ing. It also would explain why so many people relapse after they leave rehab. There is no longer the structure and (involuntary) discipline to prevent them from drinking other than what they can generate on their own. Unfortunately, this is often not enough particularly as more time goes by and more alcohol "attacks" occur.

It was during this time of hospitalization (overall about two weeks from major symptoms to discharge) that I started to develop this pro-gram in general and this Level in particular. At every turn, when my pain medication started to wear off (particularly when there were hours until my next dose), *I would blame the agony on alcohol—over and over and over again.* And *it worked*—I came to view alcohol more often as a cause of misery than I did a means of pleasure. Ever since, I try at every opportunity to mentally associate *any* pain I have with alcohol.

You don't have to be in the hospital for this to work, but in my opinion you do have to be in major pain or at a minimum extremely uncomfort-able, "ideally" for a significant period of time. In essence, this is another version of aversion therapy discussed in Level 11. That's the key for this (hopefully) last detox: *associate the pain and misery of it, and all pain and misery you experience—with alcohol. Break* any lingering associa-tion alcohol has with fun or pleasure, and *replace it* with discomfort and even agony! This "re" association might come easy, or take much "prac-tice," but it if you can do it you will find it a *very* effective deterrent to many kinds of alcohol attacks.

If you decide to try the any of the above, *consult your doctor first.* While it is hard for me as a non-medical person to conceive of any illness where your doctor *wants* you to continue drinking, it is certainly possi-ble. Perhaps for example he or she might worry that possible side effects of *not* drinking, such as DTs[4], may introduce too much risk into the treat-ment prescribed for you for your illness.

OTHER TRICKS TO HELP DETOX

Of course, it may be quite a while before you get sick, or you may not get sick at all (the ultimate good news-bad news scenario). In that case, the best advice is to go back to Level 5 and try again. Perhaps use a medically supervised approach (if you tried to do it yourself before), or use a different facility if the first one did not work or you. Also reread Level 11, to see if it may provide additional insights, and perhaps (at your own risk) try that approach again if you haven't already.

It may be you are the sort of person that just needs some of the most unorthodox approaches to problem solving for them to work on you. If so, my research found a variety of other tricks and tips that *may* help with your Detox process. I have not personally tried any of these and so cannot vouch for their effectiveness or even safety, but one may give you additional ideas to make this your LAST Detox:

• Do it while there is something you LOVE on television, for long periods of time, such as the NCAA Tournament or the Olympics. Watching it can help you occupy your mind and channel your distress for long periods of time over multiple days. "Binging" on certain TV programs (such as Breaking Bad) may also serve this purpose and is very easy to do in the age of Netflix.

> *The last drink I had was while watching the Olympic Hockey finals at 5am last Sunday. I have been exercising every day since and feeling pretty good.*
> Guest Keith, alcoholism.about.com

• If you are going to detox yourself, do it (*with someone else with you*) in a remote location and/or where alcohol is not sold within at least 100 miles (e.g. at least a couple hour's drive one-way). This distance can provide a great way to resist urges if it is a gigantic pain in the ass to get it (and very likely for someone to notice you being gone). Make sure medical treatment is *not* far away if you use this approach.

• Drink lots of fluids. Try to "taper off" to beer.[5]

> *I've detoxed over 7 times, 3 of them were fully successful, with two of those successfully being medically treated and supervised.[6] If you are detoxing, stay calm and make sure you have someone with you, at least in the house so you can be checked on frequently. Taper off the alcohol if you can to the*

point where you are only drinking beer, and if you are already only drinking beer see if you can get yourself down to a place where you're not having the shakes. Keeping hydrated is most important. Drinking Gatorade or putting very light salt in your water will help your cells retain it. If you have the ability, try to exercise. Get out into the sun or outside and try to stretch and move around. Eating is most difficult, though if possible will help you rebound and means you are on the road to recovery Stay positive and if you really can't handle it then it's no worry. If all else fails get yourself to the emergency room.[7]

Guest jd, alcoholism.about.com

- Try to get into a rhythm on how you start and end your day.

I have been starting each day with hot water and lemon juice and taking melatonin at night to help me sleep. I feel lucky that my withdrawal symptoms haven't included shakes, or vomiting.[8]

Guest Wine lover, alcoholism.about.com

- Give up alcohol for Lent.

I am a 65-year-old woman who has drank most of her life and has quit more times than I can tell. Lent is coming up and I will try one more time to quit for good.

Guest J, alcoholism.about.com

- Ask your doctor about drugs, including various vitamin supplements. Note: Level 11 discusses medications specifically targeting alcoholism, including alcohol withdrawal. This bullet refers mainly to other prescribed medicines (such as anxiety medicines, below, blood pressure drugs, and so on) that can help address specific withdrawal side effects. Consult your doctor, obviously.

The morning of the 2nd and 3rd day after I stop is the hardest. Severe tingling, anxiety, nervousness. Like a panic attack. I take a mild sedative (low dose Xanax)[9] by 9am, and that will eliminate the withdrawal symptoms. After 4 or 5 days of no drinking, my system seems to function OK and I don't need the benzodiazepine meds. But let me tell you, those attacks are very real and very scary!

Drinker06798, alcoholism.about.com

- Exercise intensely; including hiring a personal trainer (it will likely be less than the cost of your booze).

- Juicing!

> *Juicing and drinking lots of water daily helps cleanse the body and liver of toxins. Research juicing for detox of the liver [such as] juicing 2 beets, 1 apple, 3 celery, small piece of ginger, one dandelion root . . . .juicing helps with getting to sleep. Juice daily at least twice a day.*[10]
>
> Guest Jazmine, alcoholism.about.com

Again, please consult your doctor before trying any of the above (except for maybe the Lent and Juicing ideas). It is unlikely that any single one of these might be the magic bullet that helps you succeed when everything else failed, but you never know!

If you are *still* drinking after all the previous Levels (including this one), but you see *strong* signs of improvement and potential for stopping drinking entirely, then you have a great chance of succeeding completely. If you have *not* seen much improvement by now, I strongly encourage you to go back to Level 1 and literally start over. This time with *much* more attention to detail, in particular in Level 2 where you identify your triggers.

The next and final Level in The Conquer Program: Level 13—Develop Your Defense Progressions—is where we put together all of what you've learned so far in an even more powerful way to complete your fortifications against the attacks of alcohol.

LEVEL 13

Develop Your Defense Progressions

We are almost at the end! By now you should feel that you have a whole bunch of ways to defend against alcohol attacks, and have already successfully used at least some of them in a variety of circumstances. You have either completely stopped drinking (ideally), or greatly reduced the number and severity of any drinking relapses (great but not best), or at a minimum have become more aware of *why* you drink and started cutting down—at least a few less drinks a day (far from ideal but at least some progress). These last two— moderation and relapses—were discussed at length in Level 11 (with more on relapses later in this Level).

You Think You Have Made Progress, BUT . . .

. . . you still feel there is a lot more you can do. Maybe you are still drinking, and/or just not comfortable with what you have learned about yourself so far.

If so, go back and re-read this book, or at least Level 2—Know Your Triggers. That Level is the heart and soul of the Conquer Program. I recommend *all* readers do this at least once. I fully recognize that there is a lot of "stuff" in this program, and re-reading it at least once is probably going to be helpful in many ways. Level 2 in particular has a ton of info, and many of the tips included for each trigger have nuances that you may or may not have picked up upon first read.

Besides picking up on elements you missed, or identifying helpful nuances to a particular tip, you will also see humor and interesting facts that will make it even more entertaining (and thus more apt to stick in your mind) the second time around!

While you may feel you have a better handle on what makes you drink and how you can defend against alcohol attacks, you may also feel you lack ways to get *all* your tips and defenses *to work together.* Tips and defenses should be optimally structured, grouped together, integrated and coordinated, to get them to work their best in the worst of circumstances and *all* circumstances in general. That is the goal of Level 13, and is where much of the power of the Conquer Program can be brought to bear to defend against the most stubborn, most varied, most intense alcohol attacks.

From a different perspective, the Level defenses, tips, and related ideas and discussions can be viewed as kinds of pieces of a jigsaw puzzle: well-defined, uniquely shaped, and clearly intended to connect to other pieces where it may or may not be obvious how; but most importantly intended to form a complete picture once put together. The complete picture is what this Level is all about—fitting all the piece parts together, to form one set of integrated and optimized defenses. For many readers, this is where the full power of the Conquer Program comes to bear.

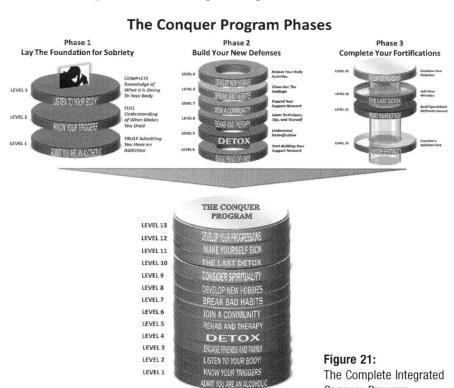

Figure 21:
The Complete Integrated Conquer Program

Let's re-review the underlying philosophy of The Conquer Program. At its core is that **no one single** method, idea, tool, tip, level, or approach will work *all* the time, for *all* triggers, for *all* situations and circumstances. You **must** have multiple defenses. But just having multiple defenses will not be enough sometimes. In these circumstances/situations, how you *structure* the defenses may be even more critical than the strength of any *individual* defense.

What do I mean by structure? Mostly it has to do with the *order* that you think and/or do the defenses. When being attacked by alcohol— e.g. in the form of a trigger—what do you do to resist? Do you call so and so first, work on Hobby #3, go to a meeting, or jump online to website B? Which one will be the most effective way of not drinking *right now* for the situation or feelings I'm dealing with *right now* and how I think I am most vulnerable *right now?*

And what happens if that first method doesn't work? *"I called so and so and still feel like drinking." "I did Hobby #3 for an hour and still feel like drinking." "What do I do next? And what after I do those and I still feel like drinking?"* Addressing these challenges is where the concept of defense progressions comes in—to methodically yet intuitively structure all your defenses in the order right for you.

However, before we get to how you develop your progressions, it is critical to understand how "sobriety" is not just a general, same-thing-all-the-time-to-all-people state of mind and body. It *will* change significantly over the first year, as will likely your triggers, your defenses, and your defense progressions. In some ways, it will be reversing the "evolution" of your stages of alcoholism, but much faster.

THE STAGES OF ALCOHOLISM AND SOBRIETY

Stages of alcoholism: why haven't these been discussed before?

That you could have "evolved" from a normal, drinking-occasionally-just-for-fun person to an alcoholic was discussed extensively in Level 1, and was an important part of getting you to admit you are an alcoholic. But since then our focus has been getting you sober *now*, we have very understandably been trying to get you to understand your current triggers so you can build the best defenses for them *now*.

As we start building this last—and in many ways best—Level of defense, it becomes more important to understand how your triggers evolved over time. In addition to defending against your triggers as they currently exist, we are going to try to reduce their intensity and even *eliminate* some of them entirely. Like rolling back time to before you started using alcohol as a crutch for life.

To be able to do so requires understanding in more detail your trigger history. I creatively break them down into three stages: Early, Middle and Late Alcoholism.

Early, Middle, and Late Alcoholism

This is not as long a section as you might expect as the reality is very simple. For many alcoholics, we likely had only a handful of triggers when we first passed the point of being an alcoholic. Since then our triggers "evolved" the longer we drank. More were added, many became more intense, and their relative priorities changed as we came to use booze as a crutch for more and more of our problems. Ultimately, they collectively blew up our lives.

There is an interesting mix of opinions and research on the "stages" of alcoholism. Many define them in terms of severity of health problems, such as the stages of liver disease. Others have varying numbers of stages, including four (*www.alcoholic.org/research/the-stages-of-alcoholism/*), five (*http://alcoholselfhelpnews.wordpress.com/2008/05/24/5-stages-of-alcoholism/*), and even seven (*www.carontexas.org/treatment-programs/assessment/seven-stages-of-alcohol-addiction*) and eight (*www.my-alcoholic-addict .com/stages-of-alcoholism.html*) stages that have a mix of mental and physical descriptions to them. While I don't disagree with any of the sources I've included above, I don't think we need to overthink it. Just three stages will do the trick.

Early Alcoholism

Early Alcoholism is the period where we started drinking for reasons other than "Fun," where our frequency and volume of drinking became such that we became physically dependent on alcohol. Instead of dealing with the normal stresses of life head-on, we started to use alcohol to help us "relax" and "forget" about them. Early alcoholism can last anywhere from several months to several years, with the longer timeframes being particularly applicable to functional alcoholics.

Early Alcoholism was likely the period when you had only a few triggers. After all, you were just getting into the alcoholic game. However, *it is likely that at least some of those early triggers have carried over into your present life*. For me, the desire to Escape has been there since my earliest drinking days and still exists today. The Times of Day trigger has been around almost as long. While these types of long-lived triggers may not always be the top priority in terms of intensity, it is important to recognize their "longevity" so you can put extra effort into how you develop their defense progressions. These long-lived triggers may well be the ones to be the biggest danger later in sobriety.

Early Alcoholism is when you first became physically dependent, yet you were still able to function as a normal human being in terms of a job, money and relationships. You likely did not drink *every* day, even with the physical dependency. The volume of alcohol was also not as great—at least compared to later years. Whether you were able to be a "functioning" alcoholic (see Level 1) determined whether you stayed in this stage for many years (as I did) or passed to the next stage relatively quickly.

Middle Alcoholism

Middle Alcoholism is where we gave up any pretense of drinking for Fun, and started finding more reasons (e.g. triggers) to drink. Our volumes increased, as did the number of days of the week that we drank and the amount of time we spent drinking each day. This stage is often highlighted by drinking *every* day, and by a visible deterioration in our relationships—particularly our intimate ones. Problems also started appearing in our job performance, and we may have started feeling (at least a little) guilty about our drinking. We likely made some attempts to stop or at least moderate our drinking, with no success of course. We might have even tried some AA meetings and even a rehab stint. In hindsight this is where things really started going bad, though we did not realize it at the time. Cracks started to appear in the cool façade of functioning alcoholics, and friends and relatives started to express worry about you drinking too much.

Middle Alcoholism does not last as long as Early Alcoholism as our downward spiral starts to accelerate towards the really bad stuff.

Late Alcoholism

Late alcoholism is where your alcoholism has become obvious to everyone around you—including *yourself*—and you (finally) seriously started to think about quitting. Odds are that many of you reading this book are in this stage of alcoholism. You are starting to be downright scared of your drinking, but the Fear of Quitting is even stronger (see Level 2 for much more on this trigger). In this last stage, you may also start experiencing many health problems (see Level 3), and in general you have the most— and most intense—triggers that you have ever had in your life. Relationships have deteriorated beyond repair or nearly so. Your life is clearly going down the road to ruin.

Figure 22 below illustrates my personal trigger evolution, reflecting many of the characteristics described above for each stage. There is a form in Appendix B to chart your personal trigger evolution history.

Example of Alcoholism Triggers Evolution

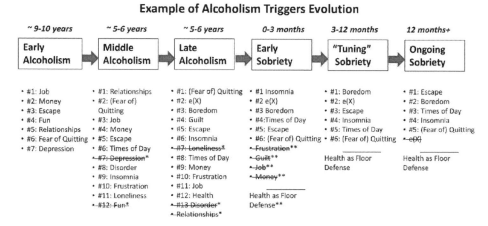

Figure 22: The Author's Stages of Alcoholism and Sobriety*[1]

The *good news* is that we can reverse this process in sobriety—at least in part—and do it much faster than it took to get to "grow" your triggers to begin with! As it was helpful to understand your trigger evolution, so it is helpful to understand how your sobriety will evolve going forward.

One thing I did not appreciate at all until I finally was sober for a long time was how *different* I felt the longer I was sober, particularly in *and within* that first year. Others have told me the same thing. I think it is one (more) thing that traditional treatment programs do not warn us sufficiently about, yet can be critically important to understand the risks we might encounter in that first year. While it is important to understand how our alcoholism changed over the years in terms of understanding our triggers and how we got into this mess, it is even more important to understand how our sobriety can evolve. This knowledge will help us endure some of the tougher times during the first year of sobriety, as well as even prevent a relapse on a longer-term basis.

To do this, we separate sobriety into three (3) distinct stages within the Conquer Program, defined by time and distinct changes/improvements in mindset:

• *Early Sobriety*—Zero to 3 months. I call this the "personal fog" stage, as your head often feels stuffed with cotton, or lost in a fog bank.

• *"Tuning" Sobriety*—3 months to 12 months. This is about getting your defenses just right.

• *Ongoing Sobriety*—12 months+. This is about managing ongoing sobriety, particularly periodically refreshing your trigger list and defenses.

Early Sobriety

The first three months or so will be the most difficult for many people, primarily in getting used to the physical changes that come with new sobriety. Fogged heads, disjointed thought processes, occasional shakes and upset stomachs, problems sleeping, frequently feeling like shit, and in general getting back on your feet mentally and physically will be preoccupying you. There is no way around it—for many of you this will *not* be in any way enjoyable.

Assuming you were still drinking or had very recently stopped while you have been reading this book, you are early in Early Sobriety. Hence, your understanding of your triggers is still very new, and there may well be a chance you haven't correctly identified all your triggers at the moment. This is why I strongly recommend rereading Level 2 *at least* once.

While I could not find any reliable statistics on the frequency of relapses within certain time frames of getting sober, the anecdotal evidence and common sense suggests that these first few months are the most likely for relapse. Other programs operate on this assumption. For example, AA recommends attend *"90 meetings in 90 days"* in your first 3 months of sobriety and distributes actual coins for 30, 60, and 90-day sobriety "anniversaries."

Recognizing this, first go back and reread Level 2 if you haven't already. As you go through the rest of *this* Level, in particular the (soon to be discussed) 9 steps for developing your defense progressions (called the Conquer Progressions Development Process), pay especially close attention to Step #8—Develop a Generic Trigger Defense. A "generic trigger defense" is just what it sounds like: a way of defending against most types of alcohol attacks, if only for a little while. This step is intended to protect you against any triggers not successfully identified previously—or at least buying you enough time to let the particular circumstances causing you to want to drink to dissipate.

Most triggers will have some circumstances where they don't last very long. You get Angry over something relatively trivial. You have an argument and start Yelling at your partner. You are forced to attend a party and endure Social Situations, Proximity and Smell—all these will go away with a bit of time. The trick is not giving into the temptation to drink while they are at their worst. This is the core purpose of the generic defense, until you can develop stronger, more specific defenses.

"Tuning" Sobriety

With 3 months or so of sobriety under your belt, you can relax a bit (just a little) and start focus on "tuning" your defenses. It is almost a certainty that the defenses you developed the first time for a given trigger can be improved. Much of this tuning is related to better understanding the Related Triggers' defenses (see Step #3), as well as ordering, testing, and adjusting your defenses (Steps #6 and #7). *Important note: this does not mean that you will only do certain steps in one phase and not another. You will do all steps in each phase, multiple times. The steps highlighted are ones that are of particular importance during that phase of sobriety.*

What is "testing?" Testing is *deliberately* putting yourself in trigger situations where you can see how well your defenses hold up. If Proximity is a big trigger, go into the liquor section of your grocery store. If Smell or Social Situations are triggers, then go to a bar. And so on.

Of course, doing so without any backup could be high risk. In those situations, you may want a trusted friend to accompany you in case your defenses turn out to be inadequate. He or she can then also sit down with you to help you figure out how to adjust your defenses.

The Tuning stage can last as short as a few weeks, but much more likely several months, particularly as you test, adjust, test and adjust your defenses again and again. Gradually, dealing with a trigger situation without temptation will become second nature to you. When you have reached this point, you will have successfully finished the Tuning stage.

But that does not mean you are done. While you no longer have to worry frequently about succumbing to a trigger and relapsing, you should *not* let your guard down, nor assume your tuned defenses will continue to work "as-is" forever. No matter how long you are sober, you will never be able to let your guard down entirely in your ongoing, everyday life.

Ongoing Sobriety

Once you have your entire trigger defenses finely tuned—likely somewhere around the one-year mark—you can consider yourself a pretty seasoned and successful veteran of the Conquer Program. Does that mean your victory is complete? Unfortunately, the answer is no; you will *never* completely rid yourself of this disease, as there is no cure. The best way to keep a conquered enemy from rising up to hurt you is to keep your defenses strong and be on the lookout for new methods of attack.

One way of self-inflicting a relapse in ongoing sobriety is succumbing to the Overconfidence trigger.[2] You haven't drunk in a year; you are feeling great, and then WHAM you are drinking. How could that happen? Sometimes because you became a bit too cocky, such as going into a high-risk trigger situation unprepared for several triggers to hit you at once. Maybe it is attending a holiday office party (which can include associated related triggers of Smell, Taste, Proximity, Social Situations, Job issues, and Peer Pressure to name a few). You may even go so far as to think you could actually take one drink with no harm. *Just one drink is not going to happen—alcoholics **cannot** stop at just one.*

More likely the biggest danger time for you in ongoing sobriety is if and when your life's circumstances change. You get a new job, lose a job, get married, have a child, get divorced, move to a new city, a close relative passes away—these kinds of major Changes in life can have a huge impact on your triggers and/or your defenses. Changes don't have to be one or two big ones; they can be several smaller ones that cumulatively add up to major Change over a short period. For those reasons it is recommended you periodically refresh all your defense progressions every 3 months or so (every calendar quarter, the beginning of a new season, etc.) using the 9 Steps discussed shortly.

You should plan on adopting this approach for the rest of your life. It is a small price to pay to spend several hours a few times a year making sure your defenses are optimized. The motivation could not be bigger—it's your life and happiness at stake here.

What Do You Do If You Relapse?

First, don't panic! Odds are it is no big deal, relatively speaking. Second, stop drinking (again) if you haven't already. Go back to Level 5 or Level 12 and detox again. If you had some significant sobriety (e.g. at least a few weeks) under your belt before you relapsed, *and* your relapse is a day or two and not weeks, then the detoxing process should not be too bad.

The most important thing, of course, is to figure out *why* you relapsed, and how you can prevent doing so by adjusting your defenses and/or progressions. Figuring this out will likely be harder to do than the detox since your first pass through this program did not result in preventing the relapse to begin with.

So, you need to redouble your efforts by rereading Level 2 and figuring out exactly where you "went wrong." I use that term because other people might do so, but in reality it wasn't "wrong," it was just "inadequately identified and defended" (not as catchy though).

Relapses and The Stage of Sobriety

You might also factor in what stage of sobriety you were in when the relapse occurred to figure out where things when "wrong." If you were still in the Early Sobriety stage, it is possible you did not like how you felt physically and/or mentally. Such as feeling lethargic or your head was stuffed with cotton and you could not think. Early Sobriety is probably the trickiest stage to relapse in as there is no real good way of dealing with it other than being confident that it *will* get better.

If you were in the Tuning Sobriety stage, then odds are that is your issue—your defenses were not "tuned" correctly. Here is where you will need to revisit the tuning steps of Steps 6 and 7 of the Conquer Progression Development Process and adjust, test, and readjust your defenses and their order and structure.

If you relapse in Ongoing Sobriety, e.g. after a year, this ironically might be a bigger cause for concern than a relapse during the earlier stages. Presumably if you had reached one year and more of sobriety and then you relapsed, something significant (and probably bad) happened in your life. Besides going back to Level 2 to revisit all the triggers, you might reread this entire book to remind yourself why you were a drunk and why you do not want to go back to being one. Perhaps you got complacent (e.g. the Overconfidence trigger in Level 2), or a major event in your life shook up key foundations of your life (e.g. Change). It is critical to get to the *detailed* reason(s) that you relapsed, in any stage but in particular in Ongoing Sobriety. Revisit the whole program and individual defense Levels, of course, but you may also want to consider seeing a therapist (e.g. Level 6) to discuss this sudden change of events in your life. From all this, you can then readjust your defenses and your progressions.

The overall key point is that a relapse is not some indicator of failure, hopelessness, impending doom, nor does it mean you have to go back to the beginning like none of your efforts mattered. The Conquer Program is all about building up your defenses against *all* the attacks of alcohol. If one attack snuck through your newly rebuilt and generally solid defenses, you have to plug the hole, *not* raze the fortress to the ground and start over.

Developing progressions will help plug these holes and prevent others from happening.

THE CONCEPT OF PROGRESSIONS

While perhaps seeming like a bit of a weird word and an even weirder concept, in reality *everyone* has been doing progressions in some form all their lives. It is what we do in everyday life in "reading" and responding to complex situations, such as driving a car or even walking and talking and eating (particularly at the same time). We are taking in the situation(s) around us, and acting/reacting accordingly with the options (e.g., often defensive in nature) available, which could constantly be changing. This is similar to reacting to treacherous driving conditions or complex social/job situations where you have to "keep on your toes" to deal with the ever-changing and often unforgiving environment.

For example, in bad road conditions we may constantly veer or change lanes, accelerate or brake, look in the mirrors, use turn signals, and look in all directions so fast that it seems we are doing it all at the same time. We may use similar techniques but in a completely different order depending on the conditions. We "read" the situation and immediately implement a set of actions to keep us safe from that situation while changing the radio station the whole time!

Here "reading" means seeing, hearing, touching, reading, and maybe even smelling and tasting[3] the situation. All of our senses are constantly at work in "reading" our situation, and sending information to our brain to process and act/react accordingly.

For many of these everyday activities we don't *consciously* think about when we are doing them—our *subconscious* does. It took education, training, and experience to get these kinds of activities to become embedded in our subconscious, so we do them automatically or nearly so. This kind of automatic reading and responding to threatening circumstances—such as what we do when we drive in dangerous traffic conditions or walk on uneven and slippery terrain—is what we seek to also achieve in dealing with the threats of alcohol.

The general concept of progressions can be learned and applied at any age by anyone. One example where "reading the progression" is used is in (American) football with the quarterback "reading" the opposing players and consciously AND subconsciously analyzing and adapting to the circumstances of the play (more info at *"Reading The Progression"*[4]). The Conquer Program draws on this concept (without your being a football fan or player) so you can retrain/rewire your mind and body in how it deals with the threat of alcohol.

Of course, the football analogy does not translate directly to defending against alcohol trigger attacks. For one thing, there are more than 11 possible triggers (attackers on the opposing side) that can come at you. There is also lots more on the bench just waiting to drive your head into the turf! More weapons too—an attack can be not just physical but mental, emotional, and environmental. They can vary by time of day, day of the week, month, season, even year. Or even hourly! Your defenses can vary too—some of the time you might be in full pads and protection coverage and other times running around in your shorts.

So how do you develop *your* defense progressions with the seemingly endless possible ways to be attacked by alcohol?

DEVELOP *YOUR* DEFENSE PROGRESSIONS

While the concept of progressions might seem like it might include dozens or even hundreds of possibilities to deal with all the different ways and times that triggers can manifest themselves, *simplicity* is the key. If you can't remember—and eventually *instinctively and intuitively* know—what to do in a certain type of trigger situation, it's not going to do you any good much of the time.

To help with this, I've developed a 9-Step process; creatively called the Conquer Progression Development Process (CPDP). The *very* good news is that you have probably done most if not all of these steps—and if you haven't, you have learned enough that doing them should be relatively straightforward.

The result is a trigger-based process that provides you with a checklist of things to do and/or think about, in the best order, so that collectively they defend you against *all* types of alcohol attacks. The CPDP individual steps are listed below and shown in Figure 23 in easy process flow form:

- Step 1—Inventory and Prioritize Your Triggers
- Step 2—Identify Your "Floor" Defenses
- Step 3—Identify Related Triggers
- Step 4—Identify Key "Tips"
- Step 5—Identify Key Levels of Defense; Get *Specific!*
- Step 6—Order Your Tips and Defenses
- Step 7—Test and Adjust your Tips and Defenses
- Step 8—Develop a "Generic" Trigger Defense Progression
- Step 9—Periodically Refresh *Everything*

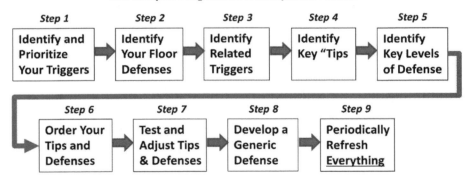

Figure 23: The Conquer Progression Development Process

Step #1—Inventory and Prioritize Your Triggers

In this step, you list of all your *major, direct* triggers. As described in Level 2, "major" triggers are those that *really* make you want to drink, *more often than not*. "Direct" means that they usually occur independent of any others, and *frequently* set off a chain reaction of other related triggers.

How "frequently" is defined is up to the individual. A rough rule of thumb is that it (a Related Trigger) happens at least 1 in every 5 times that the major trigger occurs, such as Boredom sometimes causes you to feel Loneliness. If a Related Trigger happens very frequently (half of the time or more) that may mean it should be a major trigger by itself, so perhaps you should think about perhaps making it one.

Less frequently than 1 in 5 *may* indicate that it is not that "related" and/or worth the time/aggravation/risk to defend against if it doesn't happen often—that's what "floor" defenses and generic progressions (discussed shortly) are for among other reasons. At the end of the day you have to use your best judgment, but above all trust what your gut says to you. To me my "gut instinct" is just my brain having worked something out that I can't describe just yet.

The first time you pass through the triggers discussion you may very well have a lot of triggers, say ten, fifteen, or even more. This number should not be surprising at all. Over the course of the stages of sobriety and ever-increasing alcohol consumption, we are likely to associate alcohol with "dealing with" more and more triggers as time goes on.

List *all* of your triggers—even if you are not sure of some. Then go through each trigger discussion again to see if it *really* is applicable to you according to the terms "significantly" and "directly" as defined above.

Try to get this list down to between 5 and 12 triggers if you can. There is nothing magical about this range. However, if you have fewer than five, you may not be breaking down the triggers in sufficient detail. A great example: "Stress" may be two or three more specific ones such as your Job, Kids, and Money problems. More than twelve may be difficult to "manage" on an ongoing, long-term basis. That said, more triggers are much better than fewer ones. It only takes *one* undefended trigger to screw things up, particularly early in sobriety.

Prioritizing these triggers may be very helpful as you think through things and possibly eliminate (or even add) certain triggers. What is prioritizing? It is just what it sounds like: which triggers hit you the worst? More specifically, it is those triggers whose *severity* and *frequency* make them the worst one's for you in terms of desire to drink. Is Boredom #1 in terms of the severity and frequency, or is it #4? Does Depression top all other contenders, or is it more the desire to Escape from the pressures of everyday life? Is Stress really at the top, and if so what *kind* of Stress?[5] Think about these priorities, but don't *over*-think it. Odds are your first thought of your #1 trigger will truly be your top priority. Prioritizing other triggers might require a bit more thought. If you are uncertain about whether a trigger is a major one or not, the easiest thing to do is place it at the bottom and come back to it later.

Step #2—Identify Your "Floor" Defenses

"Floor" Defenses are those that are effective for most if not all of your triggers. These defenses will vary *greatly* by person. I have two floor defenses: my health (e.g., Level 3—Listen to Your Body!) and my children (e.g., Level 4—Engage Friends and Family).

I know pretty definitively that if I start drinking again, I'm going to bite the dust pretty quickly. Maybe after a few drinks (maybe even one drink) or after I do it for a few weeks or even months. I always keep this in the back of mind when I start to get tempted. I even have used it a few times when I've been very tempted to drink, and none of the tips or other defenses for that particular trigger in that particular circumstance and time seemed to work. Hence, the idea of fear of death as being a "floor." You can also view a floor defense as a kind of defense of last resort.

● ●

Fear of Death as a Floor Defense

While many nonalcoholics may view fear of death as a floor for practically anybody, this is *not* necessarily the case for alcoholics. As discussed in the suicide section in Level 3, many alcoholics are consciously or unconsciously trying to drink themselves to death. Even those without an active death wish—but with serious health problems that alcohol will dangerously impact—while we may know *logically* that we shouldn't drink, *emotionally* we might not give a shit at times. Thus, it is good to have at least a second floor defense.

● ●

Another floor for me is my children. They put up with a tremendous amount of crap growing up during my alcoholism and turned out great despite it. I know that they are proud that I was able to pull myself out of this deep shit hole (via this program), but I also know they would be extremely disappointed if I fell back into it. To me this is the very last thing I want to happen, so I use the thought of them being happy as a "floor" defense. Since it is even more important to me than my health, I have it as second floor defense supporting even the fear of/possibility of imminent death.

Each person is different, but you *have* to have at least one floor defense; two if possible for the reasons described above. No reason *not* to have more than that, though I personally only have two that seem to be common to many of my triggers, and together *all* of my triggers. Spirituality may be another floor trigger besides your health and family, but it could be something else entirely. There is no right answer, other than *whatever works best for you.*

Step #3—Identify Related Triggers

Once you've identified your floor defenses, it is time to get to work on what defenses work best for your individual triggers. Before we address "Tips"—practical things to do and/or think about instead of drinking—and the specifics of Key Levels of Defense, it is essential to understand the *Related* Triggers to the *direct* ones that you identified in Step #1.

Most trigger discussions in Level 2 include key Related Triggers, and at the end of every section is a summary list of possible Related Triggers (RT for short) for that major trigger. These RTs are ones that I consider a strong possibility for most alcoholics; there may well be others not listed that are applicable for you. Try to identify which RTs are relevant to you for that particular trigger. Some are more obvious than others. For example, Boredom often leads to Loneliness; Job problems cause Money concerns and physical Stress; Powerlessness and Social Situations can cause Anxiety; Relationships can cause Sexual concerns (and vice versa), and so on. Note it is very possible that one or two you feel are related are not on the list. Do not feel you are limited to what you can select from—indeed, try to figure out if there are ones *not* on the list; it may help you think through the trigger more comprehensively.

Once you have identified these Related Triggers, try to prioritize them in order of impact (how much they make you want to drink), and frequency (how often they occur).

Step #4—Identify Key "Tips"

For nearly all the triggers in Level 2 there are several "Tips" for dealing with the trigger without alcohol. These tips range from common-sense ideas that may need refreshing in your mind to highly unusual ones that seem to work for some people some of the time. There are no "right" or "wrong" tips—just ones that work or don't work for *you*. Consider them all; even try them all—you may never know for sure what will work for you or unless you try. Odds are you will discover that at least a handful of very unlikely tips will have a major positive impact.

However, even some of the best ideas may not work for practical reasons. For example, having a pet is considered a great way of dealing with certain triggers such as Loneliness. Assuming you don't have an allergy and love pets, it may still not work for you at this time or at all. In the case of pets, they can come with a cost, and not just a financial one. They can, for example, contribute to Disorder (e.g., messes, smells, etc.) that may be a major trigger for you, or are just not practical for your lifestyle (traveling a lot, etc.).

The key point is that while some tips may be common sense/no-brainers, there are others that need considerable thinking through all the advantages and disadvantages before you commit, particularly if once you commit, it will be very hard to undo.

For the most part, though, most of the tips are take-it-or-leave-it. Try them, and if they don't work, then no harm-no foul. And don't limit yourself to what is listed/described—odds are that for every one listed, there are several others that might work. Do your own research, bounce ideas off of friends, family, community members; it's not that they are scarce—they just might require some digging and experimenting! Online forums are a great place for finding new ideas specifically for alcohol-related problems.

As you'll see in Step #6, the order of defenses can be particularly important, with one key consideration being how much time, energy, and/or concentration they require. In general, the *more* of any of those requires, the better the tip idea.

Step #5—Identify Key Levels of Defense; Get *Specific!*

At the end of each trigger discussion is a list of Key Defense Levels. These are ones that (in my opinion) have high potential for helping you defend against the particular trigger attack. Some of them, such as Engage Friends and Family, are fairly straightforward, "just" requiring you to find the *right* friend or family member for that particular trigger who can understand where you are coming from and have at least some time and a sympathetic ear.

Why the distinction between "Tips" and "Key Level of Defenses"? Two reasons. First, many of the tips may not be applicable for your situation, general lifestyle, and/or personality. So you might not use many of them, or even any of them (I urge you to try to use at least one tip though).

In contrast, at least one Key Defense Level should be applicable for *all* of you in one form or another. As such, I list them separately and after Tips. You have to have *at least one* Defense Level in *any* defense progression; otherwise the progression will be very weak. You would go directly from a tip to your floor defenses, which frankly you only want to use as a last resort (or at least not all the time). Again, the essence of the concept of progressions is that no one method/tip/approach/defense will work all the time for all situations, AND that many of them will weaken an alcohol attack that will in turn increase the odds of the next one working.

That said, a Key Defense Level may well require a great deal of experimentation, time, and/or practice to get "right." Level 9—Develop New Hobbies is one of these. Unless you have a number of hobbies that you know will work for you because of past experience, you'll have to invest some effort and even money to figure out if they work, and *how* they work—as well as when, where, and why they work. Get to as much specificity and detail as you can, down to days, times, environments/situations, and of course the specifics of the trigger and related triggers.

A few Levels are "optional" in some way. Level 10—Consider Spirituality is optional because it is impossible to "make" anyone become spiritual—you have to do it yourself. It may not work at all, or you may be totally against even trying.

Level 11—Make Yourself Sick of Alcohol, is very tricky, and *very* optional in that it—depending on *how* you do it—can actually be physically risky. It is also not that applicable for many triggers, but can be *very* applicable for a few, particularly Escape (getting numb), Proximity, Smell, and Taste. To repeat—be very careful how you do this Level if you choose to do so.

A similar situation exists with Level 12—The LAST Detox, particularly the (optional!) idea of detoxing while you are ill with something else. Depending on the situation, illness, and medical support environment, this can be very risky. The "good" news is that I can't think of any medical situation where continuing to drink while you are ill could be considered beneficial in any way,[6] *but leave that decision to your doctor.*

Step #6—Order Your Tips and Defenses

Since there are possibly several tips and at least one defense that should be applicable to you for every trigger, one big challenge is the order in which you try to do them. Each person is different. The same trigger with the same best tips and defenses may need to be in a different order may not be the same even if everything else is essentially the same.

Great you say. So how do I figure out which comes first, second, third, and last?

First—Order Your Floor Defenses. In Step 2, you identified at least one floor defense. If you have more than one, order these first and put them last in your trigger defense checklist (in Appendix B).[7] For me, Health (likely death) is the next to last one, with my children (pride/disappointment/happiness) underlying everything. These are shown visually in the Examples of Progressions section discussed shortly.

Select One Tip and One Level of Defense. These are ones you intuitively (if possible) *know* will be the *most* effective for you. Each progression will have the following sub-sections:

- Tips
- Key Defense Level(s)
- Floor Defense(s)

Try if at all possible to have one of each, and again you must have at least one Key Defense Level and one Floor Defense. In general, I recommend—at least at first—trying all of your tips before you start on your Key Defense Levels. If after trying them you want to fine-tune their order because they work better for you then by all means do so.

Don't overthink the tips and defenses. They may be the first one to pop into your head. Or ones that you think of after some thought. Or even ones that come up when you talk them over with friends or family members who know you best. Ideally these should make sense intuitively to you, but it is fine if they are not—*as long as they work.*

If you don't intuitively know the most effective individual defense, consider the following "tests" of those tips/defenses:

- *Which one is most likely to weaken the attack the most?* In other words, which has the best chance of success to repel the attack *by itself?* After all, why do a bunch of things when one will work? Put these first in their respective sub-section.[8]

- *Which will take the most out of you physically and/or mentally?* This might seem counter-intuitive; after all you are trying to *strengthen* your defenses, not weaken them! However, this is where the frequent desire to "numb yourself" (discussed in detail in Level 11) comes into play. Numbing yourself is part of the buzz/rush/numb/checkout continuum described in that Level. There is no question that we all want to "numb" ourselves sometimes—on occasion, some of the time, a lot of the time, or even *all* of the time—to the pain/pressure/discomfort of triggers. We can't do it with alcohol anymore obviously, but another, even better way, is to exhaust ourselves—mentally and/or physically.

  If, for example, you listed Exercise as one of your Tips or Hobbies, consider putting that first. Draining excess energy that you otherwise might use to dwell/focus/obsess about your trigger situation will help you greatly with this "numbing" process. Perhaps do a game that requires total concentration, or re-read some of the more complicated/boring chapters in this book,[9] or even balance your frigging checkbook. Supplement it with a nice (nonalcoholic) beverage such as tea or whatever helps you relax (See Level 8 for more on tea). "Drain that negative energy" might sound like a cliché, but that is exactly what I'm talking about here.

- *Which one(s) are the most distracting and/or time-consuming?* For many triggers, they are at their strongest *right now in the heat of the situation,* and quickly drop in intensity. Anger and Frustration are great examples of triggers where their intensity diminishes greatly with time, sometimes in as little as a few minutes. If you can wait them out, they will very likely become less intense; maybe not the underlying reasons, but how they make you want to drink *right now.* If you can find things that will take you at least a couple of hours to do—and even be very distracting—these are excellent candidates to put first.

- *Combine all of the above.* A strong, numbing, distracting, time-consuming tip/ defense combination is the nirvana of alcohol repellents! Even a tip/defense that is "just" fairly strong, somewhat numbing, partially distracting, and lasts just 15 minutes or so may well be sufficiently strong to help defend against many of your trigger situations.

Third—Repeat the previous step for all other tips and defenses. This may sound like a lot of work, and it can be. But it also can be kind of fun, in game-playing kind of way as you try to figure out the best ways to outsmart your evil opponent—alcohol! It is kind of like playing the game *Risk,* just at a personal level.

Be prepared for some of your initial efforts to not work or work well. The result may or may not be the final, best version for you, which is the reason for Step #7.

Step #7—Test and Adjust Your Tips and Defenses

In Missouri, where I currently live, there is no end to the opportunities to test my defenses. I swear *every* fucking store that has *any* consumable goods has a huge liquor section, and many seem to feature huge end-displays dedicated to vodka.[10] For the most part, I am (now) able to ignore these displays pretty easily. On a minority of occasions I get curious about how the pricing has changed, and occasionally I do get pretty annoyed that there are so many damn liquor displays waiting to throw themselves in my face every time I turn around. What's wrong with potato chip displays like the old days? But in the spirit of "making lemonade out of lemons" I use these displays to continually test/adjust my defenses (particularly against the Proximity trigger).

> One of the places where we hold meetings in a basement is about 4 doors down from our town's liquor store. We get a lot of laughs over that one. I learned from the beginning that trying to avoid walking by there was harder than just walking by and waving to the gals that work there. They know I'm in the program and every now in then come out to ask how I'm doing. It sort of gives me a safety net to keep them posted on my continued sobriety. They have even joked with my husband and I that Jack Daniels sales have gone down since we joined AA.
>
> Terri, alcoholism.about.com

Use these kinds of "tests" to determine the strength of any given tip/defense as well as their order. Do them in "safe" environments at first (like in the testimonial above), and then progress to tests that are more and more difficult and have less and less of a safety net. Such "safety net" environments include making sure you are with a trusted friend/family member, being in a situation where it is logistically impossible to give in to temptation (such as a passenger in a car), and deliberately not carrying enough money to buy booze. There are many other types of safety nets, limited only by your imagination!

Unfortunately, the best tests are those in real life, where your trigger is pounding you full force with little in the way of safety nets. It will take some trial and "error" (this does *not* include actually relapsing) to get the best mix of defenses. Just try to identify and have ready as many tips/defenses as you can that you know will work *at least a bit,* which, along with your floor defenses, should do the job until you can find better tips/defenses and/or better ordering structures.

Adjustments can take many forms as well. You may well find that a tip/defense you thought would work great works hardly at all. Don't feel wedded to it if doesn't work! Sometimes you may be *very* surprised with what works and what does not. Don't get frustrated; it can be kind of fun (sometimes) to discover how you mind actually reacts to unusual ideas!

Also consider what I call "side" or "overlay" defenses. These are kinds of thoughts/philosophies that I think at the tail end of every individual Tip/Defense for certain triggers. One example of this is about my e(X) as a trigger. As an "overlay" to each tip/defense, I try always to remember *"It is not my job to make her happy anymore. It is my job to make me happy."* This may take a lot of practice, but can be very effective once you get the hang of it.

Step #8—Develop a "Generic" Trigger Defense Progression

The above defense progressions will, hopefully, work for you most of the time, and even the *vast* majority of the time. But it is almost a certainty that they will not work *all* of the time—life throws too much crap at you for that to happen.

It is almost a certainty that even if you identify hundreds of defenses and dozens of progressions for dozens or hundreds of trigger/Related Trigger combinations, there will *always* be at least a few that you miss. Murphy's Law[11] is a law for a reason.

> *One of the scariest things about cravings for me is that they can appear out of nowhere. Things may be going well for me in recovery but the urge to drink or use drugs pops into my head. Very frustrating.*
> anonymous

Since it is pointless on so many levels[12] to try to plan/develop/implement dozens of progressions, you need to develop at least one "generic" progression. A generic progression is a "catch all" set of tips/defenses that will deal with unanticipated trigger episodes, ones that you *did* think about but are so unusual that they might as well be brand new triggers, or happen when you are just completely unprepared for them. You might also view them as another kind of "floor" defense—whatever the best way is for you to think about it *instantly* when such situations as the above occur.

In addition, as discussed earlier in this Level, there are triggers "events" that do not last a long time—perhaps as little as a few hours or even minutes. This is when you just need to buy some time to let *time* take care of the problem. Perhaps some road rage, or an argument with your girlfriend, or a bad Reminder on the radio that causes you to get really Depressed. These are all examples of trigger circumstances that will go away with a bit of time. These kinds of events are particularly dangerous in the Early Sobriety stage previously discussed, when you haven't really tested and adjusted your defenses, or you even missed the trigger entirely.

Super-simplicity is the key here. 2–4 tips and/or defense level specifics at most. You just need enough to let you get your bearings and regroup when faced with totally unanticipated trigger events (being fired is a "great" example)—followed by your floor triggers. One generic progression might be:

#1—Do a general "mini-meditation" (breathing, catchy phrases/
   philosophies)

#2—Call a Family Member (who depends on the situation, default
   to parent/sibling)

#3—Take a Walk, Exercise (what type depends on the situation
   and *immediate* opportunity)

#4—Have an overall philosophy to remember (such as "count
   your blessings," or "things could be worse," etc.)

#5—Floor Defense #1

#6—Floor Defense #2

All you are doing is buying time so you can get your act together to develop a new progression specific to that new/unusual/out-of-the-blue trigger and/or circumstance, *fast*.

Step #9—Periodically Refresh *Everything*

One of the steps in AA that I never fully understood until I started writing this chapter was their Step 10: *"continue to take personal inventory of ourselves."* I now can see the benefit to that concept, (greatly) adapted for this Level. Even if/when you finally find the "perfect" set of Tips/Defenses/Progressions for your triggers, you can count on their not staying perfect for any significant length of time. Alcoholism is patient; you can be sober for many years, thinking you are just fine, when it will try to strike again seemingly out of the blue. If your defenses are not up-to-date, an attack may succeed. As the late, great Robin Williams described his addiction to alcohol:

> *"It waits. It lays in wait for the time when you think, 'It's fine now, I'm O.K.' Then, the next thing you know, it's not O.K. Then you realize, 'Where am I? I didn't realize I was in Cleveland.' "*[13]

To avoid this complacency and to be ready to defend against alcohol attacks at any time, it will be very important to "refresh" everything in this Level, particularly all of the previous eight steps, at least a few times a year, *for the rest of your life.* A good rule of thumb is to refresh once a month early in sobriety, and then about every 3–4 months after that.

You should also refresh *immediately* when you have major changes in your life, as those changes could mess with some stable dimensions of your life that you never thought of when you originally put together your defense progressions. Say it with me one more time: Murphy's Law. "Good" examples of out-of-the-blue changes in your life is a sudden firing; a spouse blindsiding you and leaving overnight for someone else; the sudden death of parent, sibling, or child; a sudden diagnosis of cancer, etc. While all of these can be covered somewhat by other triggers (e.g. Job, Relationships/eX, Extreme Emotions, etc.), it is the suddenness and unexpectedness of these events that can really threaten to overcome whatever existing defenses you might have.

● ●

Remember . . .

. . . most of the activities in this program will take time and practice to refine and "optimize." Besides obviously being worthwhile, it *will* get easier and easier to do. With enough refinement, time, and practice, you may not have to *do* all of the tips/defenses in your progressions; you may merely need to *think* about them, consciously or even sub-consciously. That is the nirvana end-goal of this program—that not only do not have to obsess about not drinking, you don't have to even *think* about not drinking—indeed being able to *ignore* alcohol as irrelevant to your new life.

● ●

I characterize the result of this Level, and The Conquer Program as a whole, as equating a glass, can, or bottle of alcohol with a can of motor oil. Thinking about alcohol should become as insignificant to you as passing by a display of oil in the store. You will have taught your mind and body—with the help of ALL the tips, Levels of defense, and progressions that you have built—to react to the thought of alcohol just as it would to the thought of opening, smelling, and drinking that can of motor oil . . . by turns disgusted, incredulous, contemptuous, nauseous, and perhaps even a bit amused, but with the bottom line of it being *irrelevant* to your life now and forgotten by the time you get to the next aisle! When you are finally able to reach this kind of state and everyday reaction to alcohol, you will know as a whole that you have Conquered Your Alcoholism!

EXAMPLES OF PROGRESSIONS

Instead of hypotheticals, I use my personal progressions both as examples of the result and also the 9-Step process shown again in Figure 24 below. Important note: the triggers and their relative priority are those I had at the time I got sober via the Conquer Program, not as they exist today. That these triggers evolve over time is an important point discussed in more detail shortly.

Overall Process

The Conquer Progression Development Process

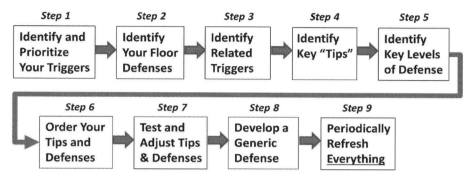

Step 1	Step 2	Step 3	Step 4	Step 5
Identify and Prioritize Your Triggers	Identify Your Floor Defenses	Identify Related Triggers	Identify Key "Tips"	Identify Key Levels of Defense

Step 6	Step 7	Step 8	Step 9
Order Your Tips and Defenses	Test and Adjust Tips & Defenses	Develop a Generic Defense	Periodically Refresh Everything

Figure 24: The Conquer Progression Development Process

Step #1: Identify and Prioritize Your Triggers

Example of Alcoholism Triggers Evolution

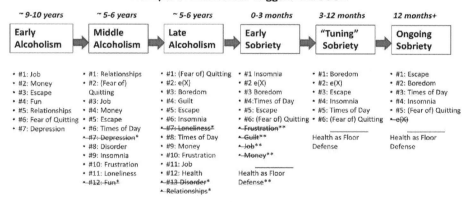

~ 9-10 years	~ 5-6 years	~ 5-6 years	0-3 months	3-12 months	12 months+
Early Alcoholism	Middle Alcoholism	Late Alcoholism	Early Sobriety	"Tuning" Sobriety	Ongoing Sobriety

Early Alcoholism	Middle Alcoholism	Late Alcoholism	Early Sobriety	"Tuning" Sobriety	Ongoing Sobriety
• #1: Job	• #1: Relationships	• #1: (Fear of) Quitting	• #1 Insomnia	• #1: Boredom	• #1: Escape
• #2: Money	• #2: (Fear of) Quitting	• #2: e(X)	• #2 e(X)	• #2: e(X)	• #2: Boredom
• #3: Escape		• #3: Boredom	• #3 Boredom	• #3: Escape	• #3: Times of Day
• #4: Fun	• #3: Job	• #4: Guilt	• #4:Times of Day	• #4: Insomnia	• #4: Insomnia
• #5: Relationships	• #4: Money	• #5: Escape	• #5: Escape	• #5: Times of Day	• #5: (Fear of) Quitting
• #6: Fear of Quitting	• #5: Escape	• #6: Insomnia	• #6: (Fear of) Quitting	• #6: (Fear of) Quitting	~~• e(X)~~
• #7: Depression	• #6: Times of Day	~~• #7: Loneliness*~~	~~• Frustration**~~		
	~~• #7: Depression*~~	• #8: Times of Day	~~• Guilt**~~	Health as Floor Defense	Health as Floor Defense
	• #8: Disorder	• #9: Money	~~• Job**~~		
	• #9: Insomnia	• #10: Frustration	~~• Money**~~		
	• #10: Frustration	• #11: Job			
	• #11: Loneliness	• #12: Health	Health as Floor Defense**		
	~~• #12: Fun*~~	~~• #13 Disorder*~~			
		~~• Relationships*~~			

* I finally realized I was not drinking in the slightest for fun anymore; Depression dropped out once I started taking medicine for it; Loneliness came after I moved cross-country, then dropped after I moved back near my kids. Disorder dropped out when I moved out of the marital house; Relationships issues transferred to e(X) after the divorce.
** Guilt went away after I stopped worrying about it; various causes of Frustration seemed to go away with sobriety; Job and Money issues no longer seemed important as I was dealing with early sobriety. I was able to turn Health worries into a successful floor defense.

Figure 25: The Author's Stages of Alcoholism and Sobriety

At the time I stopped drinking for good, I had 10 active major triggers, shown in the Early Sobriety column of Figure 25 above. During Early Sobriety I was able to eliminate four of these, resulting in six remaining. Alphabetically, those were:

- Boredom
- Escape

- Insomnia
- Times of Day

- (Fear of) Quitting
- e(X)

The four I dropped I did for a variety of reasons. Upon writing the Frustration trigger in this book, I realized it was no longer a major trigger, but instead a (very strong) Related Trigger connected to my e(X), as was Money. Both however had been full-fledged major triggers while we were still married, as was the overall Relationship. But it wasn't until I was sober and started thinking clearly about triggers did I realize I now only became frustrated or worried about money when a situation involved my eX.

This experience illustrates an extremely important point: that it is essential to think through and distinguish between what are truly your independent major triggers versus (often strong) Related Triggers. For some triggers, particularly close interpersonal ones (e.g. Relationships, Relatives, and eX), not clearly identifying which is which may prevent you from getting at key causes of your drinking, resulting in misplaced or totally missing defenses.[14]

One of the other two dropped triggers, my Job, also ceased to be an issue for me during Early Sobriety. I decided that getting sober was more important than anything else at that time. I also had the good fortune to have the support of my mother during this period, which also coincided with the start of some major medical problems. Soon after (during Tuning Sobriety), fortunes in my business picked up, as did eventually my health (in Ongoing Sobriety)—excellent omens for good things starting to happen in sobriety. It is also indicative of how important it *can* (not necessarily will) be for you to alleviate as much worry about your Job (and the Related Trigger Money) situation as you can going into any sort of treatment program. Far easier said than done, I know.

Guilt however was a different story. It had been a very significant trigger for many years until I finally concluded that the best way (really the only way) for effectively dealing with it was to not feel guilty *at all,* as it would be a key relapse trigger if I did not.[15] This defense is repeated several times in the Guilt trigger section in Level 2.

Health went from a trigger to being a floor defense as noted earlier and discussed more in Step #2.

I then prioritized the remaining six triggers. I did this by considering how hard they hit me, and how frequently. The results and the reason(s) they were where they were in Early Sobriety and how they subsequently evolved are as follows:

1. **Insomnia**—This (in hindsight) was a significant trigger for me most of my alcoholism life, shooting to #1 very early in my sobriety. It probably would still be except for the tips and ideas in Appendix A, which, unfortunately, I had to test personally to overcome my inability to sleep. These tips ideas enabled me to drop it from my #1 trigger to #4. But it still plagues me from time to time.

2. **e(X)**—It wasn't until I got sober that I fully understood the impact my eX had had on my drinking life (including while we were still in a Relationship), particularly when you factored in the Related Triggers. Through this program was I not only able to diffuse her as a major trigger, by the time I hit Ongoing Sobriety I was able to remove her entirely from my trigger list! However, I use my eX as the key example in the remainder of this section as that trigger (in some form) was such a major one for much of my life. It also is one many of you can likely relate to as well.

Guilt, as I mentioned, was originally on my Early Sobriety list (as #3) and then dropped off entirely once I figured out my defenses. This is noteworthy in that it does not mean that only your lowest priority triggers are the only ones that can be purged relatively quickly.

3. **Boredom**—The huge impact this trigger had on my life was not apparent until after I was sober for a few months, as my head cleared and I became aware of how much time I had previously used up by drinking. It became particularly acute after my major surgery (near the start of Tuning Sobriety), as I physically could not do much nor did I have much energy. As a result, I was bored out of my gourd, and in fact decided to use some of that time to test many of the tips/defenses listed in that section. But even before then (and when I was drinking) it was a significant trigger, particularly in the years after my divorce when I moved across the country and did not know anyone in the area. While #1 on my current Ongoing Priority list, it is likely to drop down in priority after my next "review" as my defense progressions continue to adjust/improve and my life continues to fulfill in new, positive ways.

4. **Escape**—This trigger was and continues to be a general desire that I have to defend against. No particular trigger may be hitting me particu-

larly strongly that day, but several smaller ones combine to say "Escape, Escape." First I try to narrow the real reason to a specific trigger if I possibly can (usually some variation of the ones below) and use their tips/defenses; if not I use my Generic Progression. Escape is particularly notable in that I've had this trigger since Day 1 of my drinking, and I will likely have to worry about this trigger for the rest of my life.

5. **Times of Day**—This trigger hit me every day between 5:30 pm and 9 pm for nearly all my drinking life—for reasons I still do not fully understand. It still does to a degree (e.g., though not every day), and I have to be ever alert for it, though it is gradually waning in impact when it does occur. This will likely gradually go away in time as I narrow the time window within which it hits me (see that trigger discussion on how I do this).

6. **(Fear of) Quitting**—This enormous fear (unfortunately not fully understood until I got sober and stayed that way) has always lurked in the background nearly all my drinking life. Every time I would make a serious attempt at stopping it would *easily* shoot to #1. This fear sabotaged many attempts to stop, and I'm certain contributed to the failures of others. I keep it on my list due to my fear of its re-emergence—a kind of sign of respect. I no longer have any progressions for it since I *have* quit, but I include one in other examples later that I wish I had thought through and took to heart during those attempts.

I strongly urge you to go through your list of triggers several times before moving on to the next step. Your initial list will likely resemble but not be an exact copy of your original list. Pay particular attention in making sure what you identify as a major trigger is not in reality "just" a Related Trigger for something else.

Step #2—Identify Your Floor Defenses

As noted earlier, you should if at all possible have at least one floor defense. If you can't figure out what it is, I'd encourage you to talk with family members and/or friends who know you best.[16]Again, my health and my children are my floor defenses, shown in Figure 26. I can count on either of them to intuitively leap to mind for most triggers, and both are valid defenses for *all* of my triggers.

Example Floor Defenses

Tip/Defense	Description	Time	Duration	Comment
Listen to Your Body!	Booze = Death	Booze = Death	Booze = Death	Booze = Death
Engage Friends and Family	Remember My Children	Remember My Children	Remember My Children	Remember My Children

Figure 26: Author's Floor Defenses

Figure 27 shows the results after the first two steps.

Identifying and Prioritizing Triggers and Floor Defenses

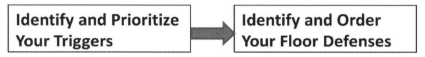

Identify and Prioritize Your Triggers	Identify and Order Your Floor Defenses

- Boredom (#3)
- Escape (#5)
- ~~Frustration~~
- ~~Guilt~~
- Insomnia (#1)
- ~~Job~~
- ~~Money~~
- (Fear of) Quitting (#6)
- Times of Day (#4)
- e(X) (#2)

- Health (Fear of Death)
- Children

Figure 27: Steps 1 and 2 of the CPDP Process

Step #3—Identify Related Triggers

Steps 3 to 7 are done for each major trigger. To illustrate this, I use my e(X) trigger, as it has been a major trigger in some form for several years (both pre and post sobriety). More importantly it provides good examples of the usefulness of all these steps. It will also probably be an experience easy to relate to for many of you.

For Related Triggers, the selection process with my eX was pretty easy, and the results included three obvious Related Triggers (RT for short): Frustration, Guilt and Money. Nearly every time I talked with her, if there was any dispute, there never seemed to be any way to resolve the issue without a bunch of bullshit (in my opinion, and probably hers too). Even when I laid-out what I thought was a very logical resolution to whatever the issue was, my eX usually would not agree, or at least not without major modifications. To say I was Frustrated by this is a gross understatement.

In addition, she would seemingly always bring out what I called the "Guilt Card," saying how I had destroyed the family, that all of our problems were 100% my fault, etc. etc. etc.[17] I *hated* this but ultimately found a way to very effectively deal with it specifically with her, but also more generally—Ignore It. This tip/approach is discussed in great detail in the Guilt trigger section.

Many of those interactions had to do with Money: how much was I sending her, when, why not more, why not sooner, etc. Any answers that displeased her, of course, resulted in the Guilt Card being played and Frustration with her ability to remember and understand the situation.

As a final note, while I list these RTs alphabetically here (and shown in Figure 28), they did happen to be in order of most impactful and frequent to least. This RT prioritizing is important, as you want your highest priority ones (and their tips) immediately after your primary tips.

Step #4—Identify Key Tips

From the descriptions of the e(X) tips in that section, I then selected those that seemed to have the most impact. In general try to select at least one tip; there is no maximum.

In the case of my e(X), the tip that seemed to do the job was Never Talk Live, which is a variation of the "Create New Boundaries" tip. Since the vast majority of the time the live conversation would degenerate into disputes, arguments, and laying on of Guilt-trips, the most logical solution was to not do it! It is far, far harder to do those things via text. I use email if the topic requires a lengthy explanation or "discussion."

After you have identified key tip(s) for the trigger, do this for your prioritized RTs, using one or more of the tips in the applicable trigger sections. For Frustration, I selected the same tip I used for the primary tip: Never Talk Live. For Guilt, I selected "Ignore Guilt." For Money, I selected "Plan and Communicate in Advance." I put these immediately under the primary trigger tip, in the order (for the RTs) that occur most frequently and/or with the strongest impact.

For each tip I spelled out *exactly* what I would do in that tip, and how, via a description. I also spelled out when I would do it (e.g., the *date*/time/frequency), and how long I would do it (the duration). Figure 28 shows the tips so far for my eX trigger. Figure 28 shows the tips so far for my eX trigger and its related triggers.

Tip/Defense	Description	Time	Duration
#1/Primary Tip: Create New Boundaries (Never Talk Live)	Text and email for everything (not emergencies)	Always	As short and infrequent as possible
(RT - Frustration) Never Talk Live	Same as above	Always	Same as above
(RT - Guilt) Ignore, ignore, ignore	Never let her lay guilt-trip on you even via the above	Always	Always
(RT - Money) Explain schedule/situation in advance (via text)	Explain in advance money situation if not usual plan	Once a month or quarter	Write/send check

Figure 28: Author's eX Trigger Tips

Step #5—Identify Key Levels of Defense; Get *Specific!*

At the end of each trigger discussion is a list of Key Defense Levels. These are ones that (in my opinion) have high potential for helping you defend against the particular trigger attack. There are four listed for e(X): Break Bad Habits, Engage Friends and Family, the Therapy part of Rehab and Therapy, and Develop New Hobbies. I didn't go to therapy for this, as I thought I (by now) knew pretty well why my eX was a trigger.[18] Develop New Hobbies was easy to drop off the list. For much of our marriage, we didn't do a lot together hobby-wise[19] or even activity-wise that didn't involve children, so I had no hobby associations that needed to be avoided/ignored/broken.

When it came to Bad Habits, I realized that I would react very fast when she would "push my buttons," which was quite often, and frequently brought Frustration and Guilt along for the ride. In addition to recognizing those related triggers and their associated tips, I realized that *reacting* to what my eX said was a bad habit as well. It either resulted in my responding exactly like she wanted me to or it would easily turn innocent topics into disputes and unpleasantness. My method for breaking this habit was ignoring the offending communication if possible, and waiting for the next day to respond if not.

My eX trigger Key Defense Levels are shown in Figure 29:

Tip/Defense	Description	Time	Duration
Break Bad Habits	Don't react; ignore or minimize issues	As applicable	As often as possible
Engage Friends and Family	Vent to mom, sisters, children (on select issues)	Variable	If above tips or defenses fail

Figure 29: Author's eX Trigger Key Defense Levels

Step #6—Order Tips and Defenses

My eX trigger tips and defenses were easy to put in order, as there was only one tip for eX itself, and only one per related trigger, plus my already ordered floor triggers (you might want to possibly consider re-ordering your floor triggers, depending on the trigger). My Boredom progression example (shown later) is a better example of the considerations for ordering tips/defenses based on priority, frequency and schedule.

But there is another factor besides priority, frequency, and schedule. There is also the *philosophy* of the tip or defense. An excellent example is with my eX primary tip and my tips for Frustration and Guilt. The philosophy for those tips was *never* to let her get to me with those triggers. This includes avoiding if at all possible *opportunities* for her to do so, through *never* talking live and *ignoring* any ways she managed to succeed slipping them in otherwise (e.g., text and email).

Step #7—Test and Adjust Tips and Defenses

The ways of testing each tip/defense will vary greatly depending on the tip, your personality, the opportunities to test, and what "safety nets" you have available in case it doesn't work. That is not as complex as it sounds, and it is *essential* to optimizing your defenses to work in *your* everyday world.

For example, until I settled on "Never Talk Live" as a Create New Boundaries approach, I tried another version—to talk live, but keep it short. It did not work much of the time, so my "safety net" was to hang up if I started to get Frustrated and particularly if it would morph into Anger. After enough of those episodes I finally settled on Never Talk Live, which I *always* use, which works great.[20]

Adjusting tips/defenses themselves is not just with respect to specific variations of tips, but when, where, and how you do them (more on this in the Boredom example). Adjusting also includes other types of "adjustments" or other nuances you need to consider or even keep track of, shown in the Comment column shown in Figure 30 below:

Tip/Defense	Description	Time	Duration	Comment
#1/Primary Tip: Create New Boundaries (Never Talk Live)	Text and email for everything (not emergencies)	Always	As short and infrequent as possible	Make sure you tell him/her that is what you are doing e.g. (never talking live)
(RT - Frustration) Never Talk Live	Same as above	Always	Same as above	Hide Frustration even via text (ok via email)
(RT - Guilt) Ignore, ignore, ignore	Never let her lay guilt-trip on you even via the above	Always	Always	Maintain <u>direct</u> contact with children to prevent manipulation
(RT - Money) Explain schedule/situation in advance (via text)	Explain in advance money situation if not usual plan	Once a month or quarter	Write/send check	Maintain log for tax reasons and avoid disputes (e.g. plan ahead)

Figure 30: Author's Adjusted Tips for the eX Trigger

For example, for my primary eX tip I needed to make sure she knew about this new boundary. For Frustration, I resolved never to show it even via texts (it would just generate more and worse texts). If I had to do so, I would only vent the Frustration via email where I could anticipate her reactions and short-circuit them. For Guilt, I knew she delighted in controlling the information about me (particularly my medical situation) to my children so I resolved always to tell them first before I told her. For Money, I wanted to make sure I kept a clear record of everything I gave her so I could minimize disputes come tax time; otherwise they would turn into major disputes, Frustration, accusation throwing . . . you get the idea—massive trigger episodes. The result is shown in Figure 31.

e(X) Spouse/Partner Trigger Defense Progression Example

Tip/Defense	Description	Time	Duration	Comment
#1/Primary Tip: Create New Boundaries (Never Talk Live)	Text and email for everything (not emergencies)	Always	As short and infrequent as possible	Make sure you tell him/her that is what you are doing e.g. (never talking live)
(RT - Frustration) Never Talk Live	Same as above	Always	Same as above	Hide Frustration even via text (ok via email)
(RT - Guilt) Ignore, ignore, ignore	Never let her lay guilt-trip on you even via the above	Always	Always	Maintain <u>direct</u> contact with children to prevent manipulation
(RT - Money) Explain schedule/situation in advance (via text)	Explain in advance money situation if not usual plan	Once a month or quarter	Write/send check	Maintain log for tax reasons and avoid disputes (e.g. plan ahead)
Break Bad Habits	Don't react; ignore or minimize issues	As applicable	As often as possible	Ignore if possible; otherwise do not respond immediately; wait a day
Engage Friends and Family	Vent to mom, sisters, children :(on select issues)	Variable	If above tips or defenses fail	Different person(s) depending on issue
Listen to Your Body!	Booze = Death	Booze = Death	Booze = Death	Booze = Death
Engage Friends and Family	Remember My Children	Remember My Children	Remember My Children	Remember My Children

Figure 31: Author's eX Defense Progression

Step #8—Develop a "Generic" Defense Progression

Again, the purpose of a generic progression is to fill the gaps in your other trigger defense progressions and protect you when something hits you out of the blue and/or for whatever reason you were not prepared to deal that makes you want to drink.

Simplicity is key here as is instinctiveness, intuition, easy to do, and do *fast*. Here I did a mix of philosophy, tips/defenses, and (always) my floor defenses.

Generic Progression Example

Tip/Defense	Description
General "Mini" Meditation	Take several deep breaths; remember *shit happens.* Reflect with a non-alcoholic calming beverage (hot tea)
Call Family Member Y	"Y" depends on situation (knowledge of situation, physical proximity)
Take A Walk, Exercise	Go to Gym if possible and nearby, otherwise take a walk
Mini-Meditation: Count My Blessings	Particularly when that situation hasn't happened before/happened often
Listen to Your Body!	Booze = Death
Engage Friends and Family	Remember My Children

Figure 32: Author's Generic Progression

Again, the goal here is doing what works for you—*now and without thinking*—so you can regroup and prepare a specific defense progression for what caught you off guard. *Not* drinking in the meantime.

Step 9—Periodically Refresh *Everything*

As I discussed above, my trigger priorities as they exist now are not the same ones I had when I was initially getting sober, or the ones I had in Tuning Sobriety. It is *essential* that you refresh/redo everything at various points in your life. Some ideas:

• *While Still Drinking*—If you are still drinking by this time in the Conquer Program, obviously something or things are still not working. Rework this entire 9-step process, and perhaps even redo the entire program until you can get to the point where you can stay sober. This might be an iterative process, meaning you get some triggers right the first time, but others (including ones you didn't identify the first time) may take multiple tries.

- *Early Sobriety (0 to 3 months)*—Be on the *constant* lookout for ways you can improve/change/add to your tips/defenses and your progressions. Even if you have nailed your triggers, it is almost a certainty that you will need several tries to get all the more subtle nuances of your defenses exactly right. You want them as bulletproof as possible! As a practical matter revisiting them *once a week* is a good target.

- *"Tuning" Sobriety (3–12 months)*—The "tuning" means that by this time you will have an excellent handle on your triggers and a very solid handle on what tips and defenses seem to be working for each trigger. During this time, you need to revisit your progressions *monthly*. Odds are that improvements that were not identifiable or even needed during Early Sobriety will become more so with the passage of time.

- *Ongoing Sobriety*—After a year of sobriety you have very likely nailed down pretty much everything *in general* you need to stay sober for quite a while. But that doesn't mean do nothing; life will continually change, and so will you. Revisit *everything* every 3 months or so, *or immediately* after a major life change (good, bad, or just very significant). This evaluation includes what your floor defenses are and how your generic progression is structured.

OTHER EXAMPLES OF PROGRESSIONS

I selected my eX progression above because I thought it was one most people could relate to in at least some form. However, all triggers are different and additional examples may help you better understand the program. Again, there is no single "right" way—*only what works best for you*.

Boredom

As mentioned earlier, Boredom is a good example of things to think about when ordering your tips and defenses. For both, you will likely need to test them frequently to get the right order and "schedule."

When first organizing Tips and Defenses, select the one you think will have the most impact, most frequently of use, and/or has a very specific timeframe in which it can be done. This will need some playing around with (e.g., testing and adjusting). For example, Exercising has the greatest impact for me for a variety of reasons, but there is only so much you can do on any given day. I love to read but can only read when I'm not working. I also like to watch shows/series I haven't seen before[21], but have to be in a watching-TV mood.

I finally chose "Vary Everything" as my first tip as it could apply to almost anything at any time. When I say everything, I mean *everything*. Food, stores/restaurants, types of exercises I do at the gym, where I walk. Exercise was second as it is a very important activity for several reasons, particularly since it is also used in two of my other triggers (Escape and Times of Day). Read Books and Watch TV Shows I put 3rd and 4th, respectively, as I like to read more than I like to watch TV.

Next I ordered my Key Defense Levels. Develop New Hobbies was

Boredom Trigger Defense Progression Example

Tips/Defense	Description	Time	Duration	Comment
Tip 1: Vary Everything	Do same things different ways	Variable	Each type at least once a week	Example: Mix types of restaurants
Tip 2: Exercise	Walk, Exercise	Tues (Yoga);Thurs & Sun (gym); walk others	1-2 hours	Generally early evening (sync w/ Times of Day trigger)
Tip 3: Read various books	Reading	Before Bed	30-60 minutes	Read multiple books at "same" time
Tip 4: Watch new shows/movies	Watch new (old) TV show series	Variable	1 hour	Keep "pipeline" of shows/series/movies
Develop New Hobbies	Bowling	Wed Evening	4 hours	Try out different bowling balls
	Gardening	Saturday	1 hour	Seasonal
	Writing (Journaling)	Multiple times a week, as needed	30 minutes	Start/continue book
	Facebook	Variable	15 minutes/day	Watch privacy
Join a Community	Go to AA, Al-Anon meetings	Mon 7 pm (Al-anon); Thurs 7:30 pm; others	2 hours (incl. travel time)	Cycle through others (by day, time, type of meeting, town)
	Online	Variable	15 minutes/day	Try different ones
Listen to Your Body!	Booze = Death	Booze = Death	Booze = Death	Booze = Death
Engage Friends and Family	Remember My Children	Remember My Children	Remember My Children	Remember My Children

Figure 33: Author's Boredom Progression

the strongest for me, with Join a Community being a kind of "gap filler" to safely and easily kill time when I needed to do so. Within Develop New Hobbies, I put bowling first, not because it was the most impactful but because it had a very set day and time. I like Gardening since it gets me outdoors, but it also has very set times I can do it (time of year, weather). I enjoy writing (and do it as well as part of my "day job") but I can do that practically anytime, so I slotted that third in my Defenses. I finished with reading/posting on Facebook as a filler and a general connection with my family.[22]

I continue my "vary everything" them within Join a Community, going both to AA and Al-Anon meetings at different times and places (and hence different people). I use online community resources as "filler." I completed the progression with my floor defenses, with the overall result shown in Figure 33 above.

Escape

The desire to Escape has been my most consistent trigger my entire alcoholic life and is my #1 trigger in longer-term sobriety. The progression I developed is multi-faceted, mixing a combination of mind and body defenses.

The first mental defense is raw knowledge, trying to figure out what were the key underlying triggers. So much of the time (*not* all of the time), the urge to get away mentally (including numbing yourself) is caused by other specific major triggers.

That said, I recognized that often my desire for Escape was a bunch of little stresses[23] and concerns that added up into a big ball that screams "Escape!" Exercise is my #1 defense in this case, as it takes the edge off the various mental and physical stresses.

I often drink herbal tea in situations where I used to drink alcohol. In theory, it has ingredients that help relaxation.[24] There is more on this in Level 8. I also try to escape *physically* when I can. This can be done many ways, from taking a long hot shower to hikes to truly relaxing getaways.

Finally, I modified my Floor triggers—particularly my Listen to Your Body! defense. The Escape trigger is one that can be complex, confusing, or even vague for some people in some situations where the root cause can't be clearly identified. This is when your floor defenses become particularly important, in case more specific ones fail in a peculiar situation. With mine added to the above tips, the result is shown in Figure 34.

Escape Trigger Defense Progression Example

Tips/Defense	Description	Time/Duration	Comment
"Diagnose" underlying triggers	Understand root cause(s) of the desire for Escape	As Needed	Likely to be a mix of common ones (e.g. Job) and ones that vary daily
Exercise	Walks, different forums and types of exercise	Everyday or as needed	Releases Endorphins; takes edge off various forms of Stress
Break Bad Habits	Substitute herbal tea for alcohol	As needed	Mix ingredients, try different varieties
Develop New Hobbies	Do things to physically Escape	Long relaxing showers; Try new activities and hobbies; Regularly go away on long weekends; Take truly relaxing vacations	For getaways and vacations – do a mix of tested/familiar destinations and activities and some totally new ones.
Listen to Your Body!	Booze = Death	Booze = Death	Booze = Death
Engage Friends and Family	Remember My Children	Remember My Children	Remember My Children

Figure 34: Author's Escape Progression

(Fear of) Quitting

How you deal with the Fear of Quitting depends *greatly* on the underlying triggers, which will obviously vary by person. It is probably safe to say that underlying this fear is one or more of the more common triggers: Boredom, Change, Escape, Fun, Guilt, Insomnia, and some version(s) of Stress (e.g., Job, Kids, Money). Unfortunately it is also likely that at least one of these will be with you well after you are sober, and you are instinctively aware of this likelihood. You can greatly reduce this fear with planning in advance what your post-drinking daily life might be like. Uncertainty of the future breeds fear, but knowledge of it provides power.

A progression (really a process) I highly recommend is shown in Figure 35 on the following page.

Fear of Quitting Defense Progression Example

Tips/Defense	Description	Comment
"Diagnose" underlying triggers	Understand root cause(s) of the Fear	Likely to be several; try and prioritize
Project ways of dealing with them without alcohol	Read high priority trigger tips & defenses, and quickly pick out obvious ones	Reduces fear of the unknown, of life without alcohol
Go through "Floor Defense" process	Figure out your "catch-all" safety net	Can be very calming and/or provide a great goal and motivation
Understand the Process, and Plan	Understand what is coming at you, particularly Detox. Select Rehab and/or Therapy	Having the knowledge and a plan will be greatly comforting, even if it doesn't seem that way at first.
Avoid last minute hiccups; Just do it!	Don't do a last binge, and don't overthink everything – just start it	Getting cold feet will be likely – don't give in to it!

Figure 35: Author's Fear of Quitting Progression

Times of Day

Times of Day has been a trigger for me as long as I can remember, and I still do not fully understand why. In any event, it is a relatively simple one in concept: I have always had a desire to drink between the times of 5:30pm and 9pm.[25] I can't think of any related triggers.

The solution to this is pretty obvious but may be pretty challenging to execute day-in and day-out: do something else during that time period, with a low possibility of alcohol coming into the picture. My Times of Day progression is shown in Figure 36 on the following page.

You may note a couple of interesting things here. One is that I do not have a place for dinner during this time. This is because I use dinner as "filler" for whatever holes I have in my 5:30–9:00 pm vulnerable period. The second is that I try to "coordinate" those tips/defenses with other trigger progressions as they have some in common, and it is a great way of addressing more than one Trigger.

Times of Day Trigger Defense Progression Example

Tips/Defense	Description	Time	Duration	Comment
Tip 1: Exercise	Walk, Exercise	Tues (Yoga);Thurs & Sun (gym); walk others	1-2 hours, starting no earlier than 5:30 pm	Coordinate with other progressions (Time of Day) & specific hobby times
Tip 2: Old activities at new times	Run Errands	Immediately before/after exercise	30 minutes – 2 hours (including driving/parking)	Bunch up, OR spread out depending on TOD needs
Develop New Hobbies	Bowling, Yoga, Disc Golf	Do only during evenings if possible	2-4 hours	Use as anchor and do others around them; coordinate with other triggers
Listen to Your Body!	Booze = Death	Booze = Death	Booze = Death	Booze = Death
Engage Friends and Family	Remember My Children	Remember My Children	Remember My Children	Remember My Children

Figure 36: Author's Times of Day Progression

This concludes Level 13 and Phase 3 overall. I realize that the defense progressions in Level 13 may appear a bit daunting at first; for that reason I hope these examples of Progressions I have used in my life can be of benefit to you. To help you further with this process, there are a number of checklists/forms in Appendix B to help you with all of the concepts and steps discussed in this Level, as well as most of the Levels in The Conquer Program overall.

More broadly, the various concepts of Phase 3 may or may not be difficult for some people to adopt. Becoming spiritual, doing aversion therapy, using unusual approaches to detox, and incorporating defense progressions into your everyday life—all or parts may seem unusual and may well require multiple re-readings to digest fully and implement.

However, do not think of this as a chore. Rather, it can be extremely interesting, even *fun*, as you incorporate the unconventional into your steadily stronger defenses, with Level 13 optimizing how you put all your tips and defenses into the ultimate personal fortress!

Conclusion

I started to write this conclusion in the typical style of rehashing and summarizing all the levels and key messages that you just spent a lot of time reading and hopefully far more time doing, and in reminding you why you should stop drinking and what you can look forward to if you do. Instead, let's summarize the most critical points:

• Unless you convince yourself you are an alcoholic, *no* program will help you;

• Understanding *your* triggers is absolutely essential to the success of this program;

• No *one* defense will guard against *all* alcohol attacks, *all the time;* thus

• Building *multiple* defenses, personalized to your life's circumstances, is the key to you staying sober in the long-term.

In the end, sometimes great summarizations can come from strange places:

If you're an addict, it controls your life and your life becomes uncontrollable. It's boring and painful, filling your system with something that makes you stare at your shoes for six hours.

—SINGER/SONGWRITER JAMES TAYLOR

James Taylor is a well-known poet, but sometimes even better characterizations of life can come from the rank-and-file:

"I felt like Walking Death."[1]

Instead of ending on such a negative, I think there is a far better perspective on the whole deal:

"Sober people are the bravest people I've ever met. They are authentic and compassionate, and they exist in the truth. It is a beautiful, beautiful place to live. Come join us. It's amazing here."[2]

APPENDIX A

Learning to Sleep in Early Sobriety

THE CHALLENGE

Well, that's the trick, isn't it? Now that you are sober and not wholly consumed with drinking and struggling not to drink, it's time to live the rest of your life. Hopefully, many of the topics and tips discussed in this book will help. But of course you have your job (hopefully), family and friends (hopefully), and other "normal" aspects of living that were warped or non-existent during your drinking days. So what else is there to discuss that will be applicable to all conquering alcoholics?

Wait for it . . . Sleeping!

For me, the most difficult aspect of successfully conquering my alcoholism was getting and staying asleep. I also had to deal with nightmares that often occurred even when I did not drink (see the Insomnia section in Level 2 for more information). Like many active alcoholics, going to sleep and passing out were close cousins. When I became sober, I had to figure out new ways of sleeping in a "normal" fashion that would allow me to function during "normal" hours.

As it turns out, this was a *very* difficult task, and frankly one I still have not mastered completely many moons after becoming sober. For some, it can also be a very *dangerous* task, in that frustration in getting to sleep on a regular and consistent basis can lead to some very bad habits, particularly drug abuse or even relapse. But the good news is that there is a fair amount of research in this area and a fairly rich set of options you can try. Hopefully, one or more will work for you.

First, why is post-drinking sleep so problematic?

The most obvious answer, of course, is that alcohol has been influencing, even dictating, the addict's sleeping pattern for many years. It can take the mind and body time to adjust to, or even create, a sleep cycle that is not chemically induced. Unfortunately, this is an unavoidable fact for the vast majority of alcoholics.

Another factor is lingering discomfort due to withdrawal, even long after drinking has stopped. In addition, newly found clarity can cause newly found or previously heavily suppressed anxiety such as worrying about the future. Even "new" ailments can occur generated by the body in its newly detoxed state, such as restless leg syndrome or full body itching (my personal favorite). One of the biggest issues is nightmares.

Nightmares

Nightmares are a big problem for many people, particularly for alcoholics who suffer from Insomnia because of the *fear* of nightmares.

● ●
What Are Nightmares?

Nightmares are vividly realistic, disturbing dreams that rattle you awake from a deep sleep. They often set your heart pounding from fear. Nightmares tend to occur most often during rapid eye movement (REM) sleep, when most dreaming takes place. Because periods of REM sleep become progressively longer as the night progresses, you may find you experience nightmares most often in the early morning hours.

The subjects of nightmares vary from person to person. There are, though, some common nightmares that many people experience. For example, a lot of adults have nightmares about not being able to run fast enough to escape danger or about falling from a great height. If you've gone through a traumatic event, such as an attack or accident, you may have recurrent nightmares about your horrifying experience.

Though nightmares and night terrors both cause people to awake in great fear, they are different. Night terrors typically occur in the first few hours after falling asleep. They are experienced as feelings, not dreams, so people do not recall why they are terrified upon awakening.[1]

● ●

I mean, who can look forward to "resting" if it actually turns out to be the worst part of the day? I had this problem off and on over the years when I would make attempts to stop drinking. There is no magical solution, and frankly you should expect some *very* strange dreams/nightmares in early sobriety as your brain and body adjust to its new life. Bear in mind it *will* get better—it "just" takes time. There are many sources of information on nightmares, from theories on what causes them to dissecting various types, such as *http://sleep.lovetoknow.com/Types_of_Nightmares*.

"Relapse" Dreams

To add to the difficulties of sleeping after you stop drinking, it is common to have an occasional relapse dream. Indeed many people (including me) consider this a form of a nightmare. During sleep, you once again experience what it is like to be using alcohol or drugs. In the dream, you may be enjoying the experience or it may have all the qualities of a nightmare where you are fighting against something, in this case alcohol. Either way it can be exhausting.

It is common to wake up from this type of dream with feelings of guilt as if you *wanted* to have such an experience. Some may even view it as an omen that they are about to relapse in reality. It is important that people realize that such dreams are a normal part of a new life of sobriety.

According to *alcoholrehab.com*,[2] relapse dreams may occur for any number of reasons such as:

• Addicts usually have been abusing alcohol or drugs for many years, making these substances an important part of their life. It is, therefore, understandable that the substances involved will continue to influence dreams.

• Dreams are often be inspired by random events that occurred during the day. If those events remind you about the past, then this may trigger material for a dream. Since the past time period usually involved drugs or alcohol, it "comes along for the ride."

• The subconscious may continue to associate alcohol or drugs with reward and pleasure. These subconscious ideas then become material for dreams.

• There seems to be a tendency for people to have more relapse dreams when they are going through a particular stressful time in their life. If the alcoholic is not dealing well with the stress, the mind may turn to drinking in its dreams having learned in the past to associate stress "relief" with alcohol. Better stress coping mechanisms in awake hours may help mitigate these kinds of relapse dreams.

It has been suggested that relapse dreams can be *beneficial* in a number of ways. If a person wakes up feeling disquieted by the dream, this can be a positive sign. This reaction is evidence that they are taking getting sober seriously and that they cherish their sobriety. It can be a good reminder of what might lay in store if they do not do the right things in the future. It may motivate them to redouble their efforts, and this is always going to be a good thing.[3]

Sometimes these relapse dreams could be a sign that something is not quite right. It will be then up to the individual to evaluate their current situation to see where they could be going wrong. In these circumstances, it may make sense to discuss this specific topic with a therapist.[4]

Sleep "Hygiene"

Practicing good "sleep hygiene" can help prevent sleep deprivation, which in turn is one of the factors that can bring on nightmares in adults. What is it? Put simply it is making your bedroom a relaxing, tranquil place that is reserved for sleep and sex, so that you don't associate it with stressful activities.[5] It also includes practices such as:

• Going to bed at the same time each night and rising at the same time each morning.

• Making sure your bedroom is a quiet, dark, and relaxing environment, which is neither too hot nor too cold.

• Making sure your bed is comfortable and use it only for sleeping and not for other activities, such as reading, watching TV, or listening to music. Remove all TVs, computers, and other "gadgets" from the bedroom.[6]

GENERAL TIPS TO IMPROVE SLEEPING

There are things that people can do to increase their chances of getting a good sleep at night. Many of these are just common sense, but they become much more important in a post-drinking world because of the body's sensitive state. These include:

The Bed

Your bed may be causing some of your most obvious and immediate issues, and it is good to get that part of your sleeping situation in place before chasing some of the more difficult ones. Ideas include:

- **Get a new bed.** Strongly consider investing in a new bed. If your old bed is actually *old*, odds are it probably smells *bad* from alcohol whether you realize it or not. The bed also probably does not having the support you want/need now that you will: A) not be thrashing around, and/or B) lying like a log in a drunken stupor in the exact same place for hours and hours.

I do not use the word "investing" lightly. Invest the time, energy and money that you would in buying a car to buy this new bed (make it new—*not* used—God knows where it has been). A new bed may help a *huge* amount—depending on the state of your old bed—in getting to sleep faster, staying that way, and even reducing/diminishing post-sobriety nightmares. I did this after several months of fitful sleep and noticed an almost immediate improvement.

There is no one "right" bed—it is very, very personal in terms of what it needs to support, how it does it, even down to the size and materials. For these kinds of purchases, I strongly advise consulting Consumer Reports (*www.consumerreports.org*), as they do a great, unbiased job on these kinds of large, dozens-to-choose-from physical purchases. An online subscription is cheap ($30) and well worth the money, or you can go to the local library and reference back copies (and maybe even online access) for free.[7]

- **Experiment with sleeping positions.** Figure out what head and body positions (one head position can have multiple body positions, and vice versa) work best for you, both in terms of getting to sleep and "managing" nightmares. There is no single best way for this in terms of position combination or finding out which one works best for you. It is trial and error. This was extra challenging for me in that concurrent with getting sober I had intestinal surgery, which prevented me from my favorite positions that were based on my lying on my stomach.

- **Look for "props" to help you.** This can include full-body pillows to wrap your arms and legs around, and even a pillow on your forehead/eyes can sometimes help.[8] Pillows in general can be very important.[9]

The Room

People often discount the general setup of their bedroom, both tangible and intangible. This is a mistake. Ideas include:

- **Pay attention to the sleeping room temperature.** I have found that sleeping in too warm temperatures can cause a problem getting to sleep. Too cold temperatures (without being prepared for them) can cause you to wake up prematurely. Cold air can be very helpful for slowing down your metabolism. The concept of "cold air" dorms in colleges is based on this premise, e.g., cooling down the raging hormones of youth to get them to fall asleep.

- **Focus the room on sleeping.** Avoid having (or watching) a TV or any other type of entertainment (excepting sex) in your bedroom. This mentally reinforces the idea that going to bed is about going to sleep (and sex). Most if not all TV shows are designed to be stimulants—NOT make you fall asleep (advertisers get cranky at that sort of thing).

Sleeping "Prep"

Good sleeping starts before you get into bed, or even enter the room. This includes:

- **Sleep Hygiene.** Diligently practice good "sleep hygiene" (discussed earlier), particularly by developing a sleeping schedule and stick to it. This means deciding on an appropriate time to go to bed and to wake up.

- **Relaxing environment.** Create a relaxing environment prior to going to bed putting you in the right mood for sleep. This could mean dimming the lights and listening to relaxing music.[10] I like listening to a book on tape section that I've listened to before. It provides something I can use to occupy my mind but at the same time introduces a degree of repetition (e.g., boredom) that helps me drift off to sleep. White noise such as air filters or even gadgets built for that specific purpose can be very relaxing and can drown out nighttime noises (very helpful if you live in a city environment).

- **Relaxing Drinks.** Drink certain kinds of liquids known to be helpful in dealing with sleep disorders, such as hot milk or chamomile tea. Some people advocate hot chocolate, but for some the caffeine and/or sugar that hot chocolate contains can defeat the purpose. A number of teas, several with relaxation, anxiety reduction, and sleep benefits are discussed in Level 8.

- **Stretching.** Perform stretching exercises as a stress reducer and relaxer. This is *greatly* underappreciated as a stress reliever. Consider practicing relaxation techniques such as meditation and yoga (discussed shortly).

- **Attention to Detail.** Don't neglect the "little" things. These are ones that are normally associated with going to sleep, and by themselves might seem negligible but can add up. Little things include changing into bed clothes (or removing your clothes), turning off the lights, letting the dog out, locking up, running the dishwasher, brushing your teeth, etc. All things you would normally do, *but* if you wait until *just* before you go to bed they won't have time to impress upon your sub-conscious that it is really time to go to sleep. If you do them about 30 minutes to an hour before you are in bed and turn off the last light, it allows more time to impact your sub-conscious. In fact. if possible you should start getting ready for bed at least 1 hour before actually getting into bed.

That's silly you say? Why? It's not any different than your triggers sub-consciously making you want to drink—you have likely been associating them for years. There's no law that says you can't use association for positive purposes! Getting ready for bed sends a real message to your brain to get ready for sleep. And even if doing this will only help you get to sleep a little bit faster, it will still be *helping.* You may find it to be consciously relaxing as well—providing you with a kind of sense of order or completeness to the day.

Daily Habits

Things that you do, or don't do, during the day can have a significant impact on the ability and overall quality of sleep. These include:

- **Avoid day-time napping.** Pretty self-explanatory, but hard to do, particularly after a crappy night of sleep. Avoid it if at all possible.

- **Pay *particular* attention to medication side effects.** If you are like most people, you never pay attention to the side effects of your doctors' prescriptions (or Over The Counter medicines). Unless you doctor is very aware of your sleeping problems (not to mention alcohol problems), then odds are he won't pay much attention to the side effects either! But they can be huge. As alcoholics when we were taking medicines while we were drinking, the very strong odds are we didn't care at all about them[11]. Indeed, any meds that caused insomnia would likely be blasted through by some form of passing out. But in sobriety their sleep-disrupting effects can be very significant.

I had to learn this the hard way because of the medicine I had taken periodically in the past (prednisone), which for me really screwed up my sleep in sobriety.[12] Since I had taken it many times over the years (while drinking), it didn't dawn on me to check the side effects. After three weeks of extremely poor sleep (particularly waking up in the middle of the night and not being able to get back to sleep), I checked—and there it was! Sleeping became much easier almost immediately after I stopped taking it.[13]

• **Avoid all caffeinated drinks.** Do this from the late afternoon onwards.

> *Ya it's weird to get used to going to sleep and waking up when you been used to passing out and coming to. I found that a brisk walk and cutting down on the coffee we inhale when we stop drinking [helps a great deal]. Try to get a routine around bedtime just like you would for your kids, if you have them: healthy supper, brisk walk, hot shower/bath, read a story or watch a little TV and lights out same time every night. Get up at the same time whether you slept through the night or not and eventually your body will begin to relax on its own at bedtime :)*
>   *Hot chocolate helps sometimes.*
>
> newbee1, dailystrength.org

• **Avoid eating in the couple of hours before going to bed.** If you like to eat large meals, try to do it as early in the evening as you can. Perhaps even changing your biggest meal from dinner to breakfast or lunch will yield surprising results.

• **Get as much fresh air as you can.** It can greatly calm the mind for some people. This can range from doing as many activities such as exercise as you can outdoors to sleeping with the window open.

Sleep Interruptions

Odds are it will be quite some time before you sleep through the night without interruptions. When this happens, consider:

• If you wake up from a nightmare, you may have a strong chance of returning to it if you immediately go back to sleep. Get up, go the bathroom, get a drink of water, etc., so you take a break of 2 to 5 minutes (no more). A break will allow your brain to "forget" the nightmare yet still keep it sleepy enough to go back to sleep relatively easily. If *that* doesn't work, resign yourself to maybe 1–2 hours of doing something else. I often find doing that allows me to go back to sleep (if you have that luxury) and get some of the best sleep that I *ever* get in the next 2–4 hours. Otherwise, it often blows up my day with nightmare exhaustion.

• Don't lie in bed for hours fruitlessly trying to sleep. If you can't get to sleep relatively quickly (*particularly* if you have slept for a few hours but wake up in the middle of the night), get up and do something relaxing like reading a book, or boring like working on paperwork.

• A nuance on the previous two points. If you find that you are doing either or both of them frequently, try to make yourself *more* tired. This could mean deliberately staying up for the rest of the night/day if you wake up in the middle of the night. Exercise whenever and wherever you can. You are trying to exhaust your mind and body.

Staying awake on purpose may be pretty unpleasant at first, particularly mid-day when you are dying for a nap from being up for 10–12 hours after only a few hours of sleep. Grind your teeth and get through it. You are essentially trying to retrain your mind (and body) to make the most out of the sleep that you get, and make it stop waking you up! The process may take several days or even weeks, but at the end of it you will sleep like a normal person. Try the other stuff first though.

All of the above are pretty commonsensical (at least they are once you read them) and just require awareness of and diligence in establishing and following new patterns in your newly found sober-sleep-seeking-self. I had to try most of the above to get to the best mix and timing for me. Then more effort to get them all in the right nightly pattern—one I still have not perfected[14]. But I'm getting there!

Two methods for relaxation and sleep preparation that many people swear by are meditation and yoga. It is worthwhile diving into detail about why and how these work, since if you are like me you regarded them as mildly crackpot concepts that had California-crazy written all over them. I'll be the first to admit this was very unfair, and that they *do* work.

SPECIAL METHODS

Meditation

Level 6 introduced the concept of using mediation as an alternative treatment approach for addiction, and discussed in detail various types of meditation. Here we focus on using it specifically for problems getting to sleep. While opinions abound, many believe there are two main ways that meditation can help with sleeping: 1) gear shifting and 2) diversion.

Gear Shifting

Many people (including me) feel that the routines and ritual of sleep preparation are as vitally important as the act (e.g. actually getting into bed, turning the lights off) of going to sleep itself. When you are putting away the dinner dishes, letting the dog out before bed, locking the doors, turning out the lights—you are essentially performing a type of meditation (e.g. moving meditation, discussed earlier), even if you don't realize it as being helpful to your process of getting to sleep. You are in effect down-shifting gears; going from a higher speed gear to a lower one, eventually towards a very low mental and physical speed where you can fall asleep.

Adding an additional, active mediation element even earlier in the process can be helpful as well. A fifteen-minute or half-hour session in the middle of the evening can slow the heart rate and make you feel sedate.

Diversion

Some of the big problems people have trying to get to sleep is rehashing the day's events, or thinking about what you need to get done, or worrying about problems you need to solve. None of those is going to help you go to sleep—quite the opposite. When you are lying there wondering how to slip off, try various elements of the meditation types discussed in Level 6 and their various techniques, such as breathing exercises to help you get to sleep. Here, you could fill your mind with a mental visualization of your breath coming and going, perhaps even counting your breaths. This can divert a restless mind, and even help you stop thinking altogether, which is the nirvana of going to sleep.

Yoga

Yoga is an ancient Indian practice that has been around since at least 3000 BC. In recent decades, it has become fashionable in Western countries as a means to promote health, but it is also a spiritual path. The word *yoga* is Sanskrit for *yoke,* which means *union between mind, body and spirit.*

While Yoga claims many benefits, such as improved physical fitness, flexibility and strength, there are two main benefits that are relevant for alcoholics: 1) as a hobby, particularly as a form of exercise, and 2) as a way of helping you sleep.

Yoga's poses and stretches can provide a surprisingly effective workout to help you drain excess energy and serve as an enjoyable hobby. Yoga may work well as a defense for triggers such as Anxiety and various forms of stress, particularly physical Stress as defined in this book. Exercise in most any form is considered helpful to sleeping, and Yoga certainly qualifies.

More directly, Yoga's breathing techniques (also known as *pranayama*) can help in relaxing your body and making it more ready for sleep.[15] *Prana* is a Sanskrit word that means life force, and *ayama* means extending or stretching. Thus, the word "pranayama" translates to the "control of life force." It is also known as the extension of breath. Research shows that a regular practice of controlled breathing can decrease the effects of stress on the body and increase overall physical and mental health. Common sense also would suggest that when a simple sigh at the end of a long day can be relaxing, something much more practiced should provide much greater benefits.

There is a variety of breathing techniques that are known to reduce stress, aid in digestion, improve sleep, and cool you down. Below are four pranayama exercise areas worth considering, a brief How-To for each, and relevant links.

• *Nadhi Sodhana aka Anuloma Viloma.* Also known as alternative nostril breathing, it is a very relaxed, balancing breath that is used to help calm the nervous system by increasing the amount of oxygen taken into the body.

How to do it: Nadhi sodhana can be done seated or lying down. To start, empty all the air from your lungs. Using the thumb of your dominant hand, block your right nostril and inhale through your left nostril only.

Be sure to inhale into your belly, not your chest. Once you are full of breath, seal your left nostril with the ring finger of the same hand, keeping your right nostril closed, and hold the breath for a moment. Then release your thumb and exhale through your right nostril only. Be sure to exhale all the breath out of the right side and pause before inhaling again through the same side. Seal both nostrils once you've inhaled on the right side and exhaled through the left side. A complete cycle of breath includes an inhalation and exhalation through both nostrils. If you're just starting out, you can do a four-count inhale, holding your breath for four to eight counts, then exhale for four counts. Perform up to ten cycles and notice how your body responds. You may feel more relaxed and calm in both your mind and body.

When to do it: Nadhi sodhana is a calm, soothing breath that can be done any time of day. Try practicing this technique when you are anxious, nervous, or having trouble falling asleep.[16]

• *Kapalabhati Pranayama.* Kapalabhati is an invigorating breath that can build heat in the body. I have not tried this for sleeping as it seems a bit counter-intuitive. Indeed it is more for when you are feeling sluggish or cold, but I include it here for completeness.

How to do it: Start by sitting in a comfortable seat with a tall, straight spine, and exhale completely. Inhale briefly through both nostrils, then sharply exhale (again out of your nose) while pulling your navel in toward your spine. The exhalation is short and quick, but very active, while the inhalation is short and passive. Again, pull your navel in as you exhale and soften it on the inhalation. Do one round of 30 (counting your exhalations) and rest for a minute with some deep breaths in between. Repeat. If this seems strenuous, start with 15 and gradually work your way up.

When to do it: Kapalabhati is great to do in the morning if you're feeling chilly or sluggish. You may also try it when you're feeling congested or bloated, but don't try it on a full stomach. Avoid this technique if you are pregnant, or suffer from blood pressure issues or heart conditions.[17]

• *Ujjayi Pranayama.* Ujjayi means victorious breath; it's also referred to as ocean breath due to the sound it creates. Ujjayi encourages full expansion of the lungs, and, by focusing your attention on your breath, can assist in calming the mind.

How to do it: Find a place where you can sit comfortably with a straight spine. Take a steady breath in through both nostrils. Inhale until you reach your lung capacity; maintain a tall spine. Hold your breath for a second, and then constrict some of the breath at the back of your throat, as if you were about to whisper a secret, and exhale slowly through both nostrils. This exhalation will sound like an ocean wave or gentle rush of air. You should feel the air on the roof of your mouth as you exhale. Repeat up to 20 times.

When to do it: This breath can be practiced for up to 10 minutes any time of day. Try it with an asana practice (yoga postures or poses) as well.[18]

• *Sitali Pranayama. Sitali* also means cooling, which explains the effect it can have on your mind and body. This breath encourages clearing heat with coolness. It's especially helpful during the summer and in hot climates.

How to do it: Roll your tongue until the outer edges touch, forming a tube. If you can't curl your tongue, make an oval shape with your mouth, keeping your tongue flat. Inhale through your mouth, taking in all the air that you can. It may make a hissing sound. After inhaling, bring the tip of your tongue to the roof of your mouth and seal your lips. Feel the coolness of the inhalation in your month then exhale through your nose. Repeat five to ten times or as needed.

When to do it: If you're feeling overheated, irritable, or find yourself waiting impatiently in hot weather, sitali is a great tool to try to cool off and relax![19]

Helpful Tips for getting started on any of these techniques include:

• *You be the judge.* If you feel any discomfort or lightheadedness, stop immediately and return to normal breathing. Consult an instructor for guidance and supervision.

• *Never force or restrict your breath.* Don't compromise the quality of the breath. Do the best that you can. The more you practice, the longer you'll be able to perform the exercises, and eventually, you'll be able to use more of your lung capacity.

• *Patience and practice.* Pranayama should be done with great care and awareness. Try to stay focused on the journey, not the destination! Over time, you will start to notice the benefits of the practice.

- *Precautions.* If you are pregnant, or suffer from diabetes, high or low blood pressure, heart conditions, epilepsy, or vertigo, please consult your health care provider before performing any of these breathing exercises.[20]

Sleep Aids (Prescription and Over the Counter)

There are a number of sleep aids—primarily prescription, but also over the counter (OTC)—that purport to help getting you to sleep. Before I provide a brief overview of some of them, there are two key considerations: 1) again; I am *not* a doctor, and 2) I do *not* recommend using them in any case.

Why the second point? As I introduced in Level 9, it is possible that you may have what is called an "addictive personality," such that you may be more susceptible to another addiction besides alcohol. There is no way of knowing: no "test" for such a thing, if it truly exists. Since by definition sleep-aids induce chemical changes in the body, I think you are just begging for trouble if you use these often. Even if they do not have any addictive chemical in them, it is still a Bad Habit waiting to happen.

Another more murky concern is how you will react to them. I found this out the hard way. Once when leaving an event, I took the sleep aid *Zolpidem* (brand names Ambien, Intermezzo, Stilnox, Stilnoct, Sublinox, Hypnogen and Zolsana), thinking I'd be ready for bed when I got home. Big mistake. I was weaving all over the place and badly reacting to road signs and such that I got pulled over by the police (that had never happened during my drinking days). Fortunately, I got off with just a moving violation, but they could easily have hauled me in for something more serious. The scary part was that I *knew* I was driving badly, and could do nothing to correct it. It wasn't as if I was falling asleep; it was that my mind, motor reflexes, and coordination were completely bonkers.

Alcoholics may be tempted—particularly those with many (lucky) years of driving after (or while) drinking without incident—to drive, operate machinery, etc. after taking a sleep aid. Trust me: that "experience" means *nothing*.

Prescription Sleep Aids

There are many, so I'm not going to try and synthesize a list from multiple sources. Best to hear it from the best (I think) and most well-known online medical source: WebMD.

TABLE 7: SLEEPING PILLS: THE PROS AND CONS[21]

Drug(s) How It Works	Duration of Effects	Side Effects	Dependence Risk
Diphenhydramine			
Acts on histamine receptors in the brain to cause drowsiness.	4–6 hours (sleepiness may last longer)	Daytime sleepiness; confusion and difficulty urinating in older people.	Low
SELECTIVE GABA MEDICINES: Ambien (zolpidem tartrate), **Ambien CR** (zolpidem tartrate extended release), **Lunesta** (eszopiclone), **Sonata** (zaleplon)			
Binds to a specific type of GABA receptor in the brain.	6–8 hours	Usually few. Memory disturbances, hallucinations, behavior changes possible.	Medium (usually low)
SLEEP-WAKE CYCLE MODIFIERS: Rozerem (ramelteon)			
Stimulates *melatonin* receptors in the brain area that controls the sleep-wake cycle.	4–6 hours	Headache, drowsiness, dizziness. Uncommonly, problems with sex drive. Loss of menses or problems getting pregnant.	Low
BENZODIAZEPINES: Ativan (lorazepam), **Halcion** (triazolam), **Restoril** (temazepam), **Valium** (diazepam), **Xanax** (alprazolam)			
Binds to general GABA receptors in the brain.	Varies (from 4 hours to more than 12)	Sedation, loss of muscle coordination, dizziness, habit-forming.	Higher
TRICYCLIC ANTIDEPRESSANTS: Adapin (doxepin), **Aventyl** (nortriptyline), **Elavil** (amitriptyline), **Pamelor** (nortriptyline), **Sinequan** (doxepin), **Trazodone** (desyrel)			
Binds to multiple brain receptors including acetylcholine; sedating.	Not well studied	Low at usual doses for insomnia. Dizziness, blurry vision, difficulty urinating, cardiac arrhythmias possible. **Trazodone** can cause prolonged, painful erections.	Low

An additional excellent resource describing sleep aids can be found at *www.webmd.com/sleep-disorders/insomnia-medications*. One warning on this website that I did not take to heart (and almost paid dearly for it, beyond the $150 ticket) was: *"All insomnia medications should be taken shortly before bed. Do not attempt to drive or perform other activities that require concentration after taking an insomnia drug because it will make you sleepy."* It should have added *"and stopped by the police."* Talk to your doctor if you are interested in these, as some of these obviously need special knowledge to be used correctly, and depending on the specific composition and dosage may need a prescription. AND if you already take other drugs there may be ugly complications. Whole books can (and are) written on these medicines/chemicals.

Over the Counter Sleep Aids

Most of the above sleeping pills are *antihistamines*. They work well but can cause some drowsiness the next day. They're often safe enough to be sold without a prescription. However, if you're taking other drugs that also contain *antihistamines*—like cold or allergy medications—you could inadvertently take too much.

I was glad to find that WebMD did not reject the notion of natural sleep aids. Their suggestions include:

NATURAL INSOMNIA REMEDIES:
Foods, Herbs, and Supplements

- **Melatonin** is a hormone that helps regulate the sleep/wake cycle, an internal pacemaker that controls the timing and our drive for sleep. It causes drowsiness, lowers body temperature, and puts the body into sleep mode.

  Research on melatonin in people with insomnia is mixed. Some research shows that taking it restores and improves sleep in people with insomnia. Other studies show that melatonin does not help people with insomnia stay asleep. *It is not regulated by the FDA and can have problems with purity. You should only use it under close supervision by a doctor.*

- **Warm milk.** You can put a tasty spin on your grandmother's natural insomnia remedy by sipping warm milk before bed. Almond milk is an excellent source of calcium, which helps the brain make melatonin. Plus, warm milk may spark pleasant and relaxing memories of your mother helping you fall asleep.[22]

- **Sleepy-time snacks.** The best sleep-inducing foods include a combination of protein and carbohydrates, says Shelby Harris, PsyD. She's the director of the behavioral sleep medicine program at the Sleep-Wake Disorders Center at Montefiore Medical Center in Bronx, N.Y.

  Harris suggests a light snack of half a banana with a tablespoon of peanut butter, or a whole wheat cracker with some cheese. Eat one of these snacks about 30 minutes before hitting the hay.

- **Magnesium** apparently plays a key role with sleep. Research has shown that even a marginal lack of it can prevent the brain from settling down at night. You can get magnesium from food. Good sources include green leafy vegetables, wheat germ, pumpkin seeds, and almonds. *Check with your doctor before taking magnesium supplements.* Magnesium can interact with many different medications, and too much of it can cause serious health issues.

- **Lavender.** Lavender oil is calming and can help encourage sleep in some people with insomnia, research shows. "Try taking a hot bath with lavender oil before bed to relax your body and mind," Harris says.

- **Valerian root.** This medicinal herb has been used to treat sleep problems since ancient times. "Valerian can be sedating and may help you fall asleep," says Tracey Marks, MD, an Atlanta-based psychiatrist.

  Research on the effectiveness of valerian for insomnia is mixed. Marks says if you try valerian as a sleep remedy, be patient. It can take a few weeks for it to take effect. *Talk to your doctor before taking valerian and follow label directions.*

- **L-theanine.** This amino acid found in green tea leaves may help combat anxiety that interferes with sleep. A 2007 study showed that L-theanine reduced heart rate and immune responses to stress. It is thought to work by boosting the amount of a feel-good hormone your body makes. It also induces brain waves linked to relaxation. *Talk to your doctor before taking it.*[23]

One exception to my distaste for mind-modifying sleep aids is herbal sedatives, which may be a good transition "tool" for some in my view.[24] Some herbal teas specifically market themselves as nighttime relaxation/sleep beverages, and some of their ingredients are supported by the WebMD overview above (See Level 8 for more information on these teas).

Regardless, try to **avoid making it or any substance a long-term method for getting and staying sleeping—at some point, you need to go** *au naturel* **in my opinion.**

APPENDIX B

The Conquer Program Checklists

Appendix B provides a number of checklists and templates to help you with many of the Levels in the Conquer Program. I suggest you make at least one copy of each one, and use them as you read each applicable Level to identify, develop, and adjust the appropriate information. (Remember, at its core this book is a "How To" book, so don't be shy about marking it up too). For electronic (and print book) readers, go to http://www.conqueryouraddiction.com/Templates.html to download and print these documents in PDF format.

The checklists and templates include:

LEVEL 1—Admit You Have an Addiction to Alcohol
Checklist 1a: The Conquer Program Levels
Checklist 1b: The Conquer Quiz Checklist and Scorecard

LEVEL 2—Know Your Triggers
Checklist 2a: Possible Triggers Checklist
Checklist 2b: Drinking Triggers History and Target Checklist

LEVEL 3—Listen to Your Body!
Checklist 3: Health Problems Checklist

LEVEL 4—Engage Friends and Family
Checklist 4: Friends and Family Selection Checklist

LEVEL 7—Join a Community
Checklist 7: Community Schedule and Checklist

LEVEL 8—Break Bad Habits
Checklist 8: Bad Habits Checklist

LEVEL 9—Develop New Hobbies
Checklist 9: Possible Hobbies Checklist

LEVEL 13—Develop Your Defense Progressions
Template 13a: Trigger Defense Progression Template
Template 13b: Generic Progression Template

CHECKLIST 1A: THE CONQUER PROGRAM LEVELS

Level	Description	Date Started	Date Completed	Comments
1.	Admit You Are an Alcoholic			Score:____/45; See Conquer Quiz Scorecard
2.	Know Your Triggers			See Drinking Trigger checklist
3.	Listen to Your Body!			See Alcoholic Health checklist
4.	Engage Friends and Family			See Friends and Family Selection checklist
5.	Detox			Supervised or unsupervised?
6.	Join a Community			See Join a Community checklist
7.	• Rehab—Inpatient			
	• Rehab—Outpatient			
	• Therapy (Type)_____			
8.	Break Bad Habits			See Bad Habits checklist
9.	Develop New Hobbies			See Hobbies checklist
10.	Consider Spirituality			
11.	Make Yourself Sick of Alcohol			Optional
12.	The Last Detox			Optional
13.	Develop Your Defense Progressions			See Progression examples and templates

CHECKLIST 1B: THE CONQUER QUIZ CHECKLIST AND SCORECARD

#	Sign of Alcoholism	Yes/ Agree	Points Possible	Points Awarded	Comments/ Explanation
1	Personality Changes (Nasty Drunk)		1, 2 or 3		1 point if once a month; 2 if twice a month; 3 points if more than twice a month OR police have had to come to your home responding to drunken arguments. In this case you may require Anger Management, specialized counseling.
2	Personality Changes (Other)		1		While subjective, it includes regularly (while drinking) acting very uncharacteristically, e.g., very loud when you are normally quiet, vice versa, etc.
3	You plan Day/Night around Drinking		1		Includes drinking "trumping" all other non-drinking responsibilities on a frequent basis.
4	You rotate place of alcohol purchases		1		You do this deliberately, and regularly
5	You are a Binge Drinker		1, 2 or 3		When you drink, you drink very heavily (more than 4–5 drinks in 2–3 hours, depending on gender/body weight). 2 times a month is 1 point; 3–4 times a month is 2 points; 5 or more times a month is 3 points.
6	You say "I can stop anytime I want to" frequently; defensive when people comment on usage		1		Usually comes up in "you are drinking too much" arguments. 1 point if you say at least once every two months.

#	Sign of Alcoholism	Yes/ Agree	Points Possible	Points Awarded	Comments/ Explanation
7	You drink in the morning		1 or 2		Meaning you drink before lunchtime. 2 points if you do it at least once a month.
8	Can't drink alone, coerce people to drink with you; or strong desire to drink alone		1		Depends on personality; indicator of extremes .
9	Irritable when drinking time nears or goes past; Always start drinking at certain times		1		Sign of physical dependency
10	You hide booze		1 or 2		2 points if you start forgetting where you hide them
11	You smell from alcohol		1, 2, or 3		Once a week, 1 Point. Twice a week, 2 points. Pretty much all the time: 3 points.
12	You sneak and lie about booze		1		You do this more than twice a month
13	You can't sleep without alcohol		1		Consider counting as 1 point if you can sleep but usually have very bad nightmares
14	Usually last to leave bar/party		1		You do this more often than you don't
15	You have alcoholism in your family		1 or 2		Parents 1 point; plus grandparents 2 points
16	You think you do certain things "better" drunk. You are more fun and interesting.		1		Particular emphasis on the word "think." It is subjective, so be honest (if you can).

#	Sign of Alcoholism	Yes/ Agree	Points Possible	Points Awarded	Comments/ Explanation
17	Your appearance has changed dramatically		1		This is subjective, but compare recent photos with photos of parent(s) at your age.
18	Not drinking is a major occasion or accomplishment		1		You go to bed pleased with yourself that you didn't drink that day.
19	Poor airplane behavior with respect to drinks		1		Regularly (more often than you don't). Usually drinking more than 2 drinks on one flight counts as well.
20	Spend time planning/ getting alcohol "fix" when you are out-of-town		1 or 2		2 points if you pre-plan your alcohol purchase before you leave town.
THE BIG FIVE					
21	2 or more DUIs		3		Counts even if you get case dismissed for non-alcohol causes or technicalities
22	Job Loss due to alcohol		3		Definite Yes if on-the-job drinking is cited as cause. Can be subjective but be honest.
23	Marriage Loss due to alcohol		3		Definite Yes if cited in divorce documents
24	Financial Loss due to alcohol		3		Includes spending over $300/month on alcohol purchases that *you* consume
25	Health Problems due to alcohol		3		See Listen to Your Body! Checklist
	TOTAL		**45**		

CHECKLIST 2A: POSSIBLE TRIGGERS CHECKLIST

Trigger	Major?	Related Triggers	Specifics/ Comments	Tips/ Defenses
Anger				
Anxiety				
Boredom				
Change				
Depression				
Escape				
Envy				
Extreme Emotions (Grief)				
Frustration				
Fun				

LEVEL 2—Know Your Triggers

Trigger	Major?	Related Triggers	Specifics/ Comments	Tips/ Defenses
Guilt				
Health (Pain)				
Holidays (& special occasions)				
Hungry				
Insomnia				
Job				
Kids				
Loneliness				
Media				
Mid-Life Crisis				
Money				

Trigger	Major?	Related Triggers	Specifics/Comments	Tips/Defenses
Music				
Noise				
Disorder				
Overconfidence				
Peer Pressure (Friends)				
Powerlessness				
Proximity				
Quitting (Fear of)				
Relatives				
Relationships				
Reminders				
Sex				

Trigger	Major?	Related Triggers	Specifics/Comments	Tips/Defenses
Smell				
Social Situations				
Stress (Physical)				
Taste				
Times of Day				
Tired				
Unfun/Uninteresting				
Victim (Abuse, Self-Esteem)				
Weather				
(e)X Spouse/Partner				
Yelling (Confrontation)				
Zeal (Excitement)				

CHECKLIST 2B: DRINKING TRIGGERS HISTORY AND TARGET CHECKLIST

Trigger	Early Alcoholism (Yrs. ___ to ___)	Middle Alcoholism (Yrs. ___ to ___)	Late Alcoholism (Yrs. ___ to ___)	Today	Target (Within 1 Year from Now)
Anger					
Anxiety					
Boredom					
Change					
Depression					
Escape					
Envy					
Extreme Emotions					
Frustration					
Fun					

Trigger	Early Alcoholism (Yrs. ___ to ___)	Middle Alcoholism (Yrs. ___ to ___)	Late Alcoholism (Yrs. ___ to ___)	Today	Target (Within 1 Year from Now)
Guilt					
Health					
Holidays					
Hungry					
Insomnia					
Job					
Kids					
Loneliness					
Media					
Mid-Life Crisis					
Money					
Music					

Trigger	Early Alcoholism (Yrs. ___ to ___)	Middle Alcoholism (Yrs. ___ to ___)	Late Alcoholism (Yrs. ___ to ___)	Today	Target (Within 1 Year from Now)
Noise					
Disorder					
Overconfidence					
Peer Pressure					
Powerlessness					
Proximity					
Quitting (Fear of)					
Relatives					
Relationships					
Reminders					
Sex					
Smell					

LEVEL 2—Know Your Triggers

Trigger	Early Alcoholism (Yrs. ___ to ___)	Middle Alcoholism (Yrs. ___ to ___)	Late Alcoholism (Yrs. ___ to ___)	Today	Target (Within 1 Year from Now)
Social Situations					
Stress					
Taste					
Times of Day					
Tired					
Unfun/Uninteresting					
Victim (Abuse, Self-Esteem)					
Weather					
(e)X Wife/Partner/etc.					
Yelling (Confrontation)					
Zeal (Excitement)					

CHECKLIST 3: HEALTH PROBLEMS CHECKLIST

Condition/ Disease	Year Started	Severity (1–10)	Your Symptoms	Defense Action Taken/ Doctor's Comments
Alcoholism—Family History (at least 2 generations)				
Anxiety (e.g., GAD)				
Bad Breath (chronic)				
Breast Cancer (incl. Family History)				
Cancer—Other (incl. Family History)				
Cardiomyopathy				
Chronic Fatigue Syndrome				
Crohn's Disease				
Dementia (incl. Family History)				
Depression (incl. Family History)				

Condition/ Disease	Year Started	Severity (1–10)	Your Symptoms	Defense Action Taken/ Doctor's Comments
Digestive Problems				
Fetal Alcohol Syndrome [1]				
Fibromyalgia				
Gallstones				
Gastritis				
Gum Disease				
Heart Problems (incl. Family History)				
Heartburn (chronic)				
Hemorrhoids				
Hormonal Imbalance				
Hypertension				

Condition/ Disease	Year Started	Severity (1–10)	Your Symptoms	Defense Action Taken/ Doctor's Comments
Jaundice				
Irritable Bowel Syndrome				
Liver Disease				
Lung Disease				
Memory Problems				
Menopause Problems				
Metabolic Syndrome				
Oral Cancer				
Pancreatitis				
Panic Attacks				
Post Traumatic SD (PTSD)				

Condition/ Disease	Year Started	Severity (1–10)	Your Symptoms	Defense Action Taken/ Doctor's Comments
Restless Leg Syndrome				
Schizophrenia				
Sexual Dysfunction				
Skin Problems				
Suicidal Thoughts				
Tinnitus				
Ulcerative Colitis				
Ulcers				
Wet Brain				
Other				

CHECKLIST 4: FRIENDS AND FAMILY SELECTION CHECKLIST

Criteria	Person 1	Person 2	Person 3	Person 4	Comments
Are not judgmental and can be objective					
Have a basic understanding of alcoholism as a disease					
Are fairly patient					
Are not gossips					
Are decent listeners					
Are willing to dedicate a reasonable amount of free time for you					
Will be there in an emergency.					
TOTAL					

Possible Rating Schemes: For each person and criteria, rate them either with an X (the person with the most X's "wins"), or if you want to be more elaborate, give them a 1 (low), 2 (med), or 3 (high), for how well they meet the criteria. The person with the highest score wins. You can select more than one person of course, but they need to expect to dedicate a large amount of time to you over the coming months.

CHECKLIST 7: COMMUNITY SCHEDULE AND CHECKLIST

Meeting	Monday	Tuesday	Wednesday	Thursday	Friday	Saturday	Sunday

List the meeting group or name you can remember, and then list the time(s) for each meeting by day. Use those days/times to populate the progression you use these meetings for (e.g., Boredom), and as a handy reference if you start to get "itchy" (thinking about drinking too much), anxious, or otherwise feeling a bit vulnerable to alcohol. You might also program them in as a destination in your GPS unit or phone application you can easily get there no matter where you are when you start to feel this way. Also consider getting a sponsor (if your community has that concept). Recognize that they might not understand you wanting them as a sponsor if you are following another program (e.g., this one), and not theirs.

CHECKLIST 8: BAD HABITS CHECKLIST

Bad Habit	Severity/Frequency	Method for Breaking	Comments
Alienating others			
Attention-seeking behavior			
Chronic lateness, procrastination			
Constantly complaining, being argumentative			
(Excessive) cursing			
Eavesdropping			
Freeloading			
Gossiping			
Impulsive behavior to the point of recklessness			
Interrupting			

LEVEL 8—BREAK BAD HABITS

Bad Habit	Severity/Frequency	Method for Breaking	Comments
Lying, exaggerating			
Monopolizing the conversation			
Nitpicking, being critical and controlling			
(Deliberate and excessive) non-conformity, often for its own sake			
Reacting quickly and often without thinking to various things, often with bad consequences			
(Not) smiling when the situation clearly calls for it			
Whining			
Others			

CHECKLIST 9: POSSIBLE HOBBIES CHECKLIST

Hobby	Trigger(s) Addressed	Specifics
AA (e.g., attending meetings), Antiques, Art/Arts and Crafts, Astrology, Astronomy		
Ballet/Ballroom/Belly Dancing, Beadwork/Beading, Biking, Bird watching, Bowling, Bug Hunting (finding computer programming errors), Bumper Stickers (creating)		
Camping, Candle Making, Carpentry, Cave Exploration, Clubs and Lodges (join and be active), Coaching, Collecting (e.g., coins, stamps, autographs, etc.), Cooking, Crocheting		
Dancing (many sub examples), Driving, Dog Training, Drawing/ Sketching		
Embroidery, Engraving, Exercise (many sub examples)		

Hobby	Trigger(s) Addressed	Specifics
Fantasy Sports, Fashion Designing, Feng Shui, Fishing, Floral Arrangements, Foreign Language (Learn one)		
Games (Computer/non-Computer —many sub examples and can be combined with others such as Clubs), Gardening, Genealogy, Glass Etching, Golfing		
Hiking, Horse Riding, Hunting		
Ice Skating, Internet (Surfing), Irish Dancing		
Jamming/Jarring, Jewelry Making, Journaling, Judo		
Kayaking, Kickboxing, Knitting		

Hobby	Trigger(s) Addressed	Specifics
Latin Dances, Leather Working		
Martial Arts (many sub examples), Magic (learn), Meditation, Meetings, Models (Build), Movies, Music (many sub examples)		
Online Hobbies (Blogging, Chatting, Dating, Games, Music, Social Networking), Organize (Filing, Closets, etc.), Origami		
Painting, Paper Crafts, Pets (many sub examples), Photography, Pool (e.g., Billiards)		
Quilting		
Racing, Radio (Ham), Reading, Recipe Collecting, Renovation, Rock/Mountain Climbing		

Hobby	Trigger(s) Addressed	Specifics
Sailing/Boating, Sand Art, School (Go back to), Scale Modeling, Scrapbooking, Sculpting, Sewing, Skating, Skiing, Singing, Sudoku, Sports (many sub examples), Stained Glass (making), Swimming		
Teaching, Toy Making, Traveling, Trekking, Tutoring		
Video Creation (e.g., YouTube), Volunteer Work (many sub examples)		
Web Site (Create, Edit), Wood Carving/Woodworking, Writing (many sub examples)		
Yoga		
Zoos (Visit, volunteer)		

Trigger Defense Progression Template

Tips/Defense	Description	Time	Duration	Comment

Generic Progression Template

Tip/Defense	Description

Website Resources

This book references numerous resources to help you Conquer Your Alcoholism. Those and more are listed here. While many are clearly intended as a marketing tool for the site's product or services (or to attract advertisers), the ones listed seem to do a good job of providing important information relevant to the section they are listed under.

Alcoholism General Information

- About.com (alcoholism): *www.alcoholism.about.com*

- American Medical Association: *www.ama-assn.org/ama*

- American Society of Addiction Medicine: *www.asam.org*

- Center for Disease Control (CDC): *www.cdc.gov/alcohol/fact-sheets/ alcohol-use.htm*

- Cigna Substance Abuse Information and Webinars: *www.cigna.com/ healthwellness/behavioral-awareness-series/coping-with-substance-abuse*

- DARA (Drug and Alcohol Asia) Web site: *http://alcoholrehab.com/alcohol-rehab/*

- "Science of Addiction and Recovery" *www.addictscience.com*

- The Mayo Clinic: *www.mayoclinic.com*

- Medhelp.org (as best as I can tell a competitor to Web MD): *www.medhelp.org/posts/Alcoholism/*

- The National Council on Alcoholism and Drug Dependence: *www.ncadd.org*

- Web MD: *www.webmd.com*

- Wikipedia (general information source, particularly definitions): *www.wikipedia.org*

Alcoholism Support Programs (for Family and Friends)

- Al-Anon Family Groups: *www.Al-anon.alateen.org*
- Families Anonymous: *familiesanonymous.org*
- Nar-Anon Family Groups: *www.nar-anon.org*

Alcoholism Treatment and Related Programs

- Alcoholics Anonymous World Services: *www.aa.org*
- Cocaine Anonymous: *www.ca.org*
- Co-Dependents Anonymous World Fellowship: *www.coda.org*
- Do It Now: *www.doitnow.org* (drugs and alcohol publications at *www.doitnow.org/pages/alcohol.html*)
- Dual-Recovery Anonymous: *www.draonline.org/*
- (Over)Eaters Anonymous: *www.oa.org/*
- Faces and Voices of Recovery: *www.facesandvoicesofrecovery.org*
- Gamblers Anonymous: *www.gambleranonymous.org* ?
- LifeRing Secular Recovery: *http://lifering.org/*
- Narcotics Anonymous World Services: *www.na.org*
- Rational Recovery: *www.rational.org*
- Recovery Dynamics: *www.kellyfdn.com/*
- Salvation Army: *www.salvationarmyusa.org*
- Secular Organizations for Sobriety (SOS): *www.sossobriety.org*
- SMART Recovery: *www.smartrecovery.org*
- Substance Abuse and Mental Health Services Administration treatment finder: *www.samhsa.gov/treatment/*
- The Addiction Recovery Guide: *www.addictionrecoveryguide.org/holistic/meditation_spirituality*
- Underearners Anonymous: *www.underearnersanonymous.org/*
- Women for Sobriety: *www.womenforsobriety.org*
- *Links to other "Anonymous" Programs: www.ipass.net/a1idpirat/ anonymousrecoverygroups.html*

Anxiety, Depression and Alcohol

• Alcohol and Depression: *www.webmd.com/depression/alcohol-and-depresssion*

• Depression and Alcohol: *http://alcoholism.about.com/od/depress/Depression_and_Alcohol.htm*

• Depression and Alcoholism: Five Tips for Recovery— *http://psychcentral.com/lib/2010/depression-and-alcoholism-five-tips-for-recovery/*

• Depression and Alcoholism: *www.learn-about-alcoholism.com/depression-and-alcoholism.html*

• Depression and Alcoholism: *www.professional-counselling.com/alcoholism-and-depression.html*

• General Anxiety and Depression Information: *www.anxiety-and-depression-solutions.com*

• Social Anxiety Support: *www.socialanxietysupport.com*

Bad Habit Breakers

• (Deliberately) alienating others—*http://essentialsoffabulous.com/blog/how-to-win-friends-and-stop-alienating-people/*

• Attention-seeking behavior (Look at me! Look at me!)— *www.wikihow.com/Tell-if-You-Are-Self-Absorbed*

• Chronic lateness, procrastination—Lateness: *www.webmd.com/balance/features/help-chronically-late*; Procrastination: *www.huffingtonpost.com/2013/03/20/8-tricks-to-stop-procrastinating_n_2916484.html*

• Constantly complaining, being argumentative—Complaining: *http://women.webmd.com/features/how-i-stopped-complaining-week*; Argumentative: *www.wikihow.com/Stop-Being-Argumentative*

• (Excessive) cursing—*www.wikihow.com/Stop-Swearing*

• Eavesdropping—*http://everydaytipsandthoughts.com/thoughts-for-thursday-how-do-you-handle-eavesdroppers/* (this is from the person being eavesdropped on perspective)

• Freeloading—*http://abcnews.go.com/GMA/MellodyHobson/friends-family-financial-freeloaders/story?id=8756440* (from the perspective of the person whom a freeloader has victimized)

- Gossiping—*http://tinybuddha.com/blog/how-to-stop-gossiping-and-creating-drama/*

- Impulsive behavior to the point of recklessness—*www.ehow.com/how_8631725_stop-being-impulsive.html*

- Interrupting—*www.divinecaroline.com/life-etc/culture-causes/conversation-killers-how-stop-interrupting-others*

- Lying, Exaggerating—Lying: *www.wikihow.com/Stop-Lying*; Exaggerating: *www.greatschools.org/parenting/behavior-discipline/1487-stop-exaggerating.gs* (focused on stopping children from exaggerating, but good in general)

- Monopolizing the conversation—*www.drphil.com/articles/article/93*

- Nitpicking, being critical and controlling—Nitpicking: *www.webmd.com/sex-relationships/features/happy-marriage-no-nitpicking* (in marriage); Being Critical and Controlling: *www.drphil.com/articles/article/93*

- (Deliberate and excessive) non-conformity, often for its own sake—*http://blogs.clc.co.nz/LearningStyles/archive/2011/06/24/dealing-with-non-conformist-learning-styles.aspx* (on children's learning issues)

- (Not) smiling when the situation clearly calls for it—*http://online.wsj.com/article/FA16266C-700C-43A2–9754–16BB0E6F7A5D.html#!FA16266C-700C-43A2–9754–16BB0E6F7A5D*

- Whining—*http://childparenting.about.com/od/behaviordiscipline/a/Child-Discipline-How-To-Stop-Whining-In-Children.htm* (about stopping children from whining)

Blogs, Forums, Chats and Other Alcoholism Information Sources

- About Alcoholism: *http://alcoholism.about.com*
- Alcoholism Coach: *http://alcoholismcoach.com*
- Binge Drinking: *www.cdc.gov/alcohol/fact-sheets/binge-drinking.htm*
- eHow Health: *www.ehow.com/ehow-health/*
- Klean Life (Information on Addiction): *www.kleanlife.com*
- Med Help: *www.medhelp.org/*
- Sober Recovery: *www.soberrecovery.com*
- The Fix (about Addiction and Recovery): *www.thefix.com*

Drug Abuse Information

- Drug Abuse General Info: *www.drugabuse.com*

- Substance Abuse and Mental Health Services Administration treatment finder: *www.samhsa.gov/treatment/*

Hobby Information

- Conventional Hobbies: *www.buzzle.com/articles/list-types-of-hobbies/*

- Finding others who share your interests: *www.meetup.com*

- Pets info: *www.kleanlife.com/therapy/pets-natural-stress-relievers/*

- Unusual Hobbies: *www.thehobbyfiles.com/static_html/sitemap.htm#HL*

Inpatient Rehab Centers

- A General Index of Treatment Centers: *www.theagapecenter.com/Treatment-Centers/index.htm*

- Betty Ford Center: *www.bettyfordcenter.org*

- Drug and Alcohol Rehab Asia: *http://alcoholrehab.com/ebrochure/DARA_eBrochure_1112_Final.pdf*

- Harvey House: *www.addictionadvisor.co.uk/Clinic/Harvey#.UYKejLQo43s*

- Hazelden: *www.hazelden.org*

- Promises Addiction Treatment Center: *www.promises.com*

- Recovery Connection (a Rehab Finder service essentially): *www.recoveryconnection.org*

- Schick Shadel Hospital: *www.schickshadel.com*

- Silver Hill Hospital: *www.silverhillhospital.org*

Intervention Approach Information

- Assistance In Recovery Intervention Model: *http://a-i-r.com/interventions/air-intervention-model/*

- The Community Reinforcement Approach and Family Training (CRAFT) intervention: *www.robertjmeyersphd.com/craft.html*

Outpatient Treatment Resources
(Resource links below may include some
Inpatient information/links to Inpatient Centers)

- New York State OASAS (Office of Alcoholism and Substance Abuse Services): *www.oasas.ny.gov/pio/needhlp.cfm*

- Oxford House: *www.oxfordhouse.org*

- Rehab Treatment Centers by State (majority are outpatient): *www.theagapecenter.com/Treatment-Centers/index.htm*

Therapy Resources

- Association for Behavioral and Cognitive Therapies: *www.abct.org*

- Therapy Styles Overview: *http://alcoholrehab.com/alcohol-rehab/rehab-therapist-styles/*

Miscellaneous Websites and Resources

- Drink Focus *drinkfocus.com*

- Alcoholic Drink.net *alcoholicdrinks.net*

- Wikipedia articles *www.Wikipedia.com*

- International Center for Alcohol Policies Tables *icap.org/table*

- International Center for Alcohol Policies *icap.org*

- History of Alcoholic Beverages *potsdam.edu/hansondj*

- History of Alcohol *nicks.com.au*

Endnotes

Introduction

1 *www.samhsa.gov/*; the study itself is at *www.samhsa.gov/data/NSDUH.aspx*. Samhas. "National Survey on Drug Use and Health." Accessed April 6, 2014.

2 The New York Times. "Effective Addiction Treatment." Accessed March 7, 2014. *http://well.blogs .nytimes.com/2013/02/04/effective-addiction-treatment/*.

3 Both of these drove my editor nuts, but I am convinced they are critical for overall usability.

4 NIAAA. "Alcohol Use Disorders." Accessed May 16, 2014. *www.niaaa.nih.gov/alcohol-health/overview-alcohol-consumption/alcohol-use-disorders.* .

5 The transparent connecting tube in Figure 4 is intended to illustrate how all Levels are connected/integrated in a central defensive core around the alcoholic.

6 There are several types of therapies used in addiction treatment, some that are more suited to the Conquer Program than others. If you tried therapy before but did not do so with any focus on identifying why you drank (e.g. your triggers), then it may be worthwhile trying it again.

7 *National Institute on Alcohol Abuse and Alcoholism* (NIAAA). "What Is A Standard Drink." Accessed May 27, 2014. *www.niaaa.nih.gov/alcohol-health/overview-alcohol-consumption/standard-drink/*. They define a "drink" as a half an ounce of alcohol (e.g., one 12-oz. beer, one 5-oz. glass of wine, or one 1.5-oz. shot of distilled spirits).

8 Some math: The same drink of alcohol hits females twice as hard as males. Put another way, it takes a male twice as much alcohol to achieve the same "effect" (states) as a female. Since the definition of binge drinking is nearly the same for males (5 drinks/2 hours) as females (4 drinks/2 hours), it follows that males are more likely to binge, particularly in efforts to reach a "numb" state. While this analysis has some holes (it assumes males seek desired "states"—particularly being "numb," in the same proportions as females), it is consistent with the fact that males make up 2/3rds of all alcoholics.

9 This is my opinion, but one backed up by a great deal of experience and observation as well as the math above. Among other factors, alcoholism develops in significant part because of the building up of tolerance to alcohol, which in turn results in you drinking more to achieve the same effect (state). To do this generally means cramming in more and more drinks into shorter and shorter time periods, to the point of effectively binging much of the time. There are no studies that I can find that *specifically* correlate binge drinking to alcoholism with hard research and statistics, though nearly all view it as a dangerous practice that often *leads* to alcohol abuse.

10 *Her Best Kept Secret* by Gabrielle Glaser. July 2013. Simon & Schuster. Pages 18/19.

11 Euphoria: *A mental and emotional condition in which a person experiences intense feelings of well-being,*

elation, happiness, excitement, and joy. Dysphoria is defined (both are from Wikipedia.org) as: *a state of feeling unwell or unhappy; a feeling of emotional and mental discomfort as a symptom of discontentment, restlessness, dissatisfaction, malaise, depression, anxiety or indifference.* **In effect, Dysphoria is the *opposite* of Euphoria.**

12 This is what killed the drummer for Led Zeppelin.

13 Notre Dame Office of Alcohol and Drug Education. "Acute Alcohol Intoxication." Accessed May 15, 2014. *http://oade.nd.edu/educate-yourself-alcohol/acute-alcohol-intoxication/*.

14 The Wall Street Journal. "Why She Drinks: Women and Alcohol Abuse." Accessed May 15, 2014. *http://online.wsj.com/article/SB10001424127887323893504578555270434071876.html*.

15 *Her Best Kept Secret* by Gabrielle Glaser. July 2013. Simon & Schuster.

16 *Her Best Kept Secret,* page 28.

17 There are numerous studies that support this conclusion. This particular reference comes from pages 27–28 in Gabrielle Glaser's book. A note on this book and other similar ones: they have been meticulously researched and footnoted accordingly. For example, this passage includes specific reference in its footnotes (page 192) to its original source *"Women and Alcohol: What You Need to Know,"* Harvard Health Publications, accessed September 12, 2012, www.helpguide.org/harvard/women_alcohol.htm. In general I will not include these root references in my citations (they can be easily obtained), otherwise we will all go nuts with the footnote process.

18 Huffington Post. "For Women: Alcohol Dependence Twice As Deadly." Accessed March 27, 2014. *www.huffingtonpost.com/2012/10/17/women-alcohol-dependence-death_n_1973713.html*.

19 Alcohol Problems & Solutions. "Drinking: Men and Women are Unequal. Accessed June 2, 2014.

www2.potsdam.edu/hansondj/HealthIssues/1055861926.html).

20 HealthGuide.org "Women and Alcohol: The Hidden Risks of Drinking." Accessed May 27, 2014. *www.helpguide.org/harvard/women_alcohol.htm*.

21 Women For Sobriety. Accessed March 27, 2014. *http://womenforsobriety.org*.

22 While I disparage self-help books in general in various places in this book, that doesn't mean they are worthless. The ones mentioned here are decided not so, particularly if you are looking for the female viewpoint.

Level 1

1 DARA Thailand. "Recognize a Functioning Addict." Accessed February 26, 2014. *http://alcoholrehab .com/alcohol-rehab/recognize-a-functioning-addict/*.

2 DARA Thailand. "Recognize a Functioning Addict." Accessed February 26, 2014. *http://alcoholrehab .com/alcohol-rehab/recognize-a-functioning-addict/*.

3 The New York Times. "Pat Summerall, Star Kicker With Giants and a Calm Voice on TV, Dies at 82." Accessed February 26, 2014. *www.nytimes.com/2013/04/17/sports/football/pat-summerall-star-with-nfl-giants-and-on-tv-dies-at-82.html?pagewanted=all&_r=0*.

4 National Institute on Alcohol Abuse and Alcoholism. "Alcohol Use Disorders." Accessed February 26, 2014. *www.niaaa.nih.gov/alcohol-health/overview-alcohol-consumption/alcohol-use-disorders*.

5 Sober Recovery. Alcoholism Drug Addiction Help and Information. Accessed February 26, 2014. *www.soberrecovery.com/forums/alcoholism/180591-problem-drinking-vs-alcoholism.html*.

6 ABC News. "Laura Bush Reveals How George W. Stopped Drinking." Accessed May 5, 2014. *http://abcnews.go.com/Politics/laura-bush-reveals-george-stopped-drinking/story?id=10552148*.

7 But even that statement was not strictly true. While GWB may well have decided that it was time to put his wild youth behind him, he still needed some help. Accounts varied, but it seems like this "help" was in the form of some (subtle?) pressure from Laura mixed with spirituality. Whatever the

help was, it seemed to be just gentle reinforcement to a firm decision that he made on his own and was able to follow through on successfully.

8 I now believe I have always lacked the ability to control alcohol, being an infrequent binge drinker from my teens. It was only after I had "built up" my tolerance in increasingly heavy drinking in my late 20's and crossed the line into physical dependence that I reached a critical point. From there it was off to the alcoholism races.

9 The Hartford Institute for Geriatric Nursing, New York University, College of Nursing, Alcohol Use Screening and Assessment for Older Adults. Accessed August 13, 2014. *http://consultgerirn.org/uploads/File/trythis/try_this_17.pdf*.

10 Fox News. "Are You An Addict?" By Dr. Nicholas Kardaras.

Accessed June 25, 2014. *www.foxnews.com/opinion/2013/02/09/are-addict/?intcmp=HPBucket*.

11 Intervention Support. "How Much Does An Intervention Cost." Accessed July 22, 2014. *www.interventionsupport.com/how-much-does-an-intervention-cost/*.

12 Intervention Resource Center. "Family Intervention." Accessed July 25, 2014. *www.interventioninfo.org/research/family.php*.

13 Intervention Support. "The Best Venue To Hold An Intervention." July 21, 2014. *www.interventionsupport.com/blog/the-best-venue-to-hold-an-intervention/*.

14 This is my opinion. Indeed, the limited research on interventions appears somewhat biased towards supporting the notion of professional interventionists (and authored by them). In any event, it does not distinguish between in-denial alcoholics and those who had previously indicated a significant awareness of their problem.

15 I have no statistics to prove this assertion, but it is common sense that if an addict has been through one intervention (an extremely unpleasant experience for all concerned) they will undoubtedly bolt at the slightest sign of another.

16 Rehabilitation treatment centers ("Rehab") are well within their rights to eject a patient who violates their rules. Rule violations vary by facility but, usually, include refusing treatment, violence, distracting other patients, violating curfews, and of course continuing to use. Rehab is discussed in great detail in Level 6.

17 The rate of recidivism in Rehab is 60% (e.g. 6 out of 10 people in Rehab have been there before). It is no stretch to think that the likelihood of relapse will be worse for people who did not want to be there in the first place, and in particular those thinking they did not have a problem to begin with.

18 Again, no statistics but plain common sense.

19 Why this might sound flippant or even stupid, it is well established in the psychiatric field that men do indeed have a problem asking for help as compared to women. See *http://psychcentral.com/blog/archives/2014/03/23/why-men-dont-ask-for-directions/* for a quick but good summary on this.

20 This does happen, more than you might think. When an alcoholic gets into self-introspection, a conclusion that they have an addiction may be undone by countless factors, such as going without a drink for a few days without major problems, being around people who say "you aren't an alcoholic!," etc.

21 Most programs will last approximately a month, but some may go for much longer periods, usually in 1-month increments (e.g. 60, 90 days). Some, like The Salvation Army, require a 6-month commitment.

22 Betty Ford Center. "Family." Accessed August 19, 2014. *www.bettyfordcenter.org/family-and-children/family/index.php*.

23 Enabler: A person who by their actions makes it easier for an alcoholic to continue their self-destructive behavior by providing money or other forms of practical support, and/or by rescuing or insulating the alcoholic from bad situations or results caused by their alcoholism.

24 Intervention Support. "How Many People Should Be Included In An Intervention?" Accessed July 24, 2014. *www.interventionsupport.com/blog/how-many-people-should-be-included-in-an-intervention/*.

25 Intervention Resource Center. "Family Intervention." Accessed July 25, 2014. *www.interventioninfo .org/research/family.php*.

26 This was my personal situation. Unfortunately, I did not realize how unpleasant I was until family members told me after I got sober. I am sure they told me while I was drinking, but I either didn't believe them or didn't care. Probably both.

27 If someone starts humming Lynyrd Skynyd's *"That Smell"* around you, you know you have some major problems.

28 KHITS963. "Interview with Joe Walsh." Accessed March 13, 2014. *www.k-hits.com/musicnews/ Story.aspx?ID=1926199*.

29 Key Motivating Factor: You can lose a large amount of weight if you give up alcohol and avoid replacing it with something equally high in calories. I estimate consumed 2500 calories a DAY in alcohol. Within 4 months after quitting alcohol, I lost over 40 pounds. Although some of that undoubtedly was due to other medical issues, there is no doubt eliminating my entire daily recommended calorie intake in alcohol contributed mightily—not to mention the retained water weight! That bloated feeling disappeared as did my sickly, flushed look.

30 Personal Note: I did not have any DUIs or arrests, but I attribute that primarily to being mainly a home drinker and some dumb luck.

Level 2

1 National Alliance on Mental Illness. "Dual Diagnosis: Substance Abuse and Mental Illness." Accessed May 14, 2014. *"www.nami.org/Template.cfm?Section=By_Illness&Template=/TaggedPage/TaggedPageDisplay.cfm&TPLID=54&ContentID=23049*.

2 Another way of thinking about multiple defenses and their progressions is that they are successive "safety nets" to catch you before you hit the ground. If the first net rips, it has at least slowed your descent, and so on through each subsequent net until one of them holds, and you can climb back up.

3 eX—refers to (e)X wife, husband, or partner. I define an eX as someone with whom you have had a serious, monogamous relationship with for *at least* two years. All others are covered under the Relationships trigger.

4 AlcoholRehab.com. "Anger and Alcohol Rehab." Accessed May 21, 2014. *http://alcoholrehab.com/alcohol-rehab/anger-and-alcohol-rehab/*.

5 Blood Pressure. "High Blood Pressure and Anger." Accessed May 22, 2014. *www.blood-pressure-updates.com/bp/high-blood-pressure/causes-symptoms/high-blood-pressure-and-anger.htm*.

6 Mayo Clinic. "High Blood Pressure (hypertension)." Accessed May 22, 2014. *www.mayoclinic.com/ health/blood-pressure/AN00318*.

7 Social Anxiety Support. "Self-Harm Coping Mechanisms." Accessed May 22, 2014. *www.socialanxietysupport.com/forum/f33/self-harm-coping-mechanisms-183993/*.

8 No, it is not plastic explosive; it is modeling clay.

9 AlcoholRehab.com. "Alcohol Induced Anxiety." Accessed May 22, 2014. *http://alcoholrehab.com/alcohol-rehab/alcohol-induced-anxiety/*.

10 The New York Times. "Anxiety In-Depth Report." Accessed February 28, 2014. *http://health.nytimes .com/health/guides/symptoms/stress-and-anxiety/print.html,*

11 The New York Times. "Anxiety In-Depth Report." Accessed February 28, 2014. *http://health.nytimes .com/health/guides/symptoms/stress-and-anxiety/print.html,*

12 The Wall Street Journal. "A Better Way To Treat Anxiety." Accessed February 28, 2014. *http://online.wsj.com/article/SB10001424127887323475304578503584007049700.html*.

13 Discussed in Level 6—Rehab and Therapy

14 Psych Central. "Normal Worry Versus Generalized Anxiety Disorder." Accessed May 22, 2014. *http://psychcentral.com/lib/normal-worry-versus-generalized-anxiety-disorder/00073.*

15 There are numerous studies that support this conclusion. This particular reference comes from pages 27–28 in Gabrielle Glaser's book, discussed earlier in the Phase 1 introduction.

16 Philippians 4:6 *"Do not be anxious about anything, but in every situation, by prayer and petition, with thanksgiving, present your requests to God."*

17 The Wall Street Journal. "A Better Way To Treat Anxiety." Accessed May 22, 2014. *http://online.wsj.com/article/SB10001424127887323475304578503584007049700.html.*

18 Source: *http://forum.wordreference.com*

19 AlcoholRehab.com. "Rehab and Boredom." Accessed May 22, 2014. *http://alcoholrehab.com/alcohol-rehab/rehab-and-boredom/.*

20 Listen to books on tape while commuting. This can drain away Job stress, and combined with driving, can be relaxing.

21 United States Marine Corp Officer Candidate literature

22 Early Recovery from Addiction Blog. "Fear of Change." Georgia W. Accessed on February 26, 2014. *http://earlyrecovery.wordpress.com/2010/09/24/fear-of-change/.*

23 Early Recovery from Addiction Blog. "Fear of Change." Georgia W. Accessed on February 26, 2014. *http://earlyrecovery.wordpress.com/2010/09/24/fear-of-change/*

24 Exact source of this version is not exactly known, but its history can be found at *http://en.wikipedia.org/wiki/Serenity_Prayer.*

25 Oxford Dictionaries. "Depression." Accessed August 14, 2014. *www.oxforddictionaries.com/us/definition/american_english/depression.*

26 Better Health Channel. "Depression." Accessed August 14, 2014. *www.betterhealth.vic.gov.au/bhcv2/bhcarticles.nsf/pages/Depression_different_types.*

27 WebMD. "Alcohol and Depression." Accessed August 14, 2014. *www.webmd.com/depression/alcohol-and-depresssion.*

28 HelpGuide.org. "Dealing With Depression." Accessed August 14, 2014. *www.helpguide.org/mental/depression_tips.htm.*

29 Washington Post. "New study offers evidence of a link between staying up late and risk of depression." Accessed August 14, 2014.

www.washingtonpost.com/national/health-science/new-study-offers-evidence-of-a-link-between-staying-up-late-and-risk-of-depression/2013/09/30/f6596518–29d8–11e3–8ade-a1f23cda135e_story.html?hpid=z5.

30 One example among *many: www.socialanxietysupport.com/forum/f33/depression-loneliness-isolation-and-sad-2074/*

31 I added Feng Shui to the hobby list in Level 9 as a result of this research on Disorder. If you really think about it, it is just an extension of the time and effort people put into arranging their furniture.

32 eHow. "Messy House & Depression." Accessed May 2, 2014. *www.ehow.com/about_6595538_messy-house-depression.html.*

33 Wikipedia. "Time Management." Accessed May 2, 2014. *http://en.wikipedia.org/wiki/Time_management.*

34 Visitors to my website *www.conqueryouraddiction.com* during this time were painfully aware of this, as I kept dragging out the completion date. Again, thanks for your patience!

35 A special shout out to Pink Floyd.

36 Defined as: *A mental and emotional condition in which a person experiences intense feelings of well-being, elation, happiness, excitement, and joy. (Wikipedia.org)*

37 Strangely this did not matter by time zone.

38 You may or may not choose to include nicotine in this list.

39 RSS refers to having breaking "news" sent to your mobile phone. TMZ.com is an online website that seems to have the latest and greatest celebrity gossip.

40 One type of belittling that is entirely Guilt-free and with no praying required is snooty wine-drinkers at parties talking about its "bouquet" and "nose" and "charm." It is a safe bet they have absolutely no idea what the hell they are talking about.

41 AlcoholRehab.com. "Dealing With Grief In Recovery." Accessed August 14, 2014. *http://alcoholrehab.com/alcohol-rehab/dealing-with-grief-in-recovery/*.

42 SocialAnxietySupport.com. "Self-Harm Coping Mechanisms." Accessed August 14, 2014. *www.socialanxietysupport.com/forum/f33/self-harm-coping-mechanisms-183993/*.

43 Essentially, a floor defense is something that will help inhibit your desire to drink in all drinking circumstances (e.g. triggers). Examples are worrying about your health or concern about what your children will think if you relapsed.

44 Foundations of Mental Health Nursing. "Adjustment Variations and Disruptions." Page 255. Accessed August 14, 2014. *http://books.google.com/books?id=ShKgSO8U3-QC&pg=PA255&lpg= PA255&dq=frustration+and+alcoholism&source=bl&ots=3wdb6gE443&sig=TwLhi19ayXcvwgnIC4qo6qdvJv8 &hl=en&sa=X&ei=EU0XUbXRMeWujALK7YHgCw&ved=0CDUQ6AEwAA#v=onepage&q=frustration%2 0and%20alcoholism&f=false*.

45 Most Al-Anon meetings are "open," meaning anyone can attend. In contrast, most Alcoholics Anonymous meetings are "closed," meaning they are intended for alcoholics only. But neither have any test or membership sign up, so in reality *anybody* can attend, assuming a meeting is not gender-specific.

46 Mind Tools. "Managing Your Emotions At Work." Accessed August 14, 2014. *www.mindtools .com/pages/article/newCDV_41.htm*.

47 Like ones for a certain flexible garden hose, match.com, and Wi-Fi security cameras, which seem to get through no matter what I do.

48 SocialAnxietySupport.com. "Self-Harm Coping Mechanisms." Accessed August 14, 2014. *www.socialanxietysupport.com/forum/f33/self-harm-coping-mechanisms-183993/*.

49 Canoeroots Magazine. "The Three Types of Fun." Accessed August 14, 2014. *www.rapidmedia .com/departments-canoeing/item/839-types-of-fun.html*.

50 Vulture. "Cougar Town: The Most Pro-Alcohol Show on TV." Accessed May 17, 2014. *www.vulture.com/2010/09/cougar_town_drinking.html*.

51 Euphoria: *A mental and emotional condition in which a person experiences intense feelings of well-being, elation, happiness, excitement, and joy. (Wikipedia.org)*

52 This is my *personal* interpretation of the effects that BAC level has according to The University of Notre Dame. See Level 11 for much more detail.

53 A *Catch-22* is a paradoxical situation from which an individual cannot escape because of contradictory rules. Or this could be the "What came first, the chicken or the egg?" scenario. In any event it is very likely there are many things you wanted to try but had never done so, purely because you *had never done them before*. People are strange.

54 Ok, Stephen King is not a humorist, but in my view he is one of the best fiction writers ever, and highly entertaining. And he also had major substance abuse problems when he was younger, so in that

sense he is inspirational. Separately, I also thought "The Exorcist" was hilarious, so my taste might be suspect.

55 AlcoholRehab.com. "Addiction and Guilt." Accessed August 15, 2014. *http://alcoholrehab.com/alcohol-rehab/addiction-and-guilt/*,

56 PainAction. "Alcohol and Pain." Accessed August 15, 2014. *www.painaction.com/members/article.aspx?id=5048.*

57 I am NOT a fan of using one chemical (drugs) to combat an addiction to another chemical (alcohol). It's just begging for (a new kind of) trouble in my view. But a doctor's order supersedes everything when it comes to health issues.

58 Mayo Clinic. "Exercise Helps Ease Arthritis Pain and Stiffness." Accessed August 20, 2014. www.mayoclinic.org/diseases-conditions/arthritis/in-depth/arthritis/art-20047971.

59 University of California San Francisco. "Alcohol May Trigger Serious Palpitations in Heart Patients." Accessed August 15, 2014. *www.ucsf.edu/news/2012/06/12071/alcohol-may-trigger-serious-palpitations-heart-patients.*

60 One example is Valentine's Day. According to Wikipedia (*www.history.com/topics/valentines-day*) it is named for a 5th century martyr and has roots going back to Roman times. I'm sure your date will love it.

61 Bright Eye. "Low Blood Sugar Levels Cause Alcohol Cravings." Accessed August 15, 2014. *www.brighteyecounselling.co.uk/alcohol-drugs/low-blood-sugar-levels-cause-alcohol-cravings/.*

62 The Hypglycemia Support Foundation. "Hypoglycemia and Alcoholism." Accessed August 15, 2014. *http://hypoglycemia.org/august-2011-hypoglycemia-alcoholism/.*

63 Mayo Clinic. "Anorexia Nervosa." Accessed October 4, 2014. www.mayoclinic.org/diseases-conditions/anorexia/basics/definition/con-20033002.

64 KleanLife. "Drunkorexia: A New Eating Disorder?" September 26, 2013. Accessed May 1, 2014. *http://kleanlife.com/2013/09/26/drunkorexia-new-eating-disorder/.*

65 About.com. "Alcohol Relapse and Craving." Accessed May 1, 2014. *http://alcoholism.about.com/cs/alerts/l/blnaa06.htm.*

66 National Eating Disorders Association. "Substance Abuse and Eating Disorders." Accessed August 18, 2014. *www.nationaleatingdisorders.org/substance-abuse-and-eating-disorders.*

67 *www.nytimes.com/2013/05/14/nyregion/council-speaker-opens-up-about-her-struggles-against-bulimia-and-alcoholism.html?pagewanted=all&_r=0*

68 Dopamine is a neurotransmitter that helps control the brain's reward and pleasure centers.

69 Psychology Today. "Your Brain on Alcohol." Accessed February 26, 2014. *www.psychologytoday.com/blog/you-illuminated/201006/your-brain-alcohol.*

70 Mayo Clinic. "Diseases and Conditions—Insomnia." Accessed February 26, 2014. *www.mayoclinic.com/health/insomnia/DS00187/DSECTION=causes*

71 AAAS ScienceNetLinks. "Alcohol and Its Impact on the Brain." Accessed February 26, 2014. *http://sciencenetlinks.com/lessons/alcohol-and-its-impact-on-the-brain/*

72 NIAAA. "Sleep, Sleepiness, and Alcohol Use." Accessed February 26, 2014. *http://pubs.niaaa.nih.gov/publications/arh25-2/101-109.htm.*

73 WebMD. "Nightmares in Adults." Accessed February 26, 2014. *www.webmd.com/sleep-disorders/guide/nightmares-in-adults.*

74 Think the weasely jerk in *Miracle on 34th Street.*

75 Alcoholism is recognized as a disability under the Americans with Disabilities Act ("ADA"); see *www.gshllp.com/60-second-memos/alcoholism-in-the-workplace-why-employers-need-to-be-careful-when-mak-*

ing-employment-decisions-involving-alcoholic-employees. Gonzalez, Saggio & Harlan. "Alcoholism in the Workplace." Accessed February 26, 2014.

76 NCADD. "Alcohol in the Workplace." Accessed February 26, 2014. *www.ncadd.org/index.php/learn-about-alcohol/workplace/204-workplace.*

77 About.com. "Construction Tops List of Industries with Problem Drinking." Accessed February 26, 2014. *http://alcoholism.about.com/od/work/a/bles050920.htm* .

78 About.com. "Construction Tops List of Industries with Problem Drinking." Accessed February 26, 2014. *http://alcoholism.about.com/od/work/a/bles050920.htm* .

79 I even had to cut a Christmas vacation short because my project manager thought I "might be needed." I wasn't, and he never said one thing even remotely close to an apology, nor did his boss. Assholes to be sure, but they are (or least were) rampant in that industry.

80 Wikipedia. "Identify Formation." Accessed August 15, 2014. *http://en.wikipedia.org/wiki/Identity_formation.*

81 Adapted from *www.linkedin.com/today/post/article/20130709152707–5799319-the-top-10-reasons-people-hate-their-job.*

82 The Wall Street Journal. "Office Stress: His vs. Hers." Accessed August 15, 2014. *http://online.wsj.com/article/SB10001424127887324678604578340332290414820.html.*

83 The Wall Street Journal. "Stressed at Work? Reflect on the Positive." Accessed August 15, 2014.. *http://online.wsj.com/news/articles/SB10001424127887324202304579053242044377758?mg=reno64-wsj&url =http%3A%2F%2Fonline.wsj.com%2Farticle%2FSB10001424127887324202304579053242044377758.html.*

84 The Wall Street Journal. "Why She Drinks: Women and Alcohol Abuse." Accessed August 16, 2014. *http://online.wsj.com/article/SB10001424127887323893504578555270434071876.html?mod=trending_now_3.*

85 NCBI. "Can your children drive you to drink? Stress and parenting in adults interacting with children with ADHD." Accessed August 15, 2014. *www.ncbi.nlm.nih.gov/pubmed/10890826.*

86 *Arthritis Today,* March-April 2013 issue, page 53

87 AlcoholRehab.com "Alone With Addiction." Accessed August 16, 2014. *http://alcoholrehab.com/alcohol-rehab/alone-with-addiction/.*

88 AlcoholRehab.com. "Dangers of Loneliness in Recovery." Accessed August 16, 2014. *http://alcoholrehab.com/alcohol-rehab/dangers-of-loneliness-in-recovery/.*

89 AlcoholRehab.com. "Dangers of Loneliness In Recovery." Accessed August 20, 2014. *http://alcoholrehab.com/alcohol-rehab/dangers-of-loneliness-in-recovery/.*

90 Be VERY aware that these online forums, such as "support" groups on Facebook.com, and in particular those where you can't be anonymous are NOT private—*not anywhere close to it.* Everything you post on Facebook and Twitter is monitored by people other than your "Friends" —total strangers looking for objectionable content, by legions of advertisers, and often by total strangers just looking to snoop.
     The general rule of thumb is "if you don't want the world to see it, don't post it on the internet." SO, if you do not want the world to know you are an alcoholic, do NOT post anything related to your problems with alcohol on Facebook or any forum that can be personally linked with your identity.

91 *www.goodreads.com/book/show/16130272-her-best-kept-secret,* July 2013, Simon & Schuster, page 34

92 Despite my rant immediately above.

93 This is almost an impossible task these days, but that doesn't mean you shouldn't try, particularly if you subscribe to the premise (as most do) that there is a significant genetic risk associated with alcoholism.

94 A&E announced in 2013 that they had canceled the series with the series finale airing on July 18,

2013. In August 2014, *LMN* announced the revival of the series with a new season premiering in 2015. So you can catch back episodes (there were over 180 over 13 seasons) on LMN and/or A&E.

95 Wikipedia. "Elliott Jaques." Accessed October 4, 2014. *http://en.wikipedia.org/wiki/Elliott_Jaques*.

96 ABC News. "New Middle-Age Crisis: Drinking Over 50." Accessed August 17, 2014. *http://abcnews.go.com/GMA/MensHealthNews/story?id=8341707*.

97 NY Times. "Rise in Suicides of Middle-Aged Is Continuing." Accessed August 17, 2014. *www.nytimes.com/2010/06/06/us/06suicide.html?_r=2&ref=us&*.

98 "Psychology Today. Rise in Suicides of Middle-Aged Is Continuing." Accessed August 17, 2014. *www.psychologytoday.com/blog/21st-century-aging/201007/new-mid-life-crisis*.

99 The Wall Street Journal. "Why She Drinks: Women and Alcohol Abuse." Accessed August 17, 2014. *http://online.wsj.com/article/SB10001424127887323893504578555270434071876.html*.

100 Huffington Post. "Midlife Crisis:10 Warning Signs." Accessed August 17, 2014. *www.huffingtonpost .com/2011/10/17/midlife-crisis-warning-signs_n_1009997.html*.Note: these are not in order of frequency or priority.

101 About.com. "Alcohol and the Elderly Seniors Drinking Mostly Unreported, Undiagnosed, or Ignored." Accessed August 18, 2014. *http://alcoholism.about.com/cs/elder/a/aa981118.htm*.

102 The New York Times. "In Midlife, Boomers are Happy—And Suicidal." Accessed August 18, 2014. *www.nytimes.com/2010/06/13/weekinreview/13cohen.html*.

103 That don't include the previous bullet points, e.g., affairs, expensive toys.

104 I just saved you a million dollars in grant money with that synopsis; please send a check to the publisher referencing this book, thank you.

105 AlcoholRehab.com. "Tinnitus and Alcohol Abuse." Accessed August 18, 2014. *http://alcoholrehab.com/alcohol-rehab/tinnitus-and-alcohol-abuse/*.

106 AlcoholRehab.com. "Surviving The Pink Cloud in Recovery." Accessed August 18, 2014. *http://alco-holrehab.com/alcohol-rehab/pink-cloud/*.

107 SoberRecovery.com. "Ten Chips Down." Accessed August 18, 2014. *www.soberrecovery.com/ forums/substance-abuse/119730-pink-cloud.html*.

108 The best definitions I found for Peer as it relates to this trigger are: a) a person who is equal to another in abilities, qualifications, age, background, and social status; and b) something of equal worth or quality. (Source: *dictionary.reference.com*)

109 Youth Communication. "Can't Afford To Follow." Accessed August 18, 2014. *www.ycteenmag.org/ topics/peer+pressure/Can't_Afford_to_Follow.html?story_id=NYC-2007–03–04*.

110 Curiosity, family drinkers, and easy access to alcohol, to name a few.

111 About.com (Teen Advice). ""How To Say No To Drinking." Accessed August 18, 2014. *http://teenad-vice.about.com/od/drugsalcohol/ht/how_to_say_no_to_drinking_alochol.htm*.

112 Having attended hundreds of AA meetings, one of the things I am always struck by is how *old* the males are. My theory is that most of them refused to admit they were powerless over alcohol until their lives totally blew up.

113 The Wall Street Journal. "Why She Drinks: Women and Alcohol Abuse." Accessed August 18, 2014. *http://online.wsj.com/article/SB10001424127887323893504578555270434071876.html*.

114 Primarily in the Hungry, Sex, and Victim discussions.

115 Two qualifiers: First, AA subscribes to the "powerless over alcohol" concept, which noted earlier may be at odds for some people with trying to become more powerful in general. Second, while AA leads with the Higher Power concept in its 12-steps, it quickly falls into many God references.

116 Adapted from sources including: Oprah. "5 Ways to Feel Less Powerless." Accessed August 20,

2014. *www.oprah.com/spirit/How-to-Feel-Less-Powerless-Deepak-Chopra*, and Huffington Post. "Overcoming Powerlessness." Accessed August 20. 2014. *www.huffingtonpost.com/anne-naylor/self-help-overcoming-powe_b_582950.html*.

117 It continues to amaze me on how many relationships seem to be built (or at least created) by a shared love of drinking.

118 Don't underestimate the advantage of living in "dry" areas, far away from places that sell alcohol.

119 The Wall Street Journal. "Wrappers as Weight-Loss Aid?" Accessed June 20, 2014. *http://online.wsj.com/article/SB20001424127887323846504579073510272072246.html?mod=ITP_personaljournal_1*

120 You the nonalcoholic might be tempted to extend this logic to open bottles, e.g., measuring the levels of say a wine or whisky bottle. Do NOT try this. A trick learned early by most alcoholics is to drink a small portion, and then fill the bottle back up to the original level with water. Most people won't notice the dilution.

121 I concede that it might *seem* to make the first day or so "easier" if, in fact, you are nursing a severe hangover and don't want to even think about alcohol. Then again, you may desire a "hair of the dog." Most importantly, you are just dragging out the detoxification process. Why add 2–3 days of additional hard detox for the "benefit" of one last binge? You will be glad you did not, trust me.

122 In such cases if they do have a major impact, they are likely to be other triggers, such as Anger or Loneliness.

123 Be careful, as many of them are crazy/full of shit

124 Referred to as "Former" with a capital in the rest of this section.

125 They mean recovering from your breakup, not alcoholism "recovery," which is a term I strenuously avoid.

126 Besides being very cruel and maybe even dangerous, it can be made fun of: *www.cracked.com/video_18386_if-breakup-ballads-were-more-realistic-and-way-crazier.html*.

127 This advice comes from an eHarmony post (see two footnotes from now for link).

128 This obviously assumes you don't have unavoidable common interests—e.g., children, a business together, etc.

129 Adapted from eHarmony. "The Do's and Don'ts of Dealing with Your Ex." Accessed August 18, 2014. *www.eharmony.com/dating-advice/about-you/the-dos-and-donts-of-dealing-with-your-ex/#.UhalIz-qm5g;* many other sites essentially boiled down to the same things. I further adapt some of these specifically for the eX trigger later in this Level.

130 This anecdote also illustrates how fragile people can be when returning to the "outside world" after inpatient rehabilitation stints. Do *not* assume that someone has been "cured" just because they went to rehab—in fact, treat them the opposite for a time—that they could relapse at any time for the slightest reason—because they might.

131 Adapted from *www.thesurvivorsclub.org/family/support/family-stress-during-holidays*. The Survivors Club. "TSC's Holiday Survival Guide: Surviving Family During the Holidays." Accessed April 6, 2014.

132 Odds are that some memories may be totally destroyed, so there is nothing to actually reach. There is no predicting what will have been totally destroyed versus what has just had the "linkages" to them destroyed.

133 Do this only if it doesn't cause a major Guilt-trip.

134 Great you say! I don't want to remember the things I did while drinking (e.g., they dredge up many triggers). But not all of them may be bad, and even bad ones may help reinforce your determination to stop drinking.

135 That's the best description for me; the medical term is "forming new neural pathways."

136 I even included it under a different label: Horny. That wasn't being flippant or gross; in rehab the "H" in the drinking trigger acronym H.A.L.T (Hungry, Angry, Lonely, Tired) is often replaced by "Horny."

137 If not earlier. Who knows what thoughts about body image comes into the mind of a child when they play with a Barbie, GI Joe, a Transformer, or other massively enhanced doll.

138 *Drinking: A Love Story,* Caroline Knapp, Bantam Dell 1996, page 83

139 TimeToast. "Perceptions of Body History Throughout History." Accessed April 6, 2014. *www.time-toast.com/timelines/40315.*

140 *Drinking: A Love Story,* Caroline Knapp, Bantam Dell 1996, pages 83–84

141 Excerpt from *A Women's Guide to Sex and Recovery,* published by the Do It Now Foundation (*www.doitnow.org*)

142 I'm not being flippant when I say males can be pretty insensitive jerks much of the time. Particularly about sex.

143 Excerpt *from A Women's Guide to Sex and Recovery,* published by the Do It Now Foundation (*www.doitnow.org*)

144 This particular testimonial demonstrates the impact of Reminders as a related trigger.

145 Some smells can be quite relaxing. This area is known as *Aromatherapy.* Aromatherapy uses the oils from certain plants to create aromatic compounds to sooth anxious nerves.

146 You think??? Sometimes the obtuseness of the medical/psychiatric professions drive me nuts.

147 Social Anxiety Support. "Drinking to get "ready for people"/anxiety and alcohol." Accessed April 6, 2014. *www.socialanxietysupport.com/forum/f33/drinking-to-get-ready-for-people-anxiety-and-alcohol-453545/.*

148 I work in the wireless industry in my "real" job, and am personally disgusted with how mobile technology has eroded basic manners over the last few years. But there is no question it can be a boon for alcoholics in difficult social settings.

149 Helpguide.org. "The Effects of Stress Overload and What You Can Do About It." Accessed April 6, 2014. *www.helpguide.org/mental/stress_signs.htm.*

150 This can be interpreted in some situations as triggering Zest/Zeal, e.g., an increase in excitement and/or energy levels.

151 The Wall Street Journal. "Office Stress: His And Hers. "Accessed May 28, 2014. *http://online.wsj.com/article/SB10001424127887324678604578340332290414820.html.*

152 Helpguide.org. "The Effects of Stress Overload and What You Can Do About It." Accessed April 6, 2014. *www.helpguide.org/mental/stress_signs.htm.*

153 Helpguide.org. "The Effects of Stress Overload and What You Can Do About It." Accessed April 6, 2014. *www.helpguide.org/mental/stress_signs.htm.*

154 Healthguide.org. "Stress Management: How To Reduce, Prevent, and Cope With Stress." Accessed May 28, 2014..*www.helpguide.org/mental/stress_management_relief_coping.htm.*

155 Healthguide.org. "Relaxation Techniques For Stress Relief." Accessed May 28, 2014. *www.helpguide.org/mental/stress_relief_meditation_yoga_relaxation.htm .*

156 Healthguide.org. "5 Steps To Reduce Stress and Bring Balance To Your Life." Accessed May 28, 2014. *www.helpguide.org/toolkit/quick_stress_relief.htm.* This link is a bit more obvious in its marketing.

157 Healthguide.org. "Stress Symptoms, Signs, & Causes." Accessed May 28, 2014. *www.helpguide.org/mental/stress_signs.htm.*

158 Having not played tennis in 30 years, I have no idea where it came from . . .

159 The Wall Street Journal. "A Top Hospital Opens Up TO Chinese herbs As Medicines." Access May 28, 2014. *http://online.wsj.com/news/articles/SB10001424052702303626804579509590048257648.*

160 BrainFacts.org. "Senses and Perception: Taste and Smell." Accessed May 14, 2014. *www.brainfacts.org/sensing-thinking-behaving/senses-and-perception/articles/2012/taste-and-smell/.*

161 OneCraftyMother.com. "In Which I Answer The Question I Get The Most." Accessed May 28, 2014.*www.onecraftymother.com/2011/06/in-which-i-answer-question-i-get-most.html.*

162 I recognize 7 pm is probably too early a cutoff for most people; it is my personal cutoff due to intestinal issues that can be caused by eating any later.

163 See Level 11 for more information on these kinds of teas

164 Join a Community, Engage Friends and Family, and Develop New Hobbies

165 Probably the only ones that thought you *were* fun/interesting were your drinking companions, and they likely did not remember much of what they did themselves while drinking, let alone most of your antics. Even if they did, odds were many were "cringe-worthy" once you sobered up.

166 The Telegraph. "Helen Mirren Is Right: alcoholics aren't funny, they're boring." Accessed May 28, 2014. *http://blogs.telegraph.co.uk/news/andrewmcfbrown/100053707/helen-mirren-is-right-alcoholics-arent-funny-theyre-boring-unless-played-by-dudley-moore-in-arthur/.*

167 Billboard. "Mary J. Blige Discusses Sexual Abuse & Alcoholism on 'Behind the Music'." Accessed May 28, 2014. *www.billboard.com/articles/columns/the-juice/469019/mary-j-blige-discusses-sexual-abuse-alcoholism-on-behind-the-music.*

168 National Institute of Alcohol Abuse and Alcoholism. "Alcohol Abuse as a Risk Factor for and Consequence of Child Abuse." Accessed October 6, 2014. *http://pubs.niaaa.nih.gov/publications/arh25–1/52–57.htm.*

169 Adapted from NIAAA Publications. "Alcohol Abuse as a Risk Factor for and Consequence of Child Abuse." Accessed March 5, 2014. *http://pubs.niaaa.nih.gov/publications/arh25–1/52–57.htm),* including the types of abuse.

170 LA Times. "Abuse in childhood common among alcohol addicts, study finds." Accessed March 5, 2014. *http://articles.latimes.com/2012/mar/15/news/la-heb-trauma-alcohol-20120315.*

171 Vera House Inc. "Survivor Stories." Accessed March 5, 2014. *www.verahouse.org/domestic-violence-sexual-assault/survivors/survivors-stories.*

172 NIAAA. "Alcohol Abuse as a Risk Factor for and Consequence of Child Abuse." March 5, 2014. *http://pubs.niaaa.nih.gov/publications/arh25–1/52–57.htm.*

173 Guilt is probably the most powerful related trigger listed; the Victim is often made to feel Guilty about their supposed "role" in the abuse, even though it is completely the fault of the abuser.

174 AlcoholRehab.com. "Addiction and low self-esteem." Accessed June 19, 2014. *http://alcoholrehab .com/alcohol-rehab/addiction-and-low-self-esteem/.*

175 Wikipedia. "Self-pity." Accessed June 19, 2014. *http://en.wikipedia.org/wiki/Self-pity.*

176 Note, this testimonial had numerous spelling and grammatical errors (which have been cleaned up for publication)—so much so that I greatly question the "highly performing" and "ok in the morning" assertions.

177 Note for ANY online support groups listed in this book you should carefully research their applicability for you. Some, if not most, of them have some sort of advertising or service they are trying to sell, which may or may not skew what help they might provide.

178 Jared Akers. "Self-Pity And Overcoming Low Self-Esteem." Accessed March 5, 2014. *http://jaredakers.com/self-pity-and-overcoming-low-self-esteem/.*

179 The Wall Street Journal. "Which Country Drinks The Most?" Accessed August 22, 2014. *http://online.wsj.com/articles/alcohol-which-country-drinks-the-most-1408705249?mod=trending_now_1.*

180 Mayo Clinic. "Seasonal Affective Disorder Definition." Accessed March 5, 2014. *www.mayoclinic.com/health/seasonal-affective-disorder/DS00195.*

181 SparkPeople. "The Symptoms Of Seasonal Affective Disorder." Accessed March 5, 2014. *www.sparkpeople.com/resource/wellness_articles.asp?id=131.*

182 Mayo Clinic. "Seasonal Affective Disorder (SAD) Symptoms." Accessed March 5, 2014. *www.mayoclinic.com/health/seasonal-affective-disorder/DS00195/DSECTION=symptoms.*

183 The Wall Street Journal. "Longest, Darkest Winters Spark Odd Mood Boosters." March 4, 2014. *http://online.wsj.com/news/articles/SB10001424052702303801304579407720715302420?KEYWORDS=lighte n+up+during+the+longest+darkest+winters&mg=reno64-wsj&url=http%3A%2F%2Fonline.wsj.com%2Farticle%2FSB10001424052702303801304579407720715302420.html%3FKEYWORDS%3Dlighten%2Bup%2B during%2Bthe%2Blongest%2Bdarkest%2Bwinters.*

184 For example, for many years I had recurring dreams of tornados from my childhood life since Alabama is in tornado country. I don't think it contributed to my alcoholism, but such experiences could well be the cause for those where Weather *is* a significant trigger.

185 For example, if another trigger is Boredom and one of your major interests is an outdoor daylight activity, then living in a dark, rainy place for half the year may result in increased Boredom for half the year. If you can afford it, you might move to the desert or Florida during the winter months, or alternatively save all your vacation time to spend solely during the winter months.

186 A Relationship is another person with whom you: A) Have or had a romantic connection to (which may or may have included sex); B) With whom you are/were monogamous—or otherwise some kind of real or inferred commitment—such as not dating other people and/or only having sexual relations with; and C) A and B has lasted/did last at least several months.

187 This was the case according to my ex-wife; I believe it was far more complicated than that.

188 Everyday Health. "Is The Seven Year Itch Real?" Accessed March 5, 2014. *www.everydayhealth .com/emotional-health/is-the-7-year-itch-real.aspx.*

189 That study did not assess specific factors that caused the divorce; it likely assumed that unique factors in any one divorce would average out. HOWEVER, I would hypothesize that when alcoholism comes into play during one of these "rocky" cycles (like in the 16–20 years range), this is when many marriages with an alcoholic break up. That period is when my marriage hit the rocks and divorce was initiated. Another research topic!

190 I have noticed that as more time progresses, AND the defenses I've established have continued to be refined, that my eX is becoming less and less of a major trigger—to the point of likely dropping in priority in the near future.

191 I found this surprisingly difficult to adopt. Logically I knew this—I mean, I obviously did not make her happy (since she divorced me), so why do I think I would/could/should be able to do so after the divorce? But emotionally it was much more difficult.

192 They mean recovering from your breakup, not alcoholism "recovery."

193 And giving potential ammunition to his/her lawyer if a divorce settlement hasn't been finalized, or has to be revisited.

194 Adapted from eHarmony.com. "The Dos And Donts of Dealing With Your Ex." Accessed March 5, 2014. *www.eharmony.com/dating-advice/about-you/the-dos-and-donts-of-dealing-with-your-ex/#.UhaIlz-qm5g;* many other sites essentially boiled down to the same things.

195 She certainly takes that view.

196 One article (*Now hear this: Screaming at teens probably will backfire—www.usatoday.com/story/ news/nation/2013/09/04/teen-behavior-parents-discipline/2724361/*) disputes the notion that yelling is a helpful parenting tool to use with teenagers.

197 About.com. "Children of Alcoholics can become frightened of angry people." Accessed June 8,

2014. *http://alcoholism.about.com/od/adult/a/Children-Of-Alcoholics-Can-Become-Frightened-Of-Angry-People.htm*.

198 About.com. "Dealing with conflict in recovery." Accessed June 8, 2014. *http://alcoholrehab.com/alcohol-rehab/dealing-with-conflict-in-recovery/*.

199 Introduced in the Escape trigger and discussed in more detail in Level 11—Make Yourself Sick

200 Euphoria: *"A mental and emotional condition in which a person experiences intense feelings of well-being, elation, happiness, excitement, and joy."* Source: Wikipedia.org

201 Dysphoria is defined (also from Wikipedia.org) as: *a state of feeling unwell or unhappy; a feeling of emotional and mental discomfort as a symptom of discontentment, restlessness, dissatisfaction, malaise, depression, anxiety or indifference.* In effect it is the *opposite* of Euphoria.

202 Choose Help. "Creating Sober Excitement—Beating the Blahs to Beat Relapse." Accessed March 4, 2014. *www.choosehelp.com/recovery/creating-sober-excitement-2013-beating-the-blahs-to-beat-relapse#ixzz2e FBYWZKR.*

203 This may sound very strange to many people and particularly hard for nonalcoholics to understand. In my personal case, excitement and the rush/buzz that came with alcohol seemed to raise my blood pressure, and so (I now understand) I drank more to quickly get to the numb state where the depressant effects slowed me down physically and mentally.

204 NCBI. "Dopamine release in ventral striatum during Iowa Gambling Task performance is associated with increased excitement levels in pathological gambling." Accessed March 4, 2014. *www.ncbi.nlm.nih.gov/pubmed/20883460.*

205 SmartNBored (an attention deficit disorder portal). Gambling: Excitement Could Lead to Addiction." Accessed March 5, 2014. *http://smartnbored.com/Gambling-Excitement-Could-Lead-to-Addiction.html.*

206 Choose Help. "Creating Sober Excitement-Beating The Blahs To Beat Relapse." Access March 5, 2014. *www.choosehelp.com/recovery/creating-sober-excitement-2013-beating-the-blahs-to-beat-relapse.*

207 Unfortunately most sports venues specialize in enticing large numbers of people to buy vastly overpriced drinks (particularly professional baseball games). Be sure you can deal with situations like the person next to you deciding to kick over a beer at your feet. Otherwise go to sporting events where alcohol is not front and center, such as tennis or golf tournaments, or non-professional teams in other sports.

208 WebMD. "Caffeine's Effect On Blood Pressure." Accessed March 5, 2014. *www.webmd.com/hypertension-high-blood-pressure/news/20020517/caffeines-effect-on-blood-pressure.*

209 As you will see, in the same way your triggers have grown in number and intensity over time, it is possible to reverse those numbers and intensity the longer you are sober.

Level 3

1 I had sores all over my back and lower legs, which *never* healed when I was drinking. They healed when I finally stopped. Unfortunately, I still have some scarring.

2*Scaredtodeath1*, at MedHelp.org. Accessed August 22, 2014. *www.medhelp.org/tags/health_page/506/Alcoholism/Stories-from-people-whove-seen-how-bad-it-can-get—end-stage-stories?hp_id=127.*

3 Many of the testimonials in this section and others throughout this book come from *www.about.com*, specifically *www.alcoholism.about.com*. It has many areas for people to post their feelings and experiences about a wide range of topics, including many sub-topics regarding alcoholism. I recommend it to any alcoholic looking to share or commiserate with other alcoholics, or just to know that you are not alone. It is also an excellent resource for information about alcoholism in general.

4 I try to cite the source of *all* testimonials in this book. When I just use "anonymous," it means I came across it in my initial research but when I went back to double-check it was no longer to be found; possibly deleted. The majority of testimonials that I can source were posted clearly under pseudo names

or incomplete names (e.g., first name, and maybe a last initial). I redact any others that I think might possibly be too close to their full/real name.

5 Personally I believe my first drink was at age 12. BUT I did not start *consistently* drinking heavily until my mid to late 20s.

6 The Guardian. "Memory loss can begin from age 45, scientists say." Accessed April 10, 2014. *www.guardian.co.uk/science/2012/jan/06/memory-loss-begins-at-45-says-study.*

7 Everyday Health. "Is The Seven-Year-Itch Real?" Accessed April 10, 2014. *www.everydayhealth.com/emotional-health/is-the-7-year-itch-real.aspx.*

8 True for me personally.

9 With agreement by my doctor, of course.

10 I am pretty sure this is the book: *www.bloggernews.net/116490*

11 NIAAA. "Alcohol Use and the Risk of Developing Alzheimer's Disease." Accessed March 4, 2014.

http://pubs.niaaa.nih.gov/publications/arh25-4/299-306.htm

12 NIAAA. "Genetics of Alcohol Use Disorders." Accessed March 1, 2014. *www.niaaa.nih.gov/alcohol-health/overview-alcohol-consumption/alcohol-use-disorders/genetics-alcohol-use-disorders.*

13 NIAAA Publications. "Spotlights on Special Populations." Accessed March 1, 2014. *http://pubs.niaaa.nih.gov/publications/arh22-4/253.pdf.*

14 Bear in mind that these articles/reports referencing various studies on alcoholism practically never define *what* alcoholism really means. The studies often go into gory detail, but in medical jargon. So it's kind of all or nothing—they just assume everybody knows what it means.

15 About.com. "Alcohol and Tolerance." Accessed March 3, 2014. *http://alcoholism.about.com/cs/alerts/l/blnaa28.htm.* Much more on tolerance to alcohol in Level 5—Detox

16 NIAAA. "A Family History of Alcoholism." Accessed March 4, 2014. *http://pubs.niaaa.nih.gov/publications/FamilyHistory/famhist.htm.*

17 Google. Accessed March 3, 2014. *www.Howistoppeddrinking.org* via Google images.

18 NCBI. "Treatment of Alcoholic Liver Disease." Accessed March 3, 2014. *www.ncbi.nlm.nih.gov/pmc/articles/PMC3036962/.*

19 DARA Thailand. "Alcoholic Liver Disease." Accessed March 1, 2014. *http://alcoholrehab.com/alcohol-rehab/alcoholic-liver-disease/.*

20 Google Images. Accessed March 3, 2014. *http://pubs.niaaa.nih.gov* via Google images.

21 NIAAA Publications. "Alcohol's Damaging Effect on the Brain." Accessed March 1, 2014. *http://pubs.niaaa.nih.gov/publications/aa63/aa63.htm.*

22 NIAAA Publications. "Blackouts and Memory Lapses." Accessed March 1, 2014. *http://pubs.niaaa.nih.gov/publications/aa63/aa63.htm.*

23 It was so bad one of my sisters got me a pink "Hello Kitty" wallet.

24 That's the best description for me; the medical term is "forming new neural pathways."

25 Think of memories as data stored on your computer. Your computer may breakdown or malfunction in some way, but that does not mean your data (memory) was lost. There is just something preventing you from accessing (or seeing) it.

26 That does not mean that you will not have permanent memory loss. My family is constantly telling me things I did while I was drinking that I can't remember, even if I try. But frankly for most of those, I don't try very hard.

27 Alzheimer's Society. "What is Korsakoff's syndrome?" Accessed March 27, 2014. *www.alzheimers.org.uk/site/scripts/documents_info.php?documentID=98.*

28 MedicineNet.com. "What Is Pancreatitis?" Accessed April 16, 2014. *www.medicinenet.com/pancreatitis/page2.htm#what_is_pancreatitis.*

29 WomensHealthandCare.com. "Pancreatic Symptoms You Should Know." Accessed August 23, 2014. *www.womenshealthandcare.com/pancreatic-cancer-symptoms-2/.*

30 Macmillan Cancer Support. "Types of Pancreatic Cancer." Accessed April 16, 2014. *www.macmillan.org.uk/Cancerinformation/Cancertypes/Pancreas/Symptomsdiagnosis/Types.aspx.*

31 How Stuff Works. "How Does Alcohol Affect Skin?" Accessed April 16, 2014. *http://health.howstuffworks.com/skin-care/beauty/skin-and-lifestyle/alcohol-affect-skin.htm.*

32 MediaIndia.net." Alcohol Exacerbates Skin Diseases and Psoriasis." Accessed August 23, 2014. *www.medindia.net/news/alcohol-exacerbates-skin-diseases-and-psoriasis-86525-1.htm.*

33 Adapted from: Livestrong. "Facial Skin Problems Related to Alcohol." Accessed March 3, 2014. *www.livestrong.com/article/28364-facial-skin-problems-related-alcohol/,* and (including image) at: MedIndia. "Alcohol Exacerbates Skin Diseases and Psoriasis." Accessed March 3, 2014. *www.medindia.net/news/healthinfocus/Alcohol-Exacerbates-Skin-Diseases-and-Psoriasis-86525-1.htm.*

34 NCBI. "Suicide Risk Associated With Drug and Alcohol Dependence." Accessed April 16, 2014. *www.ncbi.nlm.nih.gov/pubmed/1932152.*

35 For this reason many advocates of suicide barriers have been gaining credibility in recent years, such as those wanting barriers on the Golden Gate Bridge (see *www.nytimes.com/2014/03/27/us/suicides-mounting-golden-gate-looks-to-add-a-safety-net.html?_r=0*). Of course nearly all skyscraper observation towers already have such barriers to prevent suicides as well as prevent drunken idiots throwing stuff off to injure or kill people below.

36 Net Doctor. "Alcohol and Depression." Accessed April 16, 2014. *www.netdoctor.co.uk/diseases/depression/alcoholanddepression_000486.htm.* Note: I personally have questions about the scientific viability of studies that seek cause and effect from alcoholism, particularly depression. Do clinically depressed people seek out alcohol to dull the feeling, or do alcoholics become depressed due to its being a depressant? However, there is no question that Depression and alcohol abuse can be a deadly combination.

37 Hubpages.com. "An Alcoholic Suicide!" Accessed April 10, 2014. *http://wendim.hubpages.com/hub/He-Said-He-Didnt-Drink-That-Much.* Wendi M. is author cited.

38 Boogieman, from MedHelp. "Alcoholic Community." Accessed April 17, 2014. *www.medhelp.org/posts/Alcoholism/End-stage-stories/show/505316.*

39 Jml1986, from MedHelp. "Alcoholism End Stage Stories." Accessed April 17, 2014. *www.medhelp.org/posts/Alcoholism/End-stage-stories/show/505316.*

40 Universal Pain Scale Faces, numerous sources

41 I am a not a medical doctor. This is a common sense adaptation of pain/symptoms that may be helpful for you and maybe your doctor if you have never confided in him/her about your drinking. If nothing else, it may help you to admit to yourself how much physical damage your drinking is doing.

Level 4

1 Catharsis—*"the purification and purgation of emotions—especially pity and fear"* (Wikipedia.org)

2 Make sure you fully understand your privacy policies and settings on whatever online forum you use. Facebook, for example, seems to take perverse delight in changing them every few months. They have a vested interest in making your information as *public* as possible—that is how they make their money! But they (grudgingly) have controls that will make your posts difficult to see by non-friends. But as far as Facebook's own monitoring people and software, as well as advertisers—forget it. They *will* see what you post.

Level 5

1 There are an amazing amount of "definitions" about detoxification from alcohol. Many of which I think are full of crap. For instance, Wikipedia has it as: *"the abrupt cessation of alcohol intake coupled with substitution of cross-tolerant drugs that have effects similar to the effects of alcohol in order to prevent alcohol withdrawal. As such, the term "detoxification" is somewhat of a misnomer since the process does not in any way involve the removal of toxic substances from the body."* I have so many problems with this so-called definition that I consider it in total to be complete and absolute bullshit. An excellent example of don't-believe-everything-you-see on the Internet.

2 Addiction Advisor. "Chapter One: Are You Physically Addicted to Alcohol?" Accessed April 18, 2014. *www.addictionadvisor.co.uk/stay-sober/alcohol-help_a104.shtml#.UgZdoG2qm5g.*

3 When I found this analysis a *huge* light went on in my head. This goes a long way of explaining why many people (including me) will often continue to drink even if nothing is "triggering" them or even when they don't really want to otherwise—they were/are trying to replicate that initial "buzz" or "rush" that comes with that first drink. Which *cannot* be done.

4 Adapted from About.com. "Addiction and Tolerance." Accessed April 18, 2014. *http://alcoholism.about.com/cs/alerts/l/blnaa28.htm.*

5 One drink is defined as a 12-ounce bottle of beer, a 5-ounce glass of wine, or a 1 1/2-ounce shot of liquor.

6 MedLine Plus. "Alcoholism and Alcohol Abuse." Accessed April 18, 2014. *www.nlm.nih.gov/medlineplus/ency/article/000944.htm.*

7 Since lack of control and the inability to "manage" alcohol is a cornerstone of alcoholism, the odds are that you will *not* be able to stop drinking for *any* length of time. If you *can,* you may "just" be a problem drinker and not an alcoholic. See Level 1 for more on this distinction.

8 In my view, "serious" means not drinking for at least two weeks. Many inpatient treatment programs (which may or may not include detox) last four weeks (28 days). In theory, it only takes a few (2–5) days to remove all alcohol from your body. Of course, your body and mind will continue to react to its absence for *quite* some time—ranging from weeks to months to even years, *depending on the person* and their post-drinking activities (e.g., diet, exercise, et al.).

9 Burning Tree. "What are the Dangers of Detoxing Yourself from Alcohol?" Accessed February 26, 2014. *www.burningtree.com/dangers-detoxing-alcohol/.*

10 Wikipedia. "Delirium tremens." Accessed February 27, 2014. *http://en.wikipedia.org/wiki/Delirium_tremens.*

11 Some medically supervised detox programs are done in "traditional" hospitals, whereas others are done in dedicated substance-abuse facilities with full or part-time medical staff and associated equipment, which often call themselves hospitals.

12 CHCE Research. "ASAM Pyramid." Accessed April 18, 2014. *www.chce.research.va.gov/apps/PAWS/pdfs/asam.pdf.*

13 I consider both of these sub-levels to be inpatient care, whereas AMAS seems to reserve the term inpatient for actual hospital settings. I view any place where you formally check-in, stay multiple nights, and have your actions monitored and/or controlled 24/7 to be "inpatient," at least with respect to addiction services.

14 Before 2014, when this book was first published, any assumption of insurance for substance abuse services (in the U.S.) was a big one on two fronts: 1) in assuming you had insurance at all, and 2) that it covered substance abuse rehabilitation. The Affordable Care Act (ACA) made this simple (and much better for alcoholics) in that it enabled (relatively) low cost insurance, excluded preexisting conditions (alcoholism included), and mandated substance abuse coverage. However the extent of the coverage will vary by insurance carrier/plan, what facilities are covered in the plan/are in network and the type of treatment desired (inpatient, outpatient, medical intensity, etc.).

15 It can be astonishing what alcoholics will drink, particularly when they are detoxing and desperate for a drink.

16 Suicide is generally not a high risk for alcoholics in detox, but is a significant one for drug users.

17 This was synthesized from numerous sources, including my own. Your experience may be very different, particularly in how structured your entire day is and what restrictions you have (or don't have) in terms of activities like working, exercise, and outside contact, as well as wakeup and bedtime/lights out (no that is not a joke—they may literally turn off the lights in your room).

18 This kind of free time is much more likely to occur in Rehab (e.g., after you have fully detoxed). During detox you are much more likely to spend that time sleeping, reading, or just vegetating in general.

Level 6

1 All Rehabilitation programs want you to be detoxed before you start their programs. As discussed in Level 5, some (but not all) inpatient programs offer Detox services. Therapy can occur before, during, and/or after Detox. Many alcoholics are introduced to meetings such as Alcoholics Anonymous during inpatient Detox or in Rehab.

2 Narconon. "Grim Statistics on Repeated Drug Treatment Admissions Reveal Importance of Asking Right Questions before Rehab." *http://news.narconon.org/repeated-drug-treatment-admissions/*.

3 While I am not a lawyer, I strongly suspect that if you are kicked out of Rehab and were under a court order to be there in the first place, you would be in violation of that order and would incur the consequences.

4 The fact that AA meetings have so permeated rehabilitation programs and assumed a significant role as the "leading" type of alcoholism treatment is a major bone of contention for me. As you will see in Level 7—Join a Community, while being part of community support group is strongly encouraged in the Conquer Program, AA itself as a *standalone* program is *vastly* overrated, to the point of being a disservice to alcoholics by assuming a level of success by nonalcoholics that is just not supported by the facts.

5 I'm not about to pretend it will be easy to take sick time for alcohol rehabilitation without other people at work knowing. Indeed it may be impossible. The good news nowadays is there is far less a stigma than it used to be, and cannot be used in itself as a reason for dismissal under federal law. If you have exhausted your vacation or sick time, check into taking a leave of absence using Family Medical Leave Act (FMLA), discussed later in this Level.

6 Remember the caution mentioned in Level 5 (Detox) about befriending other patients. However, this is less a cause for concern the farther into rehab you and your fellow patients get. Still, be wary, as you do get a strange cast of characters sometimes. Also some will be under court-order to be there—hardly a character recommendation.

7 The New York Times. "In Russia, Harsh Remedy For Addiction Gains Favor." Accessed March 4, 2014. *www.nytimes.com/2011/09/03/world/europe/03russia.html?pagewanted=1*.

8 With Mental Health Parity Rules, cost and day limits aren't allowed unless those limits are also on other types of illnesses.

9 Healthcare.gov. "Essential Health Benefits." Accessed October 15, 2014. *https://www.healthcare.gov/glossary/essential-health-benefits/*.

10 Although not all plans have to cover EHB, all plans that do contain any EHB must remove annual dollar and lifetime dollar limits for those services, including Large Group (insured and ASO) plans. Individual grandfathered plans must remove lifetime dollar limits, but not annual dollar limits. Author's note: the fine print on the ACA is absolutely incredible, and not in a good way.

11 Employment Practice Solutions. "Navigating the FMLA, the ADA, and Substance Abuse Issues." Accessed October 14, 2014. *www.epspros.com/NewsResources/Newsletters?find=48110&printver=true*.

12 US Department of Labor. "The Family and Medical Leave Act." Accessed October 13, 2014. *www.dol.gov/whd/regs/compliance/1421.htm*.

13 Electronic Code of Federal Regulations. *"Title 29 ? Subtitle B ? Chapter V ? Subchapter C ? Part 825."* Accessed October 14, 2014. *www.ecfr.gov/cgi-bin/text-idx?c=ecfr&sid=abbd92cdff37c5d32de741cc5 ccc1e81&rgn=div5&view=text&node=29:3.1.1.3.54&idno=29#se29.3.825_1119*.

14 Legal Action Center. "The Americans with Disabilities Act: A Summary of Alcohol and Drugs and AIDS Provisions." Accessed October 15, 2014. *http://lac.org/doc_library/lac/publications/ada.pdf*.

15 U.S. Commission of Civil Rights. "Chapter 4-Substance Abuse under the ADA." Accessed October 15, 2014. *www.usccr.gov/pubs/ada/ch4.htm*.

16 The ADA takes particular pains to point out and limit protections for *current* illegal drug use, e.g. current drug users do not in any interpretation have a "disability."

17 Legal Action Center. "The Americans with Disabilities Act: A Summary of Alcohol and Drugs and AIDS Provisions." Accessed October 15, 2014. *http://lac.org/doc_library/lac/publications/ada.pdf*.

18 Society for Human Resource Management. "EEO: Disability: Are employees undergoing treatment for drug and alcohol addictions covered under the ADA?"Accessed October15, 2014. *www.shrm.org/templatestools/hrqa/pages/adadrugsandalcohol.aspx*.

19 Faegre Baker Daniels. "ADAAA Final Regulations: Frequently Asked Questions." Accessed October 15, 2014. *www.faegrebd.com/14146*.

20 Some of you might notice that a premise about this program is that the so-called "experts," (certified or otherwise) are not enough to get you sober. So why bother with certification? First, certification can separate the competent from the quacks, and second it is not because they are bad; it is because *by themselves* the knowledge they impart are not enough long-term.

21 I have already been attacked by such people.

22 Adapted from Serenity Lane. "How To Select a Treatment Center for Alcohol & Other Drug Dependencies." Accessed May 6, 2014. *www.serenitylane.org/articles/treatment_selection.html*.

23 Other than the fact that I did not stop drinking. But again, I believe that was because I was expecting the treatment to be the one and only defense I would ever need, which, if you really think about it, is a ridiculous expectation to have.

24 To this day I don't know clearly how much my Depression caused my drinking versus how my drinking caused my Depression. I do know once I stopped drinking, I did not need depression medicine anymore. However, by that time I had pretty much fully gotten over my marriage breakup and related issues, so it is not clear.

25 SAMHSA National Registry of Evidence Based Programs and Practices. "Alcohol Behavioral Couple Therapy." Accessed April 18, 2014. *www.nrepp.samhsa.gov/ViewIntervention.aspx?id=3*.

26 Learn-About-Alcoholism. "Types of Alcoholism Therapy." Accessed April 18, 2014. *www.learn-about-alcoholism.com/types-of-alcoholism.html*.

27 About.com. "Cognitive Behavior Therapy for Addiction." Accessed March 10, 2014. *http://alcoholism.about.com/od/relapse/a/cbt.htm*.

28 Learn-About-Alcoholism. "Types of Alcoholism Therapy." Accessed April 18, 2014. *www.learn-about-alcoholism.com/types-of-alcoholism.html*.

29 Arguably an example of building a broader support group.

30 NIAAA. "Motivation Enhancement Therapy Manual." Accessed April 18, 2014. *http://pubs.niaaa.nih.gov/publications/ProjectMatch/match02.pdf*.

31 Learn-About-Alcoholism. "Types of Alcoholism Therapy." Accessed April 18, 2014. *www.learn-about-alcoholism.com/types-of-alcoholism.html*.

32 Wall Street Journal . *"Still Hung Up on Your Past? A Therapy Says 'Let It Go.'"* August 27, 2013.

Accessed April 19, 2014. Again, it is my interpretation that lists the applicable triggers for each individual category.

33 There are even other categories, like "psychiatric nurse" that have their own practices. It can get confusing.

34 The exception is the concept of Aversion Therapy, which I have done twice on my own, *not* under medical direction/supervision. This concept and my experiences are discussed in more detail in Level 11—Make Yourself Sick, and Level 12—The LAST Detox. These Levels are completely optional in The Conquer Program and are at your own risk.

35 Like showing the patient gruesome images of terrible car crashes caused by drunken drivers.

36 Team Lib. "The Essential Handbook of Treatment and Prevention of Alcohol Problems." Page 12. Accessed April 22, 2014. *http://robinsteed.pbworks.com/w/file/fetch/52176344/TreatmentAndPreventionOf AlcoholProblems.pdf.*

37 Web MD. "Disulfiram." Accessed May 13, 2014. *www.webmd.com/a-to-z-guides/disulfiram.*

38 DailyStrength.org. "Alcoholism Support Group—Antabuse?" Accessed April 22, 2014. *www.daily strength.org/c/Alcoholism/advice/13982916-antabuse.*

39 Wikipedia.org. "Quitters, Inc." Accessed April 20, 2014. *http://en.wikipedia.org/wiki/Quitters,_Inc..*

40 Psychology Today. "What Does Hypnosis Really Feel Like?" Accessed April 23, 2014. *www.psychologytoday.com/blog/hypnosis-the-power-trance/200907/what-does-hypnosis-really-feel.*

41 Alcoholrehab.com. "Hypnosis As An Addiction Treatment." Accessed April 23, 2014. *http://alcohol-rehab.com/alcohol-rehab/hypnosis-as-an-addiction-treatment/.*

42 AltMD. "Meditation for Addiction-What is Meditation?" Accessed March 10, 2014. *www.altmd.com/Articles/Meditation-for-Addiction.*

43 NCBI. "Drug addiction, love, and the higher power." Accessed March 24, 2014. *www.ncbi.nlm.nih.gov/pmc/articles/PMC3185195/.*

44 Source study supporting this assertion could not be found.

45 NCBI. "Mindfulness-based relapse prevention for substance use disorders: a pilot efficacy trial." Accessed March 24, 2014. *www.ncbi.nlm.nih.gov/pubmed/19904665.*

46 Journal for Addictive Medicine. "Mindfulness Meditation for Alcohol Relapse Prevention: A Feasibility Pilot Study." Accessed March 24, 2014. *http://journals.lww.com/journaladdictionmedicine/ Abstract/2008/09000/Mindfulness_Meditation_for_Alcohol_Relapse.9.aspx.*

47 Unfortunately I could not find the source study for this assertion.

48 NCBI. "Mindfulness meditation and substance use in an incarcerated population." Accessed March 24, 2014. *www.ncbi.nlm.nih.gov/pubmed/16938074.*

49 Bulleted point source: NCBI. "Use and assessment of complementary and alternative therapies by intravenous drug users." Accessed March 24, 2014. *www.ncbi.nlm.nih.gov/pubmed/12765213.* Overall source for study information: NeuroSoup. "Meditation's Role in Drug Addiction Recovery." Accessed March 24, 2014. *www.neurosoup.com/meditations-role-in-drug-addiction-recovery/.*

50 Spiritual Healing For You. "Types of Meditation." Accessed March 17, 2014. *www.spiritual-healing-for-you.com/types-of-meditation.html.*

51 My research indicated that while meditation seems to have the same (relatively small) percentage of scammers and over promisers typical of many self-help areas (weight loss being an example), Transcendental Meditation seems to attract more than its share of rip-off artists. See *http://intentions.wordpress.com/2008/05/23/transcendental-meditation-cults-scams-and-you/*, Wordpress. "Alternative Mental Health Recovery." Accessed March 27, 2014.

52 The overview of the five categories of meditation comes from: Spiritual Healing For You. "Types of Meditation." Accessed March 10, 2014. *www.spiritual-healing-for-you.com/types-of-meditation.html.*

53 Dhamma.org. "Vipassana Meditation." Accessed March 26, 2014. *www.dhamma.org/en/about/vipassana*.

54 AltMD. "Meditation for Addiction." Accessed March 10, 2014. *www.altmd.com/Articles/Meditation-for-Addiction*.

55 Gaiam Life. "Mediation and Visualization." Accessed April 22, 2014. *http://life.gaiam.com/article/meditation-and-visualization*.

56 For Dummies.com. "Types of Mindfulness Meditation." Accessed March 26, 2014. *www.dummies.com/how-to/content/types-of-mindfulness-meditation.html?cid=RSS_DUMMIES2_CONTENT*.

57 From SalvationArmyUSA.org. "Addiction Recovery (Adult Rehabilitation Centers)." Accessed April 22, 2014. *http://centralusa.salvationarmy.org/usc/rehabilitation*: "In some areas programs have developed that serve women with addictions, but for the most part the ARC ministry is focused on men dealing with alcohol and drug addictions."

58 Adapted from Wikipedia.org. "The Salvation Army." Accessed March 10, 2014. *http://en.wikipedia.org/wiki/The_Salvation_Army*.

59 Most rehab programs have some level of trigger-related discussions (though not nearly as comprehensive and structured as this program), which will allow you an opportunity to explore deeper into some of them, such as the rehab favorite H.A.L.T. (Hungry, Angry, Lonely, Tired).

Level 7

1 In 1990, AA GSO, the governing organization overseeing all "autonomous" meetings, published an internal memo for the employees of its corporate offices. It was an analysis of a survey period between 1977 and 1989. The results were in absolute contrast to the public perception of AA: "*After just one month in the Fellowship [meaning AA,] 81% of the new members had already dropped out. After three months, 90% have left, and a full 95% have disappeared inside one year!*" (Kolenda, 2003, Golden Text Publishing Company). Source: Sober Forever. "Hazelden Treatment Center and AA Statistics-Belief versus Fact: What is the truth about AA's success rate?" Accessed March 17, 2014. *www.soberforever.net/hazelden-treatment-center-and-aa-success-rates.cfm*.

2 The Wall Street Journal. "Why She Drinks: Women and Alcohol Abuse." Accessed March 17, 2014. *http://online.wsj.com/article/SB10001424127887323893504578555270434071876.html*.

3 Wikipedia. "Alcoholics Anonymous." Accessed April 24, 2014. *http://en.wikipedia.org/wiki/ Alcoholics_Anonymous#Program*.

4 Spiritual River. What Is The Success Rate of Recovery in AA?" Accessed March 17, 2014. *www.spiritualriver.com/what-is-the-success-rate-of-recovery-in-aa/comment-page-3/*. Would the statistics be different if done today (a whole 10 years later)? Not likely. Having attended AA meetings since well before that study, I can attest that practically *nothing* has changed about the AA approach. Even the Big Book seems stuck in the 1950s (despite subsequent editing), with a strong (and highly annoying) orientation towards a stereotypical working man alcoholic/stay-at-home non-alcoholic dutiful wife mindset. No wonder there are so few women in AA!

5 You can *always* spot someone in AA who has been ordered there by the court. They look at the clock like they are trapped in the high school chemistry class from hell, and immediately rush to the person opening the meeting to get their paperwork signed. It's hilarious.

6 A big reason I use stories/testimonials so much in this book is that they are very interesting and relatable. They are a great reason to go to meetings occasionally even if you are not an AA person, particularly on speaker night.

7 Alcoholics Anonymous. "The Twelve Steps Of Alcoholics Anonymous." Accessed March 17, 2014. *www.aa.org/en_pdfs/smf-121_en.pdf*.

8 It is my opinion that long-term alcohol use has a deadening effect on the libido. So you might be pre-

pared for some long forgotten urges after you have been sober for a while. More on this in the Sex trigger discussion in Level 2.

9 The Wall Street Journal. "Why She Drinks: Women and Alcohol Abuse." Updated June 21, 2013. Accessed April 23, 2014. *http://online.wsj.com/news/articles/SB10001424127887323893504578555527 0434071876?mg=reno64-wsj&url=http%3A%2F%2Fonline.wsj.com%2Farticle%2FSB10001424127 887323893504578555270434071876.html.*

10 The Wall Street Journal. "Why She Drinks: Women and Alcohol Abuse." Accessed March 18, 2014. *http://online.wsj.com/article/SB10001424127887323893504578555270434071876.html.* Paragraph 20.

11 How you might "become" spiritual is discussed in great detail in Level 10—Consider Spirituality.

12 Attempts mostly consisted of several spurts of dedicated months with lapses in between. Since I developed this program, I go fairly regularly, about one meeting every couple of weeks. I also attend Al-Anon meetings periodically.

13 AA also has a list of "Promises," (see *www.singaporeaa.org/PDFs/The_AA_Promises.pdf,* from Singapore AA. "The AA Promises." Accessed March 17, 2014.), where in Promise #3 it says "We will not regret the past nor wish to shut the door on it." In general I have no issues with these promises and have personally experienced most of them—I just didn't use AA to achieve them.

14 During a number of "step" meetings—ones that focus on reading from The Big Book, a number of people noted that they had practical difficulty with this step, primarily in that they often did not realize they were wrong until well after the fact (sometimes months) when it was too late to bring up the topic again without looking strange.

15 The Big Book does describe in various places how doing this will help the alcoholic.

16 Silkworth.net-Your Global Resource For A.A. History. "12 Step History Reflections." Accessed March 17, 2014. *http://silkworth.net/dickb/12stephistory5.html.*

17 The Washington Post. "Live Q & A." Accessed March 17, 2014. *http://live.washingtonpost.com/dear-prudence-140317.html?hpid=z4.*

18 Wikipedia. "Rational Recovery." Accessed March 18, 2014. Last updated February 9, 2014. *http://en.wikipedia.org/wiki/Rational_Recovery.*

19 Rational Recovery. "Frequently Asked Questions." Accessed March 18, 2014. *http://rational.org/index.php?id=33.*

20 SOS Sobriety. "SOS Principles." Accessed March 18, 2014. *www.sossobriety.org/MeetingInfo/SOS_Principles.pdf.*

21 Women For Sobriety. "WFS "New Life" Acceptance Program." Accessed March 19, 2014. *http://womenforsobriety.org/beta2/new-life-program/13-affirmations/.*

Level 8

1 Be careful of course; many of these people are blithering idiots, but even they might give you some ideas.

2 Adapted from Mark's Daily Apple. "6 Tea Ingredients That Can Help You Unwind, Relax, and Chill Out." Accessed April 30, 2014. *www.marksdailyapple.com/6-tea-ingredients-that-can-help-you-unwind-relax-and-chill-out/#axzz2cvbuzKYy.* Most of these ingredients are also available in tablet form, usually at specialty vitamin stores.

3 I qualify these statements in that this is what the marksdailyapple.com article asserts as research (including some links)—I have not done the back research myself. The article goes into some detail on variations in harvesting and using the ingredients. Some of these ingredients come with various warnings, such as not combining with alcohol (ha ha) or using them if you are pregnant. Kava Kava seems to have the most concerning side effects of all the ingredients listed here. *www.webmd.com* has information on most of these ingredients including side effects.

4 While most people are aware of non-alcoholic beer, they don't know about such wine. One such brand is Fre (*www.frewines.com/*), which is actually "alcohol-removed" wine but still has a trace amount. I know one person whose doctor forbids him to drink. He likes this wine (that comes in a variety of whites and reds) and it seems to help when he has a "craving."

5 See the links in the marksdailyapple.com article for more detail. Level 11 discusses the nature and role of GABA receptors and dopamine in more detail, particularly their possible role in alcoholism.

6 Wikipedia. "Adaptogen." Accessed March 19, 2014. *http://en.wikipedia.org/wiki/Adaptogen*.

7 NCIB. "The natural products magnolol and honokiol are positive allosteric modulators of both synaptic and extra-synaptic GABA(A) receptors." Accessed March 19, 2014. *www.ncbi.nlm.nih.gov/pubmed/22445602*.

8 More info on these can be found at *www.doctoroz.com/videos/best-teas-stress-and-anxiety*. In addition, a new category of drinks targeted at relaxation has emerged, as described at *http://online.wsj.com/article/SB10001424052702304373104579109283589583074.html*.

Level 9

1 Planning your alcohol purchases is a question in the Conquer Quiz in Level 1.

2 This way of "disguising" your alcohol purchases is also part of The Conquer Quiz in Level 1.

3 Yoga is described in more detail in Appendix A (as a way of helping you sleep).

4 The New York Times. "Yes, Running Can Make You High." Accessed April 28, 2014. *www.nytimes.com/2008/03/27/health/nutrition/27best.html?_r=0*.

5 Daily Mail. "Cheers! Drinking DOES Release The Feelgood Factor In Our Brains." Accessed May 6, 2014. *www.dailymail.co.uk/health/article-2085320/Drinking-DOES-make-feel-happy-Alcohol-triggers-endorphins-brain.html*

6 While I was convalescing from surgery, I "bowled" many games on the WII U Sports Club game. It is surprising good exercise. There are a number of other active-type games and, of course, regular fitness programs available on most game systems, though WII with its special controller seems to have the most.

7 Promises Treatment Centers. "Pets: Natural Stress Relievers." Accessed May 1, 2014. *www.promises.com/articles/therapy/pets-natural-stress-relievers/*.

8 Wikipedia. "Addictive Personality." Accessed May 6, 2014. *http://en.wikipedia.org/wiki/Addictive_personality*. I find this to be a circular definition but essentially accurate.

9 Even this assertion is more anecdotal than scientific. I could find no statistics. The closest was a study that said illicit drug use *concurrent* with alcohol use (i.e., during or within 2 hours of last alcohol use) being somewhere in the 5 to 12 percent range of alcohol users (sources: SAMHSA. "Concurrent Illicit Drug and Alcohol use." Accessed May 5, 2014. *www.samhsa.gov/data/2k9/alcDrugs/alcDrugs.htm*, and the NIH. "Simultaneous and Concurrent Polydrug Use of Alcohol and Prescription Drugs: Prevalence, Correlates, and Consequences." Accessed May 5, 2014. *www.ncbi.nlm.nih.gov/pmc/articles/PMC1761923/*). Of course, *using* drugs and alcohol at the same time does not mean you are *addicted* to one or the other, let alone both. For what it is worth, my observation in AA meetings seems to indicate a lower percentage of people (about 1 in 20) who say they are both a drug and alcohol addict.

10 Saluidfy. "Addictive Personality Disorder: When Addictions Rule Our World." Accessed August 27, 2014. *http://voxxi.com/2013/10/23/addictive-personality-disorder/*.

11 AlcoholRehab.com. "Addictive Personality." Accessed August 27, 2014. *http://alcoholrehab.com/drug-addiction/addictive-personality/*.

12 This may be a particular temptation for those with the Boredom and Escape triggers who have used drugs in the past with no signs of addiction to those drugs.

13 The new—and perhaps scary—reality of trying to find something to do to fill those hours is the core purpose of Level 9 (Develop New Hobbies).

14 I use this word in quotes, as they certainly do not meet our definition of addiction described in Level 1. Obsessiveness or habitual behavior might be better descriptions.

15 Many alcoholics report that they have a fixation on wanting to put something in their mouth for a long time after stopping drinking, a phenomena I discussed in Level 8. This wanting something in your hand/mouth feeling may last for many months, and may gradually go away or seemingly vanish overnight. Don't sweat it, as no one will notice as they are preoccupied with their own fascination with coffee and soda.

16 I use this term very loosely, as the "addiction" here does not meet our royally-fucking-up-your-life definition introduced in Level 1. An emerging "bad habit" is a better term.

17 There are two casinos near me, with dramatically different styles. I was almost immediately put off by the cheesy one (cheesy advertising, decorations, etc.), while the more elegant one took some time. But when I started recognizing employees (and they recognized me), and I started to see familiar faces in the crowd, that's when it really hit home that I was going too much, as well as getting bored seeing the same types of people over and over again. So in essence I did a boredom-version of aversion therapy.

18 But make that decision after you have completed this book. They very well may provide key insights that you did not get the first time that you will get now that you have the knowledge derived from this book.

Level 10

1 Wikipedia. "Religion and Alcohol." Accessed March 15, 2014. *http://en.wikipedia.org/wiki/Religion_and_alcohol*.

2 My Recovery. "The Double-Edged Sword of Religion and Alcoholism." *www.myrecovery.com/Spirituality-in-Recovery/david-briggs-the-doubled-edged-sword-of-religion-and-alcoholism.html*.

3 Huffington Post. "The Double-Edged Sword of Religion and Alcoholism." Accessed March 15, 2014. *www.huffingtonpost.com/david-briggs/charlie-sheen-circus-and-_b_836934.html*.

4 Labeling these organizations, particularly AA, as a quasi-religious organization is sure to raise questions and controversy. There have been numerous articles written on the topic, ranging from the opinion that it was "merely" spiritual to it being very, even unpleasantly religious in nature. A good overall analysis can be found at Silkworth. "Spiritual not Religious." Accessed March 15, 2014. *www.silkworth.net/zips/SpiritualnotReligious.doc*.

5 Exception: I did attend several sessions of Strawberry Ministries near where I live. I went into those sessions *extremely* skeptical, having lived in Texas during the Evangelistic hell of the '80s and '90s. But I found them to be very well done, effectively blending spirituality themes, biblical teachings, sophisticated presentations, and even interactive visual aids and music to deliver some very good teachings on dealing with addiction from a spiritual perspective.

6 Interestingly the specific term "higher power" is not used in the 12 steps themselves, and not often in the AA "Big Book." The exact source of the term is unknown, but AA is widely credited for its common usage and reach.

7 See Level 7 for a critique of why AA overall did not work for me along with a broader analysis.

8 While I totally understand the appeal of "handing over," I personally have a hard time doing it, as it seems like you are completely absolving yourself of responsibility for the problem and/or solution, and hoping "someone else" will take care of it for you. That said—do whatever works for you!

9 Adapted from AlcoholRehab.com. "Higher Power In AA." Accessed May 1, 2014. *http://alcoholrehab.com/alcohol-rehab/higher-power-in-aa/*.

10 For a variety of reasons. One is while that chapter is reasonably written, the majority of the Big Book is heavily God-oriented, making the chapter seem small in comparison. Another is because in practice most of the 12 steps explicitly reference God, even if qualified with "as we understood him." Finally, it is more difficult to find meetings where references to God or spirituality are specifically avoided as part of the group philosophy.

11 *Never* in meetings have I encountered anything remotely pressuring you to do so. It is very easy to attend many meetings without making a sound except for perhaps the closing Serenity Prayer. But even then, you can just mumble and no one will notice or care. Your sponsor may or may not ask you about it in private.

12 For a view on being in AA without using a higher power, see *http://aaagnostica.org/2012/11/25/without-a-higher-power/*. AAAgnostica. "Without A Higher Power." Accessed May 1, 2014.

13 AlcoholRehab.com. "Spirituality and Rehab." Accessed May 1, 2014. *http://alcoholrehab.com/alcohol-rehab/spirituality-and-rehab/*.

14 The working kind of Job, not the scripture dude.

15 I'm sure I'm going to upset a lot of people by saying that, but that's sure what it looks like to me, an "outsider."

16 http://en.wikipedia.org/wiki/Religious_text#cite_note-7

17 I only cite this link since it seems to do a reasonable job of doing a high-level comparison of different religions/spiritual approaches. My guess is the authors' beliefs are skewed in a particular direction, but it is not obvious from the chart.

18 This is a phrase meaning that in times of extreme stress or fear, such as in war, all people will believe in, or hope for, a higher power. Its origin is from World War II or possibly WWI (it is not clear), where soldiers would dig holes in the ground to take cover in during bombings (to avoid shrapnel from nearby hits) or gun battles.

19 As a feeling—*an experience of sudden and striking realization*; in religion—*the appearance of a deity to a human* (source: Wikipedia.org)

20 Scientific American. "The Science Behind Dreaming." Accessed April 30, 2014. *www.scientificamerican.com/article/the-science-behind-dreaming/*.

21 If God exists, these guys better hope to hell that He has a sense of humor.

22 See Newsweek. "Proof of Heaven: A Doctor's Experience With the Afterlife" Accessed March 15, 2014. *www.thedailybeast.com/newsweek/2012/10/07/proof-of-heaven-a-doctor-s-experience-with-the-afterlife.html*.

23 If you really want to inject great humor into the topic of spirituality, there are a number of general fiction titles that do this. One is *"Lamb"* by Christopher Moore, which takes an extremely funny look at what Jesus' life might have been before he started preaching. I've always wondered what Jesus did in his first 30 years, and this book is as good a take as any while being absolutely hilarious. I hope He has a sense of humor, otherwise people like Moore and his readers (including me) are in deep trouble.

Level 11

1 Again, the author is *not* responsible for anything you do or experience from executing any aspect in The Conquer Program, particularly Levels 11 and 12. I can't repeat this enough, particularly in the opinion of my lawyers.

2 For those of you who have never played Monopoly, this is where you get sent back to start the game at the beginning spot on the board ("Go") without the usual benefit of collecting money when you do so.

3 These concepts *were* introduced briefly in Level 2, particularly for the Escape trigger where certain aspects of "buzz-rush" are central to understanding and dealing with that trigger.

4 Except of course Pink Floyd's *Comfortably Numb*.

5 Notre Dame Office of Alcohol and Drug Education. "What is Intoxication?" Accessed March 2, 2014. *http://oade.nd.edu/educate-yourself-alcohol/what-is-intoxication/*.

6 Wikipedia. "Euphoria." Accessed March 2, 2014. *http://en.wikipedia.org/wiki/Euphoria*.

7 Dysphoria is defined (also from Wikipedia.org) as: *a state of feeling unwell or unhappy; a feeling of emotional and mental discomfort as a symptom of discontentment, restlessness, dissatisfaction, malaise, depression, anxiety or indifference.* In effect it is the *opposite* of Euphoria.

8 Notre Dame is very careful to qualify the distinction and differences between intoxication/blood alcohol content and how you *act* when you have been drinking. It notes that that there are many factors that can determine your behaviors and effects when drinking, including: food intake before drinking, strength of drink, body weight/type, gender, rate of consumption, *functional tolerance* (defined in Level 5), medications, illness, and fatigue.

9 A British term for being buzzed/numb/about to checkout as far as I can tell.

10 My interpretation and mapping of the term to the BAC level.

11 Same logic—my personal interpretation and mapping of "buzzed" to those BAC levels.

12 I think it is safe to assume that once north of say 0.15% BAC, you are well into "checkout" territory no matter how "good" your tolerance level is.

13 Consistent with our earlier discussions about how alcohol hits women harder, a comparison of the tables shows the BAC for a woman is higher than for a man, *for the same bodyweight.* For a 120-pound man,1,2,3, and 4 drinks results in a BAC of .03, .06, .09, and .12, respectively. In contrast a 120-pound woman with the same number of drinks results in a BAC of .04, .08, .11, and .15.

14 Steven F. Groce, Attorney at Law. "How Much Can You Drink and Still Be Legal?" Accessed March 2, 2014. *http://attorneydwi.com/bacperdrink.html*. No lack of irony/surprise here that this came from a DWI attorney website.

15 I'm not sure how it would have made a difference, but it could have in some way. For one thing, I would have made that first drink last a *lot* longer than the 10 seconds before I took the next one. I would have (at least tried to) slow down my drinking to prolong the "buzzed" state. I'll never know now. But since I lack the ability to stop once I've started it would not have made a lasting difference in my drinking volumes anyway.

16 *Urbandictionary.com* has Buzzkill as: *Something that spoils or ruins an otherwise enjoyable event, esp. when in relation to ruining a drunken or drug-induced high.* So it is massively ironic that alcohol has its own built-in buzzkill.

17 Drummer for Led Zeppelin died in his own vomit after drinking "40 measures of vodka in 12 hours," resulting in a bladder sample of alcohol level of 276 milligrams per hundred milliliters (Source: Ultimate Classic Rock. "John Bonham Dies." Accessed May 9, 2014. *http://ultimateclassicrock.com/john-bonham-dies/*). Bear in mind this was taken an unknown amount of time after he died, so his BAC level at time of death was very likely much higher.

18 The official coroner report released on 26 October 2011 explained that Winehouse's blood alcohol content was 416 mg per 100ml (0.416%), with the verdict of dying of "misadventure." Some of her relatives dispute that verdict (but not the BAC). Maybe for legal contract/insurance reasons.

19 Since one of our premises of the disease of alcoholism is that it has destroyed your ability to have any degree of "control" over how you drink—e.g., knowing when to stop—knowing the above is *very* unlikely to help you "moderate" your drinking—even if you precisely calculate how many drinks it takes for you to achieve your desired effect.

20 Note: This section is a synthesis of multiple medical/scientific studies and theories' regarding the impact alcohol has on us—particularly the brain. I make no guarantees that this synthesis is accurate, particularly in light that *all* of the source studies make clear that *their* theories are unproven, lacking definitive, conclusive evidence. Thus by definition any drugs and/or treatments based on these theories cannot be certain as to why and how they may be effective, if they are at all.

21 There are actually other ways to "ingest" alcohol, such as via a vapor and even rectally, which besides being incredibly dangerous (you absorb all the alcohol into the bloodstream almost instantly) is creepy beyond belief.

22 Facts and Details. "Alcoholic Drinks, The Brain and Addiction." Accessed May 9, 2014. *http://factsanddetails.com/world/cat54/sub347/item1564.html*. This also scientifically explains what most alcoholics learn early on—you get drunk faster on an empty stomach.

23 How It Works. "Why Do We Get Drunk?" Accessed May 9, 2014. *www.howitworksdaily.com/science/why-do-we-get-drunk/*, which was derived from *www.bettyfordcenter.com* center for alcoholism publications.

24 This subsection is my own interpretation and theory based on all the medical research I came across. Like everything else in this section, it is based on *theories*.

25 *Cold Spring Harbor Laboratory-DNA Learning Center.* "The Serotonegic System." Accessed March 2, 2014. *www.dnalc.org/view/813-The-Serotonergic-System.html*.

26 Neurotransmitter Review. "Serotonin's Role In Alcohol's Effects On The Brain." Accessed July 30, 2014. *http://pubs.niaaa.nih.gov/publications/arh21–2/114.pdf*. Page 4.

27 Ethanol = Ethyl Alcohol = Alcohol in alcoholic beverages in layman's terms.

28 Taken verbatim from Oxford Journals. "Alcohol and Alcoholism." Accessed May 10, 2014. *http://alcalc.oxfordjournals.org/content/36/1/22.full*. I added the bolding.

29 Mail Online. "Cheers! Drinking DOES release the feelgood factor in our brains." Accessed May 10, 2014. *www.dailymail.co.uk/health/article-2085320/Drinking-DOES-make-feel-happy-Alcohol-triggers-endorphins-brain.html#ixzz31HsVYho5*.

30 I find no end to the irony that this is a study driven in part by a founder of a major winery.

31 Mail Online. "Cheers! Drinking DOES release the feelgood factor in our brains." Accessed May 10, 2014. *www.dailymail.co.uk/health/article-2085320/Drinking-DOES-make-feel-happy-Alcohol-triggers-endorphins-brain.html#ixzz31HsVYho5*.

32 This is not strictly true. At least some aversion therapy programs actually have you drink alcohol *in coordination* with taking Disulfiram/Antabuse. However, they require you to have detoxed before you start their program.

33 Wikipedia. "Acamprosate." Accessed May 12, 2014. *http://en.wikipedia.org/wiki/Acamprosate*.

34 About.com. "Medications For Alcoholism." Accessed May 12, 2014. *http://alcoholism.about.com/od/meds/a/meds.htm*.

35 And many do not. Hence the large divide on if/how to use torture with terrorists, e.g. waterboarding to state an extreme example.

36 My experience in trying to obtain aversion therapy had it in the $15,000—$20,000 range—not something the average alcoholic can cough up. I have no idea how Obamacare will impact such programs.

37 Wikipedia. "Ivan Pavlov." Accessed May 11, 2014. *http://en.wikipedia.org/wiki/Ivan_Pavlov*.

38 This is not so crazy an idea if you really think about it. For years your mind (via your desire for alcohol) has been inflicting damage on your body with only feeble attempts (e.g., occasional vomiting, hangovers that went away after a few hours) by your body to get *back* at the mind (a kind of revenge is one way to think about it), or via longer-term problems that were so slow to develop and easily attributed to other factors that they really did not influence your mind much—certainly not enough to change the way it thought about alcohol!

What I'm proposing here is really something in-between—a more constant communication and cooperation between mind and body. And a much more positive relationship, in contrast to the pure negative of the mind throwing alcohol into a body that doesn't want it, and the body's negative attempts to get back at the mind through hangovers and death-inducing conditions. It might help if you think about yourself in two distinct parts—your head (versus) your body.

39 Of course you don't have to have colon problems to do this, but (in my opinion) you *do* need some sort of *recent* agonizing pain. The "problem" with physical pain is that the mind does not retain a memory of it, which normally is obviously a good thing but works against this kind of approach—hence the pain needs to be still lingering in your memory (or better yet, still occurring. This is the point of Level 12—The Last Detox).

40 One interesting side effect is that I can detect the words "liquor" "wine" or "beer" in any sign on a street or in a store without trying.

41 For me it was Southern Comfort and Gin. I was violently ill from both—SC in college when I drank a whole bottle, and gin the first time I ever tried it. I've never touched either again even when nothing else was available.

42 Mayo Clinic. "Food Allergies: Understanding Food Labels." Accessed August 30, 2014. *www.mayoclinic.com/health/food-allergies/AA00057.*

43 It *may* be that this whip-sawing back and forth between concentrated heavy drinking and detoxes is what helped me finally achieve my aversion to alcohol—I have absolutely no way of knowing. As far as I know, this rapid-fire get drunk/detox/repeat has never been tried before, at least in a clinical setting. A great research topic!

44 I also became "sick" of wine—particularly the smell and taste of white wine—many years earlier. But in that case I believe it was from the sheer volume of drinking. I don't remember exactly when or how it happened, but one day after one of my usual very heavy consumption of wine the night before, the smell and taste started making me sick to my stomach. I rarely had more than a glass or two after that. Unfortunately I switched to vodka for the heavy alcoholic lifting.

45 Of course there were many times when I had these effects *individually,* but not very often all at the *same* time. Perhaps experiencing these multiple times in a relatively short period are one of the reasons this approach worked for me—again, I just don't know.

46 Since my last "test," I have not attempted to taste, let alone swallow, alcohol. I do not know what will happen. It's possible that I could have "1 or 2" beers without a problem. But I very much doubt it, since I am convinced that I do not have the ability to control drinking once I start. I see no point in pushing my luck. I will say that "virgin" drinks and nonalcoholic beers do not have an impact on me. However, I do not have them very often, as I view doing so as another version of pushing my luck.

47 There are very few hospitals/clinics providing this kind of "formal" treatment program. The testimonials I found were hospital specific (naming names), so I do not cite them here for legal liability reasons. Some people said it was very effective, others not so much. One prominent advocate is Pat O'Day, a prominent broadcaster and announcer in the U.S. Pacific Northwest who is the key spokesman for Schick Shadel Hospital (Source: Wikipedia. "Pat O'Day." Accessed May 13, 2014. *http://en.wikipedia.org/wiki/Pat_O'Day).*

Level 12

1 Level 11 was optional and its effectiveness depended *greatly* upon the individual. If you tried making yourself physically sick along the lines of how the author did it, it may or may not have worked—it was far from guaranteed. Another possibility is that it *partially* worked; you now find that you are less tempted to drink than you were before, but you are still doing it (perhaps drinking less, avoiding certain kinds of drinks, or even drinking a bit reluctantly). In that case, Level 12 may help complete the aversion process you started.

2 Why not just jump to this Level? Because there are very significant risks associated with *any* detox, and those who have never done it before may not have any idea how their mind and body will react—which may in some cases be dangerous and even be life-threatening (hence doing medically supervised detox is *highly* recommended).

3 And yes, the pain medications they gave me for my colon problems didn't hurt in taking my mind off detox in the rare instances when I thought about it. And no, I did not become addicted to those

medications. If you are worried about becoming addicted to pain meds, I strongly urge you to express this concern (and your drinking history) to your doctor, who will then take extra special care in prescribing them. See also a very specific discussion on the potential for other addictions in Level 9.

4 Delirium tremens—See Level 5 for more information. Obviously this assumes your doctor *knows* you are an alcoholic. If not, tell him/her. NOW. Pick up the phone NOW.

5 I would imagine that this is effective only your alcoholic beverage of choice was something much stronger, and you didn't really care for beer. But that is just a guess; other scenarios are possible. Perhaps "tapering off" to a beverage (regardless of alcohol content) that you hated, like some gross wine? You could then possibly tie it to some of the lessons of Level 11, making you sick of alcohol in the process.

6 A perfect illustration of if at first you don't succeed: try, try again! Applicable for detox, certainly. However his definition of a successful detox might leave something to be desired if he had to try again and again. But I believe he was trying to say he fully detoxed without drinking and stayed sober for at least some meaningful amount of time.

7 I found numerous testimonials about tapering, about 50/50 in terms of success. But this most likely refers to only a narrow detox time window; as an alcoholic they very likely subsequently ratcheted their drinking back up shortly thereafter.

8 I have no idea if any of this has a medical basis for avoiding shakes or vomiting. Whatever works though!

9 I found numerous testimonials describing a wide range of drugs for anxiety (such as Librium) that were prescribed (and seemed effective), so there are apparently many options. What might work for you, of course, will need to be determined by your doctor.

10 Juicing seems to emphasize detoxing as a big part of its sales pitch. I don't know how true that is, but it should certainly help with any potential vitamin deficiencies, a common problem with alcoholics.

Level 13

1 *Footnotes by Stage include *Middle Alcoholism:* Depression appeared early in this stage (arguably I had it for years) and came under control when I started taking depression medicine. It was during this time that I stopped kidding myself that I drank to have Fun. *Late Alcoholism:* Loneliness became a trigger after I moved far away from my children, and went away after I returned 4 years later. Disorder as a trigger had (in hindsight) first appeared in Middle Alcoholism; it disappeared once I got my own apartment. During this stage my Relationships trigger turned into the eX trigger with separation and divorce. *Early Sobriety:* Job and Money worries went away with a new job situation; Guilt and Frustration as major triggers in their own right went away as my defenses solidified and as I improved how I dealt with my eX. *Tuning Sobriety:* Insomnia dropped in intensity and as a priority as many of the ideas documented in Appendix A started to work. *Ongoing Sobriety:* My eX ceased to be a major trigger as my defenses were completed and tuned.

2 A version of this is called the "Pink Cloud," and is discussed in the Overconfidence trigger section in Level 2.

3 The five senses. I wouldn't even rule out a *"sixth sense."*

4 Smart Football. "Teaching a Quarterback Where To Throw the Football." Accessed May 2, 2014. Smart Football. "Teaching A Quarterback Where To Throw The Ball." Accessed May 24, 2014. *http://smartfootball.com/quarterbacking/reading-grass-versus-reading-full-coverages-or-keying-specific-pass-defenders.*

5 It bears repeating that "Stress" in the Conquer Program denotes a specific kind of physical stress. Other kinds of "stress" are most likely other triggers such as Job stress, Relationship stress, etc.

6 I'm sure there are, but just can't think of any.

7 See Appendix B for all the checklists.

8 This is in contrast to floor triggers, where you want your most effective floor trigger *last*—as in last resort.

9 Hopefully there will be few of these! More seriously, consider re-reading a boring book that you never finished because you kept dropping off to sleep. An already proven solution to your Insomnia!

10 My personal arch-nemesis.

11 Murphy's Law: What *can* go wrong *will* go wrong.

12 Not this program's Levels. "Levels" like time, energy, focus required, $, etc.

13 *The New York Times.* "Robin Williams, Oscar-Winning Actor, Dies at 63 In Suspected Suicide." Accessed August 11, 2014. *www.nytimes.com/2014/08/12/movies/robin-williams-oscar-winning-comedian-dies-at-63.html?hp&action=click&pgtype=Homepage&version=LargeMediaHeadlineSumCentered&module =photo-spot-region&region=photo-spot&WT.nav=photo-spot&_r=0* .

14 My experience also illustrates a sometimes complicating factor in separating a major trigger from a related one: when what is now a Related Trigger used to be a major trigger in the past, or vice versa. In fact, it is very possible for the same trigger to be both "major" or "related" over the course of your alcoholism life.

15 I felt, and still do, that AA is wrong, or at least premature, in its "making amends" steps in very early sobriety. Far better to start that process well after you have a long time (e.g., many months if not years) of sobriety behind you and all your defenses and defense progressions defined, in place, and well tested, because it will not be easy once you start "making amends" or its equivalent.

16 Doing so may even *be* a floor defense.

17 A shout-out to Yul Brenner in *The King and I.*

18 When I was in Therapy, I did vent a lot about my (then) wife. However, it did not seem to do any good with respect to my drinking, which I attribute to a lack of understanding on my part about the importance of triggers and understanding their root causes.

19 Free marriage advice—make yourselves do at least one hobby together.

20 I know it irritates the hell out of her, but that is just too bad. *That* is part of "It is not your (my) job to make her happy anymore." And a corollary to that is "I don't have to make myself unhappy in the slightest because of her."

21 Or know I saw before but don't remember any of the details.

22 I don't really care for Facebook (particularly as its ads get more intrusive and privacy controls get weaker), but it is the best game in town (currently) for maintaining connections with my extended family.

23 stress——uncapitalized—is used as a collective term for Stress that can be caused by many things. These include general Anxiety, Change, Job, Money, Relationships, etc. that individually are very minor triggers that day but in total add up.

24 Even if they don't, it has a great placebo effect.

25 On every day but Sunday, and regardless of time zone. Weird I know . . .

Conclusion

1 Anonymous after a meeting in Missouri sometime in 2012

2 One Crafty Mother. "In Which I Answer The Question I Get Most." Accessed May 24, 2014. *www.onecraftymother.com/2011/06/in-which-i-answer-question-i-get-most.html*, final two paragraphs

Appendix A

1 WebMD, "Nightmares In Adults." Accessed September 7, 2014. *www.webmd.com/sleep-disorders/guide/nightmares-in-adults.*

2 DARA Thailand. "Dreams About Relapsing." Accessed March 3, 2013. *http://alcoholrehab.com/alcohol-rehab/dreams-about-relapsing/.*

3 Personally I do not feel like I've "benefited" when I have relapse dreams. I wake up exhausted. But I see their point.

4 DARA Thailand. "Dreams About Sleeping." Accessed March 3, 2014. *http://alcoholrehab.com/alcohol-rehab/dreams-about-relapsing/.*

5 Web MD. "Nightmares in Adults." Accessed March 3, 2014. *www.webmd.com/sleep-disorders/guide/nightmares-in-adults.* Additional Note: If sex is a stressful activity—which it can be, particularly in terms of getting your heart rate up and in turn making it difficult for some to quickly go to sleep afterwards—then you have another area to consider how you might want to modify when/how you do it.

6 Center for Disease Control. "Sleep and Sleep Disorders-Sleep Hygiene Tips." Accessed March 3, 2014. *www.cdc.gov/sleep/about_sleep/sleep_hygiene.htm.* This last bullet is likely to be very hard to do, and I am not at all sure I agree with it. Reading and/or listening to music in particular can be very effective for making you sleepy in my opinion. The point is to try different things—you might be surprised how effective they are even if they don't seem logical. Sleep research has many more questions than answers at this point it seems.

7 One trick is to buy "floor models," as you can get discounts up to 50% on "old" models, which when it comes to beds generally does *not* mean that the new models are actually any better.

8 There are special "pillows" that are literally designed for just your eyes. Kind of like mini-sandbags. You can buy them in specialty yoga accessory stores.

9 This can include the number of pillows, the type of pillows (hard, soft, tempurpedic, etc.), whether they are hypoallergenic, the type and quality of pillowcases they are in, how well and rapidly they absorb or disperse heat, and even their arrangement prior to and during sleep. Enough variables/possible combinations to make you lose sleep…

10 Make sure you have some way of having the music end after say 30 minutes to an hour. I've found that the same music that puts me to sleep can wake me up if left on too long.

11 Including the warnings that said, "Don't take with alcohol."

12 It also caused "severe facial swelling." Meaning I blew up to look like Yoda.

13 To point out the obvious, do not stop taking the medication until you consult with your doctor.

14 Experiment; what you are used to may not necessarily be what works best for you as you try to establish new sleeping patterns.

15 Yoga requires physical movement, which some forms of meditation do not use.

16 One Life. "The Power of Breathing: 4 Pranayama Techniques Worth Practicing. Accessed September 7, 2014. *www.onemedical.com/blog/live-well/breathing-pranayama-techniques/.*

17 One Life. "The Power of Breathing: 4 Pranayama Techniques Worth Practicing. Accessed September 7, 2014. *www.onemedical.com/blog/live-well/breathing-pranayama-techniques/.*

18 One Life. "The Power of Breathing: 4 Pranayama Techniques Worth Practicing. Accessed September 7, 2014. *www.onemedical.com/blog/live-well/breathing-pranayama-techniques/.*

19 One Life. "The Power of Breathing: 4 Pranayama Techniques Worth Practicing. Accessed September 7, 2014. *www.onemedical.com/blog/live-well/breathing-pranayama-techniques/.*

20 One Life. "The Power of Breathing: 4 Pranayama Techniques Worth Practicing. Accessed September

7, 2014. *www.onemedical.com/blog/live-well/breathing-pranayama-techniques/*.

21 WebMD. "Sleeping Pills: The Pros and Cons." Accessed May 7, 2014. *www.webmd.com/sleep-disorders/features/sleeping-pills-pros-cons*.

22 WebMD says this. Seriously.

23 WebMD. "Living With Insomnia: Get A Good Night's Sleep." Accessed May 14, 2014. *www.webmd.com/sleep-disorders/living-with-insomnia-11/natural-solutions*.

24 I emphasize "in my view." I could be totally off base on any effectiveness of these *chemically*, but I have personally found them effective *mentally*. Could be a placebo-type effect, but if so, who cares?

Appendix B

1 STOP drinking if you are pregnant and see a doctor *immediately*.

About the Author

 **D. H. Williams** is a management consultant with a focus on wireless technology. Prior to launching his own firm, he worked for some of the world's leading management and technology strategy consulting firms, helping companies develop leading technology strategies and cutting-edge products and services in the United States, Europe, and Asia.

Mr. Williams has been published and quoted by leading magazines and newspapers on various technical topics. He has authored several technical books and has one patent pending. He has a BS in Electrical Engineering from a top-five school and an MBA from a top-twenty school, from which he graduated first in his class.

Despite his impressive resume, by the time Mr. Williams finally conquered his alcoholism, he had lost multiple jobs and had developed life-threatening health problems. During his twenty-plus year "career" as a hard-core alcoholic, Williams achieved many of the "benefits" of alcoholism: foreclosure and bankruptcy, divorce, unemployment, and major health problems—e.g., Four of the "Big Five" (amazingly he had no DUIs or arrests). He began to develop The Conquer Program during a major medical scare and perfected it over the course of a year, including a great deal of personal testing against a wide variety of alcohol temptations and attacks. *All* were successfully rebuffed. In addition to this book, Mr. Williams is the creator and President of *ConquerYourAddiction.com*, a website dedicated to The Conquer Program and more generally helping people in their fight against alcoholism and other addictions.

Made in the USA
Monee, IL
14 September 2022

12932912R00359